W9-BYP-096

COUNSELING AND PSYCHOTHERAPY THEORIES IN CONTEXT AND PRACTICE

COUNSELING AND PSYCHOTHERAPY THEORIES IN CONTEXT AND PRACTICE

SKILLS, STRATEGIES, AND TECHNIQUES

JOHN SOMMERS-FLANAGAN

RITA SOMMERS-FLANAGAN

JOHN WILEY & SONS, INC.

Library of Congress Cataloging-in-Publication Data:

Sommers-Flanagan, John, 1957–
    Counseling and psychotherapy theories in context and practice: Skills, strategies, and techniques / John Sommers-Flanagan and Rita Sommers-Flanagan.
        p. cm.
    Includes bibliographical references and index.
        ISBN 0-471-21105-2 (cloth)
    1. Counseling. 2. Psychotherapy. I. Sommers-Flanagan, Rita, 1953– II. Title.

BF637.C6S69 2004
158'.3—dc21

                                                                                        2003053841

Printed in the United States of America.
10 9 8 7 6 ′

Contents

Preface

One morning, long ago, John woke up and decided he wanted to write a book on theories and techniques in counseling and psychotherapy. He thought, "Of all the classes I teach, I love teaching theories and techniques best, so I should write a textbook."

John then began using a cognitive self-instructional problem-solving strategy (see Chapter 8). He identified the problems associated with existing theories and techniques textbooks and formulated possible solutions. John decided, like any smart solution-focused therapist, that talking about problems associated with other texts was a poor use of his time (see Chapter 11). So instead he constructed a reality wherein his new textbook was greeted with instructor satisfaction, student interest, and personal fulfillment.

Because of her uncanny powers of observation (an important nonspecific factor in psychotherapy outcome—see Chapter 1), Rita noticed John's positive construction of reality and associated writing frenzy. She tried to help him deconstruct his perspective by asking, "John, what are you doing?" Upon hearing his answer, she moaned, "Are you crazy? That's a huge project. And, I might add, there are quite a few theories books out there already. Besides, I'd like to spend a little quality family time together in the coming years. After all, what is life really about, anyway?" (See Chapter 5 for help understanding this existential crisis.)

Eventually, by appealing to Rita's strong ethical standards, John got his way. Rita came to believe she could weave in her feminist and multicultural sensitivities to help this book fill an important niche in the somewhat crowded theories textbook market.

Overall, we've done our best to produce a book that's fun, interesting, interactive, practical, cutting-edge, and provocative, and that gives new life to theories of counseling and psychotherapy. Students who reviewed the manuscript especially enjoyed the bursts of innovation and creativity we tried to integrate into the text. In particular, they loved the imaginary group therapy session with many great historical and contemporary theoretical characters included at the end of Chapter 13. We hope innovation and creativity are two qualities that characterize our approach to writing this book.

WRITING STYLE AND OVERALL APPROACH

Students sometimes claim that counseling and psychotherapy theories textbooks are, in fact, an excellent treatment for insomnia. To address this issue, we tried to write this book with great enthusiasm. To help keep students awake and alert, we've incorporated basic adult learning principles and used a more informal writing style. Each chapter

- Is written in a student-friendly and engaging style
- Includes numerous interactive questions for reflection

- Integrates short pieces written by active scholars and practitioners (other than ourselves) to increase the diversity of voice and perspective

Many times we've asked ourselves, why should college and university instructors adopt this book? One way we addressed this question was to ask students and professors to review the evolving manuscript and provide suggestions. Generally, students asked that we emphasize a practical approach to learning about theories. Consequently, each chapter includes sections on how to prepare for doing therapy from a particular theoretical perspective and how to prepare clients to participate in such therapy.

In contrast, professors were more likely to suggest that we briefly and articulately describe the history and context underlying each therapeutic approach. These suggestions led us to consult a variety of historical works so we could, whenever possible, accurately paint the historical and cultural background accompanying each approach.

TEXTBOOK HIGHLIGHTS AND PEDAGOGICAL TOOLS

While we were writing this text, Rita was appointed Director of the Women's Studies Program at the University of Montana. She has since spent many long nights contemplating the true meaning of the word *pedagogy*—which caused us to integrate an exceptional array of diverse pedagogical tools into this text.

Contextual emphasis. In every chapter, we have contextualized the theories, so you get exposure to the dramatic historical influences on the thinker(s), researcher(s), and practitioner(s) who created or contributed to the theoretical orientation under discussion.

Practitioner Commentary. To increase the quality of this book and provide a broader and deeper perspective for each theory, we shamelessly bothered our friends, colleagues, and noted experts in the field—both current practitioners and academic types—for their opinions and insights into psychotherapy theory and technique. We asked them to write as if they were talking with a small group of graduate students about theories and techniques of counseling and psychotherapy. The results were everything we had hoped for. From the provocative contributions of the renowned Italian constructivist Giorgio Nardone, to the crisp and scholarly essay by Judith Beck on why she is a cognitive therapist, these practitioner commentaries educate and inspire. The full list of contributors, along with their biographical information, follows this preface.

Ethical Highlights and Multicultural Perspectives. Rather than artificially separating and compartmentalizing ethical and cultural issues and then relegating them to separate chapters, we've woven an exploration of these issues into every chapter. Our hope is to facilitate more integrated thinking about ethical and cultural issues—and perhaps stimulate a few lively class discussions along the way. Every chapter includes a "Multicultural Perspectives" section and boxed material titled "Ethical Highlights."

Putting It in Practice. To help prepare young therapists for a real world where pressure from managed mental health care requires an emphasis on practical and concrete application of theoretical principles, this text strongly emphasizes technical applications of each theory. Emphasizing techniques was one of our main goals in writing this book because we recognize that novice mental health and human service providers are expected to quickly know the pragmatics of providing treatment to clients in need. Every chapter includes boxed material titled "Putting It in Practice."

TEXTBOOK ORGANIZATION AND OVERVIEW

This text includes 13 chapters covering 12 different theories and approaches to counseling and psychotherapy.

In Chapter 1, we provide an overview and foundation for studying the great theories of therapy. The chapter includes information about the history, empirical research, and ethical principles that form a foundation for the practice of counseling and psychotherapy. Additionally, we include information on how students can explore their own personal theory and how broad social and cultural factors, including the Zeitgeist, Ortgeist, and Poltergeist, can shape and form how we think about various therapeutic approaches.

Chapters 2–13 focus on specific theoretical and therapeutic approaches. These theories and approaches include

Chapter 2: Psychoanalytic, brief analytic, object relations, and interpersonal approaches

Chapter 3: Individual psychology: the therapeutic approach of Alfred Adler

Chapter 4: Jung and the practice of analytical psychotherapy

Chapter 5: Existential theory and therapy

Chapter 6: Carl Rogers: person-centered theory and therapy

Chapter 7: Behavioral theory and therapy

Chapter 8: Cognitive theory and therapy

Chapter 9: Choice theory and the new reality therapy

Chapter 10: Feminist theory and therapy

Chapter 11: Constructivist theory and therapy

Chapter 12: Multicultural and non-Western theories

Chapter 13: Integrative theories of counseling and psychotherapy

Every text has limited scope, and this text is no exception. The first and biggest omission from our list of theories is family systems theory. To be honest, we left it out primarily because every psychology and counseling program we know has an entire course on family systems theory. Therefore, we rationalized that it might be more important to devote time to covering less commonly studied theoretical perspectives, such as Jungian and constructivist theory, both of which usually receive little specific coverage in most graduate programs. Additionally, we only obliquely address interpersonal theory and the impressive contributions of Harry Stack Sullivan within the context of psychoanalytic theory (Chapter 2) and eclectic/integrational theory (Chapter 13).

Chapters 2–13 follow, more or less, a consistent format. In addition to periodic "Questions for Reflection" and "Putting It in Practice" boxes, major chapter sections include

- An introductory statement
- Historical context and biographical information
- Theoretical principles
- A section on the practice of each theoretical approach, which includes information on self-preparation, client preparation, assessment strategies, and specific techniques

- An extended case example
- Therapy outcomes research
- Multicultural perspectives
- Ethical highlights
- Practitioner commentary
- Concluding comments
- Student review assignments
- Recommended readings and resources

THE USE OF CASE EXAMPLES

As we discuss briefly in Chapter 2, using case examples to illustrate theoretical principles and therapy techniques can be problematic. Although a well-described case is unarguably an excellent teaching tool, it is also just one case and obviously not representative or illustrative of the magnificent diversity inherent in conducting therapy with individuals.

Consequently, we decided against the format of providing a single case to represent the plurality of people and problems that therapists face in the real world. Instead, although we still use extended case examples to illustrate therapeutic procedures and process, in an effort to individualize therapy to fit specific clients and problems, we provide different case examples for each chapter. We think this approach is a better reflection of competent and ethical practice than other pedagogical alternatives.

AN EMPHASIS ON RELEVANCE

We don't really like admitting this, but as instructors, we've occasionally had graduate students sincerely confide to us that adding to their knowledge of psychotherapy theories doesn't seem very relevant in their day-to-day professional lives. "After all," they complain, "most of the theorists are dead, most of the theories seem dead, and it's hard to imagine using free association, dream analysis, Pavlovian conditioning, and other theory-derived techniques in our professional settings."

The point of studying the concepts in this book is not always direct application, although we hope application is not far away. Our hope is that you take the time to understand the history and diversity in theories of why humans suffer psychologically and what will bring about change, relief, growth, development, and even self-actualization. This book is only a small slice of that history and diversity, but we cover the majority of the theories from the turn of the century forward that have developed within Western European culture. We admittedly cover many theories you won't agree with, and many you could use more often. But trust us. It is far better to know and then reject a given approach than to have no exposure to it at all. Surveying and sampling each theory in this text will help you develop your own personal approach and theory of counseling and psychotherapy.

Speaking of sampling theories, one way to approach learning theories is a strategy that we heartily endorse called the "swallow it whole" approach. This approach requires jumping head first into each theory in each chapter. When you come to the person-centered chapter, pretend you've experienced a person-centered conversion, and then, when you move on to behavior therapy, change your persona. Use the psychological technique of being "as if" (see Chapters 3 and 11) to get into the heads and hearts of those who really believe the stuff of the theory, and then try to enact it. Pretend you are, in fact, Jean Miller Baker, or Carl Rogers, or (if you have no rules about swearing at your house) Albert Ellis. Suspend judgment and give the whole theory, or at least some key techniques, a try from the inside out. Try your best to see how you could tackle a given problem or irritation in your life through the strategies implied in the theory.

Another approach to learning theories, for the more oppositional among us, is to learn a theory well enough to convincingly and intelligently refute it. This will require knowing a number of theories, and knowing your own worldview pretty well. You can't just say "I don't believe in object relations theory and therapy because of its link to Freud, and Freud was sexist." Only undergraduates with undeclared majors can get away with this. Instead, you need to understand a theory well enough to know where it breaks down. Try this: "Behavioral theory can be used effectively to change troubling behaviors, but I find I am more existential in orientation, preferring to work from the perspective of human freedom, meaning-making, and responsibility."

LEARNING IN THE FUTURE

In our therapy work with individuals, couples, and groups as well as in our teaching, we've discovered and rediscovered the obvious truth that learning continues long after the therapeutic and teaching activities end. To facilitate continued student development into the future we've included periodic "Questions for Reflection" in each chapter and end each chapter with a series of student review assignments. These questions and review assignments are designed to promote and provoke a lingering of student thinking and interest even after the text has been set aside.

Finally, we should mention that adopting this text provides access to an on-line Instructor's Manual to assist professors in teaching their theories courses. The Instructor's Manual includes sample syllabi geared toward teaching theories from the psychology and counseling fields (including APA and CACREP-based objectives), chapter outlines, additional lecture topics, classroom activities and suggested assignments, procedures for conducting small-group oral examinations, and a test bank with multiple-choice and short-answer test items. Additionally, you may contact the authors for consultation or to provide feedback at john.sf@mso.umt.edu.

ACKNOWLEDGMENTS

Many colleagues and friends helped this book come into being. In addition to the names you'll see in the "Contributors" section, we offer our special thanks to Bernie Balleweg, Ph.D., and Marianne Spitzform, Ph.D.

Our daughters, Rylee Sommers-Flanagan and Chelsea Elander, have voluntarily (but not always quietly) allowed us to expose them to many theoretical experimentations and conversations. They've been most patient and supportive.

Our editor, Tracey Belmont, and the other professionals at John Wiley and Sons continue to be inspirational, helpful, trustworthy, and affirming.

This book would not exist if not for our many students over the years. Your laughter, your learning, and your feedback inspire us to keep on thinking, learning, and writing.

Contributors

The following mental health professionals contributed Practitioner Commentaries, Ethical Highlights, or Multicultural Perspectives to this textbook. Their written contributions greatly enhanced, deepened, and broadened this book's story of theory and therapy. Their contributions also enriched the learning process for us, and we thank them for their insight and wisdom.

Judith Beck, Ph.D., is the director of the Beck Institute for Cognitive Therapy and Research in Philadelphia and clinical associate professor of psychology in psychiatry at the University of Pennsylvania. She is the author of *Cognitive Therapy: Basics and Beyond* (Guilford Press) and the forthcoming book *Cognitive Therapy for Challenging Patients* (Guilford Press). Dr. Beck is a distinguished founding fellow and president of the Academy of Cognitive Therapy. Her Practitioner Commentary, "Why I am a Cognitive Therapist," is featured in Chapter 8 (cognitive therapy).

L. Sherilyn Cormier, Ph.D., is a professor in the Department of Counseling, Rehabilitation Counseling, and Counseling Psychology at West Virginia University. In this role she specializes in teaching and supervising master's and doctoral students. She is the author or coauthor of several textbooks related to counseling practice, including *Interviewing Strategies for Helpers* (Brooks/Cole). She does a lot of training related to clinical supervision issues. She experiences "flow" when engaging with students, supervisees, bike riding, walking, boating, and reading! Her Practitioner Commentary, "Four Cornerstones of Being a Therapist," is featured in Chapter 6 (person-centered therapy).

Suzanne Comingo Griffith, Ph.D., is professor of counseling and psychological professions at the University of Wisconsin, Superior. She publishes in the area of women's issues, especially the intersection of race, gender, and class, and actively works to improve the psychological climate. Her Practitioner Profile, "The Personal is Political," is featured in Chapter 10 (feminist therapy).

Daniel Eckstein, Ph.D., is president of Encouraging Leadership Inc. in Scottsdale, Arizona. He is also director of organization development for the Adler School of Professional psychology in Toronto and adjunct faculty in counseling psychology for Capella University in Minneapolis. Dr. Eckstein is the author of eleven books, including *Psychological Fingerprints: Lifestyle Assessment and Intervention, Leadership by Encouragement,* and *Raising Respectful Kids in a Rude World.* His web page is www.encouragingleadership.com. His Practitioner Commentary, "Encouragement and Adlerian Psychology," is featured in Chapter 3 (Adlerian therapy).

Claudette Kulkarni is a psychotherapist in private practice and at Persad Center (a mental health agency serving the "sexual minority" and HIV/AIDS communities and their families), in Pittsburgh, Pennsylvania. She is the author of *Lesbians and Lesbianisms: A Post-Jungian Perspective,* and "Radicalizing Jungian Theory" in *Contemporary Perspectives on Psychotherapy and Homosexualities.* She is a contributing editor to *The Round Table Review.* Kulkarni's Multicultural Perspective, "On Being a Lesbian Jungian," is featured in Chapter 4 (Jungian therapy).

Kurt L. Kraus, Ed.D., is an associate professor in the Department of Counseling at Shippensburg University of Pennsylvania. His professional interests include the application of existential and phenomenological perspectives to counseling, counselor education, clinical supervision, and research. Kurt likes to play outdoors. He and his family live in Carlisle, Pennsylvania. His Practitioner Commentaries, "Your Emerging Personal Theory" and "Existential Musings," are featured in Chapter 1 (an introduction) and Chapter 5 (existential therapy).

Mark Kuras, Ph.D., is a clinical psychologist and a Jungian analyst. He is on faculty at the College of Physicians and Surgeons at Columbia University Medical School and at the C.G. Jung Institute of New York. He is an associate Editor on the *Journal of Jungian Theory and Practice.* He maintains a private practice in New York City. His Practitioner Commentary, "The Jungian Dynamic Unconscious," is featured in Chapter 4 (Jungian therapy).

Ellen Hawley McWhirter, Ph.D., obtained her doctorate from Arizona State University. She is an associate professor of counseling psychology at the University of Oregon. Her teaching includes practicum and vocational counseling, and her scholarship focuses on empowerment and the vocational development of adolescents of color. She is coauthor of *Youth at Risk,* Pacific Grove, CA: Brooks/Cole. Her Practitioner Commentary, "Experience Your Theory," is featured in Chapter 1 (an introduction).

Scott T. Meier, Ph.D., is professor and codirector of training of the Program in Counseling/School Psychology, Department of Counseling, School, and Educational Psychology, State University of New York at Buffalo. Meier is the author or coauthor of four books, including *The Elements of Counseling* (Brooks/Cole), and 40 journal articles. He is a licensed psychologist who received his Ph.D. in counseling psychology from Southern Illinois University, Carbondale, in 1984. His Practitioner Commentary—"The Future (of Behavior Therapy) Is Feedback!"—is featured in Chapter 7 (behavior therapy).

Kurt D. Michael, Ph.D., is an assistant professor of psychology at Appalachian State University and is in independent practice. He was trained at the University of Colorado, Boulder; Utah State University; and Duke University Medical Center, and he holds a Ph.D. in clinical psychology. His Practitioner Commentary, "A Winding (and Serendipitous) Road to Integration," is featured in Chapter 13 (Integrative Therapy).

Professor Giorgio Nardone, Ph.D., is director of the Centro di Terapia Strategica (Center for Strategic Therapy), the only official representative for Italy of Mental Research Institute of Palo Alto, California, and director of the Postgraduate School of Brief Strategic Therapy in Arezzo. He is also professor of brief psychotherapy at the Postgraduate School of Clinical Psychology, University of Siena, Italy. With a Ph.D. in educational science from the University of Siena, he holds the title of specialist in clinical psychology at the School of Medicine, University of Siena. He has published many articles and 14 books translated in many foreign languages. His systematic and effective models for treating phobic and obsessive disorders and eating disorders are followed by many psychotherapists all around the world. Nardone's books include *The Art of Change: Strategic Therapy and Hypnotherapy Without Trance* (Jossey-Bass), *Brief Strategic Solution-Oriented Therapy of Phobic and Obsessive Disorders* (Jason Aronson), and *Brief Strategic Therapy* (Jason Aronson). His Putting It in Practice, "Applying Strategic-Constructivist Techniques to Yourself," and his Ethical Highlight, "Constructive Ethical Principles," appear in Chapter 11 (Constructive Therapy).

Brent Richardson, Ph.D., is an assistant professor in counseling at Xavier University in Cincinnati. He is the author of *Working with Challenging Youth* (Brunner/Routledge). His Ethical Highlight, "Pay Attention to What You Pay Attention To," is featured in Chapter 12 (Multicultural Theory).

Natalie Rogers, Ph.D., is a pioneer in expressive arts therapy. She is an author, artist, psychotherapist, and group facilitator. She founded the Person-Centered Expressive Therapy Institute, California, and has taken this training to Europe, Russia, Latin America, and Japan. She is author of *Emerging Woman* (1980) and *The Creative Connection: Expressive Arts as Healing* (1993). She is the daughter of the humanistic psychologist Carl Rogers. An interview of her is featured in Chapter 6 (person-centered therapy).

Felix Salomon, Ph.D., received his doctorate in clinical psychology from Long Island University, Brooklyn, New York. During the past 25 years, Dr. Salomon cofounded and was the first president of the Phoenix Psychoanalytic Study Group and chaired the Arizona State Psychological Association Ethics Committee. Currently, Dr. Salomon is in independent-private practice in Phoenix, Arizona. His Ethical Highlight, "Maintaining a Safe Container," is featured in Chapter 2 (psychoanalytic theory).

David Scherer, Ph.D. (Clinical Psychology, University of Virginia), is an associate professor of counseling and an assistant professor of psychiatry at the University of New Mexico. He is a family systems theorist and specializes in research and interventions with children, adolescents, and families. His Practitioner Commentary, "Integrational, Not Eclectic," is featured in Chapter 13 (integrative therapy).

Susan Simonds, Ph.D., has her doctorate in clinical psychology from The Fielding Institute, a master's degree in creative arts therapy from Hahnemann University, and a bachelor's degree with distinction in Chinese language and literature. She is the author of *Depression & Women: An Integrative Approach to Treatment* (Springer, 2001) and *Bridging the Silence: Nonverbal Modalities in the Treatment of Childhood Sexual Abuse* (Norton, 1994). Her Practitioner Commentary, "Finding My Own Eclectic Feminist Theory," is featured in Chapter 10 (feminist therapy).

Marianne Spitzform, Ph.D., completed her training in clinical psychoanalysis with the Colorado Center for Psychoanalytic Studies and received her doctorate in psychology from the University of Montana. She is in private practice in Missoula, Montana. Her Practitioner Commentary, "Why I Became a Psychoanalyst," is featured in Chapter 2 (psychoanalytic therapy).

Tamara J. Suttle, M. Ed., is a licensed professional counselor in Castle Rock, Colorado, specializing in the gay, lesbian, bisexual, and transsexual communities. Her services include the use of interactive drama and games as well as traditional psychotherapy with individuals, couples, and groups in a variety of settings including conferences, workshops, and retreats. Her Practitioner Commentary "Why Adlerian Theory" is featured in Chapter 3 (individual psychology).

Luis A. Vargas, Ph.D., is an associate professor and director of the clinical psychology predoctoral internship program in the Department of Psychiatry at the University of New Mexico School of Medicine. He has written many articles and several books, including *Working with Culture* (San Francisco: Jossey-Bass) and *Working with Latino Youth* (San Francisco: Jossey-Bass). His Practitioner Commentary, "Reflections of a Process-Oriented Contextualist," is featured in Chapter 13 (multicultural theory).

Robert E. Wubbolding, Ed.D., is professor emeritus at Xavier University, director of training for the William Glasser Institute, and director of the Center for Reality Therapy in Cincinnati. He has taught reality therapy from Korea to Kuwait and from Singapore to Slovenia. Over the years, he has been a high school counselor, elementary school counselor, and halfway house counselor for ex-offenders. He has authored over 125 articles and essays, 17 book chapters, and 10 books—including the most comprehensive book on reality therapy: *Reality Therapy for the 21st Century.* His Practitioner Commentary, "The Interface Between Choice Theory and Reality Therapy," is featured in Chapter 9 (reality therapy).

Kazuo Yamashita, M.S.W., is an assistant professor at Kanasai University of Social Welfare in Japan. His Multicultural Highlight, "My PCA Experience in Japan," is featured in Chapter 6 (person-centered therapy).

COUNSELING AND PSYCHOTHERAPY THEORIES IN CONTEXT AND PRACTICE

Chapter 1

INTRODUCTION TO PSYCHOTHERAPY AND COUNSELING THEORY AND TECHNIQUE

We need to do more than collect a recipe book of psychological procedures; we need to understand human suffering and how best to treat it. Neither the history of other disciplines nor that of our own suggests that applied psychology can advance rapidly as a discipline without a comprehensive worldview and theory.

—S. C. Hayes, K. D. Strosahl, and K. G. Wilson, *Acceptance and Commitment Therapy: An Experiential Approach to Behavior Change* (1999)

Leave your theory, as Joseph his coat in the hand of the harlot, and flee.

—Ralph Waldo Emerson

My first act of free will shall be to believe in free will. . . .

—William James

A theory is not built on observation. In fact, the opposite is true. What we observe follows from our theory.

—Albert Einstein

IN THIS CHAPTER YOU WILL LEARN

- The historical context and origins of counseling and psychotherapy
- Different ways of defining counseling and psychotherapy
- The definition of a theory
- About the evaluation and effectiveness of modern therapy
- Essential ingredients and common factors associated with therapy effectiveness
- Essential ethical issues for therapists
- How to develop your own personal theory
- A quick review of the theories covered in this book
- About the authors' biases
- The influence of the Zeitgeist, Ortgeist, and Poltergeist on counseling and psychotherapy

Theories are essentially a set of speculations that seem to explain empirical facts. A sound and accurate psychological theory should give a practitioner confidence in what he is doing and why he is doing it. A good theory of human behavior should generate more effective methods of treatment. Yet many psychological theories, like most religious taboos, prevent practitioners from engaging in helpful activities.

—Arnold Lazarus, *Behavior Therapy and Beyond*

BACKGROUND AND OVERVIEW

The drama imbedded in theories of human pain, suffering, change, and development rivals anything Hollywood has to offer. These theories are revealed in great literature, in myth, in religion, and in our dominant political and social systems. They directly influence the ways we treat each other, including our definitions of mental health and mental illness, as well as our ideas about helping, rehabilitation, and even culpability for distress. What makes people tick? What messes up their minds, lowers their productivity, destroys their fragile relationships? What makes or breaks an individual? What causes one person to live a simple and cheerful life, while another claws his or her way ruthlessly to the top? What makes some people come out stronger after facing tragedy or hardship, while others are weakened or destroyed?

If you've come this far in your studies of psychology and counseling, you know there's no single answer to these questions. It's commonplace for mental health professionals to strongly disagree with each other on just about every topic under the sun. Therefore, it should be no surprise that this book—a book about the major theories and techniques of psychotherapy and counseling—will contain stunning controversies and conflict. This book itself may be controversial. Often, there are vast disagreements among individuals claiming to believe in the same theory. In the following pages, we'll do our best to bring you more than just the basic theories about how humans change; we'll also bring you some of the excitement associated with the history and practice of these theories and techniques of human motivation, functioning, and change.

HISTORICAL CONTEXT

Every human practice or set of beliefs has its own particular historical context. This is also the case for psychotherapy and its close relatives: counseling, therapy, and general mental health consultation. Unfortunately, history is an imperfect, subjective account of the past. As the old African proverb states, "Until lions have their historians, all tales of hunting will glorify the hunter" (quoted in Tallman & Bohart, 1999, p. 91).

Modern psychology originated in Western Europe and the United States in the late 1800s. During that time, women and other minorities were generally excluded from higher education. Consequently, much of the history of psychotherapy is written from the perspective of privileged white men advocating a particular theory (usually while trashing someone else's). This tendency, so dominant in psychology over the years, led, as recently as the 1980s, to the sarcastic comment "In psychology, even the rats are white and male."

Despite the limitations of historical analysis, we begin our exploration of contemporary theories and techniques of counseling and psychotherapy with a look back in time to the possible origins of psychotherapy and related professional activities.

The Father of Psychotherapy?

Many theories books make the metaphoric claim that Sigmund Freud is the father of modern psychotherapy. Although there is truth to this claim, it's impossible to give a single individual the credit—or blame—for an enterprise as huge as psychotherapy.

If it were possible to bestow such a title, Freud would be a leading candidate. But Freud had professional forebears as well. For example, back in the late 1890s, the Frenchman Pierre Janet claimed that some of Freud's early work was not original but, instead, supported his (Janet's) previous findings:

> We are glad to find that several authors, particularly M. M. Breuer and Freud, have recently verified our interpretation *already somewhat old*, of subconscious fixed ideas with hystericals. (Janet, 1894/1901, p. 290, italics added, quoted in Bowers & Meichenbaum, 1984)

Clearly, as we can see from this and other information, Pierre Janet believed *he* was developing a new theory about human functioning, a theory that Freud was simply helping to validate. Not surprisingly, Janet had conflicts with Freud, and he wasn't alone. Freud's interest in inner conflict was outpaced perhaps only by his tendency toward external, interpersonal conflict. With regard to the conflict between Janet and Freud, Bowers and Meichenbaum (1984) state: "It is clear from their writings that Freud and Janet had a barely concealed mutual animosity, though each, at times, paid respect to the work of the other" (p. 11).

Legitimate questions remain regarding who, in the late nineteenth century, initially began the work leading to the development of the psychotherapy and counseling movements in Western Europe and, later, the United States. Further, it is inappropriate to attribute the origins of either the theories or practices of counseling and psychotherapy exclusively to Western European men. Some certainly played important roles in naming and furthering various theories of psychopathology and psychotherapy, but it's unlikely that any theory exists that doesn't draw many truths and tenets from earlier human practices and beliefs.

Bankart (1997) articulates this point about historic discovery:

> My best friend has a bumper sticker on his truck that reads, "Indians Discovered Columbus." Let's heed the warning. Nineteenth-century European physicians no more discovered the unconscious than John Rogers Clark "discovered" Indiana. Indeed, a stronger argument could be made for the reverse, as the bumper sticker states so elegantly. (p. 21)

In thinking about Bankart's comment, we're struck by the possibility that Freud, Breuer, and Janet may have been "discovered" by this interesting entity, the human unconscious. Of all the theorists discussed in this book, we think Carl Jung would most appreciate the concept of an active unconscious seeking to discover humans (see Chapter 4).

Alternative Historical-Cultural Realities: Three Perspectives

The history of counseling and psychotherapy is neither one-dimensional nor linear. There are many examples of psychotherapy and counseling that precede Janet and Freud, although these practices may not have been so named. For the most part, early treatments for human distress and disturbance consisted of a combination of medical-biological, spiritual, and psychosocial procedures. As you'll discover as you read through the various theories, there is a tendency for old explanations and treatments of mental disturbance and distress to be discovered, rediscovered, and recycled through the ages. Sometimes the same treatment technique has even been rediscovered and implemented based on an alternative theory of therapy.

The Biomedical Perspective

One rather extreme example of this recycling and rediscovery involves trephining and lobotomies. Early archeological finds of Stone Age cave dwellers provide evidence of a treatment procedure now called trephining. This procedure involved using a stone tool to chip away at a human skull until a circular opening was established. It is believed, in the absence of written documentation, that this opening was created by a shaman or medicine man, to release an evil spirit from the afflicted individual's brain. Evidence indicates that some patients survived this crude procedure, living for many years afterward (Selling, 1943).

Only about half a million years later, a similar procedure, the prefrontal lobotomy, emerged as a popular treatment for the mentally disturbed in the United States. This medical procedure was hailed as a great step forward in the treatment of mental disorders. It was described in *Time* magazine in 1942:

> After drilling a small hole in the temple on each side of the skull, the surgeon then inserts a dull knife into the brain, makes a fan-shaped incision through the prefrontal lobe, then downward a few minutes later. He then repeats the incision on the other side of the brain. . . . (p. 42, as cited in Dawes, 1994, p. 48)

Although neither lobotomies nor trephining is currently in vogue, scientists and practitioners are still trying to find effective ways to intervene directly in brain functioning. Electroshock therapy and various drugs designed to change the function and balance of neurotransmitters are commonly advocated for various forms of human mental distress. It's clear that for a very long time humans have understood that changing the functioning or structure of the brain will change thinking patterns, mood, and behavior. The biological perspective is an important area for research and treatment. Although the responsible therapist keeps abreast of developments in this area, the focus of this text is on nonbiological explanations for human behavior and on non–biologically based interventions.

The Religious/Spiritual Perspective

The clergy, shamans, mystics, monks, elders, and other religious and spiritual leaders have been sought for advice and counsel over the centuries. It was reported that Hild of Whitby (an abbess of a double monastery in the seventh century) possessed prudence of such magnitude that not only ordinary folk, but even kings and princes, would come to ask her advice about their difficulties (Petroff, 1986). For many Native American tribes, spiritual authority and spiritual practices still hold as much or more salience for healing than do most forms of counseling or psychotherapy (D. Wetsit, personal communication December 17, 2001). The same holds true for many native or indigenous people, as well as those of Western European descent who have strongly held religious commitments. Many Asian and African cultures also believe that spiritual concerns and practices are intricately related to psychological matters.

We readily acknowledge the healing potential in spiritual practices and beliefs. Religious and spiritual leaders often have great wisdom, compassion, and insight into the human condition. Some theories we'll cover in this text are more open than others to inclusion of the spiritual dimensions of humanity. However, once again, we won't directly address spiritual practices in the context of the dominant theories of psychotherapy, except in Chapter 12.

Any therapist worth his or her salt will take into account a client's biological condition and spiritual beliefs and concerns when providing treatment. Of course, therapists will vary in the relative weight they give to these dimensions. But the task at hand is to understand the theories of psychotherapy and counseling that draw primarily from the psychosocial perspective.

The Psychosocial Perspective

Just as trephining dates back about 500,000 years, humans have probably also understood, from a time prior to recorded history, that verbal interactions and relationship alterations can change thinking patterns, mood, and behavior. At the very least, we know that for centuries wise healers from many cultures and traditions used psychological and relational techniques that, upon close inspection, look very familiar to current theoretically driven strategies for helping people with psychological change and healing. Typical examples include Siddhartha Gautama (563–483 B.C.), better known as the Buddha and the Roman philosopher Epictetus (50–138 A.D.), both of whom are considered forebears to contemporary cognitive theory and therapy.

A less cited example, from the tenth and eleventh centuries, is Avicenna (980–1037 A.D.), a great figure in Islamic medicine. The following case description illustrates Avicenna's rather modern, albeit unorthodox, approach to treating mental and emotional disorders:

> A certain prince . . . was afflicted with melancholia, and suffered from the delusion that he was a cow . . . he would low like a cow, causing annoyance to everyone, crying "Kill me so that a good stew may be made of my flesh," [and] . . . he would eat nothing. . . . Avicenna was persuaded to take the case. . . . First of all he sent a message to the patient bidding him be of good cheer because the butcher was coming to slaughter him. Whereas . . . the sick man rejoiced. Some time afterwards, Avicenna, holding a knife in his hand, entered the sickroom saying, "Where is this cow that I may kill it?" The patient lowed like a cow to indicate where he was. By Avicenna's orders he was laid on the ground bound hand and foot. Avicenna then felt him all over and said, "He is too lean, and not ready to be killed; he must be fattened." Then they offered him suitable food of which he now partook eagerly, and gradually he gained strength, got rid of his delusion, and was completely cured. (Browne, 1921, pp. 88–89)

Based on this description, Avicenna might well be considered one of the very first individuals to practice strategic or constructivist therapy (see Chapter 11).

DEFINITIONS OF COUNSELING AND PSYCHOTHERAPY

Over the years, many students have asked us questions similar to the following: "I love working with people and so I want to do counseling. Should I get a Ph.D. in psychology, a master's degree in counseling, or a master's in social work?"

This question usually brings forth a lengthy response from us, during which we not only explain the differences between the various degrees, but also discuss additional career information pertaining to the Psy.D. degree, psychiatry, school counseling and psychology, and psychiatric nursing. Generally, this discussion leads to the confusing topic of the differences between counseling and psychotherapy. If time permits during these discussions, we also like to throw in some of our thoughts about the meaning of life.

Sorting out the differences between mental health professional groups can be difficult. When responding to the question "In relation to being a successful therapist, what are the differences between psychiatrists, social workers, and psychologists?" Jay Haley wrote: "Except for ideology, salary, status, and power the differences are irrelevant" (Haley, 1977). This response accurately captures the fact that each of these professional tracks, including professional counseling, despite differences in ideology, salary, status, and power, can produce exceptionally successful therapists.

In this section we explore three confusing and sometimes conflict-ridden questions: What is psychotherapy? What is counseling? And what are the differences between the two?

What Is Psychotherapy?

Anna O., an early psychoanalytic patient of Breuer, referred to the treatment she received as "the talking cure." This is an elegant, albeit vague description of psychotherapy. Technically, it tells us very little, but at the intuitive level, it embraces a great deal of the definition. Anna O. is proclaiming something that most people readily admit: That is, talking, expressing, verbalizing, or somehow sharing one's pain is, in and of itself, potentially healing. Of course, this definition does not and should not satisfy contemporary psychotherapy researchers, but it does provide an historic and foundational frame to consider.

There are many other definitions of this thing we call psychotherapy. According to the Random House dictionary, the definition is simply "The treatment of psychological disorders or maladjustments by a professional technique, as psychoanalysis, group therapy, or behavior therapy" (1993, p. 1561). In contrast, the definition of counseling reads, "Professional guidance in resolving personal conflicts and emotional problems" (Random House unabridged dictionary, 1993, p. 460).

Taken alone, or even in combination, Anna O.'s and Webster's definitions of psychotherapy are inadequate for the purposes of this textbook. In the following paragraphs, we'll try to improve upon these efforts. However, before moving on, we should pause and reflect on the opening statement made by Corsini and Wedding, in the introduction of their 600-plus-page sixth edition of "Current Psychotherapies." They state: "Psychotherapy cannot be defined with any precision" (Corsini & Wedding, 2000).

Despite Cornsini and Wedding's rather pessimistic view, we have a number of favorite definitions of psychotherapy, some of which are imprecise, but others that nearly reach the standard of scientific precision.

1. "A conversation with a therapeutic purpose" (Korchin, 1976)
2. "The purchase of friendship" (Schofield, 1964)
3. "[A] situation in which two people interact and try to come to an understanding of one another, with the specific goal of accomplishing something beneficial for the complaining person" (Bruch, 1981)
4. "When one person with an emotional disorder gets help from another person who has less of an emotional disorder" (J. Watkins, personal communication, October 13, 1983)

5. "Psychological treatment of emotional problems in which a trained person deliberately establishes a professional relationship with the patient in order to: (a) remove or modify or retard existing symptoms; (b) mediate disturbed patterns of behavior; (c) promote positive personality growth and development" (Wolberg, 1995)

What Is Counseling?

In some settings, an evaluative or judgmental distinction is made between the practice of counseling and psychotherapy. In fact, Alfred Adler, whom we'll get to know much more intimately in Chapter 3, might claim that counseling has an inferiority complex with respect to its slightly older sibling, psychotherapy (Adler, 1958). Or, perhaps more accurately, it could be claimed that psychotherapy has a superiority complex with respect to its younger rival, counseling. Either way, at some point you may notice or experience a judgmental-sounding side to the distinction between psychotherapy and counseling.

Overall, counselors have struggled with the definition of their craft in ways similar to psychotherapists. Consider, for example, this quotation:

> Counseling is indeed an ambiguous enterprise. It is done by persons who can't agree on what to call themselves, what credentials are necessary to practice, or even what the best way is to practice—whether to deal with feelings, thoughts, or behaviors; whether to be primarily supportive or confrontational; whether to focus on the past or the present. Further, the consumers of counseling services can't exactly articulate what their concerns are, what counseling can and can't do for them, or what they want when it's over. (Kottler & Brown, 1996)

As with the term *psychotherapy*, a good definition of *counseling* is hard to find. Here is a sampling of counseling definitions:

1. "Counseling is the artful application of scientifically derived psychological knowledge and techniques for the purpose of changing human behavior" (Burke, 1989).
2. "Counseling is a helping relationship that includes someone seeking help and someone willing to give help who is trained to help in a setting that permits help to be given and received" (Cormier & Hackney, 1987).
3. "Counseling consists of whatever ethical activities a counselor undertakes in an effort to help the client engage in those types of behavior that will lead to a resolution of the client's problems" (Krumboltz, 1965).
4. "[Counseling is] an activity . . . for working with relatively normal-functioning individuals who are experiencing developmental or adjustment problems" (Kottler & Brown, 1996).

With both lists of definitions in mind, we turn now to the question of the differences between counseling and psychotherapy.

What Are the Differences between Psychotherapy and Counseling?

Patterson (1973) has answered this question directly by claiming: "There are no essential differences between counseling and psychotherapy." Of course, Patterson's comment could be taken to mean that although there are no essential differences between counseling and psychotherapy, there are *unessential* differences.

> On this issue, we find ourselves in step with Corsini and Wedding (2000): Counseling and psychotherapy are the same qualitatively; they differ only quantitatively; there is nothing that a psychotherapist does that a counselor does not do. (p. 2)

Both counselors and psychotherapists engage in the same behaviors—listening, questioning, interpreting, explaining, advising, and so on. However, often they do so in different proportions.

Generally, psychotherapists are less directive, go a little deeper, work a little longer with individual cases, and charge a higher fee. In contrast, counselors are slightly more directive, work more on developmentally normal—but troubling—issues, work more overtly at the surface, work more briefly with individual clients, and charge a bit less for their services. Of course, in the case of individual counselors and psychotherapists, each of these rules may be reversed, because, for example, some counselors may choose to work longer with clients and charge more, whereas some psychotherapists may choose to work more briefly with clients and charge less. Additionally, although it used to be the case that counselors worked with less disturbed clients and that psychotherapists worked with more disturbed patients, now, perhaps because obtaining services from master's-level counselors or social workers is generally less expensive, counselors often work more than psychotherapists with clients who have extensive personal and family problems.

Questions for Reflection

What are your thoughts on the differences and similarities of counseling and psychotherapy? In your community and at your university are counseling and psychotherapy considered with equal (or unequal) reverence? Go back and review the nine different definitions of counseling and psychotherapy we have given. Which definition did you find most appealing? Which one did you find least appealing? Before proceeding, list what you consider to be the most important parts of a comprehensive definition of counseling and psychotherapy.

A Working Definition of Counseling and Psychotherapy

At the very least, there are strong similarities between the practice of counseling and psychotherapy. At the most, they may be considered virtually identical procedures. Because the similarities vastly outweigh the differences, for the purposes of this book, we will use the words *counseling* and *psychotherapy* interchangeably. And sometimes we will insert the word *therapy* as a third, perhaps less divisive, alternative.

After you review the various definitions for counseling and psychotherapy, we wish we could provide you with an exact, elegant, formulaic definition for these terms, or the activity they represent. However, the best we can offer is a working definition based, more or less, on a compilation of the preceding definitions.

For the purposes of this text, we define counseling and psychotherapy as a process that involves

*a trained person who practices the artful application of scientifically derived principles for es-
tablishing professional helping relationships with persons who seek assistance in resolving
large or small psychological or relational problems. This is accomplished through ethically
defined means and involves, in the broadest sense, some form of learning or human development.*

It's also important to distinguish between the concepts of *therapy* and *therapeutic.* A
therapist in Syracuse, New York, locally renowned for his work with other therapists,
told us that he believed life itself was therapeutic (J. Land, personal communication,
March 16, 1986). We've all had therapeutic experiences with a friend, spouse, or relative. However, by our definition, these experiences would not qualify as therapy. Therapy entails a relationship established for a specific purpose, protected by both a professional knowledge-base and a set of ethical principles. Further, our definition, as well
as most definitions of therapy, does not fit any self-administered forms of therapy, such
as self-analysis or self-hypnosis.

WHAT IS A THEORY?

As long as we're making our way through elusive definitions, we may as well attempt to
define the word *theory.* A theory is defined as "a coherent group of general propositions
used as principles of explanation for a class of phenomena" (Random House unabridged dictionary, 1993, p. 1967).

Basically, a theory involves a gathering together and organizing of knowledge about
a particular object or phenomenon. In psychology, theories are used to generate hypotheses about human thinking, emotions, and behavior. Most of us, as a function of
being the social creatures that we are, build our own personalized theories about human behavior. These personal theories guide the ways in which we observe and evaluate others. This makes all of us theorists (or potential theorists) even though our thinking is not as explicit (or as detailed—or perhaps as tedious) as that of most famous
psychological theorists.

Within the context of psychotherapy and counseling, a theory needs to accurately
describe, explain, and predict a wide range of therapist and client behaviors. A theory
also needs to have relevance to its domain. For example, a good theory should clearly
explain what causes client problems (or psychopathology) and offer ideas or specific
strategies for how to alleviate these problems. Additionally, a good theory will help us
predict client responses to various therapy techniques. Specifically, these predictions
should help us know what techniques to use, how long therapy normally will last, and
how a particular technique is likely to affect a particular client.

Despite their strong eclectic or integrational orientation, Prochaska and Norcross
(2003) describe the importance of psychological theory for the practice of psychotherapy and counseling:

> Without a guiding theory . . . , clinicians would be vulnerable, directionless creatures
> bombarded with literally hundreds of impressions and pieces of information in a single
> session. Is it more important to ask about color preferences, early memories, parent rela-
> tionships, life's meaning, disturbing emotions, environmental reinforcers, thought pro-
> cesses, sexual conflicts, or something else in the first interview? (Prochaska & Norcross,
> 2003, pp. 5–6)

One of the greatest tasks of a theory is to provide therapists with a clear model or foundation from which they can conduct their professional service. To be without a theory, to be a "vulnerable, directionless creature," is something most of us would just as soon avoid.

Some psychological theorists believe their particular theory can and should be used to predict and control human behavior (Skinner, 1971). This is a fear Hollywood capitalizes on occasionally, with films such as *A Clockwork Orange.* There is no doubt that to some degree this is a goal of many theories. However, as British psychologist David Smail writes, we should be concerned when prediction and control become the goal of psychological theory:

> [T]he prediction and control of human behavior is, as an aim of human inquiry, no new phenomenon: it expresses an intellectual aspiration as old as magic, and restates a practical interest dear to the hearts of tyrants ever since time began. (Smail, 1984, p. 47)

Although Smail's concerns are important to consider, most theories in this book were primarily derived to explain and address suffering and to facilitate human healing, growth and development.

Questions for Reflection

As you read through this text, we will regularly remind you to step back and evaluate whatever theory we are currently discussing. In each chapter, be sure to ask yourself how well the theory assists you in understanding and helping clients through and beyond their personal problems. In addition, consistently try to ask critical questions about the theories. As Smail might ask, "How does each theory potentially tyrannize clients?"

MODERN THERAPY: DOES IT WORK?

In 1952, Hans Eysenck published a bold and controversial article titled "The Effects of Psychotherapy: An Evaluation." In the article, he claimed that after over 50 years of therapy, research, and practice no evidence existed attesting to its beneficial effects. He stated that "roughly 2/3 of a group of neurotic patients will recover or improve to a marked extent within about two years of the onset of their illness [in the absence of treatment]" (Eysenck, 1952, p. 322). Further, he compared this natural recovery rate with rates produced by traditional psychotherapy and reported that

> patients treated by means of psychoanalysis improved to the extent of 44%; patients treated eclectically improved to the extent of 64%; patients treated only custodially or by general practitioners improved to the extent of 72%. There thus appears to be an inverse correlation between recovery and psychotherapy. (p. 322)

As you can imagine, Eysenck's article created significant defensiveness among psychotherapy researchers and practitioners. Supporters of psychotherapy complained that Eysenck's conclusions were based on poorly controlled studies; they clamored that he didn't address severity of diagnosis issues; and they moaned that the measures of improvement used in the studies he reviewed were generally poor and crude. Overall, Eysenck's critics were correct—his review was indeed flawed. Of course, a primary reason for this was because so many of the existing studies of counseling and psychotherapy effectiveness were also flawed. The truth is, despite the fact that psychotherapy researchers and practitioners in the 1950s believed psychotherapy was more effective than no treatment, they had not adequately gathered scientific evidence to support their beliefs.

A Celebration of Effectiveness

Despite the outrage raised by Eysenck's article, it's easy to see in retrospect that he provided the entire field of psychotherapy with a much-needed reality check. In response, counseling and psychotherapy research began to flourish. More studies were conducted and better outcome measures were developed. Hubble, Duncan, and Miller (1999) recently reflected on the progress in psychotherapy research with undaunted optimism and confidence:

> The uncertainties loosed on the clinical and counseling disciplines by Eysenck and like-minded critics have now been set aside. Therapy works. . . . More than 40 years of outcome research make clear that therapists are not witch doctors, snake oil peddlers, or over-achieving do-gooders. . . . Study after study, meta-analyses, and scholarly reviews have legitimized psychologically based or informed interventions. Regarding at least its general efficacy, few believe that therapy need be put to the test any longer. (1999, pp. 1–2)

Hubble and associates are not alone in their positive evaluation of therapy. The scientific literature is replete with statements extolling therapy's virtues. Just to give you a broader sense of these views, we provide additional published comments on therapy effectiveness:

- "It was established in the 1980s that counseling and psychotherapy are remarkably efficacious" (Ahn & Wampold, 2001, p. 251).
- "'Do people have fewer symptoms and a better life after therapy than they did before?' This is the question that the CR [Consumer Reports] study answers with a clear 'yes'" (Seligman, 1995, p. 973).
- "Spanning six decades, reviews of psychotherapy outcome research document the empirical evidence supporting the effectiveness of psychotherapy" (Asay & Lambert, 1999, p. 23).

Obviously, the prevailing view among mainstream researchers and practitioners is that therapy is a potent and positive process that consistently contributes to the recovery of clients who engage in treatment. Nonetheless, there are dissenters.

Is Psychotherapy Harmful?

Despite apparent statistical evidence, several therapy critics make strong arguments against its efficacy. These arguments are both philosophical and empirical. In his critique of therapy, Jeffrey Masson (1988) presents his philosophical argument against therapy:

Although I criticize many individual therapists and therapies, my main objective is to point out that the very *idea* of psychotherapy is wrong. The structure of psychotherapy is such that no matter how kindly a person is, when that person becomes a therapist, he or she is engaged in acts that are bound to diminish the dignity, autonomy, and freedom of the person who comes for help. (p. ix)

Masson believes that counseling or psychotherapy, in any form, constitutes an oppressive process. It is oppressive because the imbalance of power between therapist and client gives therapists the authority to judge—and sometimes even condemn—their clients' thoughts, behaviors, and feelings as unacceptable. He states:

[W]hen somebody who has been stigmatized as "mentally ill" staunchly maintains his or her own vision in the face of social disapproval, this courage is considered by therapists as further proof of the illness. Psychotherapy is still a living legacy to its forebear: a confining institution. (Masson, 1988, p. 9)

These are powerful accusations. Although it would be easy and comforting to those of us who practice therapy to blithely dismiss his perspective, we believe it's crucial to acknowledge and explore Masson's position and the possibility that therapy may be— at least sometimes, and perhaps unintentionally—a destructive force in the lives of clients. We encourage you to read more complete critiques of counseling, psychotherapy, and diagnosis (see Recommended Readings and Resources at the end of this chapter). Moreover, Masson's philosophical opposition to therapy is not the only existing argument that therapy can be harmful to clients (see Putting It in Practice 1.1: Psychotherapy and Sexual Abuse).

Questions for Reflection

On the one hand, psychotherapy researchers are celebrating the effectiveness of therapy. On the other hand, Masson is claiming that therapy—as a discipline— is fatally flawed. Consider both perspectives. Which perspective do you find more convincing? Could psychotherapy research findings and Masson's view both be valid at the same time?

Are Psychotherapy Researchers and Practitioners Objective?

There are many angles to consider before you wholeheartedly join in celebrating the effectiveness of counseling and psychotherapy. Consider this: Could the scientists who research therapy efficacy and effectiveness be influencing the results of their studies due to their positive bias toward or belief in therapy effectiveness? Who determines the operational definitions of therapy success? For what reasons was the study conducted? Is it possible to quantify human distress, create a control group, and then quantify relief or healing? The difficulties of meaningful therapy outcome research, and the ongoing possibility of researcher bias should always be taken seriously.

Although the preponderance of scientific evidence supports the likelihood that therapy is more effective than no treatment, we encourage you to watch for potential flaws in the scientific research and in the research paradigm. As noted by Messer and Wachtel (1997), "the criteria employed in . . . research are covertly value laden, reflecting definitions of therapeutic success more congenial to some approaches than others" (p. 22). The fact is that scientific research is a reductionistic process, one that often leaves out the measurement of many important variables because they're impossible to fit within the currently popular research paradigm. Each theory chapter in this text will have a section summarizing what we know about its efficacy. You'll notice that the more straightforward theories have more outcome research than the richer, more complex theories. This is especially true if the theory limits itself to addressing a narrow, more easily defined set of human problems. We will revisit this issue and the issue of empirically supported or validated treatments throughout this text.

WHAT HELPS CLIENTS: COMMON FACTORS OR SPECIFIC TECHNIQUES?

Now that we've explored the more radical arguments that therapy is a damaging process and that all therapy research may be too biased to provide objective information, we can turn to a more central contemporary argument in the research literature. Namely, what are the active ingredients in therapy that help clients recover?

Specific Techniques

The question of the potency of specific techniques was addressed in the 1970s and 1980s, when researchers began claiming that distressed individuals who receive therapy are consistently better off than those who do not receive therapy (Lambert & Bergin, 1994). In particular, in 1977, Mary Smith and Gene Glass developed a new statistical method for evaluating the efficacy of therapy. Their approach, meta-analysis, pools together and obtains an overall average effect size obtained from outcome measures across a diverse range of therapy research studies. Smith and Glass published their landmark review, titled, "Meta-analysis of psychotherapy outcome studies." In this study, Smith and Glass evaluated 375 outcome studies and reported that the average outcome study "showed a .68 standard deviation superiority of the treated group over the control group" (Smith & Glass, 1977, p. 756). At that time, they concluded that the average client treated with psychotherapy was better off than 75% of clients who received no treatment. Later, upon expanding their study to 475 outcome studies and publishing the results in a book, they concluded that the average treated person was better off than 80% of the untreated sample (Smith, Glass, & Miller, 1980).

Not surprisingly, the work of Smith and her colleagues didn't clear up one of the biggest debates in therapy research. That is, they found that different therapist theoretical orientation and different techniques did not produce different results.

This finding, which is consistent with previous and later research, has led many researchers to what has been dubbed "the Dodo bird effect," named after the Dodo bird in Alice's Wonderland who cheerfully proclaims, "Everybody has won and all must have prizes" (Luborsky, Singer, & Luborsky, 1975).

Adherents to particular theoretical orientations are, to put it mildly, sometimes reluctant to concede that all forms of therapy produce relatively equivalent results. For example, despite the research, behaviorists continue to believe behavior therapy is superior, cognitive therapists cite evidence of the power of their approach, psychoanalytic or psychodynamic therapists contend their approach is superior, and solution-oriented therapists scoff at the entire group for spending far too much time and energy arguing and focusing on problems when there are solutions just waiting to be discovered around virtually every corner.

As the debate over which theories and techniques are most effective for different problems and different clients has raged, another school of thought among therapy researchers and practitioners has emerged (Frank, 1961, 1973; Frank & Frank, 1991). This perspective de-emphasizes the importance of specific therapy techniques, pointing instead to several common therapeutic factors associated with all therapy approaches as the best explanation for why most research studies indicate that different approaches to therapy are generally equivalent in efficacy.

Common Therapeutic Factors

What causes therapeutic change? In the 1870s, Anton Mesmer, then famous for "mesmerizing" or hypnotizing patients would have claimed that his method—which involved purple robes, rods of iron, and magnetic baths—produced therapeutic change due to shifting magnetic fields or "animal magnetism." More recently, psychoanalysts would emphasize the merits of insight, the behaviorists, classical or operant conditioning, and Carl Rogers, "a certain type of relationship."

Lambert (1992) conducted an empirical analysis of common therapy factors. In his review, he identified the following four common factors and estimated how much each factor typically accounts for therapeutic change (Lambert, 1992).

- Extratherapeutic change (40%)
- Therapeutic relationship (30%)
- Expectancy (placebo effects; 15%)
- Techniques (15%)

Extratherapeutic Change

Lambert (1992) defines extratherapeutic change variables broadly. They include client factors such as severity of disturbance, motivation, capacity to relate to others (and the therapist), ego strength, psychological-mindedness, and the ability to identify a single problem to work on in counseling, as well as "sources of help and support within their environments" (Asay & Lambert, 1999, p. 33). For example, many clients who experience spontaneous remission (sudden improvement without therapy) do so because of positive support from important people in their lives. Lambert contends that extratherapeutic change factors account for about 40% of what causes clients to succeed in therapy.

Therapeutic Relationship

There are two main ways that the therapeutic relationship seems to generate positive therapy results. First, as Rogers (1942a) posited, when therapists are able to connect with clients using the core conditions of unconditional positive regard, empathy, and congruence, positive therapeutic outcomes are facilitated (see Chapter 6). These conditions can also be viewed as therapist attitudes that are perceived as helpful by clients. Second, as Freud originally formulated, the therapeutic alliance, characterized by an attachment between therapist and client based on working together, also seems to be a relationship ingredient that fosters client improvement. This alliance or bond between therapist and client has been identified as an important therapeutic component in many studies (Gaston, 1990). Lambert estimates that therapeutic relationship factors account for about 30% of the variation in therapy outcomes.

Expectancy

Frank (1961) originally defined this therapeutic variable as hope. Essentially, vastly different procedures can all be viewed as including positive expectation or hope as an active therapeutic ingredient. Obviously, as a potential positive change factor, hope is complex and can be used and abused. Interestingly, controlled research studies indicate that clients treated with placebos (an inert substance without any inherent therapeutic value) are better off than 66% of clients who receive no treatment. Lambert estimates that expectation, hope, and placebo factors account for 15% of the variation in therapy outcomes.

Techniques

Asay and Lambert (1999) point out that many studies minimize the importance of theories and techniques as an important active therapy ingredient:

> For those convinced of the singular abilities of their models [theories] and related interventions, the results have been disappointing. Overall, in the many comparative studies completed to date, little evidence to suggest the superiority of one school or technique over another has been obtained. (p. 39)

This is not to say that technique is unimportant to therapeutic success. In fact, most therapy research involves comparative studies—studies that pit one therapy approach and set of techniques against another. Consequently, although it's definitely difficult to show different efficacy rates based on different techniques, doing counseling or psychotherapy without a theoretical model and techniques is difficult to imagine. Overall, Lambert estimates that 15% of treatment outcomes variation is due to the specific techniques employed.

Techniques or Common Factors? The Wrong Question

Empirical research would suggest that a common factors model provides a better explanation for treatment success than specific treatment models. If so, perhaps we should abandon the study of theory and technique and focus instead on teaching students how best to employ the common factors to enhance therapeutic outcomes. Although a case might be made for doing just that, before you toss out this book in favor of a common factors approach, consider this: At this point, it's impossible to separate common factors from the various theoretical approaches. Each theoretical approach includes within it all of the therapy-related common factors. Therefore, having a reasonable theory and using it faithfully is one of the best ways for you to (1) develop a positive working relationship, (2) create expectancy or placebo effects, and (3) have a fistful of techniques to use with your clients.

Quite simply, it's hard for us to imagine doing therapy without theory and technique. As Frank (1973) noted, it's crucial for therapy to include a "myth" or rationale.

> [A]ll psychotherapies are based on a rationale or myth which includes an explanation of illness and health, deviancy, and normality. If the rationale is to combat the patient's demoralization, it must obviously imply an optimistic philosophy of human nature. This is

clearly true of the rationales underlying most American psychotherapies, which assume that aggression, cruelty, and other unattractive forms of human behavior result from past hurts and frustrations. (p. 327)

Even the most basic technique of role induction (that is, informing the client about how a particular therapy model works) implies that you have a procedure or rationale to tell the client about. Imagine, for a moment, the common factors therapist who provides her client the following role induction at the beginning of therapy:

"The counseling I offer is based on extensive empirical research. About 40% of your cure will come directly from you. If you're motivated, your problems aren't too big, and you've cultivated some helpful friends and family, then we're in good shape. Another 30% of your cure comes from us developing a positive therapeutic relationship . . . so let's work together and try to like each other. Then, the other 30% of your cure is equally based on how well I can get you to have hope that this procedure will help you and on the particular counseling techniques I'll be using. Does that make sense to you? Okay, good. So I think the best place for us to start is by getting right to work on establishing a positive therapeutic alliance. Is that okay with you?"

The preceding therapy scenario is like trying to make a meal out of ketchup, chutney, salsa, mayonnaise, garlic, mustard, basil, onions, and pickle relish. Generally speaking, although condiments, herbs, and garnishes are fine, they work much better if you have something to put them on.

Questions for Reflection

Now that you've seen the scientific review of four main common factors, reflect on your personal view of what helps people benefit from therapy. Which of the four common factors do you personally think is most important? Do you agree with our point about common factors approaches to therapy being similar to condiments without content? Do you think you need to have a theory to have a technique, or is it possible to employ a technique without having an underlying theory?

ETHICAL ESSENTIALS

And now, here's some unsettling news. The act of reading this book and pursuing your studies will contribute to your loss of innocence. For example, in many states, "Good Samaritan" laws allow untrained bystanders who witness an accident to try to help without fear of being sued for doing something wrong. But these laws don't extend to trained medical personnel. If bystanders trained in medical procedures help someone at an accident, they are practicing medicine and are expected to use their professional judgment wisely. If they don't, they can be held liable for their mistakes.

Similarly, you will soon no longer simply be an armchair philosopher, a good friend, a kind coworker, or even an understanding son or daughter. If you're reading this book, you're most likely on your way to obtaining credentials in the wonderful world of mental health professionals. Soon you'll be a professional helper, change-agent, listener, diagnostician, adviser, and healer. Even when off duty, you'll be accountable to certain ethical guidelines. This should motivate you to engage in a careful reading of the ethical codes of the profession you're aspiring toward. In fact, you should be so motivated that you might even postpone reading the rest of this chapter until you've obtained and read your professional code (although tearing yourself away from this book will undoubtedly require a rather hefty amount of delay of gratification).

A good ethics code defines the professional knowledge base, describes the activities sanctioned in the profession, and provides a clear picture of the boundaries of professional activity. A good code has three main dimensions: It is educational, aspirational, and judicial (Elliott, 1986). As you read the code for your profession, see if you can discern these three components.

Because this is a theories book, what follows is a bare-bones consideration of very basic ethical issues. Your professional training should include a class or seminar in applied ethics, and ethical issues should be a common discussion topic in your classes and supervision.

Confidentiality

Confidentiality implies trust. When clients come to therapy, they will wonder if they can trust the professional to keep what they've said private. If you work as a mental health professional, you will be expected to hold what your client says to you in strict confidence.

Many professions assume client confidentiality. In fact, honoring confidentiality boundaries is often seen as part of the definition of what it means to be a professional, in fields ranging from architecture to law to various forms of business consulting (Sommers-Flanagan, Elliott, & Sommers-Flanagan, 1998). When a client can assume his or her business will be kept private, the client has probably engaged the services of a professional of some sort.

Confidentiality is central to counseling and psychotherapy. The mental health professional creates a safe environment wherein the client can disclose and work on the deepest, most vexing, or most confusing aspects of life. Of course, there are limits to confidentiality, and these limits should be clearly spelled out to the client before counseling begins. Within those limits, the counselor is expected to keep the contents of the counseling relationship and even the fact that there *is* a counseling relationship absolutely confidential.

Why is confidentiality so important? The theories you will read about in this book vary in their claims regarding why things go wrong for people and what should be done to fix them. They also vary in the degree to which they value the confidential setting and the relationship between client and practitioner. But, as noted in our review of the common factors research, the practice of counseling and psychotherapy is essentially an interpersonal enterprise, in which the professional relationship is foundational. If the therapist does not have the client's confidence, trust is impaired. All the fancy theories and techniques in the world cannot make up for an absence of trust.

Practically speaking, you need to keep the identity of your client confidential, you need to keep therapy notes and videotapes secure, and you cannot discuss the content of therapy sessions in ways that identify your client. You also need to research the limits of confidentiality legally and ethically in your state, province, or region, and in the context of the clinic or lab in which you work. You should provide a list of these limits to your clients and go over them verbally as well (see the section in this chapter on informed consent).

Multiple Roles

Although it may be neither wise nor easy for teachers to have their own sons and daughters in class, or for physicians to treat their own children, these activities are not considered unethical. However, mental health professionals, because the very essence of their work entails a relationship with strict boundaries and expectations, are highly encouraged to work only with people they don't know from other contexts. Further, once you're a person's therapist, you should consider that relationship to be the dominant relationship, and not seek, or even allow, any other relationships with the client to develop—including friendship, romance, or business.

Why is this ethical guideline in place? There are several reasons:

- There is always a *power differential* between client and therapist. Counseling is sometimes called a one-way intimacy. The client is in need and has sought the help of a trained, ethical professional. In offering the help, the professional is implicitly or explicitly acknowledging expertise or authority. Therefore, the professional is in the position of power and could use this power (consciously or unconsciously) to inappropriately meet personal needs, especially if another type of relationship is formed.

- Offering professional counseling to family members and friends imperils relationships at many levels. Imagine the following scenario: A friend of yours wants to quit smoking. When you tell him hypnosis sometimes works for smoking, he asks if you'll hypnotize him. You agree. Unfortunately, you're now in a no-win situation. If the hypnosis works, then your relationship is forever changed. Maybe he'll start asking you for more help, or maybe he'll feel indebted to you. On the other hand, if it doesn't work, then your relationship will be transformed in different ways. And worst of all, while under hypnosis he may share intimate details of childhood abuse or other trauma that would place you in a very uncomfortable position, for obvious reasons.

- If you have a social or familial relationship with someone before or after you have a therapy relationship, the client will know more about you than when the relationship was strictly therapeutic. This new knowledge can make both clients and therapists uncomfortable.

It's hard to find a good therapist in film or on television. Year after year, we've come to dread watching films that include a therapist character. If you watch therapists on the screen, you're likely to assume that all therapists are reckless, unprofessional risk-takers who nearly always establish multiple roles and violate relationship boundaries. You're also likely to assume from television and film that therapists cannot resist their sexual impulses and therefore often end up in bed with their clients (or their client's husband, wife, sibling, etc.). In truth, therapist-client sexual relations occur in a vast minority of therapy cases. Even so, therapist-client sex occurs far too often in the real world because, as Pope (1990a) has discussed, therapist-client sex always constitutes sexual abuse of clients (for more on this, see Putting It in Practice 1.1).

On a lighter note, as you begin learning about theories and techniques associated with mental health work, it will be natural for you to try out minor therapeutic–like things with friends or family members. We certainly did, and we're happy to report that we didn't do any lasting damage that we're aware of. But there are dangers. Engaging in nondirective, active listening with someone who is accustomed to having lively, inter-

Client Harm: The Sexual Abuse of Therapy Clients

Believe it or not, in the 1960s and 1970s, some mental health professionals claimed that sexual contact between therapist and client could be therapeutic (McCartney, 1966; Shepard, 1972). Even worse, prior to the landmark legal case Roy vs. Hartogs (1975) the courts generally avoided psychotherapy-sex cases, in part because of the belief that mentally unbalanced women were merely fantasizing sexual relations with their esteemed psychotherapists. As late as 1978, the highly regarded author and psychotherapist M. Scott Peck wrote, "Were I ever to have a case in which I concluded after careful and judicious consideration that my patient's spiritual growth would be substantially furthered by our having sexual relations, I would proceed to have them" (Peck, 1978, p. 176). Despite the fact that Peck concludes his commentary on this issue with the statement "I find it difficult to imagine that such a case could really exist" (Peck, 1978, p. 176), he leaves open the possibility of sexual contact between therapist and client as being beneficial.

In more recent years, hundreds of substantiated and successful legal proceedings against therapists have led all mental health professional groups to establish crystal-clear ethical guidelines prohibiting sexual contact between mental health practitioners and clients (Welfel, 2001). For example, the American Counseling Association (1995) ethical guidelines state that "Counselors do not have any type of sexual intimacies with clients and do not counsel persons with whom they have had a sexual relationship," and prohibition of sexual relations is unequivocal in the American Psychiatric Association (APA) ethical guidelines: "Sexual activity with a current or former client is unethical" (APA, 1993).

Based on research, legal precedent, and anecdotal information, the bottom line is that sexual contact between therapist and client is harmful. Unfortunately, over the years, too many therapists have, in Peck's words, *imagined* their sexual touch was healing; or, in psychoanalytic terms, they *rationalized* that they could help clients through sexual contact. It wasn't until the 1980s that Kenneth Pope began referring to sexual contact between therapist and client as what it is: sexual abuse of clients (Pope, 1988).

Sexual contact between therapist and client constitutes sexual abuse for two main reasons. First, the relationship between therapist and client is characterized by a power imbalance. The therapist has more power and prestige and charges clients for services. Second, research has shown that sexual contact between therapist and client causes clients significant psychological and emotional damage (Pope, 1988, 1990b).

Despite new and strict ethical guidelines and evidence attesting to its harmfulness, sexual abuse of clients continues. The good news is that client sexual abuse rates have decreased (although it's difficult to determine if the decrease is real or simply a function of decreased reporting of sexual incidents by therapists and clients).

In conclusion, the following question is directly relevant to the issue of potential client harm: If we as therapists are prone to exploiting and abusing clients sexually, might we also be prone to exploiting clients in other ways? Of course, the answer to this question is affirmative. There is always the potential for therapists to exploit clients. From our perspective, exploitation of clients is not only a disservice, but the royal road to client harm.

active exchanges with you will not go unnoticed (see Chapter 6). One of our friends told us that she was very relieved when we finally got over our "exclusively Carl Rogers" stage, and she could hear a direct, bossy opinion from us again.

Overall, it's best to restrain your impulse to practice therapy techniques on innocent bystanders—with the possible exception of trying out various listening strategies.

Competence and Informed Consent

A central tenet of any professional code is competence: The practitioner must have the knowledge to perform whatever service the profession offers (R. Sommers-Flanagan, 2001). As a student, you're not expected to be completely competent yet. However, you are expected to strive toward competency by obtaining training and supervision from knowledgeable instructors and supervisors. The provision of effective therapy is both art and science. You learn the *science* by reading, studying, thinking, and doing good literature-based and applied research. This learning never ends. Most ethics codes and state licensing boards encourage or mandate continuing professional education; the ethical practitioner is a lifelong learner (Welfel, 2001).

You learn and develop the *art* of psychotherapy in at least three ways. First, you learn by engaging in a journey of knowing and improving yourself. This means seeking personal therapy, pursuing other healthy life activities, and being as honest as you can possibly be about your needs, shortcomings, fears, and failures. June Singer (1973) warns:

> It only takes a little insight to recognize that the goals of many of today's "gods" in the high places of psychotherapy are to create man in their own image. . . . The danger is that the psychotherapist who has not had analysis himself tends to get *his* way confused with *the* way, and consequently in his work finds himself living out his own unconscious needs through the patient and using the patients to prove his own efficacy as a therapist. This is, of course, an ego trip. (p. 14)

Second, having supervisors and peer supervision with people whom you can watch and listen to and talk to about doing therapy helps you learn the art of therapy. Third, the art of applying therapy techniques and strategies comes with practice, feedback, and more practice.

Closely related to competence is an important ethical concept referred to as *informed consent*. Informed consent refers to clients' rights to know about and consent to the ways you intend to work with them. Clients have the right to know your training status and the supervision arrangements you have. They also should have some idea about the techniques you use and why you've chosen them, and they should have some indication about the length of time counseling might last. Involving your client in these topics, both in dialogue and by providing a written statement, is an empowering act for both of you (Corey, Corey, & Callanan, 2001).

Additional Ethical Issues

There are, of course, many more ethical issues to grapple with as you develop professionally. Most authors in this area adamantly point out that ethics codes are just a rudimentary attempt to hold practitioners to high standards of care (Corey et al., 2001; Pope & Vasquez, 1998; Welfel, 2001). Unfortunately, ethics codes have become increasingly legal in orientation, and sometimes they serve protective rather than proactive functions. Being a truly ethical practitioner requires ongoing attention to the heart of the profession. It will require trusted colleagues, a good problem-solving model, ongoing reading and education, and sometimes a willingness to ask painfully hard questions.

EMERGENCE OF PERSONAL THEORY

We've written this book because we want you to know about the major contemporary theories of counseling and psychotherapy. If you want to become an excellent therapist, then it makes sense for you to closely study the thinking of some of the greatest minds in the field. We cover 12 of the most comprehensive and practical theories in existence. We hope you will absorb each theory as thoroughly as you possibly can, and try to experience it from the inside out. Make it a goal to read at least a little bit of original writing by theorists in the area. Suspend doubt, and try thinking like the theorists do—if only for a short time.

Beyond this thorough exploration of the existing theories, another goal we have is for you to discover which theory or theories fit best for you. And finally, we want you to do the thinking and exploration necessary to understand and further develop your own theory of human functioning and change. In some ways, you might say that we want you to develop a 13th theory. Corsini and Wedding (2000) state this position with clarity:

> [I]f [you] go into the fields of counseling and psychotherapy, then the best theory and methodology to use has to be [your] own! [You] will not be either successful or happy using a method not suited to [your] own personality. The really successful therapist either adopts or develops a theory and methodology congruent with his or her own personality. (p. 13)

We recognize that some of you reading this book may already have considerable knowledge and experience about counseling and psychotherapy theories. You may already have your favorite theory. However, even if you have very little knowledge and experience, you undoubtedly have at least some theoretical or philosophical perspectives about what makes people tick and how and why they tend to suffer, change, or stay the same. Therefore, before you explore the theories put forth by the experts, we encourage you to take at least a brief look at your own implicit or natural psychological theories about people.

Your First Client and Your First Theory

Pretend that this is the first day of your career as a therapist. You have all the amenities: a tastefully decorated office, two comfortable chairs, a graduate degree, and a client.

You also have everything that any scarecrow, tin man, or lion might yearn for: a brain full of knowledge about how to provide therapy, a heart full of compassion for a diverse range of clients, and a fistful of courage for facing the challenge of providing therapeutic services. But do you have what it takes to help a fellow human being climb out of the pit of despair? Do you have the judgment to apply your knowledge in an effective way?

You walk to the waiting room. She's there. She's your first client ever. You greet her. The two of you walk back to the office.

In the first 20 minutes of your interview, you learn quite a lot about your client: She is a 21-year-old college student who is experiencing apathy, insomnia, no romantic interest, carbohydrate cravings, an absence of hobbies, and extremely poor grades. Based on this very basic information, you decide to classify her as depressed and proceed with treatment. But the question is: How do you proceed? Do you focus on her thoughts and how they might be depressing her? Do you help her get a tutor in hope that improving her grades might improve her overall condition? Do you explore her history on the assumption that some childhood trauma needs to be understood and worked through? Do you have her role play and rehearse possible solutions to her problems? Do you just listen, based on the assumption that listening well is healing in and of itself? Do you help her recast herself and her life into a story with a positive ending to help her construct a more adaptive identity? Do you ask her to alternate sitting in different chairs—speaking from different perspectives to explore her present feelings of success and failure? (See Table 1.1 for a brief review of the theoretical perspectives included in this book).

Obviously, you have many choices for how to proceed with therapy, depending upon your theoretical orientation. Here is our advice: Don't get stuck too soon with a single theoretical orientation. It's unlikely that all humans will respond to a single approach. As suggested in Practitioner Commentary 1.1, take time and experiment before deciding on your chosen theory.

PRACTITIONER COMMENTARY 1.1

Your Emerging Personal Theory

As noted in the preface, while writing this book we asked professional therapists and scholars to contribute their thoughts on issues ranging from ethics, to theory, to technique, to multiculturalism. We've sprinkled the comments of these wise colleagues throughout the text in the form of Practitioner Commentaries. In this first installment, Dr. Kurt Kraus of the Department of Counseling of Shippensburg State University in Pennsylvania shares his thoughts on theories:

> I am afraid that students are encouraged to identify their emerging theoretical identity way too early. Students write papers for professors of Introduction to Counseling and Survey of Theoretical Approaches espousing their growing theoretical identities. Nonsense! Take time to learn about mental health professionals who have practiced for many years, study their contributions, write about them and their experiences, their beliefs, their skills, the benefits and liabilities inherent in their practices. Only after you have explored the journeys of many others can you really begin to make a decision about your own. Heck, you are only beginning; how dare we imply that you should know where you want to be? (K. Kraus, personal communication, August, 2002)

Another colleague who teaches theories of counseling and psychotherapy to graduate students, Janice DeLucia-Waack of the State University of New York, Buffalo, gives the following advice to her students: "I tell my students that I don't expect or even want them to get married to any particular theory while they're taking my course. However, I DO tell them that I expect them to do some serious dating with a theory or two before the semester is over" (J. DeLucia-Waack, personal communication, April, 2002).

Table 1.1   A Summary of 12 Major Theoretical Perspectives

Psychoanalytic/psychodynamic/object relations theory. Freud was mostly neutral or pessimistic about the nature of humans. Therapies derived from psychoanalytic theory hold the common belief that human personality and behavior are powerfully shaped by early childhood relationships. Classical Freudians believe humans are primarily pleasure-seeking creatures dominated by sexual and aggressive impulses.

Contemporary object relations theorists emphasize that humans are driven by human relationship and attachment needs, rather than instinctual drives. Psychopathology develops from conflicted, maladaptive, or inadequate parent-child interactions. The overriding goal of therapy is to bring maladaptive unconscious relationship dynamics into consciousness. Therapy process involves an exploration of past relationships, development of insights into current relationship dynamics, and an application of this growing insight to contemporary relationships. Therapy is effective because the therapist accurately interprets or gives the client feedback about conflicted issues outside the client's awareness and relationship patterns, including transference reactions and dreams.

Adlerian/individual psychology theory. In contrast to Freud, Adler was an optimist. Individual psychology considers each client to be a unique, whole individual who strives toward completion and toward achieving his or her idiosyncratic, fictional personal goals. Psychopathology develops when clients construct a belief system or lifestyle that is maladaptive, inaccurate, and dysfunctional. The goal of therapy is to help clients develop a more adaptive lifestyle. This is accomplished when the therapist helps clients have insight into the "basic mistakes" imbedded in their lifestyle. Once this insight is attained, clients are naturally motivated to change in positive ways, and therefore more directive techniques, including guidance and advice, can be used. Therapy is effective because of a friendly, collaborative relationship, insight into maladaptive aspects of the lifestyle, and education about how to remediate the maladaptive lifestyle.

Jungian/analytic theory. Jung's background and interest in mystical traditions strongly shaped his view of humans as having a vast and mysterious potential within their unconscious. The primary goal of Jungian analysis is to bring the unconscious and conscious minds together into a constant dialogue. Analytic theory is optimistic about the nature of humans and society. Human problems, neuroses, or complexes are viewed as stemming from unresolved conflicts residing in the unconscious. Effective therapy occurs when the therapist engages the client, both his or her conscious and unconscious mind, a process that helps the client not only work through difficult issues, but also sail forward into creative and growthful actions.

Existential/Gestalt theory. Existential and Gestalt approaches to therapy are derived primarily from existential philosophy. Overall, existentialists have a wide range of different views of the nature of humans and the nature of reality. Some existentialists are optimistic, whereas others focus on nihilism and meaninglessness. Some are very religious, and others are antireligious. The existential approach emphasizes that individuals must grapple with core life issues such as death, freedom, isolation, and meaninglessness. Anxiety is viewed as a part of normal human experience. Psychopathology arises when the individual avoids, rather than confronting and coping with, life's core issues. Existential therapists can be alternatively gentle and confrontive as they strive to develop a deep and authentic relationship with clients. Therapy is effective because, within the context of an authentic relationship, clients are able to begin facing the reality of death, freedom, isolation, and meaninglessness.

Person-centered theory. Developed by Carl Rogers, person-centered therapy is an optimistic, humanistic, and existential approach to therapy. Person-centered theory posits that each individual has within him or her a capacity for dramatic and positive growth. This growth is stymied and psychopathology arises when clients, usually in childhood relationships, begin to believe they are not worthwhile or lovable unless they meet specific behavioral conditions. In person-centered therapy, clients can talk about the past, present, or future, because it is basically a nondirective

(*continued*)

Table 1.1   Continued

therapy wherein the therapist trusts the client's capacity for growth and therefore follows his or her lead, discussing whatever he or she believes is important. Person-centered therapy is effective when therapists help clients recapture their natural propensity for growth by establishing a therapy relationship characterized by therapist congruence or genuineness, unconditional positive regard or prizing of the client, and accurate empathy.

Behavioral theory. In the tradition of John B. Watson, behaviorists believe deeply in the importance of basing all therapeutic approaches on scientific research. Behaviorists view humans as neither inherently positive or negative, but simply a function of their environment. Psychopathology is directly caused by maladaptive learning, either from the classical or operant conditioning model. Behavior therapy essentially consists of relearning, so the focus of therapy is primarily on the present. The past may be discussed briefly to enhance motivation and the future may be discussed in order to establish goals, but the therapy process and work occur in the present. Therapy is effective because the therapist teaches the client to apply basic behavioral learning principles both within and outside of therapy.

Cognitive theory. Cognitive theory and therapy are usually used in combination with behavioral approaches and also have a neutral perspective on the nature of humans. Cognitive theory emphasizes that it's not what happens to individuals that causes them distress, but what they think or believe about what happens to them that causes distress. Maladaptive or irrational thinking styles and beliefs about the self produce psychopathology. Cognitive therapy primarily uses teaching or educational approaches with clients. Therapy is effective because clients learn new and more adaptive or rational ways of thinking about themselves and their lives.

Reality therapy/choice theory. Choice theory, as developed by William Glasser, holds that individuals are responsible for choosing their thoughts and behavior, which directly influence their feelings and physiology. All humans are viewed as being motivated to satisfy one or more of their five basic needs: survival, love and belonging, power, freedom, and fun. Psychopathology develops because clients choose to restrain anger, want to receive help from others, or are choosing to avoid important issues. Reality therapy focuses exclusively on the present. Therapy is effective because the therapist forms a positive therapy relationship with the client and then teaches the client choice theory from within the context of that relationship.

Feminist theory. Feminist theory was developed by women to address the social and cultural oppression and unequal treatment of women. Implied in the feminist perspective is the tendency for humans who wield more power to use that power to oppress and suppress those with less power. Feminists view psychopathology as arising from social, cultural, and masculine-based power inequities. Recognition of these inequities and the empowerment of women and minorities are the major focus of feminist therapy. Effective therapy is based on a strong, mutual, supportive, and empowering relationship between therapist and client. When therapy is effective, clients are empowered to use their strength and inner resources to further and deepen mutual relations in their lives.

Constructivist theory. Constructivist theory emphasizes the power of language, information processing, and cybernetics in influencing human behavior and change. This theory takes no position regarding the innate goodness or badness of humans. Humans are shaped by the way they construct reality, which directly influences human behavior, problem-solving strategies, and human emotions. Psychopathology is a function of each individual client's construction of reality. Constructivists use both direct and indirect strategies to help clients change. They focus on the future, solutions, and reshaping the narrative or story the client is living. Therapy is effective when therapist and client have a conversation or dialogue and co-create a reality wherein the client engages in positive, solution-focused strategies for constructing and maintaining his or her world.

Table 1.1   Continued

Multicultural and Eastern theories of therapy. Multicultural theory focuses on the power of culture in influencing human behavior, emotions, and values. This theory takes no position on the innate goodness or badness of humans and generally accepts and tolerates diverse culturally sanctioned behaviors. Psychopathology varies depending upon cultural experiences and beliefs. Multiculturalists tailor their approaches to clients' cultural orientation. Many multicultural approaches acknowledge and embrace religious and spiritual perspectives. There are no clear explanations for why clients benefit from therapy and spiritual counseling approaches are distinctly nonempirical in their orientation.

Integration/eclectic theory. Psychotherapy and counseling integration acknowledges the potential positive contributions of all theoretical orientations to effective therapy. No single theory is viewed as more correct or inherently better than any other. Three approaches to weaving together diverse theoretical perspectives are emphasized. First, a common factors approach to therapy is used to develop therapy approaches based on what active ingredients work across a wide range of theoretical approaches. Second, technical eclecticism emphasizes using the best treatment technique available, given a particular client and a particular problem. Third, theoretical integration seeks to weave together two or more therapy systems to create a more effective hybrid system. The nature of humans, psychopathology, and theoretical constructs shifts, depending upon the approach being employed. Effective therapy is characterized by positive outcomes.

It takes a long time to fully understand and become proficient at even one well-articulated theory. We're asking you to give them all serious thought and to try out at least three or four of them, while at the same time staying authentic to your own gifts, skills, and leanings. Further, we believe you will eventually—perhaps much later—develop your own ethical amalgamation of theory and technique, based on research, experience, and your clients' needs.

Questions for Reflection

At first glance, which theoretical approaches do you find most appealing? Are you more inclined toward the scientific security of behaviorism or more attracted to the relationship emphasis of person-centered therapy? As you explore the various theories throughout this book, start thinking about which approach you'd like to date, but as DeLucia-Waack suggests, try to avoid prematurely eloping with one of the approaches.

OUR BIASES

When soliciting guidance for writing this book, we asked a number of prominent scholars and respected practitioners to answer the question "What criticisms do you have regarding current theories of counseling and psychotherapy books?" In response, we received the following advice from the renowned Italian strategic/constructivist therapist, Giorgio Nardone:

> Very often, while going through some current theory books, I have come across great contradictions. While declaring that the text would not be following a particular preferred psychological approach, already from the very first lines, one can easily deduce the authors'

point of view, carefully embedded within the presented pages. Even the choice of the text's layout and the ample space given to certain approaches and not to others reveal the authors' un-discussible preference. I believe it would be more correct if the authors would simply declare their own perspective, while maintaining a respectful position in the exposition of other theories.

It is impossible to be absolutely "objective" or "neutral" in writing a book. However, the reader will surely understand and accept this preference and moreover he/she will undoubtedly appreciate the authors' honesty. (G. Nardone, personal communication, July, 2002)

At this point, you've already met several of our biases, but based on the advice and inspiration of Dr. Nardone, we thought we should provide you with a more formal and explicit introduction.

Our Theoretical Roots

At this point, we've been eclectic so long it seems like we both must have been born eclectic. However, after closely reading about Dr. Nardone's appreciation for honesty, we decided to look deeper and explore our possible biases. After all, telling you that we're eclectic doesn't tell you much about our deeper preferences, tendencies, and biases.

In a sense, it's true that we were born and raised eclectic. In graduate school, we both attended a staunchly generalist program. Our clinical psychology faculty at the University of Montana in the 1980s included a psychoanalytic/hypnoanalytic professor, a cognitively oriented professor, a person-centered professor, and two behaviorists. John went to a strictly psychoanalytic predoctoral internship at a medical center in New York in 1985, and Rita went to a family systems–oriented child and family clinic in Oregon in 1988. After licensure, John spent time teaching, working as a health psychologist in an industrial setting, in private practice, and as director of a nonprofit organization dedicated to parent education. Rita has consulted with two different Vet Centers, established a part-time private practice, and taught the past 12 years as a professor of counselor education. During this time period, we lived in Montana, New York, Washington, Oregon, Belize, Central America, and Northampton, England.

John's favorite theoretical figures are Carl Rogers, Alfred Adler, and Irving Yalom. Rita casts her votes for Carl Rogers, Viktor Frankl, and Jean Baker Miller. John loves to quote Freud and Rita loves to hate Freud, considering him antithetical to her feminist beliefs.

Our generalist background makes us slow to jump on contemporary bandwagons. For example, we're especially cautious about any purportedly new theory or technique that claims remarkable recovery rates for psychologically distressed individuals. Hopefully, this doesn't mean we're not open to new ideas. We're just reluctant to believe that having clients hum a few tunes while practicing thought field therapy will cure their longstanding personal problems.

Balance and Uncertainty

We have a strong bias against certainty. Several years ago we attended a workshop conducted by the great structural family therapist and theorist Salvador Minuchin. The subtitle of his presentation was "Don't be too sure." We agree. No theory holds the key to all problems. No theory entirely explains what it means to be human. When we get too sure about our theory, we close ourselves off to different perspectives of reality; even worse, being too sure places us in danger of forcing the client to fit the theory, rather than the other way around.

We also tend to be skeptical about empirical research. You probably started getting that impression as you read earlier sections in this chapter. The biggest problem with research is that it's tremendously difficult to conduct studies that truly reflect what happens in the real therapy offices of practitioners around the world. As W. Silverman (1996) stated, "Efficacy studies do not reflect models and they do not represent psychotherapy as practiced in the field" (p. 210).

On the other hand, we definitely value counseling and psychotherapy research—we just try not to overvalue it. When a particular form of treatment makes great claims of effectiveness in the absence of empirical research, we become very suspicious.

Theory versus Technique

Despite the minimal evidence supporting the importance of technique, we're big fans of therapy techniques. In our *Tough Kids, Cool Counseling* book, we wrote about our belief that, especially for children, techniques, properly implemented, facilitate and deepen the therapeutic relationship (Sommers-Flanagan & Sommers-Flanagan, 1997). This is perhaps our biggest bias, and we hope that in admitting it we meet the high standards of Dr. Nardone. We believe that the primary purpose of using different therapy techniques is to help build therapy relationships. Overall, after therapy is long over with, we believe clients are much more likely to remember and benefit from a warm, supportive, collaborative, and interesting relationship. And we're not afraid to use a few techniques, from a place of honesty and integrity, to build a relationship that we hope clients will remember (see Practitioner Commentary 1.2 for a discussion of the importance of experiencing your theory).

Questions for Reflection

Okay, now that we've bared our theoretical souls, maybe you should follow suit and take a look at your personal biases. Even if you don't want to go that deep, at least consider our biases and reflect on where you stand on the issues we've raised. What are your theoretical roots? Where do you stand on the issue of balance and uncertainty? What do you think and how do you feel about using specific techniques to further the therapy relationship?

THE ZEITGEIST, THE ORTGEIST, AND THE POLTERGEIST

The Zeitgeist is defined as "the spirit of the time." It refers to the fact that more often than would be predicted by chance, more than one individual makes a significant discovery at around the same time. This spirit of the time explains why Pierre Janet and Sigmund Freud, in France and Austria, could both independently discover the existence of the unconscious at about the same time. In other words, in the late 1890s, the Zeitgeist was such that the unconscious was ready to be discovered.

The Ortgeist refers to the "spirit of the place." It also explains Freud and Janet and

---

PRACTITIONER COMMENTARY 1.2

Experience Your Theory

The following practitioner commentary was contributed by Ellen Hawley McWhirter. She is an associate professor in the counseling psychology department at the University of Oregon.

I was fortunate to be provided with very good theoretical training during both my master's and doctoral programs. In addition to reading basic theories texts, for example, we were required to read Rogers, Ellis, Freud, Adler, and other theoreticians' original works. However, it was not reading about theories that helped me move from being able to describe theories to being able to describe what I do in consistent theoretical terms. It was the combination of practicing, trying out, and receiving supervision on my attempts to live out theory in my sessions. When I was completing my predoctoral internship, I had a wonderful supervisor who allowed me to sit in on her sessions, and who conducted supervision in a way that paralleled the way she did therapy (although supervision never felt like therapy). That exposure might not have even changed what I did on the outside; I'm not sure. But it radically changed the way I felt on the inside: It was like finally finding a shoe that fit just right. What is ironic is that I had never read Teyber [the author of *Interpersonal Process in Psychotherapy*] and didn't know what to call her way of doing therapy. When I began teaching practicum myself, I read Teyber's book and realized that my supervisor had been doing interpersonal process [see Teyber, 1997]. The more I read, the more it fit. This theory more than any other is consistent with things I believe about human change processes and about how to facilitate those processes. Now I require that text for all students in practicum, regardless of their preferred theory, because it promotes self-reflection and in-session process that enriches their growth and their sessions.

---

the discovery of the unconscious. Perhaps the Ortgeist spirit was operating in Europe in the late 1890s. Bankart (1997) speaks of the Zeitgeist and Ortgeist in relation to Freud: "A genuine understanding of Freud's psychoanalysis, for example, requires (and at the same time provides) a reasonably deep understanding of middle-class life in turn-of-the-century Europe" (Bankart, p. 8).

Similarly, recently on the National Public Radio show "The Writer's Almanac," Garrison Keillor quoted the plainspoken philosopher Eric Hoffer's perspective on Freud:

> Ah, don't talk to me about Freud. Freud lived in a tight little circle in Vienna, and inside that tight little circle was another tight little circle, and inside that tight little circle was still *another* tight little circle. What applies to that poor man, Freud, does not necessarily apply to me. (Keillor, 2002)

A Poltergeist is a mischievous spirit or ghost. We include reference to it here because, in our experience, conducting psychotherapy or counseling sometimes includes mysterious and mischievous surprises. An example of a poltergeist is given in the famous Harry Potter book series:

Peeves the Poltergeist was worth two locked doors and a trick staircase if you met him when you were late for class. He would drop wastepaper baskets on your head, pull rugs from under your feet, pelt you with bits of chalk, or sneak up behind you, invisible, grab your nose, and screech, "GOT YOUR CONK!" (Rowling, 1997, p. 132)

As a therapist, you should be prepared for the unexpected. Sometimes your clients will say and do outrageous things. At other times, you will suddenly feel the urge to say or do something inappropriate. For whatever reason, sitting privately with another individual for long periods of time can produce unusual and profound experiences. Just when you least suspect it, your VCR will malfunction or you'll abruptly feel like crying or you'll feel fidgety and want to leave the room or the clock hanging on the wall in your office will stop or your client will tell you something absolutely outrageous. Our point is: Don't be surprised when you feel surprised.

Overall, we hope as you explore the theories in this book and as you come to know contemporary perspectives in counseling and psychotherapy, that you'll keep the Zeitgeist, Ortgeist, and Poltergeist in mind. What spirits of time, place, and mischief are operating right now? What will be the next big discovery and next big scandal in the field of counseling and psychotherapy?

CONCLUDING COMMENTS

In this chapter we've taken you on a very quick tour of major issues in counseling and psychotherapy. From historical context to contemporary research to ethical essentials, the field of counseling and psychotherapy is filled with amazing and interesting information. We wish you the best as you begin to explore the main theories of therapy in greater depth.

STUDENT REVIEW ASSIGNMENTS

At the end of each chapter, rather than providing a traditional summary, we offer you an opportunity for a more interactive review.

Critical Corner

In this section, we have included some extremely critical statements about counseling and psychotherapy designed to provoke a response in you. If you like, you can write your response to the criticisms in the space provided.

1. Most of the psychological theories reviewed in this book were developed by privileged, White, and European or American males. Given the narrow origins of these theories, how can the information provided be useful to you as a developing mental health professional?
Response:

2. Smith, Glass, and Miller (1980), in their extended meta-analysis of therapy outcome studies, concluded that the average person treated in therapy was better off

than 80% of the untreated sample. Of course, they neglected to comment on the inverse fact that average untreated person was better off than about 20% of the treated clients. What does this inverse statement suggest? Are there large numbers of treated therapy clients who are getting worse? Or are some untreated clients somehow spontaneously getting better?

Response:

3. In this chapter we've suggested that you begin to explore different theories and that, in the end, perhaps the best theory will be your personal theory. Is this a valid suggestion? Might you be better off simply adopting a particular theory and hanging in there with it, despite its limitations? Wouldn't you be better off just knowing one theory very well, rather than knowing a little bit about many different perspectives?

Response:

Reviewing Key Terms

- The biomedical perspective
- The religious/spiritual perspective
- The psychosocial perspective
- Trephining
- Meta-analysis
- The Dodo bird effect
- Extratherapeutic change
- Confidentiality
- Informed consent
- Zeitgeist
- Ortgeist
- Poltergeist

Review Questions

1. What is the difference between a therapeutic experience and a therapy experience?
2. Who was Hans Eysenck and why is he important to the evolution of psychotherapy and counseling?
3. What are the common factors and their relative importance as described by Lambert (1992)?
4. Why is sexual contact between therapist and client now referred to as sexual abuse of clients?
5. What are the limits of confidentiality in therapy?

RECOMMENDED READINGS AND RESOURCES

Please feel free to explore the following resources.

Lead Theory Journals

There are hundreds of journals related to counseling, psychotherapy, mental health, social work, and psychology. The following list is only partial, but it represents some of the mainstream journals in the previously mentioned areas.

- *American Journal of Psychotherapy*
- *American Psychologist*
- *Journal of Consulting and Clinical Psychology*
- *Journal of Counseling and Development*
- *Journal of Counseling Psychology*
- *Journal of Mental Health Counseling*
- *Journal of School Psychology*
- *Journal of Social Work Practice*

- *Professional Psychology*
- *Psychological Bulletin*
- *Psychotherapy*
- *School Psychology Quarterly*
- *School Psychology Review*
- *Social Work*
- *Social Work in Health Care*
- *Social Work Research*
- *The Counseling Psychologist*
- *The School Counselor*

Books and Articles: Ethics Codes

American Association for Marriage and Family Therapy. (1991). *Code of ethics.* Washington, DC: Author.

American Counseling Association. (1995). *Code of ethics and standards of practice.* Alexandria, VA: Author.

American Psychiatric Association. (1993). *Principles of medical ethics with annotations especially applicable to psychiatry.* Washington, DC: Author.

American Psychological Association. (2002). Ethical principles of psychologists and code of conduct. *American Psychologist, 57,* 1060–1073.

National Association of Social Workers. (1993). *Code of ethics.* Silver Springs, MD: Author.

Books and Articles: Ethics and Theories Readings

Bankart, C. P. (1997). *Talking cures: A history of Western and Eastern psychotherapies.* Pacific Grove, CA: Brooks/Cole.

Corey, G., Corey, M. S., & Callanan, P. (2001). *Issues and ethics in the helping professions* (6th ed.). Belmont, CA: Brooks/Cole.

Eysenck, H. J. (1952). The effects of psychotherapy: An evaluation. *Journal of Consulting Psychology, 16,* 319–324.

Frank, J. D. (1961). *Persuasion and healing.* Baltimore: Johns Hopkins Press.

Haley, J. (1977). A quiz for young therapists. *Psychotherapy, 14*(2), 165–168.

Hubble, M. A., Duncan, B. L., & Miller, S. D. (Eds.). (1999). *The heart and soul of change.* Washington, DC: American Psychological Association.

Kottler, J. A., & Brown, R. W. (1996). *Introduction to therapeutic counseling.* Pacific Grove, CA: Brooks/Cole.

Luborsky, L., Singer, B., & Luborsky, L. (1975). Comparative studies of psychotherapies: Is it true that "Everybody has won so all shall have prizes"? *Archives of General Psychiatry, 32,* 995–1008.

Mahoney, M. (1991). *Human change processes.* New York: Basic Books.

Masson, J. M. (1988). *Against therapy: Emotional tyranny and the myth of psychological healing.* New York: Atheneum.

Pope, K. S., & Vasquez, M. J. T. (1998). *Ethics in psychotherapy and counseling: A practical guide* (2nd ed.). San Francisco, CA: Jossey-Bass/Pfeiffer.

Welfel, E. R. (2001). *Ethics in counseling and psychotherapy* (2nd ed.). Pacific Grove, CA: Brooks/Cole.

Videotapes

Corey, G., Corey, M. S., & Walters, T. (1998). *Ethics in action: Student version and workbook* [Videotape]. Pacific Grove, CA: Brooks/Cole.

Training Opportunities and Web Sites

The following web sites will connect you with specific professional mental health associations. These associations are excellent resources for obtaining cutting-edge information about what's happening in your field of interest. They also often list upcoming training opportunities. Most of these web sites include information on ethical codes and principles associated with each professional group.

American Association of Marriage and Family Counselors (web site: www.aamft.org)

American Counseling Association (web site: www.counseling.org)

American Psychological Association (web site: www.apa.org)

National Association of Social Work (web site: www.naswdc.org)

Chapter 2

PSYCHOANALYTIC, BRIEF ANALYTIC, OBJECT RELATIONS, AND INTERPERSONAL APPROACHES

A man like me cannot live without a hobby-horse, a consuming passion—in Schiller's words a tyrant. I have found my tyrant, and in his service I know no limits. My tyrant is psychology.

—Sigmund Freud, 1895, in a letter to W. Fliess

IN THIS CHAPTER YOU WILL LEARN

- The history and context of psychoanalysis, including Freud's seduction hypothesis
- Theoretical principles of classical psychoanalytic theory
- The evolution and development of psychoanalytic theory and practice, including developments leading to ego psychology, object relations, and self psychology
- The difference between one-person and two-person psychology as it applies to psychoanalytic theory and practice
- Basic methods and techniques of psychoanalytically oriented therapy
- Client selection criteria for engaging in brief psychoanalytic psychotherapy
- About the efficacy of psychoanalysis and psychoanalytic therapy
- About a contemporary psychoanalytically derived treatment, interpersonal psychotherapy for depression

---

Sigmund Freud has maintained his place as the central figure in psychotherapeutic thinking since the early 1900s. For his psychoanalytic and neo-analytic followers, he is still an icon of brilliance. For others, he is an object of disdain, frequently viewed as a symbol of much that is wrong with psychology, psychiatry, psychotherapy, and counseling. The fact that speaking his name in public continues to produce strong emotional and intellectual reactions is a testament to his widespread influence. Let us begin with a brief examination of his childhood and personal history, because, frankly, Freud himself wouldn't have it any other way.

BIOGRAPHICAL INFORMATION: SIGMUND FREUD

Sigmund Freud was born in Freiberg, Moravia, in 1856. He was the firstborn in a family with three boys and five girls. His father, a wool merchant, has been described as very authoritarian, his mother as protective and nurturing. Due to financial limitations, the family lived together in a small apartment.

Freud's intellectual potential was obvious early on. For example, he and a friend taught themselves Spanish because they wanted to read *Don Quixote* in its original language. His parents did what they could to support his intellectual appetite, and Freud ended up feeling he was a favored child. He obtained his medical degree from the University of Vienna with the goal of becoming a research scientist. Given his later fascination with psychosexual development and the unconscious sexual meaning of many behaviors, it's of special interest that he spent time searching for the testes of the eel in his first major research project.

Freud was unable to continue being a research scientist due to financial needs. Consequently, he went into the private practice of neurology.

As a neurologist, Freud was exposed to the disorder "hysteria," which affected a significant number of European women in the late nineteenth century. This disorder included unexplained symptoms of numbness, paralysis, and tremors. During a visit to France, he became familiar with the work of Jean Charcot, who was using hypnosis to *produce* hysterical symptoms. This convinced Freud that the same procedure might be used to treat hysteria. Subsequently, Freud found he could use hypnosis to get his patients to talk about important incidents that they didn't recall when awake. After experimenting with hypnosis and reporting that it made him feel like "a miracle worker," Freud began working with Viennese physician Josef Breuer. Breuer was successfully treating hysteria symptoms by having patients talk about emotionally laden childhood experiences. In the early 1880s Breuer worked extensively with Anna O., discussing her hysteria symptoms and treatment in great detail with Freud. Together, they published *Studies in Hysteria* in 1895 (Breuer & Freud, 1955). Eventually, Freud became even more impressed with this "talking cure" than he had been with hypnosis. And the rest, as they say, is history.

HISTORICAL CONTEXT

As we suggested toward the end of Chapter 1, psychological theories are generally a product of the prevailing Zeitgeist and Ortgeist. Bankart (1997) states:

> To fathom Freud's near-obsession with the sexual foundations of emotional distress is also to come to a fuller awareness of the sexual repression and hypocrisy in the lives of the Austrian middle class at the turn of the . . . [nineteenth] century and the effect of this repression on the mental health of adolescents and young adults during the time when Freud derived his theories. (p. 8)

One of the best illustrations of the historical context of psychoanalysis is the dramatic story of Freud's development and subsequent recanting of the seduction hypothesis. This story captures his psychoanalytic thinking along with the social dynamics of his time. It's also simply an incredible story (see Masson, 1984, for a more detailed version). As you read this section, keep in mind that, at Freud's time and in Freud's place, sex was more than just a dirty word; it was verboten.

The Seduction Hypothesis

In 1885, Freud went to France to study under the famous neurologist Jean Charcot. The research of Jeffrey Masson, former projects director of the Freud Archives, indicates that it is likely during his time in France, Freud visited the Paris Morgue, observing autopsies of young children who had been brutally physically and sexually abused (Masson, 1984). This exposure to the grisly reality of child abuse combined with subsequent years of careful listening to women suffering from hysteria resulted in conclusions Freud could not dismiss. As Masson notes,

> In 1895 and 1896 Freud, in listening to his women patients, learned that something dreadful and violent lay in their past. The psychiatrists who had heard these stories before Freud had accused their patients of being hysterical liars and had dismissed their memories as fantasy. Freud was the first psychiatrist who believed his patients were telling the truth. These women were sick, not because they came from "tainted" families, but because something terrible and secret had been done to them as children. (p. xviii)

Eventually, Freud presented a paper titled "The Aetiology of Hysteria" at the Society for Psychiatry and Neurology in Vienna (Freud, 1896). During this, his first major presentation to professional colleagues, he outlined a stunning and controversial hypothesis:

> I therefore put forward the thesis that at the bottom of every case of hysteria there are one or more occurrences of premature sexual experience, occurrences which belong to the earliest years of childhood, but which can be reproduced through the work of psychoanalysis in spite of the intervening decades. (Freud, 1896, cited in Masson, 1984, p. 263)

Freud reported on 18 cases (12 women and 6 men), all of which included childhood sexual abuse. Freud made a connection between childhood sexual abuse and subsequent psychopathology that would not be seriously acknowledged for many decades. This analysis provided an early formulation of the contemporary diagnosis of Post-Traumatic Stress Disorder and/or Dissociative Identity Disorder (APA, 2000):

> Our view then is that infantile sexual experiences are the fundamental precondition for hysteria. . . . [I]t is they that create the hysterical symptoms, but . . . they do not do so immediately, but remain without effect to begin with and only exercise a pathogenic action later, when they have been aroused after puberty in the form of unconscious memories. (Freud, 1896, cited in Masson, 1984, p. 272)

Freud's correspondence with his friend Wilhelm Fliess, a physician from Berlin, reveals Freud's great compassion for his clients—clients who had been horribly victim-

---

Questions for Reflection

A thorough examination of Freud's original seduction hypothesis—the hypothesis that childhood sexual abuse produces later psychopathology—is often overlooked or neglected in psychology textbooks. Why do you suppose Freud's early thinking on this issue is so often ignored? Also, speculate on what powerful forces could have caused Freud to recant the seduction hypothesis.

ized as children. Further, he continued to believe his clients' stories of sexual abuse until around September 1897 or possibly the early 1900s (depending upon which version of the story is more accurate).

Recanting the Seduction Hypothesis

Imagine yourself alone with a great and horrible insight. This was Freud's situation. Aside from some remarkably open and engaging letters he wrote to Fliess, Freud was more or less professionally isolated for a time after the presentation of his 1896 paper. Masson (1984) describes the reception Freud received after presenting his hypothesis:

> The paper . . . met with total silence. Afterwards, he was urged never to publish it, lest his reputation be damaged beyond repair. The silence around him deepened, as did the loneliness. But he defied his colleagues and published "The Aietology of Hysteria," an act of great courage. (pp. xviii–xix)

Five days after presenting his paper, Freud wrote about the experience to Fliess. Freud's pain and anger are obvious:

> [My] lecture on the aetiology of hysteria at the Psychiatric Society met with an icy reception from the asses, and from Kraft-Ebing [the distinguished professor and head of the Department of Psychiatry at the University of Vienna] the strange comment: "It sounds like a scientific fairy tale." And this after one has demonstrated to them a solution to a more than thousand-year-old problem, a "source of the Nile!" They can all go to hell. (Schur, 1972, p. 104, cited in Masson, 1984, p. 9)

Freud's reputation plummeted. His insights were countered by professional insults. He again wrote to Fliess: "I am as isolated as you could wish me to be: the word has been given out to abandon me, and a void is forming around me" (Masson, 1984, p. 10).

His private practice in decline and his professional life in a shambles, Freud began what has been described as "his lonely and painful self-analysis" (Prochaska & Norcross, 2003, p. 29). His two-year self-analysis included uncovering memories of yearning for his mother and equally powerful feelings of resentment toward his father (Bankart, 1997).

Eventually, Freud abandoned his seduction hypothesis in favor of his theory concerning the Oedipal conflict and its associated seduction and power fantasies. In the process, he also abandoned his belief in the truths his patients shared with him. Whatever your present opinion of Freud might be, his effort to find the truth could not have been a pleasant process and, most likely, caused him significant psychological distress and damage.

Eventually, in 1925, long after he recanted the seduction hypothesis, he reflected on his struggle:

> I believed these stories, and consequently supposed that I had discovered the roots of the subsequent neurosis in these experiences of sexual seduction in childhood. . . . If the reader feels inclined to shake his head at my credulity, I cannot altogether blame him. . . . I was at last obliged to recognize that these scenes of seduction had never taken place, and that they were only fantasies which my patients had made up. (Freud, 1925, cited in Masson, 1984, p. 11)

The official story line most often used to represent Freud's change of heart goes something like this: Freud had to abandon his earlier views about child seduction and sexual abuse to discover the more basic truth of the power of internal fantasy and of spontaneous childhood sexuality. In a letter to Masson, Anna Freud makes this point perfectly clear:

> Keeping up the seduction theory would mean to abandon the Oedipus complex, and with it the whole importance of phantasy life, conscious or unconscious phantasy. In fact, I think there would have been no psychoanalysis afterwards. (A. Freud, personal communication, September 10, 1981, cited in Masson, 1984, p. 113)

Questions for Reflection

Take a moment to reflect on Anna Freud's comment. Do you think if Freud had retained his belief in the seduction theory there "would have been no psychoanalysis afterwards?" Even further, are the following four factors mutually exclusive?

1. The reality of child sexual abuse
2. The power of internal fantasy to produce psychological symptoms
3. The spontaneous developmental nature of childhood sexuality
4. The presence of the Oedipal conflict as an observable developmental reality

Would it be possible to reconstruct a psychoanalytic theory including all four preceding factors?

PSYCHOANALYTIC THEORETICAL PRINCIPLES

Freud's theory is one of what P. Miller (1983) refers to as the "giant theories" of developmental psychology (p. 108). If you've studied basic psychology, you've undoubtedly read about Freudian theory. One of our psychoanalytic colleagues refers to classical Freudian theory as a "museum theory," not so much because it belongs in a museum (although a case can be made for that as well), but because classical Freudian theory is a *one-person* intrapsychic model that treats the client as a separate, individual artifact to be systematically and objectively examined. In contrast, modern analytic theory treats the therapy encounter more as a *two-person* field, wherein the therapist's and client's intrapsychic and relationship *interactions* help shed light on patterns that may be troubling the client (Benjamin, 1990; Renik, 1993; Ringstrom, 2001).

Given the museum nature of classical Freudian theory, our coverage of this material is brief. Resources on classical Freudian and contemporary psychoanalytic theories are listed at the end of this chapter.

The Dynamic Approach

Freud's dynamic approach to human psychology is known as *drive theory* or *instinct theory.* He believed humans are filled with mental or psychic energy. This energy comes from two essential sources: Eros (energy associated with life and sex) and Thanatos (energy associated with death and aggression).

In constructing his theory, Freud applied available information from the field of physics to the human mind, using physical models to describe how psychic energy is built up, transformed, connected to certain images, distributed, and discharged. But, as Brenner (1973) pointed out, "Psychic energy is a term for a psychological concept, not a physical one" (p. 20). Parallel physical processes may exist, but they have yet to be pinpointed.

The hypothesis of psychic determinism underlies the dynamic approach. Brenner (1973) states: "in the mind, as in physical nature . . . nothing happens by chance, or in a random way. Each psychic event is determined by the ones which preceded it" (p. 2).

Freud's psychic determinism proposes an underlying psychological explanation for your every emotion, thought, impulse, and behavior. This is why from the psychoanalytic perspective there are no accidents. If you oversleep, you're probably avoiding something or someone. If you go out and party too hard, maybe you're expressing antagonism toward your parents' demands for responsible behavior. If you forget your professor's name, perhaps somewhere deep inside you have an aggressive impulse toward her. Or she may remind you, in some unconscious way, of someone you felt sexual feelings for and so you defend against your sexual impulse by not recalling her name.

The concept of psychic determinism is probably the main reason that some people feel extremely uncomfortable talking to psychology or counseling majors. For example, if you go to a party and someone asks, "Are you analyzing me?" you can blame Freud and his concept of psychic determinism.

Eros and Thanatos are the two basic drives that energize behavior. Freud referred to Eros-related energy as *libido,* whereas Thanatos- or destructive-related energy was unnamed. Based on Freudian drive (dynamic) theory, every impulse has an *origin, aim, object,* and *intensity.* An impulse always *originates* from some place in the body. For example, in very young children, most pleasure (or libidinal) impulses arise from the oral region. This is why young children put everything into their mouths. Their *aim* (or goal) is to obtain oral gratification.

If we stick with the small child example, the baby experiences libidinal impulses and aims toward obtaining gratification. At the same time, the pressure or *intensity* of gratification/pleasure need is building. This puts the baby on a mission to find an *object* that will allow him or her to discharge tension and obtain pleasure. In many cases, for the baby, the *object* will be the mother's breast or a bottle. Obviously, the identification of an oral need, the building up of pressure to meet that need, and the discharge of oral tension and resulting gratification is an oft-repeated cycle in a baby's life. For Freud, if the cycle does not flow smoothly due to parental overindulgence or withholding, there can be a fixation and later unconscious acting out, or repetition compulsion, of the pathological cycle during adulthood.

The Topographic Approach

The territory of the psychoanalytic mind is divided into three interrelated regions: the unconscious, the preconscious, and the conscious. Freud described this situation:

> Let us therefore compare the system of the unconscious to a large entrance hall, in which the mental impulses jostle one another like separate individuals. Adjoining this entrance hall there is a second, narrower, room—a kind of drawing-room—in which consciousness, too, resides. But on the threshold between these two rooms a watch-man performs his function: he examines the different mental impulses, acts as a censor, and will not admit them into the drawing-room if they displease him. (Freud, 1963, p. 295)

Freud believed that human consciousness is an "exceptional rather than a regular attribute" (Brenner, 1973, p. 2). In other words, there is much more going on at the unconscious level than at the conscious.

Because awareness of our basic, primitive sexual and aggressive impulses might disrupt our daily lives, our brain protects us from them. As we will see later, the main purpose of psychoanalytic therapy is to help us slowly become aware of unconscious impulses. By bringing unconscious impulses to awareness, we're better able to manage them, because even when they are outside awareness, primitive impulses can still act on us in an indirect and destructive manner.

For example, if a young man has an unresolved Oedipal conflict with his father, he may be overly aggressive and competitive in his daily life. His lack of awareness of the origin, aim, intensity, and object of these impulses allows for their escalation. As a consequence, some night when out with a few friends, he might become belligerent toward a police officer and end up in jail. Alternatively, if the young man had been through a psychoanalytic form of therapy, he might recognize the source and nature of his competitive and combative impulses and therefore control their expression and avoid time in jail.

The Developmental Stage Approach

In recent years concern about early "brain development" has been emphasized in the popular press and in the schools. For many, this emphasis seems like common sense, but back in the early 1900s, the idea that adult functioning is shaped by early childhood experiences was groundbreaking. Freud was the first to outline a developmental theory explaining how early childhood experiences influence later adult functioning.

P. Miller (1983) describes Freud's developmental stages clearly:

> Each stage is defined in terms of the part of the body around which drives are centered. The eye of the storm shifts from the oral to the anal to the phallic area during the first five years. Then a period of latency in middle childhood is followed by the genital stage of adolescence. Each stage presents new needs that must be handled by the mental structures. The way in which these needs are met (or not met) determines not only how sexual satisfaction is achieved, but also how the child relates to other people and how he [sic] feels about himself. He develops characteristic attitudes, defenses, and fantasies. Unresolved conflicts in any stage may haunt the person throughout his lifetime. (pp. 125–126)

Freud's developmental theory is relatively straightforward. All children progress through four different developmental stages as well as a latency period. Progress through the stages is driven by biological maturation—which forces the individual to confront demands inherent within each stage. At each stage, if parents are overly indulgent or withholding, the child can end up with fixations or complexes associated with the stage. A fixation or complex is an unresolved unconscious conflict. Freud's traditional developmental stages are

- Oral: birth to 1 year old
- Anal: 1 to 3 years old
- Phallic: 3 to 5 years old
- Latency: 5 to 12 years old
- Genital: adolescence to adulthood

Most contemporary psychoanalysts don't find much value in Freud's original developmental stages. As one of our psychoanalytic colleagues put it, "Freud's stages don't really match up with reality; they're not really taken seriously any more" (Spitzform, personal communication, February, 2003).

On the other hand, Freud's general premise that individuals experience developmentally specific arrests that can be unfrozen via psychoanalytic treatment remains alive and well within psychoanalytic circles. Contemporary analysts consider a variety of developmental theories when working with clients (see Erikson, 1963; Mahler & Pine, 1975; Stern, 1985).

The Structural Approach

The structural approach of Freud's theory involves the interrelationships of the well-known concepts of id, ego, and superego. As discussed previously, powerful, unconscious forces flow through the body and mind. If not for the structural components of Freud's system, human behavior would be completely dictated by primal sexual and aggressive forces or drives. However, because primal forces flow through the id, ego, and superego, humans learn to constructively manage their urges; we learn to wait, to watch, and to control ourselves.

The *id* is the seat of biological desires. As a structural entity within the human personality, it functions on the *pleasure principle* and *primary-process thought.* Freud described the id as "a chaos, a cauldron full of seething excitations" (Freud, 1964, p. 73).

For the most part, id impulses are outside awareness or unconscious. However, it's possible to glimpse these impulses in society—as in cases when individuals seek immediate sexual or aggressive gratification. Additionally, we can view id impulses within ourselves via dreams, fantasies, flashes of instinctual desire, and powerful urges toward pleasure-seeking behavior. Primary process thought, another facet of id functioning, is characterized by hallucination-like images of fulfilled sexual or aggressive desires.

In many ways, the id is the mother of the *ego.* Because it's impossible to continuously have one's desires gratified, it becomes necessary to deal with frustration by learning to wait for what you want. Although the id is a powerful seething cauldron of desire, the ego has potent resources of its own. Specifically, ego functions include memory, problem-solving ability, and rational or logical thought processes. These functions are defined as *secondary thought processes* and directly aid us in coping with or defending against powerful sexual and aggressive drives.

The *superego* develops around the time when children resolve their Oedipal issues and begin strongly identifying with parents and parental demands or expectations. There are two parts of the superego: First, there is the *conscience.* The conscience develops as a function of parental prohibitions. When mom, dad, or another adult authority figure says, "No!" or "Stop that!" or administers stern punishment, these admonitions are internalized within the child's psyche and later used by the child (and, in later years, by the adult) to self-punish or prohibit unacceptable impulses. Essentially, the conscience becomes the inner source of punishment which is why children of extremely strict and punitive parents often end up with neurotic guilt as adults.

Second, the superego is also composed of the *ego-ideal.* In contrast to the negative, punishing quality of the conscience, the ego-ideal is a positive desire to emulate adult standards of conduct. For example, when parents model healthy, rational, and functional behavior, the child strives to be like those parental figures. Using the language of behavioral psychology, the conscience is an inner presence that uses a "stick" or punishment as a motivator, while the ego-ideal is a similar presence that uses a "carrot" or reinforcement as a primary motivator.

Overall, the ego essentially acts as a mediator within the structure of the human personality. It must contend not only with the id's primitive impulses, but also with admonitions and expectations of the superego, and the reality of the external world. This is no easy task, and therefore the ego often must use defense mechanisms as a means of dealing with battling forces.

Defense mechanisms are designed to ward off unacceptable id impulses that are at odds with superego standards or that would result in problems within the real world. They have four primary characteristics:

- They are automatic: Individuals learn to reflexively use particular defense mechanisms.
- They are unconscious.
- They ward off unacceptable impulses.
- To a greater or lesser extent (depending upon the defense mechanism employed) they distort reality.

From an applied perspective, most therapies are ego supportive in that they aim to help the ego—a rational and logical thinking entity—deal more effectively with primitive desires, internalized parental and societal standards, and the real world. A list and brief description of eight common ego defense mechanisms is included in Table 2.1.

Psychopathology and Human Change

Based on psychoanalytic theory, psychopathology arises from early childhood experiences. Further, Freud believed that psychopathology existed on a continuum, with even relatively healthy individuals showing occasional signs or symptoms of pathology. This portion of his theory has been referred to as the "normal-abnormal continuum" and is described by Miller:

> In an abnormal personality, psychological processes are exaggerated or distorted. A melancholic patient has an overly strong superego. A sadistic killer has a strong, uncontrolled aggressive drive. An amnesiac must repress all of a painful past. Yet every normal personality has traces of melancholia, sadism, and unaccountable forgetting. (P. Miller, 1983, p. 128)

The building blocks of psychopathology were described in the preceding sections. To summarize, there are several key issues pertaining to psychopathology and human change that have remained constant in the field of psychoanalytic theory and therapy. First, the theory and therapy remain focused primarily on early childhood experiences as the origin of psychopathology. Second, early childhood experiences that produce pathology are not completely understood, recalled, or dealt with in a conscious manner. Consequently, repetitive and dissatisfying patterns exist in relationships, and changing these patterns feels beyond the client's control. Third, a cornerstone of human change continues to be some form of insight- or consciousness-raising experience. Fourth, human change is not an instantaneous process; it requires a working through

Table 2.1   Ego Defense Mechanisms

Defense Mechanism	Description and Example
Repression	Repression involves forgetting an emotionally painful memory. When a client has repressed a memory, there may be behavioral evidence that it exists, but the client genuinely has an absence of recall: "Hmm. Nope. I don't remember anything unusual about my childhood. In fact, I don't recall much at all."
Denial	In contrast to repression, denial is usually expressed with more force. Its essence is captured by Shakespeare's famous line about "protest[ing] too much." Clients using denial often say, "No way, that's not true" and repeat their denial forcefully.
Projection	Projection occurs when clients push their unacceptable thoughts, feelings, or impulses outward, onto another person. A client may accuse someone else of anger, while denying his or her own: "I'm not mad about anything; you're the one who's pissed off!"
Reaction formation	If it is too dangerous to directly express aggression toward someone, the individual may behave in an excessively loving way. This is reaction formation. The inverse example occurs when it is unacceptable to express sexual attraction and therefore the individual behaves in ways suggestive of hatred or distaste toward the person toward whom he or she really feels an attraction.
Displacement	Displacement occurs when the individual shifts the aim of sexual or aggressive impulses from a more dangerous person or activity to a less dangerous person or activity. Aggressive displacement is characterized by the colloquialism of "kicking the dog." Sexual displacement occurs when sexual feelings are aroused by a forbidden object and displaced onto a more acceptable object.
Rationalization	Humans are notorious for rationalizing or intellectualizing away primordial impulses. Rationalization occurs when clients use excessive explanations to account for their behavior. For example, if a student makes an impulsive, hostile comment to someone in class, he or she might spend a significant amount of time explaining and justifying the comment.
Regression	Regression involves going back to an old, less sophisticated method of doing things. Traumatized children often regress to wetting the bed or pooping in their diapers rather than using their more advanced toileting skills. Adults who are skillful communicators may regress to shouting and physical altercation rather than controlling impulses and letting go of an argument.
Sublimation	Sublimation is one of the most constructive defense mechanisms. It occurs when primal sexual or aggressive energy is channeled into positive loving or vocational activities. For example, sexual energy is often sublimated into creative tasks and aggression into hard work (e.g., house cleaning, yard work).

process where consistent practicing of new ways of understanding inner impulses and contemporary human relationships occurs.

Freud's Theory in Action: Implications for Psychotherapy

Freud's theory has grand implications for psychotherapy. This should come as no surprise, because his theory is derived from listening to and observing patients in analysis (including himself, in self-analysis). Here we offer a short list of the main implications of his theory for psychotherapy and counseling:

- Clients are not fully aware of the complete struggle through the psychosexual developmental stages. Nevertheless, clients are affected daily by the traces of unconscious memories left over from childhood.

- In particular, unconscious memories are acted out and acted on, rather than directly recalled. If a client had difficulties in the oral developmental stage, you're likely to hear him or her regularly talk about oral-related issues (e.g., eating, biting, talking, yelling, drinking, sucking). This client will also behave, depending on the particular nature of the oral fixation, in ways that are either oral-dependent or oral-aggressive.

- Because clients bring developmental baggage into therapy with them, they will invariably project their old child-caretaker (parent) relationship dynamics onto the therapist. This tendency is referred to as *transference* (we discuss this in greater detail later).

- Because therapists bring their developmental baggage into therapy with them, the same projection process can occur in the opposite direction. When therapists project their childhood relationship patterns onto the client, it is called *countertransference.*

- Similar to defense mechanisms, transference and countertransference tend to be unconscious, automatic, and repetitive. They are also characterized by inappropriate intensity, frequency, and duration.

- The repetitive quality of inappropriately applying old relationship dynamics to new relationships is often described as *repetition-compulsion.* For example, a man who has felt criticism from his mother will continually try to reenact the childhood situation so he can eventually obtain approval. Unfortunately, he is often doomed to failure because he repeatedly chooses to reenact this dynamic with women who are similar to his mother and therefore unlikely to offer him approval.

- Because therapy is threatening, clients often resist therapy. Traditionally, resistance is defined as virtually anything the client does to oppose the psychoanalyst's goals, and it frequently takes the shape of defense mechanisms. A common defense within the therapy is regression, which is manifest as an intense form of transference.

- For therapy to succeed, resistances and transference must be understood, usually through some form of interpretation. When this process proceeds smoothly, the client's ego or self is strengthened and greater insight can be tolerated because of greater ego control.

We will return to a review of psychoanalytic methods following a discussion of expansions and revisions associated with classical Freudian psychoanalysis.

EVOLUTION AND DEVELOPMENT IN PSYCHOANALYTIC THEORY AND PRACTICE

As we've seen, Freudian theory originally focused on biological or somatic instinctual sexual and aggressive drives as the primary motivational factor influencing behavior. But this is not the end of the story. Pine (1990) has identified four primary stages of development in psychoanalytic thinking:

- Drive
- Ego
- Object
- Self

Interestingly, one of the most important psychoanalytic expansionists was also named Freud. We now turn to the story of Anna Freud (Sigmund's youngest daughter) and her influence on the development of ego psychology.

Anna and the Ego

One of the ways Sigmund Freud controlled the growth of psychoanalytic theory and therapy was to insist that all his disciples submit to a course of psychoanalysis by the master. During this early period of psychoanalysis, the behavior of individual analysts was not under the scrutiny of state licensing boards and professional ethics codes. Thus, Freud was able to take what we would now consider the most unusual step of accepting his youngest daughter, Anna, into analysis. As Bankart (1997) states, Anna was barely out of her teens when she began analysis, and "From those days until the end of her life, Anna had room for only one man in her life, and that man was her father" (p. 183).

Anna was one of the few practicing psychoanalysts ever to be without an official professional degree. She was, in virtually every sense of the phrase, "home schooled."

In many ways, Anna Freud ushered in a new generation of psychoanalysis. As you may recall, Sigmund Freud based his theoretical propositions about child development on his intensive study of adults through psychoanalysis. In contrast, Anna Freud studied children directly, through psychoanalysis. She listened as children told about their dreams and fantasies. Perhaps more importantly, she discovered how to observe children's unconscious mental processes through play. Although she never directly disputed her father's belief in the dominance of id impulses in human development and functioning, she did change the psychoanalytic focus from the study of instinctual drives to a study of ego development. She is best known for her work with children and her theoretical writing on ego defense mechanisms.

Psychoanalytic Ego Psychology

Beginning in about the 1930s, psychoanalytic ego psychology began officially claiming a portion of the original psychological landscape for the ego. These theorists did not completely break with Freud; rather, following Anna Freud's lead, they extended his ideas, eventually emphasizing that certain ego functions were inborn and autonomous of biological drives (Hartmann, 1958; Rapaport, 1951). These ego functions include memory, thinking, intelligence, and motor control. As Wolitzky and Eagle (1997) state,

"Following . . . ego psychology, there was now room in psychoanalytic theory for behavior and functions relatively autonomous of the vicissitudes of drive" (p. 44). In addition, the greater emphasis on ego functioning as apart from and interacting with id impulses brought the interpretation of ego defenses to the forefront of therapeutic intervention.

The new focus on ego had ramifications for both psychoanalytic theory and practice. A profound development during this period came from one of Anna Freud's analysands and followers, Erik Erikson.

Like Anna Freud, Erik Erikson had little formal academic training. Nonetheless, perhaps because he was an artist with exceptional observational skills, he managed to outline a highly regarded and oft-cited theory of human development. In his eight-stage epigenetic theory of development, Erikson (1963) deviated from Freudian developmental theory in two key ways: He emphasized psychosocial development instead of psychosexual development, and he emphasized the continuous nature of development into old age, rather than ending his theorizing, like Freud, in early adulthood. Erikson's eight stages of development are summarized in most introductory and developmental psychology textbooks. For a glimpse into the ever-evolving nature of developmental theories, we recommend viewing Joan Erikson's (Erik's wife) video on the ninth stage of human development (Davidson, 1995).

Object Relations

In the 1950s, object relations theorists began conceptually reformulating traditional psychoanalytic theory. Specifically, whereas traditional Freudian theory focuses primarily on parent-child dynamics during the Oedipal crisis, object relations theory focuses on the dynamics and motivation captured within the context of earlier parent-child relationships. These dynamics are referred to as pre-oedipal.

The most profound shift in psychoanalytic thinking brought about by object relations theorists is captured by Fairbairn's statement "libido is object seeking, not pleasure seeking" (1952, p. 82). To embrace this perspective means that human behavior is no longer fueled by instinctual drives for sexual and aggressive gratification; instead, behavior is directly influenced and motivated by the desire for interpersonal relationships and human connection. Wolitzky and Eagle (1997) comment, "In contrast to Freud's psychic world which is populated by unconscious wishes and defenses against those wishes, Fairbairn's psychic world is populated by internalized objects and internalized object relations" (p. 56).

Object relations theorists believe humans mentally internalize both a representation of self and a representation of early caretaker figures (St. Clair, 2000). These internalized self and other representations are then carried within the individual into adulthood. If during early childhood an object relationship was characterized by trauma or destructive interpersonal patterns, remnants of these early self-other relationship patterns can continue to dominate and adversely affect a client's relationships. Consequently, a major goal of object relations therapy is to "exorcise" the old maladaptive internalized representations and replace them with healthier representations (Fairbairn, 1952). Essentially, object relations therapy attempts to "replace the 'bad object' with a 'good object'" (Wolitzky & Eagle, 1997, p. 59). In some ways, this process is very similar to Alexander and French's (1946) concept of the corrective emotional experience. The therapist acts as a good object, and through this experience the client is able to replace the original bad internalized parent object.

The different theoretical foundation in object relations therapy makes the focus of interpretive work in object relations therapy different from traditional Freudian analysis. In particular, whereas Freudian analysis focuses on Oedipal conflicts over sexual and aggressive wishes and drives, object relations therapy focuses on relationship wishes and pre-Oedipal interpersonal dynamics as played out in the regressive analytic situation. As a "good object," the therapist makes distinct efforts to respond empathically to client struggles. Althea Horner (1998) states, "Once we have ascertained the core relationship conflict as it is manifest in the treatment relationship, it is important that it be laid out in a manner that communicates empathy" (p. 14).

Self Psychology

The fourth phase of psychoanalytic evolution centers on the theoretical writings of Heinz Kohut (1971, 1977, 1984). In contrast to the preceding theoretical perspectives, Kohut considers needs for self-cohesiveness and self-esteem to be the overarching motivations that fuel human behavior. His focus is not on instincts, ego, or even object relations, but instead on the development of healthy narcissism within individuals.

Along with his focus on the development of a healthy or cohesive self, Kohut focuses on self-defects and the noncohesive self. He believes that self-defects and noncohesion stem from early childhood experiences. In particular, he emphasizes that the development of a "cohesive self requires the parental provision of empathic mirroring and the later availability of a parental figure permitting idealization" (Wolitzky & Eagle, 1997, p. 67).

Practically speaking, Kohutian self psychological psychotherapy proceeds on the basis of the following process:

- Due to early childhood developmental defects, the client quickly establishes a mirroring and idealizing transference within the therapy situation.
- This mirroring and idealizing transference is both regressive and progressive; it seeks to reengage a mirroring and ideal object in order to repair and build up its psychic structure.
- The major fear of the client is retraumatization by the therapist; this fear produces resistance.
- The therapist interprets the resistance.
- The therapist is imperfect and therefore will inevitably fail at providing for the client's wish and need for perfect empathy and will not be a perfect figure for idealizing.
- The client will then retreat from intimacy with the therapist.
- If the therapist's deficiencies and failures are not of traumatic proportions, then this retreat can be interpreted in conjunction with the therapist's acknowledgment of his or her failures.
- These failures, if handled well, will be "optimal failures," and then "new self structure will be acquired and existing ones will be firmed" (Kohut, 1984, p. 69).

Wolitzky and Eagle (1997) summarize the Kohutian therapeutic unit: "For Kohut, empathic understanding and the repeated working through of optimal failures in empathy constitute 'the basic therapeutic unit' of treatment" (p. 69).

Continuing Theoretical Developments

To this point in our discussion, the evolution of psychoanalytic thinking might be described, following Pine (1990), as a progression of focus from drive to ego to object to self. Unfortunately, although Pine's distinctions are helpful, the evolution of psychoanalytic thought has not been quite so simple and linear. In fact, Gedo (1979) described the progression of psychoanalytic thought as "piecemeal patching" rather than an organized effort at theoretical evolution (p. 9). This section briefly describes two alternative theoretical developments.

Around the time of ego psychology and its development, Karen Horney's work, following Adler's lead, began focusing on how social and cultural factors can powerfully affect personality development (Horney, 1950). In particular, Horney articulated many early feminist critiques of Freudian theory (see Multicultural Perspective 2.1 for a taste

---

MULTICULTURAL PERSPECTIVE 2.1

Karen Horney versus Freudian Orthodoxy: The Battle of the Sexes

Karen Horney grew up in an era when both men and women feared the dangers of female emancipation. As Otto Weininger wrote in *The Emancipated Woman,* "All women who really strive for emancipation are sexual intermediate forms. . . . [A]ll the so-called important women are either strongly masculine or imprinted by man or overestimated" (Quinn, 1987, p. 103).

Despite the odds, Karen Horney obtained her medical degree in 1911. This was the same year she gave birth to her first child, Brigitte.

Alfred Adler may have been the first Freudian disciple with feminist leanings (see Chapter 3), but as a woman herself and therefore an authority on the matter, Karen Horney was able to take the battle of the sexes to new and exciting depths.

She did not believe in Freud's theory of penis envy, and she did not believe that women were naturally inferior beings. Although she was immersed in traditional psychoanalytic thinking early on, she eventually found her voice and began strong arguments against masculine formulations of female sexuality and development. She wrote:

> How far, has the evolution of women, as depicted to us today by analysis, been measured by masculine standards and how far therefore does this picture fail to present quite accurately the real nature of women?

And further:

> [I]f we try to free our minds from masculine mode of thought, nearly all the problems of feminine psychology take on a different appearance.

She then turns the tables on penis envy:

> When one begins, as I did, to analyze men only after a fairly long experience of analyzing women, one receives a most surprising impression of the intensity of this envy of pregnancy, childbirth, and motherhood, as well as of breasts and of the act of suckling.

Finally, she interprets male behavior from a new, feminine perspective:

(continued)

MULTICULTURAL PERSPECTIVE 2.1 (continued)

> Is not the tremendous strength in man of the impulse to creative work in every field precisely due to their feeling of playing a relatively small part in the creation of living beings, which constantly impels them to an overcompensation in achievement?

Later in her career, she increased the volume of her claims of a male inferiority complex.

> One of the exigencies of the biological differences between the sexes is this: that the man is actually obliged to go on proving his manhood to the woman. There is no analogous necessity for her. Even if she is frigid, she can engage in sexual intercourse and conceive and bear a child. She performs her part by merely *being,* without any doing—a fact that has always filled men with admiration and resentment. (Horney, 1932, pp. 348–360)

Whether you are a woman or a man, the ideas of Karen Horney are worth reading. She was steady and forthright in her views. She accepted some of what psychoanalysis had to offer and rejected other psychoanalytic assumptions, especially erroneous assumptions about the nature of women. She is a role model for all of us, at least with regard to the need to look long and hard at the perspectives of both women and men, before formulating a complete psychology of humanity.

---

of her opposition to Freudian views of female sexuality). Horney's work has generally been labeled "neo-Freudian."

Alternative theoretical developments have often resisted theoretical purity, striving instead for integration. For example, Margaret Mahler's formulations are something of an amalgamation of different theoretical perspectives. She includes components of drive, ego, object relations, and self psychology within her writings. Her observations of mother-child interactions, in combination with the attachment research and writings of John Bowlby and Mary Ainsworth, have provided the foundation for contemporary attachment-based models of psychotherapy (Ainsworth, 1969; Bowlby, 1978, 1988; Hughes, 1998).

Practical Modifications: Short-Term and Time-Limited Psychoanalytic Psychotherapy

Very early in the psychoanalytic movement, discussion began on how to shorten treatment duration. The first psychoanalyst to push for more active and directive therapy was probably Sandor Ferenczi (Ferenczi, 1920, 1950), one of Freud's closest friends. Ferenczi claimed that because all therapy techniques were more or less suggestive, his proposal to be more active was an acceptable option.

Over the years, many other analysts have recommended modifying the psychoanalytic procedure to speed the therapeutic process. Notably, Alexander and French (1946) experimented with methods of time-limited psychoanalysis through the Chicago Institute of Psychoanalysis. They developed a procedure called the *corrective emotional experience,* which was designed to speed the curative therapeutic process. Alexander and French recommended that analysts adopt a compensatory role toward clients. If the client suffered from an overly critical parent and therefore, due to the transference phenomenon, expected criticism from the analyst, then the analyst would instead adopt a very positive and supportive role. This manner of interacting was supposed to produce a corrective emotional experience, thereby reducing the length of time required for a complete analysis.

In direct contrast, other theorists have advocated a sort of role-playing by the analyst wherein he or she purposely acts in ways to further the transference. This might involve an analyst's behaving in a cold and critical manner toward the patient who had cold and critical parents. As Horowitz and colleagues (1984) state,

> The technique of "seeding," or manipulating, the transference has the apparent advantage of accelerating its development and the possible disadvantage of traumatizing the patient, causing him to feel manipulated or to disavow his own contribution. (p. 6)

Another alternative strategy for reducing time needed for analysis was advocated by French (1958) and Balint, Ornstein, and Balint (1972). These theorists recommended that analysts stop short of conducting a complete analysis and instead focus their work on one significant conflict or problem. This modification in the analytic process has come to be known as *focal psychotherapy.*

There are a number of major figures with their own particular approach to time-limited psychodynamic or psychoanalytic therapy:

- David Malan: intensive brief psychotherapy
- Peter Sifneos: short-term anxiety-provoking psychotherapy
- Habib Davanloo: broadly focused short-term dynamic psychotherapy
- James Mann: time-limited psychotherapy
- Lester Luborsky: the Core Conflictual Relationship Theme method
- Hans Strupp and Hanna Levenson: time-limited dynamic psychotherapy
- Gerald Klerman and Myrna Weissman: short-term interpersonal psychotherapy

Simply adding up the modifications to psychoanalytic technique as promoted by the proponents of briefer analytic therapy provides an overview of where the field is now. Psychoanalytic therapy is more active and directive, more focused on establishing a healing relationship, and more focal or limited in its breadth of goals.

The following points summarize the modifications suggested for shortening psychoanalytic therapy by the previously listed theorists and practitioners.

- Use a rigorous initial evaluation and selection process to screen out individuals who are unable to tolerate an intensive short-term psychoanalytic treatment procedure (see Putting It in Practice 2.1 for an outline of selection criteria for acceptance into brief psychoanalytic psychotherapy).
- Fix the time limit or number of sessions from the outset of therapy.
- Relate surface symptoms to an underlying, core, repeating relationship conflict (in Luborsky's terms, the core conflictual relationship theme).
- Choose, with the client, a mutually agreeable and reasonable focus for therapy.
- Actively and repeatedly use confrontation, clarification, and interpretation to establish *triangles of insight* (this concept is explained further later in this chapter).

===== **Putting It in Practice 2.1** =====

Selection Criteria for Brief Analytic Psychotherapy

When I (John) worked as a recreational therapist at a psychiatric hospital in 1980, a woman who had made an extreme suicide attempt was admitted. She had slashed her arm so severely that she was in a cast and under constant watch by the nursing staff. This woman had been in psychoanalysis. The rumor quickly swept through the hospital staff; the woman had been a poor choice for a psychoanalytic patient.

Although this rumor may or may not have been true, it illustrates the fact that psychoanalysis—and its close relative, psychoanalytic psychotherapy— may not be the best form of therapy for all patients. Because of undesirable outcomes such as the one described, selection criteria have been developed for prospective psychoanalytic psychotherapy patients. Proponents of brief analytic therapies have been most clear and aggressive in promoting specific selection (or inclusion and exclusion) criteria for admittance into psychoanalytic psychotherapy. The following criteria are usually evaluated during the course of a trial psychotherapy interview.

1. Does the patient describe the presence of a meaningful intimate relationship in the past? The relationship should include shared intimacy, emotional involvement, and trust.
2. Does the patient have above-average intelligence (as reflected by the ability to learn new things about him- or herself)?
3. Is the patient able to tolerate anxiety, guilt, anger, and depression without acting out with aggression toward others or toward him- or herself?
4. Is the patient psychologically minded? In other words, can the patient actively consider psychological and emotional causes for behavioral and physical problems?
5. How does the patient respond to trial interpretations? Because brief analytic therapies involve active and sometimes aggressive interpretation of client behavior, the patient must demonstrate an ability to handle these interpretations without becoming excessively angry or depressed or defensive.
6. Does the patient have a circumscribed or manageable central complaint? If the problems are vague and difficult to define, the patient does not qualify.
7. Does the patient have a strong motivation for change and resources to match this motivation? Psychoanalytic therapy requires a financial and time commitment.
8. Is the patient willing to commit to the psychoanalytic process wherein his or her behavior and words in the session will be consistently scrutinized, analyzed, confronted, and interpreted by the therapist?

The Intersubjectivity, Two-Person Psychology, or Relational Psychoanalytic Movement

Psychoanalysis, as discussed thus far, reflects Freud's original image of a thoroughly analyzed, dispassionate, objective psychoanalyst expertly interpreting derivatives of the client's unconscious mind in order to eradicate maladaptive childhood fixations and neuroses. Renik (1993) describes the classical Freudian position in these terms: "The image of the analyst as detached psychic surgeon, dissecting the patient's mental operations in an antiseptic field" (p. 553).

Currently, we are in the midst of a paradigm shift in psychoanalysis. The new paradigm is usually referred to as *two-person psychology* (Balint, 1950; Ghent, 1989), although *intersubjectivity* and *relational psychoanalysis* are other commonly used terms (Benjamin, 1990). Two-person psychology emphasizes that the psychoanalyst is always subjective:

> Instead of saying that it is *difficult* for an analyst to maintain a position in which his or her analytic activity objectively focuses on a patient's inner reality, I would say that it is *impossible* for an analyst to be in that position *even for an instant:* since we are constantly acting in the analytic situation on the basis of personal motivations of which we cannot be aware until after the fact, our technique, listening included, is *inescapably* subjective. (Renik, 1993, p. 560)

Within the theoretical realm, abandonment of one-person psychology by psychoanalysts began in full force in the 1980s. Many psychoanalysts, following the lead of French psychoanalyst Jacques Lacan, began viewing two-person psychology as "the most fertile line of thought traced out since Freud's death" (Lacan, 1988, p. 11).

In two-person psychology the analyst is viewed as participant-observer. Again, Renik provides an articulate summary:

> Consider an analogy from physics. Let us say that we want to ascertain the exact temperature of a glass of water. As soon as we introduce a thermometer into the water, we alter the temperature we want to measure. (Renik, 1993, pp. 561–562)

This line of thinking parallels the paradigm shift from Newtonian physics to Einsteinian physics. Consequently, the inherent relativity and subjectivity of the psychoanalyst is now an important focus of study in and of itself.

This new perspective has dramatic implications for psychoanalysis and psychoanalytic psychotherapy. The therapist and client are now often referred to as the psychoanalytic couple. This means the analyst no longer has the authority to make "interpretations" of his client's unconscious derivatives. Instead, interpretations are cast as an alternative viewpoint for the client to consciously consider while making up his or her own mind. Moreover, not only is the client's enactment of transference considered important therapeutic information, but so is the analyst's enactment of countertransference. In fact, many writers are beginning to strongly recommend greater psychoanalyst spontaneity and countertransference enactment (Benjamin, 1990; Renik, 1993; Ringstrom, 2001; Spezzano, 1996). Finally, in a move seemingly in contradiction with classical Freudian analysis, there is a growing call for analysts to become more emotionally involved with their clients: "If the analyst does not get emotionally involved sooner or later in a manner that he had not intended, the analysis will not proceed to a successful conclusion" (Boesky, 1990, p. 573).

Questions for Reflection

For psychoanalysis, two-person psychology changes everything. How do you think this new perspective might affect traditionally authoritative activities such as dream interpretation? Remember, the analyst is no longer an unquestionable authority, but instead is a partner in exploring the client's personal and interpersonal unconscious and conscious dynamics. From your perspective, does the two-person psychology model make psychoanalytic approaches more or less acceptable?

THE PRACTICE OF PSYCHOANALYTIC THERAPY

Reading this short chapter on psychoanalytically oriented therapy will not provide you with the requisite skills and experiences to go out and conduct such therapy. However, this chapter can help you keep psychoanalytic or psychodynamic principles and techniques in mind as you provide therapy services.

Psychoanalytic Principles and Therapy Methods

Numerous specific methods for conducting therapy are derived from Freud's psychoanalytic theory and are outlined directly in his original works and the writing of others (Brenner, 1973; Fenichel, 1945); Freud, 1966). As suggested in the preceding discussion of theoretical modification of Freud's theories, there have been changes in the ways in which psychoanalysts use many of Freud's original ideas. The following section describes standard methods, techniques, and concepts that continue to be emphasized and employed to some extent by contemporary psychoanalytically oriented therapists.

Overall, the methods and techniques of psychoanalytic therapy have the following goals:

- To make the unconscious conscious or increase client awareness
- To help the client develop greater ego-control or self-control over unhealthy or maladaptive impulses
- To help the client dispose of maladaptive or unhealthy internalized objects and replace them with more adaptive internalized objects
- To repair self-defects through mirroring, presenting a potentially idealized object, and expressing empathy during optimal therapeutic failures

The Basic Rule

Traditional psychoanalysts begin each session the same way. They tell the client, "Say whatever comes to mind." This is the basic rule in psychoanalysis, and a variation of this approach is used in most psychoanalytically oriented therapies. The basic rule is designed to facilitate emergence of unconscious impulses and conflicts. To use the basic rule, the analyst adheres to the following guidelines. In some ways, optimal conditions for analysis are similar to those for meditation.

All external stimuli are minimized. To let unconscious impulses and conflicts rise to consciousness, distractions must be minimized. This is one reason why Freud used a couch. If the analyst has the client lie on a couch and then sits behind it, the client cannot see him; the distracting stimulus of the analyst's facial expressions is eliminated. With the elimination of the analyst's real facial expressions, greater emphasis can be placed on what facial expressions (or thoughts and feelings) the patient imagines the analyst is experiencing.

The patient's internal stimuli are minimized. When free associating, it's best not to be too hungry or thirsty or physically uncomfortable. For example, if clients come to analysis hungry, thoughts about food will flood into their free associations. Similarly, if the client is physically uncomfortable, it will distract from the free association process. Also, as described in Ethical Highlight 2.1, sometimes potential leaks in confidentiality associated with reporting information to insurance companies can inhibit the free association process.

Cognitive selection or conscious planning is reduced. Free association is designed, in part, to counter intentional or planned thought processes. For example, if a client comes to therapy with a notepad and a list of things to talk about, psychoanalytically oriented practitioners might interpret this behavior as resistance. You may wonder, "How could the client's planning for the session be viewed as resistance?" The answer

---

ETHICAL HIGHLIGHT 2.1

Maintaining a Safe Container

The following ethical commentary was contributed by Felix Salomon of Phoenix.

I have found the following to be the most vexing conflict between our ethics code and psychoanalytic theory. Specifically, the American Psychological Association code of ethics (APA, 2002) requires that we recognize "that the extent and limits of confidentiality may be regulated by law or established by institutional rules" (Standard 4.01, p. 1066).

On the other hand, psychoanalytic theory informs us that in order for therapy to have a reasonable chance for success, the therapist must become a "safe container" for all the patient's communications (Bion, 1962). This implies that the therapist must provide not only a "nonleaking" container by providing confidentiality, but also an impenetrable container regarding any third-party attempts at intrusion (Bollas & Sundelson, 1995). The superficial conflict lies in the patient's conscious awareness that written records, as well as oral reporting—insurance companies demand to know clinical details and to pass on the continuation of mental health benefits—may be publicized under certain circumstances, ranging from the "accidental" to the "legally required." The much more significant conflict lies in the patient's unconscious editing and censoring of potentially important material that would substantially affect the quality of the therapeutic effort. This, I believe, results in a pervasive subversion of the therapy if the therapist adheres to the APA code of ethics. I feel it also has several other far-reaching implications for other ethical areas (for example, it places the therapist in the position of needing to be dishonest on behalf of the patient: at times overpathologizing, at other times underpathologizing, and engaging in other questionable selective reporting practices).

is that conscious planning is a defense for warding off or keeping control over prim-itive sexual and aggressive and other conflict-ridden impulses. Traditional psychoan-alytic theory presumes that these warded-off impulses are adversely affecting the client and need to be brought to consciousness. For contemporary theorists, client list-making might be an interpersonal control strategy deserving collaborative explo-ration; awareness might be enhanced rather than the unconscious motives uncov-ered.

Interpretation

Traditional analysis views the unconscious as so charged with conflictual material that even free association doesn't allow the analyst direct access. Instead, ego defenses, de-signed to protect clients from their own unconscious knowledge, distort information rising up from the unconscious. Therefore, in analytic terms, the best the therapist can hope for is to work with *derivatives* from the unconscious. Depending upon the ana-lyst's particular perspective, the derivatives may reflect primarily instinctual conflicts or primarily relationship or attachment conflicts.

The Freudian analyst's job is to listen for and interpret unconscious derivatives. This process is anything but simple. The analyst cannot just sit back and make interpreta-tion after interpretation of unconscious derivatives. Fenichel (1945) states the reason for this: "The unprepared patient can in no way connect the words he hears from the analyst with his emotional experiences. Such an 'interpretation' does not interpret at all" (p. 25).

Fenichel is saying that analysts must prepare clients before using interpretation. Proper client preparation involves steps described in the following sections.

Developing a Therapeutic Alliance

Mentioned in Chapter 1 as a common factor contributing to positive therapy outcome, the therapeutic alliance was first discussed by Freud (1958, 1966). He emphasized that a reality-based attachment between analyst and client was crucial and needed to coex-ist with the positive or negative transference distortions occurring simultaneously. Later, Zetzel (1956) was the first to actually use the term "therapeutic alliance." Con-sistent with Freud, she believed that if clients had early parent-child interactions char-acterized by trust and affection, their ability to develop a positive therapeutic alliance was enhanced. Overall, it's easier to defensively disregard input from someone—even potentially helpful input—when you don't like the source of the feedback.

Role Induction

When clients are left without information about how psychoanalytic therapy proceeds, they often feel confused or annoyed. This is especially the case if you use interpretation as a therapy technique. To use interpretation more collaboratively, you might say some-thing like this:

> As I do therapy with you, I may notice some patterns. These patterns may be linked to your early childhood relationships, your relationship with me, or your descriptions of your re-lationships outside therapy. Is it okay with you if I occasionally mention these patterns so we can explore them together and then hopefully come to a better understanding about how they might affect your life?

Timing

Once a therapeutic relationship has been established and role induction information provided, then interpretation becomes a potential therapy tool for the analyst. However, even then, the effective analyst proceeds carefully. Again, Fenichel (1945) articulates this point:

> Since interpretation means helping something unconscious to become conscious by naming it at the moment it is striving to break through, effective interpretations can be given only at one specific point, namely, where the patient's immediate interest is momentarily centered. (p. 25)

Obviously, timing is essential. Here are several tips for timing interpretations:

- Watch for when the client is just a step away from becoming aware of something new.
- Wait for the client to show positive regard for you.
- Wait until you can say the interpretation clearly and articulately; if the interpretation is muddled in your mind, it probably won't be helpful.
- Wait until you have enough data to support your interpretation; in other words, you should be able to clearly and briefly explain, based on your observations of the client and what he or she has said, why you're pointing out particular patterns and connections.

To make matters even more complex, good timing isn't everything. If you're conducting psychoanalytic therapy, you also need to know what to interpret.

What to Interpret

When it comes to what to interpret, there are three main choices from the traditional psychoanalytic menu. Do you interpret the client's ego defenses? Do you interpret the client's underlying wish and inner conflict about the wish? Or do you interpret the transference relationship? For now, keep in mind that the general rule is to interpret defensive processes or resistance before interpreting underlying conflict or transference. Later in this chapter we use an in-session dialogue and commentary to help you understand how interpretation of resistance and interpretation of transference usually proceeds.

Transference

One of the unique and most lasting contributions of Freud's work was his discussion and analysis of transference (Luborsky et al., 1985). In the past half century, over 3,000 books and professional journal articles have been published on transference phenomena (Kivlighan, 2002). As Kivlighan (2002) states, "From a strictly classical stance, transference is a client distortion that involves re-experiencing Oedipal issues in the therapeutic relationship" (p. 167). Gelso and Hayes (1998) provide a more modern definition of transference that goes beyond Oedipal issues:

> *The client's experience of the therapist that is shaped by the client's own psychological structures and past and involves displacement, onto the therapist, of feelings, attitudes and behaviors belonging rightfully in earlier significant relationships.* (p. 51, italics in original)

More than anything else, transference is characterized by inappropriateness. As Freud stated, transference "exceeds anything that could be justified on sensible or rational grounds" (Freud, 1958, p. 100). This is because transference involves using an old map to try to get around on new terrain, and, simply put, it just doesn't work very efficiently (Sommers-Flanagan & Sommers-Flanagan, 2003). Consequently, one way to detect transference is to closely monitor for client perceptions and treatment of you that don't fit correctly. Of course, to effectively monitor for inaccuracies in your client's perceptions, you must know yourself well enough to identify when your client is treating you like someone you aren't.

In one clinical case, I (John) had a client accuse me of being the most insensitive man she had ever had the displeasure of meeting. Eventually, after becoming fed up with her perception of my nonresponsiveness, she shouted, "I bet if I cut open your arms, I'd find wires, not veins."

Fortunately, as it turns out, this woman was having a transference reaction toward me. In her past, the consistent pattern was for men (including her father) to be relatively unresponsive until finally erupting into a sometimes abusive rage toward her. And this was precisely what she was waiting for and finding so frustrating. From the corrective emotional experience and object relations perspective, my nonaggressive response to her may have been considered healing.

Countertransference

Countertransference was originally defined as the therapist's tendency to see the client in terms of his or her own previous relationships. In that sense, it's the same as transference, but it occurs only when the transference is directed from the therapist toward the client. Freud conceptualized countertransference as a negative factor in therapy: "Recognize this counter-transference . . . and overcome it," he counseled, because "no psychoanalyst goes further than his own complexes and internal resistances permit" (Freud, 1957, p. 145).

As stated elsewhere, "Countertransference . . . consists of emotional, attitudinal, and behavioral responses that are inappropriate in terms of . . . intensity, frequency, and duration" (Sommers-Flanagan & Sommers-Flanagan, 2003, p. 116). When working with clients, it's helpful to pay attention to your own emotions, thoughts, impulses, and behaviors. For example, during a session you may notice that you feel irritated or annoyed with a client. If you're the sort of person who occasionally feels annoyed with others, your feelings may not require much additional scrutiny—other than simply noting they've come up. However, when your annoyance is strong (intensity), comes up often (frequency), and sticks with you for a considerable length of time (duration), then you may be suffering from countertransference.

As you may have guessed, in the case where I (John) was accused of being emotionally unresponsive and "robotic," there was also evidence of countertransference. Specifically, as my client progressively increased the volume of her complaints about me, I found myself in a quick emotional retreat. The fact is that I've never been comfortable with highly intense emotional demands aimed toward me, and my typical response is emotional distancing and escape. Clearly, her transference had pushed my buttons. In a way, she was absolutely right: Although I didn't have wires for veins, I was becoming more and more emotionally unresponsive toward her. It was a case of transference-induced countertransference and illustrates how psychoanalytic psychotherapy is a two-person or intersubjective process.

Moving beyond Freud, contemporary psychoanalytically oriented clinicians broadened the definition of countertransference to include all therapist emotional-cognitive-physical reactions to the client. This means that the therapist's reaction need not be viewed as a sign of personal unresolved conflicts. Using this conceptualization, many writers emphasize at least two potential beneficial aspects of countertransference (Beitman, 1987; Pipes & Davenport, 1999).

First, awareness of countertransference reactions can help therapists obtain a deeper understanding of their own personal issues. When therapists struggle with this deeper awareness, it can give them greater compassion for the client. Second, if the therapist's reaction to a client is unusual, it may have much more to do with the client than the therapist. For example, if you're feeling afraid of a client, it may be that he or she is subtly saying or doing something threatening; consequently, your reaction to the client can help you glimpse how the client usually affects other people. This glimpse can provide you a foundation from which to make a transference interpretation.

From the two-person psychology frame within psychoanalytic theory, even if your reaction to a client is not unusual, it still may represent a sort of countertransference response. The key question to keep in mind is "Who am I being asked to be in this situation?" (M. Spitzform, personal communication, January, 2003).

Triangles of Insight

Earlier we discussed the issue of what the psychoanalytic therapist should interpret. Now we'll focus on a common approach to interpretive material. Later we'll look more closely at this process through case examples.

Beyond resistance, psychoanalytic therapists often focus their interpretations on *triangles of insight*. These insight triangles are either primarily conflict-based or transference-based.

The conflict-based triangle of insight includes (1) the client's wish, aim, or drive; (2) the threat or imagined threat that makes the direct gratification of the wish impossible; and (3) the defensive compromise. Although in traditional Freudian analysis the client's wish has either sexual or aggressive roots, in an object relations model the client's wish might have an interpersonal focus. For example, a young man might wish for greater emotional and physical distance from his mother. However, because when he was growing up his efforts toward individuation were met with abandonment from his mother, he finds himself feeling too anxious and too guilty to assert his independence needs directly. Then, although he feels confused when his mother places demands on him, he denies and minimizes the issue by stating, "Oh it's just my mom being my mom; I don't really like it, but there's nothing else I can do." Using the triangle of insight model, an interpretation might focus on one or more of these issues: (1) "You wish you could have a little more independence or be a little more assertive with your mother, (2) but you don't say or do anything because you're afraid you'll hurt her or she'll just turn away from you in anger, and (3) you've been trying to shrink the problem by saying it's no big deal, but you still end up feeling anxious, guilty, and confused more often than you'd like."

The transference-based triangle of insight includes (1) observations based on the transference relationship, (2) the client's reports of his early childhood relationship dynamics, and (3) the client's reports of his contemporary, outside-of-therapy relationships. In the case described in the preceding paragraph, to facilitate insight, the therapist (who happens to be a woman who is about 20 years older than the client) might say,

(1) "Sometimes in here I feel you pulling away in a sort of charming way; you laugh and joke, but you seem to want to keep me away from knowing more personal or intimate things about you;" (2) "You've told me before about how your mom would cling to you until finally you'd break free and then she'd punish you by being unavailable, and this seems connected to (3) how hard it is now for you to really open up to a woman, because you fear she'll clamp onto you and never let you out of her sight." The transference triangle of insight may emerge and repeat itself in the client's dreams and waking narratives (Popp, Diguer, Luborsky, Faude, et al., 1996).

Dream Interpretation

Freud considered dreams to be the royal road to the unconscious. He believed that client dreams constituted the best access he could get to repressed, unconscious, instinctual drives. Unfortunately, as it turns out, even Freud's royal road is fraught with potholes and speed bumps.

Although dreams provide access to the unconscious, similar to client free association material, they consist of unconscious derivatives and require interpretation to produce insight. This fact, once again from the classical psychoanalytic perspective, gives the psychoanalyst the authority to provide accurate and therapeutic interpretations. In some ways client dreams are a temptation for the psychoanalyst to project his or her own issues and conflicts onto ambiguous dream symbols and material. Certainly, one might conclude that Freud, because of his own interest (and perhaps preoccupation) with sexual issues, might have been inclined to overinterpret or misinterpret client dream images as representing sexual instinctual drives. Additionally, based on his own theory, his own phallic (achievement) issues might have led him to insist to clients that his interpretations (rather than the clients') were sacred and correct.

This may be why therapists from a psychoanalytic orientation often have a reputation for giving out authoritarian, symbol-based interpretations of dream content. For example, in textbook descriptions of psychoanalytic dream analysis, if a male client dreams of struggling while climbing a tree, the tree trunk is interpreted as a penis and his struggle represents his problems associated with feeling sexually adequate. Similarly, a woman client with the same dream is told that she's experiencing penis envy and that her efforts to climb to the top are symbolic of her wish to become a man.

In reality, contemporary psychoanalytic dream work does not rely on authoritarian, symbol-based, analyst-centered interpretations. Instead, it is a deeply personal and interactive process. Levy (1984) briefly describes the dream analysis process:

> Using dreams to their fullest advantage requires that the patient be encouraged to free associate to dream elements. The patient must be an active collaborator in dream interpretation in order to avoid a sense of speculation. . . . Whenever possible, the patient's own ideas should be sought so that he becomes familiar with unconscious mechanisms that are sometimes most clearly seen in dream material. (p. 48)

This description should be a reminder that psychoanalytic dream analysis, as currently practiced, is an interactive process, emphasizing the client's reactions to and impressions of the dream's meaning. Although the analyst's perspective and interpretations are important, the method involves asking clients to free associate to their dreams, and then a collaborative exploration of responses ensues.

Preparing Yourself to Do Psychoanalytically Informed Therapy

It's very unlikely (not to mention unethical) for beginning therapists to rush out and start conducting traditional psychoanalytic therapy. Consequently, as an initial step toward weaving psychoanalytic principles and techniques into your therapy sessions, we've provided a short list of practical tips.

- *Strongly consider getting psychoanalytically oriented psychotherapy for yourself.* Ellen McWhirter, a professor in counseling at the University of Oregon with a strong interest in the interpersonal process approach to therapy, gave the following suggestion for counseling and psychotherapy students: "Get experience as a client. There is always room for further growth and insight, and I firmly believe that nothing helps us assist clients more than learning what it's like to be a client, whether the therapist we see is excellent or mediocre. In addition, therapy is a wonderful way to learn about and move through blindspots [and] figure out what our weaknesses are and where we are likely to be vulnerable, and [it] can teach us humility. Humility also comes from our own struggles, and there's nothing like falling down and getting up again to help us appreciate the courage and strengths of our clients" (E. McWhirter, personal communication, August 17, 2002).
- *When in doubt, don't forget the basic rule.* From time to time simply tell your client to say whatever comes to mind, or ask something like, "What's passing through your mind right now?" Then, just sit back and listen for struggles, wishes, or other important themes. A few minutes of free association is acceptable, even from a managed care perspective.
- *Use noncritical, mutual exploration as a general technique.* This approach is useful in teaching clients the psychoanalytic model and in demonstrating that everything emerging from the client—even blatant resistance—is worth looking at. The main point is to be able to do this in a collaborative manner, without blaming the client for his or her performance in therapy.
- *Pay attention to your client's childhood baggage and possible transference.* Whether you directly discuss it or not, your client's current behavior is strongly influenced by early childhood experiences. Pay attention to ways in which your client interacts with you. If the interaction is particularly intense, repetitive, and unusual, you may be observing a transference reaction.
- *Pay attention to your own childhood, interpersonal baggage, and possible countertransference.* Be sure to recognize that you are a subjective participant observer within an interpersonal relationship. This suggests that you should educate yourself on how you and other therapists might respond to particular clients (for example, you might respond differently to clients with Borderline Personality Disorder or Post-Traumatic Stress Disorder). Also, getting feedback on your interpersonal style from friends, family, and supervisors is essential. As Karen Horney suggested in her book *Self-Analysis,* "It is frequently declared that analysis is the only means of furthering personality growth. . . . That is not true. Life itself is the most effective help for our development" (Horney, 1942).

Preparing Your Client to Engage in Psychoanalytically Informed Therapy

Psychoanalytic therapy is definitely not for everyone. For clients to effectively use this form of therapy, they need to be keenly interested in psychological, interpersonal, and family of origin issues. Additionally, psychoanalytic therapy approaches should not be used unless you have given your client full disclosure about how therapy generally proceeds. For example, we know of one analytically oriented therapist who began sessions—even his initial session with new clients—by simply looking expectantly at the client. This look was designed to begin the free association process, but without explanation, it often became an immediate obstacle that might have been easily overcome had he provided clients with information about his approach.

The best preparation for clients is to provide them with informed consent and role induction. Informed consent was discussed in Chapter 1. Role induction is a procedure through which therapists tell clients about how therapy works. It occurs most formally at the beginning of therapy, but it also continues on an intermittent basis throughout therapy. Lester Luborsky (1984) recommends that preliminary socialization interviews for psychoanalytic therapy be provided by a professional who won't be providing the therapy. Although this can be complicated to arrange, Luborsky believes socialization yields shorter therapies with better outcomes. Here's an example of a therapy socialization statement pertaining to interpretation:

> We try to kid ourselves, and it's your therapist's job to make you aware of when you are kidding yourself. The therapist is not going to try to tell you what he or she thinks but will point out to you how two things you are saying just don't fit together. You know, feelings have to add up, kind of like two and two are four, but we like to kid ourselves sometimes that they are five. (Orne, 1968, cited in Luborsky, 1984, p. 195)

The preceding role induction statement informs the client that the therapist will be pointing out logical and emotional inconsistencies in the client's verbalizations. Similarly, role induction can be used to inform clients of the therapist's particular procedures or theoretical perspectives. Here we provide an example of role induction for psychoanalytic dream work.

> The dream, as you remember it, can be thought of as a reflection of certain thoughts, feelings, wishes, and fantasies in you, perhaps stirred up by recent experiences of yours, which are represented in the dream in ways that make them either more acceptable to you or so disguised that they are at first unrecognizable. We can learn a great deal about you by understanding what these hidden trends are, as well as by seeing how and why you disguise them. (Levy, 1984, p. 47)

Assessment Issues and Procedures

Traditionally, psychoanalytically oriented clinicians use two primary assessment procedures. First, they use clinical interviewing. Second, they use projective testing with their clients. Projective tests used by analytic therapists include the Rorschach Inkblot Test, the Thematic Apperception Test, free association to specific words, and human figure drawings. Because they value direct interaction with clients and generative assessment procedures (in which the client generates information from his or her imagination), psychoanalytic therapists are often unimpressed by objective, psychometrically based questionnaires or assessment procedures.

For example, during a 2-hour weekly assessment seminar on my (John's) psychoanalytic internship, the supervisors spent 10 minutes reviewing results from the Wechsler Adult Intelligence Scales and the Minnesota Multiphasic Personality Inventory (MMPI) and 1 hour and 50 minutes talking about the Rorschach and human figure drawings. One supervisor in particular especially enjoyed turning the MMPI profile up-side down and sideways to make fun of objective testing procedures. Although this be-havior was a bit over the top, we interns had long stopped caring about his MMPI jokes. This was because he had already won our respect and admiration; in one of the first cases presented in the seminar, he accurately concluded that a woman he'd never met had been sexually abused solely on the basis of her first response to Card 1 on the Rorschach (this is a true story and not a tongue-in-cheek comment).

Unless you've received adequate training and supervision, you should avoid using projective assessment strategies. However, as we have noted, analytic therapists also use clinical interviewing assessment techniques. Probably the most valuable and prac-tical of the interviewing assessment procedures for graduate students in psychology and counseling is the screening interview used to determine whether an individual client is appropriate for psychoanalytically oriented treatment (see Putting It in Prac-tice 2.1).

APPLICATION: CASE EXAMPLES

Althea Horner, a contemporary object relations practitioner and theorist, has com-mented on the educational use of case examples. She states: "Because no two people are alike (being as idiosyncratic as their fingerprints or their DNA), as much as specific cases elucidate they can also mislead when applied to other situations" (Horner, 1998, p. xv). With Horner's warning in mind, we now proceed to a series of case examples de-signed to help you think about therapy process from a psychoanalytic perspective.

Analysis of Resistance

In traditional psychoanalysis, it's standard procedure to interpret defense before con-flict. The reason for this rule is basic. If you interpret underlying conflict first, then the client will simply use preexisting defenses to deny your insightful interpretation. For ex-ample, if you tell your client that the reason for her silence is fear of rejection, then she's likely to withdraw from you by using more silence. Instead, if you interpret the defense first, by opening up a discussion of how she uses silence to protect herself, then she may be able to begin using less distorting defenses, giving both you and her a clearer glimpse of the underlying conflicts and a better chance of understanding and accepting your eventual deeper conflict interpretations.

Defenses don't promptly disappear upon interpretation. In fact, especially when used in an authoritarian manner, interpretations can cause clients to react defensively. Consider this example:

Client: There's absolutely nothing about my past that causes me any trouble. I hated my older brother, but he's dead now. There's no point in talking about that. The past is over. It doesn't do any good to talk about it.

Therapist: I've heard you say this before. You close down an entire subject for dis-cussion when, very possibly, there could be something uncomfortable worth talking about. It's like you put up a wall and say, "There's nothing there, end of subject." [Therapist makes interpretation of denial.]

Client: There really *is* nothing in my past to talk about! [Client persists in using denial to ward off an exploration of potentially difficult experiences.]

Analytic therapists don't expect instant change. Clients have been using the same or similar defensive styles for years, and one interpretation isn't enough to produce insight and change. Psychoanalytic therapy takes time; defensiveness will persist, but eventually, when it is identified and interpreted repeatedly, clients begin having greater understanding and greater voluntary control over their defensiveness than before.

Case Example 1: An Initial Interpretation of Resistance

Resistance can emerge at any time during psychotherapy, but it occurs somewhat more often early in therapy as a means of avoiding discussions of emotionally uncomfortable material. As in the following example, an early interpretation of this sort of resistance usually comes in the form of a gentle observation combined with gentle encouragement for the client to engage in a mutual self-observation process.

> **Therapist:** I have noticed, and wonder if you have, that as intensely as you re-member and talk about your struggles with your father, thoughts and memories about your mother rarely appear for us to look at.
>
> **Patient:** I don't think I'm hiding anything. She was always around, right in the middle of things, sort of. (Levy, 1984, p. 76)

This interpretation illustrates the straightforward nature of many early interpretations. The therapist simply points out what the client is talking about freely and what he is not talking about freely. It's not unusual for this type of observation to generate additional therapeutic material. Levy (1984) reports that the client followed this interpretation with some "forced comments" about his mother, quickly returning to more detailed discussions of his father. Subsequently, another gentle, explorative interpretation was used.

> **Therapist:** Despite trying to talk more about your mother, you return to your father as though you can't allow yourself to tell me more about your feelings toward her.
>
> **Patient:** I feel you want to force me to have an Oedipus complex, whatever that is. The thought of my having sexual feelings toward my mother is disgusting. I was very close, too close to her, maybe, as a child. But it was her doting on me. And it was never sexual. I do remember the way she would wear pajamas around the apartment. But that's all. (Levy, 1984, p. 76)

In this second interpretation, the therapist "portrays the patient's resistance as a struggle with himself that involves an internal prohibition" (Levy, 1984, p. 77). Shortly afterward, the client began talking about vivid memories relating to his curiosity about his mother. Therapy was then able to move forward in a more comprehensive manner—as the client began talking about his uncomfortable feelings about his mother as well as the feelings he had been describing toward his father.

Case Example 2: Analysis of Resistance Leading to Transference Material

This example emphasizes the importance of exploring resistance as something valuable—something to be explored together by therapist and client to pursue the possible meaning of the resistance. In this case, the client falls silent. The therapist had observed the following pattern during the past several sessions: His client was having difficulties speaking freely and usually followed these struggles with apologies and scathing self-critique. The bracketed information that follows is in the original text.

Patient: I'm sorry. I feel like I don't have anything to say. [Silence, lasting a minute or two.]

Therapist: Let's try to understand the silence together and see what it tells us about you.

Patient: I just seem to run out of things to say. [Silence.]

Therapist: When you run out of things to say, how do you begin to feel?

Patient: I feel stupid. In fact, often, in the car on the way over here I worry about whether I'll have enough things to talk about to fill the time.

Therapist: You feel stupid.

Patient: After I've told you the news since my last appointment, I can't think of anything important to tell you. My mind wanders to dumb things, what to cook for dinner, my hair, stupid things like that.

Therapist: You label your more personal thoughts dumb or stupid. What does that bring to mind?

Patient: My parents. They were always telling me I was stupid, that my opinions were stupid if they were different from theirs.

Therapist: So when you are silent, you keep more personal things to yourself. I think you may do this to ward off the possibility that I, too, may find your more personal thoughts stupid, even if that doesn't consciously occur to you.

Patient: You know, I do worry that you'll think I'm stupid, although I never put that together with being silent. Stupid was a word my mother used constantly. She still does, whenever I don't do things her way. (Levy, 1984, p. 82)

This case illustrates how exploration of resistance (silence) can produce transference material and insight. The transference issue revealed will not magically disappear, but its emergence provides the client and therapist with new and clearer information that should lead to further work on the client's internalized harsh and critical self.

Case Example 3: Exploration and Interpretation of Transference

In a case with a dynamic very similar to the preceding example, a psychoanalytic therapist explores and interprets a transference reaction.

Patient: So it was really interesting that I have all these rules I live by, and statements coming from other people. Yet I depend on myself to interpret all the rules. I never bother to ask for help, or understanding from the point of view of the person who set the rule at any given time.

Therapist: How are you thinking about it—in terms of the sessions and things like that? What sort of things were you thinking about?

Patient: Hmm. Because I'm doing . . . if I even could ask you questions, I mean.

Therapist: If you could?

Patient: Uh-huh. Not in terms of whether or not it's allowed. But also in terms of like whether or not you can even answer them.

Therapist: What did you think?

Patient: I think I'm the only one who can answer my questions. I mean, ultimately, I guess. It's almost like asking the questions would be kind of a waste of time. Sometimes, too, I know when I get in conversations with other people, I somehow touch upon questions that I'm asking myself, although I don't directly come out and say it. I think I really weigh whatever they say too heavily. I really get carried away with their answer . . .

Therapist: Mm-hmm.

Patient: . . . and forget about the focus of mine, my own answer.

Therapist: So do you think that plays out in here? Where you may want help, but you won't ask for it, or you kind of expect it from me, or something from me, but . . .

Patient: Yeah.

Therapist: . . . maybe are reluctant to let it happen.

Patient: Yeah.

Therapist: In what way? How do you think it plays out? (Jones, 2000, pp. 181–182)

Later in the therapy session, the client and therapist try to connect the client's reluctance to ask questions in therapy to a past experience.

Patient: Not really being able to ask questions almost feels like when I was living with my stepmother. It means smarter or stupid. I mean being smart like acting up or I think "you're being dumb," that I didn't have any common sense. But I should be able to figure myself out.

Therapist: You might have felt really hurt by those things because you might have just been asking the questions because you didn't know and you wanted to be helped.

Patient: Yeah.

Therapist: Maybe some of that is happening now. Because one of the first things you said, you kind of were wondering if you could ask me questions. And it sounds like you're kind of afraid to ask me questions, for some of the same reasons.

Patient: Yeah. (cries quietly for a minute, blows nose) I mean I can't ask questions, or feel like I can't ask questions. I mean, my employer and my friends, I feel like I'm bugging them. (two minute silence) Can I ask questions?

Therapist: What would stop you from asking questions?

Patient: I don't know.

Therapist: You know I can't promise that I would answer every one of them. But I'm kind of curious as why you think you couldn't.

Patient: Mm. (pause) Because they seem like—I'm not sure they lead to anything.

Therapist: Yeah, but that's a different point, whether or not they lead anywhere is, you know, open to see, but something stops you . . .

Patient: Mm-hmm.

Therapist: . . . from even getting to the point of feeling like you can ask me a question. I mean independent of whether I answer it or whether or not it leads somewhere. I think it provokes some feelings inside you, that old feeling you said. (pause) Feelings of being what—being smart or being called stupid, or feeling like you're bugging somebody.

Patient: Mm-hmm. (pause) Also, I don't know. I've got to use your common sense to answer questions. I'm not using my common sense. (silence) I feel like I'm trying to get everyone else to live my life if I can't answer my own questions. (silence) Sometimes I think I do all kinds of dumb things, so I can find answers without having to ask anyone.

Therapist: So it may be less painful perhaps, to do those things rather than to put yourself in the position of asking people questions.

Patient: Yeah.

Therapist: Well, it sounds like you're struggling with some of that in here. You have given me lots of information or lots of cues that you really want to ask me some questions but are hesitant to.

Patient: It still doesn't feel right. It seems like I am not supposed to ask questions.

Therapist: Well, what's interesting about that is, I've never said anything to that effect. I don't remember any rule like that being talked about, yet it feels that way to you. Like you were saying before, it's one of these rules that you've come up with about how you and I relate; one of the rules you've come up with is, you don't ask questions.

Patient: Yeah.

Therapist: But it sounds like the same thing is happening in here that sometimes happens outside of here. Like you're saying with your friends and with your boss and maybe with your stepmother. (E. E. Jones, 2000, pp.183–184)

This case illustrates several psychoanalytic procedures. First, the therapist is working on establishing a transference-related triangle of insight, and he provides an interpretation for that triangle in his last statement. Second, this example shows how psychoanalytic therapists will sometimes withhold a response to a client in the service of deepening and exploring transference. About midway through the dialogue, the client asks, "Can I ask questions?" but the therapist does not directly provide an answer. The purpose of withholding a direct answer is to further nurture the developing transference reaction. Third, it demonstrates how psychoanalytic therapists keep exploring process dynamics through clarification, empathy, and interpretation.

Questions for Reflection

When the client asked, "Can I ask questions?" the therapist could have responded in many different ways. Consider the following alternative responses to the client's question and speculate on how each alternative might be conceptualized from a psychoanalytic or object relations perspective. Also, speculate on how the alternative responses might change the direction of the therapy and how it might affect the client.

Client: Can I ask questions?

Alternative 1: Yes, absolutely. You can ask me questions whenever you'd like.

Alternative 2: I noticed that was a question right there. How did it feel for you to ask it?

Alternative 3: What do you imagine would happen if you asked me a question?

Additional Psychoanalytic Techniques

The preceding case examples illustrate the traditional psychoanalytic technique of interpretation. There are other, less commonly discussed techniques, such as catharsis or abreaction and the hypnoanalytic affect bridge, both of which may be explored should you have a strong interest in learning more about psychoanalytic therapies (Watkins, 1971; Watkins & Watkins, 1997).

THERAPY OUTCOMES RESEARCH

Over the years, classical Freudian psychoanalysis has been the focus of much criticism from empirical researchers. Recall that in Eysenck's initial review of psychotherapy outcome, psychoanalysis was rated as less effective than either eclectic therapy or no treatment (Eysenck, 1952). Despite these criticisms, to date, there still have not been any systematic, well-controlled outcome studies published attesting to the efficacy of psychoanalysis (Fonagy et al., 1999). In fact, prior to his death, Merton Gill, a renowned psychoanalyst, noted that "[psychoanalysis is] the only significant branch of human knowledge and therapy that refuses to conform to the demand of Western civilization for some kind of systematic demonstration of its contentions" (Gill, 1994, p. 157).

There has been some less rigorous scientific research attesting to the effectiveness of classical psychoanalysis. In particular, Fonagy and colleagues (1999) report on data from 4 case studies, 13 naturalistic, pre-post, or quasi-experimental studies, 9 experimental studies, 9 follow-up studies, and 6 process-outcome studies. Fonagy describes the research:

> Notwithstanding these . . . severe [methodological] limitations, many of the studies are impressive: they report results which other psychotherapies have not been able to achieve, particularly with intractable disorders; some show very long-term benefits; results tend to be highly consistent across studies; and some include samples larger than those of most better controlled treatment trials. So whereas it is true that the outcome of psychoanalysis is not established, some suggestive conclusions may be drawn: Psychoanalysis benefits the majority of those who are offered this treatment . . . and brings the functioning of a clinical group to the level of the normal population. . . . Longer treatments have better outcomes . . . and intensive psychoanalytic treatment is generally more effective than psychoanalytic psychotherapy . . . although its superiority is sometimes only apparent on long-term follow-up. . . . Psychoanalysis can lead to a reduction in health care related use and expenditure . . . which is maintained for some further years. . . . Long-term psychoanalytic therapy can reduce symptomatology in severe personality disorder . . . and these improvements are largely maintained. . . . Psychoanalysis may also be an effective treatment for severe psychosomatic disorders. (Fonagy, 1999, pp. 4–5)

Overall, although well-controlled outcomes research is sorely lacking, the existing literature is mostly positive (Fonagy & Target, 1996; Knight, 1941). There are also many relatively famous individuals (including the son of the great behaviorist John B. Watson) who have personally testified to the benefits of their experience in psychoanalysis (see Chapter 7).

Short-term or time-limited psychoanalytic psychotherapy and various forms of psychodynamic therapy have been the focus of considerable controlled research. The overall findings have been summarized via various meta-analyses. All of these summaries have indicated that psychoanalytic or psychodynamic therapies are at least slightly more effective than no treatment. More specifically, comparisons between psychoanalytic and behavioral/cognitive approaches have produced somewhat variable results, with claims ranging from (1) psychoanalytic and behavioral approaches are approximately equivalent in effectiveness (Smith, Glass, & Miller, 1980) to (2) psychoanalytic approaches are slightly less effective than behavioral/cognitive approaches (Shapiro & Shapiro, 1982) and (3) psychoanalytic approaches, while more effective than no treatment, are substantially less effective than behavioral/cognitive treatments (Weisz, Donenberg, Han, & Weiss, 1995).

More recently, three forms of brief psychodynamic therapy have received endorsement from the APA's Division 12 Task Force on Promotion and Dissemination of Psychological Procedures (Chambless et al., 1998) as "probably efficacious." These treatments and their supporting research studies include

- Brief dynamic therapy for opiate dependence (Woody, Luborsky, McLellan, & O'Brien, 1990)
- Brief dynamic therapy for depression (Gallagher-Thompson & Steffen, 1994)
- Insight-oriented marital therapy (Snyder & Wills, 1989; Snyder, Wills, & Grady-Fletcher, 1991)

In recent years, a treatment approach for depressed adults and adolescents derived from interpersonal psychiatry and object relations theory has received extensive research attention (DiMascio et al., 1979; Klerman, Weissman, Rounsaville, & Chevron, 1995; Mufson, Moreau, Weissman, & Klerman, 1993). This treatment, interpersonal psychotherapy for depression, was evaluated in the large scale National Institute of Mental Health (NIMH) Collaborative Study. In this extremely well-controlled scientific study, interpersonal psychotherapy was more effective than a placebo control and equally as effective as antidepressant medication (imipramine) and cognitive-behavior therapy (Elkin et al., 1989). Based on Beck Depression Inventory scores for the patients who completed the study, the recovery rates were 51% for placebo treatment, 65% for cognitive-behavior therapy, 69% for imipramine treatment, and 70% for interpersonal psychotherapy (see Putting It in Practice 2.2 for a more detailed description of interpersonal psychotherapy). The strong empirical research supporting the efficacy of interpersonal therapy for depression resulted in its being listed as a "well-established" empirically validated therapy by the APA's Division 12 Task Force on Promotion and Dissemination of Psychological Procedures (Chambless et al., 1998) and as a "probably efficacious" treatment for bulimia (Fairburn, Jones, Peveler, Hope, & O'Conner, 1993).

Overall, as usual, we recommend that you take the preceding research findings with a grain of salt. This is because of the challenges inherent in conducting systematic research on something as precarious and subjective as human mental and emotional problems. One such challenge, referred to by Luborsky and colleagues as the *allegiance effect,* suggests that the researcher's therapy preference or allegiance is a strong predictor of outcome study results (Luborsky et al., 1999). Specifically, Luborsky and colleagues reported that about two thirds of the variation in outcome differences between psychotherapy techniques was accounted for by the researcher's theoretical allegiance. The implications are obvious. Most psychotherapy researchers are behavioral and cognitive in their orientation. Consequently, it's no surprise that most research reviews end up attesting to the efficacy of cognitive-behavioral approaches over psychoanalytic approaches.

Putting It in Practice 2.2

Interpersonal Psychotherapy for Depression

Sometimes psychotherapy research progress chugs along so slowly that one wonders whether there's any movement happening at all. This has especially been the case with regard to efficacy research on psychoanalysis.

In contrast, a rather new, short-term, and focal approach to treating depression has quickly emerged and established itself as an effective therapy. This approach, developed by the late Gerald Klerman of Harvard University and a group of associates from Yale University, is called *interpersonal psychotherapy for depression*. It was developed in the 1970s and empirically validated in the 1980s.

Interpersonal psychotherapy has its roots in the interpersonal psychiatry of Harry Stack Sullivan and the attachment theories of John Bowlby and Mary Ainsworth (Ainsworth, 1969; Bowlby, 1977; Sullivan, 1953). It is unique in that it was designed, not as a general psychotherapeutic approach, but as a specific treatment for depression. Klerman and colleagues describe the approach in contrast to psychodynamic approaches:

> Both interpersonal and psychodynamic approaches are concerned with the whole life span, and both consider early experience and persistent personality patterns important. In understanding human transactions, however, the psychodynamic therapist is concerned with object relations while the interpersonal therapist focuses on interpersonal relations. The psychodynamic therapist listens for the patient's intrapsychic wishes and conflicts; the interpersonal therapist listens for the patient's role expectations and disputes. (Klerman, Weissman, Rounsaville, & Chevron, 1984, p. 18)

Interpersonal psychotherapy is a rarity. It has quickly established itself as an effective treatment for depression in both adults and adolescents (Moreau, Mufson, Weissman, & Klerman, 1991; Weissman, Markowitz, & Klerman, 2000). It focuses on diagnosing and treating the various interpersonal problems associated with depression. These include grief, role disputes, role transitions, and interpersonal deficits. Because it focuses on real interpersonal relationships instead of internalized object relations, it is one step removed from a psychoanalytic form of treatment, but it is certainly rooted in and guided by some psychoanalytic principles and is a testament to the potential empirical success that could be awaiting other forms of treatment. We will return to the practice of interpersonal psychotherapy for depression and other conditions in Chapter 13.

For those of you interested in understanding why someone would undertake psychoanalytic training in this era of briefer therapies and managed-care, a short essay from a clinical psychoanalyst is provided in Practitioner Commentary 2.1.

CONCLUDING COMMENTS

Anyone whose collected works fill 24 volumes is likely to have—as we psychoanalytically informed mental health professionals like to say—achievement issues. Dr. Freud would probably accept this interpretation. He himself stated that "A man who has been

PRACTITIONER COMMENTARY 2.1

Why I Became A Psychoanalyst

Marianne Spitzform

What possessed me to train in clinical psychoanalysis at a time when managed care, with its emphasis on brief, symptom-focused treatment, was spreading through the country? I've always been fascinated by the ways we humans relate to each other and this planet we live on—what motivates and what frightens, and the ways we meet suffering and try to find happiness. And there is the simple fact that for certain kinds of learning about oneself, no other tool is as refined and elegant and powerful as psychoanalysis. A psychoanalytic approach helps the client see the ways he or she views the world and facilitates change in harmful or outmoded patterns of relationships with others and with him- or herself. It is characterized, of course, by its tracking of unconscious process, adaptive and maladaptive defenses, and its reliance upon free association. But this method of inquiry into the human mind and spirit offers in addition two unique features that are absent or minimized in other clinical techniques. Psychoanalysis values emotions and the ways we experience, express, and think about them, and it specifically trains its practitioners to be aware of the emotional impact the client is having upon the analyst in the clinical situation. No other methodology has studied, written about, and experientially explored the complexity of the therapeutic relationship with the sophistication of psychoanalysis. In everyday work, whether or not I am engaged in psychoanalysis, the depth and scope of this way of thinking about human experience is something I value and use whether in brief once a week treatments or those that are more intensive. I guess the short answer to the question why I became a psychoanalyst is that training in, and practice of, this method offers a fascinating glimpse into the workings of the human mind, as well as a powerful agent for healing.

the indisputable favorite of his mother keeps for life the feeling of a conqueror, that confidence of success that often induces real success" (E. E. Jones, 1961, p. 6).

Judging solely by his own theoretical perspective, Freud clearly suffered from some Oedipal conflicts, and these were, in part, manifest in his intense striving for recognition. When, initially, his potential for greatness was unrecognized by his peers (his paper "The Aetiology of Hysteria" was poorly received) he responded with anger. Eventually, it may have been his penchant for stature that contributed to, or caused him to recant his seduction theory.

In 1937, two years before Janet's death, Edouard Pichon, Pierre Janet's son-in-law, wrote to Freud, asking him to visit with Janet. Freud responded:

No, I will not see Janet. I could not refrain from reproaching him with having behaved unfairly to psychoanalysis and also to me personally and never having corrected it. He was stupid enough to say that the idea of sexual aetiology for the neuroses could only arise in the atmosphere of a town like Vienna. Then when the libel was spread by French writers that I had listened to his lectures and stolen his ideas he could with a word have put an end to such talk, since actually I never saw him or heard his name in the Charcot time: he has never spoken this word. You can get an idea of his scientific level from his utterance that the unconscious is une façon de parler. No I will not see him. I thought at first of sparing him the impoliteness by the excuse that I am not well or that I can no longer talk French and he certainly can't understand a word of German. But I have decided against that. There is no reason for making any sacrifice for him. Honesty the only possible thing; rudeness quite in order. (Bowers & Meichenbaum, 1984; E. E. Jones, 1961, pp. 633–634)

In the end, there is no reconciliation for Freud. He is tormented by his resentment. In fact, one might hypothesize that he was tormented by his unconscious—an unconscious well informed of the compromises he made with his clients' truth in the name of his own self-interest. In contrast to what Fritz Perls (Chapter 5) later claimed about guilt (that it is often resentment in disguise), the case of Freud seems to argue otherwise: Sometimes a guilt complex is just a guilt complex.

STUDENT REVIEW ASSIGNMENTS

Please read and respond to the following student review activities.

Critical Corner

The following critical statements about psychoanalytic approaches to therapy are designed to be provocative. You may or may not agree with them. Please read and consider the statements and then write your response to the criticisms in the space provided.

1. Traditional psychoanalysis is based on the interpretation of unconscious conflicts and unconscious maladaptive relationship patterns. This approach is inherently defective because it relies on another completely fallible human being with his or her own unconscious conflicts and problems to make accurate interpretations. Comment on how this approach can ever have any legitimacy. Does the contemporary psychoanalytic two-person psychology model offer any improvement in this regard?
    Response:

2. Presently, many would agree that psychoanalytic theory is an overly intellectual and impractical approach to helping clients. As Gedo (1979) has suggested, it has become a piecemeal patchwork of different theories and approaches. Isn't it time to throw out Freud's psychoanalytic theory and to begin again with a more practical, contemporary approach? Isn't that why interpersonal psychotherapy of depression is gaining popularity?
    Response:

3. Some critics might argue that psychoanalytic drive theory and even more contemporary object relations and self psychology reformulations of psychoanalytic theory are blatantly sexist. Consider Karen Horney's criticisms. What do you think of the possibility of men having pregnancy, childbirth, breast, and mother-

hood envy? How would acknowledgment of these important social and cultural influences affect traditional psychoanalytic theory?
Response:

4. After over 100 years of psychoanalysis, there is still little or no hard scientific evidence attesting to its efficacy. How can an approach to therapy rationalize its existence without any scientific data to support its practice?
Response:

5. Traditional psychoanalytic forms of therapy have "making the unconscious conscious" or "insight" as their primary therapy goal. Some critics claim there is no scientific evidence of the unconscious. Where do you stand on this issue? Are there unconscious processes that affect interpersonal relationships?
Response:

6. Traditional psychoanalytic theory is strongly deterministic. Similar to behavioral approaches, psychoanalytic therapies minimize client choice and personal responsibility. After all, if behavior is psychologically determined, then is there any possibility of human choice as a method of change? Do you agree that psychoanalysis is needed for any true and lasting personal change to occur?
Response:

Reviewing Key Terms

- The seduction hypothesis
- The Oedipal conflict
- Unconscious
- Preconscious
- Conscious
- Id
- Ego
- Superego
- Repression
- Denial
- Projection
- Reaction formation

- Displacement
- Rationalization
- Regression
- Sublimation
- Repetition-compulsion
- Ego psychology
- Object relations theory
- Self psychology
- Corrective emotional experience
- Focal psychotherapy
- Selection criteria
- The basic rule

- Role induction
- Transference
- Countertransference
- Interpretation
- Triangles of insight
- Two-person psychology or intersubjectivity
- Projective assessment
- Dream interpretation
- Interpersonal psychotherapy of depression

Review Questions

1. Describe Freud's seduction hypothesis as outlined in his famous paper "The Aetiology of Hysteria." According to Anna Freud, why did Freud have to recant the seduction hypothesis?

2. What are the four primary characteristics of ego defense mechanisms?

3. Describe what Fairbairn (1952) means when he states: "Libido is object seeking, not pleasure seeking." What does this statement mean with regard to the primary motivation for humans?

4. Both *corrective emotional experience* and *seeding the transference* were suggested as methods for speeding up psychoanalytic therapy. What is the difference between these two concepts or approaches?

5. How might the requirement of reporting client information to insurance companies interfere with the basic rule in psychoanalytic therapy?

6. What is a triangle of insight? Draw two triangles, one with a conflict-based triangle of insight and the other with a transference-based triangle of insight.

7. What are the main differences between one-person and two-person psychology as it applies to psychoanalytic theory and practice?

8. What are the main differences between interpersonal psychotherapy for depression and psychodynamic therapy?

RECOMMENDED READINGS AND RESOURCES

The following readings are provided for your further study.

Leading Psychoanalytic Journals

Reviewing the following journals will keep you up-to-date with the latest discourse in psychoanalytic theory and practice.

- *Contemporary Psychoanalysis*
- *International Journal of Psychoanalysis*
- *Journal of the American Psychoanalytic Association*
- *Journal of Psychoanalytic Psychology*
- *Psychoanalytic Dialogues*
- *Psychoanalytic Psychology*
- *Psychoanalytic Quarterly*
- *The Psychoanalytic Review*

Books and Articles

Erikson, E. H. (1963). *Childhood & society* (2nd ed.). New York: Norton.

Fonagy, P., Kachele, H., Krause, R., Jones, E., Perron, R., & Lopez, L. (1999). *An open door review of outcome studies in psychoanalysis.* London: International Psychoanalytical Association.

Freud, S. (1949). *An outline of psychoanalysis.* New York: Norton.

Freud, S. (1964). *New introductory lectures on psychoanalysis* (J. Strachey, Trans., Vol. 22). London: Hogarth Press.

Greenberg, J. R., & Mitchell, S. A. (1983). *Object relations in psychoanalytic theory.* Cambridge, MA: Harvard University Press.

Horner, A. J. (1998). *Working with the core relationship problem in psychotherapy: A handbook for clinicians.* San Francisco: Jossey-Bass.

Jones, E. E. (2000). *Therapeutic action: A guide to psychoanalytic therapy.* Northvale, NJ: Jason Aronson.

Klerman, G. L., Weissman, M. M., Rounsaville, B. J., & Chevron, E. S. (1984). *Interpersonal psychotherapy of depression.* New York: Basic Books.

Klerman, G. L., Weissman, M. M., Rounsaville, B. J., & Chevron, E. S. (1995). Interpersonal psychotherapy for depression. *Journal of Psychotherapy Practice & Research, 4*(4), 342–351.

Levy, S. T. (1984). *Principles of interpretation.* New York: Jason Aronson.

Luborsky, L. (1984). *Principles of psychoanalytic psychotherapy: A manual for supportive-expressive treatment.* New York: Basic Books.

Mahler, M. B., & Pine, F. (1975). *The psychological birth of the human infant: Symbiosis and individuation.* New York: Basic Books.

Masson, J. M. (1984). *The assault on truth: Freud's suppression of the seduction theory.* New York: Farrar, Straus, and Giroux.

Mitchell, S. A. (1997). *Influence and autonomy in psychoanalysis.* Hillsdale, NJ: Analytic Press.

Pine, F. (1998). *Diversity and direction in psychoanalytic technique.* New Haven, CT: Yale University Press.

St. Clair, M. (2000). *Object relations and self psychology: An introduction.* Pacific Grove, CA: Brooks/Cole.

Stern, D. N. (1985). *The interpersonal world of the infant.* New York: Basic Books.

Strupp, H. H., & Binder, J. L. (1984). *Psychotherapy in a new key.* New York: Basic Books.

Wallerstein, R. S. (1986). *Forty-two lives in treatment: A study of psychoanalysis and psychotherapy.* New York: Guilford Press.

Weissman, M. M., Markowitz, J. C., & Klerman, G. L. (2000). *Comprehensive guide to interpersonal psychotherapy.* New York: Basic Books.

Videotapes

Carlson, J., & Kjos, D. (2000). *Object relations therapy with Dr. Jill Savege Scharff* [Videotape]. Boston: Allyn & Bacon.

Davidson, F. (1995). *Old age I: A conversation with Joan Erikson* [Videotape]. San Luis Obispo, CA: Davidson Films.

Freedheim, D. K. (1994). *Short-term dynamic therapy* [Videotape]. Washington, DC: American Psychological Association.

Karon, B. P. (1994). *Effective psychoanalytic therapy of schizophrenia and other severe disorders* [Videotape]. Washington, DC: American Psychological Association.

Training Organizations and Web Sites

The American Psychoanalytic Association has a helpful web site with information on training programs, workshops, and graduate training programs: www.apsa.org. It also includes a literature search feature as well as a Freud quotation contest.

There are dozens of full-text, cutting-edge psychoanalytic articles at psychematters.com. This web site also includes a listing of events and conferences and a detailed list of state, national, and international psychoanalytic associations, institutes, and societies.

The International Psychoanalytic Association (IPA) web site is at www.ipa.org.uk. The IPA is the world's largest psychoanalytic accreditation and regulatory body. It has over 11,000 members, and its web site is available in four languages (English, French, German, and Spanish).

The National Psychological Association for Psychoanalysis (NPAP) is at www.npap.org. This organization is the training institute for non-medical psychoanalysis.

Information on publications and training opportunities in interpersonal psychotherapy is at the International Society for Interpersonal Psychotherapy web site: www.interpersonalpsychotherapy.org.

A comprehensive list of psychoanalytic journals can be found at the Dallas Society for Psychoanalytic Psychology's web site: www.dspp.com/links/psypubs.htm.

Chapter 3

INDIVIDUAL PSYCHOLOGY: THE THERAPEUTIC APPROACH OF ALFRED ADLER

In a word, I am convinced that a person's behavior springs from his [or her] idea. . . .
As a matter of fact, it has the same effect on one whether a poisonous snake is actually
approaching my foot or whether I merely believe it is a poisonous snake.

—Alfred Adler (1964a)

IN THIS CHAPTER YOU WILL LEARN

- Alfred Adler's contributions to individual psychology
- The history and context of individual psychology
- Theoretical principles of individual psychology
- The central position of encouragement and discouragement in the development of psychological well-being
- The four stages of Adlerian therapy
- Basic methods and techniques of Adlerian therapy
- How and why the individual's lifestyle guides daily functioning
- The results of outcomes research on Adlerian therapy
- The ubiquitous influence of Adler's thinking on subsequent psychological theories

---

We've often wondered about Alfred Adler. Officially, he is the founder of individual psychology. But where did he come up with his radical ideas? As this chapter unfolds, you'll find his beliefs were so out of step for the early twentieth century that he seems an anomaly: He's like a man from the future who somehow landed in the middle of Freud's inner circle in Vienna.

Adler's psychology was far ahead of its time. He wove an understanding of cognition into psychotherapeutic process nearly four decades before Albert Ellis and Aaron Beck officially launched the cognitive therapy movement in the 1950s and 1960s. This chapter's opening quotation captures Adler's ability to articulate, in simple terms, how belief and perception can powerfully shape human emotional experience. In his historical overview of the talking cure, Bankart (1997) claims that "Adler's influence on the developing fields of psychology and social work was incalculable" (p. 146). This chapter is an exploration of Alfred Adler's individual psychology and his incalculable influence on modern counseling and psychotherapy.

BIOGRAPHICAL INFORMATION: ALFRED ADLER

Adler was the second of six children born to a Jewish family on the outskirts of Vienna. His older brother was brilliant, outgoing, and handsome, and also happened to be named Sigmund. In contrast, Alfred was a sickly child. He suffered from rickets, was twice run over in the street, and experienced a spasm of the glottis. When he was three, his younger brother died in bed next to him (Mosak, 1972). At age four, he came down with pneumonia and later recalled his physician telling his father, "Your boy is lost" (Orgler, 1963, p. 16). Another of Adler's earliest memories has a similar sickly, dependent theme:

> One of my earliest recollections is of sitting on a bench bandaged up on account of rickets, with my healthy, elder brother sitting opposite me. He could run, jump, and move about quite effortlessly, while for me movement of any sort was a strain and an effort. Everyone went to great pains to help me, and my mother and father did all that was in their power to do. At the time of this recollection, I must have been about two years old. (Bottome, 1939, p. 30, quoted in Bankart, 1997, p. 131).

In contrast to Freud's childhood experience of being his mother's favorite, Adler was more encouraged by his father. Despite his son's clumsy, uncoordinated, and sickly condition, Adler's father Leopold, a Hungarian Jew, deeply believed in his son's innate worth. When young Alfred was required to repeat a grade at the same middle school Freud had attended 14 years earlier, Leopold was his strongest supporter. Mosak and Maniacci (1999) capture the nature of Adler's response to his father's support:

> His mathematics teacher recommended to his father that Adler leave school and apprentice himself as a shoe-maker. Adler's father objected, and Adler embarked upon bettering his academic skills. Within a relatively short time, he became the best math student in the class. (p. 2)

Adler's love and aptitude for learning continued to grow, and he studied medicine at the University of Vienna. After obtaining his medical degree in ophthalmology in 1895, he met and fell in love with Raissa Timofeyewna Epstein, and he married her in 1897. She had the unusual distinction of being an early socialist and feminist who maintained her political interests and activities throughout their marriage (Hoffman, 1994).

HISTORICAL CONTEXT

Freud and Adler met in 1902. According to Mosak and Maniacci (1999), "Legend has it" that Adler published a strong defense of Freud's *Interpretation of Dreams,* and consequently Freud invited Adler over "on a Wednesday evening" for a discussion of psychological issues. Thereafter, "The Wednesday Night Meetings, as they became known, led to the development of the Psychoanalytic Society" (p. 3).

Adler was his own man with his own ideas before he met Freud. In fact, prior to their meeting he had already published his first book, titled *Healthbook for the Tailor's Trade* (Adler, 1898). In contrast to Freud, much of Adler's medical practice was with the working poor. Early in his career he worked extensively with tailors and circus performers.

In February 1911, Adler did the unthinkable. As president of Vienna's Psychoanalytic Society, he read a highly controversial paper at the group's monthly meeting. The essence of this paper, "The Masculine Protest," was deeply at odds with Freudian theory. Instead of focusing on biological and psychological factors and their influence on excessively masculine behaviors in males and females, Adler emphasized the power of culture and socialization. He claimed that women were socially coerced into an underprivileged social and political position. Further, he noted that some women who reacted to this cultural situation by choosing to dress and act like men were suffering not from penis envy, but from a social-psychological condition he referred to as *the masculine protest.* Finally, he also claimed that the overvaluing of masculinity was driving men and boys either to give up and become passive or to engage in excessive aggressive behavior. In extreme cases, males who suffered from the masculine protest began dressing and acting like girls or women.

The response of the Vienna Psychoanalytic Society members was perhaps even more extreme than the response of Freud's colleagues upon his reading "The Aetiology of Hysteria" to the Vienna Psychiatric Society in 1896. Bankhart (1997) describes the scene:

> After Adler's address, the members of the society were in an uproar. There were pointed heckling and shouted abuse. Some were even threatening to come to blows. And then, almost majestically, Freud rose from his seat. He surveyed the room with his penetrating eyes. He told them there was no reason to brawl in the streets like uncivilized hooligans. The choice was simple. Either he or Dr. Adler would remain to guide the future of psychoanalysis. The choice was the member's to make. He trusted them to do the right thing. (p. 130)

Undoubtedly, Freud must have anticipated the outcome. The group voted for Freud to lead them. Adler left the building quietly, joined by the Society's vice president, William Stekel, and five other members. They moved their portion of the meeting to a local café and established The Society for Free Psychoanalytic Research. The Society moved even farther from its psychoanalytic roots by quickly changing its name to The Society for Individual Psychology. The focus of this new group included the groundbreaking acknowledgment that human functioning was not only biologically based, but also powerfully influenced by social, familial, and cultural factors. Bankart (1997) summarizes the perspective of the Society for Individual Psychology: "Their response to human problems was characteristically ethical and practical—an orientation that stood in dramatic contrast to the biological and theoretical focus of psychoanalysis" (p. 130). For a contemporary practitioner's perspective on the ethical and practical nature of individual psychology see Ethical Highlight 3.1.

Adler's break with Freud gives us a glimpse of the shape of his theory and approach to counseling and psychotherapy. Adler identified with the common people. He was, surprising as it seems for his time, also a feminist. These leanings likely reflect the influences of his upbringing and his marriage. They reveal his compassion for the sick, the oppressed, and the downtrodden. For Adler, the key to psychological health and well-being can be summed up in a single word: encouragement. In contrast, the road to psychological ill health is paved with discouragement.

ETHICAL HIGHLIGHT 3.1

Why Adlerian Theory?

It can be challenging for beginning theories students to select a single therapy approach to focus on and learn more thoroughly than all the others. However, to really plunge into and get to know a single theory and therapy may be the most ethical way to begin as a therapist. Tamara G. Suttle writes of her experience of choosing Adlerian theory and therapy.

I was initially trained in a university that required adherence to a specific theory—any theory of choice. I opted for Adlerian. Out of that experience, I would like to note two things.

The first is that I (and my fellow students) balked repeatedly at being pigeonholed into one specific theory. At the time, we thought it to be incredibly limiting. However, almost immediately upon leaving school and beginning clinical work in the real world, I found that the value of having that "road map" of one single theory was evident over and over again. Each time I got lost, my Adlerian theory told me exactly where to go.

And, related to this, Adlerian theory taught me that the primary reason to gather (and spend time on) a client's history is only to understand the impact it has on today and his or her future. History in and of itself is not significant. The moral of the teaching, then, is not to wallow in the history but rather to use it. This understanding helped me to find the balance in working with my clients.

When a doctor once said to Adler: "I do not believe you can make this backward child normal," Dr. Adler replied: "Why do you say that? One could make any normal child backward; one should only have to discourage it enough!" (Bottome, 1936, p. 37)

Before turning to an examination of Adlerian theoretical principles, let's look at one more quotation, perhaps his most powerful, about the state of gender politics during his lifetime:

All our institutions, our traditional attitudes, our laws, our morals, our customs, give evidence of the fact that they are determined and maintained by privileged males for the glory of male domination. (Adler, 1927, p. 123)

It's hard not to wonder if perhaps Raissa Epstein may have had a few pointed discussions with Alfred Adler—and more than just a little influence on his thinking.

Questions for Reflection

What are your thoughts on Adler's allegiance to feminism? Do you suppose he became more of a feminist because he married one? Or did he marry a feminist because he already had strong leanings in that direction?

THEORETICAL PRINCIPLES

Adler and his followers have written about the theoretical principles of individual psychology extensively. Much of the material that follows is derived from Adler (1956a, 1958), Dreikurs (1950), Mosak (1989), and Mosak and Maniacci (1999).

The Whole Person

Adler did not believe in dichotomies or in breaking the individual into different functional parts. Instead, he emphasized unity of thinking, feeling, acting, attitudes, values, the conscious mind, the unconscious mind, and more. His entire theoretical system, individual psychology, was named after the Latin word *individuum,* meaning "complete, whole, indivisible" (Parrott, 1997). As Mosak and Maniacci (1999) state, "For Adler, the question was neither 'How does mind affect body?' nor 'How does body affect mind?' but rather 'How does the individual use body and mind in the pursuit of goals?'" (pp. 73–74).

   Adlerian holism is in direct contrast to Freud's reductionistic psychological models. Adler did not believe in Freud's tripartite id-ego-superego psychology. This may be why many consider him to be the first true proponent of ego psychology—because he believed the whole person made decisions for which he or she was completely responsible. The idea of an id entity or instinct separately pushing for gratification from inside a person was incompatible with Adler's basic beliefs about holism.

Striving with Purpose

A central proposition of individual psychology is that humans actively shape themselves and their environments. We are not merely passive recipients of our biological traits or simply reactors to our external environment. There is a third element—beyond biology and the environment—that influences and directs human behavior; Adler referred to this third force as "attitude toward life" (Adler, 1935, p. 5). Attitude toward life is composed of a delightful combination of individual human choice and individual sense of purpose.

   In a very practical sense, for Adlerians, everyday behavior can be analyzed with respect to its purpose. When an Adlerian therapist notices a maladaptive quality to her client's behavior patterns, she wonders why that behavior occurs. Of course, she doesn't interrogate her client with aggressive questions like "Why did you do that?"—but she remains interested in the purpose of her client's behavior.

   This concept of striving with purpose has been especially helpful in child psychology and parenting. Specifically, Rudolph Dreikurs applied the concept of purposeful striving to children when he identified "the four goals of children's misbehavior" (Dreikurs, 1948; see Putting It in Practice 3.1).

Striving for Superiority

Adler's most basic human motive, for children and adults, has been identified in the literature as striving for superiority. This doesn't mean Adler believed humans inherently try to demonstrate their interpersonal superiority by dominating one another. Instead, his emphasis was that individuals strive for a perceived plus in themselves and their lives. Mosak and Maniacci (1999) apply this concept to a clinical situation:

Why Children Misbehave

In keeping with Adler's philosophy of a practical psychology for the common person, his followers frequently applied his principles to everyday situations. Rudolph Dreikurs identified the four goals of children's misbehavior, a practical concept that has, for many years, aided parents in their understanding of children's misbehavior.

Children, like all humans, have a motivation toward growth and personal development. Unfortunately, if they don't have a sense of growth—usually through feeling *useful* and feeling that they *belong*—they're often motivated by less positive goals. In his book *The Challenge of Parenthood,* Dreikurs (1948) identified the four main goals of children's misbehavior:

1. To get attention
2. To get power or control
3. To get revenge
4. To display inadequacy

The key point is that children do not behave randomly; they are purposeful. Children want what they want. When we discuss this concept in parenting classes, parents respond by nodding with insight. Suddenly they understand that their children, like them, have particular goals toward which they strive. The boy who is "bouncing off the walls" is truly experiencing, from his perspective, an attention deficit. Perhaps by running around the house at full speed he'll get the dose of attention he craves. At least, doing so has worked in the past. His parents undoubtedly feel annoyed and may therefore end up giving him attention for misbehavior.

The girl who refuses to get out of bed for school in the morning may be trying to obtain much-needed power. Maybe she feels ignored, or like she doesn't belong in the family, and so her best alternative is to grab power whenever she can. In response, her parents are likely to feel angry and activated—as if they're in a power struggle with someone who's not pulling any punches.

The boy who slaps his little sister may be seeking revenge. Everybody's always talking about how cute his sister is and he's sick and tired of being ignored, so he takes matters into his own hands. His parents are likely to feel scared and threatened; they don't know if their beautiful little daughter is safe from her vengeful brother.

There's also the child who has given up. Maybe she sought attention before, or revenge, or power, but now she has thrown her hands up in despair and is primarily displaying her inadequacy. This isn't because she's inadequate, but because her striving for excellence, for completion, has—in her eyes—failed miserably. This child is acting out the concept of learned helplessness (Seligman, 1975). Her parents probably feel anxiety and despair as well. Or, unfortunately, as is often the case, they may finally begin responding to her with the attention and inclusion she wished for, thereby reinforcing her behavior patterns and her self-image of inadequacy.

When teaching about the goals of children's misbehavior, we often include the following caveat: Children who misbehave may also be responding to their more basic biological needs and physical state. Therefore, the first thing for parents to check is whether their child is hungry, tired, or in physical discomfort. After checking these essentials, they should move on to evaluating the underlying purpose of their child's behavior.

How can self-mutilation move someone toward a plus situation? Once again, that may be a "real" minus, especially in the short-term situation. Long-term, however, that person may receive attention, others may "walk on eggshells" when near that person (so as to not "upset" him or her), and he or she may gain some sense of subjective relief from the act, including a sense of being able to tolerate pain. (p. 23)

As you can see from the preceding example, within the individual there is opportunity for both interpersonal gain and individual developmental gain. This is one of the inner pushes that fuels the Adlerian psyche. But it should be emphasized that when it comes to basic human nature and potential, Adler is like Switzerland. He is neutral. He does not believe in the innate goodness or innate destructiveness of humans. Instead, he believes we are what we make ourselves; we have within us the potential for goodness and evil.

If you look at it in an interpersonal context, striving for individual superiority can take on a western, individualistic quality. Fortunately (for humanity), this was not Adler's perspective. He viewed individualistic superiority striving as a sign of psychopathology. And, as we'll discuss later in this chapter, he also articulated concepts of community feeling and social interest as innate positive or prosocial motivations.

Additionally, we should point out that the term *superiority* is an oversimplification of Adler's writings. Heinz Ansbacher articulated a more comprehensive and accurate view of Adler's concept of striving for superiority in a published interview:

The basic striving, according to Adler, is the striving for Vollkommenheit. The translation of Vollkommenheit is completeness, but it can also be translated as excellence. In English, only the second translation was considered; it was only the striving for excellence. The delimitation of the striving for excellence is the striving for superiority.

Basically, it all comes from the striving for completeness, and there he said that it is all a part of life in general, and that is very true. Even a flower or anything that grows, any form of life, strives to reach its completeness. And perfection is not right, because the being does not strive—one cannot say to be perfect—what is a perfect being? It is striving for completeness and that is very basic and very true. (Dubelle, 1997, p. 6).

Ansbacher's clarification helps us to see that there is much more to Adler than superiority striving. Adler (1956b) also provides us with more information about superiority striving when he states, "The fundamental law of life is to overcome one's deficiencies" (p. 48). This is the flip side of superiority and another way to look at the concept of completeness.

Phenomenology

After reading the quote from Ansbacher about flowers and completeness and humans and individuality, we can't help but head down the road toward existentialism. You may be wondering, was Adler an existentialist? Did he, in some ways, predate modern existentialism?

The answer is that Adler was indeed an early existentialist; the concept of phenomenology is a central assumption of individual psychology. In fact, Adler was writing about experiences of neuroses at around the same time and in about the same place as Edmund Husserl, the founder of the school of phenomenology (see Mosak, 1999).

An Idiographic Approach

For Adler, general statements about humans and human psychology are helpful, but of limited use. Ansbacher's statement about a flower growing to completeness is an excellent example. Although it's an accurate statement about flowers in general, it tells us nothing about the particular completeness associated with a daisy, a rose, or a sunflower. Similarly, if you read about sunflowers in a book, the statements contained therein may tell you a lot about sunflowers in general, but not much about the particular sunflower plant that you're trying to grow in your shady garden in upstate New York. In Adler's words, "a human being cannot be typified or classified" (Adler, 1935, p. 6).

Individual psychology is all about the psychology of the single, unique, whole individual. Therefore, being given general or nomothetic information about schizophrenia is only minimally helpful in our study of an individual who happens to have the diagnosis of schizophrenia. In the practical, sensible manner common to Adlerian approaches, it's more important that we meet and spend time with clients than it is for us to provide a diagnostic label.

Soft Determinism

At this point, it should come as no surprise to hear that Adler is not deterministic in his psychological approach. In other words, he's not one to emphasize the causal determinants of human behavior. An old story of Mulla Nasrudin, a mischievious but wise and perhaps mythical figure from Turkey, articulates soft determinism. The story is titled *Moment in Time.*

> "What is fate?" Nasrudin was asked by a scholar.
> "An endless succession of intertwined events, each influencing the other."
> "That is hardly a satisfactory answer. I believe in cause and effect."
> "Very well," said the Mulla, "look at that." He pointed to a procession passing in the street.
> "That man is being taken to be hanged. Is that because someone gave him a silver piece and enabled him to buy the knife with which he committed the murder; or because someone saw him do it; or because nobody stopped him?" (Shah, 1966, p. 110)

Soft determinism is the midpoint between deterministic, cause-and-effect thinking and nondeterminism, which assumes no causal connections. In the Nasrudin story, we can add a number of other influential factors that may or may not have contributed to the man's committing a murder and going to be hanged. Perhaps he experienced child abuse, or was deeply hurt by the person he murdered, or believed he had no other recourse, or . . .

From the individual psychology perspective, human behavior is a function of a combination of influences. There is usually not a single, direct *causal* factor that produces a single behavior. Instead, there are many influences or *contributing* factors.

Adler believed every individual is responsible for his or her behavior. People have the freedom to choose from a range (sometimes a quite limited range) of behavioral options. Although the Adlerian position holds individuals responsible for their behavior, it doesn't blame individuals for their misdeeds. Instead, Adler holds open the possibility that an individual may not completely understand or be conscious of the potential consequences of her actions. Mosak and Maniacci describe this position: "People are not to be blamed, but to be educated" (1999, p. 19).

As implied by the preceding quotation, Adlerian theory is hopeful and optimistic. If you think about Adler and his life, his hope and optimism seem well founded. To begin as a young boy who was pronounced lost, who flunked a year of middle school, and who was hit by various vehicles in the street, and to end up as one of the most influential psychological thinkers of all time—how could he not grow up to be an optimist?

Social Interest and Community Feeling

Humans are born into an interpersonal context. As a consequence, the development of each individual personality is shaped by interpersonal factors. This is why Adlerians place so much emphasis on understanding the individual within the context of the family constellation.

The interpersonal nature of humans leads to what Adler refers to as community feeling. When an individual experiences a deep sense of connection to others—an awareness of being a member of the human community—he or she is experiencing community feeling.

Social interest, or *Gemeinschaftsgefuhl,* is community feeling in action. For Adler, the development of social interest or a sense of social responsibility is a goal of therapy for many clients. As an individual's social interest develops, so does the capacity for empathy and altruism. Psychologically healthy individuals are those who feel a sense of communion with others and who strive to take action to help other humans. As Mahatma Gandhi is quoted as saying, "Consciously or unconsciously, every one of us does render some service or other. If we cultivate the habit of doing this service deliberately, our desire for service will steadily grow stronger and will make, not only for our own happiness, but that of the world at large" (Boldt, 1999, p. 59).

Lifestyle: The Early Cognitive Map

Although we know that Adler became an optimist, we don't know exactly when and how he became an optimist. It just so happens that the theory of individual psychology provides us with reasonable hypotheses about when and how Adler came to have such a positive view of humanity. The theory suggests that Adler developed a lifestyle characterized by optimism. He probably became an optimist, at the very latest, before age 8 or 9, and more likely by age 5.

Adler was deeply influenced by Hans Vaihinger, a philosopher who wrote a book titled *The Psychology of "As If"* (Vaihinger, 1911). According to Vaihinger, we each create our own world and then live by the rules we've created. This world is necessarily subjective and essentially fictional—in the sense that it's based on our implicit and explicit personal beliefs rather than objective fact. This is why Adlerians sometimes refer to a client's *fictional goals* or *fictional finalism* as a future-oriented concept that influences an individual's present behavior. Obviously, Vaihinger's philosophy is based on a cognitive psychological model; it strongly contributed to the cognitive flavor of Adler's individual psychology and his formulation of the lifestyle concept, as we can see from this anecdote of Adler's:

> Perhaps I can illustrate this [lifestyle concept] by an anecdote of three children taken to the
> zoo for the first time. As they stood before the lion's cage, one of them shrank behind the

mother's skirts and said, "I want to go home." The second child stood where he was, very pale and trembling and said, "I'm not a bit frightened." The third glared at the lion and fiercely asked his mother, "Shall I spit at it?" The three children really felt inferior, but each expressed his feelings in his own way, consistent with his style of life. (1931, p. 50)

An individual's style of life (also referred to as lifestyle) is both conscious and unconscious. It is a subjective cognitive map of how the world works. If as a child you learned from your father's example that men are harsh, critical, and to be feared, you will likely carry that schema with you for many years afterwards. At times, you may be conscious of this belief, but you also may avoid being around men or respond to men in ways outside of your awareness.

The concept of lifestyle is similar to transference, only broader. It includes your general conceptions about yourself, how the world works, and personal ethical convictions—not just interpersonal dynamics. Your entire being is guided by your lifestyle. Lydia Sicher, an early Adlerian, claimed that even the apparently nonsensical behavior of psychotic patients can be understood through an understanding of their lifestyle:

> To the person not acquainted with the life history and life-style of this woman, her utterances would probably seem completely confused and incoherent, just as dreams seem when one tries to interpret them according to their content rather than in the light of their psychological purposes. To one fully acquainted with her life history and life-style, everything she said can be construed in connection with actual experience and real people. (Sicher, 1935, p. 55)

For an Adlerian, the future is now. This is because your conception of the future is a strong influence on your everyday behavior. In addition, the future is then. This means that your future was established, to some degree, by your early childhood experiences. The overall theoretical construct operating here is continuity. Humans are characterized by continuity; the past, present, and future are all closely intertwined.

An individual's personal continuity or lifestyle may be more or less adaptive. Some people hold onto beliefs about the self, world, and others that cause them emotional pain and distress. Adler has referred to these beliefs as "basic mistakes," and these cognitive mistakes are an obvious target of therapy. As you might expect, Adler is hopeful and optimistic about the possibility for helping individuals change their cognitive maps through therapy or through therapeutic life experiences. Despite the fact that we are characterized by continuity, change is also possible. We will examine Adlerian approaches to lifestyle assessment and analysis later in this chapter.

Questions for Reflection

What continuities do you notice in your view of yourself and your life? This next question is harder: What basic mistakes do you make over and over again? As you reflect on your answer to this question, you should be reassured, because Adler believed that we all make basic mistakes repeatedly in our lives—it's only a matter of whether the mistakes are large or small.

A summary of the theoretical assumptions associated with individual psychology is included in Table 3.1.

Table 3.1   Theoretical Assumptions of Individual Psychology

Theoretical Assumption	Description
Holism	Humans are a single complete unit—a whole that cannot and should not be divided into separate parts.
Superiority striving	Humans strive; we are active, creative, and persistent in our drive to move toward completion and excellence. We can become discouraged and resigned due to unfortunate life circumstances, but our natural state is forward moving.
Purpose	Human behavior is purposeful. We move toward specific goals in life. In this sense, humans are driven by hopes for the future, rather than instinctual forces from the past. Adler referred to the endpoint of our future purposeful striving as *fictional finalism* because the endpoint is each individual's subjective fiction.
Community feeling	In addition to striving for completion and excellence (also called superiority), humans also strive to connect socially, both with individuals and with the community in general. The specific manifestation of this motivating factor is referred to as *social interest.* If humans strive for superiority without a community-feeling motive, they are likely to become driven, selfish, and arrogant in pursuit of their goals.
Idiography	Although general information about humans can be helpful, every individual is unique. Therefore, to really understand an individual, a couple, or a family, you must work with that individual, couple, or family.
Phenomenology	Individual experience is a subjective fiction based on each individual's perception. The individual actively creates and adapts his or her own personal reality.
Soft determinism	Adlerians believe in the power of biology and the environment to influence human behavior. However, biology, environment, and other significant factors do not directly cause specific behaviors to occur; instead, behavior is determined by a myriad of influencing factors.
Freedom to choose	Humans are free to choose their behavior from a limited set of options. Humans are also fully responsible for their choices, although they may make uneducated choices due to bad information or a lack of information. Therefore, education can help facilitate healthy, free choice and personal responsibility.
Early cognitive map	The individual map each of us uses to navigate through life is established in childhood. This map, referred to as *lifestyle,* is our personality: It gives us our continuity and tells us about ourselves, others, and how the world works. The map can be deficient in some ways, but it can be modified through therapeutic, educational experiences, including counseling or psychotherapy.
Optimism	Adler was an optimist. Although he believed that basic human nature was neutral, he was hopeful that the pull toward community feeling and the drive toward completeness would help individuals live together peacefully and happily.

Tasks of Life

Adlerian theory is not just a psychological theory of the individual; it also includes assumptions about the demands the world places on individuals. Adler (1956a) claimed that all individuals must face three interrelated life tasks or challenges:

- Work or occupation
- Social relationships
- Love and marriage

Later, Dreikurs and Mosak (1966, 1967; Mosak & Dreikurs, 1967), both of whom worked directly with Adler, identified two additional life tasks within the individual psychology framework:

- Self
- Spirituality

Finally, another Adlerian theorist and practitioner, Dinkmeyer, identified a sixth task (Dinkmeyer, Dinkmeyer, & Sperry, 1987):

- Parenting and family

These six tasks constitute the challenges of life.

When clients come to therapy, they almost always come because they have had difficulty with one or more basic life tasks. The difficulties arise from inaccuracies, mistakes, and maladaptive perceptions associated with their lifestyles. Therefore, the overarching goal of therapy is to help clients adjust or modify their lifestyles in ways that help them more effectively complete their life tasks.

Work or Occupation

Adler believed the best way to solve the life task of work or occupation was by solving the second life task, social relationships, through "friendship, social feeling, and cooperation" (Adler, 1958, p. 239). If a person is unable to work cooperatively, divide labor responsibilities, and maintain friendly relations, he or she is likely to struggle in the area of work. Here is an example of how Adler described one particular work or occupational problem and its origin:

> There are some people who could choose any occupation and never be satisfied. What they wish is not an occupation but an easy guarantee of superiority. They do not wish to meet the problems of life, since they feel that it is unfair of life to offer them problems at all. These, again, are the pampered children who wish to be supported by others. (Adler, 1956a, p. 429)

In this excerpt, Adler is clearly linking the past to the present. He believes that the client who was pampered as a child will have occupational difficulties. However, if the client can have experiences, inside or outside of therapy, that help to change the assumption that life should offer no problems at all, then the occupational problem will not necessarily extend into the future.

Social Relationships

Adler was a strong proponent of positive social relationships. As has been noted, he felt that establishing healthy social relationships was the key to solving the work or occupational problem. In essence, humans are interdependent. Lydia Sicher emphasized the centrality of this concept in the title of her classic paper "A Declaration of Interdependence" (Sicher, 1991). It is only when we accept this interdependence and develop empathy and concern for others that social relationships can prosper.

Following Adler's lead, Dreikurs (1950) articulated the importance of belonging. Everyone needs to belong to some social group, whether it be family, club, school, team, or musical group. This need mimics the reality that everyone is a member of the human race.

Some clients come to therapy because they have social relationship problems. This fact is the cornerstone of many therapeutic approaches. If you think back to the previous chapter, the brief psychodynamic therapy approaches of Luborsky (1984) and Strupp (Strupp & Binder, 1984) are both based on identifying the client's core conflictual relationship theme or dynamic relationship conflict. Of course, from the Adlerian perspective, clients' social problems stem from inappropriate expectations, beliefs, and interpersonal habits imbedded in their individual lifestyles.

Love and Marriage

Some theorists refer to this life task as *love* and others refer to it as *sex* (Mosak, 1999). For the purposes of our discussion here, we're using Adler's original terms, *love* and *marriage* (Adler, 1956a).

Adler's writing and speaking about love and marriage were reportedly quite popular during his lifetime. Should you explore his original work in this area, you will find his writing very accessible, possibly even romantic. A brief excerpt of his original work follows, with the male-oriented language of his time included:

> [E]ach partner must be more interested in the other than in himself. This is the only basis on which love and marriage can be successful.
>
> If each partner is to be more interested in the other partner than in himself, there must be equality. If there is to be so intimate a devotion, neither partner can feel subdued nor overshadowed. Equality is only possible if both partners have this attitude. It should be the effort of each to ease and enrich the life of the other. In this way each will be safe; each will feel that he is worthwhile and that he is needed. The fundamental guarantee of marriage, the meaning of marital happiness, is the feeling that you are worthwhile, that you cannot be replaced, that your partner needs you, that you are acting well, and that you are a fellow man and a true friend. (Adler, 1956a, p. 432)

Many clients come to therapy with intimacy problems, both sexual and nonsexual. For Adlerians, the road to recovery for these clients is the same as we have suggested previously: Modify the lifestyle, develop empathy for others (community feeling), and take decisive action by thinking and acting differently in everyday life.

Self

Dreikurs and Mosak (1967) and Schulman (1965) have written about the life task of self. They note that this task was implied, but not fully developed, in Adler's original work. Essentially, this task emphasizes that everyone has a relationship with himself or herself. Not surprisingly, the nature of your relationship with yourself is established during childhood.

Mosak and Maniacci (1999) describe four dimensions of the self life task:

- *Survival of self:* Am I taking good care of my physical self? Am I taking good care of my psychological self? Am I taking good care of my social self?
- *Body image:* Is my perception of my body reasonable and congruent with my actual body?
- *Opinion:* What is my opinion of me? To evaluate this in an interview, Adlerians often ask clients to complete the incomplete sentence, "I _____ me" (Mosak & Maniacci, 1999, p. 107).
- *Evaluation:* Some clients have various extreme perspectives of the self. From the object relations perspective, the question would be "Am I good or am I bad?"

The optimal resolution of the self task is characterized by good self-care, an accurate perception and expectations of one's body, a reasonably accurate and positive opinion of oneself, and a balanced view of oneself as not overly good or overly bad.

Spirituality

Much of Adler's writing focuses on the need for community feeling, social interest, and cooperation. This is even the case with regard to some of his writing about religion. He stated: "The most important task imposed by religion has always been, 'Love thy neighbor'" (Adler, 1958, p. 253).

Mosak and Maniacci (1999) describe five specific issues related to the spirituality task. As individuals grow up and face life, they must approach and deal with each of these issues:

- *Relationship to God:* Does the individual believe in God? If so, what kind of God does he or she perceive? If not, then what does he or she believe in?
- *Religion:* Addressing the issue of organized religion is different from addressing the issue of God. Does the individual embrace religious belief or avoid it? How are guilt and repentence dealt with (Mosak, 1987)?
- *Relationship to the universe:* Mosak and Maniacci state that "Some individuals see humans as simply another animal. Others see humans as the pinnacle of God's creation" (p. 108). This concept is interwoven with religious beliefs, but it can also be somewhat separate. The question is: What is the nature of the relationship of humans to the rest of the world and the universe?
- *Metaphysical issues:* Most individuals have beliefs about heaven, hell, reincarnation, karma, salvation, and so on. How individuals view these issues is a function of lifestyle, and an individual's lifestyle must conform to beliefs in this area.
- *Meaning of life:* A special emphasis is placed on the importance of finding meaning in life. Adlerians believe that healthy individuals lead meaningful lives in cooperative relationship to other members of the human community.

Parenting and Family

Giving birth to and raising children, and functioning as a family, are extensions of the love and marriage task discussed previously. However, these things also constitute a task in and of themselves. Some individuals function as single parents and raise children outside marriage. Individual parents also develop strong feelings and beliefs about how children *should* be raised. How individuals face the parenting and family task is both a function of and a challenge to the lifestyle.

Psychopathology and Human Change

Adlerians define psychopathology as "discouragement," but of course there's much more to it than that.

The discouraged individual is one who is unable or unwilling to approach and deal with essential life tasks. With regard to psychopathology and life tasks, Adler stated:

> The three problems of life which I have already described must be solved somehow or other by every human being for the individual's relationship with the world is a three-fold relation. . . . [W]hoever can make friends with society, can pursue a useful occupation with faith and courage, and can adjust his sexual life in accordance with good social feeling, is immune from neurotic infection. But when an individual fails to square himself with one or more of these three inexorable demands of life, beware of feelings of abasement, beware of the consequent neurosis. Schizophrenia is the result of a failure in all three directions at once. (Adler, 1964a, p. 20)

In the case of mental dysfunction, one or more of the life tasks have become overwhelming. This is where the concept of discouragement fits in. The person struggling to adequately face a life task becomes discouraged. He or she feels inferior or unable to successfully manage the life task demands, and therefore symptoms arise.

Symptomatic patients are suffering from the effects of their inaccurate or mistaken lifestyles. Due to early childhood experiences, the lifestyle is dysfunctional. Symptoms become an answer to the question "What shall I do if I cannot successfully manage this life task?" From an Adlerian perspective, symptoms help individuals avoid facing life tasks for which they feel ill-prepared or inadequate. Here are some examples:

- If I steal, then I won't have to work so hard at an occupation, and I won't have to communicate, cooperate, divide labor, or perform other basic social functions needed in the workplace.
- If I become depressed, I can communicate my anger and dissatisfaction indirectly. I will be taken care of and thereby in control of the household.
- If I become anxious, I will not have to approach one or more of the basic life tasks. Perhaps I can avoid marriage or work. If I collapse from anxiety, surely someone will rescue me from the demands of life.

Adler articulated his formulation of many different mental disorders. Here is an example of his rather blunt description of the etiology of anxiety problems: "Anxiety neurosis is always symptomatic of a timid attitude towards the three problems of life, and those who suffer from it are invariably 'spoiled' children" (Adler, 1964, p. 6).

Mosak (1989) also makes a clear statement about psychopathology from the Adlerian perspective when he says, "poor interpersonal relationships are products of misperceptions, inaccurate conclusions, and unwarranted anticipations incorporated in the life-style" (p. 86). Of course, this statement brings us back to the concept of discouragement. The maladaptive lifestyle and its associated interpersonal dysfunctions cause the client to experience disappointments, feelings of inferiority, and eventually discouragement.

THE PRACTICE OF ADLERIAN THERAPY

In his time, Adler's approach to human psychology was criticized as being based on common sense. Although we agree that individual psychology sometimes seems like common sense, we find Adlerian therapy to be a sensitive and complex process, requiring rigorous training to do it well. Therefore, if you happen to be interested in practicing Adlerian therapy well, we include several recommendations at the end of this chapter.

Preparing Yourself to do Therapy from an Individual Psychology Perspective

To prepare yourself to practice Adlerian-oriented therapy with role playing or practicum clients, it may help to hear some advice directly from Adler. He stated that "The first rule in treatment is to win the patient; the second is for the psychologist [mental health professional] never to worry about his own success: if he does so he forfeits it" (Adler, 1964a, p. 73).

Questions for Reflection

Why does Adler warn us not to worry about our success as a therapist? What happens or what might happen if you begin thinking about and worrying about your success with a client from the beginning of therapy? Think about the emphasis in individual psychology on superiority striving. Do you think Adler might be trying to tell therapists to put aside their own superiority issues and, instead, just try to create a positive relationship with the client?

Adler also provides another example of how important it is for therapists to avoid the superiority trap:

> A girl of twenty-seven came to consult me after five years of suffering. She said: "I have seen so many doctors that you are my last hope in life." "No," I answered, "not the last hope. Perhaps the last but one. There may be others who can help you too." Her words were a challenge to me; she was *daring* me not to cure her, so as to make me feel bound in duty to do so. This is the type of patient who wishes to shift responsibility upon others, a common development of spoiled children. . . .
>
> It is important, by the way, to evade such a challenge as the one I have recorded here. The patient may have worked up a high tension of feeling about the idea that the doctor is his "last hope," but we must accept no such distinction. To do so would prepare the way for grave disappointment, or even suicide. (Adler, 1964, pp. 8–9)

As illustrated by this example, Adlerian therapy is a deeply interpersonal, interactive process. Bear in mind that Adlerians believe transference is a function of the lifestyle. Watch for it when you begin doing therapy. Mosak (1989) states:

> The patient may feel misunderstood, unfairly treated, or unloved and may anticipate that the therapist will behave accordingly. Often the patient unconsciously creates situations to invite the therapist to behave in this manner. (p. 85)

As an Adlerian therapist, one of your main goals is to counter the client's unhelpful lifestyle-based expectations. This is similar to the concept of corrective emotional experience (Alexander & French, 1946).

General Therapeutic Strategy

Therapeutic strategy from an Adlerian perspective can be boiled down to a few simple components. Use these as a general guide:

- Be a friendly, supportive model for your clients.
- Use encouragement to help clients have more success potential and faith in themselves.
- Help clients have insight into their style of life and fictional finalism.
- Help clients modify their basic mistakes using a broad range of educational procedures

Client Preparation, Assessment Issues, and Therapy Process

Counseling or psychotherapy is a friendly and collaborative process consisting of four phases (Dreikurs, 1969). These phases include

- Forming the therapeutic relationship
- Lifestyle assessment and analysis
- Interpretation and insight
- Reorientation

Next, we briefly describe the four phases. Later, in sections on assessment and therapy techniques, we provide more detailed discussion of the specific activities of the Adlerian therapist.

Forming the Therapeutic Relationship

Recall Adler's first rule: Win the patient. This is the essence of client preparation from the Adlerian perspective.

The relationship between Adlerian therapists and their clients is egalitarian and characterized by effective listening and caring. Therapist and client sit on chairs of equal status and look more or less directly at one another. Of all types of therapists, Adlerians may seem most like a friendly teacher or business consultant whose business it is to help the individual negotiate life more successfully.

Therapy is conducted collaboratively. The therapist takes steps to enhance collaboration and to communicate interest in the client as a person. Bitter and colleagues describe how an Adlerian counselor might open a first session:

> We often start an interview with "What do you want me to know about you?", rather than, "What brought you in?" or "What did you want to talk about today?" Meeting and valuing the person is essential to positive change; the relationship may not be everything that matters, but [it] is *almost* everything that matters. (Bitter, Christensen, Hawes, & Nicoll, 1998, p. 98)

Clients are encouraged to be active participants in therapy. Although the therapist is in a teaching role, the client is an active—as opposed to passive—learner.

Alignment of Goals

One way the therapist shows the client respect is by working hard to understand the client as a person and the client's goals for therapy. In particular, for therapy to have a chance to proceed successfully, therapist and client must align their therapeutic goals.

Although client and therapist goals for therapy should be aligned, the Adlerian therapist has preset ideas about appropriate therapy goals. Mosak (1995) includes the following goals as appropriate for Adlerian therapy:

- Fostering client social interest or community feeling
- Helping clients overcome their feelings of inferiority and discouragement
- Helping clients change the basic mistakes imbedded in their lifestyle
- Shifting client motivation from a self-focused superiority to a more adaptive community focus
- Helping clients believe and feel like they are equals in their relationships
- Helping clients to become contributing members to society

Mosak's goal list further articulates how clients and their problems—consistent with Adlerian theory—are viewed as inseparable units. Consequently, the therapist is unlikely to formulate a "problem list" with the client. The problem and the person are one entity and need not be separated, except for specific therapeutic purposes.

Focusing on the Positive

Adlerians focus on the person and his or her strengths as well as problems. For example, it's common to ask about positive personal qualities (e.g., "What were some of your best traits as a child?" and "Tell me a story about one of your childhood successes"). This is not to say that talking about problems and difficulties is avoided, as in solution-oriented therapy approaches. Instead, the therapist shows interest in the whole person, both problems and strengths. Overall, the goal is to establish an environment characterized by encouragement.

Initial Lifestyle Interpretations

One of our old supervisors with an Adlerian-humanistic bent used to insist, "Tell your client something you've learned about him toward the end of the first session" (H.A. Walters, personal communication, December, 1983). The purpose of this early interpretation is to further the connection between therapist and client and begin the process of a deeper analysis of problems than the client has participated in previously. Because it occurs so early in counseling, this first interpretation is really more of a guess than an interpretation, and it should be phrased as such. It also prepares the client for the Adlerian approach and further interpretations and techniques offered later in therapy. An example of an initial lifestyle interpretation is included in this chapter's case example.

Lifestyle Assessment and Analysis

Several approaches to lifestyle assessment are available to the Adlerian therapist. Although some practitioners use client questionnaires and formal testing procedures (Stein, 2002), the main four assessment strategies are:

- The family constellation interview
- The question

- Earliest recollections
- Dream analysis

The Family Constellation Interview

The family constellation interview is a particular approach to obtaining pertinent information about the client's childhood experiences that shaped lifestyle development. Topics covered in a family constellation interview include descriptions of each family member, descriptions of how the different family members interacted with one another, how each family member was viewed by the client (in relation to the client), who fought, who didn't fight, and more. Adler also considered birth order to be a strong predictor of lifestyle (see Putting It in Practice 3.2). In particular, he emphasized that every individual family member within a family is born into a different family; this is because with the addition of a new family member, the family dynamics always change and a new family is born.

An example of a family constellation interview, leading to interpretation and client insight, is included in this chapter's extended case example.

After reading these brief descriptions of lifestyle possibilities stemming from birth order, discuss with your classmates or friends whether or not you think they hold true. Also, don't forget to include in your discussion some of the unique ways your position in your own family unfolded, because, as Adler suggested, your unique experience is much more important than simple birth order.

The Question

In order to obtain information about the purpose of the client's symptoms, the therapist asks the client "the Question." The Question is "How would your life be different if you were well?" It also can be phrased differently: "What would you be doing in your life if you no longer had your symptoms (problem)?" The question is a straightforward method for determining if the client is obtaining special treatment or *secondary gain* for having problems.

After asking the question, the individual psychology practitioner listens closely for activities or relationships that the client might resume should his or her problems be resolved. In this way, the therapist is determining which life tasks the client may be avoiding by virtue of his or her symptoms.

Questions for Reflection

How do you think "the Question" might help in formulating a treatment approach for an individual client? What if the question were posed to you? What would your answer be?

Earliest Recollections

Adler considered the significance of early memories to be one of the most important discoveries of individual psychology. Adlerian therapists use early recollections as powerful tools for understanding the client's lifestyle and fictional goals.

The early recollection is seen as not so much a memory as a projection. It is a continuity or message from the past, still active in the client's present life. The accuracy of

Birth Order and Lifestyle

Popular psychology has often oversimplified the Adlerian concept of birth order. At the worst, there are those who use birth order, like an astrological sign, to describe an individual's personality and to predict human behavior. This occurs despite the fact that, as early as 1937, Adler was cautioning against using a simplistic birth order approach to understanding lifestyle development. He states:

> There has been some misunderstanding of my custom of classification according to position in the family. It is not, of course, the child's number in the order of successive births which influences his character, but the *situation* into which he is born and the way in which he *interprets* it. (Adler, 1937, p. 211).

With this clear caution in mind, we will now describe birth order tendencies reported by individual psychology adherents over the years. The bottom line is that birth order *is* important, but that it's completely dependent upon the individual's interpretation of his or her family position and situation. (Please note that, despite our use of gendered pronouns, we do not wish to imply that these characteristics are linked more to one sex than to another—except, of course, in the two final categories.)

Child's Position	Lifestyle Characteristics
Oldest	This child may be initially spoiled and later dethroned. She may be bossy, strict, and authoritarian; it's as if she has a right to power. She also may feel exceptionally responsible for others. The oldest child may strongly identify with father because she turns to him for support after the birth of the second child.
Second	He always has an older rival, and this may make him competitive. The challenge is for him to develop a unique identity, so he may end up being a rebel. There is often an unfulfilled wish to be bigger, stronger, smarter, and more capable.
Middle	She is likely to be even-tempered, developing a sort of "take it or leave it" attitude. She may become overly sensitive to the plights of others who are overlooked or underprivileged. She can feel cheated out of her position of privilege and harbor resentments, sometimes quietly manipulating others to achieve her ends. She also may have trouble finding her niche in life.
Youngest	He is never dethroned, and so he may feel he should be treated like royalty. He's likely to have unrealistic aspirations. He dreams of being bigger and more powerful than everyone else, but usually doesn't have the follow-through to achieve these dreams. This may make him chronically frustrated, and consequently he could choose to stay the baby.
Only	This child has plenty of attention from both parents and therefore feels special, especially liking attention from adults. There may be problems with peer relationships due to lack of experience with give and take and tolerance. May believe she should be "taken care of."
Only boy among girls	He may need to prove he's a man, but he is also likely to be sensitive to feminine issues. He may be treated like a hero and therefore hold high expectations of himself. He also may have strong expectations that everyone will immediately recognize his special qualities and feel deep disappointment when he's treated just like everyone else.
Only girl among boys	She may become either overly feminine or a tomboy, trying to compete with her brothers. She also may feel she has a special designation and, depending upon her relations with her brothers, may expect abuse from males or may expect them to be her protectors.

the memory is much less important than the existence of the memory. If the memory exists, then it's an active expression of the client's living lifestyle. It's no surprise that the memory is twisted into a shape that corresponds with the client's thoughts, feelings, and attitudes toward him- or herself and life. If the memory was not important *in the now,* there would be no purpose for the client to remember it.

The best memories for lifestyle interpretation are clear, occur before age 8 or 9, and describe a specific incident or situation that the client experienced as a child. A general report, such as "We always went to the beach for our vacations," is not useful. However, it becomes useful if the client describes a specific memory: "One time when we were at the beach I remember being afraid of the waves. I had to hold my mother's hand and didn't go out in the water with my sisters."

Sweeney (1989) identifies a list of questions to help therapists judge the meaning of the memory:

- Is the individual active or passive?
- Is he or she an observer or participant?
- Is he or she giving or taking?
- Does he or she go forth or withdraw?
- Is he or she alone or with others?
- Is his or her concern with people, things, or ideas [or animals]?
- What relationship does he or she place himself or herself in with others? Inferior? Superior?
- What emotion does he or she use?
- Are detail and color mentioned?
- Do stereotypes of authorities, subordinates, men, women, old, young, reveal themselves?
- Prepare a "headline" that captures the essence of the event. [For example, in the memory of being afraid of waves, the headline might read: BOY MISSES OUT ON FUN DUE TO FEAR OF WAVES!]
- Look for themes and an overall pattern.
- Look for corroboration in the family constellation information (adapted from Sweeney, 1989, pp. 217–218).

Dream Analysis

With regard to dream analysis, Adler's approach remains consistent with his theory. Generally, dreams represent an effort by the individual to solve immediate life problems. Additionally, the dream and the dreamer are viewed as a unique, connected, and cohesive unit. This natural connection between dream and dreamer, and the fact that everyone is a unique individual, makes it problematic to interpret a dream unless you know the dreamer and the dreamer's life situation.

In contrast to Freud, Adler doesn't interpret dream images as having generic symbolic meaning. This cookbook approach to dream interpretation goes against the essence of Adlerian theory; each individual and his or her personal experience deserves a fresh look, uncontaminated by stereotypic symbolic interpretations.

Dreams, like human behavior, are purposeful. Adler said, "Sleeping is another kind of waking" (1964a, p. 161). He discussed the continuum of consciousness and unconsciousness represented by dreams:

In dreams, therefore, we never find any other tendencies or movements that those manifested in the style of the waking life. . . . We cannot oppose "consciousness" to "unconsciousness" as if they were two antagonistic halves of an individual's existence. The conscious life becomes unconscious as soon as we fail to understand it—and as soon as we understand an unconscious tendency it has already become conscious. (p. 163)

The key to Adlerian dream interpretation derives from the following question: "What function might this dream serve in the dreamer's overall life?" Adler's answer is that the dream is both a metaphorical expression of a problem and a self-deception. It's a self-deception because having thoughts and feelings in the form of a dream allows individuals to distance themselves from their own thoughts and feelings. Adler describes a man who was experiencing marital difficulties and who had lost faith in women. The man had the following dream: "I was in a battle in the streets of a city, and in the midst of the shooting and burning many women were thrown into the air as if by an explosion" (Adler, 1964, p. 165). In this dream the man has feelings of anger and horror and an image depicting the annihilation of women. Adler connected this theme to the man's marital woes. Essentially, as long as the man dreams of anger and "a battle" he minimizes his conflicts with his wife and doesn't engage in a full relationship with her. The solution is to understand the meaning of the dream within the context of the man's lifestyle and then help him to approach and successfully address the thoughts and feelings in his waking life. Interestingly, Adler posits that "the more an individual's goal agrees with reality the less a person dreams," and "Very courageous people dream rarely, for they deal adequately with their situation in the day-time" (pp. 163-164). However, before those of you who cannot recall your dreams begin feeling too superior, Adler leaves open the possibility that individuals who cannot remember their dreams may be forgetting them for less than positive reasons: "[T]he absence of dreams may be a sign that an individual has come to a point of rest in his neurosis and has established a neurotic situation which he does not wish to change" (Adler, 1936, p. 13).

Questions for Reflection

Adler emphasizes the avoidance function of dreams. That is, if you dream about it, perhaps you don't have to deal with it in your waking life. What do you think of this approach to dreams? Also, what do you think of Adler's comment that courageous people don't recall many dreams?

Toward the conclusion of the assessment phase of therapy, an Adlerian becomes able to identify a client's "basic mistakes." Five examples of basic mistakes are identified by Mosak (1995):

- Overgeneralization: There is no fairness in the world, or I'm always the one who has to take care of everything.
- False or impossible goals: I have to be the boss to be acceptable, or others should always take care of my needs.
- Misperceptions of life and life's demands: The world is against me, or the world is my oyster.
- Denial of one's basic worth: I totally suck, or no one could ever love me.

- Faulty values: A set of values at odds with social interest; I must win and be the best no matter how much it hurts others.

Interpretation and Insight

Insight is central to Adlerian therapy. However, it's conceptualized somewhat differently from the way it is in psychoanalytic psychotherapy. For Adlerians, there's a strong link between insight, motivation, and action. Insight implies action, because if you think about it, most people get motivated to change after discovering maladaptive lifestyle patterns and assumptions in themselves. Insight that does not produce action or efforts toward change is not true insight, but a sign that a client is playing at therapy, rather than taking it seriously.

Insight is generally achieved through interpretation, although many of the techniques we will describe are also in the service of deepening insight. The purpose of interpretation is to demonstrate continuity of an inaccurate, maladaptive lifestyle; it's not important to show a causal connection between past and present. Once this continuity is revealed in a way the client can understand, the final phase of therapy, reorientation, has begun.

Reorientation (Specific Therapy Techniques)

Individual psychology practitioners do not shy away from using specific techniques in the service of therapy process and outcome. This is because they believe it requires more than an analysis of problems and insight to facilitate positive change. In particular, because therapy is all about new learning—in the broadest sense of the term—using specific, action-oriented, techniques that facilitate client learning is not only an acceptable practice, but a desirable one as well. Mosak (1989) captures this Adlerian attitude toward the therapist's role and function: "There comes a time in psychotherapy when analysis must be abandoned and the patient must be encouraged to act in lieu of talking and listening. Insight has to give way to decisive action" (p. 91).

In honor of Adler, Mosak, and other individual psychology proponents, we now turn to a review of several techniques used by Adlerian therapists.

The Future Autobiography

For the Adlerian, the future guides and shapes our everyday behavior. Given this assumption, the future autobiography is an excellent technique for helping clients reshape their view of the future.

This technique is especially useful for clients who like to write. However, it can be adapted for clients who like to draw or for clients who like to tell stories.

You can proceed with this technique in at least two ways. However, because Adlerians support counselor creativity, you may find a way to use this technique in a manner different than we describe here.

First, this technique can be used as an assessment tool. Give your client the following assignment:

> "Everyone has a life story. So far, yours has a past and a present, and if I asked you to, you could write me a great story about everything you've experienced up to today. That would be tremendously interesting, but I'd like you to do an even more interesting writing project. Between now and next week, write a story about the rest of your life. Make it as de-

tailed or as sketchy as you want. The point is for you to look at who you are right now and project your life into the future—as you want it. In other words, finish your life story in the way you would like it to go. We can look at it together next week."

As an assessment procedure, the future autobiography can help identify your client's fictional life goals and determine whether those goals are facilitating or hampering his or her daily functioning. Additionally, a discussion of the client's future autobiography can help your client take greater conscious responsibility for directing and shaping his or her life.

The future autobiography can also be used in a more purely therapeutic manner. If this is your preference, use it *after* you've gathered information about your client's past and lifestyle. Then, because you have an initial grasp or understanding of your client's basic beliefs about the world, self, and others, you can coach your client to write a realistic and adaptive future autobiography. For example, you might ask your client to address one of the basic mistakes within the context of this assignment:

"We've been talking about how you think you need to be perfect all the time. This belief causes you no end of anxiety. As an assignment for this week, write a 'future autobiography.' In other words, just write the rest of your life story, from here on out. And as you do that, keep this in mind: Write a story in which you're not perfect, one in which you make mistakes but, overall, live in an acceptable and loving way in the world. Okay?"

The future biography assignment directly addresses the lifestyle and fictional finalism concepts. It can be modified for clients who prefer not to write. Either an oral future biography or a pictorial future biography can be assigned.

Creating New Images

Clients naturally have images of themselves in the past, present, and future. As with most Adlerian techniques, this procedure can be used in many different ways. In some cases, the therapist may try to use a short phrase to visually and metaphorically capture a client's behavior, attitude, or value. I (John) have found this technique useful in my work with adolescents, perhaps because they love feedback, especially feedback that is unusual, compelling, sarcastic, and in the form of a sound bite.

A 15-year-old boy consistently criticized his mother's wealth. He didn't respect how she chose to spend her money. He liked to dress in ragged T-shirts and ripped-up baggy pants, and he hung out with friends whose parents had little extra money. He claimed he was embarrassed to bring his friends over to his mother's nice home. However, this boy also regularly complained that his mother didn't provide him with enough money. This inconsistency raised the possibility that the boy was trying to control his mother and get everything he wanted for himself. To create a new image in therapy, I commented, "You know what, I think you're a closet spoiled rich kid. You want to have money, you just don't want anybody to know about it." This image of "a closet spoiled rich kid" helped the young man more directly acknowledge the financial expectations and conflicts associated with his lifestyle.

This technique can also be used to encourage clients to actively develop new and more adaptive self-images. After analyzing your client's early recollections and basic mistakes, you can simply work to come up with a "new visual" (as our artistic friends like to say). This new visual is an image that is self-generated and used to replace old more negative, disturbing, or maladaptive self-images.

Acting "as If"

Clients (and all humans for that matter) often wish for traits they don't have. For example, some people wish for greater self-confidence. In contrast, others may wish they were calm instead of nervous and edgy. Still others wish they could focus, get organized, and follow through on a project.

The "as if" technique is used when clients express a desire to be different. When this wishing occurs, you can initiate the process by asking: "What if you were self-confident? How would that look?" Then, if your client shares an image of self-confidence with you and it seems a positive step toward adjustment, you might suggest: "For the rest of our time today and throughout this week, how about if you try acting as if you were filled with self-confidence." Of course, there's always the possibility that your client will balk at this suggestion and claim that acting self-confident would be phony. Your job at that point is to encourage your client to try it anyway. Mosak (1989) gives an example of encouragement in this situation: "[E]xplain that all acting is not phony pretense, that one can try on a role as one might try on a suit" (p. 91).

This technique is primarily experimental. It gives clients permission to see how it feels to try on new ways of being. By engaging in these experiments and then talking about them in therapy, clients gain new perspectives and new motivation for behaving in different, more adaptive ways.

The Push-Button Technique

Adler believed that under every feeling there is a cognition (Mosak, 2000). Based on this theoretical assumption, Mosak described a therapy technique he referred to as the "Pushbutton Technique" (Mosak, 1985, p. 210). The technique is designed to help clients have greater emotional control. Mosak outlines how to introduce this technique to clients:

> This is a three-part experiment. Please close your eyes and keep them closed until all three parts are over. First, I'd like you to dig into your memory and retrieve a very pleasant memory—a success, a beautiful sunset, a time when you were loved—and project that in front of your eyes as if you were watching it on a TV screen. Watch it from beginning to end and attach to it the feelings you had when the incident occurred. Go! Remember how wonderful it was! When you are through, hold up a finger to signal that you are through, and we'll go on to the next part. . . .
>
> Now I'd like you to fish back in memory and retrieve a horrible incident. You failed. You were hurt or ill. Life screwed you. Someone died. You were humiliated. Watch that one from beginning to end as if it were on TV and attach to it the feelings you had at the time the incident occurred. Go! Remember how terrible it was! When you are through, hold up a finger to signal that you are through and we'll go on to the last part. . . .
>
> Now I'd like to go into your memory and retrieve another pleasant memory. If you can't come up with another pleasant memory, go back to the first pleasant memory you had. Watch it on the TV screen from beginning to end and attach to it the feelings you had when the incident occurred. Go! Remember how wonderful it was! When you are through, please open your eyes. (1985, pp. 211–212)

The push-button technique is an ABA reversal experimental design that teaches clients the power of thoughts and images over feelings. After the client experiences affective changes with this procedure, you can make the point, "It's no wonder that depressed people feel depressed. It's because they're consistently thinking depressing thoughts." In the end, the therapist sends the client home with two make-believe push buttons (one happy and one sad) and the following persuasive statement:

> [I]f you come back next week and are *still* depressed, I'm going to ask you to explain why you *choose* to continue to feel depressed when you have the happy button at your disposal. We'll find out what your investment in being depressed is. (Mosak, 1985, p. 212)

In this example, you've seen Mosak's approach to using the push-button technique in a session with a depressed adult. However, this technique can also be applied to children and adolescents in therapy and as a general emotional education technique in schools (see Sommers-Flanagan & Sommers-Flanagan, 1997, 2001).

Spitting in the Client's Soup

Clients frequently avoid or evade demands and responsibilities associated with basic life tasks. The concept of spitting in the client's soup is a metaphor for spoiling the client's use of a particular avoidance or neurotic strategy. After all, who can enjoy eating his soup after someone has spat in it? Here's an example of the technique.

A 30-year-old unemployed man recently separated from his wife and returned home to live with his parents. His wife asked him to join her for couples counseling, but he declined, agreeing instead to attend individual therapy. When asked by his counselor about his progress in his active employment search, he stated, "I'm stepping back from that right now. I need to get my ducks in a row, and then I'll get back out there." The counselor then spat in the client's soup by observing, "This is your old pattern of avoiding things when you think you won't be unconditionally accepted. It's what you choose instead of facing your wife in counseling, and it's what you do to talk yourself out of meeting with possible employers." Of course, this soup-spitting technique is used within the context of a friendly therapeutic relationship.

Catching Oneself

Self-awareness and self-control are at the foundation of Adlerian theory. The technique of catching oneself is designed to help clients become aware of their maladaptive behavior patterns and goals. To use the technique, the therapist coaches the client on how to catch himself when he or she slips into old, unhelpful behaviors. For example, a college basketball player came to therapy because of problems with his explosive temper during practice. His coach had issued an ultimatum: "Deal with your anger more constructively or leave the team." The first step of his therapy involved having this young man catch himself when he began thinking or acting in ways that usually led to his angry outbursts. Because, for this client, the primary dynamics related to his anger were perfectionism and blame, he was given the following instructions:

> "During this session and throughout the week, we'll focus on your tendency to think you need to be perfect and then blame others when you aren't perfect. That's the beginning of your slippery slope toward anger. Your job is to simply notice when you're not performing perfectly and thinking critically about yourself. Just notice it, catch yourself, and think— ah, there it is again, that tendency to criticize myself. Also, notice when you shift from self-criticism to blaming others for your performance. Again, just notice it; there's no need to do anything about it for now."

As you may have noticed, the technique of catching oneself is a historical predecessor of behavioral and cognitive self-monitoring (see Chapters 7 and 8).

Task Setting and Indirect Suggestion

Adler employed an interesting, engaging, but not always direct therapy style. In the next section we talk about his most indirect strategy: namely, paradoxical instructions. However, as in the following excerpt, he sometimes used both a direct task-setting strategy and an indirect or suggestive method for implementing it. This style reminds us of the renowned hypnotherapist Milton Erickson, who mastered this approach and become famous for it several decades after Adler's death (see Chapter 12).

In this case, Adler is discussing a task-setting procedure he uses with depressed patients:

> After establishing a sympathetic relation I give suggestions for a change of conduct in two stages. In the first stage my suggestion is "Only do what is agreeable to you." The patient usually answers, "Nothing is agreeable." "Then at least," I respond, "do not exert yourself to do what is disagreeable." The patient, who has usually been exhorted to do various uncongenial things to remedy this condition, finds a rather flattering novelty in my advice, and may improve in behavior. Later I insinuate the second rule of conduct, saying that "It is much more difficult and I do not know if you can follow it." After saying this I am silent, and look doubtfully at the patient. In this way I excite his curiosity and ensure his attention, and then proceed, "If you could follow this second rule you would be cured in fourteen days. It is—to consider from time to time how you can give another person pleasure. It would very soon enable you to sleep and would chase away all your sad thoughts. You would feel yourself to be useful and worthwhile."
>
> I receive various replies to my suggestion, but every patient thinks it is too difficult to act upon. If the answer is, "How can I give pleasure to others when I have none myself?" I relieve the prospect by saying, "Then you will need four weeks." The more transparent response, "Who gives *me* pleasure?" I encounter with what is probably the strongest move in the game, by saying, "Perhaps you had better train yourself a little thus: do not actually *do* anything to please anyone else, but just think about how you could do it!" (Adler, 1964a, pp. 25–26)

Adler is marvelously engaged with his client. He has thought through the typical responses and is acting with the client—as in a "game." Although you might make the case that he is being ingenuine during this exchange, you can also make the opposite argument. Perhaps Adler is being so much himself that he's able to let out his playful, artistic, and Socratic self—all in an effort to move the patient away from depression and toward community feeling.

Paradoxical Strategies

Many different authors have written about paradoxical strategies, but Adler was one of the first (see also Frankl, 1967, and Dunlap, 1933). The concept of paradox in therapy generally involves prescribing the symptom. Specifically, if your client is overly self-critical, you might suggest that she negatively analyze and criticize herself at even a higher rate and intensity during the coming week.

Although there is some empirical evidence supporting paradoxical approaches, they're generally considered high-risk techniques (Hill, 1987). Consequently, when we use paradox, we generally use it in moderation. For example, with a 43-year-old woman who "worries constantly," we don't generally tell her to "worry more," but instead tell her to take 20 minutes twice daily to sit down or pace as she worries intensively. Often, the positive outcome of a paradoxical prescription is the interesting phenomenon of clients feeling more in control than they did previously. Paradoxical strategies are covered in more detail in Chapter 5.

Advice, Suggestion, and Direction

The Adlerian therapist offers advice freely. Of course, he or she does so only within the context of a friendly, collaborative, positive relationship.

Corsini (1998) offers a description of a directive, advice-giving technique he refers to as "I'll Betcha." He claims that this technique is a form of turning the tables on the client, and in that sense it contains paradoxical qualities (but seems much less risky than prescribing a symptom). He states:

> [This technique] is called "I'll Betcha." It goes as follows: Say that I suggest that a client do a particular thing to achieve a particular end and the client says it will not work. I will persist and finally will say, "I'll betcha it will." Then I outline the bet—always for exactly $2.00. If the client accepts my bet, the conditions are the following: He or she is to do exactly what I say. If it does not work, he or she wins the bet; if it does work, I win the bet. I have made about 50 such bets over the years and have not lost one. The interesting part is that my opponent decides whether it worked or not. (Corsini, 1998, p. 54)

Offering advice, suggestions, and direction are generally associated with the reorientation stage of counseling. This is because, by this time, the client has already been provided with interpretations, and therefore insight and motivation are present. The motivation ignited through insight is the motivation for excellence and a drive toward improving one's lot in life. It's hard to think of a better time to offer a client a bit of helpful advice.

APPLICATION: CASE EXAMPLE

In this section we've included excerpts of a demonstration family constellation interview H. Mosak conducted with a 17-year-old girl. This is a marvelous interview, and we recommend that, if possible, you read it in its entirety (Mosak, 1972; see also Sweeney, 1989).

In the first excerpt, Dr. Mosak is asking the client, Ann, about her perceptions of her older sister, Debbie. As he gathers information, he occasionally shifts to connecting with the client through gentle interpretations:

Dr. M.: What kind of child was Debbie when you were growing up?

Ann: She was *very* studious all the time. . . . Well, from my point of view she was a goody-goody. . . . It's hard to talk about your own sister.

Dr. M.: Especially if you have to say such nice things about her.

Ann: No, she was *very* reliable and *very* responsible . . . and *very* talkative.

Dr. M.: Did she get into trouble at school for that?

Ann: Occasionally.

Dr. M.: So, while she was a goody-goody, she still got into trouble occasionally. She wasn't quite perfect. What else was she like?

Ann: Well, she always tried to please my parents. And she was *very* sensitive. You know like she cried easily . . . that's about all.

Dr. M.: I'm going to invite you, Ann, to look at all of this on the blackboard. If you had one word to describe your sister, what word would you use? Let me give you an incomplete sentence. She was . . .

Ann: Responsible, I guess.

Dr. M.: That's a good word.

Ann: I can't do it all in one word.

Dr. M.: I can. Would you like to hear my one word?

Ann: Yes.

Dr. M.: She was *very* . . . (Audience laughter). How does that sound?

Ann: Very good. (Ann and audience laughter).

In this excerpt you can see the approach used by Adlerians to obtain family constellation information. As Dr. Mosak collects information, he's also consistently validating the client's perspective. He embodies an Adlerian therapist: He is friendly, supportive, and perceptive.

Children often compete with each other to find their own successful niches within the family value system. Each child needs to belong and be valued for his or her unique attributes. Even very young children can sense if they have a chance at being the "successful" one in the family on a particular dimension. This is why a second child who follows an academically successful sibling usually chooses to develop her own, different successful attributes (e.g., she may become the class clown). Without special efforts by the parents to encourage a younger child, it can be too threatening for her to compete with an older and smarter child in the area of academic success (or athletic or musical prowess, etc). Without parental support, the younger child has inferiority issues stimulated whenever she tries hard in the area in which the older child excels, and discouragement ensues.

Next, Dr. Mosak continues to identify Ann's unique status in the family and how it relates to her conception of herself.

Dr. M.: Who's the most industrious, and who the least?

Ann: Debbie, the most; me, the least.

Dr. M.: Who's the "goodest," and who rebelled openly?

Ann: Debbie was the "goodest," and I was the rebel.

Dr. M.: Proudly?

Ann: Yep!

Dr. M.: Who was the covert rebel, never fought openly, just did what he wanted?

Ann: Sam.

Dr. M.: Who demanded his own way, and who got it?

Ann: I demanded it, and Debbie got it.

Dr. M.: And Sam?

Ann: Sam got his way also.

Eventually, Dr. Mosak paints the picture of Ann as what he refers to as a "reverse puppet." This means that Ann has inaccurately defined defiance toward her parents as freedom. For her, to continue to exist in her family she had to be the opposite of her sister Debbie. Consequently, she turned into a tomboy who did poorly academically—which was exactly the opposite of what her parents wanted her to do. Of course, a reverse puppet is still a puppet, because it isn't free to do what it wants, but only the defiant thing. Ann still desperately wants her parents' acceptance and approval—she just wants it in an area where she has some measure of hope for success.

There is much more to this interview than we can include here. Dr. Mosak goes on to connect Ann's feelings of weakness and inferiority to her mother's weakness and her father's dominance. He also engages the professional audience to support and encourage Ann's potential new perception of her qualities of creativity and sensitivity as positive traits, rather than signs of weakness. In the end, he offers her an initial lifestyle interpretation.

Dr. M.: We can see, Ann, why you would not believe in yourself, growing up the way you did. I guess if I grew up in that spot, I would feel pretty much the way you feel. The question is, is it necessary now? Or do you want to stop being a "reverse puppet" and decide what *you* want to do in life? Not, "what *they* want me to do which I will not do." That's the issue you and your counselor will have to work out together. Is there anything else you would like to add, ask, or comment on?

Ann: I think you are just remarkable. I mean the way you can . . . (Audience laughter and applause).

Dr. M.: Thank you, you are very kind. Other than that . . .

Ann: I guess I didn't realize that I was the victim of, what I was suffering from, I think I can accept myself a lot easier now.

Dr. M.: You are suffering from the ignorance that you are a good, competent person. You *are* competent, you are good, but you are too busy looking at Debbie and your mother, and judging yourself negatively, instead of deciding what you want to do. (These excerpts from Mosak's interview are quoted in Sweeney, 1989, pp. 268–286.)

In his interpretation, Mosak is compassionate, supportive, encouraging, and hopeful. He is so much of these qualities that the client can easily digest the less positive interpretive feedback—that she is a reverse puppet who doesn't believe in herself—without becoming defensive.

Mosak's interpretation explicitly articulates what many psychodynamic interpretations imply: he asks the client if she wants to change her old, outdated, way of thinking about and being in the world. Mosak asks Ann, "The question is, is it necessary now? Or do you want to stop being a 'reverse puppet' and decide what *you* want to do in life?" If the timing is right, based on Adlerian theory, the client, because she has within her the basic motivation to strive toward excellence and completion, will answer this important therapy question with, "Absolutely, yes! I want to change!" This answer—this articulation of the client's motivation—leads directly to the reorientation phase of Adlerian therapy.

Mosak's work with Ann was limited to a single consultation session. If we had access to additional therapy interactions with Ann and her individual psychology practitioner, they would focus primarily on action, encouragement, and support (see Practitioner Commentary 3.1 for more detailed information on encouragement). The following techniques could be applied to Ann and her situation, based on her family constellation interview.

- *Acting as if.* "During this next week, Ann, I'd like you to act 'as if' you're completely competent and good. As you practice this new way of thinking about yourself, notice the ways you feel, think, and act differently. Also, notice what activities spark your interest."

PRACTITIONER COMMENTARY 3.1

Encouragement and Adlerian Psychology

by Daniel Eckstein

Daniel Eckstein is president of Encouraging Leadership Inc. in Scottsdale, Arizona. He is also an adjunct professor for Capella University, Minneapolis, and counseling director of organization development for the Adler Professional Schools Inc. in Toronto. You can learn more about him and encouragement at his web site, www. encouragingleadership.com.

Thirty years ago, I saw noted psychiatrist Harold Mosak do a lifestyle demonstration. Since then I have utilized early recollections, metaphors, and the idea that all behavior is purposeful or goal-directed as adjunctive interventions in addition to a formal lifestyle assessment.

But if I had to choose just one Adlerian concept most dear to me, it would be the idea of encouragement. While this is not a concept exclusive to Adlerians, the book *Leadership by Encouragement* (Dinkmeyer & Eckstein, 1996) has taken me to many other countries with the profoundly simple idea Adler noted of building on strengths and not weaknesses. This is a major theme of the contemporary positive psychology movement too.

Encouragement is a process whereby one focuses on an individual's resources to build that person's self-esteem, self-confidence, and feelings of worth. Encouragement involves focusing on any resource that can be turned into an asset or strength. Adlerian psychiatrist Rudolf Dreikurs (1950) said that humans need encouragement like plants need water. He believed that every person with whom one comes in contact feels better or worse according to how others behave toward him or her.

The value of encouragement is often taken for granted or missed completely because it tends to be private, not public. And although there are identifiable words and ways that express encouragement, it is best manifested by an attitude that nonverbally communicates caring and compassion.

To encourage requires a subtle shift of focus. Clients are too often bombarded with shortcomings and the deficiencies of their birth, their parents, their culture, their organization, and, of course, themselves. Encouraging individuals have the ability to perceive a spark of divinity in others and then act as a mirror that reflect that goodness to them.

The greatest counselors are the ones who truly inspire others to seek more out of life, the ones who help us to remember our dreams, the ones who touch our hearts with a phenomenal ability to see beauty in all things. They inspire others to new heights because of their ability to assist them in seeking, and ultimately believing, that each person in the home will indeed discover ultimately his or her own personal dreams.

In the past few years I and my colleague Phyliss Cooke have interviewed almost 500 people by simply asking them, "Who encouraged you and how?" We have found seven re-occurring ways people encourage others. They are included here, along with sample quotations from the people interviewed.

PRACTITIONER COMMENTARY 3.1 (continued)

1. *Role modeling.* Both the fear of consequences and anticipation of rewards seem influential in adopting a role model. The importance of fear of consequences in adopting a role model is illustrated by the following statement, from coach to teenager: "I'm going to chew you out and you'd better come back tomorrow for more . . . that's how life is!" Anticipation of rewards is illustrated by this statement: "I was constantly praised and encouraged for small achievements and I learned the importance of token rewards: smiles, hugs, kind words."

2. *Seeing strengths and abilities.* When specific talents, skills, and personal qualities are mentioned, encouragement happens. "She noted my tennis skills." "She complimented my writing talent."

3. *Supporting over the long haul (consistency).* People report that mottos to live by and consistent positive feedback from birth are encouraging. "Numerous positive statements through my formative years is [sic] the basis of my self confidence."

4. *Seeing people as special.* If one person sees an individual as special, in spite of many others who didn't, the individual feels encouraged.

5. *Supporting during crises.* It is deeply encouraging when you have someone in your corner during difficult times. "I'm in your corner, and I always will be!" "I was unfairly accused and he stood by me."

6. *Supporting what people are interested in.* When an individual's unique interests or assets are acknowledged as the foundation for positive development, the individual feels encouraged. "She encouraged me to capitalize on my love for children." "Life is too short not to enjoy it . . . ; be your own person."

7. *Encouraging career choices.* Individuals are encouraged when others articulate and support specific career choices and attributes. "Since she said I had a gift for math and I would do well in the subject, I explored careers with this talent in mind." "I knew I wanted to be a nurse and she helped me get into a school after I was rejected by the first one."

- *Spitting in the client's soup.* When the therapist notices Ann talking about her sister or mother, he or she might comment, "It seems like one of your favorite ways to avoid deciding what you want to do is to keep the spotlight on your mom and sis."

- *Creating new images.* "Until now, you've had an image of your sister on a pedestal. It's like you're down below, looking up at her. Let's make a new and more useful image for you. What if you saw both you and your sister on the same level? Try to imagine it. How does it feel?"

Overall, the purpose of Adlerian therapy is to help the client develop a more adaptive lifestyle. As noted previously, a variety of active techniques can be used to facilitate positive change. Adler sums up the modest nature of therapy goals for Ann or other Adlerian therapy recipients: "Our method enables us to replace the great mistakes by small ones. . . . Big mistakes can produce neuroses but little mistakes a nearly normal person (Adler, 1964a, p. 62).

THERAPY OUTCOMES RESEARCH

Adlerian concepts have been written about for nearly a century, and individual psychology has certainly lived up to Adler's hopes for producing a useful psychology: Professionals and teachers around the globe have applied the principles of individual psychology within educational settings, for parent education, and for group, family, couple, and individual therapy. Even further, numerous contemporary approaches to therapy borrow extensively from individual psychology, including, but not limited to, cognitive-behavior, solution-focused, existential, and reality therapy.

Despite the prominent use of Adler's concepts, empirical research attesting to the efficacy of Adlerian approaches is sparse. Early research reviews, based on only four empirical studies of Adlerian psychotherapy, indicate that the procedures are slightly more effective than placebo treatment. In several studies, Adlerian therapy was shown to have efficacy similar to psychoanalytic and person-centered therapy (Smith et al., 1980).

A number of studies have been conducted on the efficacy of paradoxical techniques in therapy. In a meta-analysis of these studies, paradoxical intention was shown to have a .99 effect size (Hill, 1987). This suggests that the average client treated with paradoxical approaches is better off than about 84% of clients not receiving treatment. Overall, this is a fairly strong outcome and slightly better than the .80 effect size typically attributed to psychotherapy in general (Smith et al., 1980). An alternative meta-analysis of paradoxical techniques was similarly positive (Shoham-Salomon & Rosenthal, 1987).

Overall, there is a surprising lack of controlled empirical studies directly evaluating Adlerian therapy. This makes it difficult to say conclusively whether Adlerian therapy is effective. At this point, logic and the minimal amount of existing research support its efficacy, but additional research is needed. It is hoped that the contemporary Adlerian brief therapy movement will produce more controlled research on its effectiveness in the near future (Bitter, Christensen, Hawes, & Nicoll, 1998).

MULTICULTURAL PERSPECTIVES

Adler is a friend of the individual. He was the first modern psychotherapist to emphasize how social and familial factors shape and contribute to individual problems. He was particularly sensitive to women's issues and often made a point of outlining the challenges women face in a male-oriented society. He stated:

> It is a frequently overlooked fact that a girl comes into the world with a prejudice sounding in her ears which is designed only to rob her of her belief in her own value, to shatter her self-confidence and destroy her hope of ever doing anything worthwhile. If this prejudice is constantly strengthened, if a girl sees again and again how women are given servile roles to play, it is not hard to understand how she loses courage, fails to face her obligations, and sinks back from the solution of her life's problems (quoted in J.B. Miller, 1973, p. 41).

Because of its focus on the individual as a unique entity deserving time, attention, and compassion, Adlerian therapy is well suited to individuals from various cultural backgrounds. This therapeutic approach, emphasizing a friendly, respectful, and collaborative relationship, could feel comfortable to many different types of clients. The fact that Adler based much of his theoretical work on his practice with individuals of lower socioeconomic status makes it well suited to the common person.

From a multicultural perspective, a central criticism of Adlerian therapy is its emphasis on insight as a primary factor in generating behavior change. Sue and Sue describe the problem with insight-oriented approaches from a multicultural perspective:

> [I]nsight is not highly valued by many culturally diverse clients. There are major class differences as well. People from lower socioeconomic classes frequently do not perceive insight as appropriate to their life situations and circumstances. . . . For the individual who is concerned about making it through each day, this orientation proves counterproductive. (D. W. Sue & D. Sue, 2003, pp. 109–110)

Although we appreciate the multicultural perspective on insight as articulated by Sue and Sue (2003), it seems like their description of insight-oriented therapy approaches is more consistent with classical psychoanalytic formulations. In contrast, as described in this chapter, the Adlerian approach emphasizes the connection between insight, motivation, and action, rather than intellectual insight.

CONCLUDING COMMENTS

In the end, there is little debate about the significance of Adler's contribution as a person, theorist, and practitioner to the fields of counseling and psychotherapy. Even Albert Ellis, not typically one to lavish praise on anyone, has written a tribute to Alfred Adler, in which he refers to him as the "true father of modern psychotherapy" (Ellis, 1970, p. 11). Similarly, Ellenberger (1970) wrote, "It would not be easy to find another author from which so much has been borrowed from all sides without acknowledgement, than Adler" (p. 645).

Indeed, you will find that Adlerian psychology is everywhere. Sometimes he is cited; other times he is not. One possible explanation for Adler's omnipresence in modern counseling and psychotherapy is that he employed a psychology of common sense. And so it has been only a matter of time until the rest of the field began catching up with him.

We leave you with two of our favorite Adlerian quotations:

"Everything can also be different" (Adler, 1936, p. 14).
"Everything is a matter of opinion" (Adler, 1912/1983, p. 1).

STUDENT REVIEW ASSIGNMENTS

Please read and respond to the following review assignments.

Critical Corner

The following critical statements about individual psychology are designed to be provocative. Please write your response to the criticisms in the space provided.

1. Much of individual psychology is based on concepts such as lifestyle and the individual's subjective fictional goals. These concepts are at best elusive, and at worst fictional. Comment on how a modern psychological theory could base itself on such unscientific concepts.
Response:

2. The Adlerian family constellation and, in particular, birth order, is too flexible for practical evaluation. For example, birth order research has been flatly negative—in that birth order, in and of itself does not adequately predict individual personality or behavior. However, Adler's belief in the individual's unique interpretation of birth order and family position makes it impossible to systematically evaluate these theoretical influences on human behavior.
Response:

3. As a theory, individual psychology is somewhat loose and poorly organized. Adler spent more time lecturing and talking about therapy cases than writing out his ideas into a coherent and integrated theory. Although no one claims his ideas are poor, it's obvious from reading Adler that his theory is underdeveloped. In fact, individual psychology is more like the pasting together of a number of common-sense ideas about humans than a formal theory of personality or psychotherapy.
Response:

4. One of the cornerstones of Adlerian therapy is that insight produces motivation for change. Do you think that's true? Is there any empirical evidence to support the contention that insight produces motivation?
Response:

5. Individual psychology is an overly optimistic and naive approach to therapy. For example, Adlerians advocate the use of a variety of superficial techniques to produce lasting human change. Do you really think that individuals experience lasting change when told to act "as if" they are confident?
Response:

6. In this chapter Adler has been characterized as a strong feminist. However, he also wrote that the woman's proper place is in the home, raising children, and that's where his wife spent most of her time. Consequently, from a feminist perspective, although Adler may have been a feminist in his time, he can hardly be viewed as a man who was completely liberated from the trappings of masculine domination.
Response:

Reviewing Key Terms

- The masculine protest
- Holism
- Purposeful striving
- Superiority striving
- The idiographic approach
- Soft determinism
- Social interest
- Community feeling
- Phenomenology
- Tasks of life

- Fictional goals or fictional finalism
- Lifestyle
- The four goals of children's misbehavior
- The four stages of Adlerian therapy
- Family constellation
- The question
- Birth order
- Early recollections
- Dream analysis

- Basic mistakes
- Future autobiography
- Creating new images
- Acting "as if"
- Push-button technique
- Spitting in the client's soup
- Catching oneself
- Task-setting and indirect suggestion
- Paradoxical strategies
- I'll betcha

Review Questions

1. According to Dreikurs, what two psychosocial needs should be fulfilled to alleviate children's pursuit of the four goals of misbehavior?
2. Adler emphasized the importance of "winning the patient." What does he mean by this, and what is the other major point he makes about the attitude of the therapist during therapy?
3. From the Adlerian perspective, discuss the relationship between insight and motivation.
4. Answer the following question as briefly as you can: How do Adlerians propose that individual clients overcome their basic mistakes?
5. Identify and operationally define one Adlerian concept that you think should and could be evaluated using modern quantitative scientific research methods.
6. For an Adlerian, what causes psychopathology?
7. Discuss the suitability of Adlerian therapy for ethnoculturally diverse clients. Which of the techniques discussed in this chapter do you think would be appropriate and/or inappropriate for clients of specific ethnocultural backgrounds?

RECOMMENDED READINGS AND RESOURCES

The following resources provide additional information on Adler and Adlerian therapy.

Lead Adlerian (Individual Psychology) Journals

- *Journal of Individual Psychology*
- *The Quarterly: Publication of the Adlerian Psychology Association of British Columbia*
- *Individual Psychology: Journal of Adlerian Theory, Research & Practice*
- *International Journal of Individual Psychology*

Books and Articles

Adler, A. (1927). *Understanding human nature.* Garden City, NY: Garden City Publishing.

Adler, A. (1956). *The individual psychology of Alfred Adler.* New York: Basic Books.

Adler, A. (1958). *What life should mean to you.* New York: Capricorn.

Adler, A. (1964b). *Social interest: A challenge to mankind* (J. Linton & R. Vaughan, Trans.). New York: Capricorn.

Bottome, P. (1939). *Alfred Adler, apostle of freedom.* London: Faber and Faber.

Bottome, P. (1962). *The goal.* New York: Vanguard Press.

Eckstein, D. (1999). An early-recollections skill-building workshop. *Journal of Individual Psychology, 55*(4), 437–448.

Ellis, A. (1970). Tribute to Alfred Adler. *Journal of Individual Psychology, 26,* 11–12.

Mosak, H. H. (1985). Interrupting a depression: The pushbutton technique. *Individual Psychology, 41,* 210–214.

Mosak, H. H., & Kopp, R. R. (1973). The early recollections of Adler, Freud, and Jung. *Journal of Individual Psychology, 29,* 157–166.

Mosak, H. H., & Maniacci, M. P. (1999). *A primer of Adlerian psychology: The analytic-behavioral-cognitive psychology of Alfred Adler.* Philadelphia: Taylor & Francis.

Orgler, H. (1963). *Alfred Adler: The man and his work.* New York: Mentor Books.

Sicher, L. (1991). A declaration of interdependence. *Individual Psychology, 47*(1), 10–16.

Sommers-Flanagan, J., & Sommers-Flanagan, R. (2001). The three-step emotional change trick. In H. G. Kaduson & C. E. Schaefer (Eds.), *101 more favorite play therapy techniques* (pp. 439–444). New York: Jason Aronson.

Sweeney, T. J. (1998). *Adlerian counseling: A practitioner's approach* (4th ed.). Philadelphia: Accelerated Development.

Vaihinger, H. (1911). *The psychology of "as if."* New York: Harcourt, Brace and World.

Videotapes

Carlson, J. (1997). *Brief integrative Adlerian couples therapy* [Videotape]. Framingham, MA: Microtraining and Multicultural Development.

Carlson, J., & Kjos, D. (2000). *Adlerian therapy with Dr. James Bitter* [Videotape]. Boston: Allyn & Bacon.

Carlson, J., & Kjos, D. (2000). *Adlerian therapy with Dr. Jon Carlson* [Videotape]. Boston: Allyn & Bacon.

Training Organizations and Web Sites

Extensive information about Alfred Adler and the practice of individual psychology can be obtained from the following web sites and training institutes.

North American Society of Adlerian Psychology (web site: www.alfredadler.org)

Adler School of Professional Psychology (web site: www.adler.edu)

Alfred Adler Institute of Northwest Washington (e-mail: HTStein@att.net)

Alfred Adler Institute of San Francisco (e-mail: DPienkow@msn.com)

Alfred Adler Institute of New York (web site: www.alfredadler-ny.org/alfred.adler.htm)

The International Committee for Adlerian Summer Schools and Institutes (ICASSI) (e-mail: PeteHMSU64@aol.com)

Chapter 4 ——————————————————————————

JUNG AND THE PRACTICE OF ANALYTICAL PSYCHOTHERAPY

The serious problems in life, however, are never fully solved. If ever they should appear to be so it is a sure sign that something has been lost. The meaning and purpose of a problem seem to lie not in its solution but in our working at it incessantly. This alone preserves us from stultification and petrifaction.

—Carl Gustav Jung, *The Portable Jung* (Campbell, 1971, pp. 11–12)

IN THIS CHAPTER YOU WILL LEARN

- The history and context of analytical (or Jungian) psychotherapy
- Theoretical concepts of personality described by Jung
- Methods and techniques of Jungian therapy
- Strategies for working with dreams from a Jungian perspective
- The multicultural strengths and weaknesses of Jung's theory
- Ethical considerations associated with Jung's ideas
- Key terminology of Jungian theory and therapy

Jungian theory appeals to deep thinkers, dreamers, the spiritually open, and the psychologically adventurous. This is probably because Jung himself embodied these traits. He traveled, delved into the mystical, and experimented in concrete ways with making his unconscious conscious—he even built his own castle, out of stones, by hand. There are some fairly esoteric aspects to a full-blown Jungian approach to understanding and helping people. On the other hand, some of his thinking has become as common and useful as standard gardening tools. Human fascination with dreams, culture, and the collective and mysterious forces that motivate, frighten, thrill, and fulfill us guarantees that Jung's ideas will continue to hold intrigue long into the future.

BIOGRAPHICAL INFORMATION: CARL JUNG

Carl Gustav Jung, named for his paternal grandfather, was born in Kesswil, Switzerland, in 1875 and died in Zurich in 1961. His parents had previously lost two boys in infancy, so Carl was an only child until the birth of his sister, 9 years later. As a youngster, Jung remembered struggling with many fears and insecurities. His mother, a housewife, became ill and had to be away for a significant period of time while Jung was 3 years old. The young boy experienced this absence as a terrible and frightening abandonment. Jung's father, a clergyman, was invested in his son's intellectual development, teaching him Latin at an early age. Jung reported that his mother was also intellectually oriented, often reading to him of exotic world religions. According to June Singer (1973), young Carl Jung was resistant to certain traditional subjects, and he learned to have fainting spells in order to stay home from school. At one point he overheard his father stating that his son was quite disabled and would probably never lead a normal life. This inspired Jung to overcome his malingering tendencies, and he returned to school, determined to succeed.

Jung considered careers in archaeology and theology before settling on medical training, which he completed in 1900. However, he continued to develop his interest in spiritual and psychic phenomena, working with Eugene Bleuler at a mental hospital in Zurich, and later with Pierre Janet in Paris.

A cousin of Jung's displayed unusual psychic abilities at an early age. At age 15, she "channeled" the spirits of dead relatives and performed various séances that Jung attended and studied at length. In fact, his interest in these phenomena were so strong that he completed his dissertation in the area.

Jung married Emma Rauschenbach in 1903, and the couple had four daughters and one son. Although Jung lived most of his life in Switzerland, he traveled extensively to feed his avid curiosity about differing human cultures and practices. Carl Jung began corresponding with Sigmund Freud in 1906 and traveled to Vienna with his family in 1907 to spend a week socializing and meeting with Freud and members of the Viennese psychoanalytic circle. The two spent 13 straight hours together after the Wednesday gathering of Freud's group, tremendously enjoying each other's intellectual company. We detail the development and ending of their relationship in the next section.

HISTORICAL CONTEXT

Freud, Jung, and Adler were contemporaries, acquainted with each other, living in similar worlds, and using similar terminology to explore and articulate relatively new ideas about human functioning that were circulating during their time. However, there are vast differences in their family lives and professional exposures. Jung's father, a clergyman, and his grandfather, a medical doctor, were both reported to be intellectual and politically radical. Jung's mother delighted in reading him stories of faraway lands and unusual belief systems. Jung's cousin conducted convincing séances. And Jung himself was drawn to the mysteries of life, culture, and the paranormal. Jung's world was far larger than his native Switzerland. He traveled to many distant lands, including Uganda, Kenya, New Mexico (to visit with Indians there), Tunis, and Algiers. He read extensively in religion, mythology, folklore, philosophy, and theology.

Jung and Freud

Similar to Adler, Jung had a professional life that preceded his contact with Freud. Also similar to Adler, following a few years of close contact with Freud and psychoanalysis, Jung severed all ties with Freud. However, unlike Adler, Jung was not expelled from the Psychoanalytic Society. Instead, for the most part, Jung emotionally and psychologically liberated himself from Freud's influence.

In 1909, Freud considered Jung to be like an eldest son and the crown prince of psychoanalysis. At almost the same moment, Jung began to question Freud, the "father." In a dramatic exchange, Jung revealed to Freud his interest in the paranormal, an interest that moved Freud to respond with "That is sheer bosh" (Jung, 1965, p. 155). Jung also proposed the possibility of a "psychosynthesis" that created future events as a balancing force to psychoanalysis. In late summer of 1912, Jung sailed to New York and gave a lecture series at Fordham University. These lectures began clearly distinguishing his form of psychoanalysis from Freud's. He was in the process of completely reformulating the psychoanalytic construct of psychic energy or libido from a sexually based source of psychic energy to a more general source of psychic energy, a process that was simultaneously threatening and disappointing to Freud.

Jung was aware of Adler's earlier exit from the Psychoanalytic Society. Although he was critical of Adler and his followers, Jung's emotional response to Freud was leading him down the same road. He was struggling to manage his ambivalence toward Freud. On December 18, 1912, he wrote the following powerful letter to the man who had anointed him the crown prince of psychoanalysis.

Dear Professor Freud:
May I say a few words to you in earnest? I admit the ambivalence of my feelings towards you, but am inclined to take an honest and absolutely straight forward view of the situation. If you doubt my word, so much the worse for you. I would, however, point out that your technique of treating your pupils like patients is a *blunder.* In that way you produce either slavish sons or impudent puppies (Adler-Stekel and the whole insolent gang now throwing their weight about in Vienna). I am objective enough to see through your little trick. You go around sniffing out all the symptomatic actions in your vicinity, thus reducing everyone to the level of sons and daughters who blushingly admit the existence of their faults. Meanwhile you remain on top as the father, sitting pretty. For sheer obsequiousness nobody dares to pluck the prophet by the beard and inquire for once what you would say to a patient with a tendency to analyze the analyst instead of himself. You would ask him: "Who's got the neurosis?"

You see, my dear Professor, so long as you hand out this stuff I don't give a damn about my symptomatic actions; they shrink to nothing in comparison with the formidable beam in my brother Freud's eye. I am not in the least neurotic—touch wood! I have submitted *lege artis et tout humblement* to analysis and am much the better for it. You know, of course, how far a patient gets with self-analysis: not out of his neuroses—just like you. If ever you should rid yourself entirely of your complexes and stop playing the father to your sons and instead of aiming continually at their weak spots take a good look at your own for a change, then I will mend my ways and at one stroke uproot the vice of being in two minds about you. Do you *love* neurotics enough to be always at one with yourself? But perhaps you *hate* neurotics. In that case how can you expect your efforts to treat your patients leniently and lovingly not to be accompanied by somewhat mixed feelings? Adler and Stekel were taken in by your little tricks and reacted with childish insolence. I shall continue to stand by you publicly while maintaining my own views, but privately shall start telling you in my letters what I really think of you. I consider this procedure only decent.

No doubt you will be outraged by this peculiar token of friendship, but it may do you good all the same.

With best regards,
Most sincerely yours, Jung (quoted in Bankart, 1997, pp. 155–156)

Freud's response to Jung was less outrage than disappointment. But in the end, he was unable to tolerate Jung's angry critique and his promise of a friendship characterized by a brutal bluntness. An excerpt of Freud's letter in response to Jung captures his effort to minimize his personal emotional damage and move on. It reads:

> I propose that we abandon our personal relations entirely. I shall lose nothing by it, for my only emotional tie with you has long been a thin thread—the lingering effect of past disappointments—and you have everything to gain, in view of the remark you recently made in Munich, to the effect that an intimate relationship with a man inhibited your scientific freedom. I therefore say, take your full freedom and spare me your supposed "tokens of friendship." (Bankart, 1997, p. 156)

Jung's response was brief and carried within it the seeds of his interest in and aptitude for predicting the future. He wrote:

> I accede to your wish that we abandon our personal relations, for I never thrust my friendship on anyone. You yourself are the best judge of what this moment means to you. "The rest is silence." (Bankart, 1997, p. 156)

With that formidable phrase, the Freud-Jung correspondence officially ended. And Jung's plunge into the depths of his own psyche deepened.

Post-Enlightenment

The Enlightenment period in history is also referred to as the Age of Reason. Jung's intellectual development was strongly influenced by post-Enlightenment thinking. Like many other thinkers of his time, he began exploring concepts and experiences beyond the reasonable and rational. In contrast to Freud's positivistic, mechanistic, scientific, and materialistic approach to human psychology, Jung embraced mystical and religious symbols and experiences.

By some measures, Jung is the most multiculturally oriented of the early theorists. His exposure to the wisdom of other cultures led him to an openness about ideas. He saw overarching patterns as well as distinctive features in the myths and religions he explored. Although Jung may not have framed it as such, his thinking also has surprising feminist applications that we'll discuss in the next section. Unfortunately, though, Jung's philosophies also reflected a belief that not all people had the gifts necessary to achieve full individuation. In fact, he, like Plato, envisioned a relative minority of individuals who, given the proper opportunities, could be both the political and moral leaders of humankind (Pietikainen, 2001). Further, he hypothesized possible racially specific collective unconscious patterns that could be construed as constituting greater or lesser sophistication. For a period of time in the early to mid-1930s, Jung's work and certain beliefs about archetypal energies came under Nazi influence, although many claim that Jung went along more for expedience than heartfelt agreement with Nazi philosophy. He abandoned this association long before it began to display its horrific manifestations. He moved back (figuratively and in reality) to his neutral Switzerland and distanced himself from the politics and racial discrimination of that era.

THEORETICAL PRINCIPLES OF JUNGIAN PSYCHOLOGY

Whereas Freud was methodical, pessimistic, and preoccupied with unconscious, conflict-ridden, instinctual drive states, Jung was impressionistic, optimistic, and preoccupied with unconscious forces, mystery, myth, and symbol. His overarching emphasis was on the great potential and creative energy residing within individuals and society. Both Jung and Freud believed the key to psychological healing and growth involved making the unconscious conscious, but for Freud, the unconscious was a cauldron of primitive impulses needing to be tamed and subdued. For Jung, the unconscious was the source of both great peril and great wisdom—to be approached respectfully, hopefully, and with a listening attitude. As Yoram Kaufmann (1989) points out, "[a]nalytical [Jungian] psychotherapy is an attempt to create, by means of a symbolic approach, a dialectical relationship between consciousness and the unconscious" (p. 119).

Jungian analyst Alex Quenk takes issues with this statement. He writes,

> A dialectical or compensatory relationship between consciousness and unconsciousness is a given aspect of our psyche. It does not need to be 'created'; it is an inherent part of us. Jungian psychotherapy explores, explicates, and enables us to be more aware of this dialectical aspect. (personal communication, December, 2002)

In his *Collected Works,* Volume 7, Jung (1966a) wrote the following, certainly underlining the importance of this dialectical relationship:

> A psychological theory, if it is to be more than a technical makeshift, must base itself on the principle of opposition; for without this it could only re-establish a neurotically unbalanced psyche. There is no balance, no system of self-regulation, without opposition. The psyche is just such a self-regulating system. (p. 92)

Although the term *spiritual* is currently both popular and overused, Jung's open attitude toward explanations that elevated and transcended biologically based drive states led Petteri Pietikainen (2001) to write:

> What is remarkable about the development of Jung's analytical psychology is that he spiritualised [sic] the world of nature, the world of drives and instincts. . . . In contradistinction to Freud, who had naturalized the world of spirit and reduced even the loftiest of ideas to the level of elementary drives, Jung proposed that there are spiritual and ethical values that manifest themselves as drives. (p. 5)

Jung called his theory and therapy "analytical psychotherapy" to distinguish it from Freud's psychoanalysis. However, perhaps because analytical psychotherapy has stayed very closely aligned with Jung, the terms *Jungian* and *analytical* are used inter-

---

Questions for Reflection

One of the most basic questions about human nature is this: Are humans born with more natural tendencies toward the good (community spirit, kindness, creativity, compassion) and therefore the role of parents, therapists, and society is to encourage and enhance these good inborn tendencies, *or* are humans born with more natural tendencies toward the destructive (selfishness, lawlessness, aggression, egocentricism), and therefore the role of parents, therapists, and society is to limit, discipline, reign in, and overcome these natural but dominant tendencies? Freud and Jung seem to stand on opposite sides of this debate. Where would you stand? Most people want to stand somewhere in the middle, but if you had to lean one way or the other, which way would it be? How might this influence the ways you work with people seeking to change?

changeably. It is important to understand that the word *analytical* does not insinuate a close relationship to the concept of analysis. The reason this is important is that psychoanalysis has come to mean, in common parlance, an analysis of the *un*conscious. Jung was very clear that one should not simply attempt to analyze the unconscious, stating, "Indeed it would be a most reprehensible blunder if we tried to substitute analysis of the unconscious for the well tried conscious methods" (Jung, 1954a).

Theory of Personality

If Jung is right in thinking that creative energy comes from making the unconscious conscious, then he must have been well acquainted with his own unconscious, as he was certainly a creative thinker and writer. His construction of the human personality is uniquely his, even though some of the terms may seem familiar. The following are important and particular definitions of terms Jung used in his explanations of human functioning.

Unconscious

This is the vast pool of forces, motives, predispositions, and energy in our psyches that is, at any given time, unavailable to our conscious mind but, when sought, can offer balance and health. Jung wrote:

> The unconscious as we know can never be "done with" once and for all. It is, in fact, one of the most important tasks of psychic hygiene to pay continual attention to the symptomatology of the unconscious content and processes, for the good reason that the conscious mind is always in danger of becoming one-sided, of keeping to well-worn paths and getting stuck in blind alleys. (Campbell, 1971, p. 159)

Jung divided the unconscious into two entities. The *personal unconscious* is particular to each individual and is material that was once conscious. It contains information that has been forgotten or repressed but that might be made conscious again, under the right circumstances. When dreams and fantasies are of a personal nature, Jung believed they represented the personal unconscious.

The *collective unconscious* is a shared pool of motives, urges, fears, and potentialities that we inherit by being human. Jung believed this part of the unconscious was far larger than the personal unconscious and that it was universally shared by all members of the human race. When dreams and fantasies contain impersonal material that seems unrelated to personal experiences, Jung believed they emanated from the collective psychic substrate, the collective unconscious. Jung believed that the collective unconscious consisted of universally shared myths and symbols, common to all humans. Another way to understand this concept is offered by Erich Kahler (1989):

> "Collective unconscious," as used by Jung, seems to me a misleading term. I prefer to call the same psychic zone "generic unconscious" because the word collective presupposes a number of separate individuals who assemble together. Archaic groups . . . did not form through collection or being collected. . . . This distinction is all the more important since in recent times, under the impact of modern collectives—political parties, unions, associations of all kinds—there has developed a truly collective unconscious which will have to be clearly set apart and considered in its own specific character. (pp. 7–8)

Complexes

Freud, Adler, and Jung all used this term. For Jung, a complex was a swirling pool of energy generated in the unconscious. The energy whirls and circles because there is something discordant and unresolved in the person's life. Jung claimed that one could think of complexes as challenging obstacles—therefore, complexes weren't necessarily negative, but their effects might be. If you had a difficult or an absent father, and you haven't worked out that loss, you might not be as neutral and balanced about the concept of "father" as your peers. You might not react in what are considered normal ways to father figures. You might fight ferociously, or run in fear from certain emotional triggers that have to do with fathers, although you might not be aware that you do so. You also might not be able to explain your emotions or actions to yourself. In short, you might have a father complex. The possible complexes are as diverse as human experience. Jung placed great importance on complexes, stating, "The via regia [royal road] to the unconscious, however, is not the dream, [as Freud claimed,] but the complex, which is the architect of dreams and of symptoms" (Jung, 1946, p. 101).

Archetypes

The collective unconscious contains patterns and ordering principles that are essential components of the common human experience. Jung called these patterns archetypes (pronounced ark´-a-types) and believed they gave form and energy to our unconscious enactments of basic human dramas. The concept of Archetypes is not particularly easy to grasp. You might try thinking of them as electrical potential—a great deal of energy can be accessed in the right circumstances, should the valences be correct. This archetypal energy will take form as circumstances and individual propensities match up. Jung (1946) wrote that

> the archetype as an image of instinct is a spiritual goal toward which the whole nature of man strives; it is the sea to which all rivers wend their way, the prize which the hero wrests from the fight with the dragon. (p. 212)

Jungian analyst and author Alex Quenck states, "[t]o focus on the presumptions underlying any person's behavior, belief or dream is to explicate the archetypal explanatory principles that are at their base." (A. T. Quenk, personal communication, 2002). Jung and Jungian practitioners and theorists have named many archetypal images. We'll define some of the most common, but many fascinating books explore the notion of archetypes and specific ones in much greater depth. You'll find some of these books mentioned at the end of the chapter.

1. The *persona* is the archetype that takes and/or changes form where situation meets person. Jung believed that healthy people adapt to the social demands around them. Our persona enables us to hold our inner selves together while interacting with the diverse distractions, temptations, provocations, and invitations the world offers us. Many have described persona as being analogous to skin, in that our skin provides containment, shape, and an informative and somewhat permeable boundary between our inner workings and the substances and sensations in the outer world. Our persona is the mask we wear, or the set of behaviors we engage in to accomplish what is expected in a given relationship. Our professional persona is and should be somewhat different from our persona at a party or our persona when spending time with loved ones.

   When a persona is too loose, there is too little common ground between behaviors and personality in different settings. From the outside, this might make someone look phony and inconsistent. From the inside, the person might struggle to have any sense of who he or she really is. When a persona is too tight, one cannot seem to stop being a certain way, even when the situation demands a very different set of behaviors. The businesswoman who can't leave work at the office and the doctor who can't stop doctoring are examples of the tight persona. In dreams, we get hints about struggles with persona when symbols like houses or other shelters or coverings are featured. Jung (1950) wrote, "The persona is that which in reality one is not, but which oneself as well as others think one is" (p. 61).

2. The *shadow* is that aspect of our psyche we have either never known or have repressed. It contains aspects of ourselves that we've been unable to accept. It is compensatory, or in direct, reciprocal relationship with the persona. Most people who consciously believe themselves to be relatively nice and caring have shadows that are not all that nice. But Jung also hypothesized that if our personas were mean, unworthy, inadequate types, then our shadow might contain kind, upright, caring aspects. Either way, the shadow dwells deep in the unconscious.

   One way to glimpse your shadow is to notice people who really, *really* bother you. Jung believed that we project our shadow archetypes onto other people and then over-react to that projection, as if it were something we were highly allergic to (Kaufmann, 1989). The projection isn't inaccurate, just overblown. The person we believe to be horribly dishonest and self-serving probably is dishonest and self-serving. But if you didn't fear the same traits in yourself, you would be much more balanced in your response to this person. There are some similarities between the concept of the shadow and Freud's concept of id. However, consistent with Jung's buoyancy and optimism, therapeutic work is aimed not at controlling our shadow, or shaming it, or robbing it of energy (Bly, 1988). Instead, it is to understand and embrace it. We'll talk more about this in the section on application. In dreams, the shadow often shows up as the same sex as the dreamer. It is usually an unsavory or frightening character of some sort.

3. The archetypes of *anima* and *animus,* as concepts, have a great deal in common with the Chinese concepts of yin and yang, the feminine and the masculine principles present in all humans. In men, Jung believed there existed a feminine image, "an imprint or archetype of all the ancestral experiences of the female, a deposit, as it were, of all the impressions ever made by woman" (Jung, 1954b, p. 198). Similarly, a male imprint exists in women. Jungians believe that all humans are potentially androgynous, but that for most, one side comes to dominate over the other, thus causing the other to be sublimated or unconscious. When properly functioning, a male's anima enables him to be caring, connected, and emotionally spontaneous and available, and a female's animus enables her to be strong, directive, active, disciplined, and aggressive (Rybak, Russell-Chapin, & Moser, 2000). In men's dreams, the anima manifests as a female. In women's dreams, the animus archetype manifests as a male.

4. The *Self* is one of the most intriguing and spiritually laden archetypes. It is the central, organizing archetype, the archetype of awareness of being. Jung wrote of the Naskapi Indian tribe, a tribe that believes within each person there resides the Great Man—an internal embodiment of all wisdom and truth. This is the Self archetype. Many faith systems and philosophies believe that there is a divine or enlightened potentiality within all humans. Jung would say these are ways of imagining the Self. Further, Jung believed that this Self within us, when fully realized, helped us connect with the spiritual around us—the larger spiritual truths. Jung once said, "[i]f I didn't know that God exists, I would surely have to invent him" (quoted in Bankart, 1997, p. 164).

There are many other archetypes that analytical therapists use in their work. These include the warrior, the hero, the great mother, the innocent, and the trickster, to name a few. Various archetypes—organizing, unconscious patterns—emerge intermittently during a person's life. When they emerge, they are thought to be important messages and guiding influences from the unconscious (Pearson, 1989).

Personality Types

Jung believed that our personalities are organized by certain mental functions and attitudes that determine the ways in which we habitually or preferentially orient ourselves. The two basic attitudes he identified were (1) Extraversion, an orientation to the outer world of people, things, and activities, and (2) Introversion, an orientation to the inner world of concepts, ideas, and internal experience. Jung (1966a) wrote:

> Introversion is normally characterized by a hesitant, reflective, retiring nature that keeps itself to itself, shrinks from objects, is always slightly on the defensive and prefers to hide behind mistrustful scrutiny. Extraversion is normally characterized by an outgoing, candid, and accommodating nature that adapts easily to a given situation, quickly forms attachments, and, setting aside any possible misgivings, will often venture forth with careless confidence into unknown situations. In the first case obviously the subject, and in the second the object, is all-important. (p. 44)

Extraverts tend to enjoy interacting with people frequently, have many friends and acquaintances, and are at ease in and energized by social interactions. Introverts have a smaller circle of friends, enjoy spending time alone, and may feel some unease in social interactions. They rejuvenate with alone time, rather than by hanging out with their buddies. Jung believed that although individuals could behave in both Extraverted and Introverted ways, there is a tendency for one way or the other to feel more real, comfortable, and energizing.

He also believed that at midlife, the attitude that had been repressed or subjugated might assert itself, so that the dominant attitude, in some instances, would recede and the nondominant attitude would become more prominent. In fact, there is some empirical research that suggests that switching from Introversion to Extraversion (and vice versa) is not unusual in middle adulthood (Bradway & Detloff, 1996).

Perhaps in noting this switching tendency, Jung was simply observing the phenomenon often described as the midlife crisis! For instance, if one of the authors of this book failed to do the psychological work necessary to mature, to bring his shadow into consciousness and acceptance, to make friends with his anima, and to seek his wiser, higher Self as he approaches age 50, he might be in danger of seeing his introversion take a back seat (literally) as he drives around in his new red sports car, purchased to chase women and draw attention to his starved Extraverted side. (Of course, because that author is deeply involved in his psychological work, consistently bathing in his creative unconscious and moving steadily toward individuation, such immature behaviors are virtually impossible.)

Ah, yes. Well, getting back to Jung. . . . Along with the defining attitudes of Introversion and Extraversion, Jung identified four functions, two of which he believed were "irrational," in that they do not involve evaluation or judgment. He called these nonrational functions *Sensation* and *Intuition.* Another way to think of these functions involves their role in perception (Quenk, 2000). These are the perceiving functions. Sensation is the function that notices the real world around us and establishes the fact that something exists. Intuition is the function that guesses or surmises the origins and direction of things and ideas. People tend to trust one or the other of these functions more fully as their source of information.

Sensation-trusting people take in information through their senses. They notice and are informed by the world around them. They, like the people of Missouri (the show-me state), are the kind of people who need to see it to believe it. Intuition-trusting people are more likely to make inferential leaps pertaining to cause and effect. They take in the details around them, but their reality is informed more by their sense of possibility than their sensation of reality. These are the kind of people who believe there is more to a situation than meets the eye; they trust their impression of what's underneath, or between the lines, and they often rely on hunches or guesses about what may happen next.

Jung's rational functions were called *Thinking* and *Feeling.* Another way to think of these functions is the role they play in judgments we make. Thinking and Feeling are the judging functions, influenced not by perception, but by reflection. People who have a Thinking preference apply specific, logical, linear principles in their analyses of the information they've taken in via their perception functions—either sensing or intuiting. Thinking is an objective function, not influenced by values or concerns about well-being. People who prefer Thinking are not consumed by issues of harmony and welfare, and will not usually consider things based on these aspects.

Feeling judgments are informed by an assessment of values and the potential impact of choices on individuals and groups of people. People who prefer the Feeling function will take into account the values, concerns, and welfare of themselves and of those around them. They have the ability to operate empathically with others, and although they are able to conceptualize issues objectively and logically, they will lean toward decisions and outcomes that establish harmony and uphold group or individual values (Quenk, 2000).

Katharine Briggs and Isabell Briggs Myers have expanded and elaborated on Jung's notion of human psychological types derived from orientations and functions. Their work resulted in the popular Myers-Briggs Type Indicator, a standardized psychological assessment questionnaire commonly known as the MBTI (Myers, 1955). Briggs and Myers added a third pair of opposites they believed was implied by Jung in his original theorizing. They called these additions *Judging* and *Perceiving* attitudes or orientations. These last two opposites apply only when individuals are interacting with the outside world—regardless of whether they are by nature Introverted or Extraverted. Someone who prefers to use a Judging attitude will use one of the two Judging functions (Thinking or Feeling) when interacting with others. The person who prefers a judging function desires to reach conclusions quickly and efficiently. These people do not welcome interruptions or diversions from the task at hand, and prefer to work with a well-thought-out plan (Quenk, 2000).

As opposed to the Judging attitude, the Perceiving attitude involves the habitual use of one of the perceiving functions, Sensing or Intuition, when interaction with the outside world (Quenk, 2000). Individuals who prefer a Perceiving attitude cope very well with interruptions and diversions from a given plan. They are spontaneous and flexible, and they handle both change and pressure fairly well. They are energized by new information and prefer to have more rather than less going on.

With the two attitudes (Introversion and Extraversion) and the three contrasting function sets, the Myers-Briggs Type Indicator has sixteen possible personality types as outcomes. In addition to categorizing individuals on the basis of their psychological typology, the MBTI also provides information to respondents regarding how extreme

---

Putting It in Practice 4.1

The Myers-Briggs Type Indicator

Isabell Briggs Myers and Katharine Briggs developed what has become known as the Myers-Briggs Type Indicator. Because it is a psychological test that is nonpathologizing (i.e., all scores are acceptable and only indicate individual differences) and holds great commonsense appeal, it has become very popular for a wide range of uses, many of which have not been empirically tested for validity. One of the problems that occur when complex concepts are translated into simpler terms is that much richness is lost. On the other hand, Briggs and Myers have made some of Jung's ideas well-known and popular. If you plan to use the MBTI clinically, we highly recommend you read Naomi Quenk's *Essentials of Myers-Briggs Type Indicator Assessment* (Quenk, 2000) as well as the literature that comes with the assessment instrument. We also recommend that you take the MBTI yourself and talk over your results with a professional experienced in using this instrument. The typologies and the instrument are deceptively simple at first glance. But before taking the MBTI, read back over the brief descriptions of the attitudes and functions and make a guess as to which way you lean in each pairing. Are you more Introverted or Extraverted? Are you guided more by what you actually see, or what you sense as possibilities? Do you allow your head (and the facts accumulated therein) or your heart (and the value systems imbedded there) to be more of an influence in your decision making? When dealing with the outside world, are you more planful, organized, and efficient, or are you more likely to be spontaneous, creative, and oriented to what's happening in the moment?

---

their scoring patterns are. For example, although one individual might be categorized as an Introvert with an extremely high Introversion score, another person might be categorized as an Introvert because his Introversion score was only one point higher than his Extraversion score. Both Jung and Myers and Briggs observed that there is wide variation in the development and maturity of type, so people obtaining the exact same type could be quite different in their personalities and in the level of effectiveness and centeredness they experience internally and in the world.

Theory of Psychopathology

Jungians believe that people come to counseling because they are summoned there by their unconscious. Something needs attending to; something isn't right in the person's life, or development and the unconscious will send troubling messages until the person pays attention and addresses what is awry. People seek help due to a vague, unspecified unhappiness or discontent. In addition, they come simply out of a wish to know themselves better—to lead richer, more fulfilled lives. Of course, people come to Jungian therapists for all the usual reasons as well, and most counselors who utilize Jungian techniques will approach the problems from a Jungian perspective when appropriate.

In the film *A Matter of Heart* there are a number of video clips of Jung's former analytic patients as they provide commentary about him and his therapy approach (Whitney, 1985). In one excerpt, the writer Mary Bancroft discusses a particularly intense interaction she had with Jung. After she asked why everyone was so mean to her, he responded by asking, "Why are you being so mean to everyone else?" After hearing this, she became so angry that she stormed out of therapy, vowing never to return. However, after over a year of being out of analytic therapy and regularly writing and sending angry letters to Jung, she woke up one morning and reported the following:

> Suddenly I realized. Surely he really hit it. And so I phoned Ms. Schmidt [Jung's secretary] ... and I asked if I could have an appointment and she laughed and said, "Oh yes," she said, "Professor Jung told me to save some time for you, he thought you'd be calling shortly." (Whitney, 1985)

Questions for Reflection

Consider the preceding anecdote. How could Jung foresee the fact that his former client would be calling him soon? What explanation do you think Jung would use to explain his remarkable intuitive abilities? Do you think this prediction was presumptuous on Jung's part, or is it possible he knew his patients that well?

The normal and healthy trajectory for human life, according to Jungians, is toward individuation and transformation—a journey that continues throughout life. The first half of life is spent finding out who we are, asserting, jostling for position. The second half is integrating—pursuing our callings and gifts, not frittering away our energies where we don't fit or aren't welcome (Singer, 1973). We move through our lives, energized and guided by the archetypes that emerge at the right time from our unconscious (Pearson, 1989). Sometimes we get trapped or frightened and need assistance in sorting out the messages and troubles. This isn't pathology in the sense of deviance or illness, but rather simply a case of a troubled soul's having wandered off the path.

As you can see, Jung's perspective on psychopathology is not consistent with contemporary emphases on diagnosable mental conditions currently in vogue within the mental health field. This may be why, when clients came to him for analytic therapy, he sometimes responded by stating: "Oh, I see you're in the soup too" (Whitney, 1985).

Questions for Reflection

What are the potential strengths and/or weaknesses of envisioning mental distress and illness as signals of distress, or urgings to listen, emanating from the unconscious?

THE PRACTICE OF JUNGIAN THERAPY

Jung believed that humans follow a journey toward individuation (a term he coined in 1916; Jung, 1938). This is an inner journey toward completeness, or authenticity, and it takes shape at the beginning of the second half of life. At this time, adults become aware of the limits we endure when we seek to meet the social demands around us through our persona—demands that can easily become restrictive or even destructive if our persona possesses us. We begin to admit to ourselves our imperfections, childish longings, hypocrisies and dissatisfactions. Described below are four stages of the journey identified by various authors. Jung himself was never this discrete, seeing the journey as fluid, and believing, as the quote at the beginning of this chapter illustrates, that we never fully arrive.

Aspects of the Journey

The following sections will describe in more detail the various aspects of the journey toward individuation.

Persona and Authenticity

In the individuation journey, it becomes necessary that we drop the more obvious facades and strive to be genuinely ourselves, no matter what the social demands might be. The questions posed in this effort might be "Who am I, really? Deep down, at my core, who am I? When all the fluff and posturing and superficial masks are taken away, who am I?" Many of us suffer from the sense that people don't know us—they don't know our deepest selves, and they've assumed we're something we're not. For many, there is concern that we don't measure up, that we have pretended to be far more competent than we are, and that we will someday be found out. For others, there is the belief that we've been undervalued and misunderstood, held down, and denied a chance to develop. Getting our persona to feel congruent with our inner experiences is the task of persona-level work.

Making Peace with the Dark Side

In the journey toward individuation, at some point, we must realize we have a shadow—our very own dark side—and begin the work of understanding and incorporating this regressed and repressed part of ourselves into consciousness. In working with our shadow, the job is to resolve the opposites we embody and to make peace with longings and urges we've pushed aside or denied. It's important to learn to use the creative energy present in our shadow.

Integrating the Anima/Animus

The work of integrating the anima/animus aspect carries us even deeper into union and wholeness: It involves getting in touch with the opposite-sex archetype each of us embodies. Jungians believe that truly individuated human beings are comfortably androgynous (Rybak et al., 2000). They have achieved the union of apparently opposite (male and female) internal identities. Bankart (1997) writes:

> We see in this aspect of Jung's theory the tremendous impact of Eastern philosophical and religious teachings on the development of his thinking. . . . I fear, however, that for most Westerners the task Jung proposes is very challenging. Keep in mind that most of Jung's patients were in late middle age, a time in life when these concepts may meet with less rigorous resistance from a Western-trained intellect. (p. 172)

Transcendence, Wholeness, Fully Conscious Living

Jung believed that psychotherapy moves us toward a sort of spiritually whole place where one encounters, welcomes, and brings to full consciousness the God Within, the Wise Old Man, or the Great Mother. The Self is consciously known and honored, leading to a transcendent sense of self-actualization, or psychic wholeness. Needless to say, Jung didn't expect many people to actually fully achieve all aspects of the journey toward individuation. Notions of transcendence can be glimpsed in the concepts of enlightenment from Buddhist philosophy (see Chapter 12) and in the work of humanistic thinkers and theorists Carl Rogers and Abraham Maslow (self-actualization).

Preparing Yourself to do Therapy from a Jungian Perspective

Authentic Jungian analysis is a long-term, serious undertaking that by definition can only occur with a certified Jungian analyst. Obtaining certification requires academic training, study, analysis, and supervision provided at one of the few accredited Jungian Institutes (see resources listed at the end of the chapter). However, many therapists use Jungian techniques and perspectives when working with clients, and it is doubtful that Jung would have protested this effort to integrate his concepts into counseling. He believed therapy was a relationship between a therapist who had acquired a certain level of self-awareness and a client who was seeking to increase his or her self-awareness.

Jung believed in an important division between the first half of life and the second. His own interest was especially focused on the struggles and potentials present in the second half of life, and his analytic work was often with the population in that time of life. Consequently, Jungian analysis is sometimes thought to be most applicable with well-adjusted adults who have lived productive younger lives but are now bored and listless or feel that their lives lack meaning. It's also seen as an approach geared toward people who've experienced radical changes in well-being during midlife (Kelleher, 1992). However, Jungian techniques and concepts are also useful with younger populations who are seeking self-understanding, direction, and meaning in their lives.

Jungian analysis has individuation (transcendence or self-actualization) as its ultimate goal. However, Jung believed that in smaller doses therapy could serve as education, as a process of acquiring deeper self-knowledge, or as a force that could enable clients to change their personality structure. He resisted any rigid doctrine or regime and was known for a wide variety of assignments and techniques, some of which he made up on the spot, responding at an intuitive level to what he believed the client needed. Jung wrote, "Learn your theories as well as you can, but put them aside when you touch the miracle of the living soul" (Jung, 1954a).

Jung believed that therapy was an assisted conversation between the client's conscious and unconscious. This communication takes place on a symbolic level, with one of the primary modes of communication being the dream. James Harbeck (2001) writes, "What we humans by habit take to be ourselves is only a rather narrow area of focus on the surface of a much larger Self" (p. 13). At the very least, to work within a Jungian frame, you need to believe in the unconscious and the vast, mostly unexplored terrain in our souls. You need to believe in the symbolic and communicative quality of dreams, daydreams, visions, and things that go bump in the night.

Jungians also pay attention to life's irrational irritations, attractions, fears, and joys, believing that there is rich symbolic information contained therein. They also pay attention to a concept Jung called *synchronicity,* by which he meant coincidences, or noncontrolled happenings that matched up with other happenings, or needs, and resulted in an answer, or in new knowledge (Marlo & Kline, 1998; Singer, 1973). Examples might include a client having a dream that was extraordinarily similar to a dream the therapist had, or an answer to an important dilemma simply appearing, or other seemingly psychic happenings, like premonitions that come true.

For events to be considered synchronistic, they cannot simply seem coincidental: They must also include an enhanced sense of meaning for the effected parties (Storm, 1999). Jung was intrigued with such things for many years. He reported that his interest in this area was first piqued by visits he had with Albert Einstein, who made Jung aware of the possibilities of relativity in time and space, and thereby opened the door for his ponderings of synchronicity (Singer, 1973).

Questions for Reflection

Think of coincidences in your life that seemed too good (or too bad) to be true, and that cause you to rethink certain beliefs you've held. What kinds of attributions do you usually make about such things? Luck? Karma? Accidents of fate? Random events? God or the Goddess? Can you tolerate the notion of synchronicity—the idea that things (at least sometimes) happen for a reason, and that if you are receptive, you'll learn what the reason is? Most of us are uncomfortable with either extreme—the idea of a completely random universe in which there is no meaning other than what meaning each individual makes, or the idea that everything, even the tiniest event, has meaning if we could only "get it." Where do you fall on this continuum? Can you comfortably let people function in this realm in much different ways than yourself?

Preparing your Client for Using Jungian Concepts

Clients who seek out a professional who uses Jungian techniques are often people who've read about Jung or know about some of the treatment approaches that use a Jungian framework. They are eager to explore their existential angst, or their troubled soul, within the therapeutic conversation and to know the importance of their dreams, fantasies, and fears. However, others are just curious or come for all the other reasons people seek counseling. Ethical Highlight 4.1 provides an excerpt that might be included in a general informed consent document for a counselor who uses Jungian techniques and methods.

The use of Jungian techniques can be especially helpful with clients who remember and are intrigued or troubled by their dreams. Often, clients working with analytical therapists are asked to keep dream journals and to write down other impressions that come to them during the week. Clients are expected to be as open, spontaneous, and self-observant as they can be while in therapy. However, Jung was very respectful and hesitant to do more or go deeper than the client wanted or needed. In this regard, he wrote:

> It would be a dangerous prejudice to imagine that the analysis of the unconscious is the one and only panacea which should therefore be employed in every case. It is rather like a surgical operation and we should resort to the knife when other methods have failed. So long as it does not obtrude the unconscious is best left alone. (Jung, 1966b, p. 186)

Assessment Issues and Procedures

Jungians generally do not use formal assessment procedures and are not likely to diagnose problems or psychopathology as disease or defect. In this, they have much in com-

=== **ETHICAL HIGHLIGHT 4.1** ===

Aspects of Informed Consent

Jungian analysis is a very particular form of therapy. There are approximately 2,500 Jungian analysts available worldwide. A Jungian analyst would have a very particular form of informed consent. However, many eclectic therapists use Jungian techniques, so the following comments might serve well for that purpose. Of course, they are only an excerpt of what would be a more general informed consent form.

In our work together, you will be the expert, and I will be a guide. The problems and struggles that bring you to therapy are important messages to you. They signal where you need to pay attention to your life and development as a human being. I hope you will keep track of and talk about things that bother you and things that come into your mind over and over again. Also, your dreams and fantasies may have keys to understanding. Life is a journey toward fulfillment and maturity, but it is full of challenges and obstacles too. In my work with you, I will be open and spontaneous—using techniques that seem to hold promise in helping you achieve insight, growth, and comfort with yourself. I will encourage you to be spontaneous, open, and attentive to your own inner life, dreams, daydreams, fantasies, and the things that seem to bother you more than they should. Keeping dreams and thoughts in a journal can be useful in helping you remember the details and, later, work with me to identify themes and meanings.

mon with those who practice existential therapies. However, Jung's theories provide a rich language and set of images to work with in understanding human ways of being and distresses.

As mentioned earlier, the Myers-Briggs Type Indicator is based on Jung's conception of attitudes and functions that vary from individual to individual and that combine to create unique personality types. There are sixteen different type combinations possible. Each is described in very positive, affirming language. Typologies are often used to explain how people who are well-intended can end up in serious conflict without understanding why. The Jungian philosophy of having a nonpathologizing approach to psychological types is well articulated in the title of a popular Jungian typology book, *Gifts Differing* (Myers & Myers, 1997).

Jungians see all of life as a journey, so they will engage in an ongoing assessment of archetypal manifestations and conflicts reflected in the client's dreams and life struggles. Dreams provide not only the working material of the analysis, but also a sort of yardstick for how things are going. A Jungian therapist expects to be featured in an occasional dream or two of the client's, and the themes of therapy are likely to be present.

For example, a young man we'll call Ed was on a waiting list to see a Jungian therapist. The night Ed got the call that there was an opening, he dreamed that he was about to begin a long journey but had forgotten to pack enough clothing. He got to the destination, opened his scantily packed suitcase, and found there was only candy inside. Both Ed and his new therapist were delighted that his unconscious pinpointed his fears

---

PRACTITIONER COMMENTARY 4.1

The Jungian Dynamic Unconscious

The following material was contributed by Mark Kuras, a clinical psychologist and Jungian analyst from the C. G. Jung Institute of New York.

C. G. Jung and his analytical psychology occupy a mysterious position in the history of psychology and psychotherapy. Jung and Freud are the founders of depth psychology, a theory oriented around the concept of a dynamic unconscious. In essence this dynamic unconscious is a stratum of mind with its own set of intentions and related logic of association that must be probed if we aspire to a comprehensive theory of mind.

Freud and Jung broke. So as a Jungian, I am constantly asked why I followed Jung and not Freud. This question supposes that when Freud and Jung split they both created their unique and free-standing models of mind. In my opinion, it isn't Freud *and* Jung, nor Freud *or* Jung, but Freud *then* Jung.

Freud assumed that the unconscious stratum of mind that he called the *Primary Process* was a primitive form of mentation, not as advanced as the thinking occurring in the ego (the more acculturated level of mind). This makes sense when one is confronted with impulse-ridden behavior and frank delusional thinking. It becomes questionable, however, when aboriginal cultures, children, and artists are also categorized as laden with Primary Process thinking and thus are developmentally inferior.

Jung responds to this, and he finds that when the Primary Process is intimately engaged through therapeutic means, it does not appear as a primitive form of thinking, but reflects a psychological process, an instinct, that is presently dedicated to surmounting the dissociation and repressions required by the development of the acculturated ego.

Jung called this instinctual activity *Individuation.* He found that its inhibition created symptoms that, when analyzed, showed that consciousness was dangerously distant from deep, structural levels of the psyche. These levels, organized by what he called archetypes, were responsible for holding consciousness in an intimacy with the world as a whole—what one might experience as a religious dimension of psychological life.

This collective level of the mind has always been recognized as having therapeutic effects, as any reading of cultural mythology shows. This collective dimension is not, as is often assumed, a rigid two-dimensional scheme of thought and/or behavior. In our theory, it is the psychological representation of nature; its absence is implicated in symptom formation. As a Jungian, I am committed to the clinical task of piecing together, with each client, the unique and specific means required to bring consciousness to this depth of mind that makes life psychological, that protects consciousness from experiencing itself as being *only* a product of social learning. We work with dreams, and other modes of consciousness, such as Active Imagination, to temper the dominance of ego-consciousness and its associated effects on the psychological well-being of individuals and our culture as well.

of being ill prepared and lacking in the required depth to do the therapy. Very often, the initial dream reported in therapy contains information about the goal of the therapy. Often, clothing is a symbol of the persona. In this dream, Ed may have assumed he would be working on persona issues, but the dream, instead, points to the importance for him of working on enjoying the simple and ostensibly useless joys in life (A. T. Quenk, personal communication, December 2002).

Ed's therapy work progressed. A couple of months into the work, he dreamed that his mother sent him a large trunk filled with clothing he'd had as a child. The trunk was sturdy, and the clothes were in surprisingly good shape. In his dream, he took the clothes to a church rummage sale, donated them, and was thanked profusely. He felt very good about the fact that the clothes were in good shape and served a purpose in the world. In his therapy, he'd been examining all the expectations he had carried in his family of origin and how he'd outgrown them. His bitterness melted away as he saw how the expectations weren't bad: They simply weren't his anymore. His mother had sent him her idea of his persona, and it didn't fit.

Toward the conclusion of his work, many months and many dreams later, Ed dreamed that he was given a ticket to travel to an exotic country. He used the sturdy trunk of his earlier dream to pack just the right items for the journey. Then, in his dream, he suddenly wished he could take just one outfit from the outgrown collection his mother had mailed in the earlier dream. He went out into the streets, looking for the church where he had donated everything. In the bright light of day, he realized he didn't want to waste the space on an outfit that was too small, so he went back to packing, excited and happy about his upcoming trip. The dream confirmed his growing awareness that he could simply discard personas if they didn't "fit" him anymore.

This dream sequence provides both great therapy material and signs of progress in the young man's development. Jungians take dreams very seriously as they are considered central to establishing the dialectic between consciousness and unconsciousness. In this example, the dreams provided a gauge of the client's level of distress and the progress being made.

APPLICATION: CASE EXAMPLE

Different forms of therapy are necessary for clients in different stages of their journey. This case example is one written up in the *Journal of Analytical Psychology,* an excellent source for case examples and current professional Jungian dialogue. In 1996, Barbara Wharton, a Jungian analyst practicing in London, wrote of her work with a 76-year-old woman she called Ruby.

Ruby came to see Dr. Wharton because she was not getting along well with her daughter. She had been through three analyses in the course of her life, and obviously believed in their value. She brought three dreams with her to her first consultation, all with the common theme of frustration of efforts towards a goal. In one, she was intending to swim in the sea, but it dried up. In the second, she was destroying something and couldn't stop herself. The third, one she had recurrently, entailed efforts to get to a special place near the sea—a place she felt she must visit again before she died but to which, in the dream, she couldn't find the way.

Ruby told Dr. Wharton about her suicidal impulses and fantasies. The form of these fantasies suggested to Dr. Wharton that Ruby was ambivalent about life as well as death. On the one hand, Ruby longed for union with a Great Mother image, but on the other, she feared that the end of her life would be empty, without blessing or union of any sort—a final withholding from the Terrible Mother. Ruby talked at length about her various plans to kill herself. She also talked a great deal about her own mother. Themes of unpredictability, terror, and abandonment were common in these stories, but Ruby was very resistant to confronting these disappointments and fears.

As Ruby's early life story gradually came out, she remembered many instances of child abuse and neglect: humiliating and undeserved spankings in front of relatives and neighbors, and being flung against walls, shouted at, and threatened with being "skinned alive." She remembered longing to touch her mother's cheek but never daring to do so, fearing an outburst of violence. It also became clear that the man Ruby had assumed to be her stepfather, and who had sexually abused her, was in fact her biological father.

Ruby had a series of "baby" dreams, in which infants were smiling, or screamed and then started smiling. Dr. Wharton was able to identify an important positive "mother transference" as well as evidence for Ruby's defensive false self. Here's the outline of one of the dreams:

> I am a passenger in a car, holding a sleeping baby in my left arm: there is a sense of harmony and bliss. Then the baby is older and is sitting on my right. It lets out a most terrible scream that makes me jump out of my skin. Its face takes on that expression that babies get when they've been crying, the tears are still there, but they're trying to smile. (Wharton, 1996, p. 27)

As the analysis progressed, other disturbing childhood memories came to light. Dr. Wharton reports that Ruby's primary reaction to her mother's failures was one of pity. Ruby realized how fragile her mother's psyche was and, early on, took on a parentified role. This same style was reenacted, to some extent, with Dr. Wharton. However, breaks in the analysis were extremely difficult for Ruby, and they elicited a deeper, more rageful response. When Ruby was an infant her mother had been hospitalized, and at age 7 Ruby had been hospitalized. Her family did not come to see her for 6 weeks. These painful abandonments surfaced as Ruby tried to cope with breaks in analysis.

Ruby's dreams progressed, coming to feature a number of dreams with male babies and toddlers. Clearly, her animus was beginning to develop even as she became more able to express feelings such as rage, as well as pity, when she felt abandoned. These dreams also began to include religious symbolism and deep, troubling shadow aspects as well. In one dream, Ruby had a festering sore in her solar plexis. Her struggle to embrace her shadow was long and difficult.

As Ruby's analysis progressed, she had a terrifying dream in which a number of people were trapped underground as a fire broke out. They rushed to the opening, which was an iron gate, locked shut. Ruby experienced herself both inside the gate and outside, but she had no power to save the others. Ruby's work with this dream and her associations to it enabled her to finally decide she would not kill herself. She made a firm commitment to life. Some time after this, she reported a dream in which she experienced "a moment of inexpressible, wordless feeling." She reported being deeply moved and knew that "in this old and ugly body lies this Moment" (Wharton, 1996, p. 34).

At the end of the article describing her work with Ruby, Dr. Wharton writes:

> I am impressed by the drive to truly live as death draws near as a possibility, and by the energy of the Self, expressed in the patient's dreams, in fostering a new attitude towards dependency and towards the Great Mother in both her aspects. I feel that this not only represents fear of an early death-like state, but also a more positive and vital preparation for the last event in life, death itself. (1996, p. 36)

We've chosen to summarize the case of Ruby because it emphasizes the following Jungian core tenets:

- No matter how advanced one's age, there is a drive toward growth and transcendence.
- The relationship with the analyst is deep, trusting, spontaneous, and informative.
- Dreams will often provide enormous amounts of important information, far transcending what is available to the conscious mind.
- Analysis will move through the archetypal forces, beginning with struggles around persona and moving toward the deep Self- (or spiritually) related archetypes.

Specific Therapy Technique: Trusting the Dream

Jung's approach to dream work focuses on two main perspectives, the practical and the spiritual.

The Practical Perspective

Among Jung's many useful contributions to therapy and self-understanding, two that stand out are the use of the personality typologies to foster understanding and reduce interpersonal conflict, and the use of dreams to enhance personal growth and highlight important aspects of the dreamer's life and journey. Unlike Freud, Jung believed that the person who had the dream was the most likely person to ultimately understand what it meant. In this regard, he stated: "I am doubtful whether we can assume that a dream is something else than it appears to be. I am rather inclined to quote another Jewish authority, the Talmud, which says: 'The dream is its own interpretation'" (Jung, 1938, p. 28).

Of course, this statement doesn't mean Jung thought dreams were readily transparent, but rather that they contained important messages and meanings that were specific to the dreamer. He believed dreams had to do with present situations in the dreamer's life and that if the dreamer meditated on the dream long enough, the meaning would finally come.

Jung was always willing to work with patients as they sifted through their dreams, but he did not believe there was a "correct" interpretation. Instead, he believed a dream was rightly interpreted when it made sense to the dreamer and could therefore be constructively used in the journey (Faraday, 1981). Writer and Jungian therapist Polly Young-Eisendrath (1999) writes,

> To glean wisdom from interpreting our dreams, we have to remain modest in the claims we make, careful about our assertions, and well grounded in our experiences, especially in regard to the relational context when the dreams are part of an on-going therapy relationship. (p. 339)

To help in the process of dream understanding, here are a number of guidelines or suggestions compatible with a Jungian approach to dream work.

- Anyone who wants to work with dreams must find a strategy for remembering them. Most therapists recommend keeping a dream journal, in which clients faithfully write down the dream as soon as possible after dreaming it. Some avid dreamers keep a tape recorder by their beds and speak the dream into the tape recorder instead of writing it down.

- Generally, the persona archetypes will show themselves in dreams as shelter, coverings, costumes, masks, and other externally defining features of a character.
- The shadow archetype usually appears as a character of the same sex as the dreamer but of very different values and orientation. The shadow figure might be disgusting, frightening, tricky, or just mostly hidden.
- Opposite-sex figures might represent the anima or animus of the dreamer.
- The Self or God-like archetypes will be wise, older characters who have something to show or offer the dreamer.
- The overall theme and emotional valences in the dream will be somehow related to the dreamer's current life. If the dreamer dreams of persons who are close to the dreamer in real life, it may be a signal to pay attention to that relationship in the waking world.
- When faced with a difficult dream, the dreamer might ask, "How does this theme compensate for something in my waking life?"
- The dreamer can gain much meaning by having conversations with characters in the dream. Jung believed the dreamer could give voice to each character in the dream and thus produce a very helpful inner dialogue.
- Dreams can be related to one another. The dreamer can sometimes note a series of dreams that make sense together and are interrelated over weeks, months, or even years.

The Spiritual Perspective

Jung's religious upbringing and exploration of diverse religious perspectives made him especially sensitive and open to spiritual and religious possibilities. This view is especially present in his conceptualization of the meaning of dreams:

> I hold that our dream really speaks of religion and that it means to do so. Since the dream is elaborate and consistent it suggests a certain logic and a certain intention, that is, it is preceded by a motivation in the unconscious which finds direct expression in the dream content. (Jung, 1938, p. 31)

These comments suggest that Jung sees dreams as sometimes having their own intention or motivation apart from or outside of the dreamer. Even more specifically, he sometimes considers the dream to be an intentional religious message. In one of his more explicit statements about the dream as a spiritual/religious message, Jung claims that a dream is a "basic religious phenomenon and that the voice which speaks in our dreams is not our own but comes from a source transcending us" (Jung, 1938, p. 45).

Given his deeply spiritual view of dreams, it is no wonder that Jungian psychology tends to appeal to religious and spiritual individuals.

Questions for Reflection

Jung's spiritual view of dreams places yet another twist on a man and a theory that seems ever transforming. What do you make of his statements about the spiritual or religious nature of dreams? Do you resonate with or resist his idea that the voice speaking in our dreams may come from a source transcending ourselves? Do you think the source of the voice is Jung's collective unconscious . . . or is it the voice of God?

THERAPY OUTCOMES RESEARCH

Comparatively few practitioners identify themselves as practicing exclusively Jungian therapy. Therefore, outcome studies would be next to impossible to conduct. However, components of Jungian theory have been used in a number of settings. The concept of types, as measured by the MBTI, has been proven useful in certain work settings to help achieve more co-worker understanding, to guide people in choosing careers, to help couples understand their differences, and to help in leadership applications (Pajak, 2002).

The use of Jungian symbolism to understand dreams and to facilitate dialogue between our unconscious and our conscious is fairly common. Petteri Pietikainen (2001) states:

> The doctrine of the collective unconscious and its archetypes is Jung's major contribution to twentieth century intellectual culture, and while the scientific status of Jung's theory is rather feeble, to say the least, the very idea of an archetype has filtered into common usage and influenced popular psychology, especially growth-oriented therapeutic practices. (p. 5)

It is interesting to note that efficacy research is under way in Switzerland, at the Jung Institute. Swiss health authorities require that psychotherapeutic methods be effective, appropriate, and economical. Therefore, the Jung Institute is participating in a study on the practice of analytical long-term therapy sponsored by the Swiss Society of Analytical Psychology. This study is part of a larger naturalistic study, conducted by Professor Gerd Ruldof of Heidelberg and sponsored by the German Society of Psychotherapists. Information about this project is available at www.jung.edu, 2003.

It is difficult to obtain outcome data on treatments as extensive as Jungian analyses. However, it is clear that many of Jung's concepts and techniques are helpful in furthering understanding and insight into the nature of humans and their interactions.

MULTICULTURAL PERSPECTIVES

Jung had a curious, open attitude toward people from many racial and ethnic backgrounds—more so than many theorists and writers of his time. However, like these colleagues, he is guilty of many errors, omissions, misunderstandings, and blatant racist, sexist, and heterosexist biases. Multicultural Perspective 4.1 provides a rather scathing analysis of one area of multicultural trouble in Jungian theory. The analysis is offered by a practicing Jungian therapist. Although she points directly at significant theoretical difficulties, the author also helps us understand that all theories must evolve with the times and with the needs and insights of the people effected in a given era.

Jung can be credited with theories and ideas that he believed transcended traditional gender boundaries. He certainly had a global curiosity and allowed what he saw in other cultures to inform his perspectives on humanity. He can also be criticized for some of his racial and cultural attitudes, in that they were judgmental and hierarchical, as well as favoring Jung's own cultural definitions of achievement and civility. Jung repeatedly wrote that "nature is aristocratic," meaning not only that nature's gifts are distributed unevenly, but that certain races and cultures were more evolved and worthy of emulating than others. Was Jung guilty only of articulating what everyone else in his time simply believed to be true? Centuries before, Aristotle was certainly guilty of similar racist, sexist, and classist views.

=== **MULTICULTURAL PERSPECTIVE 4.1** ===

On Being a Lesbian Jungian

Claudette Kulkarni is a therapist in private practice and at the Persad Center in Pittsburgh, Pennsylvania. She is the author of Lesbians and Lesbianisms: A Post-Jungian Perspective (Routledge, 1997). We have excerpted this Multicultural Perspective from her article, posted on www.cgjungpage.org, *entitled "On Being a Lesbian Jungian: A Self-Interview." She begins:*

I am a lesbian. I am also a Jungian. Given the homophobic and heterosexist foundations of analytical psychology, I wonder some days how I can authentically be both. So, I thought I would interview myself in an attempt to find out how I manage this—and why I bother. . . . Many of Jung's constructs are heterosexist and his theory depends largely on a psyche that speaks in oppositions, the most basic of which are the so-called feminine and masculine principles. Heterosexism is, in fact, institutionalized through these Jungian constructs of contrasexuality, opposition, and complementarity. And it's not just Jung's original work that is problematic. There is an entire tradition of heterosexist work that came after him.

. . . [W]e must recognize that major portions of Jung's theory were predicated on a near obsession with the concept of 'the opposites' and elaborated by the concomitant concept of complementarity—that is, the idea that each of a pair of opposites possesses a set of qualities which supplement the elements missing from its opposite. . . . The implication, of course, is that one 'needs' the opposite list in order to complete oneself, that otherwise one will be lacking in wholeness. . . . [I]n this framework, the central or most fundamental opposition of all for Jung is the opposition between the so-called masculine and feminine principles. These two principles are said to complement each other, that is, to need each other in order to make 'a whole.'

It is an easy step from this to the concept of contrasexuality—that is, to the idea that in order to be a 'whole' person, one must be sexually involved with a member of the 'opposite' gender/sex via a projection of the contrasexual 'other' (anima or animus) onto a literal member of the 'opposite' gender/sex. Some have tried to salvage this part of Jung's theory by complicating it (e.g., by using concepts and phrases like 'the anima of the animus' or by arguing that both men and women have an anima and an animus). But this misses the point. Jung's theories on sexuality are irretrievably heterosexist and based on several assumptions: that there are only two sexes, that these are 'opposite' (rather than just different from) each other, that the qualities of one sex/gender are innate and, therefore, available only through some connection with 'the opposite sex,' that in order to be 'whole' one must have this connection with someone of 'the opposite' sex/gender. I would argue, therefore, that these heterosexist aspects of Jung's work do not need to be reformulated or salvaged. They need to be sunk.

On the other hand, Jung was intrigued and familiar with cultures vastly different from his own. His interest was sincere, and it was expressed respectfully. He clearly believed we had much to learn from any existing culture and much to learn from the histories of cultures long gone. This cannot be said of many other theorists of Jung's time. Further, many cultures other than Western culture place a far greater emphasis on the spiritual world, on dreams, and on nonlinear reasoning and meaning-making. Jung's ideas, therefore, have much multicultural appeal in certain settings.

MULTICULTURAL PERSPECTIVE 4.2

Exploring Ethical Concerns

Here are some issues often discussed about Jungian philosophy and therapy. Why do you suppose they might pose ethical concerns?

1. More than most theories in this book, Jungian therapy seems designed for the well-endowed, both materially and intellectually. Jung made it clear that he believed only certain individuals have the stamina, the intellect, and the inner discipline to reach the final, transcendental state that he envisioned as the end state of human maturity.
2. Dream work, like hypnosis, is deceptively simple. Ann Faraday (1981) writes, "Not the least significant outcome of Jung's work was to open up the possibility that some use may be made of dream interpretation by ordinary people outside the professional consulting room" (p. 125).
3. Jung believed modern humans are losing touch with the symbols and rituals of religions and spiritual practices. He believed that part of the journey toward wholeness would open the individual to spiritual or "primordial" communication and connection (Ulanov, 1997).
4. Jungian analysis can be overwhelming. By delving into dreams, impulses, images, and symbols, the average client may feel more confusion than insight. Consider the possibility that for many individuals Jungian analysis is contraindicated, because it may cause psychological decompensation.

CONCLUDING COMMENTS

Jung's analytic approach to counseling and psychotherapy is unique. C. G. Jung brings a new twist into the human psyche. In a clear break from Freud, he claims that libido is a broad, more encompassing source of psychic energy and that within the unconscious resides immense wisdom and potential. He states that "the unconscious mind is capable at times of assuming an intelligence and purposiveness which are superior to actual conscious insight" (Jung, 1938, p. 45).

At its conceptual heart, the Jungian unconscious is a respite from the negative, conflict-ridden Freudian unconscious. Yes, we are still not completely in control, and we are guided by mysterious forces we do not and, in some ways, cannot understand. But there is also an additional presence, a friendly guiding force. To make matters even better, throughout life we will have opportunities to grow, deepen, and gain wisdom by being open to what life brings.

STUDENT REVIEW ASSIGNMENTS

The following assignments will draw on what you have learned and contemplated during the chapter.

Critical Corner

The following statements are designed to provoke a response from you. Read and consider the statements about Jung's analytic psychology while recognizing that we are exaggerating criticisms to stimulate your thinking. Then write your responses to the criticisms in the space provided.

1. Jung's psychology can be discomforting. It is mysterious, conceptual, free-flowing, and difficult to understand. It openly includes the paranormal and spiritual. Consider this: If we simply eliminated this chapter from the book, would you miss it? Would anything be lost by intentionally deleting Jung's psychology from this book and the history of psychological thinking?
Response:

2. Even more than Adlerian concepts, Jungian concepts of archetypes, collective unconscious, intuition, and individuation are fuzzy and unscientific. Is there any way to scientifically evaluate Jungian psychology? Given the difficulties inherent in evaluating Jung's theory, is there any place for it within the field of modern psychology? Is there any way to justify the practice of Jungian therapy to a managed care company? Would a Jungian care about managed care standards?
Response:

3. Jungian theory essentially has no coherent explanation of psychopathology. If there is no clear definition of psychopathology, how can there be an understanding of psychological health? The Jungian perspective is nonpathologizing and does not provide adequate guidelines for defining positive functioning.
Response:

4. In the end, Jung emerges as a distinctly spiritual or religious individual. When he claims that dreams are messages from God he is moving into an antiquated theological perspective. No one who is a serious contemporary mental health practitioner suggests to clients that God may be speaking in dreams.
Response:

Reviewing Key Terms

- Individuation
- Archetypes
- Persona
- Shadow
- Anima
- Animus
- The self

- Collective unconscious
- Personal unconscious
- Synchronicity
- Transcendence
- Analytical psychology
- MBTI
- Dream analysis

- The practical perspective on dreams
- The spiritual perspective on dreams
- Personality typologies or psychological types
- Complexes

Review Questions

1. Jung's break with Freud was filled with conflict. Reread his final two letters to Freud and describe what conflicts you believe he was dealing with.
2. What is the primary and overarching goal of Jungian analysis?
3. There is no direct evidence for the presence of a creative unconscious filled with wisdom. Or is there? In his writing and speaking, Jung spoke of the wisdom of the dream. Is the dream evidence for a creative unconscious?
4. What are the two "attitudes" in Jungian personality typology?
5. What are the four functions in Jungian personality typology? Which functions are irrational and which are rational?
6. What two additional functions were added by Briggs and Myers to Jung's original typology?
7. What are the four stages of the individuation journey that characterizes Jungian analysis?
8. What is Jung's view of psychopathology?

RECOMMENDED READINGS AND RESOURCES

The following resources offer additional information about Jung and Jungian thought.

Lead Journals

- *Journal of Analytic Psychology*
- *Journal of Jungian Theory and Practice*
- *Quadrant: The Journal of Contemporary Jungian Thought*

Books and Articles

Bly, R. (1988). *A little book on the human shadow.* San Francisco: Harper.

Faraday, A. (1981). *Dream power.* New York: Berkley Books.

Jung, C. G. (1956). *Two essays on analytical psychology.* Cleveland: World Publishing.

Jung, C. G. (1964). *Man and his symbols.* Garden City, NY: Doubleday.

Jung, C. G. (1965). *Memories, dreams, reflections.* New York: Vintage Books.

Marlo, H., & Kline, J. S. (1998). Synchronicity and psychotherapy: Unconscious communication in the psychotherapeutic relationship. *Psychotherapy: Theory, Research, Practice, Training, 35*(1), 13–22.

Pearson, C. S. (1989). *The hero within: Six archetypes we live by.* San Francisco: Harper & Row.

Quenk, A. T., & Quenk, N. L. (1995). *Dream thinking.* Palo Alto, CA: Davies-Black.

Quenk, N. L. (2000). *Essentials of Myers-Briggs Type Indicator assessment.* New York: Wiley.

Sharp, D. (1991). *C. G. Jung lexicon: A primer of terms and concepts.* Toronto: Inner City Books.

Singer, J. (1973). *Boundaries of the soul: The practice of Jung's psychology.* Garden City, NY: Doubleday.

Young-Eisendrath, P. (1993). *You're not what I expected: Breaking the "he said-she said" cycle.* New York: Touchstone.

Videotapes

Segaller, S. (1989). *Wisdom of the dream: Carl Gustav Jung* [Videotape]. Chicago: Home Vision Entertainment.

Whitney, M. (1985). *A matter of heart: The extraordinary journey of C. G. Jung into the soul of man* [Videotape]. Los Angeles, CA: C. G. Jung Institute.

Training Organizations and Web Sites

International Association for Analytical Psychology (e-mail: iaap@swissonline.ch)

New York Association for Analytical Psychology (web site: www.cgjungpage.org/newyork.html)

The New Mexico Society of Jungian Analysts (web site: www.cgjungpage.org/events/santafe.html)

New England Society of Jungian Analysts (web site: www.cgjungboston.com)

Chicago Society of Jungian Analysts (web site: www.jungchicago.org)

Society of Jungian Analysts of Southern California (web site: www.junginla.org)

The Inter-Regional Society of Jungian Analysts (training web site: www.cgjungpage.org/irsja.html)

A great web site for an amazing array of Jungian writings and resources can be found at www.cgjungpage.org. This webpage was founded in 1995 to encourage new psychological ideas and conversations about what it means to be human in our time and place.

Chapter 5

EXISTENTIAL THEORY AND THERAPY

[A]ctually, I have been told in Australia, a boomerang only comes back to the hunter when it has missed its target, the prey. Well, man also only returns to himself, to being concerned with his self, after he has missed his mission, has failed to find meaning in life.

—Viktor Frankl, *Psychotherapy and Existentialism: Selected Papers on Logotherapy* (1967, p. 9)

IN THIS CHAPTER YOU WILL LEARN

- About a few key existential philosophers
- Basic principles of existential philosophy
- Theoretical principles of existential and Gestalt therapy
- The four ultimate existential concerns
- Specific techniques employed by existential and Gestalt therapists
- The scientific efficacy of existential therapy approaches
- Ethical dilemmas facing existential therapists
- Multicultural issues facing existential therapists
- How Fritz Perls addressed his unfinished business with Sigmund Freud

---

Some forms of counseling and psychotherapy, such as Freud's psychoanalysis, evolved primarily from medical practice with disturbed patients. Others, such as behavior therapy, arose from experimental psychological research. Still others, such as person-centered therapy (Chapter 6) and individual psychology (Chapter 3), have roots in clinical practice, humanistic-existential philosophy, and, to some degree, psychotherapy research. In contrast, purely existential approaches to counseling and psychotherapy are more directly and deeply linked to philosophy than any other perspective. Existentialists typically eschew scientific research because of its inauthentic artificiality. Additionally, although they practice therapy with individuals, couples, families, and groups, their approach is systematically guided by a philosophical position, rather than knowledge obtained from therapeutic practice. As Irvin Yalom, a renowned existential therapist, has stated, "I have always felt that the term 'existential therapy' reflects not a discrete, comprehensive body of techniques, but, instead, a posture, a sensibility in the therapist" (Serlin, 1999, p. 143).

KEY FIGURES AND HISTORICAL CONTEXT

The roots of existential philosophical thought are diverse. There is probably no single existential philosopher from whom all existential thinking flows. Most texts point to nineteenth-century philosophers Soren Kierkegaard and Fredrick Nietzsche as major players in the formulation of existentialism, and, in fact, Kierkegaard and Nietzsche do capture and embody the diversity of thinking inherent in existentialism.

The Danish philosopher Soren Kierkegaard (1813–1855) lived nearly his entire life in Copenhagen. Kierkegaard was devoutly religious and powerfully shaken when he discovered, at age 22, that his father had not only cursed God, but also seduced his mother prior to marriage. Subsequently, Kierkegaard's writings focused primarily on religious faith and the meaning of Christianity. Eventually he concluded that religious faith was irrational and was attainable only via a subjective experiential "leap of faith." For Kierkegaard, virtuous traits such as responsibility, honesty, and commitment are subjective choices—often in response to a subjective religious conversion. Kierkegaard did not describe himself as an existentialist, but his work is seen as precursor to the existential philosophical movement, which formally began some 70 years following his death.

In stark contrast to Kierkegaard, who had started with firm religious faith, the German philosopher Freidrich Nietzsche (1844–1900) had strongly negative feelings toward Christianity. It was he who, in his book *Thus Spake Zarathustra,* coined the phrase "God is dead." He also claimed that religion used fear and resentment to pressure individuals into moral behavior. Instead of following a religion, he believed, individuals should learn to channel their passions into creative, joyful activities. Yalom offers a fascinating view of Nietzsche's psychological suffering in a historical fiction piece titled *When Nietzsche Wept.* In this novel, Yalom weaves existential principles into a fictional therapeutic encounter between Breuer, Freud, and Nietzsche.

Kierkegaard and Nietzsche represent an interesting paradox in existential thinking. On the one hand, some existentialists are spiritually or religiously oriented or both, whereas others are staunchly atheistic. Still others claim the more agnostic middle ground.

It may be that polarized positions regarding religion within existential philosophy are predestined. After all, as Fritz Perls emphasizes in his existentially based Gestalt approach to treatment, "every psychological phenomenon . . . [is] experienced as a polarity" (1969b, p. 3). Consequently, we can view the ongoing struggle between these polarized factions within the individual—represented by the belief in God and the opposition to God—as a primary pathway toward deeper understanding of the true nature of the self. This seems an appropriate outcome of the existential struggle because, for most existential practitioners, regardless of their religious orientation, the overarching goal of therapy is to help the client discover and explore the authentic self.

Beyond Kierkegaard and Nietzsche, many other European philosophers have articulated existential philosophical principles. In particular, the works of Pascal, Husserl, Vaihinger, Sartre, Heidegger, Jaspers, and Marcel were instrumental in popularizing existential perspectives.

Rollo May: From Existential Theory to Existential Practice

Most historians credit Rollo May with formally introducing and integrating existential thought into American counseling and psychotherapy (May, Angel, & Ellenberger, 1958). After obtaining his bachelor's degree in English from Oberlin College in Ohio,

May was a missionary teacher in Greece for three years in the early 1930s. During that time he traveled to Vienna in the summer, where he happened to take some seminars from Alfred Adler. Following that experience, he returned to the United States, where he obtained a bachelor's degree in divinity, working with the existential theologian Paul Tillich at Union Theological Seminary in New York.

May gave up the life of a pastor at a New Jersey church to study clinical psychology at Columbia University. Shortly thereafter he fell ill with tuberculosis and was on the brink of death, which forced him into 18 months of treatment in a sanitarium. Eventually May returned to Columbia, where he was granted its first doctoral degree in counseling psychology (DeCarvalho, 1996). His dissertation, *The Meaning of Anxiety,* argued that anxiety was an essential component of the human condition.

Of course, May was not the first or even the main person to integrate existential thinking into psychological practice. Nearly a decade before he began studying with Adler in the early 1930s, another early existential practitioner, young Viktor Frankl, had joined Adler's inner circle (in 1926). As Gould writes, "Frankl agreed with Adler's viewpoint. Adler saw a person's freedom of choice as central . . . and . . . freedom of choice became the starting point for the development of Frankl's own theories" (1993, p. 4). Consequently, it appears that the presence of existential thought within modern therapeutic practice can be traced back at least to Alfred Adler, who had significant influence on both May and Frankl. As you may recall, Adler's view that individuals are unique beings struggling with feelings of inferiority and striving toward completion has a distinctly existential flavor (see Chapter 3).

Jean-Paul Sartre: The Existentialist Prototype

The philosophical character of existentialism is perhaps most aptly and succinctly articulated by Jean-Paul Sartre, who claimed, with bold certainty, "Freedom is existence, and in its existence precedes essence" and "Man's essence is his existence" (Sartre, 1953, p. 5).

If you're unclear about exactly what Sartre's assertions mean, you're not alone. Existial philosophy is sometimes so utterly abstract that it's difficult to distill practical implications from philosophical statements. Grasping meaning from existential philosophy is especially challenging for practicing therapists and students of counseling and psychotherapy, who are usually looking for concrete advice about exactly how to behave during a therapy session. We have only this minor reassurance for you as you embark on this chapter: In many ways, the entire purpose of existential philosophy is to struggle with individual, personal meaning. Therefore, as you grope and flail for meaning within the philosophy that embodies this chapter, you will also simultaneously be experiencing existential psychology.

Rollo May explains Sartre's statement "Freedom is existence, and in its existence precedes essence": "That is to say, there would be no *essences*—no truth, no structure in reality, no logical forms, no *logos,* no God nor any morality—except as man in affirming his freedom makes these truths" (May, 1962, pp. 5–6).

Sartre's philosophical proposition is that there are no absolute or essential truths (essences), but that we as individual human beings create our own truth and reality. His statement articulates the pure existential position. Once again, you may recognize that Adler's (Chapter 3) and Vaihinger's (1911) concepts of lifestyle and fictional finalism are consistent with this proposition; each individual constructs his or her own individual reality.

Paul Tillich discusses Sartre's second statement, "Man's essence is his existence."

There are, however, only rare moments . . . in which an almost pure existentialism has been reached. An example is Sartre's doctrine of man. I refer to a sentence in which the whole problem of essentialism and existentialism comes into the open, his famous statement that man's essence is his existence. The meaning of this sentence is that man is a being of whom no essence can be affirmed, for such an essence would introduce a permanent element, contradictory to man's power of transforming himself indefinitely. According to Sartre, man is what he acts to be (1961, p. 9).

This description speaks to another proposition of pure existential theory. That is, humans contain no permanent elements. This concept is further articulated in a popular phrase in the contemporary media, "to reinvent oneself." If you "reinvent yourself" (or even talk or think about anyone reinventing himself or herself), you're using the existentially based concepts of impermanence and emergence.

Following these lines of thought, existentialism strongly emphasizes personal choice, personal consciousness, and personal responsibility. If humans construct their own reality and are continuously capable of self-reinvention, then all behavior is owned by the individual. Sartre lays claim to the reality of human responsibility succinctly when he states: "I *am* my choices" (Sartre, 1953, p. 5).

Existentialism is, at its core, antideterministic. If you suggest to existentialists that human behavior is determined by particular factors, events, or mental processes, they are likely to recoil. This is because existentialists reject the proposition that humans are enslaved by Freudian unconscious, instinctual drives, and they reject environmental stimulus-response determinants as well. In place of instinctual and environmental causes of behavior, existentialists posit individual choice and human freedom. The past does not and cannot determine the future. This moment, this *now,* and our particular choices in this moment determine the now, and our choices in the next moment determine that moment.

But what, from a purely existential perspective, determines our daily, moment-to-moment choices? For Sartre, the answer is this: Human reality "identifies and defines itself by the ends which it pursues" (Sartre, 1953, p. 19). Of course, this theme should sound familiar because, once again, it resonates with Adler's concept of lifestyle. The following quotation from Yalom's discussion of Frankl's theories in *Existential Psychotherapy* further clarifies this common theme:

> The difference is between drive and strive. In our most essential being, in those characteristics that make us human rather than animal, we are not driven but instead actively strive for some goal. . . . "Striving" conveys a future orientation: we are pulled by what is to be, rather than pushed by relentless forces of past and present. (Yalom, 1980, p. 445)

Fritz and Laura Perls: From Existential Theory to Gestalt Experiments

Just as Rollo May is viewed as bringing existential philosophy to American psychotherapy, Fritz and Laura Perls can be seen as bringing specific therapy techniques into the domain of existential therapy. In essence, the Gestalt therapy movement is an extension of existential therapeutic thinking. Although Fritz Perls developed his own, somewhat idiosyncratic theory, his therapeutic approach is based squarely on existential principles. Therefore, despite the fact that most contemporary existential therapists do not practice Gestalt therapy, for the sake of integration, we weave Gestalt therapy principles and practice into this chapter.

In 1936, Fritz Perls met Sigmund Freud at a conference in Germany. Perls describes this meeting in his free-flowing autobiography, *In and Out the Garbage Pail:*

I made an appointment, was received by an elderly woman (I believe his sister) and waited. Then a door opened about 2 1/2 feet wide and there he was, before my eyes. It seemed strange that he would not leave the door frame, but at that time I knew nothing about his phobias.

"I came from South Africa to give a paper and to see you."

"Well, and when are you going back?" he said. I don't remember the rest of the (perhaps four-minute long) conversation. I was shocked and disappointed. (F. Perls, 1969b, p. 56)

For Perls, this meeting was ultimately invigorating and motivating. It freed him from the dogma of psychoanalytic thinking and propelled him to embrace existentialism and the development of his own approach to psychotherapy.

Laura Posner Perls was the cofounder of Gestalt therapy. She wrote several chapters of F. Perls's first major work, *Ego, Hunger, and Aggression* and introduced him to Gestalt psychology and the writings of Koffka, Kohler, and Wertheimer. She also had contact with and was strongly influenced by the existentialist theologians Tillich and Martin Buber (Buber, 1970). Although the contributions of Laura Posner Perls to the practice of Gestalt therapy were immense, she has not received much direct credit, partly due to the flamboyant extraversion of Fritz Perls and partly due to the fact that her name did not appear on many publications. She did, however, comment freely— and perhaps somewhat bitterly—on Fritz's productivity at the twenty-fifth anniversary of the New York Institute for Gestalt Therapy (an organization that she cofounded with Fritz). She stated: "Without the constant support from his friends, and from me, without the constant encouragement and collaboration, Fritz would never have written a line, nor founded anything" (L. Perls, 1990, p. 18).

Because of its strong applied orientation, we primarily focus on Gestalt therapy later in this chapter, in the section on the practice of existential therapy. For a quick look at Gestalt theoretical principles, see Putting It in Practice 5.1.

THEORETICAL PRINCIPLES

The existential theory of psychotherapy is based on existential philosophy and phenomenology. In the following sections we describe the defining principles of existential therapy.

The I-Am Experience

The I-am experience is the experience of being, of existing. For existentialists, the experience of being is often referred to as *ontological* experience (*ontos* means "to be" and *logical* means "the science of"). Literally, then, a major focus of existential therapy consists of exploring the immediate individual human experience. You might think of it as suddenly waking up and being completely tuned into what it's like to be alive, to exist, to be here right now in this particular moment in time.

It follows that existential therapy is almost always in the service of self-awareness or self-discovery. However, unlike psychoanalysts, existentialists seek to expand client self-awareness rather than interpreting client unconscious processes. This is because existentialists believe the entirety of an individual's human experience is accessible to consciousness. It's not a matter of uncovering an elusive unconscious, but a matter of elucidating the conscious.

========== Putting It in Practice 5.1 ==========

Gestalt Theory in Action

The following principles characterize Gestalt theory. However, despite the fact that these are abstract principles, the Gestalt therapist aims to put them in action.

The whole, self-regulating person. In Gestalt psychology, and in applied therapy, the whole is greater than the sum of its parts. The goal of treatment is to help the individual become aware of and own his or her entire self. All previously disowned or devalued parts are integrated into the whole person. Gestalt therapy enhances awareness, which leads to reintegration and allows the whole person to regulate and be responsible for his life.

Field theory. Every individual must be viewed within the context of his or her environment, because everything is relational. A key concept in Gestalt theory is *contact.* This term emphasizes the importance of contact between individuals and their environments. Ideally, individuals have the ability to make contact with and *taste,* and sometimes *digest,* their environments. Perls (1969a) used the metaphor of mental metabolism and resistance to contact (or defense mechanisms) to describe ways individuals might interact with their environments.

Some individuals accept anything from their environment, swallowing ideas and perspectives of others whole, without testing or tasting (introjection). Others spit parts of themselves out onto the world, refusing to own these parts (projection). Others do to themselves what they would like to do to others and so, in a sense, they chew on themselves (retroflection). Others keep their mouths shut so that nothing from the environment can get in (deflection). Finally, some individuals maintain a completely permeable boundary between themselves and the world and therefore have trouble distinguishing between themselves and the outside world (confluence). Much of Gestalt therapy involves exploring what's happening between individuals and their environment.

The figure-ground-formation process. In Gestalt perceptual psychology, an image, sound, or taste is viewed as emerging from the background and into central focus within one's awareness. This perceptual process, as applied to therapy, suggests that the primary or dominant needs of an individual will emerge into focus at any given moment. This is why Gestalt therapists believe that a client's *unfinished business* from the past will inevitably be brought into focus as therapists keep clients in the here and now.

Peeling the onion. According to Gestalt theory, for clients to fulfill their potential and achieve psychological maturity, they must peel off five distinct layers of neurosis: (1) the phony, (2) the phobic, (3) the impasse, (4) the implosive, and (5) the explosive. In the end, through awareness and integration, clients can wake up and become themselves, rather than pretending to be something they aren't. When this happens, they come in touch with an explosive and powerful source of energy.

The therapy process. We think the Gestalt therapy process can be aptly summarized in nine words that describe the therapy relationship, the therapy focus, and the therapy process: I and thou, here and now, what and how.

The Daimonic

According to Rollo May, "The daimonic is *any natural function which has the power to take over the whole person*" (May, 1969, p. 123, italics in original). *Daimon possession* has historically been used to explain psychotic episodes and is popularly referred to as *demonic possession.* However, May repeatedly emphasizes that daimonic and demonic are not the same concept, as in this response to criticism from Carl Rogers: "I never use the word demonic, except to say that this is not what I mean" (May, 1982, p. 11).

The daimonic includes both positive and negative potential. Similar to Jung's more general conception of libido, it is a form of psychic energy or an *urge* that is the source of both constructive and destructive impulses. May describes the daimonic in greater detail: "The daimonic is the urge in every being to affirm itself, assert itself, perpetuate and increase itself. . . . [The reverse side] of the same affirmation is what empowers our creativity" (May, 1969, p. 123).

Again, just as Jung emphasized the integration of the shadow archetype, May considers the harnessing and integration of the daimonic to be a central task in psychotherapy. He views psychotherapy as an activity that plumbs the depths of an individual's most basic impulses in an effort to acknowledge, embrace, and integrate every bit of being and energy into the whole person. Integrating the biological and natural daimonic urge maximizes constructive and creative behavior. May commented specifically about the need to integrate the daimonic and the danger of leaving it unintegrated:

> If the daimonic urge is integrated into the personality (which is, to my mind, the purpose of psychotherapy) it results in creativity, that is, it is constructive. If the daimonic is not integrated, it can take over the total personality, as it does in violent rage or collective paranoia in time of war or compulsive sex or oppressive behavior. Destructive activity is then the result. (May, 1982, p. 11)

The Nature of Anxiety

R. May was perhaps the first modern mental health professional to conceptualize anxiety as a good thing (May, 1977). He emphasized that it was a normal and essential byproduct of human existence. His formulation of anxiety encourages us all to view anxiety differently. We should embrace it as a part of our experience. We should explore it, experience it, engage it, and redirect it into constructive activities—we should not avoid it.

The existential perspective identifies two types of anxiety: normal anxiety and neurotic anxiety. Normal anxiety is directly proportional to the situation. It is within our awareness (not requiring repression or other defensive processes) and can be used creatively. In contrast, neurotic anxiety is disproportionate to the situation; it is usually repressed, denied, or otherwise avoided, and is not used for creative or constructive purposes. Instead, it is destructive.

For example, as you read this chapter, you may simultaneously be aware of mounting anxiety over time pressures in your life. Perhaps you need to finish reading this chapter and study for an exam in your theories class. You also need to finish writing a proposal for a research class. At the same time, you're thinking about how you should get the oil changed in your car before your weekend road trip. In addition, you haven't found anyone to take care of your dog while you're away for the weekend. The pressure is rising.

If, in response to your pressure-packed situation, you respond by functioning creatively and efficiently, you're experiencing normal anxiety. Perhaps you decide to write your research proposal on an existential topic and hire your nephew to stay at your apartment and take care of your dog. You study as efficiently as you possibly can, and then get your oil changed on the way out of town. In the end, you heave a sigh of relief. You've faced your anxiety and dealt with the situation effectively.

In contrast, if you experience neurotic anxiety, you avoid facing your anxiety-provoking situation by going out and partying with your friends, blowing off your theories exam, writing up a minimal research proposal, and taking your misbehaving dog with you on the road in your car without rechecking the oil. The key differences are (1) you deny the importance of your life demands, (2) you respond to the situation out of desperation, rather than responding with creativity, and (3) you end up increasing your chances of having difficulties down the road (literally) because you haven't responsibly maintained your self (or your vehicle).

As you can see from the preceding example, the goal of existential treatment is not to do away with anxiety, but to reduce neurotic anxiety. This is accomplished by helping clients live with and cope effectively and creatively with the normal anxiety that accompanies existence.

Normal and Neurotic Guilt

Guilt, like anxiety, has both positive and negative qualities. It may seem a bit odd, but guilt is good—normal guilt, that is. Guilt inspires people to act in thoughtful and conscientious ways. Normal guilt is sort of like a sensor: When functioning well, it alerts us to what's ethically correct and guides us toward morally acceptable behavior.

Psychopathology arises, not from the human experience of normal guilt, but from neurotic guilt. Neurotic guilt usually consists of a twisted, exaggerated, or minimized version of normal guilt. For example, when a victim of domestic abuse feels guilty for provoking her abuser, it is a twisted guilt and does not serve a productive purpose. Similarly, the abuser who feels only transient or minimal guilt after physically battering his romantic partner is neurotically denying or minimizing his responsibility for the situation. He may experience complete relief from guilt after delivering a quick apology and a dozen roses. Worse, he may relieve his guilt by blaming his partner and demanding an apology from her.

In contrast, some individuals feel massive guilt and responsibility for even the most minor, normal, human ethical transgressions. Excess guilt may make such people think they should be punished, or make restitution, or both for their unacceptable behavior. For example, after making a mistake that cost her employer several hundred dollars, a guilt-ridden employee may commit unending hours of service to her employer, church, and community in an effort to relieve herself of her guilty feelings.

The Gestalt perspective on neurotic guilt is somewhat unusual. Specifically, when clients spoke of guilt, F. Perls often asked them to turn it into resentment. For example, with the aforementioned neurotically guilty employee, Perls might ask her to talk about resentments she has toward her employer, church, and community. The Gestalt approach emphasizes that clients own the complete range of their emotions, including the resentments lurking beneath neurotic guilt.

Existential Psychodynamics

Similar to psychoanalytic theorists, existentialists believe that humans are in intrapsychic conflict with powerful forces. However, instead of helping clients cope with instinctual drives or rework internalized object relations, the existential therapist helps clients face and embrace "ultimate concerns" of existence (Van Deurzen-Smith, 1997). These ultimate concerns of existence produce anxiety that must be dealt with either directly or indirectly via defense mechanisms (although for existentialists, defense mechanisms are not an elusive, automatic unconscious process, but a style or pattern of avoiding anxiety that can and should be brought to awareness).

In his text *Existential Psychotherapy,* Irving Yalom (1980) describes four ultimate concerns relevant to psychotherapy. These concerns are

- Death
- Freedom
- Isolation
- Meaninglessness

These four ultimate concerns capture the nature of reality for existentialists. Everyone who lives is confronted with real demands and truths inherent in human existence. In turn, we are all free to choose our response to those demands and anxiety-producing truths.

Death

Yalom (1980) outlines two therapy-relevant propositions about death. First, he emphasizes that death and life exist simultaneously: "[D]eath whirs continuously beneath the membrane of life and exerts a vast influence upon experience and conduct" (p. 29). As a consequence, the possibility of death cannot be ignored. Any of us might suddenly face death in the next moment, next day, or next week—or we may live for decades more. Death is knowable and unknowable. We will die; it is only a question of when, where, and how. Death is simply part of the reality of life.

Second, Yalom claims that death is a "primordial source of anxiety" and therefore is the main source of psychopathology (Yalom, 1980, p. 29). For anyone who has directly faced death, the potential influence of death anxiety is obvious. Years ago when I (John) was prematurely and inaccurately diagnosed as having cancer spreading throughout my body, I experienced several days of anxiety that I would prefer not to repeat. The continuous whirring of death to which Yalom refers became a deafening gale. It was only after looking into the abyss of my own, possibly imminent death, that I could understand what it meant to directly encounter *death anxiety*—a phenomenon that I had previously contemplated in only the most abstract and intellectual manner. The fortunate revision of my cancer diagnosis allowed the immediate anxiety to recede, but the experience left me with a much greater appreciation of both life and death.

Despite the imposing and potentially debilitating fact that death is constantly rumbling beneath the surface of life, confronting and dealing with death is also a potentially therapeutic mechanism of personal change. Yalom (1980) summarizes his existential perspective on this issue:

> The matter can be summed up simply: "Existence cannot be postponed." Many patients with cancer report that they live more fully in the present. They no longer postpone living until some time in the future. They realize that one can really live *only* in the present; in fact, one cannot outlive the present—it always keeps up with you. Even in the moment of looking back over one's life—even in the last moment—one is still there, experiencing, living. The present, not the future, is the eternal tense. (p. 161)

The purpose of facing death for existentialists is to experience life more deeply and fully. To face death is to motivate oneself to drink with great enthusiasm from the cup of life. Obviously, this is *not* a call for morbid preoccupation about life's end, but instead a call to shed external trappings and roles and to live in the now as an individual self with freedom of choice.

Questions for Reflection

A hospice chaplain we know told us that often, when people with terminal diseases make peace with their impending death, their lives become more rich, deep, and full. In contrast, a famous Dylan Thomas poem urges, "Do not go gently into that good night. Rage, rage against the dying of the light." Peace or resistance? Rage or acceptance? Where do you find yourself?

Freedom

Generally, freedom is considered a positive condition of life, eagerly sought by many individuals. But this is not the view of the existentialist. Sartre believed humans are condemned to freedom, and existential therapists have followed suit by articulating the many ways in which freedom is an anxiety-laden burden (Sartre, 1971).

Personal responsibility is a powerful and direct implication of freedom. Viktor Frankl once claimed that because the United States has a statue of liberty on the east coast, it should have a statue of responsibility on the west coast. This is the first and primary burden of freedom. If you are free, you are simultaneously responsible. Every action becomes a choice. There is no one to blame for your mistakes. Perhaps you made a poor choice because you were misled, but the fact is that *you* were misled and therefore you were a participant in the misleading. You cannot even defend yourself by employing the pesky Freudian unconscious. As Yalom (1980) states, "To a patient, who insists that her behavior is controlled by her unconscious, a therapist says, 'Whose unconscious is it?'" (p. 216).

Complete and total responsibility is inescapable. In the end, the more freedom you experience, the more choices you have; and the more choices you have, the more responsibility you have; and having a large load of responsibility translates into a large load of anxiety.

To make matters even more daunting, you are responsible not only for your choices, but also for your *nonchoices*. This is because every choice you make represents, at the same time, the death of hundreds of other possibilities. Yalom provides an excellent personal example based on Sartre's existentialism:

> There is, as I write, mass starvation in another part of the world. Sartre would state that I bear responsibility for this starvation. I, of course, protest: I know little of what happens there, and I feel I can do little to alter the tragic state of affairs. But Sartre would point out that I choose to keep myself uninformed, and that I decide at this very instant to write these words instead of engaging myself in the tragic situation. I could, after all, organize a rally to raise funds or publicize the situation through my contacts in publishing, but I choose to ignore it. I bear responsibility for what I do and for what I choose to ignore. Sartre's point in this regard is not moral: he does not say that I *should* be doing something different, but he says that what I *do* do is my responsibility. (p. 221)

Personal responsibility is a heavy burden to carry. It is so heavy that many individuals cannot bear the weight. When the weight of personal responsibility is too heavy, individuals defend themselves with denial, displacement, and blaming. For example, when an employee underperforms, rather than claiming responsibility, he blames the situation ("I didn't have time to do a good job on the project") or a coworker ("Bob is impossible to work with. How can I be expected to produce a quality product?") or his employer ("I'm not paid enough or given enough respect to work any harder than I'm working").

Nearly everyone considers acceptance of personal responsibility to be a virtue. Sartre's "I am my choices" is roughly the equivalent of former U.S. President Harry Truman's "The buck stops here." Not surprisingly, if you meditate on this concept for a while, you're likely to end up feeling empowered, which is, of course, the reason why existentialists hammer away at the concept of ultimate personal freedom. For them, the best and most direct route to personal empowerment is awareness of personal responsibility, including fully experiencing the angst that comes along with it.

Overall, the essential point of freedom and responsibility for the existentialist is this: You, and you alone, are the author of your experiences. Don't bother pointing the finger of blame at anyone but yourself.

Questions for Reflection

Governments vary dramatically across the globe in the amount of individual freedoms available to citizens. States vary, cities vary, even families and couples vary in this domain. What makes freedom safe within a group of humans? What makes it dangerous?

Isolation

The existential assumption is that every individual is fundamentally alone. In Yalom's words, there is "an unbridgeable gulf between oneself and any other being" (1980, p. 355). This is a terrible truth; we enter life as an independent being and we take leave from life alone. This is the nature of existential isolation.

There are also other, less deep and less permeating, forms of isolation. For example, many individuals who come for therapy come because of social problems that include feelings of disconnection and loneliness. In addition, some clients experience intrapersonal isolation, in that they feel cut off from or out of touch with their sense of self. Although both of these forms of isolation are important in therapy, they are examples of surface symptoms rather than directly representative of existential psychodynamics.

The ideal or goal of existential therapy with respect to isolation is to help clients connect as deeply as possible with others while at the same time acknowledging their incontrovertible separateness. Yalom refers to this as a "need-free" relationship. Need-free relationships are unselfish relationships in which one person knows another person intimately, gives love without a personal agenda, and acknowledges the other's separateness and independence of thought. When a need-free relationship exists, both parties usually feel more alive and engaged in life (Yalom, 1980).

Martin Buber, a Jewish philosopher and theologian, has written extensively on the "I-Thou" relationship (Buber, 1970). An I-Thou relationship involves the deepest of all possible connections between two individuals. It is a completely mutual and celebratory relationship, in which both self and other are experienced fully. Unfortunately, according to Buber, legitimate I-Thou moments are rare and relatively brief. This is the relation toward which we should strive, but it is impossible to live consistently in an I-Thou connection.

The practical interpersonal problem faced by most of us is the problem of isolation versus fusion. Like a newborn baby, sometimes we luxuriate in the illusion that someone will anticipate and meet our every need. Or in the blush of a powerful infatuation, we are intoxicated by the possibility of complete fusion with another individual. Sometimes, even a brief glimpse of the reality of our existential aloneness can cause us to cling to whatever potential love object may be in our vicinity, often with less than desirable outcomes.

Yalom claims that denial is the most common way that humans deal with the conflict between being an individual and experiencing the frightening quality of existential isolation. One of the most common forms of denying isolation is through love or fusion with another individual. In his book *Love's Executioner,* Yalom (1989) complains of working with clients who are in love:

> I do not like to work with patients who are in love. Perhaps it is because of envy—I, too, crave enchantment. Perhaps it is because love and psychotherapy are fundamentally incompatible. The good therapist fights darkness and seeks illumination, while romantic love is sustained by mystery and crumbles upon inspection. I hate to be love's executioner. (p. 15)

No doubt you've sometimes been around friends, relatives, acquaintances, or clients who are desperately seeking social or intimate contact. These individuals loathe being alone, and if they're in an intimate relationship that ends, they move quickly to replace their former partner. They have not developed the inner strength, identity, and sense of completeness necessary to face the piercing anxiety associated with existential isolation. Instead, they frantically seek connection with others because doing so gives them at least a brief experience of completeness.

Earlier in this chapter we noted that the overarching goal of existential therapy is to help the client discover and explore the authentic self. We should extend that definition to include the discovery and exploration of the authentic and complete, individual self—separate from others.

When done correctly, heightening a client's awareness of existential isolation should improve his or her ability to form healthy interpersonal relationships. Similar to death anxiety and angst over the burden of personal freedom, getting in touch with and embracing existential isolation has a positive consequence. To admit and face aloneness gives us the strength to face the world and the motivation to connect in deep and meaningful ways with other individuals.

Questions for Reflection

Eastern philosophies often stress the fact that our separations are illusions. We are, in fact, all one. We are all part of the great web of life. Does this argue against accepting and embracing our isolation? Is one view or the other true, or do they somehow both speak to ultimate reality?

Meaninglessness

The classic existential crisis or existential neurosis occurs when an individual faces the question "What is the meaning of my life?" Seeking life's meaning can be an agonizing process. Consequently, it's common for many of us to just stay busy with daily activities, instead of grappling with life's biggest question. Leo Tolstoy captures the pain and torment associated with thinking too much about the meaning of one's life:

> The question, which in my fiftieth year had brought me to the notion of suicide, was the simplest of all questions, lying in the soul of every man from the undeveloped child to wisest sage: "What will come from what I am doing now, and may do tomorrow? What will come from my whole life?" otherwise expressed—"Why should I live? Why should I wish for anything? Why should I do anything?" Again, in other words: "Is there any meaning in my life which will not be destroyed by the inevitable death awaiting me?" (Tolstoy, 1929, p. 20)

Most existentialists would likely respond to Tolstoy's queries about life's meaning with something along the lines of "Life has no inherent meaning. It is up to you to invent, create, or discover meaning in your life. Your challenge is to find meaning in an apparently meaningless world."

To begin our discussion of meaninglessness, we should emphasize that, similar to the other ultimate concerns, meaninglessness should be confronted, embraced, and dealt with directly. Viktor Frankl has written of his own personal struggle with meaninglessness:

> I gladly and readily confess that as a young man I had to go through the hell of despair over the apparent meaninglessness of life, through total and ultimate nihilism. But I wrestled with it like Jacob with the angel did until I could say "yes to life in spite of everything," until I could develop *immunity* against nihilism. (see Gould, 1993, p. 9)

Of all existential theorists, Frankl has written the most about the importance of living a meaningful life. He believes the "will to meaning" is a primary motive, far surpassing the importance of Freud's pleasure principle and Adlerian superiority striving. He also emphasizes that, similar to Adler's formulations of human motivation, meaning is not a drive or push; instead it is characterized by striving or willing.

Many clients come to therapy because they are suffering from the absence of meaning in their lives. Jung, whose theory we reviewed in Chapter 4, wrote this about the preponderance of meaninglessness among clients with whom he worked:

> Absence of meaning in life plays a crucial role in the etiology of neurosis. A neurosis must be understood, ultimately, as a suffering of a soul which has not discovered its meaning. . . . About a third of my cases are not suffering from any clinical definable neurosis but from the senselessness and aimlessness of their lives. (Jung, 1953, p. 83)

Is Life Meaningful?

Frankl claims that humans have a primary motivational pull toward meaning. And yet the question remains: Is there any inherent meaning in life toward which humans can strive? On the one hand, the ever-optimistic Sartre says no: "All existing things are born for no reason, continue for no reason, continue through weakness and die by accident. . . . It is meaningless that we are born; it is meaningless that we die" (cited in Hepburn, 1965).

Fortunately, Sartre's position is not the only approach to the problem of meaninglessness. Frankl is specific about his contrasting theoretical perspective: "We do not just attach and attribute meaning to things, but rather find them; we do not invent them, we detect them" (Frankl, 1967, p. 16).

Frankl is claiming two things: First, humans have a will to meaning. Second, meaning *does* exist in the world, and it's up to us to find it. Further, Frankl emphasizes that the individual does not find meaning through preoccupation with the self. Instead, we must look outside ourselves to find meaning.

Frankl's approach to helping clients find meaning in life is logotherapy (*logos* = meaning; *therapeia* = healing). He developed this approach after being imprisoned in Nazi concentration camps in Germany. During this time, his previous beliefs in the importance of meaning to human survival were affirmed.

The key to logotherapy is to confront clients directly with the need for meaning, but not to tell them what they *should* consider personally meaningful. Logotherapy celebrates individual responsibility: Clients are completely responsible for their lives and choices regarding the pursuit of meaning. Although Frankl comes across as somewhat religious or spiritual in his writings, he consistently emphasizes that logotherapy is a secular theory and practice.

In the end, there are a number of paths toward meaning that humans can discover and through which they can thereby resolve their existential neurosis. The following possibilities are derived from Yalom (1980) and Frankl (1967):

- *Altruism:* Clients can choose to serve others through kindness and unselfishness.
- *Dedication to a cause:* Clients can dedicate themselves to political, religious, medical, familial, scientific, or other causes. The key is for the cause to take the person beyond selfishness.
- *Creativity:* Clients can choose to create something beautiful, powerful, and meaningful.
- *Self-transcendence:* Guilt, depression, personal salvation, and other self-oriented goals can be put aside to pursue selflessness.
- *Suffering:* Clients can face suffering with optimism, dignity, and integrity.
- *God/religion:* Clients can focus on serving God or their religion instead of serving self or pursuing material goals.
- *Hedonism:* Clients can choose to live life to the fullest each moment, to drink up the excitement, joys, and sorrows of daily life.
- *Self-actualization:* Clients can dedicate themselves to self-improvement, to meeting their potential.

These final two potentially meaningful pursuits are discussed by Yalom, but would not be considered suitably meaningful from Frankl's perspective because they focus exclusively on the self, rather than on something outside the self.

In summary, humans have an internal striving for meaning, meaningful pursuits exist in the world, and it is the counselor's task to confront clients with meaning.

Questions for Reflection

What messages about meaning dominate the airwaves in our culture? Watch TV or read a few magazines and fill in the blank with an answer based on their messages: The meaning of life lies in _____.

Self-Awareness

Self-awareness is central to existential therapy. Earlier, we said the goal of therapy was to help clients get in touch with their authentic self. We revised that goal to emphasize the individual's separateness. Now, consistent with the spirit of existentialist thought, we are revising the goal of existential therapy again (recall that because existence precedes essence, we are continually reinventing, revising, and updating ourselves). For now, the goal of existential therapy is to facilitate self-awareness—including the awareness of death, freedom, isolation, and life's meaning.

Existentialism and Pessimism

When we lecture on existential psychodynamics, many students justifiably complain about the inherent pessimism associated with existentialist thought, and they have a legitimate foundation for their complaints. After all, when existentialists look at life, they see the rumblings of impending death. When they contemplate freedom, they become preoccupied with the burdens of responsibility. When they consider love, they cannot stop themselves from lamenting that individual isolation is a permanent condition of life. And when they talk about the meaning of life, they are thrown into the nihilistic pit of meaninglessness and can only dig themselves out by creating their own meaning.

There's no doubt that existential philosophy has its share of depressing thoughts. On the other hand, we believe that the whole point of existential thought is not to depress, but to provide hope. Life is a struggle. Life is filled with suffering. But most of all, life is to be lived. And that makes all the difference as we face the realities of death, freedom, isolation, and meaninglessness.

Theory of Psychopathology

For existentialists, psychopathology results from failure to adequately face and integrate basic inner daimonic impulses, and from failure to acknowledge and reconcile life's ultimate concerns. Typically, neurotic or maladaptive behavior is linked to avoidance. As clients disavow natural urges and avoid ultimate concerns, they progressively or suddenly develop psychological, emotional, or behavioral symptoms. The cure generally involves facing oneself, facing life, and embracing the reality of death, freedom, isolation, and meaninglessness. This does not mean that life becomes easy. However, clients who face ultimate concerns with an integrated sense of self will experience normal anxiety and guilt, rather than neurotic anxiety and guilt.

Gestalt theory defines psychopathology in a similar manner. Specifically, when clients resist contact with the environment they are likely to experience what Gestalt therapists call *stuckness* or an inability to grow, adapt, and cope. Essentially, symptoms arise because of dysregulation in the boundary between self and environment. Psychological health is characterized by a healthy boundary between self and environment. A healthy boundary is one with both permeability and firmness. Using the mental metabolism metaphor, the healthy individual grows through biting off reasonably sized pieces of the environment, chewing on them, and then determining whether the environmental input is toxic or nourishing. If the bitten-off piece of the environment is toxic, the individual rejects it, spitting it out. If the piece of environment is nourishing, one swallows, digests, and assimilates the environmental information. To make determinations about whether one's environment is toxic or nourishing requires confidence and trust in one's taste and judgment (see also Putting It in Practice 5.1).

THE PRACTICE OF EXISTENTIAL THERAPY

Most existential practitioners are reluctant to discuss therapy techniques because technical interventions are often viewed as artificial or phony, detracting from the authentic I-Thou existential encounter. May states:

> In this country we tend to be a nation of practitioners; but the disturbing question is: Where shall we get *what* we practice? Until recently, in our preoccupation with technique, laudable enough in itself, we have tended to overlook the fact that *technique emphasized by itself in the long run defeats even technique.* (May, 1983, p. 47)

Instead of techniques, the therapeutic force or factor employed by existentialists is the therapeutic encounter. This encounter is best articulated by Buber's I-Thou relationship. The therapist is the leader in this encounter. By being with the client in the immediate moment, the existential therapist partners with the client toward self-discovery and growth. In essence, the therapy encounter facilitates creativity, the expansion of awareness or consciousness, and self-development.

Preparing Yourself to Do Therapy from an Existential Perspective

Before you try to practice existential therapy, try participating in an existentially or Gestalt-oriented activity. This activity might be a formal group therapy experience, individual therapy, or self-guided awareness exercises. An example of a Gestalt-based self-guided awareness exercise is included in Putting It in Practice 5.2.

If you plan to practice existential therapy, you need to work on two main issues: First, you need to understand and practice existential philosophy. Second, you need to sharpen the main therapeutic tool you'll be using: your *self.*

At this point, you should be familiar with the basic principles of existential philosophy. If not, you can either reread the theory section of this chapter or explore the additional readings listed at the end of this chapter; it's your choice. Existential therapy in practice is existential philosophy lived.

From a more concrete perspective, developing self-awareness and interpersonal skills will also help you practice existential therapy. The foundation of existential therapy is the human contact between you and your client. Ideally, you should seek to establish an I-Thou relationship with your client—a relationship characterized by depth, mutuality, connection, and immediacy.

The existential theme of personal responsibility has direct implications for the therapist. As the therapist, you are completely responsible for your behavior within the therapy session. Also, although you are not responsible for your client's welfare, you are responsible for the therapy process to which your client is exposed. In terms of the therapy relationship, it is your job to be alert, interested in your client, and as fully present as possible during every minute of every session. For example, if you feel bored or distracted (signs of what psychoanalysts refer to as countertransference), it's your responsibility to get reconnected and fully engaged in the process.

Beyond the therapy relationship, your focus is primarily on feedback. As therapist, your role is to provide your clients with feedback, while at the same time honoring their personal experience. Depending upon your personality style and the particular existential approach you are using, feedback you give clients may be more or less confrontational. As a therapist, Fritz Perls tended to be more in-your-face confrontational,

---

Putting It in Practice 5.2

The Gestalt "Feeling the Actual" Experiment

This is experiment 1 from *Gestalt Therapy* by F. Perls, Hefferline, and Goodman (1951). We include it here not only because it illustrates a concrete therapy technique, but also because it captures the basic philosophy of Gestalt therapy. It is written in a manner that encourages you to participate in the experiment. Later, after you have experienced it, you may want to try it with someone else, possibly a fellow student or willing practicum client (with your supervisor's permission).

The purpose of this experiment is to help you tune into what is actual and what is now. All too often, our attention is divided and we are numb to life. Alternatively, sometimes we experience anxiety or apprehension that focuses our attention, but a true experience of being in contact with the environment and with yourself is much different from a state of anxiety.

To participate in this experiment, all you need to do is follow these instructions: "Try for a few minutes to make up sentences stating what you are at this moment aware of. Begin each sentence with the words 'now' or 'at this moment' or 'here and now'" (F. Perls et al., 1951, p. 37). Start now.

How did it feel to participate in this experiment? For some, it will feel silly or awkward. For others, it may seem phony and contrived. Still others may have felt resistance or opposition to participating. As with most Gestalt experiments, your individual here-and-now reaction to the experiment is just as important as whatever you may have produced during the experiment. You are a total being, capable of both experiencing an experience and, at the same time, reacting to the experience.

If you felt this experiment to be phony, you shouldn't be surprised. Sometimes, after living disconnected from life, it's possible for it to feel like you're simply acting when, in reality, you are beginning to really experience life.

In contrast, if you felt opposed and resistant to this experiment, perhaps you're using the defense of deflection: You're avoiding contact with the environment by pulling back and being uninvolved.

Now, in the true spirit of Gestalt therapy, in this moment repeat the experiment: "Try for a few minutes to make up sentences stating what you are at this moment aware of. Begin each sentence with the words 'now' or 'at this moment' or 'here and now'" (F. Perls, et al., 1951, p. 37).

Gestalt therapy can be repetitive. But the purpose of repeating oneself is not in the service of numbness, but instead, in the service of awakening. One of Perls's most famous statements about therapy and life is "Wake up and come to your senses." This statement emphasizes the value he placed on the human physical-sensory experience. Repeatedly experiencing the mundane as well as the extraordinary as fully and completely as possible means that awareness is elevated and consciousness expanded.

whereas Rollo May was more patient and reflective. Although your purpose is to function as a mirror—giving clients feedback about who they are and how they affect you and others—your specific therapy style is an extension of who you are as a person.

Preparing Your Client

The ethical principle of informed consent mandates that therapists tell clients what to expect in therapy. There is perhaps no other form of therapy in which providing complete informed consent is more essential than the existential approach. This is because existential approaches, more than any other, include an immediate confrontational component. See Ethical Highlight 5.1 for a sample informed consent form from an existential perspective.

In addition to providing presession informed consent, initial here-and-now interactions with clients should proceed gently and educationally. This is true whether the interaction is simply feedback about personal responsibility or involvement in a Gestalt experiment. Later in this chapter we illustrate gentle, educational therapist-client interactions within the context of specific techniques and case examples.

Assessment Issues and Procedures

Existential therapists do not believe in assessment procedures. I (John) recall teasing colleagues over lunch about their possible Myers-Briggs Type Indicator scores. The resident existentialist was clearly offended. She countered with, "You wouldn't ever use a questionnaire like that with a client, would you?" When I said I might, because I thought questionnaires and personality assessment could sometimes be therapeutic, she launched into a diatribe about how using such instruments was unethical and inauthentic. Of course, she had an important point: All assessment measures fall short of measuring anything close to a real, complete person. The goal of existential therapy is not to narrow an individual's conception of self, but to expand it. As a consequence, for true existentialists, psychometric assessment procedures not only are useless, but also might be considered antitherapeutic and even unethical because they detract from the human encounter.

Despite their anti-assessment/measurement perspective, existential therapists undoubtedly use some implicit, less objective, assessment procedures with clients. Overall, the existential therapist looks for neurotic anxiety, neurotic guilt, avoidance, denial, and other signs of pathology to guide the therapeutic encounter. Additionally, the therapist might use specific questions oriented toward existential ultimate concerns to enhance client self-awareness and promote personal discovery. Examples include

- What do you want?
- What are you experiencing/feeling right now?
- Who are you?
- What do you want to say right now?
- Where do you feel that in your body?

Gestalt therapy approaches primarily utilize confrontation to facilitate client self-assessment and discovery. As will be discussed, Gestalt therapy consists of therapeutic

===== **ETHICAL HIGHLIGHT 5.1** =====

Informed Consent from the Existential Perspective

The following is an excerpt from a sample informed consent form from the existential perspective. As you read it, pretend that you're sitting in a therapist's waiting room, about to go in for your first therapy session with a new therapist.

Welcome to therapy! As you may already know, therapy is an intense, engaging, exciting collaborative process. When you arrive at your therapy sessions, be prepared for action. Of course, we'll do some talking because all forms of psychotherapy and counseling involve talking. But, in addition to talking together, you'll be directly involved in activities, experiments, and movements all designed to increase your self-awareness.

The purpose of therapy is for you to more deeply discover who you are, what you want, and how to get it. The philosophy underlying my work is that life should be lived to the fullest. This means that during our sessions we won't focus on how you can control your emotions more completely; instead, we will focus on how you can feel your feelings and experiences—both joy and sorrow—with more depth and authenticity.

During therapy, I will do my best to honor you and your personal experience and perspective. However, I will also consistently provide you with feedback about your thinking patterns, feelings, gestures, and other behaviors that may be outside your awareness. In some ways, you should think of me as a mirror, designed to help you get to know yourself better. This means that I won't be playing any social games with you or dancing around the truth of what I see. Often, I will simply tell you what I see, what I think, and the emotional reactions I have to you and your behavior.

Finally, when you come to therapy, be prepared to have emotions stirred up. Therapy is not a calm place where you come to relax and detach from the world and your personal experiences. Our purpose together is to help you face and embrace all of life, rather than running from it. Therefore, much of what we do together will be a real, authentic, mini–life experience wherein you confront the challenges of life and existence within the relatively safe confines of the therapy office. We will use therapy for practicing life, rather than for avoiding life.

As you read through the preceding excerpt, what thoughts came to mind about the therapist and therapy you are about to engage in? Did the informed consent information make you more excited about the opportunity for therapy, or did it make you want to run from the waiting room and get as far away from this therapist and this form of therapy as possible?

Regardless of your personal reaction to the informed consent information, how do you feel about the need for providing this information to clients? Is it crucial to provide this information? Or do you think it might be interesting or useful for the therapist's approach to therapy to be more of a surprise for clients? As the opportunity arises, take time to discuss the issue of informed consent with your peers or instructor.

experiments conducted in the here and now with the purpose of expanding client self-awareness. In some ways, the entire Gestalt therapy approach involves facilitation of self-assessment. It is through self-awareness that humans change. Without self-awareness, there can be no self-regulation. Bankart (1997) describes this Gestalt concept that includes both assessment and treatment components:

How does Gestalt psychotherapy help the individual become self-regulating again? Here, I think, Perls showed us the true genius of the talking cure. Perls believed that the conflicts manifest in the unconscious must be brought out of the past—out of the demilitarized zone of fantasy, dream, and memory—and into the here and now. The therapeutic session must become a living theater of the mind where dreams and impulses are lived out, usually symbolically but always immediately and fully. As awareness bursts into consciousness, the person must become the reality of what she or he is experiencing. The empty chair next to the client becomes the mother who withheld love; the foam bat placed in the client's hands becomes the sword with which she or he can "stab" the betraying father in the heart; the dream symbol is unlocked and its power unleashed to reveal the unfinished situations that prevent us from experiencing life here and now. (p. 321)

As Bankart emphasizes, the Gestalt approach pulls the long-dead, but still influential past, into the living present. This is one way an existential approach deals with assessment. Because everything is happening *now,* we can watch the client's personal issues and neurosis unfold in the therapy session.

Specific Existential Therapy Techniques

Most existential therapists reject the use of techniques. However, some existentialists, particularly Frankl and Fritz Perls, wrote extensively about interventions that can be used with clients. Interestingly, Perls referred to his techniques as "experiments," a term that captures the immediate experiential nature necessary in an existential encounter. The following techniques are derived from Frankl, Perls, and contemporary experiential therapy approaches.

Paradoxical Intention

Paradoxical intention or antisuggestion was a technique originally employed by Alfred Adler. Frankl also wrote about and used this approach. In a case example, Frankl discusses a bookkeeper who was suffering from a chronic case of writer's cramp. The man had seen many physicians without improvement and was in danger of losing his job. Frankl's approach, implemented by one of his associates, was to instruct the man to

do just the opposite from what he usually had done; namely, instead of trying to write as neatly and legibly as possible, to write with the worst possible scrawl. He was advised to say to himself, "now I will show people what a good scribbler I am!" And at that moment in which he deliberately tried to scribble, he was unable to do so. "I tried to scrawl but simply could not do it," he said the next day. Within forty-eight hours the patient was in this way freed from his writer's cramp, and remained free for the observation period after he had been treated. He is a happy man again and fully able to work. (Frankl, 1967, p. 4)

Frankl attributes the success of this approach, in part, to humor. He claims that humor is therapeutic in that it allows individuals to place distance between themselves and their situation. As a result of the new perspective facilitated by humor, the client is then able to let go of symptoms. Frankl emphasized that paradoxical intention is not a superficial technique. He considered the attitude change achieved by paradoxical intention to be of considerable depth.

Given Frankl's emphasis on humor as an underlying therapeutic force in paradoxical intention, it should not be surprising to find that he explains the mechanism underlying the effectiveness of paradoxical intention with a joke:

The basic mechanism underlying the technique . . . perhaps can best be illustrated by a joke which was told to me some years ago: A boy who came to school late excused himself to the teacher on the grounds that the icy streets were so slippery that whenever he moved one step forward he slipped two steps back again. Thereupon the teacher retorted, "Now I have caught you in a lie—if this were true, how did you ever get to school?" Whereupon the boy calmly replied, "I finally turned around and went home!" (Frankl, 1967, pp. 4–5)

Frankl claims that paradoxical intention is especially effective for anxiety, compulsions, and physical symptoms. He reports on numerous cases, similar to that of the man with the writer's cramp, in which a nearly instantaneous cure results from the intervention. In addition to ascribing the cure to humor and distancing from the symptom, Frankl emphasizes that through this technique, clients are taught to intentionally exaggerate, rather than avoid, their personal experience.

Questions for Reflection

Take a few minutes to ponder Frankl's joke. Then apply it to the treatment of mental, emotional, and behavioral problems. How might this mechanism of change work in various situations? Consider applying it to symptoms associated with depression, agoraphobia, and oppositional defiant disorder. Finally, think about a time when you experienced an annoying physical symptom that seemed beyond your control (e.g., an eye twitch, excessive sweating, or heart palpitations). Do you think that intentionally "trying" to produce the symptoms ("I'm really going to show everyone how much I can sweat!") might actually give you more control over them?

Cognitive Reframing

As a modern therapy technique, cognitive reframing probably has its origins in the individual psychology of Adler. However, Frankl also employed this technique, and later cognitive therapists such as Albert Ellis and Aaron Beck more forcefully emphasized its power as a primary therapeutic technique.

Frankl (1967) describes using a reframing technique (although he doesn't refer to it as reframing) in the following case example:

An old doctor consulted me in Vienna because he could not get rid of a severe depression caused by the death of his wife. I asked him, "What would have happened, Doctor, if you had died first, and your wife would have had to survive you?" Whereupon he said: "For her this would have been terrible; how she would have suffered!" I then added, "You see, Doctor, such a suffering has been spared her, and it is you who have spared her this suffering; but now you have to pay for it by surviving and mourning her." The old man suddenly saw his plight in a new light, and reevaluated his suffering in the meaningful terms of a sacrifice for the sake of his wife. (pp. 15–16)

This example clarifies Frankl's emphasis on confronting clients with meaning. In this case, suffering without meaning produces the psychopathology of clinical depression. But when Frankl gives the man contextual meaning for his suffering, the depression is lifted.

Specific Gestalt Therapy Techniques

Perhaps due to the eccentric, flamboyant, and extraverted personality of Fritz Perls, the Gestalt approach is much more active, confrontive, and provocative than traditional existential therapy. Before embarking on a description of Gestalt techniques, we should heed the words of Perls as he describes the use and abuse of techniques:

> A technique is a gimmick. A gimmick should be used only in the extreme case. We've got enough people running around collecting gimmicks, more gimmicks and abusing them. These techniques, these tools, are quite useful in some seminar on sensory awareness or joy, just to give you some idea that you are still alive, that the myth that the American is a corpse is not true, that he *can* be alive. But the sad fact is that this jazzing-up more often becomes a dangerous substitute activity, another phony therapy that *prevents* growth. (F. Perls, 1969a, p. 1)

In this statement, Perls makes several issues clear. First, Gestalt therapy, despite its emphasis on "experiments" or techniques, is not technique-driven. Second, the goal of therapy, and therefore of techniques, is to facilitate self-awareness and personal growth in the long run (not the short term). Third, Gestalt techniques, inappropriately used, can be phony and antitherapeutic. To these cautions we would add, consistent with Perls's theory and practice, Gestalt techniques must be employed within the greater context of an authentic, I-Thou, dialogue relationship.

Although the following techniques are designed for use with adult clients, Gestalt therapy also has been used with child and adolescent populations (Oaklander, 1978).

Staying with the Feeling

Gestalt therapy places a strong emphasis on immediate feelings. Overall, feelings are to be faced and confronted, not avoided. In some ways, from the Gestalt therapy perspective, staying with the feeling is less a specific technique than a general therapy strategy or philosophy.

Gestalt therapists use a variety of techniques to encourage clients to stay with or confront feelings they're trying to avoid. First, they use persistent, repeated questions such as "What are you aware of now?" or "What are you noticing inside yourself right now?" Second, clients can be instructed to give "voice" to their feelings and sensations (e.g., "Let your anxiety have a voice and let it speak for a while"). Third, clients can be encouraged to act on or act out their feelings in the here and now. For example, Perls often had clients pull on and "stretch" him when they felt inner tension and conflict. He believed that by acting out their feelings outside of themselves, his clients would be able to identify and reintegrate their uncomfortable or disowned feelings.

I Take Responsibility For. . .

This experiment is used to fulfill one of the basic underlying principles of Gestalt and existential therapy. As Patricia Baumgardner states, "Gestalt therapy is an existential therapy, concerned with the problems evoked by our dread of accepting responsibility for what we are and what we do" (Baumgardner, 1975, p. 9).

To use this experiment, the therapist has the client use the statement as a sort of prefix to what he or she is saying in therapy. For example, if the client is feeling bored, he or she might be instructed to say, "I'm bored and I take responsibility for my boredom." The technique is especially useful when clients are externalizing their symptoms.

Questions for Reflection

Think about how you might use this technique with clients suffering from anxiety and depressive disorders. Can you imagine having a client say, "I'm depressed and I take full responsibility for my depression?" How about "I take responsibility for my anxiety?" How does using this technique fit with your beliefs and understanding of the neurobiology of depression and anxiety?

Playing the Projection

Much of Gestalt therapy as practiced by Perls was conducted within group settings. He would routinely put group participants on the hot seat and exhort them to become involved in Gestalt experiments and give them feedback. An old supervisor of ours who was in a group facilitated by Perls noted—with some enthusiasm—that being in the hot seat was one of the most frightening and growthful experiences in his life.

Playing the projection is especially applicable to group therapy. Similar to psychoanalytic object relations theorists, Perls believed much of what happens interpersonally to be a function of projection. Therefore, when, in the therapy group, Perls noticed a group member making a statement about someone else that seemed to have much more to do with herself, Perls would ask the participant to play the projection. For example, if the participant commented that she thought Robert (another group member) was too critical of other group members, Perls might say to the woman, "Okay, I want you to take on that quality. You be critical of everyone here. Go around the room and criticize everyone."

Another way to apply this technique is to direct your client, "Tell me something especially annoying you've noticed about someone else." When the client responds with something like "I hate it when Juan is so selfish and insensitive," ask the client to act selfish and insensitive. You can also have the client amplify these selfish and insensitive feelings by having him engage in an empty-chair dialogue, with one part being selfish and insensitive and the other part being unselfish and sensitive. As the dialogue ensues, be sure to encourage the client to focus on what thoughts and feelings come up as he plays the two parts or roles. We will discuss the empty-chair technique in more detail in an upcoming section.

The Reversal Technique

This technique is designed to get clients in touch with parts of themselves that they ordinarily minimize, deny, or ignore. Consequently, passive individuals are asked to behave aggressively, exhibitionists are asked to inhibit themselves, and a person who talks least is asked to talk the most. As with the playing-the-projection experiment, the reversal technique is often employed in a group therapy context. However, it can also be modified for individual clients. As usual, the main emphasis is for clients to notice physical sensations, feelings, and thoughts that emerge as they engage in these less prominent behaviors.

The Exaggeration Experiment

In this experiment clients are instructed to exaggerate their subtle nonverbal behaviors. These nonverbals may or may not be consistent with the client's overall behavior pattern or verbal statements. Exaggerating subtle nonverbal behaviors amplifies the meaning of the behaviors—behaviors that may have been outside of awareness.

This experiment is used in conjunction with focusing and awareness instructions. For example, a client who brushes her hand past her neck might be asked to exaggerate the motion and then to focus on what she feels. In essence, the therapist says, "Make that motion again, only make it bigger. That's it, do it again, even bigger. What are you aware of now?"

The Empty-Chair Technique or Dialogue Experiment

This technique is the best known and best researched of all the Gestalt experiments (Greenberg & Foerster, 1996; Greenberg & Malcolm, 2002; Paivio & Greenberg, 1995). There are two different ways to use the empty-chair dialogue in therapy. In the first version of empty-chair, the client is instructed to play two different parts of herself, depending upon the chair in which she is seated. Typically, this approach to the empty-chair results in the client taking on the "top dog" and "underdog" polarities of her personality. For example, if a client is experiencing a neurotic conflict about getting her college assignments and projects completed in a timely manner, the following therapy interaction might ensue:

Therapist: If you're up for it, I'd like you to try an experiment with me. It involves putting your two most extreme attitudes about doing your class assignments and projects into each of these chairs. So in this chair put all your feelings and beliefs about getting your assignments done on time, and in this other chair put all your feelings and beliefs about resisting assignments. Then move back and forth between the chairs and have a dialogue. Okay?

Client: Okay. I'll try it.

Therapist: Which chair would you like to start in?

Client: I'll be in this one (moves into chair). It's the side that doesn't want to do any homework at all.

Therapist: Okay. Look at the empty chair and tell it how you feel.

Client: Homework sucks. What's the big deal? I don't know why I have to do it. I think mostly all the professors just give it because they think they have to. It's just busy work. I really, totally, don't care at all about homework. (Pause.)

Therapist: Sit in the other chair and see what comes up.

Client: What should I do?

Therapist: Look over at the chair you were just in and respond to what you heard.

Client: You're so irresponsible. If you don't do your projects, you'll get bad grades. Then you might flunk. Then you'll lose your scholarship. And then you might as well plan on flipping burgers at a fast food restaurant all your life. Is that what you want?

Therapist: Go ahead, switch again and respond.

Client: (Switches.) Of course I don't want to flip burgers. That's not the point. The point is you never want to do anything fun. And that's what I want. Flipping burgers is no fun, but neither is homework. Don't you get the fact that there's more to life than being serious and doing homework?

Therapist: You want to have some fun. What's the other side say to that?

Client: (Switching chairs.) All you ever want to do is have fun. You're total fun. Well, I'm not just a party girl. I want to make something of myself someday.

Therapist: What if you had these two try to work out a compromise? Switch seats and try that.

Client: (Switches.) How about a deal? You know I love to play, and you're totally serious. Just give me some play time. Some regular play time. Schedule time for fun and relaxation into every single day. It doesn't have to be for any longer than an hour. But during that hour I get to be spontaneous and have total fun.

Client: (Switches chairs spontaneously.) How can I trust you? Once you get out having fun, then you'll blow off all responsibility. This has happened before. You don't take life seriously. How can I trust you?

Client: (Switches chairs.) Give me a chance to prove myself. Let's make a schedule. You're right. Sometimes I'm going to want to keep having fun. Maybe I'm willing to wait a day or two and only do fun stuff two or three times a week. But I need a guarantee. I need to have you come through so I can trust you. Otherwise, we know how it's gonna be. Everything will be late. You'll be distracted by everything. If you plan some fun, you'll be able to focus.

Client: (Switches chairs.) You've got a deal. I am so sick of being distracted by everything. If you let me focus, we'll plan some fun!

This sequence is simplified, but it illustrates the Gestalt top-dog/underdog phenomenon. Perls writes about this split:

[O]ne of the most frequent splits in the human personality . . . is the topdog-underdog split. The topdog is known in psychoanalysis as the superego or the conscience. Unfortunately, Freud left out the underdog, and he did not realize that usually the underdog wins in the conflict between topdog and underdog. I give you the frequent characteristics of both. The topdog is righteous, some of the time right, but always righteous. . . . The topdog always says you should and the topdog threatens . . . However, the topdog is pretty straightforward. Now the underdog looks for the different method. The underdog says, yeh, or I promise, or I agree . . . or . . . if only I could. So the underdog is a very good frustrator. And then the topdog, of course, doesn't let him get away with it and praises the use of the rod and the self-torture game or self-improvement game, whatever you want to call it, goes on year in and year out, year in and year out and nothing ever happens. Right? (F. Perls, 1973, p. 125)

The purpose of the empty-chair technique is to help clients break out of being stuck in this self-torture game. In the preceding example, as the empty-chair dialogue proceeds, polarization occurs, but with some prompting from the therapist, a new approach is used to move toward an internal resolution. In this case, the top-dog entity that wants class assignments completed is clearly connected with an early parent figure, and the underdog is the child. The conflict represents unfinished business. By bringing the unfinished business into the here and now, the empty-chair experiment provides an opportunity to move toward resolution and to finish the unfinished business. In many cases, when this exchange occurs, it's desirable for emotions to run high, which seems to facilitate resolution (Greenberg & Malcolm, 2002).

In the second version of Gestalt empty chair, the client acts out a contemporary life conflict. For example, if a female client is in the midst of a conflict with her husband, she would be asked to play both parts of a dialogue with her husband while simultaneously examining the feelings that emerge. Although this procedure begins differently from the first version of the empty chair dialogue, it usually progresses into the same sort of top dog versus underdog dialogue previously described. The key difference is in how the dialogue is initiated. In the first case, the dialogue emerges from an inner conflict. In the second case, the dialogue emerges from an external conflict. However, considering the dynamic of defensive projection, intense conflicts are usually strongly characterized by projected parts of the self onto others. Therefore, as the client's dialogue of external conflict ensues, it begins to capture important, unfinished characteristics of the client's inner self. Eventually, disowned parts of the self can be reintegrated.

The Gestalt Approach to Dream Work

For the Gestalt therapist, dreams are to be experienced, not interpreted. Additionally, in keeping with existential philosophy, Gestalt therapists view the dreamer as 100% responsible for all dream images. Specifically, if your client dreams of a terrible monster murdering an innocent victim, both the monster and the victim are considered manifestations of the dreamer.

Perls considered dream work to be central to Gestalt therapy. He stated, "I believe the dream is really the royal road to integration," and "[a]s in psychoanalysis, the mainstay in Gestalt therapy is the dream." Moreover, he stated,

> In my opinion, the dream is much more than wish fulfillment of an unfinished situation. To me, a dream is an existential message. It can lead to understanding one's life script, one's karma, one's destiny. And the beauty of this is that once we take responsibility for our life script, for our dreams, then we are capable of changing our lives. (Baumgardner, 1975, p. 117)

There are four main steps to Gestalt dream work. First, the dreamer tells the story of the dream. Second, the dreamer "revives" the dream by changing the language: Instead of telling the dream in the past tense, he or she reports it in the present tense. Third, the dreamer becomes a director and organizes the dream as a play, moving around, setting the stage, and describing where everyone is and where every object is. Fourth, the dreamer then acts out the dream, always using the personal pronoun "I" to enhance identification with each object and character in the dream.

Overall, the goal of dream work is for the dreamer to

> [b]egin on his own to re-identify with the scattered bits and pieces of his personality, which had only been held together superficially by the expression "I." Then when the click comes, the dynamic, the *élan vital,* the life force that has been disowned and projected into others will begin to follow into his own center and he will begin to be himself again. (Baumgardner, 1975, p. 119)

Because of the centrality of dream work to Gestalt therapy, we examine it next in a case example.

APPLICATION: CASE EXAMPLE

Perls had an uncanny ability to use repetitive phrases to produce client insight. He used the "and this is my existence" technique especially with dreams, fantasies, and other repeating images. The technique is straightforward and formulaic. To use it, you simply tell the client to describe a dream image with a brief phrase and then follow the phrase with the statement ". . . and this is my existence." When introducing the technique to a client you should emphasize that it will feel silly or phony, but that the client should just let him- or herself focus on the experience. The following example illustrates the technique with a 26-year-old male who came for treatment because of anxiety connected with achievement in the academic arena.

Client: I dreamt I was racing my brother home. We were kids again. He got ahead of me and cut me off. I tackled him from behind. The next thing I knew we were all muddy and my mom was scolding us.

Therapist: Just go through the dream one thought at a time. Say it slowly and clearly. Then, after each thought, add the statement ". . . and this is my existence." I know this sounds silly and phony, but just try it and see what it feels like.

Client: I'm racing my brother . . . and this is my existence.

We're heading home . . . and this is my existence.

Therapist: That's it. Keep your focus on your body and your feelings and see what happens.

Client: He's ahead . . . and this is my existence.

I can't catch up because he's blocking me . . . and this is my existence.

I'm tackling him from behind . . . and this is my existence.

I'm muddy and a big mess . . . and this is my existence.

My mom is standing over me . . . and this is my existence.

She's telling me I'm stupid . . . and this is my existence.

And that I should leave my brother alone . . . and this is my existence.

Therapist: What's happening?

Client: I can't believe it. This dream is my life!

Therapist: What is there you don't want to believe?

Client: That I'm still competing with my brother. I'm still losing. And I'm still worried about what my mother will think.

Therapist: How do you want to change the dream?

Client: What do you mean?

Therapist: I mean you can go ahead and change the dream. It's your dream. Tell it to me again, only this time change it into how you want it to be right now.

This example illustrates several Gestalt therapy principles. First, the dreamer owns the dream, whether he wants to or not. The simple "existence" technique only amplifies reality as it is. Second, the therapist does not interpret reality for the client, but only facilitates. Interpretation is the job of the client, not the therapist. Third, as the client sinks into the process, he begins to feel connections. These connections fit into his personal reality like pieces of a puzzle. It can feel like an "aha" experience. The client's insight represents his unfinished business. For the Gestalt therapist, the unfinished business is dominating the client's life. Now, as awareness increases, the client can take control and guide his life in the present, rather than spending energy battling the unfinished business from the past. At the end of the case example, when the therapist asks the client to recreate his dream, the client is empowered to actively live his life, rather than being an automaton trudging forward without an independent spirit. For additional case material from an existential perspective we recommend Yalom's book, *Love's Executioner.*

THERAPY OUTCOMES RESEARCH

There has been no traditional outcomes research conducted on the efficacy of existential therapy per se. Although there is some published research on the effectiveness of paradoxical intention, this technique does not represent an evaluation of the whole process of existential therapy.

In defense of the lack of controlled scientific research on existential therapy, May

---
Questions for Reflection

Before reading further, speculate on why existential therapists have not produced any research to support their approach. How might the lack of research support for their approach be related to their underlying philosophy?

(1983) provides the following somewhat lengthy, but purely existential, discussion of the limitations of contemporary scientific methods.

> [T]he existential movement in psychiatry and psychology arose precisely out of a passion to be not *less* but *more* empirical. Binswanger and the others were convinced that the traditional scientific methods not only did not do justice to the data but actually tended to hide rather than reveal what was going on in the patient. The existential analysis movement is a protest against the tendency to see the patient in forms tailored to our own preconceptions or to make him over into the image of our own predilections.
>
> It is also important here to remind ourselves that every scientific method rests upon philosophical presuppositions. These presuppositions determine not only how much reality the observer with this particular method can see—they are indeed the spectacles through which he perceives. . . .
>
> The result in our day is that science gets identified with methods of *isolating* factors and observing them from an allegedly *detached base*—a particular method which arose out of the split between object and subject made in the seventeenth century in Western culture and then developed into its special compartmentalized form in the late nineteenth and twentieth centuries.
>
> [As] Helen Sargent has sagely and pithily remarked, "Science offers more leeway than graduate students are permitted to realize." (pp. 45–46)

May's commentary suggests that existential approaches to therapy should not be measured using contemporary scientific outcome studies. In fact, scientific outcome studies only represent a single perspective on the nature and effectiveness of therapy. Of course, this position may seem a cop-out by some therapy researchers. Prochaska and Norcross (2003) provide a critique of existential approaches to therapy from a behavioral perspective:

> With no controlled outcome studies, we can see why some existentialists prefer to consider their approach a philosophy about psychotherapy and not a theory of psychotherapy. But what kind of authentic philosophy would be unwilling to fall or stand on the basis of its effectiveness in helping patients overcome their pathologies? (p. 132)

Although this criticism has legitimacy from an objective scientific stance, it reminds us of the communication difficulties that often arise when individuals with much different Jungian psychological types try to communicate with each other. The existentialists are more Intuitive and Feeling in their styles, whereas the behaviorists are more Sensing and Thinking. They are so different in their approaches to viewing the world that they seem like two individuals speaking two different languages. At the very least, we should acknowledge that the existentialist's refusal to buy into the scientific research game is internally consistent with existential philosophy. Could it be that the existentialists are not afraid to measure their therapeutic outcomes but, instead, are insisting on remaining authentic to their core beliefs?

ETHICAL HIGHLIGHT 5.2

How Much Self-Disclosure is Too Much Self-Disclosure?

More than any other therapy orientation, existential therapists utilize authentic self-disclosure as a therapeutic approach. This position is in direct opposition to Freud's early advice for psychoanalysts: "The physician should be impenetrable to the patient, and like a mirror, reflect nothing but what is shown to him" (1912/2000, p. 18). In fact, many therapists who practice from the existential perspective believe the therapist should not be a mirror, but more like a window: transparent, open, and real with clients. From the existential perspective, only an open and real therapist can establish an I-Thou relationship and experience an existential encounter.

Despite Freud's opinion, many therapists use self-disclosure during the therapy hour (Simi & Mahalik, 1997). In reality, it appears that Freud also regularly disclosed personal information about himself to his clients (Goldstein, 1994). As a consequence, for most therapists the question is not whether self-disclosure is acceptable. Instead, the key questions are

- How much self-disclosure is acceptable?
- When is self-disclosure more (or less) appropriate?
- What type of information is acceptable for therapists to share with clients?

As you have the opportunity, explore these questions for yourself and in dialogue with your peers and professor.

Some Dangers of Self-Disclosure

The liberal use of self-disclosure from any therapy perspective naturally raises several ethical issues. An acquaintance of ours told us she had chosen to work with an existentially oriented counselor, but soon stopped. "I didn't really want to pay for the privilege of listening to her talk about her affairs and her marriage breaking up. We did have a few common painful life experiences, but she told me way more than I wanted or needed to know. It wasn't at all helpful."

For psychoanalytic therapists, personal disclosure places an unnecessary burden on the client. The client may feel an urge to take care of or feel sorry for the therapist, or the client may lose faith in the therapist's ability to help. We recommend that before you use self-disclosure with clients, you become conscious of exactly why you believe your client might benefit from hearing something about you and your personal life.

In keeping with the more concrete nature of Gestalt therapy, there have been a few research studies published on the efficacy of Perls's approach to treatment. However, Perls was generally against therapy outcome studies and nomothetic approaches to understanding the individual. He emphasizes that discovering what works should not and cannot be determined through research. Instead, to determine the effectiveness of an approach, the focus should be on the individual: [W]e present nothing that you cannot verify for yourself in terms of your own behavior" (F. Perls et al., 1951, p. 7).

PRACTITIONER COMMENTARY 5.1

Existential Musings

Kurt Kraus of Shippensburg State University wrote the following commentary. His thoughts about practicing counseling from an existential-phenomenological perspective are also included in the multicultural perspectives section of this chapter.

As an existentially oriented phenomenologist I am often caught, conflicted by my theoretical belief and my clients' desire for someone in my chair whose beliefs are not mine. For me, the honoring of suffering, the anxiety of limited time, and the continuous presence of opportunities for personal meaning are often the very things that clients initially wish to be rescued from. It is a conflict that I very much appreciate, one that makes for the most interesting therapeutic alliances.

I often ask myself, "How can theory help me better understand some aspect of the client with whom I am working?" And then, when I have located one or two meaningful theoretical explanations, I store them in some recess of my mind—sort of as a backdrop or a map. I then proceed with my client to construct a personal meaning for his or her experience. One thing I try to remember is that no map gets you where you want to be: Movement does. It is, at least in therapy, the actual journey that gets the client where he or she chooses to go. Learning theories is a valuable means to an end, but the path is not paved in theory; it is paved with experience.

Sometimes theory texts afford great fantasy. If I adhere to one theory I will be clear in my professional identity, "I am a reality therapist, or I am Rogerian, or I do rational emotive behavior therapy." At times through these fantasies I can be Melanie Klein, or Alexander Wolfe, or Judith Jordan. I've never held on long enough to emerge as anyone other than myself—full of doubts about the veracity of any one theory over all others. Instead I study those that fit me, content in the notion that the theories of counseling and psychotherapy are quite occasionally transmogrified through my interpretation and through my unique relationship with each and every client with whom I sit.

Perls's perspective notwithstanding, the standardized empirical research on Gestalt therapy is moderately positive. This empirical result was initially articulated by Smith, Glass, and Miller (1980) in their meta-analysis of 475 outcome studies (which also included a number of Gestalt therapy studies). Further research has consistently shown that Gestalt therapy is slightly better than placebo treatment and perhaps somewhat less effective than cognitive and behavioral treatments (Greenberg, Elliot, & Lietaer, 1994). It also has been shown to be most effective with reserved, internalizing clients who are open to participating in Gestalt experiments (Daldrup, Beutler, Engle, & Greenberg, 1988). However, before concluding that Gestalt therapy is clearly a less effective therapy, we should note that some researchers have suggested that the slightly lower effectiveness of Gestalt therapy during clinical studies can be more than accounted for by the researcher allegiance effect. In particular, the bias of cognitive and behavioral researchers may produce the aforementioned results (Elliot, Greenberg, & Lietaer, 2002).

MULTICULTURAL PERSPECTIVES

Existential therapy continues its paradoxical preoccupation with polarities with respect to its sensitivity to diversity. On the one hand, because of its emphasis on the sanctity of individual experience and discovery of the unique self, it is sometimes championed as one of the most ethnoculturally sensitive therapy approaches in existence. On the other hand, feminists and multiculturalists frequently complain that existentialism is a theory promoted by wealthy, dead, white, European men. As Prochaska and Norcross state, "Only in existentialism and the movies do people possess unlimited freedom, construct their own meanings, and execute boundless choices. Save it for the wealthy, worried well" (2003, p. 133).

Despite the scathing critique from Prochaska and Norcross, we're still willing to admit that some of our best friends are existentialists . . . and that they often work very hard at being multiculturally and gender sensitive. In fact, Vontress and his colleagues write about cross-cultural counseling cases and issues from an existential perspective (Vontress, Johnson, & Epp, 1999). This sensitivity of existentialists is also well articulated by Kurt Kraus:

> I remember a time in my career when with great anticipation I moved far away to be able to work with more clients of color-specifically Native American and African American peoples. When I found myself, White, for the first time in the minority, still experiencing life as a majority person, it dawned on me: Being well-trained and embracing a multicultural experience did not make me ready; privilege is a skin that is hard to shed.
>
> When a supervisee errantly says, "I know how you feel" in response to a client's disclosure, I twitch and contort. I believe that one of the great gifts of multicultural awareness . . . for me [is] accepting the limitations to the felt-experience of empathy. I can only imagine how another feels, and sometimes the reach of my experience is so short as to only approximate what another feels. This is a good thing to learn. I'll upright myself in my chair and say, "I used to think that I knew how others felt too. May I teach you a lesson that has served me well?" (personal communication, August, 2002)

Kraus's multicultural lesson reminds us of Yalom's discussion of existential isolation (Yalom, 1980). As individual entities traveling through human existence, we are destined to be separate from everyone else. To say "I know how you feel" is a violation of that existential reality. In some ways, it is a very direct lie. Perhaps the best thing we can communicate to our clients, regardless of their cultural background, is "I'm trying my best to understand how you feel," keeping in mind, of course, that we'll never fully succeed.

CONCLUDING COMMENTS

There is no doubt about the potential power of existential therapy and the Gestalt approach. We will revisit some of Rollo May's thinking in Chapter 6, as we explore person-centered therapy and a dialogue that occurred between Carl Rogers and May on the nature of evil. For now, as we take leave of this theoretical perspective, we reflect on the transformative power of Gestalt therapy.

In this final excerpt from *The Gestalt Approach and Eyewitness to Therapy,* Fritz Perls has switched seats with his client, and so she is now playing the role of Fritz, while Perls takes the role of a very resistant client. Finally, after battling his resistance, she moves

Perls toward a breakthrough. The following dialogue took place as a live demonstration in front of an audience.

> **Barbara:** I notice that no matter what happens, the burden returns to me. No matter what I suggest, you say no, you do it for me, I don't know how.
>
> **Fritz:** Of course. If I weren't so incapable, I wouldn't be here. This is my illness, don't you see?
>
> **Barbara:** Talk to your illness.
>
> **Fritz:** But my illness isn't here. How can I talk to my illness? And if I could talk to the illness, the illness wouldn't listen, because this is the illness.
>
> **Barbara:** I'll listen. Did someone give you the illness?
>
> **Fritz:** (Slowly) Yes.
>
> **Barbara:** Who?
>
> **Fritz:** Sigmund Freud. (There is much laughing among the group at this point.)
>
> **Barbara:** I realize that Sigmund isn't here, that he's . . .
>
> **Fritz:** But for seven years I got infected.
>
> **Barbara:** (Giggling) Oh, I'm three years above you because I spent ten years with an analyst. Don't tell me how bad it is! Could you talk to Sigmund?
>
> **Fritz:** Oh no, I can't. He's dead.
>
> **Barbara:** You've changed. That's the first time you've slipped. What are you aware of now?
>
> **Fritz:** (Soberly) A great sorrow that Freud is dead before I really could talk as man to man with him.
>
> **Barbara:** (Gently) I think you could still talk to him. Would you like to?
>
> **Fritz:** Uh huh.
>
> **Barbara:** Fine. (Pause) I'd like to listen.
>
> **Fritz:** Now I'm stuck. I would like to do it. I would like to be your patient in this situation, and uh . . . (speaking very slowly) Professor Freud . . . a great man . . . but very sick . . . you can't let anyone touch you. You've got to say what is and your word is holy gospel. I wish you would listen to me. In a certain way I know more than you do. You could have solved the neurosis question. And here I am . . . a simple citizen . . . by the grace of God having discovered the simple secret that what is, is. I haven't even discovered this. Gertrude Stein has discovered this. I just copy her. No, copy is not right. I got in the same way of living—thinking, with her. Not as an intellectual, but just as a human plant, animal—and this is where you were blind. You moralized and defended sex; taking this out of the total context of life. So you missed life. (There is quiet in the room for several moments. Then Fritz turns to Barbara.) So, your copy of Fritz wasn't so bad. (Gives Barbara a kiss) You did something for me.
>
> **Barbara:** Thank you, Fritz. (F. Perls, 1973, pp. 207–208).

Unlike psychoanalysis, existential philosophy and therapy is about much more than just isolated sexual and aggressive impulses. Existential and Gestalt approaches to therapy are about life.

STUDENT REVIEW ASSIGNMENTS

The following exercises encourage you to review and evaluate your knowledge of existential and Gestalt theory.

Critical Corner

The following critical comments about existential and Gestalt theory and therapy are designed to provoke a reaction and stimulate your reflection. Please read the comments and then write your thoughts and reactions to the criticisms.

1. Existential approaches have primarily been developed, promoted, and oriented toward White men. In fact, aside from Laura Perls, whose contributions have been relatively ignored, it's difficult to find women or minorities who were deeply involved in the development of existential thinking and therapy. Even within the domain of Yalom's four primary ultimate concerns, the absence of any reference to the birth experience—a deeply powerful ultimate experience that must be dealt with exclusively by women—is striking. As you contemplate existential theory and therapy, consider whether it is a therapy for the masses or perhaps just an approach oriented toward wealthy men who have had far too much time on their hands for deep thought and reflection. On a related note, how can existential theory and therapy become more relevant for individuals who don't have time in their daily lives for deep thought and reflection?
   Response:

2. Although existential therapists encourage individuals to embrace their deepest fears, they have not, themselves, embraced the concept of scientific or empirical evaluation of existential therapy. Could it be that existentialists are too afraid to expose their therapy approaches to scrutinizing scientific evaluation? If existentialists are interested in the complete human experience, why do they avoid and demean scientific procedures? It seems that scientific evaluation of therapy effectiveness, despite its limitations, reflects an important part of human experience—and the effort to understand and quantify therapeutic process and outcome should be recognized as having at least some validity. Comment on the existentialists' clear lack of openness to the scientific side of human experience.
   Response:

3. As noted in the chapter, existentialists are also generally opposed to standardized psychological assessment and evaluation. Can you imagine a situation in which the administration of a psychological assessment procedure might be helpful to an individual? Can you imagine this even if you look at the process from an existential perspective? Are there parts of human experience that can be accurately measured? Consider anxiety and guilt. Is it possible to measure a client's anxiety and guilt experiences and conclude whether he or she is experiencing neurotic or normal anxiety or guilt?
   Response:

4. One of the strong contemporary movements in psychotherapy and counseling practice is manualized therapy. The manualized approach is appealing because it provides therapists with clear guidelines and structure for conducting therapy. Although therapy manuals are not to be used like cookbooks, they provide therapists, both new and old, with standard procedures. How can existential or

Gestalt therapy approaches survive when they are based on spontaneity and authenticity—a foundation that is completely counter to contemporary emphases on standardization of therapy?
Response:

5. Gestalt therapy focuses on clients' body awareness and trusts the individual to make contact with the environment and move in a positive and growthful direction. As practiced by F. Perls and others, Gestalt therapy is confrontive and provocative. Consider the application of Gestalt therapy with low-functioning or psychotic clients. What might be the dangers of using an empty-chair technique with a dissociative client? What might be the dangers of having a paranoid, borderline psychotic client play his projection? Do you think the Gestalt Prayer, "You do your thing and I do mine," would be a useful philosophy to teach men and women who are in prison because of criminal behavior? In general, list and discuss with your class the potential contraindications of Gestalt therapy.
Response:

Reviewing Key Terms

- Ontological experience
- Neurotic anxiety
- Neurotic guilt
- Ultimate concerns
- Logotherapy
- I-Thou relationship
- Nihilism
- Gestalt
- Field theory
- Figure-ground-formation
- Will to meaning

- Self-regulating
- Confluence
- Retroflection
- Deflection
- Projection
- Contact
- Gestalt experiments
- Paradoxical intention
- Cognitive reframing
- Staying with the feeling
- And this is my existence

- The empty-chair dialogue experiment
- Top dog
- Underdog
- I take responsibility for
- Playing the projection
- The reversal technique
- The exaggeration experiment
- Gestalt dream work

Review Questions

1. Discuss how Kierkegaard's Christian faith and Nietzsche's atheism can be viewed as philosophical polarities that lead to a deeper understanding of the individual self.

2. Frankl openly admitted to facing nihilism and eventually discovering meaning. Did Frankl initially face nihilism before, during, or after his concentration camp experiences? Reflect on whether you believe (1) meaning naturally exists in the world or (2) individuals must create meaning in their lives.

3. What does Sartre mean by existence preceding essence? What are the implications of the opposite philosophical position, that essence precedes existence?

4. Is Frankl's will to meaning a drive or a striving? What difference does it make?

5. Gestalt perceptual principles suggest that the whole is greater than the sum of its parts. If this is the case, then why do so many Gestalt therapy techniques in-

volve breaking the individual down into fragments or parts (as in dream work or the empty-chair dialogue)?

6. Describe the figure-ground-formation process and discuss how it is related to unfinished business.

7. Is it possible for a therapist to maintain an I-Thou relationship throughout the duration of a therapeutic encounter? Discuss ways in which you, as a therapist, might try to establish and maintain an I-Thou relationship with your clients.

8. According to Yalom, facing death can motivate individuals to live life more fully. Describe how the four ultimate concerns of existential theory can be used as a positive motivation with clients in therapy.

9. What is cognitive reframing, and how did Frankl apply it to confront clients with a deeper sense of personal meaning?

10. Describe the two different ways a therapist can initiate a Gestalt empty-chair dialogue.

11. List and discuss the sorts of questions an existential and/or Gestalt therapist might use with clients to help keep them focused on their immediate experience in therapy.

12. How does the Gestalt therapist view clients' dreams? What are the four steps to dream work the Gestalt therapist employs?

RECOMMENDED READINGS AND RESOURCES

For the philosophically inclined, there's an overwhelming amount of reading that can be done on existentialism. The following list of resources is only the tip of the iceberg.

Lead Journals

- *Australian Gestalt Journal*
- *British Gestalt Journal*
- *Gestalt Review Journals*
- *Journal of the Society for Existential Analysis*
- *Review of Existential Psychology and Psychiatry*

Books and Articles

Baumgardner, P. (1975). *Legacy from Fritz.* Palo Alto, CA: Science and Behavior Books.

Buber, M. (1970). *I and thou.* New York: Charles Scribner.

Bugental, J. F. T. (1987). *The art of the psychotherapist.* New York: Norton.

Frankl, V. (1963). *Man's search for meaning.* Boston: Beacon.

Frankl, V. (1967). *Psychotherapy and existentialism: Selected papers on logotherapy.* New York: Clarion.

Frankl, V. (1978). *The unheard cry for meaning.* New York: Simon & Schuster.

May, R. (1977). *The meaning of anxiety* (Rev. ed.). New York: Norton.

May, R., Angel, E., & Ellenberger, H. F. (Eds.). (1958). *Existence: A new dimension in psychiatry and psychology.* New York: Basic Books.

Oaklander, V. (1978). *Windows to our children.* Moab, UT: Real People Press.

Perls, F. (1969a). *Gestalt therapy verbatim.* Moab, UT: Real People Press.

Perls, F. (1969b). *In and out the garbage pail.* Moab, UT: Real People Press.

Polster, E., & Polster, M. (1973). *Gestalt therapy integrated: Contours of theory and practice.* New York: Brunner/Mazel.

Sartre, J.-P. (1953). *Existential psychoanalysis* (H. E. Barnes, Trans.). Chicago: Henry Regnery Company.

Sartre, J.-P. (1971). *Being and nothingness.* New York: Bantam Books.

Tolstoy, L. (1929). *My confession, my religion, the gospel in brief.* New York: Charles Scribner.

Van Deurzen-Smith, E. (1997). *Everyday mysteries: Existential dimensions of psychotherapy.* London: Routledge.

Vontress, C. E., Johnson, J. A., & Epp, L. R. (1999). *Cross-cultural counseling: A casebook.* Alexandria, VA: American Counseling Association.

Yalom, I. D. (1980). *Existential psychotherapy.* New York: Basic Books.

Yalom, I. D. (1989). *Love's executioner.* New York: Basic Books.

Yontef, G. M. (1993). *Awareness, dialogue and process: Essays on gestalt therapy.* Highland, NY: Gestalt Journal Press.

Videotapes

Carlson, J., & Kjos, D. (2000). *Existential-humanistic therapy with Dr. James Bugental* [Videotape]. Boston: Allyn & Bacon.

Mahrer, A. (1994). *Experiential psychotherapy* [Videotape]. Washington, DC: American Psychological Association.

Yalom, I. (2002). *The gift of Therapy: An interview with Irvin Yalom* [Videotape]. Pacific Grove, CA: Brooks/Cole.

Training Organizations and Informational Web Sites

Gestalt Center for Psychotherapy and Training
26 West 9th Street
New York, NY 10011
Telephone: (212) 387-9429

Society for Existential Analysis
School of Psychotherapy and Counselling, Regent's College
Inner Circle, Regent's Park
London, England NWI 4NS United Kingdom
E-mail: spc@regents.ac.uk

Gestalt Associates Training, Los Angeles
1460 7th Street, Suite 300
Santa Monica, CA 90401
Telephone: (310) 395-6844
E-mail: ritaresnick@gatla.org

International Network on Personal Meaning (web site: www.meaning.ca)

New School of Psychotherapy and Counselling (web site: www.nspc.org.uk/index.htm). This program in Waterloo and London offers a 4-year course of study to obtain an M.A. in existential psychotherapy.

Chapter 6

CARL ROGERS: PERSON-CENTERED THEORY AND THERAPY

[I]t is the client who knows what hurts, what directions to go in, what problems are crucial.

—Carl Rogers, *On Becoming a Person* (1961, pp. 11–12)

IN THIS CHAPTER YOU WILL LEARN

- The personal and professional history of Carl Rogers
- The historical context of the development of person-centered therapy
- Basic principles of a person-centered theory of personality, psychopathology, and psychotherapy
- How to prepare yourself and your clients for a person-centered therapy experience
- Specific attitudes and strategies employed by person-centered therapists
- Contemporary modifications of person-centered therapy, including process-experiential therapy and motivational interviewing
- Multicultural issues and applications of person-centered therapy
- Ethical issues associated with person-centered therapy
- The empirical status of person-centered therapy

If Freud was a pessimist and Adler and Jung were optimists, then Carl Rogers—the primary theoretical figure of this chapter—was a super-optimist. His approach is founded on an abiding belief in the capacity for persons, when unfettered by social and familial obstacles, to develop into positive, creative, flexible, and altruistic beings. Rogers referred to this capacity as an *actualizing* or *formative* tendency. As you read about him, you will see that his belief in the positive nature of persons is unshakable.

Rogers developed a distinctive approach to therapy: He listened. He listened to clients with every ounce of respect he could muster. Additionally, in all aspects of his life, he strove to be a genuine and open person; he strove to be himself. As he interacted authentically with clients, he put himself so deeply into their world that he could feel their feelings right along with them.

At times, other theorists have viewed Rogers's optimism as frustrating and naive. For example, Rollo May, a person who regarded Rogers quite highly, once wrote to Rogers concerning his (Rogers's) extraordinarily positive view of the world's future:

> You paint a seductive and enticing picture, and anyone would like to believe it. But I recall the words of Warren Bemis in the film of you and him, when he characterized your viewpoint as "devilishly innocent." (Kirschenbaum & Henderson, 1989, p. 242)

We hope that, despite his apparent innocence, you will embrace Carl Rogers and his person-centered theory and therapy with every part of your being. As one of the best listeners ever to walk the planet, Rogers deserves to have us stop whatever else we might be doing and for the moment listen to him.

BIOGRAPHICAL INFORMATION: CARL ROGERS

Carl Ransom Rogers was born in 1902. He was the fourth of six children and was raised on a farm in Illinois. His parents were rigid fundamentalist Christians, whom Rogers later described as "absolute masters of repressive control" (quoted in Bankart, 1997, p. 292). He describes how his parents taught him to keep his distance when socializing with outsiders:

> Other persons behave in dubious ways which we do not approve in our family. Many of them play cards, go to the movies, smoke, dance, drink, and engage in other activities, some unmentionable. So the best thing to do is to be tolerant of them, since they may not know better, and to keep away from any close communication with them and live your life within the family. (Rogers, 1980, p. 28)

Rogers's family dynamics appear to have laid the groundwork for the social and personal transformation he later experienced. In many ways, Rogers as a therapist sought to create a completely accepting, permissive, and nonjudgmental therapy environment. He tried to help his clients obtain an experience that was the polar opposite of what he had experienced in relationship to his parents.

Despite his parents' distrust of intellectualism, Rogers went to college, initially following the family policy of majoring in agriculture. He also was involved in the campus Young Men's Christian Association group and was one of twelve students chosen to attend the World Student Christian Federation Conference in Peking, China (Rogers, 1961).

It was on this trip that, according to Bankhart, "Rogers appears to have become Rogers" (Bankart, 1997, p. 292). He was away 6 months. Somehow this experience produced the following changes in Rogers: (1) He rejected his parents' conservative religious ideology; (2) he decided to marry his childhood sweetheart; and (3) he decided to pursue graduate studies at the liberal Union Theological Seminary in New York City.

HISTORICAL CONTEXT

Not long after enrolling at Union Theological Seminary, Rogers transferred (across the street) to Columbia University Teachers College to study clinical psychology. His training was squarely within the domain of American academic psychology. At the time, Columbia University was inculcated with John Watson's behaviorism (see Chapter 7). Consequently, Rogers was oriented more toward the contemporary scientist-practitioner model in psychology than any theorist we have discussed to this point. His strong interest in research—he was the first person to tape-record actual therapy sessions—led some to refer to him as "the founder of psychotherapy research" (Bohart, 1995, p. 87; Rogers, 1942b).

Rogers's first clinical position was at the Adlerian-oriented Rochester Child Guidance Center. During this time, academic psychologists were staunchly behavioral, while clinicians were trained in either psychoanalytic or neo-analytic theory. Since Rogers wanted to help people (rather than work in a laboratory), he was trained in a diagnostic-prescriptive analytic approach:

> Rogers originally went to . . . Rochester . . . believing in this diagnostic, prescriptive, professionally impersonal approach, and it was only after actual experience that he concluded that it was not effective. As an alternative, he tried listening and following the client's lead rather than assuming the role of the expert. This worked better, and he discovered some theoretical and applied support for this alternative approach in the work of Otto Rank and his followers. (Raskin & Rogers, 1989, pp. 160–161)

Rogers attended a 2-day seminar with Otto Rank and learned a great deal from a Rank-trained social worker, Elizabeth Davis, whom he hired to work for him in Rochester. Ms. Davis was able to tune into and articulate clients' feelings in a way that fascinated Rogers; he credits her as the inspiration for his best-known therapeutic approach. "What later came to be called the reflection of feeling sprang from my contact with her," he noted (Rogers & Haigh, 1983, p. 7).

During his 12 years in Rochester, Rogers wove many elements of Rankian practice into his approach, including the following premises:

- Clients have creative powers.
- Therapy should help clients accept their personal uniqueness and self-reliance.
- The client is the central figure in the therapy process; the therapist only helps clients access their powers of self-creation.
- Therapists shouldn't seek to educate clients.
- Therapist shouldn't foster dependency with clients by becoming love objects.
- Therapy works when clients are able to experience the present within the therapy setting. (adapted from Raskin & Rogers, 1989)

As a young American living in the 1930s, Rogers was influenced by the social policies and person of President Franklin D. Roosevelt. Roosevelt was optimistic, empowered individuals by involving them in social and political activities, and supported the creativity of his subordinates (Bohart, 1995). At the same time, Rogers was influenced by the philosophy of John Dewey, whose statements about human development goals are similar to Rogers's goals for and attitudes toward psychotherapy: "Not perfection as a final goal, but the ever-enduring process of perfecting, maturing, refining, is the aim in living" (Dewey, 1920, pp. 176–177).

Rogers's relationship with his wife also had a powerful affect on him. Because of his sheltered childhood and poor social skills, she was the first person with whom he ever had a caring and sharing relationship. In 1980, at the age of 75, he wrote,

During the first two years of marriage we learned a vitally important lesson. We learned, through some chance help, that the elements in the relationship that seemed impossible to share—the secretly disturbing, dissatisfying elements—are the most rewarding to share. This was a hard, risky, frightening thing to learn, and we have relearned it many, many times since. It was a rich and developing experience for each of us. (Rogers, 1980, p. 32)

Honoring the Client

Consistent with his theory, Rogers gave the most credit for the development of his theory to his clients; he learned about what helped and what didn't directly from them. Rogers's first book, *The Clinical Treatment of the Problem Child* (1939), helped him obtain a professorship in psychology at Ohio State University. He subsequently published *Counseling and Psychotherapy* in 1942, which pioneered the use of audiotape recordings to study therapy and featured his nondirective psychotherapeutic approach.

Struggles with Psychiatry and Psychology

Rogers developed his client-centered approach to psychotherapy in a climate openly hostile to his ideas. He was an extremist, the most dangerous sort of radical, rapidly building a devoted following both within academia and out in the real world. He had to fight the behaviorism of academic psychology as well as the psychoanalysis that ruled the clinical world. However, one of his biggest battles was with psychiatry, a battle that he described as "an all-out war" (Rogers, 1980, p. 55).

During the 1930s and 1940s, psychiatry was adamantly opposed to letting nonphysicians practice psychotherapy. They also fought desperately to keep psychologists from assuming leadership roles within mental health agencies. At Rochester, Rogers battled with psychiatry to maintain his leadership position at the guidance clinic. Later, at the University of Chicago counseling center, he was accused of practicing medicine without a license and launched a "blistering counterattack" to earn psychologists the right to practice psychotherapy (Rogers, 1980, p. 54).

Rogers also had his battles with mainstream academic psychology. His ongoing debate with the noted behaviorist B. F. Skinner is the stuff of legend (see Chapter 7).

Overall, professional counselors, social workers, and educators have been much more open and appreciative of Rogers and his work than psychologists. He summarized his feelings about his impact on psychology by writing:

I believe an accurate statement would be that we have had very little influence on academic psychology, in the lecture hall, the textbook, or the laboratory. There is some passing mention of my thinking, my theories, or my approach to therapy, but, by and large, I think I have been a painfully embarrassing phenomenon to the academic psychologist. I *do not fit.* Increasingly I have come to agree with that assessment. (Rogers, 1980, p. 51)

Rogers has indeed been an unusual academic psychologist. He fraternized with social workers, counselors, and teachers, even publishing in their journals. He rebelled against assigning course grades, allowing students to be their own teachers and evaluators. He participated in encounter groups and expressed disdain for the time-honored traditional class lecture. In the end, however, Rogers earned significant respect from academic psychology. He was elected president of the American Psychological Association in 1946 and received a prestigious award for scientific contribution in psychology in 1956. These honors led Rogers to refer to himself as a "respected gadfly" within psychology (Rogers, 1980, p. 53).

Rogers's work has been honored and extended by his many students, some of whom we discuss in this chapter. Additionally, his daughter, Natalie Rogers, has become a significant force in integrating dance, movement, and the arts with person-centered theory and therapy (Carlson & Kjos, 2000b; N. Rogers, 1996).

The Evolution of Person-Centered Therapy

Overall, Rogers's practice of person-centered theory and principles is divided into four developmental periods.

- *Nondirective counseling.* This period began in the 1940s and was characterized by Rogers's growing aversion to directive, traditional therapy methods. His publication of *Counseling and Psychotherapy* marks this period (Rogers, 1942a).
- *Client-centered therapy.* In the 1950s Rogers changed the name of his approach from *nondirective counseling* to *client-centered therapy.* During this period Rogers published *Client-Centered Therapy* and changed his focus from nondirective technique to an honoring of the client's ability to lead the therapy process (Rogers, 1951).
- *Becoming a person.* During the 1960s, Rogers began to more clearly focus on self-development. His work was strongly associated with the human potential movement. He published *On Becoming a Person* (Rogers, 1961) and moved from academia at the University of Wisconsin to California in 1964. His other major publications during this period included *Freedom to Learn: A View of What Education Might Become* and *Carl Rogers On Encounter Groups,* reflecting his application of person-centered principles to many new situations, including encounter groups and the teacher-student relationship (Rogers, 1969, 1970).
- *Worldwide issues.* In the 1970s and 1980s, Rogers became more concerned with worldwide issues. He founded the Center for the Study of the Person in La Jolla, California, in 1968 and began dedicating much of his work to improving interracial relations and bringing about world peace. He met with Irish Catholics and Protestants, visited South Africa and the Soviet Union, and conducted cross-cultural workshops in Brazil, Dublin, and Hungary. During this period he published *Carl Rogers On Personal Power* (1977) and *A Way of Being* (1980).

As with most popular theories, person-centered principles have moved beyond a focus on the life and achievements of the original founder. Throughout his career, Carl Rogers worked with many students and inspired others who extended his thinking and person-centered theory and practice. These students and followers of Rogers include Eugene Gendlin, who developed an experiential therapy called *focusing* (Gendlin, 1981), and Leslie Greenberg, developer of process-experiential psychotherapy (Greenberg, Rice, & Elliot, 1993). Rogers also had a strong influence on the nondirective play therapy of Virginia Axline, Bernard and Louise Guerney's Relationship Enhancement Therapy (Guerney, 1977; Guerney & Guerney, 1989), and motivational interviewing strategies for persons with addiction problems, developed by William Miller and Stephen Rollnick (Miller & Rollnick, 2002).

Questions for Reflection

Do you think it is possible for a therapist to conduct truly nondirective therapy? Is it really possible to let the client take the lead during therapy hours? As it turns out, close observation of Carl Rogers doing therapy has shown that he did occasionally guide clients toward talking about particular issues. Just by choosing when to say "Uh-huh" or choosing when to nod your head, you will also subtly influence what clients say. As you continue reading this chapter try to fully accept the concept of letting go of your biases and sense of direction, letting the client talk about whatever seems important.

THEORETICAL PRINCIPLES

The person-centered approach includes a theory of personality and a theory of psychotherapy. The theory of personality, as articulated by Rogers, consists of a series of 19 propositions. It is surprisingly complex and difficult to articulate, which may be one of the reasons it is often given little attention. Even Rogers noted that his personality theory "is the most thoroughly ignored of anything I have written" (Rogers, 1980, p. 60).

Theory of Personality

As an overview, we have collapsed Rogers's 19 theoretical propositions into four core features of his personality theory.

Self-Theory

In the tradition of William James, Mary Calkins, and Gordon Allport, the person-centered theory of personality is essentially a self-theory (Bankart, 1997). Rogers postulated that every person exists within an ever-changing world in which he or she is the center. In addition, he believed that the self is not a fixed structure, but a structure in process, capable of both stability and change.

Rogers used the term *organism* to refer to the locus of all psychological experience. The organism is the entire realm of an individual's experience, while the self is the "me" portion of the organism. Rogers's self has both conscious and unconscious components.

The distinction between organism and self leaves open the possibility that an individual's self can be inconsistent with its overall psychological experience. This potential discrepancy is referred to as *incongruence.* In contrast, when the self's experiences and perceptions are consistent with the organism's total experience, there is *congruence.* Congruence between self and organism is highly desirable; it leads to adjustment, maturity, and a fully functioning individual.

Phenomenology and the Valuing of Experience

Rogers summarizes his personality theory by stating, "This theory is basically phenomenological in character and relies heavily upon the concept of self as an explanatory concept" (Rogers, 1951, p. 532). Person-centered theory places a premium on direct personal experience. Although both intellectual/rational thinking and feelings/

emotions are valued and crucial informational sources, experiencing is considered a more direct way of accurately knowing oneself and the world. Bohart states that "[e]xperiencing is the direct, nonverbal sensing of patterns and relationships in the world, between self and world, and within the self. It includes what is often called 'intuitive knowing'" (Bohart, 1995, p. 91).

In part, person-centered therapy is designed to help clients be more open to their vast array of personal or organismic experiences. True learning is best achieved through lived experience wherein the self judges whether a particular action or feeling is self-enhancing or not.

Learning and Growth Potential

Rogers believed strongly in the inherent *actualizing* or *formative* tendency in humans. Some of this viewpoint was derived from his childhood farming and outdoor experiences, as he came to see the potential for many things in nature to grow and evolve toward completeness. Additionally, he attributes this viewpoint to several writers and philosophers, including Kurt Goldstein, Harry Stack Sullivan, and Karen Horney. Rogers believed people have the capacity to learn on a moment-to-moment basis and have a formative tendency to "move toward greater order, complexity and interrelatedness" (Bohart, 1995, p. 89):

> There is one central source of energy in the human organism. This source is a . . . function of the whole system [and] . . . is most simply conceptualized as a tendency toward fulfillment, toward actualization, involving not only the maintenance but also the enhancement of the organism. (Rogers, 1980, p. 123).

Conditions of Worth

In addition to the organism's need to maintain and enhance itself, there are additional, learned needs. The main two learned needs are the need for *positive regard* and the need for *self-regard.*

As babies and toddlers grow in relationship with caretakers, two things begin happening. First, the baby begins developing a greater and greater consciousness of self. Most parents see this behavior clearly in their children at about age two, when the child's favorite words become "mine!" and "no." Second, the growing child develops a strong need for positive regard or approval. This need for positive regard—to be prized and loved—becomes so powerful that the child is almost always looking to caretakers and significant others for acceptance and approval.

Rogers describes the ideal situation:

> If an individual should *experience* only *unconditional positive regard,* then no *conditions of worth* would develop, *self-regard* would be unconditional, the needs for *positive regard* and *self-regard* would never be at variance with *organismic evaluation,* and the individual would continue to be *psychologically adjusted,* and would be fully functioning. (Rogers, 1959, p. 224, italics in original)

Unfortunately, no child's home life is ideal, so although children consistently watch and listen for approval, it does not always come. Consequently, children begin distinguishing between approved and disapproved feelings and actions. They sense and understand the *conditions of worth* present in their lives. Eventually, children internalize their caretakers' appraisals, despite the fact that these appraisals are not completely consistent with their overall organismic experiences, because the alternative is to suffer the pain of negative regard. For example, if a young girl who loves to play roughly and aggressively with other boys and girls consistently experiences disapproval from her parents when she does so, then she is forced to one of the following conclusions: (1) When I play rough I am bad (negative self-regard); (2) my parents don't like me because I play rough (negative regard from others); or (3) I don't like to play rough (denial of a desirable organismic experience). As you can imagine, none of these conclusions value the child's total organismic love of rough-and-tumble play, so she experiences incongruence in one way or another.

Over time, if children continually experience conditions of worth that are incongruous with their organismic values, a conflict or discrepancy may develop between their conscious, introjected values and their unconscious genuine values. Hall and Lindzey (1970) describe this seed of psychopathology:

> If more and more true values of a person are replaced by values taken over or borrowed from others, yet which are perceived as being his own, the self will become a house divided against itself. Such a person will feel tense, uncomfortable, and out of sorts. He will feel as if he does not really know what he is and what he wants. (p. 532)

The more individuals get out of touch with their true selves and desires, the more likely it is that psychopathology will develop. An internal battle for the definition of the self ensues. There may be a growing but vague awareness of discomfort, of something being terribly wrong. This discomfort is especially likely to arise when clients are exposed to organismically desirable feelings, actions, or opportunities.

For example, when the little girl who was negatively judged for having aggressive impulses grows up and has an opportunity for aggressive expression, all sorts of twisted internal events may take place. She may project her desires for anger expression onto others, she may become aggressive and then condemn herself, or she may let loose with her aggression but then deny that she experienced any anger or gratification. Unless her self becomes more congruent with reality, she will continually reinterpret reality to fit whatever self-picture she needs to maintain, no matter how much this violates her true experience and external reality.

Rogers also believed that individuals are capable of perception without awareness. Similar to other writers in the 1940s, he referred to this process as *subception* (McCleary & Lazarus, 1949). Subception occurs when a person unconsciously perceives a threatening object or situation. The object or situation is generally threatening because it represents an inner conflict between real desires and introjected desires. Further, subception is likely to result in visceral reactions (e.g., increased heart rate, high blood pressure, rapid respiration, and other anxiety sensations).

To summarize, Rogers's personality theory emphasizes several concepts. It is a theory of self, of experience, of striving for maintenance and enhancement of the self, and of learned needs for positive regard. It is also a theory of discrepancy, because it is the discrepancy between self and organismic experience, between what the caretakers value and what the organism values, that creates or determines psychopathology.

Theory of Psychopathology

In summarizing Rogers's theory, of psychopathology, Bohart (1995) states:

Psychological problems are neither faulty beliefs or perceptions nor inadequate or inappropriate behavior per se. As humans confront challenges in life they will periodically misperceive, operate on mistaken beliefs, and behave inadequately. Dysfunctionality occurs if we *fail to learn* from feedback and therefore remain stuck in our misperceptions or inadequate behavior. Dysfunctionality is really a failure to learn and change. (p. 94)

The *failure to learn from experience* best characterizes person-centered psychopathology. This is why person-centered therapists work so hard to help clients become more open to learning from new experiences. This is also why rigidity is considered the antithesis of psychological health. Rigidity impairs learning.

Psychopathology occurs when clients hang on to introjected parental conditions of worth instead of modifying their self-concept based on moment-by-moment, day-by-day personal experience. Since every moment is an opportunity for new learning, closing down and avoiding or ignoring these moments is pathological. Similarly, Greenberg and colleagues (Greenberg, Rice, & Elliot, 1993; Paivio & Greenberg, 1995) focus especially on the importance of openness to emotional processing in normal human functioning in their process-experiential psychotherapy approach. When clients are unaware of or unable to access important emotional information, dysfunctional behavior or interpersonal interactions result.

Theory of Psychotherapy

Rogers's theory of psychotherapy is very directly related to the tenets just noted. If psychopathology originally stems from the individual's experience of judgment or invalidation of the self by significant others, then it logically follows that a nonjudgmental atmosphere might facilitate psychological health. This premise is the foundation of Rogers's theory of psychotherapy.

Overall, the success of person-centered therapy hinges on two fundamental factors:

- The therapist must trust the client.
- The therapist must establish a *certain type* of relationship with the client.

Rogers believed that if therapists can trust clients and provide that particular relationship, then clients will be able to begin trusting themselves, consequently experiencing a steady and powerful movement toward greater personal development and psychological health. He wrote, "If I can provide a certain type of relationship, the other person will discover within himself the capacity to use that relationship for growth, and change and personal development will occur" (Rogers, 1961, p. 33).

Rogers (1957) outlined his relationship-based theory of psychotherapy in a landmark article, "The Necessary and Sufficient Conditions of Therapeutic Personality Change." He used his academic-scientific orientation to describe the essentials of effective psychotherapy:

For constructive personality change to occur, it is necessary that these conditions exist and continue over a period of time:

1. Two persons are in psychological contact.
2. The first, whom we shall term the client, is in a state of incongruence, being vulnerable or anxious.

3. The second person, who we shall term the therapist, is congruent or integrated in the relationship.

4. The therapist experiences unconditional positive regard for the client.

5. The therapist experiences an empathic understanding of the client's internal frame of reference and endeavors to communicate this experience to the client.

6. The communication to the client of the therapist's empathic understanding and unconditional positive regard is to a minimal degree achieved. (Rogers, 1957, p. 95)

Questions for Reflection

Rogers's statement about the essential ingredients of psychotherapy is very carefully worded and worth a closer look. What do you suppose he means by *psychological contact*? He seems to imply some sort of connection or intimacy. Does he mean emotional contact? Verbal contact? How does his statement that the client is in a state of incongruence relate to his theoretical principles of the real and ideal self? What is he suggesting when he says the therapist is congruent or integrated in the relationship? Further, what does he mean when he states that the therapist must *experience* unconditional positive regard and empathic understanding toward the client?

This is the essence of Rogers's belief: Person-centered therapy requires that the therapist communicate congruence, unconditional positive regard, and empathic understanding to the client. This may sound simple, but in practice, doing real person-centered therapy is anything but simple.

Because of their central importance in most forms of therapy relationships today, we will define and describe congruence, unconditional positive regard, and accurate empathy—the core conditions of person-centered therapy. Later, when we focus on how to practice person-centered therapy, practical applications of these core conditions are discussed.

Congruence

Congruence is defined as authenticity and is sometimes referred to as transparency as well. The congruent therapist is real, open, and honest. Rogers claimed, "The more that I can be genuine in the relationship, the more helpful it will be" (Rogers, 1961, p. 33). Rogers was very specific about why therapist congruence is essential. He stated, "It is only by providing the genuine reality which is in me, that the other person can successfully seek . . . the reality in him" (1961, p. 33). Counselor congruence provides a sort of grounding or reality so that clients' real selves have something to interact with.

Congruence implies that therapists should acknowledge and express both positive and negative feelings within the context of the therapy relationship. Rogers emphasized

---

Questions for Reflection

From the person-centered viewpoint, is it possible to be congruent in a way that is not therapeutic for the client? Can you come up with some examples of therapist disclosures that you believe would always be destructive? What might Rogers say about this situation?

the importance of expressing less positive feelings when he wrote, "I have found this to be true even when the attitudes I feel are not attitudes with which I am pleased, or attitudes which seem conducive to a good relationship. It seems extremely important to be *real*" (1961, p. 33).

Unconditional Positive Regard

Unconditional positive regard is also referred to as acceptance, respect, or prizing. It involves an emphasis on valuing the client as a separate person or organism whose thoughts, feelings, beliefs, and entire being are openly accepted, without any conditions. Person-centered theory holds that if the therapist can accept clients completely, then clients can begin exploring who they really are and what they really want. By accepting all of who clients are, therapists lead clients to begin accepting themselves.

Rogers describes his discovery of unconditional positive regard as a therapeutic element:

> I find that the more acceptance and liking I feel toward this individual, the more I will be creating a relationship which he can use. By acceptance I mean a warm regard for him as a person of unconditional self-worth—of value no matter what his condition, his behavior, or his feelings. It means a respect and liking for him as a separate person, a willingness for him to possess his own feelings in his own way. (Rogers, 1961, p. 34)

Rogers goes on to say that this acceptance should extend to the moment-to-moment changes and inconsistencies manifested by clients during sessions. He takes a stand against more directive interventions, such as confrontation and interpretation. It matters not whether clients claim to have a change of heart halfway through a session. At one moment they may identify only feelings of love and kindness toward someone, and at the next they may rage about the same person. To the person-centered therapist, both love and rage are important, valid, and equally worthy of attention. By simply listening and reflecting back the depth of both feelings, the therapist allows the clients to accept or modify what's been expressed. Even further, Rogers believed that complete acceptance combined with accurate empathy could lead clients to an expanding awareness or insight into previously unknown parts of the self. Hall and Lindzey (1970) note that

> [e]xplicitly recognized in Rogers' [sic] theory is the concept of an organism that has many experiences of which the person is not aware. Some of these unsymbolized experiences are denied entrance to consciousness because they are inconsistent with the self-image. If this is not repression, in the psychoanalytic sense, then the distinction between it and repression is so slight as to be negligible. The principal difference between Rogers and psychoanalysis lies in Rogers' conviction that repression can be prevented in the first place by the parents giving unconditional positive regard to the child. Or if the damage has been done, it can be corrected later by therapeutic intervention in which the therapist prizes the client. When he is given unconditional positive regard, the client eventually discovers his real self. (pp. 545–546)

Unconditional positive regard is challenging but essential in helping clients begin to accept their complete and uncensored self. It can lead to a willingness to explore very personal feelings and to a greater self-awareness.

Accurate Empathy or Empathic Understanding

Accurate empathy is the therapeutic condition that professionals most directly link to Carl Rogers and person-centered therapy. Rogers was a master at getting deeply into the client's world. Based on what he initially learned from Elizabeth Davis, Rogers became more and more capable of noticing and reflecting his clients' feelings. At times, when listening to audiotapes of his work, he seems to slip completely into the client's world, seeing and experiencing exactly what the client sees and experiences. At such times, he sometimes shifts from using a second-person pronoun ("When he left, you felt betrayed and alone") to using a first-person pronoun ("If I'm getting this right, it's almost like, here I was, wanting to be close, and then he just up and left, and I felt betrayed and alone"). This pronoun shift, apparently designed for the purpose of greater connection and identification with clients, is referred to as *walking within* and is discussed in greater depth later in this chapter.

Of the three core conditions, empathy has been most widely discussed and researched (Bohart & Greenberg, 1997; Duan, Rose, & Kraatz, 2002). Many theorists from many different theoretical orientations acknowledge the importance of empathy to psychotherapy. For example, it has been referred to as a prerequisite for therapy (Freud, 1923), a necessary condition (Bohart & Greenberg, 1997), and an enabling factor (Hamilton, 1995). It is also considered to have a variety of functions. Some say it is the basis for forming a patient-therapist bond (Kohut, 1959), others claim it dissolves client fear and denial (Barrett-Lennard, 1981), and still others promote it as a factor that provides clients with safety (Jenkins, 1997). Even behavioral, cognitive, solution-oriented, and reality therapists acknowledge the importance of empathy to positive therapeutic outcome (Beck, Rush, Shaw, & Emery, 1979; Glasser, 2000; Goldfried & Davison, 1976; Lazarus, 1997; O'Hanlon & Bertolino, 1998).

Empathy is not a simple construct and is considered by many to be multidimensional. Although some theorists have identified four components of empathy, the following three empathy components are commonly discussed in the literature (Buie, 1981; Sommers-Flanagan & Sommers-Flanagan, 2003):

- *Intellectual empathy* involves seeing the world from the client's perspective in a distant or intellectual way.
- *Emotional empathy* occurs when you naturally or spontaneously begin feeling an emotion in response to the client's words or emotional state.
- *Imaginative empathy* involves asking yourself the empathy question: "How would I feel if I were in my client's situation?" (Carkuff, 1987)

Questions for Reflection

Can you think of any drawbacks or problems with having too much empathy? Do you think therapists can get over-involved with clients and lose objectivity? What do you think about the possibility of working with someone who is similar to you? Do you think you might overidentify with the client and then project your feelings onto him or her, rather than sitting back and letting the client tell you about his or her feelings and experiences?

Though empathy is a powerful factor in psychotherapy, from a person-centered perspective, empathic understanding is not a single variable leading to a particular outcome. Instead, it is used in conjuction with the other two therapeutic conditions, congruence and unconditional positive regard. In the following excerpt, Rogers (1961) discusses the importance of experiencing and conveying *both* empathy *and* unconditional positive regard when relating to clients:

Acceptance does not mean much until it involves understanding. It is only as I understand the feelings and thoughts which seem so horrible to you, or so weak, or so sentimental, or so bizarre—it is only as I see them as you see them, and accept them and you, that you feel really free to explore all the hidden nooks and frightening crannies of your inner and often buried experience. (p. 34)

Despite all the research confirming that empathy is crucial to therapy, Natalie Rogers has commented that she believes it is still perhaps the most underestimated condition leading to positive change in therapy. For some reason, people seem to take empathy for granted and don't believe that it's the powerful cure that Carl Rogers believed it to be. She states: "The most powerful thing from the client's point of view is to be deeply heard" (Carlson & Kjos, 2000b).

Natalie Rogers echoes her father's writings from over two decades ago and implies there are at least two levels to empathic listening (Rogers, 1975). In his original theorizing, Rogers talked about a deeper empathic listening that involves "sensing meanings of which the client is scarcely aware" (Rogers, 1980, p. 142). Egan has referred to this deeper empathy as advanced empathy, or hearing "the message behind the message" (Egan, 2002). We will return to this concept later within the context of a case example.

THE PRACTICE OF PERSON-CENTERED THERAPY

Generally speaking, there are two different types of person-centered therapists. The first type is the pure or *traditional* person-centered therapist. The traditional person-centered therapist is highly nondirective, does not use assessment procedures, and does not establish any specific goals for clients. The second type, the *contemporary* person-centered therapist, is a more active and directive therapist but still adheres to an underlying person-centered philosophy. For example, Gendlin's focusing therapy, Greenberg's process-experiential therapy, and Natalie Rogers's integration of art and dance into therapy all represent slight modifications of the completely nondirective person-centered stance (Gendlin, 1981, 1996; L. S. Greenberg, 2002a; N. Rogers, 1996). Each of these approaches sometimes provides clients with suggested directions, uses at least minimal assessment procedures, and may have preplanned goals for clients. This section on the practice of person-centered therapy emphasizes the traditional person-centered approach, but it also includes examples from contemporary, more directive person-centered therapies.

Decades of psychotherapy research confirm that the relationship between therapist and client is a fundamental, active therapeutic factor (Asay & Lambert, 1999; Lambert, 1992). We firmly and absolutely believe that beginning mental health professionals should learn to practice pure person-centered therapy before including directive approaches associated with more modern person-centered therapy. Rogers's concepts, like Adler's, have been integrated into virtually every other contemporary therapeutic approach. Learning to do traditional person-centered therapy is excellent foundational training for becoming any sort of therapist you want to become.

Preparing Yourself to Do Therapy from a Person-Centered Perspective

To practice person-centered therapy, you'll need to work on your attitude! Most graduate students in counseling, social work, and psychology grossly underestimate the power of person-centered therapy. This might be a natural by-product of student impatience. Being eager to prove your worth, you may want to learn powerful behavior change techniques rather than learning how to listen to clients talk on and on about their lives. Similarly, managed mental health care strongly pushes us all toward "doing something" with clients, rather than just spending time respectfully listening to clients telling their personal stories.

Your attitude is central to person-centered work. Your job is to experience and express the three core conditions (or attitudes) of congruence, unconditional positive regard, and empathy. Don't make the mistake of confusing person-centered therapy (which is based on the proper attitude) with active listening (which is based on the proper skills). Active listening is an honorable and valuable skill, but it simply isn't an adequate substitute for adopting a person-centered therapeutic attitude. Active listening occurs when therapists and other mental health and human service professionals use specific techniques and strategies (e.g., eye contact, body posture, vocal qualities, and verbal tracking) to effectively listen (Sommers-Flanagan & Sommers-Flanagan, 2003). In contrast, person-centered therapy occurs when a therapist adopts and communicates a particular *attitude* toward a client. Of course, active listening skills are manifestations of this special attitude, but traditional person-centered therapists begin with the attitude and then display the skills.

Rogers (1961) described ideal person-centered attitudes:

> [T]he therapist has been able to enter into an intensely personal and subjective relationship with this client—relating not as a scientist to an object of study, not as a physician expecting to diagnose and cure,—but as a person to a person. It would mean that the therapist feels this client to be a person of unconditional self-worth; of value no matter what his condition, his behavior or his feelings. It would mean that the therapist is genuine, not hiding behind a defensive façade, but meeting the client with the feelings the therapist is experiencing. It would mean that the therapist is able to let himself go in understanding this client; that no inner barriers keep him from sensing what it feels like to be the client at each moment of the relationship; and that he can convey something of his empathic understanding to the client. It means that the therapist has been comfortable in entering this relationship fully, without knowing cognitively where it will lead, satisfied with providing a climate which will permit the client the utmost freedom to be himself. (pp. 184–185)

Person-centered therapy is clearly much more than using just the right amount of head nodding, eye contact, and verbal tracking with clients. Traditional person-centered therapy requires you to experience and express the proper attitude toward clients (see Putting It in Practice 6.1).

Preparing Your Client for Person-Centered Therapy

Rogers wrote about what it would be like for a client to experience the ideal person-centered therapy experience:

> For the client, this optimal therapy would mean an exploration of increasingly strange and unknown and dangerous feelings in himself [sic], the exploration proving possible only because he is gradually realizing that he is accepted unconditionally. Thus he becomes acquainted with elements of his experience which have in the past been denied to awareness as too threatening, too damaging to the structure of the self. He finds himself experiencing these feelings fully, completely, in the relationship, so that for the moment he *is* his fear, or his anger, or his tenderness, or his strength. And as he lives these widely varied feelings, in all their degrees of intensity, he discovers that he has experienced *himself,* that he *is* all these

feelings. He finds his behavior changing in constructive fashion in accordance with his newly experienced self. He approaches the realization that he no longer needs to fear what experience may hold, but can welcome it freely as a part of his changing and developing self. (Rogers, 1961, p. 185)

Putting It in Practice 6.1

Exploring Yourself as a Potential Person-Centered Therapist

In *On Becoming a Person,* Rogers (1961) posed 10 questions to those of us striving to engage in helping relationships with others (pp. 50–55). His questions, for your reflective responses, are listed below.

1. Can I *be* in some way which will be perceived by the other person as trustworthy, as dependable or consistent in some deep sense?
2. Can I be expressive enough as a person that what I am will be communicated unambiguously?
3. Can I let myself experience positive attitudes toward this other person—attitudes of warmth, caring, liking, interest, respect?
4. Can I be strong enough as a person to be separate from the other?
5. Am I secure enough within myself to permit him his separateness?
6. Can I let myself enter fully into the world of his feelings and personal meanings and see these as he does?
7. [Can] I be acceptant of each facet of this other person which he presents to me? Can I receive him as he is?
8. Can I act with sufficient sensitivity in the relationship that my behavior will not be perceived as a threat?
9. Can I free him [the client] from the threat of external evaluation?
10. Can I meet this other individual as a person who is in process of *becoming,* or will I be bound by his past and by my past?

It can be hard to explain traditional person-centered counseling to clients, especially if they're coming to therapy to obtain some professional advice and guidance. In fact, if clients are coming to counseling specifically to obtain guidance and advice, then it's probably unethical to proceed with traditional person-centered therapy without at least explaining the theory of change inherent in person-centered work. A sample description of person-centered therapy that might be included on a written informed consent form is included in Ethical Highlight 6.1.

Traditional person-centered therapy requires that you set goals for yourself, but not for your client. That doesn't mean you won't talk about goals, but from the person-centered perspective, the client's goals are the client's business.

The Therapist's Opening Statements

From the person-centered perspective, clients take the lead in the therapeutic process. Essentially, the message given to clients by person-centered therapists is "You talk and I'll listen and try my best to understand what you're experiencing in your life and in yourself." As usual, the best model for how to start a person-centered therapy session comes from Carl Rogers:

ETHICAL HIGHLIGHT 6.1

Informed Consent from the Person-Centered Perspective

The following is an excerpt from a sample informed consent form from the person-centered perspective. As you read it, pretend that you're sitting in a therapist's waiting room, about to go in for your first therapy session with a new therapist.

Client Information Form

My name is _____ and I'm looking forward to working with you in counseling. The purpose of this client information form is to provide you with basic information about your rights as a client and to tell you what to expect during typical counseling sessions.

The first thing I should say is that there is, of course, no such thing as a typical counseling session. You are unique, and the problems and challenges you're facing in your life and in yourself are unique. As a counselor, it's my job to help you express what you're thinking, feeling, and experiencing. You should think of me as a sort of companion. I will accompany you as you explore yourself, your problems, your life situation, and all of your personal experiences. Generally, I won't give you expert advice or tell you what decisions you should make in your life. Instead, because the form of counseling I provide is "person-centered counseling" I will help you focus on your own thoughts and feelings. There are two reasons why I don't offer expert advice to clients: First, you're a different person than I am, and therefore I can't and shouldn't tell you what you should do with your life. Your personal decisions are completely up to you, and I respect and trust your ability to make informed decisions about your life. Second, I also don't give out expert advice because I've discovered that clients rarely benefit from such advice. You will benefit from struggling with your own personal decisions and discovering what's right for you.

Even though I won't be giving you expert advice, that doesn't mean I won't be expressing some of my opinions or feelings during counseling. At times, when I have a strong feeling or reaction to you, I will tell you what I'm thinking or feeling as honestly as I can. I will try to openly express thoughts and feelings that I have that might be helpful as you explore what's right for you.

Being in counseling is not always easy, and it's never an emotionally neutral experience. Sometimes in counseling you may feel good because you're getting to express everything you're feeling and thinking while I'm trying my best to listen and understand all of what you're experiencing. At other times you may find yourself talking about and feeling things that are very hard and painful. Counseling is not a neutral experience because it requires you to face yourself more completely than you do in your ordinary life. It's like really scrutinizing yourself in a mirror. Even though the mirror does not judge you, as you look in the mirror you will probably judge yourself. As you explore every square inch of yourself on the inside and on the outside, you may feel both pain and joy.

If you have questions or concerns about counseling, you have the right to ask them at any time. I will do my best to respond to your questions as soon as possible. Overall, my view is that counseling is an excellent opportunity for you to explore, in greater depth, who you are, what you want, and how you want to live. I am delighted to accompany you on your journey of self-discovery.

Anything you'd like to tell me about yourself that will help me to know you better, I'd be very glad to hear. (Rogers, 1963)

Assessment Issues and Procedures

Traditional person-centered therapists do not employ standardized assessment or diagnostic procedures. Rogers wrote that "psychological diagnosis as usually understood is unnecessary for psychotherapy and may be actually be detrimental to the therapeutic process" (Rogers, 1951, p. 220).

Assessment and diagnostic procedures are seen as potentially contributing to client psychopathology. By judging or placing labels or conditions of worth onto the client, we move the locus of experiential reality further from the client as an experiencing organism. Also, when therapists diagnose or classify a client as having a particular mental disorder, it is harder for them to view the client as a unique individual. Typical behavioral and cognitive therapy texts that focus on treatments for specific disorders such as Major Depressive Disorder, Generalized Anxiety Disorder, Obsessive-Compulsive Disorder, or Post-Traumatic Stress disorder miss the whole point of therapy—which is to treat the individual, not the disorder.

Rogers also elaborated on his concerns about an inherent power imbalance linked to assessment and diagnosis:

> [There is an] imbalance of power created when the therapist is in the position to diagnose, the possibility of an unhealthy dependency developing if the therapist plays the role of expert, and the possibility that diagnosing clients places social control of the man in the hands of the few.

Despite the potential drawbacks of diagnosis, at times person-centered therapists may use diagnostic procedures solely for professional communication purposes. For example, because insurance companies require a diagnostic label for reimbursement, a person-centered therapist may provide a diagnosis. Also, when communicating with other professionals, therapists may employ diagnostic terminology, but they take care to treat the client as a unique individual who deserves respect.

Contemporary forms of person-centered therapy sometimes employ assessment procedures. For example, in Greenberg's process-experiential therapy the therapist assesses very specific areas of client functioning (Goldman & Greenberg, 1997; Greenberg et al., 1993). Goldman and Greenberg explain that they use assessment procedures in the service of idiographic case formulation, that assessments are never performed a priori, and that assessment data emerge best within the safety of a person-centered therapy environment. Greenberg's approach to assessment and therapy is described in Chapter 13.

SPECIFIC THERAPY TECHNIQUES

Given the fact that there are no traditional person-centered therapy techniques, this section should be short. However, because traditional person-centered therapy requires that the therapist experience the three core therapeutic conditions, we will discuss their practical application. As suggested in a recent interview with Natalie Rogers, we recommend that you explore the following attitudes in an experiential manner, going deeper than the superficial exposure to person-centered approaches common in the United States (see Putting It in Practice 6.2: An Interview with Natalie Rogers).

===== **Putting It in Practice 6.2** =====

Why is the Person-Centered Approach Undervalued in the United States?
An Interview with Natalie Rogers

In the following edited excerpt from two telephone interviews, Natalie Rogers discusses why person-centered theory and therapy tend to be undervalued or overlooked in the United States.

John Sommers-Flanagan (JSF): Other than the managed-care focus and an emphasis on quick fixes, can you think of any reasons why more American therapists aren't practicing person-centered therapy?

Natalie Rogers (NR): That's a good question. Most psychology students I know only get a chapter or two in the academic world, and they don't really understand in any depth what the person-centered approach is about. And, most importantly, I think they haven't experienced it. They've read [about] it and they've talked about it and they've analyzed it, but my own belief is that it really takes in-depth experiencing of the client-centered approach to know the healing power of empathy and congruence and unconditional positive regard.

JSF: So it's almost like students get more of an intellectual understanding, but you're just not seeing them get the experiential part.

NR: Even the intellectual understanding is very superficial, because they read maybe a chapter and watch the old Gloria film [Rogers, 1965]. The fact that there have been 16 books written on client-centered therapy and a lot of other books now that Carl's passed away and the research that he did is so profound . . . the in-depth research on what actually helps clients go deeper into their feelings and thoughts.

JSF: Right.

NR: You know, [how therapists can help clients go deeper into their feelings and thoughts] is hardly ever mentioned in academia as far as I know.

JSF: And what I remember from our last conversation was that you said you thought it didn't happen in the U.S. at all and maybe a little bit in Europe?

NR: . . . I think it does happen a lot more in Europe, and most particularly in the United Kingdom, Scotland and England. They have really excellent training programs in the client-centered approach, and the books that are coming out are coming out from there. You know in Germany they have a several-year, very extensive training program that's also linked in, I believe, to becoming accredited or licensed as a therapist. Things are going that particular route in Europe, but none of that is here in the States.

JSF: That seems to reflect our own emphasis on the surface or the quick fix as well in that people just really haven't gone deeper and experienced the power of person-centered therapy.

NR: Right. And then again I think the other point is that the ego needs of the therapists [appear] to be strong here. Therapists in this country seem to need to have the attitude that "I have the answers" or at least that "I know more," and it's . . . the old medical model that we still hold onto in this country a lot. The doctor knows what he needs to diagnose and treat, knows what's wrong and that there are ten steps to fix it.

(continued)

=====   **Putting It in Practice 2.1 (continued)**   =====

JSF: Right, which seems to be the opposite of the person-centered therapy of "trust the individual, trust the person."

NR: Not just seems to be, it is the opposite. So, to actually believe, to have faith in the individual, to have faith that each person has the answers within himself or herself if given the proper conditions, and that's a big if. That philosophy takes a great deal of humility on the part of the therapist.

JSF: For us to realize that we don't have all the answers for another person.

NR: Right. I kind of like the gardener metaphor. That I'm the gardener and I help till the soil and I help water the plants and fertilize the plants, and care for them. And I need to understand what the plant needs, what conditions that plant needs for it to actually grow and become its full potential. That's very different. That's what I see as one metaphor for being a therapist. I don't know all the answers, but I'm a person who creates the conditions for the person to grow.

JSF: Kind of the fertile field metaphor. So . . . what would you tell beginning therapists that would help them see the tremendous value of following person-centered principles?

NR: Well, I always ask my students to examine their own beliefs about psychotherapy and about what it is that creates psychological feelings and growth. I think it's a philosophical, spiritual belief system that we're looking at. People are using the words "methods" and "techniques," which always puts me off, because although there certainly are methods that we use, it's much bigger than that. It's a belief system about the connection between mind, body, and emotional spirit. And so I ask them what do they believe creates personal growth, and what have they experienced themselves that creates growth, and we get them to think and talk about their religious experiences, their psychotherapy experiences, their experiences in nature, and their experiences in relationships. I think they're all profound. And then when we focus in on relationships, which is what psychotherapy is about, then I want them to experience . . . from me or my colleagues in hour-long demonstrations what it means to be client-centered. So then they experience it as witnesses and they can experience it as a client.

JSF: So more students need to directly experience, or at least witness, client-centered therapy.

NR: Let me give an example. I was talking to a colleague once who had some of my training and who said that he was now using brief therapy, brief psychotherapy, and I admitted I didn't really know what that was. We decided that he'd have to give me some ideas on what that's like. So I listened to him describe the theory and practice for quite a while and questioned him about it. And as he was describing it, I was wondering, how would I feel if I were in the client's chair and this was what was being done to me. And so then I felt pretty uncomfortable, and thought, "I guess I wouldn't like it." So I asked him, "Have you ever been a client in this kind of brief therapy yourself?" And he said "No," and I thought that was inexcusable. To practice something on somebody else that you haven't experienced in-depth yourself. I think it is inexcusable. So that illustrates in a kind of negative way the point that I wanted to make. You really need to have in-depth experience of that which you are going to have other people do.

Experiencing and Expressing Congruence

Therapist congruence has particular implications for therapy and for the therapist (Sommers-Flanagan & Sommers-Flanagan, 2003). Both beginning and experienced therapists frequently struggle to communicate congruence to clients. Perhaps the most basic question is this: If I am to be congruent, do I need to tell the client about my every thought and feeling?

Of course, the answer to this question is a clear "No." That's not to say that therapists should be too inhibited or cautious about self-disclosing to clients. Instead, the point is that random or unhelpful therapist thoughts, no matter how spontaneous, need not be shared. Despite the openness and transparency of the person-centered therapist, the main aim of this openness is communicating potentially helpful information to clients. Rogers (1958) discusses this issue directly:

> Certainly the aim is not for the therapist to express or talk about his own feelings, but primarily that he should not be deceiving the client as to himself. At times he may need to talk about some of his own feelings (either to the client, or to a colleague or superior) if they are standing in the way. (pp. 133–134)

The message here is that a certain amount of censoring is necessary. In our experience, an excellent way to see how much self-disclosure is appropriate from a person-centered perspective is to listen to Rogers doing therapy or to obtain specific training in person-centered therapy. In his audio and videotaped therapy sessions, Rogers rarely self-disclosed, and when he did it was in the service of furthering the client's therapy work and not in the service of his own ego needs (see Recommended Readings and Resources). He stated:

> Sometimes a feeling "rises up in me" which seems to have no particular relationship to what is going on. Yet I have learned to accept and trust this feeling in my awareness and to try to communicate it to my client. For example, a client is talking to me and I suddenly feel an image of him as a pleading little boy, folding his hands in supplication, saying, "Please let me have this, please let me have this." I have learned that if I can be real in the relationship with him and express this feeling that has occurred in me, it is very likely to strike some deep note in him and to advance our relationship. (Rogers, 1980, p. 15)

When asked if it's ever appropriate for therapists to use techniques in therapy, Carl Rogers said yes, but only when the techniques come up spontaneously—not when they're preplanned.

Questions for Reflection

What do you think about trusting your *self* in the counseling hour? Do you think it's appropriate to base the choice of specific therapist interventions on something as unscientific and ephemeral as intuition? In Chapters 7 and 8 we'll cover therapy approaches that claim to base their therapy interventions on empirical research. Would you rather place your faith in your own judgment and intuition, what the scientific research tells you, or a combination of your intuition and the research?

The Ethics of Congruence

Perhaps the biggest ethical danger from the person-centered perspective is the tendency to use the core condition of congruence in a self-serving manner. On the other hand, in some ways, even writing about this problem seems inconsistent with person-centered theory. After all, aren't we supposed to completely trust ourselves and our clients and thereby activate our formative, self-actualizing tendency? And if we activate that positive growth-potentiating tendency, then there should be no need to worry about using congruence in a self-serving manner—right?

Although that may be true and our caution here about self-serving congruence may be ill advised, to be honest and congruent we should just go right ahead and express our concerns . . . so here goes.

We recommend, and we believe Rogers would concur, that congruence must be tempered by the therapeutic framework. Here's what we mean: In his work, Rogers always kept the client's well-being front and center in his mind. That's why he began calling his therapy approach "client-centered" therapy—because the client's needs are the main concern. Therefore, all therapist behavior must be governed by rules and guidelines designed to protect clients from harm. This means that if you briefly have an inappropriate, unhelpful, or distracting thought pass through your mind while conducting therapy, it's best to simply dismiss it.

For example, imagine you've been working with a very attractive client for about five sessions. Not surprisingly, you begin having brief but compelling sexual thoughts about this client, and sometimes these thoughts occur right in the middle of therapy. What should you do? Should you openly express these thoughts, because doing so is congruent? Consider your own thoughts about what's best to do in this situation before reading on and digesting our opinion.

The answer to whether you should ever or even occasionally disclose your sexual thoughts and fantasies to a client is never a simple one. It always requires inhibition and reflection—if only to make sure that any possible disclosure is clearly in the service of the therapy and not in the service of your own impulse gratification. In most cases, you're best served by keeping your sexual thoughts and feelings to yourself, rather than burdening your client with your sexual interests and desires. Also, as a general rule it's a good idea to be congruent in the sense that you should talk about these feelings with a trusted colleague or supervisor, but not with your client.

There is, of course, an exception to every general rule. In fact, there may be a time when it's appropriate and therapeutic for you to disclose sexual feelings to a client. It might be appropriate to disclose sexual feelings if, by doing so, you provide a constructive information or reality that's likely to benefit your client. For example, if your client's attractiveness is causing him problems in life, disclosing your thoughts might help him begin exploring his sexual signals and how they cause him trouble.

This sort of disclosure also needs to be accompanied by a particular form of ethical reassurance. Because it's always unethical to have sexual relations with clients and in most cases it's unethical to have sexual relations with former clients, you should add to your disclosure a statement similar to the following: "I want you to know I'm sharing these thoughts only because I believe it will be helpful to you in your therapy work. But I should let you know that because we have a therapist-client relationship, I would never act on these feelings."

As a person-centered therapist you need to be congruent with the essential therapy framework and ethical framework. If you cannot disclose something in a way that's highly likely to benefit the client, or if you cannot disclose it in a way that adheres to the usual and customary ethical principles of your profession, then you shouldn't make the disclosure.

Experiencing and Expressing Unconditional Positive Regard

Is it possible for anyone to ever experience unconditional positive regard for another person? After all, everyone is human, and it seems only human to judge others. Nevertheless, completely suspending judgment, accepting clients as they are, is one of Rogers's core therapeutic conditions, so we must face this challenge.

For now, let's assume it's possible, at least intermittently, for therapists to experience unconditional positive regard toward clients. There remains the problem of how to best express positive regard. Should you do it directly? Would it be appropriate to say, "I accept you completely and totally as the person you are" or "I prize and value your total being"?

Practically speaking, most therapists eventually get themselves in trouble if they directly express unconditional positive regard to clients, for two reasons. First, expressing too much positive regard can be overwhelming to clients. Clients may react by wanting to break down therapy boundaries. Upon hearing such positive, loving statements they naturally seek more closeness, perhaps a friendship or romantic relationship. Alternatively, some clients may react to direct expressions of affection with fear. These clients may try to widen the boundary between themselves and the therapist, moving rapidly away from the intimacy the therapist is so overtly offering.

Second, saying "I care about you" or "I won't judge you" can be viewed as phony or unrealistic, especially if the therapist hasn't spent much time with the client and therefore doesn't really know him or her well. These phony or unrealistic statements often backfire because eventually the client begins noticing ways in which the therapist does not care or is judgmental.

If it's inappropriate to directly express unconditional positive regard to clients, then how can therapists communicate this important message? In our interviewing book, we've detailed several ways that therapists can indirectly communicate unconditional positive regard:

> The question remains: How do you express positive regard, acceptance, and respect to clients indirectly? Here are some ideas: First, by keeping appointments, by asking how your clients like to be addressed and then remembering to address them that way, and by listening sensitively and compassionately, you establish a relationship characterized by affection and respect. Second, by allowing clients freedom to discuss themselves in their natural manner, you communicate respect and acceptance. Third, by demonstrating that you hear and remember specific parts of a client's story, you communicate respect. This usually involves using paraphrases, summaries, and sometimes interpretations. Fourth, by responding with compassion or empathy to clients' emotional pain and intellectual conflicts, you express concern and acceptance. . . . Fifth, clinical experience and research both indicate that clients are sensitive to an interviewer's intentions. Thus, by clearly making an effort to accept and respect your clients, you are communicating a message that may be more powerful than any therapy technique. (Sommers-Flanagan & Sommers-Flanagan, 2003, p. 108)

To return to our original question, is it possible for therapists to feel unconditional positive regard toward some or all of their clients? The realistic answer is, probably not. However, our original question is probably the wrong question. Rogers was an optimist and an idealist, but he was not a fool. The more important question is this: Is it possible for therapists to *try* to feel unconditional positive regard toward their clients? We think the answer to this revised question is an enthusiastic "Yes!"

| *Questions for Reflection* |

Trying to experience and express unconditional positive regard for clients is very hard. In the following situations, see if you can imagine yourself experiencing unconditional positive regard as a therapist.

- You're working with a sex offender who is talking about the gratification he gets from fantasizing sexual encounters with prepubertal children.
- You're working with a bruised and battered victim of domestic violence who insists her husband loves her and that she must go back and live with him again—for the fifth time.
- You're working with a pyromaniac. He tells you about how he masturbated after setting a local historical building ablaze.
- You're working with a teen girl. She tells you about her promiscuous sexual exploits and regular use of strangulation or the drug ecstasy to increase her sexual gratification.

From the person-centered perspective, it is absolutely essential for the therapist to experience unconditional positive regard for the client. Do you think you could experience unconditional positive regard in the preceding situations? What might prevent you from feeling unconditional positive regard? Which situations would be easier for you? Which ones would be harder?

One way to experience positive regard in these difficult situations is to begin by finding within yourself positive regard simply for the suffering human being in the room with you—not positive regard for the behaviors, but for the yearnings, longings, losses, and fears the behaviors represent. Every human being was a tiny, helpless baby once. Carl Rogers firmly believed that every human being was born with the potential to develop in positive, loving ways, given the right environment. Some of these human beings didn't have much of a chance. When doing person-centered therapy, you become their next chance, maybe their last chance, to be welcomed, understood, and accepted. Your acceptance may create the conditions necessary for them to change.

Experiencing and Expressing Empathic Understanding

Consistent with the existential-humanistic tradition, person-centered therapists do not believe it's possible for one individual to directly know and experience another individual's feelings (Rogers, 1959). As with unconditional positive regard, what appears important regarding empathy is not that therapists perfectly experience and express empathy, but that they try their best to do so. Rogers described the empathic way of being in 1975:

> The way of being with another person which is termed empathic has several facets. It means entering the private perceptual world of the other and becoming thoroughly at home in it. It involves being sensitive, moment to moment, to the changing felt meanings which flow in this other person, to the fear of rage or tenderness or confusion or whatever, that he/she is experiencing. It means temporarily living in his/her life, moving about in it delicately without making judgments, sensing meanings of which he/she is scarcely aware, but not trying to uncover feelings of which the person is totally unaware, since this would be too threatening. (Rogers, 1975, p. 4)

Entering and Becoming at Home in the Client's Private Perceptual World

Entering the client's private world requires preparation. You need to begin your encounter with your client deeply valuing an understanding of the client's perspective. You need to be open to feeling what the client feels and willing to ask the empathy question "How would I feel if I were _____ and saying these things?" (Carkuff, 1987, p. 100). Technically, the procedures employed to enter the client's world include reflection of feelings, empathic exploration, and clarification.

Being Sensitive from Moment to Moment with the Client's Changing Meanings and Emotions

Moment-to-moment sensitivity requires focused attention to your client's constantly changing way of being. In his emotion-focused or process-experiential person-centered treatment approach Greenberg and his colleagues recommend focusing on meaning and poignancy associated with the client's verbalizations (Goldman & Greenberg, 1997). For example, they recommend that as the client offers a narrative, the therapist keep his or her attention focused by continually asking internal questions such as "What is the core meaning or message that she or he is communicating?" or "What is most alive?" or "What is being felt?" (p. 408). Avoid getting stuck focusing on what the client said previously, because your focus is on the new information or the new emotion that is occurring in the now.

Temporarily Living, and Moving About Delicately, in the Client's Life

To reside in another person's life is serious business. Notice that Rogers says to do this *temporarily.* This is a subtle warning of the dangers of diving too deeply into the world of another. In 1967, Rogers wrote about an experience in which he became too involved with a client and lost his way:

> I stubbornly felt that I should be able to help her and permitted the contacts to continue long after they had ceased to be therapeutic, and involved only suffering for me. I recognized that many of her insights were sounder than mine, and this destroyed my confidence in myself, and I somehow gave up my self in the relationship. (Rogers, 1967a, p. 367)

Ideally, your goal is to have one foot inside the world of the client and one foot firmly planted in your own world, letting yourself flow into the client's being for periods of time without losing a more objective perspective on what's happening in the therapy session. As noted in Chapter 5, Martin Buber, the Jewish theologian, referred to this sort of relationship experience as an I-Thou relationship, and he emphasized that it's impossible to constantly maintain such a relationship. For a transcript of a 1957 dialogue between Rogers and Buber, see Kirschenbaum and Henderson (1989).

Sensing Deep Meanings, but not Uncovering Feelings That Are Too Far out of Awareness

Rogers sometimes talked about working on the edge of his clients' consciousness. In this regard his approach is consistent with psychoanalytic practice. Recall from Chapter 2 that psychoanalytically oriented therapists emphasize making interpretations of unconscious material at *just the right time* when an insight is about to break through. Similarly, Rogers emphasizes the importance of respecting the client's pace and comfort. As a person-centered therapist moving about gently within your client's world, if you have an impulse to tell a client about something completely outside of his or her awareness, it's probably best to hold your tongue. Even though there is room for intuitive input, your main job is to follow the client's lead, not to forge your own path.

APPLICATION: CASE EXAMPLE

In the following case example, Carl Rogers is conducting a single-session demonstration with a hospitalized young woman, known here as Mrs. P. S. (Rogers, 1963). This is a slightly abridged version of the session, with ellipsis following responses where portions were deleted. Our comments are in brackets.

Carl Rogers (CR): What'd I like is for you to tell me anything you're willing to tell me about yourself and your situation and how you feel about yourself and your situation. Or I guess another way of putting it is, anything you're willing to tell me that would help me to know you better, I'd be very glad to hear. [This is a vintage Rogers opening. His goal is clear: He wants to hear whatever she's willing to say and to get to know *her* better.]

PS: Where do you want me to start?

CR: Where ever you would like to. [Again, this is a classic person-centered response to the client's hesitation over where to begin. A fundamental component of person-centered therapy is to follow the client's lead.

PS: Well, I'll start with my childhood. When I was, uh, when I was a little girl, I had this cross eye since I was about 7 years old. And, I mean kids poked fun of me and as the years got longer and I start going into the higher grades. I mean I never had no boyfriends or anything I mean I had girlfriends but after the girls started going around with the boys I mean and the boys would tell them, don't go around with me or something like that. And actually I ended up without any girlfriends at all. And around my neighborhood there was no girls my age so I was counting on the school and they sort of let me down. And I felt just like I, I wasn't wanted.

CR: So you sort of wound up with no friends at all and am I getting it right, that you feel that was due, basically, due to your eye condition, or. . . . [As described by Wickman and Campbell (2003), Rogers commonly provided clients with "invitations for repair" (p. 179). These invitations give clients an opportunity to correct Rogers, in case his perceptions of the client's inner experience was inaccurate.]

PS: Well, probably the looks, my looks too. . . . But in my last year school I made friends with this one girl, but she wasn't a very nice girl, but I mean when she was with me she was nice. . . . And my husband, he didn't want me to go around with her because he didn't like her and like most my friends that I did have when I was a child, when I lived on the eastside kids from around the house, but that's when I was real young and they grew up and they all moved away. . . . He won't let see them or anything.

CR: So you feel, here's this one girl whom you like, even if she doesn't have a very good reputation, and you're friends from way back, but that your husband won't let you associate with them. . . . [This is a straightforward summary or paraphrase.]

PS: Yes. Like myself. I gotta, I gotta stay in the house all day long and with him not wanting me to go with my friends and he don't want me to go alone any place. I mean actually, he's the one that would take me out. I would go out with him. And then if we went dancing or any place like that or anything, he, he dance with other girls and he wouldn't even dance with me. So, then I dance with other guys too, if that's . . . two can play the game . . .

CR: If he's not really gonna pay much attention to you, then okay, you can do that too.

PS: Yeah. What's good for the gander is good for the goose.

CR: Uh huh. Uh huh.

PS: That's what I always say (5 seconds of silence). And then my home situation now, is um, well that's part of it, my husband won't let me go anyplace. But then there's my mother too. My husband's brother's staying downstairs with my mother and I just don't, I don't like the idea of it. I mean, my mother isn't married to him, and yet he acts like he's a father to my two brothers and we're living upstairs in my mother's place and even though I'm married, he tries to boss me around.

CR: So that's another thing you don't like, you don't quite like the situation your mother is in and you don't like him, because he acts like he's married to her. . . . [The client is focusing repeatedly on what she *doesn't* like, and Rogers is staying right with her.]

PS: No, she's only living on 20 dollars a month for food already and with having to have him stay there and eat and, my God, they practically eat beans all the time, it wouldn't be that bad if he wasn't there. Gotta be buying cigarettes and all that stuff. They could be saving that money for food. Actually with the little money she gets he's actually living off her.

CR: Sounds like you feel pretty resentful of that. [This is Rogers's first response that can be categorized as a "reflection of feeling."]

PS: Yes, well, I mean I don't care for it. I mean everybody's up against it, like my mother's mother.

CR: I'm sorry. I didn't get that.

PS: My mother's mother don't like it either.

CR: I see, um hmm.

PS: She don't like to have her daughter talked about by my mother's brothers and sisters.

CR: Uh huh. Uh huh. So I guess you're saying, "I'm not the only one that feels that way about her and her situation." [Notice that Rogers uses a first-person quotation—for the first time in this session—to deepen his empathic connection with this client. This procedure is sometimes referred to as "walking within." He also steers clear of his client's muddled verbal output, commenting only on the main message in the communication.]

PS: Yes. I mean, I'm not the only one, but if anybody tells her anything, she's so bull-headed and knot-headed that she, she just, if somebody tells her to do something or get away from him or something, she just stay with him. I mean she just wants to do things her own self. But, even though I'm married, she wants to try to run my life. I mean. I hate the idea of everybody telling me what to do. Even my husband, he'll tell me what to do. Even though I'm young and I'm married, I mean I'm a human being and I like to run my life myself. I mean I don't want to feel like I'm still in a baby buggy or something like that.

CR: You feel that your mother and your husband and everybody tries to run your life.

PS: Yes. That's why I feel, I was old enough to bear a baby and that's surely a lot of pain. But yet they won't let me make up my mind for myself.

CR: Here I was old enough to have a child and yet nobody thinks I can make my decisions or run my own life. Is that what you're saying? [Here he's both walking within and using an invitation for repair.]

PS: Yes. I mean like, this is when my husband and I went to California, with our little boy. . . . But, being back in the whole situation it's just not good. His mother is the kind of person who would talk behind her own brother's back. Uh, I mean her own son's. My husband has six brothers and one sister. And I mean she'll talk to one of her sons about one of her other sons. I mean, she's that kind of person. And although she don't come right out and tell me to my face that she don't like me, I know by the way she's talking about the other people behind their backs, that she's talking about me too.

CR: You feel she's just a gossip and you feel she doesn't like you.

PS: Oh, I know she don't like me (laughs).

CR: No doubt about that. [Rogers just goes right along with the client's correction of his response to her.]

PS: Oh, no doubt (11 seconds of silence). Uh, mostly that's, uh, that's the point. And my little girl she passed away a couple of months ago. And my mother did another thing. See, when my little girl was born, I asked my mother, I said, um, "How come her leg, her one leg, is turned a little bit?" and she said, "All babies are like that when they're small." She said, "You can't expect them to get up and walk right away," and I said, "I know that." And she said, "Don't worry about it" and so I didn't worry about it and then after my little girl passed away, my mother told me that my daughter was cripple. She kept it from me again. She keeps things from me like that. And, and in a way I felt responsible for my little girl's death. You know, she would be sitting down and um, well, I'd sit her up in the davenport, in the corner and I'd put her little legs in, but if I would have known she was cripple, I surely wouldn't do that. [This is a key interaction. Following Rogers's validation of her correction of his paraphrase, the client wanders into a silence and Rogers just allows the silence to be. Then the woman moves right into an emotionally significant issue. In essence, his responses to her have allowed her to go deeper.]

CR: That really concerns you that that was kept from you and it concerns you that maybe you didn't deal with her right, not, not knowing that she was crippled. . . .

PS: She let me down. I mean, my mother she, I always took the blame home. My mother always, always liked my oldest brother. I always took the blame home, whether I did something wrong or not. And I got along a lot better with my father. But, then my father passed away and then, and well actually, I mean I took most, I took all the blame I wanna say, than my brother did and now my youngest brother that's home, he's going through the same darn thing I am. He's taking all the blame home.

CR: You feel when you were home, whatever went wrong, you took the blame for it, within yourself.

PS: No, uh, my brother would say that I did this and that.

CR: I see. That's what I wasn't quite clear about, you were blamed for everything.

PS: Yeah.

CR: Whether you had done it or not. Is that . . . ?

PS: Yes I was.

CR: It isn't so much you felt you were to blame, but, but, others blamed you.

PS: I mean my brother actually got away with everything.

CR: I guess you feel that was sort of true with everybody except your father. Is that . . . That things went somewhat better between you and your father. [At this point Rogers leads the client a bit–down the track toward talking about her father.]

PS: Yes. Yes they did. I mean, I could go and he'd take me, well, my mother and my father we used to go out a lot of times, but they went sort of late you know and by that time I'd be asleep and I used to fool 'em all the times because I knew they were gonna stop at the hamburger shop. And I'd make believe I was asleep and when they'd stop and I'd say, "Oh, I'm awake, I'm awake, you gotta get me one too." And I mean, I used to have a lotta fun when I used to go out with my mother and father and mostly when I went away with my father I used to help him pile wood and I mean we had a lotta fun the neighborhood kids would come over, boys and girls and they'd help my father pile up the wood and help him cut it with a saw and after that, we'd all pile in the car and went down got an ice cream cone.

CR: Those are really kind of pleasant memories.

PS: Uh hmm.

CR: (10 seconds of silence) I don't know, but it looks as though, thinking about those things, make you feel a little bit weepy, or am I wrong? [Once again, Rogers lets the silence do its work and then tentatively comments on the client's affect.]

PS: A little bit.

CR: A little bit.

PS: I can remember, I don't exactly know how it went, but I know I was pretty young, but um, we went over by, my father, yes his brother, we went over by, it was I and David, my oldest brother. Anyway, the two guys, they decided to go out and then my mother and my aunt and my brother were there and two children, gee, I don't know if I'm getting this quite clearly. [Again, Rogers has created an atmosphere—despite the presence of cumbersome 1960s audiotaping equipment—that allows the client to continue going deeper into an early childhood memory.]

CR: It's hard to remember.

PS: But, anyhow, my father didn't come back till real late. And my mother was mad at him. And I don't know, but before I knew it, I was, I was, going with my father and it was his car and it was a stormy night. Yeah, I mean it scared the wits out of me. But my mother somehow got home ahead, ahead of us. My uncle took her home. But on that stormy night, it seemed like, I don't know, it seemed so spooky out just like I was scared we were gonna get in a crash or something. Cause daddy was drinking a little bit. And while he was driving he had his arm around me. I was standing up on the seat. I don't even know how old I was, I mean, I just.

CR: That's something that's so far back it's kind of vague and yet certain parts of it evidently are very vivid to you.

PS: Yes.

CR: You can remember his being . . . not coming back and remember your mother being angry, but mostly you can remember this spooky, wild ride with him through the storm and your fear that you might crash up and his holding you. His arm around you.

PS: Yes, even, even after a while too, when we would go out for a ride, if it would be at night time, I would be scared to ride. I would be afraid we were going over a cliff or something. I always thought we were going to a dead end and we'd go flying over the cliff.

CR: Am I getting this right, that even after that, it seemed to you as though you and your father were headed for a cliff?

PS: Yes, I mean, everybody was with us, but I mean I would sort of shut my eyes when I was driving because I was scared to look out the window cause I think well, we're going over a cliff. Or I'd be thinking that we were going to come to one and dad's not going to be able to stop or something.

CR: Just felt he isn't going to be able to manage it, he's going to go over the edge.

PS: Gee, that's funny, I never said these things before to the other doctors (16 seconds of silence). [The patient's comment at this juncture reflects the fact that Rogers is, indeed, different than the other doctors. As Natalie Rogers has put it, her father's approach uses a different language and is revolutionary (N. Rogers, May, 2003, personal communication). Thus far, he has shown deep interest in the client as a person, while showing absolutely no interest in the client's symptoms. One can certainly see why this client said things to Rogers that she'd never said to any other doctors.]

As the session continued, the client spoke about many deeply personal and deeply powerful issues. For example, she talks about wanting to be attractive to other men (despite being married); about her fear that, if she let some of her aggressive feelings out, she might accidently kill someone; and about dreams of being consumed by a dark cloud holding her down. She also discloses that her father hit her. Finally, toward the end she admits to having previously wanted pity from others, but states that she wants to start making her own decisions and no longer wants the pity from others. In one of her final apt references to her self-development, she states: "It's just like everyone's got a part of me . . . like one's got one leg the one's got one arm (laughs), just like they all got part of me and I ain't got none of myself."

If you have interest in person-centered therapy, we strongly recommend that you read and listen to Rogers on video or audiotape. At the end of this chapter, a resource list compiled by Natalie Rogers, the executor of his work, is included.

Additional Person-Centered Therapy Approaches and Techniques

To this point we've focused primarily on first-generation or traditional person-centered therapy principles and practice. As suggested earlier, Rogers's theory and approach have been integrated into the practice of most other therapies. However, in addition, his narrow person-centered approach to therapy has been expanded and extended. A specific second-generation person-centered approach, motivational interviewing, is outlined and discussed next. An additional derivative of person-centered therapy, process-experiential psychotherapy, due to its integrative nature, is described in Chapter 13.

Motivational Interviewing

Motivational interviewing was developed by William R. Miller. In his work with problem drinkers, Miller discovered to his surprise that structured behavioral treatments were no more effective than an encouragement-based control group. However, therapist empathy ratings significantly predicted positive outcomes at 6 months ($r = .82$), 12 months ($r = .71$) and 2 years ($r = .51$; W. R. Miller, 1978; W. R. Miller & Taylor, 1980). Consequently, he concluded that reflective listening and empathy were crucial in producing positive treatment effects with problem drinkers, and thus began his development of motivational interviewing.

Motivational interviewing (MI) uses person-centered therapy constructs as its foundation. However, similar to process-experiential therapy, MI builds on its person-centered foundation by adding more focused therapeutic targets and more specific client goals. Rollnick and Miller (1995) define MI as "a directive, client-centered counseling style for eliciting behavior change by helping clients to explore and resolve ambivalence" (p. 326).

Miller and Rollnick note that Rogers was collaborative, caring, and supportive—but that he was not nondirective (W. R. Miller & Rollnick, 1998). Instead of being nondirective, they note, Rogers gently guided clients to places where they were most confused, in pain, or agitated and then helped them to stay in that place and work through it. Their four central principles of MI flow from their conceptualization of Rogers's approach (W. R. Miller & Rollnick, 2002). According to these principles, it is the therapist's job to

- Use reflective listening skills to *express empathy* for the client's message and genuine caring for the client
- Notice and develop the theme of discrepancy between the client's deep values and current behavior
- Meet client resistance with reflection rather than confrontation (Miller and Rollnick refer to this as "rolling with resistance")
- Enhance client self-efficacy by focusing on optimism, confidence that change is possible, and small interventions that are likely to be successful

The most important and elegant discovery of Miller and Rollnick is that the old-school style of confronting substance-using clients actually *produces* resistance to change. Therefore, when resistance about substance use rises up in clients it should be greeted with person-centered attitudes and interventions that permit clients to claim their own ambivalence about abusing substances.

Motivational interviewing is both a set of techniques and a person-centered philosophy or style. The philosophical MI perspective emphasizes that motivation for change is not something the interviewer imposes on clients. It must be elicited, gently and with careful timing. Additionally, the ambivalence experienced and expressed by clients belong to clients. It is not the counselor's job to resolve it, but rather to reflect it and join with client as they explore and resolve their ambivalence. Motivational interviewers do not use direct persuasion. They come alongside, rather than confronting head-on.

Nondirective (Person-Centered) Play Therapy

In the 1960s, some of Rogers's students began applying his person-centered principles to the treatment of children. The result was a treatment approach without interpretation, without behavior modification, and without structure or direction from the therapist. Consistent with person-centered theory, nondirective play therapy was designed to facilitate client trust in himself or herself through the core relationship conditions of congruence, unconditional positive regard, and empathic understanding. For an excellent sample of the practice and power of person-centered play therapy, we recommend *Dibs in Search of Self* by Virginia Axline (1964).

In the following excerpt, Dibs, a 5-year-old boy, is deeply involved in sandplay when he spontaneously initiates a discussion with Axline about a card that sits outside the therapy office. One side of the card reads *"Therapy,"* and the other side displays the directive *"Do Not Disturb."* There is, perhaps, no better description of nondirective play therapy than that offered up by Dibs:

> Suddenly, he pulled his feet out of the sand, stood up, jumped out of the sandbox, and opened the playroom door. He reached up, took the card out of the holder, came back into the room, closed the door, thrust the card at me.
>
> "What is therapy?" he asked me.
>
> I was astonished. "Therapy?" I said. "Well, let me think for a minute." Why had he asked this question, I wondered. What explanation would make a sensible reply?
>
> "I would say that it means a chance to come here and play and talk just about any way you want to," I said. "It's a time when you can be the way you want to be. A time you can use anyway you want to use it. A time when you can be *you.*" That was the best explanation I could come up with then. He took the card out of my hand. He turned it to the other side.
>
> "I know what this means," he said. 'Do not disturb' means everybody please let them alone. Don't bother them. Don't go in. Don't knock on the door, either. Just let them both be. This side means *they are being.* And this side says *you let them both be*! Like that?"
>
> "Yes. Like that." (pp. 120–121)

If you're interested in applying person-centered principles to the practice of play therapy, many resources are available. Axline's *Play Therapy* is a good place to start. Additionally, Bernie and Louise Guerney and Barry Ginsberg have also applied person-centered theory to play therapy, couples therapy, and family therapy through what they refer to as *filial therapy* (L. Guerney, 2001). A variety of filial therapy resources are listed at the end of this chapter.

Finally, to help you focus on how to be person-centered with a child, we offer a summary of Axline's guidelines for play therapy. The therapist

- Develops a warm and friendly relationship with the child
- Accepts the child as she or he is, without judgment
- Establishes a feeling of permission in the relationship so that the child is free to express his or her feelings completely
- Recognizes the feelings the child is expressing and reflects these feelings back in such a manner that the child gains insight into his or her behavior
- Maintains a deep respect for the child's ability to solve problems and gives the child the opportunity to do so; the responsibility to make choices and to institute change is the child's
- Does not direct the child's actions or conversations in any manner; the child leads the way, the therapist follows
- Does not hurry the therapy; it is a gradual process and must be recognized as such by the therapist
- Only establishes limitations necessary to anchor the therapy to the world of reality and to make the child aware of his or her responsibility in the relationship

In contrast to Freud's rule of free association, "Say whatever comes to mind," the nondirective play therapist enacts the person-centered play therapy rule: "Play whatever comes to mind."

THERAPY OUTCOMES RESEARCH

Early in his life, Rogers learned to be cautious and conservative. In what turned out to be a great boon for all of us, as an adult, Rogers learned to trust himself and to face risks, not the least of which was the risk of exposing himself and his particular form of therapy to empirical scrutiny.

As the first modern scientist-practitioner, Rogers took the unusual step of empirically evaluating a phemonenological approach to psychotherapy. As you have seen in previous chapters (e.g., Chapter 5) and as you will see in coming chapters (e.g., Chapter 9), existential-phenomenological therapies generally avoid systematic empirical evaluation. Thanks to the efforts of Rogers and his followers, person-centered therapy has been empirically evaluated in many research studies.

One of Rogers's early and most ambitious studies on client-centered therapy was with hospitalized schizophrenics in Wisconsin. This study examined client-centered relationship variables in the treatment of 16 hospitalized schizophrenics. Rogers reported an interesting and unexpected finding, that the psychotic patients themselves and a group of naive college students had a more realistic perception of the quality of the therapy relationship than the therapists. He noted:

> It is a sobering finding that our therapists—competent and conscientious as they were—had over-optimistic and, in some cases, seriously invalid perceptions of the relationships in which they were involved. The patient, for all his psychosis, or the bright young college student with no knowledge of therapy, turned out to have more useful (and probably more accurate) perceptions of the relationship. (Rogers, 1967b, p. 92)

Overall, there was generally little progress reported in this treatment study. However, the finding that therapists have a skewed or biased view of the therapy relationship has remained an important contribution to psychotherapy process and outcome research. Although the therapy relationship is estimated as accounting for about 30% of positive outcomes, to be predictive of positive outcome an appraisal of the relationship must be based on ratings by the client, rather than ratings by the therapist. These results suggest that the therapist is generally not a good judge of how helpful he or she is experienced to be *by the client.* It also suggests the likelihood of method variance in psychotherapy outcome research. That is, measurements completed by clients (relationship ratings and outcomes ratings) are more likely to correlate positively with each other than they are to correlate positively with measurements completed by another person (therapist or neutral observer).

More recent research on the effectiveness of person-centered therapy has yielded consistently positive, but generally unremarkable, results. First, person-centered therapy is consistently more effective than no treatment. Second, it is marginally more effective than placebo treatment. Third, it is generally somewhat less effective than more structured cognitive and behavioral treatments. For example, in their large meta-analysis, Smith and Glass reported that client-centered therapy had an average effect size of .63, a moderate-sized effect (Smith & Glass, 1977; Smith et al., 1980). In contrast, behavioral and cognitive therapies obtained effect sizes ranging from .73 to 1.13 (Smith & Glass, 1977; Smith et al., 1980).

Other reviews have results that vary slightly, probably based on the allegiance effect more than anything else. For example, in their review of client-centered treatment versus no treatment, experiential therapists and researchers Greenberg, Elliot, and Lietaer reported an average effect size of .95 for client-centered therapy (Greenberg et al., 1994). In contrast, behaviorally oriented researchers who replicated the Smith and Glass meta-analysis with greater rigor reported effect sizes for behavioral therapies with adults in the range from .85 to 1.52 (Shapiro & Shapiro, 1982). Systematic reviews of the relative effectiveness of person-centered and cognitive and behavioral treatments for children have generally shown that person-centered therapy is more effective than no treatment or placebo treatment, but less effective than the more structured therapies (Weisz, Weiss, Alicke, & Klotz, 1987; Weisz, Weiss, Han, Granger, & Morton, 1995).

Given the empirical facts, most professionals, academics, and students conclude that cognitive and behavioral treatments are more scientifically valid than person-centered therapy. Although this may well be the case, there is, of course, another perspective. It may be that, when measured using scientifically validated clinical outcome instruments, person-centered therapy is destined to appear less effective than therapies specifically designed to change behavior, alleviate symptoms, and modify cognitions. In fact, it would be shocking to discover the opposite—that a phenomenologically oriented treatment actually outperforms structured educational treatments on specific and artificially-constructed measures of progress. As the existentialists would probably argue, it is virtually impossible for empirical research to quantify and measure people's capacity to love, accept, and prize themselves—which is the sort of outcome toward which person-centered therapy strives.

Before leaving this section on empirical evaluations of person-centered therapy, we should comment on the empirical status of Rogers's bold claim, made in 1957, that a special relationship between therapist and client is all that is *necessary* and *sufficient* for positive behavior change to occur. Most researchers have disproven, at least to their satisfaction, Rogers's claims that the relationship is necessary and sufficient. For example, Parloff, Waskow, and Wolfe (1978) state that

> the evidence for the therapeutic conditions hypothesis [as necessary and sufficient] is not persuasive. The associations found are modest and suggest that a more complex association exists between outcome and therapist skills than originally hypothesized.

In the phrasing of their statement, Parloff and associates demonstrate a lack of understanding of person-centered therapy, making the common mistake of evaluating Rogers's therapeutic conditions as "therapist skills" rather than as therapist attitudes. However, even when misconstrued as skills, Rogers's core conditions are empirically robust, though perhaps not as robust as he originally claimed. Overall, even person-centered therapists now acknowledge that Rogers's conditions, as far as they can be operationalized and measured, are not necessary and sufficient, but are best described as facilitative (Raskin, 1992).

Always the scientist-practitioner, Rogers continued to campaign for empirical research until the very end of his life. In one of his very last publications, he wrote:

> There is only one way in which a person-centered approach can avoid becoming narrow, dogmatic, and restrictive. That is through studies—simultaneously hardheaded and ten-

My PCA Experience in Japan
By Kazuo Yamashita

The following excerpt is from a native Japanese social worker. He is a member of the institute that Carl Rogers founded in La Jolla, California, the Center for the Study of the Person. He writes to share his experiences with the person-centered approach (PCA) in Japan.

When I was a student, I encountered the person-centered approach. This was in 1973. I took a class from Professor Gisho Saiko, who tried to teach us in a learner-centered way. At first he explained the reason why he chose these textbooks and his idea about this class. And then he said to students, "Whether you use these books or do not use these books, it is your choice. You can do it any way you want in this class." He put the books on the desk and never started to lecture. I was very surprised and bewildered. However, I liked teacher's atmosphere. He smiled; his eyes were so kind. I felt warmth from him and psychological safety. I asked him, "Surely can I do as I want?" He said, "Yes." I was so glad. I started to express my thoughts and feeling. It was amazing. He listened to my feelings and thoughts carefully and understood me correctly. Something happened in myself. My classmates and I had a great experience in this class. We learned a very important sense of ourselves and a self-motivated attitude toward our lives. It was the starting point of my PCA experience. I attended lots of workshops and learned about PCA and myself in Japan.

After I graduated from the university, I worked at a nursing home as a social worker. I tried to treat residents the way I had learned from PCA. I listened to their feelings carefully, understood them, and confirmed them. It was wonderful! I felt residents' satisfaction, their smiles, their liking. I was also satisfied. It was so lovely. I started a community meeting for the residents: Once a month we gathered and expressed anything we wanted to express. At first the residents were bewildered. But gradually they got used to it and shared among themselves, discussed their lives at home, and planned their recreations. Then I moved my workplace to a residential child care facility (orphanage). I treated the children in same way, and it worked well. However, in here I needed to set my limits toward the children. Thomas Gordon's (1975) skill "I message" (Parent Effectiveness Training, P.E.T.) helped me very much.

Through both of my experiences, I can say PCA works very well with Japanese people who have a relationship with me. But I had a big problem with my colleagues. Many of my colleagues did not know PCA well, so my approach—influenced by PCA—was very different from theirs. Their way is the authoritarian way; mine is the nonauthoritarian way. It was hard for me to harmonize. But I do not think this is a cultural issue.

In the 1960s Rogers's approach came to Japan. In my perception we learned it very enthusiastically. It remained in the 1970s, too. I encountered it in 1973, so I remember the enthusiasm. It tasted like a new democratic way, which we wanted, and had some similarity to Eastern culture. And Rogers's approach has been a concrete one. In my perception the initial enthusiasm has diminished and PCA is not fresh in Japan. In one way I could say it infiltrated Japanese society: There are almost no psychotherapists who do not know PCA. On the other hand, I could say this infiltration is superficial. Many other approaches have come to Japan, and Japanese people have been attracted by these approaches. However, I can say there are people who like PCA and have kept this approach in their life (including me). For those people, PCA is not a strange method, and it works with clients. It is interesting. (Yamashita, March, 2003, personal communication).

der minded—which open new vistas, bring new insights, challenge our hypotheses, enrich our theory, expand our knowledge, and involve us more deeply in an understanding of the phenomena of human change. (Rogers, 1986, pp. 258–259)

MULTICULTURAL PERSPECTIVES

In some ways person-centered therapy seems, at its core, to be a culturally sensitive therapy. After all, it is the quintessential individually sensitive treatment. This sensitivity and unconditional positive regard for individuals and their cultural beliefs and backgrounds have made person-centered therapy internationally popular. Although its use is on the decline in the United States, person-centered approaches remain popular in Japan, South Africa, South America, and in a number of European countries and the United Kingdom.

Although potentially culturally sensitive, person-centered therapy hasn't fared quite so well when it comes to being preferred by all cultures. In fact, several research studies show that African Americans, American Indians, Asian Americans, and Hispanic Americans tend to prefer active, directive, and advice-oriented counselors over passive, nondirective, and feeling-oriented counselors (Atkinson & Lowe, 1995).

In one study, Asian American students rated active and directive counselors as more credible and more approachable than nondirective counselors (Atkinson, Maruyama, & Matsui, 1978). This may be because "Asian American clients . . . value restraint of strong feelings and believe that intimate revelations are to be shared only with close friends" (D. W. Sue & D. Sue, 2003, p. 144).

Another potential limitation with regard to using person-centered approaches with diverse populations is the possibility that individuals from collectivist cultures might feel very uncomfortable with a strong emphasis on the individual and individual needs or feelings. Rogers's orientation toward self-development (e.g., helping clients *become persons*) requires paying too much attention to clients' internal locus of control. For many nonwestern cultures, paying too much attention to the self is considered inappropriate.

Person-centered approaches may be too indirect for some cultures, but in some cases they may actually be too direct. For example, if counselors are too congruent they may openly express thoughts and feeling more overtly and directly than is acceptable within some cultures. If so, instead of serving as a facilitative condition, the counselor's congruence might increase the client's anxiety and thereby impair the therapy process.

To this point, we've primarily described the limitations of person-centered therapy as an approach to counseling clients from diverse cultures. Of course, as always, there is an alternative view. Much of what Rogers emphasized in his approach was (and is) antithetical to our fast-paced, quick-fix American society. If you think for a moment about the current popularity of very brief therapy, solution-oriented techniques, managed care, and quick-fix psychopharmacological cures, you'll find little that's consistent with the values of person-centered theory and therapy. Interestingly, Rogers notes that many of his philosophical ideas have an Eastern flavor. He discusses the Taoist principle of wu-wei, sometimes referred to as the principle of non-action, and he shares several of his favorite sayings, most of which are Eastern in origin. In particular, he cites the following quotation from Lao-tse as possibly his very favorite:

> If I keep from meddling with people, they take care of themselves,
> If I keep from commanding people, they behave themselves,
> If I keep from preaching at people, they improve themselves,
> If I keep from imposing on people, they become themselves. (quoted in Rogers, 1980, p. 42)

Four Cornerstones of Being a Therapist

You may already be aware of the work of Sherry Cormier. Dr. Cormier is co-author of Interviewing Strategies for Helpers, *a well-respected book on interviewing within the mental health field. Her text, which is subtitled* Fundamental Skills and Cognitive Behavioral Interventions, *is frequently adopted in departments of psychology, counseling, and social work. So why would we include a Practitioner Commentary by someone known for her cognitive-behavioral text within this person-centered chapter? Dr. Cormier's description of her theoretical orientation is an excellent integration of the evolutionary stages of person-centered theory and therapy. Her description of herself is clearly within the spirit of contemporary person-centered therapy.*

I don't use a single or a particular counseling technique or theoretical approach with all clients, and I consider this an ethical issue. To me the one-size-fits-all approach places loyalty to a technique or an orientation above the welfare of the client. There are, however, four things that are very important to me in working with people.

The cornerstone of all of my interactions with people is respect. To me this is a fundamental quality necessary for any effective human interaction, and I try to be as respectful as possible whether I am counseling, teaching, parenting, partnering, or shopping. In this sense I am a Rogerian, in that back in 1957 Carl Rogers defined positive regard and respect as one of the three core facilitative conditions for counseling and psychotherapy.

I think respect has been an internal quality I have had with myself for a very long time. More recently, I have come to believe that breathing is another very important part of human interactions. What I mean by this is that it is important for me to pay attention to my own breathing when I am with a person. When I am tense or uncomfortable I notice my breath gets faster and more shallow. As I deepen my breath and slow it down, I feel more centered, and when I am more centered I am more fully present and more alive in the interaction. In some instances I also pay attention to the breath patterns of the other person as well. This seems to reflect both Rogerian and and Gestalt influences.

The third quality that is important to me in working with people in all kinds of interactions is intuition. This is also a much more recent development in the evolution of how I am with people.

As I have gotten older, I have recognized my capacity to be intuitive, and, perhaps more importantly, have learned to trust it. Over the years there have been instances when I have turned away from my intuition and have come to regret this. So now when I get a hunch or a feeling in my gut about a client or a person I pay attention to that for a period of time. Sometimes my intuition shows up in my dreams. If I am unclear about what the intuitive images mean, I seek consultation about them, or sometimes I draw about them in order to create meaning. This, I think, reflects both Jungian and narrative approaches.

At the same time, I am also influenced by techniques, interventions, and approaches that are evidence-based; that is, they have some sort of literature base or empirical support for their use with certain clients and certain issues. This reflects my cognitive-behavioral roots. In recent years, one such approach that I rely on greatly in all person-to-person interactions is the Prochaska, DiClemente, and Norcross stages of change model. I find myself conceptualizing clients, students, my family, my friends, and so on in terms of this model, and this conceptualization seems to help me understand and be more empathic and more patient with their process.

I have enjoyed sharing this with you. I wish each of you the very best in developing your own orientation and approaches to working with people.

As a multicultural approach, person-centered therapy has both potential benefits and potential liabilities. It may be more difficult for a white male to attempt an empathic connection with a H'mong female than for most white counselors to connect with others in their culture, even if they've behaved in seemingly reprehensible ways. Cultural empathy requires knowledge, skill, and self-awareness. Also, using person-centered attitudes can backfire because they clash with cultural values of some clients. It's hard to imagine Rogers ever blindly applying his approach to anyone, and it's even more doubtful that he would ever recommend that others do so in his name (see Multicultural Perspective 6.1 to read about a native Japanese social worker's experiences with Rogers's theory in Japan).

CONCLUDING COMMENTS

Rogers, more than anyone before or after him, understood the central role of relationship in therapy. The person of the therapist and the attitudes the therapist holds are more important than problems or techniques. We cannot generate a more apt or succinct concluding comment than that of Rogers himself:

> [T]he relationship which I have found helpful is characterized by a sort of transparency on my part, in which my real feelings are evident; by an acceptance of this other person as a separate person with value in his own right; and by a deep empathic understanding which enables me to see his private world through his eyes. (Rogers, 1961, p. 34)

STUDENT REVIEW ASSIGNMENTS

The following exercises will allow you to further explore person-centered therapy.

Critical Corner

Keep in mind that the following statements are strongly worded to provoke a response from you.

1. At the core of person-centered theory is the concept of trusting the individual. Theoretically, if an individual receives that special relationship Rogers speaks of, he or she will move naturally toward self-actualization. Basically, there are two problems with this assumption. First, it's impossible for individuals to have such an ideal environment all the time, so even if everyone had this inherent actualizing tendency, it would constantly be thwarted by real relationships in the real world. Second, with all the hate, prejudice, and evil in the world today, the evidence is certainly not in support of Rogers's rose-colored theory.
Response:

2. Rogers often saw clients for 50 or more therapy sessions. This snail's pace of change is simply unacceptable in today's economy and with the needs of the modern client. How can person-centered therapy be practical when it takes so long to establish that special type of relationship and healing environment?
Response:

3. Often cognitive and behavioral researchers use "nondirective" therapy as a control group or placebo condition to which they compare the efficacy of their therapeutic techniques. If researchers are just using this form of therapy as something equivalent to a placebo treatment, how can we justify using it as a real treatment with real people in the real world?

Response:

4. If all that people need to recover from their suffering is a kind and loving relationship, then why go to graduate school? Couldn't we just train legions of volunteers to display a saintlike, loving attitude and a lot of patience and thereby eradicate all suffering in our lifetime?

Response:

5. Person-centered therapy is fine for the worried well who enjoy and can benefit from examining themselves in perpetuity. But when it comes to treating people who have clear behavioral skills deficits or who are suffering from some sort of oppression, don't you think a more directive and problem-solving approach is necessary?

Response:

Key Terms

- Organism
- Self
- Incongruence
- Actualizing or formative tendency
- Positive regard
- Self-regard
- Subception
- Psychological contact

- Congruence
- Unconditional positive regard
- Empathic understanding
- Intellectual empathy
- Emotional empathy
- Imaginative empathy

- Traditional person-centered therapy
- Contemporary person-centered therapy
- Process-experiential psychotherapy
- Motivational interviewing

Review Questions

1. What innovative procedure did Rogers introduce to the study of psychotherapy that causes some historians to refer to him as the first modern psychotherapy researcher?
2. From the person-centered perspective, what is the main cause of psychopathology, and what is the main characteristic of psychopathology?
3. What is the empathy question (Carkuff, 1987), and what might be its uses and limits in helping therapists have empathy with their clients?
4. What are the dangers and benefits of experiencing and expressing congruence during therapy?
5. What is the person-centered perspective with regard to psychological assessment?

6. What are your thoughts on the empirical efficacy of person-centered therapy? Do you think there are some situations in which a radical person-centered approach might be more effective than a scientifically validated cognitive or behavioral approach?

7. Imagine Carl Rogers talking with Sigmund Freud. What would they say to each other? How would they treat each other? Who would come away most changed?

8. Which modern treatment modalities give Rogers credit for much of their foundation?

RECOMMENDED READINGS AND RESOURCES

The following resources provide additional information on person-centered therapy.

Lead Journals

- *Journal of Humanistic Counseling, Education and Development*
- *Journal of Humanistic Education*
- *Journal of Humanistic Psychology*
- *Person-Centered Journal*
- *Person-Centered Review*

Books and Articles

Axline, V. M. (1964). *Dibs in search of self.* New York: Ballentine Books.

Bohart, A. C., & Greenberg, L. S. (1997). *Empathy reconsidered.* Washington, DC: American Psychological Association.

Boy, A. V., & Pine, G. J. (1999). *A person-centered foundation for counseling and psychotherapy* (2nd ed.). Springfield, IL: Charles C. Thomas.

Bozarth, J. (1999). Person-centered therapy: A revolutionary paradigm. In T. Merry (Ed.), *Person-centered approach and client-centered therapy essential readers series* (pp. 59–87). Ross-on-Wye: PCCS Books.

Duncan, B. L., & Miller, S. D. (2000). *The heroic client: Doing client-centered, outcome-informed therapy.* San Francisco: Jossey-Bass.

Gendlin, E. T. (1996). *Focusing-oriented psychotherapy: A manual of the experiential method.* New York: Guilford Press.

Guerney, B. (1977). *Relationship enhancement therapy.* San Francisco: Jossey-Bass.

Kirschenbaum, H., & Henderson, V. L. (Eds.). (1989). *Carl Rogers: Dialogues.* Boston: Houghton Mifflin.

May, R. (1982). The problem of evil: An open letter to Carl Rogers. *Journal of Humanistic Psychology, 22*(3), 10–21.

Miller, W. R., & Rollnick, S. (2002). *Motivational interviewing: Preparing people for change* (2nd ed.). New York: Guilford Press.

Patterson, C. H., & Hidore, S. (1997). *Successful psychotherapy: A caring, loving relationship.* Northvale, NJ; Jason Aronson.

Rogers, C. R. (1961). *On becoming a person.* Boston: Houghton Mifflin.

Rogers, C. R. (1977). *Carl Rogers on personal power.* New York: Delacorte Press.

Rogers, C. R. (1980). *A way of being.* Boston: Houghton Mifflin.

Rogers, C. R., & Russell, D. E. (2002). *Carl Rogers the quiet revolutionary: A post-humous autobiography.* Roseville, CA: Penmarin Books.

Rogers, N. (1996). *The creative connection.* New York: Science and Behavior Books.

Thorne, B. (2002). *The mystical power of person-centred therapy: Hope beyond despair.* London: Whurr Publishers.

Audio and Videotapes

Carlson, J., & Kjos, D. (2000). *Person centered therapy with Dr. Natalie Rogers* [Videotape]. Boston: Allyn & Bacon.

Miller, W. R., & Rollnick, S. (1998). *Motivational interviewing* (Vols. 1–7) [Videotape]. Albuquerque, NM: Horizon West Productions.

Raskin, N. J. (1994). *Client-centered therapy* [Videotape]. Washington, DC: American Psychological Association.

Rogers, C. R. (1963). *Mrs. P.S.* [Audiotape]. Orlando, FL: American Academy of Psychotherapists.

You can peruse some of the other many Carl Rogers videotapes and audiotapes at www.centerfortheperson.org/videos.html.

Training Organizations and Web Sites

Center for Studies of the Person (web site: www.centerfortheperson.org)

National Institute of Relationship Enhancement (NIRE): (web site: www.nire.org)

Person-Centered Expressive Therapy Institute (web site: www.pceti.org)

Natalie Rogers has her own informational website with information about herself and Carl Rogers at www.nrogers.com.

Chapter 7

BEHAVIORAL THEORY AND THERAPY

At the time . . . , some dramatic advances in experimental method had made it possible to predict and control quite complex behavior with considerable precision. But it was only the behavior of rats and pigeons. Though I suspected that the same methods would work with men, I was not sure. . . ." [B]ehavioral engineering . . ." was still a dream.

But the dream was to come true. A technology of behavioral management is now well developed, particularly in education and psychotherapy.

—B. F. Skinner, *Walden Two* (1970, p. viii)

IN THIS CHAPTER YOU WILL LEARN

- The difference between behaviorism and behavior therapy
- John Watson's and Mary Cover Jones's early application of classical conditioning procedures to human subjects
- Who first used the term *behavior therapy* and when
- Basic principles of classical conditioning, operant conditioning, and social learning theory
- How behavior therapists view psychopathology
- Methods of behavioral assessment
- Specific behavior therapy techniques
- Ethical and multicultural issues facing behavior therapists
- About empirical research on behavior therapy

The story of behaviorism and its therapeutic application, behavior therapy, is deeply linked to the story of science in American psychology. Behaviorism and, later, behavior therapy sprang from efforts to describe, explain, predict, and control observable animal and human behavior. Behaviorism and behavior therapy are often considered reactions to unscientific psychoanalytic approaches to psychology (Fishman & Franks, 1997).

In some ways, behaviorism is philosophically opposed to psychoanalysis, and in other ways the two approaches are quite similar. The biggest difference between behaviorism and psychoanalysis is that psychoanalysts subjectively focus on inner dynamics or mentalistic concepts, whereas behaviorists objectively focus strictly on observable phenomena or materialistic concepts (Lazarus, 1971). In addition, behaviorists, by definition, utilize techniques derived from scientific research, whereas psycho-analytic techniques are usually derived from clinical practice. However, both perspectives are similar in that they are highly mechanistic, positivistic, and deterministic approaches to understanding humans. These similarities led Michael Mahoney, an influential behavioral theorist who has more recently become a constructivist (see Chapter 12), to refer to psychoanalysis and behaviorism as the yin and yang of determinism (Mahoney, 1984).

For the behaviorist, all behavior is learned. Even the most complex human behaviors are explained, controlled, and modified through learning procedures. This chapter explores the application of behaviorism to the human therapeutic enterprise.

HISTORICAL CONTEXT

There are three major historical stages in the evolution of contemporary behavioral approaches to human change:

- Behaviorism as a scientific endeavor
- Behavior therapy
- Cognitive behavior therapy

The placement of behaviorism and behavior therapy within the historical context of psychological theory development is somewhat problematic. As you may know, existential-humanistic psychology is often called the *third force* in American psychology. As a third force, existential-humanistic psychology is an alternative to psychoanalysis and behaviorism. Why, then, does this behavior therapy chapter come after the existential-humanistic chapters? Why isn't behavior therapy included earlier in this book? Or, alternatively, if behavior therapy emerged after existential-humanistic approaches, why isn't *it* referred to as the third force?

Although behaviorism as an academic and scientific approach to studying animal and human behavior began gaining popularity in the early 1900s, behavior therapy was not identified as a specific therapeutic approach until the 1950s (Lazarus, 1958; Skinner, Solomon, & Lindsley, 1953). Prior to the 1950s, most behavioral work was confined to the laboratory. Existential-humanistic philosophers and therapists consider their perspective as a third force because they contrast their theory with psychoanalytic theory and academic-scientific behaviorism as an explanation for human behavior and motivation. Applied behavior therapy came later.

Behaviorism

In the early 1900s, North American scientific psychology was on the move. Led by the ambitious John B. Watson, a new and different mechanistic view of humans was becoming more popular. This view, dubbed *behaviorism,* was in stark contrast to other prevailing perspectives. For example, although most early twentieth-century academic psychologists were interested in human consciousness and free will, and used a procedure called *introspection* to identify the inner workings of the human mind, behaviorists systematically excluded consciousness and introspection, and believed in determinism rather than free will.

Prior to Watson, William James, the innovative thinker credited with launching the field of psychology in the United States, was much more comfortable identifying himself as a philosopher than as a scientist. When, in 1889, James was told by the president of Harvard University that he would soon be appointed the first Alford Professor of Psychology at Harvard University, James allegedly retorted: "Do it, and I shall blow my brains out in front of everyone at the first mention of my name" (Bankart, 1997, p. 218). James had little regard for the scientific foundation of psychology; he claimed that it consisted of

> a string of raw facts; a little gossip and wrangle about opinions; a little classification and generalization on the mere descriptive level; a strong prejudice that we *have* states of mind, and that our brain conditions them: but not a single law in the sense in which physics shows us laws, not a single proposition from which any consequence can causally be deducted. . . . This is no science, it is only the hope of a science. (James, 1992, p. 433)

John Watson's perspective on psychology was much different. Watson believed in psychological science. He immersed himself in experimental psychology, the classical conditioning learning model as demonstrated by Pavlov's salivating dogs (Pavlov, 1906). He was aware of Thorndike's problem-solving cats and the law of effect (a precursor to operant conditioning; Thorndike, 1911). For Watson, behaviorism was far beyond "the hope of a science." His behaviorism was based exclusively on verifiable scientific data. In publishing his behaviorist manifesto in 1913, he essentially redefined psychology as a pure science: "Psychology as a behaviorist views it is a purely objective branch of natural science" (Watson, 1913, p. 158). The young field of psychology was ready for Watson and enthusiastically embraced his ideas. He was elected to the presidency of the American Psychological Association in 1915, at the age of 35.

In direct opposition to James's conceptions of free will and human autonomy, the purpose of Watson's scientific psychology, his behaviorism, was the deterministic prediction and control of human behavior. Much of his work, similar to that of Pavlov and Thorndike, focused on animal behavior. Watson viewed humans and animals as indistinguishable. His claims about the potential of behaviorism in predicting and controlling human behavior were as bold and startling then as they are now.

> Give me a dozen healthy infants, well-formed, and my own specified world to bring them up in and I'll guarantee to take any one at random and train him to become any type of specialist I might select—doctor, lawyer, artist, merchant-chief and yes, even beggar-man and thief, regardless of his talents, penchants, tendencies, abilities, vocations, and race of his ancestors. (Watson, 1924, p. 104)

From the beginning, Watson had a strong interest in the application of behavioral scientific principles to human suffering. This may have been because he experienced a nervous breakdown as a young man and had not found psychoanalysis helpful (Bankart, 1997).

Little Hans and Little Albert

Watson began testing his beliefs about the origins of human psychopathology partly as a reaction to what he viewed as ridiculous notions of psychoanalytic treatment. In 1909 Freud reported an analysis of a 5-year-old boy who experienced a profound and debilitating fear of horses. Freud explained that his patient, Little Hans, was afraid of being bitten by a horse because of unresolved Oedipal issues and castration anxiety (Freud, 1909).

In contrast, Watson sought to demonstrate that severe fears and phobias were caused not by obscure psychoanalytic constructs but by direct classical conditioning of a fear response. In his now famous experiments with 11-month-old Little Albert, Watson quickly made his point. After only five trials in which Watson and his research assistant Rosalie Raynor paired the presentation of a white rat to Albert with the striking of a metal bar, Albert developed a strong fear and aversion to white rats (Watson & Rayner, 1920). Classical conditioning was quick and efficient despite the fact that Albert had previously been a calm and happy baby who eagerly played with white rats. Even worse (for Little Albert), his conditioned fear response generalized to a variety of furry or fuzzy white objects, including a rabbit, a dog, cotton wool, and a Santa Claus mask. Although Watson had further conditioning and deconditioning plans in store for Little Albert, after the initial five trials the boy's mother apparently decided that enough was enough and removed Little Albert from Watson's experimental clutches (Bankart, 1997).

Little Peter

In 1924, Mary Cover Jones, who had studied with Watson, conducted an investigation of the effectiveness of *counter-conditioning* or deconditioning with a 3-year-old boy named *Little Peter.* It is Jones's study and not Watson's that directly and dramatically illustrated the potential of classical conditioning techniques in the remediation of psychological fears and phobias.

Jones initially documented the presence of an intense fear reaction in Little Peter (M. C. Jones, 1924). Prior to his involvement in the behavioral experiments, Little Peter exhibited fear in response to several furry objects, including rabbits, fur coats, and cotton balls. Jones proceeded to systematically decondition Little Peter's fear reaction by pairing the gradual approach of a caged rabbit with Peter's involvement in an enjoyable activity—eating his favorite foods. In the end, Peter's fear response was extinguished.

Jones's work was extensive and profound. Over time, she worked with 70 different children, all of whom had marked and specific fear responses. The children upon whom she conducted her experiments were institutionalized; her efforts were uniformly designed to eliminate their fears, not create them. Overall, her conclusions are clear and constitute the basic framework for contemporary (and scientifically verifiable) behavioral approaches to treating human fears and phobias. She stated:

> In our study of methods for removing fear responses, we found unqualified success with only two. By the method of direct conditioning we associated the fear-object with a craving-object, and replaced the fear by a positive response. By the method of social imitation we allowed the subjects to share, under controlled conditions, the social activity of a group of children especially chosen with a view to prestige effect. [Other] methods proved sometimes effective but were not to be relied upon unless used in combination with other methods. (M. C. Jones, 1924, p. 390)

As illustrated by Watson's and Jones's experiments, the behavioral emphasis on observable behavior and rejection of mentalistic concepts is well suited to laboratory research with animals and humans. Early behaviorists made many important contributions to psychological science. Overall, the highlights include

- The discovery by Pavlov, Watson, and their colleagues that emotional responses could be involuntarily conditioned in animals and humans via classical conditioning procedures
- The discovery by Mary Cover Jones that fear responses could be deconditioned by either (1) replacing the fear response with a positive response or (2) social imitation
- The discovery by Thorndike and its later elaboration by Skinner that animal and human behaviors are powerfully shaped by their consequences

Behavior Therapy

In a testament to the behavioral zeitgeist of the 1950s, three different research groups in three different countries independently introduced the term *behavior therapy* to modern psychology.

B. F. Skinner in the United States

Skinner's early work was an immense experimental project on operant conditioning with rats and pigeons in the 1930s (Skinner, 1938). At that time, his emphasis was on the extension of Thorndike's law of effect. He repeatedly demonstrated the power of positive reinforcement, negative reinforcement, punishment, and stimulus control in the modification of animal behavior. In fact, within the confines of his well-known Skinner box, he was able to teach pigeons to play ping-pong via operant conditioning procedures.

In the 1940s, Skinner began extending operant conditioning concepts to human social and clinical problems. His book *Walden Two* was a story of how operant conditioning procedures could be used to create a utopian society (Skinner, 1948). His next book, *Science and Human Behavior,* was a critique of psychoanalytic concepts and a reformulation of psychotherapy in behavioral terms (Skinner, 1953). Finally, in 1953, Skinner and his colleagues first used *behavior therapy* as a clinical term referring to the application of operant conditioning procedures to modify the behavior of psychotic patients (Skinner et al., 1953).

Joseph Wolpe, Arnold Lazarus, and Stanley Rachman in South Africa

Joseph Wolpe's interest in conditioning procedures as a means for resolving neurotic fear began with his doctoral thesis (Wolpe, 1948). Later, he conducted "experiments in neurosis production" with 12 domestic cats (Wolpe & Plaud, 1997, p. 968) and eventually established the first nonpsychoanalytic, empirically validated behavior therapy technique (Wolpe, 1954, 1958). His book *Psychotherapy by Reciprocal Inhibition* outlined the therapeutic procedure now called *systematic desensitization* (Wolpe, 1958). Wolpe recently reflected on his treatment technique:

> As the therapy procedure has evolved, the anxious patient is first trained in progressive muscle relaxation exercises and then gradually exposed imaginally or in vivo to feared stimuli while simultaneously relaxing. (Wolpe & Plaud, 1997, p. 969)

Wolpe's approach is very similar to Jones's deconditioning principle wherein a conditioned negative emotional response is replaced with a conditioned positive emotional response (M.C. Jones, 1924). Wolpe's revolutionary work attracted the attention of two South African psychologists, Arnold Lazarus and Stanley Rachman. Both contributed significantly to the behavior therapy movement. In fact, Lazarus claims the credit for first using the term *behavior therapy* in a scientific journal. He states:

The first time the terms behavior therapy and behavior therapist appeared in a scientific journal was when I endeavored to point out the need for adding objective, laboratory-derived therapeutic tools to more orthodox psychotherapeutic techniques. (Lazarus, 1971, p. 2)

Lazarus is perhaps the first mental health professional—and certainly the first behavior therapist—to openly embrace eclecticism. Early on, and throughout his career, he advocated the integration of laboratory-based scientific procedures into existing clinical and counseling practices (Lazarus, 1958, 1991). He is an adamant opponent of narrow therapy definitions or conceptualizations. Because of his broadly eclectic practices, we explore his multi-modal behavior therapy approach in Chapter 13.

Over the years, Rachman also has influenced developing behavior therapy procedures. He has been the editor of the journal *Behaviour Research and Therapy* for decades. His initial unique contribution involved the application of aversive stimuli to treating neurotic behavior, including addictions (Rachman, 1965).

Hans Eysenck and the Maudsley Group in the United Kingdom

British psychiatrist Hans Eysenck independently used the term "behaviour therapy" to describe the application of modern learning theory to the understanding and treatment of behavioral and psychiatric problems (Eysenck, 1959). Eysenck's subsequent quick publication of two edited volumes (a behaviorally based textbook of abnormal psychology and a collection of case studies in behavior therapy) led to the widespread dissemination of behavior therapy as a procedure through which surface symptoms are directly treated as a means of alleviating neurotic functioning (Eysenck, 1960, 1964).

As a consequence of the work of all these pioneering researchers and practitioners, behavior (or behaviour) therapy was born.

Cognitive Behavior Modification

Although the very thought of this would be most disturbing to early behaviorists, contemporary behavior therapy now includes and even embraces cognitive variables. For example, in the compilation *The Best of Behaviour Research and Therapy,* which includes journal articles written over 35 years, many selected articles specifically focus on thoughts, expectations, and emotions (Rachman, 1997). Clearly, behavior therapy is no longer a process that focuses exclusively on external behavior. The integration of cognitive and behavioral therapy approaches is discussed further throughout this chapter and the next.

Behavior therapy continues to evolve. This should not be surprising because, as articulated by Cyril Franks, a staunch behaviorist and associate of the late Hans Eysenck in London, behavior therapy is designed to evolve: "Above all, in behavior therapy a theory is a servant that is useful *only until better theory and better therapy* come along" (Franks & Barbrack, 1983, pp. 509–510; italics added).

THEORETICAL PRINCIPLES

Over the years there have been many formulations and reformulations of behavioral theory and therapy. For the most part, two primary convictions characterize behaviorists and behavioral theory—both then and now:

- Behavior therapists employ techniques based on modern learning theory.
- Behavior therapists employ techniques derived from scientific research.

Some behaviorists have criticized even these most basic behavioral tenets. For example, in his book *Behavior Therapy and Beyond,* Lazarus states:

> Eysenck's . . . insistence that behavior therapy denotes "methods of treatment which are derived from modern learning theory" amounts to little more than a beguiling slogan. . . .
> The danger lies in a premature elevation of learning principles into unwarranted scientific truths and the ascription of the general term of "modern learning theory" to what in reality are best described as "modern learning theories." (Lazarus, 1971, pp. 4, 5)

Lazarus's main point is that behavior therapy is based not on learning theory, but on learning theories (in the plural). He asserts that even psychoanalytic formulations of what occurs in therapy constitute learning hypotheses, many of which remain unsubstantiated.

Theoretical Models

Despite the fact that learning theory models are continually in flux and revision, we turn now to a brief description of the four main models of learning that form the theoretical foundation of behavior therapy (Fishman & Franks, 1997, p. 141).

Applied Behavior Analysis

Also referred to as *radical behaviorism,* applied behavior analysis is based on Skinner's operant conditioning principles. The radical behavioral position is straightforward: *Behavior is a function of its consequences.*

Radical behaviorism is based on *stimulus-response (SR) theory;* there are no cognitive or covert intervening variables that mediate the organism's response to a particular stimulus. Applied behavior analysis focuses solely on observable behaviors. Therapy proceeds primarily through the manipulation of environmental variables to produce behavior change.

The main procedures used by applied behavior analysts are reinforcement, punishment, extinction, and stimulus control. These procedures are used to manipulate the environment and the client's environmental contingencies. The goal is to increase adaptive behavior through reinforcement and stimulus control and to reduce maladaptive behavior through punishment and extinction. Several traditional behavior therapy techniques are directly derived from applied behavior analysis, including assertiveness training, the token economy, and problem-solving training.

In his laboratory, Skinner demonstrated that behavior is a function of its consequences (Skinner, 1938). He discovered that when a particular behavior is followed by positive reinforcement, the tendency for an organism to engage in that specific behavior is strengthened or reinforced. Similarly, when a specific behavior is followed by punishment or an aversive stimulus, the tendency for an organism to engage in that specific behavior is weakened.

In theory, and sometimes in practice, positive reinforcement and punishment concepts are simple. For example, when your cat meows at the front door and gets a bowl of tasty cat food, the likelihood of the cat's meowing again is increased. In contrast, if you spray cold water on the cat when it meows (or administer an aversive electric shock), the meowing behavior is likely to diminish (or, as sometimes occurs with punishment procedures, erratic or aggressive behaviors may develop).

Unfortunately, operant conditioning procedures are not always so simple and straightforward in real life. Take, for example, the hypothetical parents of 5- and 15-year-old girls. The parents are trying to teach their 5-year-old to tie her shoes. Therefore, whenever she engages in shoe-tying behavior they coo and clap, and when she finally gets it right they give big bear hugs and high fives. If their 5-year-old is like most girls her age she will be strongly motivated to learn to tie her shoes and will enjoy receiving the social rewards her parents are heaping on her.

At the same time, the parents are also trying to teach their 15-year-old daughter to speak to them more respectfully. Because positive reinforcement worked so well with their 5-year-old, they initially try cooing, clapping, and hugging in response to their daughter's respectful communication. Unfortunately, when they hug her, she responds by saying, "I don't want to be hugged. Just leave me alone!" After discovering that their positive reinforcement plan doesn't work with their older daughter, the parents decide to try using punishment. Together, they resolve to shout and scold her whenever she speaks disrespectfully. This time their efforts backfire even worse—she responds by shouting right back at them.

Finally, in desperation, the parents visit a counselor. When the counselor suggests using a behavioral plan, the parents roll their eyes and exclaim, "We've already tried that, and it definitely doesn't work!" In reality, the only thing the parents discovered is that simple operant conditioning is more complex than most people believe.

Neobehavioristic, Mediational Stimulus-Response Model

The neobehavioristic mediational SR model is based on classical conditioning principles. Its tenets were developed and articulated by Pavlov, Watson, Mowrer, and Wolpe.

Classical conditioning is sometimes referred to as *associational learning* because it involves an association or linking of one environmental stimulus with another. In Pavlovian terms, an unconditioned stimulus is one that naturally produces a specific physical-emotional response. The physical response elicited by an unconditioned stimulus is mediated through smooth muscle reflex arcs, so higher-order cognitive processes are not required in order for conditioning to occur. The following clinical example described by Wolpe illustrates how fear or anxiety responses are classically conditioned.

> A 34-year-old man's four-year fear of being in automobiles started when his car was struck from behind while he was waiting for a red light to change. At that moment he felt an overwhelming fear of impending death; subsequently he was afraid to sit inside even a stationary car. That the fear was purely a matter of classical autonomic conditioning (automatic response to the ambience of a car's interior) was evidenced by the fact that he had no expectation of danger when he sat in a car. (Wolpe, 1987, pp. 135–136)

In Wolpe's example, the experience of being struck from behind while waiting for a red light is the unconditioned stimulus. This stimulus automatically (or autonomically) produces a reflexive fear response (or unconditioned response). After only a single, powerful experience, the 34-year-old man suffers from a debilitating fear of impending death (a conditioned response) whenever he is exposed to the interior of an automobile (a conditioned stimulus). As Wolpe emphasizes, this scenario represents classical autonomic conditioning or learning because the man has no cognitive expectations or cognitive triggers that lead to his experience of fear when he is sitting inside an automobile. Because of the lack of cognitive processing involved in classical conditioning, when an individual experiences a purely classically conditioned fear response, often he or she will say something like, "I don't know why it is, but I'm just afraid of elevators."

Classical conditioning principles also include *stimulus generalization, stimulus discrimination, extinction, counter-conditioning,* and *spontaneous recovery.*

Stimulus generalization is defined as the extension or generalization of a conditioned fear response to new settings, situations, or objects. For example, in the preceding example, if the man begins experiencing intense fear when sitting in an airplane, stimulus generalization has occurred. Similarly, in the case of Little Albert, stimulus generalization occurred when Albert experienced fear in response to objects (stimuli) similar in appearance to white rats (e.g., Santa Claus masks, cotton balls, etc.).

Stimulus discrimination occurs when a conditioned fear response is not elicited by a new or different stimulus. For example, if the 34-year-old man can sit in a movie theater without experiencing fear, stimulus discrimination has occurred. Apparently the movie theater setting (stimulus) is different enough from the car setting that it does not elicit the conditioned response. In the case of Little Albert, stimulus discrimination occurred when Little Albert did not have a fear response when exposed to a fluffy white washrag.

Extinction involves the gradual elimination of a conditioned response. It occurs when a conditioned stimulus is repeatedly presented without a previously associated unconditioned stimulus. For example, if Watson had kept working with Little Albert and repeatedly exposed him to a white rat without a frightening sound of metal clanging, eventually Little Albert would lose his conditioned response to rats. Extinction is not the same as forgetting; instead, it involves relearning that the conditioned stimulus is no longer a signal that precedes the unconditioned stimulus.

In contrast, Mary Cover Jones's work with Little Peter is an example of successful *counter-conditioning* or deconditioning. Counter-conditioning involves new associative learning. The subject learns that the conditioned stimulus brings with it a positive emotional experience. For example, when Jones repeatedly presented the white rat to Little Peter while he was eating some of his favorite foods, eventually the conditioned response (fear) was counter-conditioned. The same counter-conditioning principle is in operation in Wolpe's systematic desensitization.

Spontaneous recovery within a classical conditioning paradigm was initially discussed by Pavlov (Pavlov, 1927). Spontaneous recovery occurs when an old response suddenly returns (is recovered) after having been successfully extinguished or counter-conditioned. For example, if, after successful counter-conditioning through systematic desensitization, Wolpe's client suddenly begins having fear symptoms associated with the interior of automobiles, he has experienced spontaneous recovery.

Social Learning Theory

Social learning theory was developed by Albert Bandura and his colleagues (Bandura & Walters, 1963). As a theoretical model, it's most accurately viewed as an extension of the operant and classical conditioning models. Specifically, social learning theory includes stimulus-influence components (classical conditioning) and consequence-influence components (operant conditioning), but it also adds a strong cognitive mediational component.

Social learning theory emphasizes two main cognitive processes. First, a significant portion of human learning is observational in nature (Bandura, 1971). For example, in Bandura's famous Bobo doll experiment, he documented the power of observational or vicarious learning as a source of behavior change (Bandura, Ross, & Ross, 1963). This process has come to be known as *modeling.* Obviously, observational learning includes a covert or private mental process that cannot be directly observed by experimenters (or therapists).

Second, social learning theory emphasizes that reciprocal interactions can occur between the individual's behavior and the environment (Bandura, 1978). This theoretical position represents a dramatic shift from traditional learning theory. Specifically, Bandura postulates that because of these reciprocal interactions, individuals are capable of self-directed behavior change. In direct opposition to Skinner and Watson, Bandura gives free will and self-determination back to the individual.

One of Bandura's most important social learning theory concepts is self-efficacy (Bandura, 1977; Bandura & Adams, 1977). Self-efficacy is defined as an individual's belief or expectation that he or she can adequately complete or master a specific situation or task. From Bandura's perspective, a primary purpose of therapy is to help clients develop and strengthen self-efficacy. For example, a client who comes to therapy to quit smoking cigarettes may initially have little confidence in his or her ability to quit. Consequently, if therapy is to be successful, it will be necessary to enhance the client's smoking cessation self-efficacy. This may come about when the therapist teaches the client self-monitoring procedures, progressive muscle relaxation, and strategies for coping with uncomfortable feelings associated with nicotine withdrawal. In other words, from Bandura's perspective, behavioral techniques can produce change indirectly; they provide the client with tools that have a positive impact on his or her belief that he or she can successfully stop smoking.

Cognitive-Behavior Therapy

The cognitive-behavioral movement in psychotherapy began in the late 1950s and became associated with mainstream behavior therapy in the 1970s. Initially, the cognitive methods that Albert Ellis and others (Phillips, 1957) employed were viewed as being outside the purview of behavior therapy. However, because behavioral psychology is based on the application of scientific principles and knowledge, behavioral scientists sought to experimentally test and validate cognitive approaches to emotional and behavior change. For example, in an early study on the effects of self-talk on mood, Velten (1968) aptly articulated the purpose of his research: "The theoretical goal of this experiment was to test the central tenet of 'semantic' therapy, that the constructions or interpretations people place upon events determine their affective responses" (p. 473). Velten's article, published in *Behavioural Research and Therapy,* became part of the scientific foundation for including cognitive processes within the behavior therapy domain.

Historically, behaviorists hold one of two views of cognitive therapy. On the one hand, most mainstream behaviorists, including the 5,000 or so members of the Association for Advancement of Behavior Therapy (AABT; founded in 1967), view all cognitive approaches, to the extent they are empirically based, as forms of behavior therapy. On the other hand, members of the Association for Behavior Analysis (the followers of B. F. Skinner) reject cognitive or cognitive-behavioral principles and approaches (Fishman & Franks, 1997).

Theory of Psychopathology

For behaviorists, maladaptive behavior is always learned and can always be either unlearned or replaced by new learning. The concept that human learning is at the core of human behavior profoundly influences how behavior therapists approach the assessment and treatment of clients. Paula Truax articulates this link between psychopathology, assessment, and treatment:

> The basic assumption in behavioral theory is that both adaptive and maladaptive behaviors are acquired, maintained, and changed in the same way: through the internal and external events that proceed and follow them. This means that behavioral case conceptualization involves a careful assessment of the context within which a behavior occurs, along with developing testable hypotheses about the causes, maintaining factors, and treatment interventions. (Truax, 2002, p. 3)

Behavior therapists also believe that psychopathology may be a function of inadequate learning or skill deficits. For example, an underlying premise of assertiveness training is that individuals who exhibit too much passive or too much aggressive behavior simply have skill deficits; they haven't learned how to appropriately use assertive behavior in social situations. Consequently, the purpose of assertiveness training (a behavioral treatment) is to teach clients assertiveness skills through modeling, coaching, behavior rehearsal, and reinforcement. Interestingly, the successful outcomes associated with assertiveness training can be explained through either classical conditioning or operant models. For example, Wolpe considers assertive behavior to be incompatible with anxiety; therefore an anxiety response is being counter-conditioned and replaced by an adaptive, incompatible response (Wolpe, 1973). In contrast, contemporary assertiveness trainers usually focus more on the contingencies—reinforcements and punishments—that establish and maintain passive, aggressive, and assertive social behavior (Alberti & Emmons, 2001).

As a means of better understanding client psychopathology, behaviorists apply the scientific method to the clinical or counseling setting. For every case, behaviorists systematically

- Observe and assess client maladaptive or unskilled behaviors
- Develop hypotheses about the cause, maintenance, and appropriate treatment for maladaptive or unskilled behaviors
- Test behavioral hypotheses through the application of empirically justifiable interventions
- Observe and evaluate the results of their intervention
- Revise and continue testing new hypotheses about ways to modify the maladaptive or unskilled behavior(s) as needed

Behaviorists are on the cutting edge when it comes to applying specific treatment procedures to specific clinical problems. More than any other nonmedical group of practitioners, behavior therapists (and cognitive-behavioral therapists) focus on demonstrating empirical support for their treatment methods. As a consequence, almost all therapy interventions that have obtained the status of "empirically supported" or "empirically validated" are behavioral or cognitive-behavioral in nature (Chambless et al., 1998). Even further, behaviorists are far ahead of all other theoretical orientations in applying specific treatment techniques to specific clinical problems (see Hersen, 2002).

THE PRACTICE OF BEHAVIOR THERAPY

To practice behavior therapy requires that you think like a scientist. When preparing for therapy, be sure to get out your clipboard, because behavior therapists take notes. You may even need some graph paper or a white board for illustrating concepts to clients. Above all, as a behaviorist, you are a teacher and educator: Your job is to help clients unlearn old, maladaptive behaviors and learn new, adaptive behaviors.

Preparing Yourself to Practice Behavior Therapy

There is an unfortunate myth about behavior therapy and behavior therapists that characterizes behaviorists as stiff, scientifically inclined individuals with little interpersonal skill or sensitivity. Sometimes behaviorists are even viewed as having little respect for individual freedom and personal dignity (Franks & Barbrack, 1983).

In reality, this myth is far from the truth. Being a behaviorist does not rule out being compassionate and sensitive. As behavior therapy has evolved, its practice has been characterized more and more by flexibility. Gone are the days when most behaviorists adhered to a noncognitive and non–clinically sensitive model of practicing behavior therapy. In fact, some reviewers contend that behavior therapists have always been warm and supportive of clients and that tales of insensitive behavior therapists applying behavior modification techniques to clients in a rote, scientific style are and always have been myths (Fishman & Franks, 1997). As Lazarus stated back in 1971, "conditioning procedures may be applied in a noncoercive context of human dignity, empathy, authenticity, and warmth" (Lazarus, 1971, p. 205). And over 25 years ago, Goldfried and Davison said, "Any behavior therapist who maintains that principles of learning and social influence are all one needs to know in order to bring about behavior change is out of contact with clinical reality" (Goldfried & Davison, 1976, p. 55).

Preparing Your Client for Behavior Therapy

Clients who come for behavior therapy may have misconceptions about what behavior therapy is all about. In extreme cases, they may expect a behavior therapist to appear dressed in a white lab coat with an M&M® dispenser for giving out positive reinforcements. Like mental health professionals with other orientations, most behaviorally oriented professionals provide written and oral explanations of their therapeutic approach. A sample excerpt from a behaviorally oriented informed consent form is included in Ethical Highlight 7.1.

Assessment Issues and Procedures

In a perfect behavioral assessment world, behavior therapists would be able to directly observe clients in their natural environment to obtain specific information about exactly what happens before, during, and after adaptive and maladaptive behaviors occur. Speaking theoretically, the main goal of behavioral assessment is to determine the external (environmental or situational) stimuli and internal (physiological and sometimes cognitive) stimuli that directly precede and follow adaptive and maladaptive client behavioral responses.

=== **ETHICAL HIGHLIGHT 7.1** ===

A Behavioral Informed Consent Form

The following is a sample excerpt from an informed consent form from the behavior therapy perspective. As you read it, pretend that you're sitting in a therapist's waiting room, about to go in for your first therapy session with a new therapist.

Client Information Form

I specialize in the practice of behavior therapy. You may have heard of behavior therapy. It's a highly effective form of therapy based on scientific research and on modern theories of learning.

My behavior therapy practice is based on the fact that humans are constantly learning. Of course, learning is a complex process. As you know from experience, humans learn everything from very basic skills, like tying shoelaces and riding bicycles, to complex emotional responses, like love, jealousy, and nervousness. Everyone has a tremendous capacity for learning.

Whether you've come to therapy because of a difficult situation, a problem relationship, or a troubling emotion, I will help you focus on unlearning old negative or unhelpful habits and learning new, more positive habits. Research has proven that behavior therapy is very helpful for many types of problems.

Sometimes people think that therapy based on learning must be boring and impersonal, but nothing could be further from the truth. In therapy, you and I will work very closely together. We'll work as a team, and we'll talk in detail about some of the hardest things you're facing in your life. Then we'll develop a plan for helping you overcome the problems and symptoms that cause you distress.

In most cases, our plan will include several different approaches to learning and to changing. Some new learning will happen right in our sessions, and some of the new learning will happen outside our sessions. That means sometimes I'll give you assignments to complete between our meetings. If you complete your assignments, then the new learning we're working on in therapy will happen even faster.

Behavior therapy is a relatively short form of therapy. You won't have to come to therapy forever; depending on your problem and your life situation, it may take only a few sessions for therapy to be successful, or it may take up to several months. Whichever is the case for you, you can count on me to talk with you openly and directly about how long therapy should take and why. That's because behavior therapy doesn't involve any big mysteries or secrets. My job is to work with you in partnership to improve your life and to change uncomfortable symptoms you're experiencing. Therefore, I will regularly explain to you exactly what we're doing and why we're doing it. And whenever you have questions, feel free to ask, and I'll do my best to answer you.

This assessment procedure is sometimes referred to as obtaining information about the client's behavioral ABCs (Sommers-Flanagan & Sommers-Flanagan, 2003):

- A = The behavior's *antecedents* (everything that happens just before the maladaptive behavior is observed)
- B = The *behavior* (the client's problem specifically defined in concrete behavioral terms; e.g., rather than being called an "anger problem," it's referred to as "yelling or swearing six times a day and punching others twice daily")
- C = The behavior's *consequences* (everything that happens just after the maladaptive behavior occurs)

For example, if a child client is disrupting class in school, the optimal assessment procedure is a school visit to *unobtrusively* observe the child at various times during the day. Through direct observation, the behavior therapist gathers data and watches for specific patterns. The child's class disruptions may be preceded by a particular stimulus (e.g., in-class reading assignments), or perhaps the therapist will discover that the child is obtaining positive reinforcement (e.g., attention from the teacher and classmates) immediately after disrupting classroom activities.

Unfortunately, direct behavioral observation is inefficient, for several reasons. First, most therapists can't afford the time required to observe clients in their natural settings. Second, many clients object to having their therapist come into their home or workplace to conduct a formal observation. Third, even if the client agreed to have the therapist come perform an observation, the therapist's presence is unavoidably obtrusive and therefore influences the client's behavior. The therapist observer is more than an observer, also becoming a participant within the client's environment—which means that an objective and natural observation cannot be obtained.

Because behavior therapists usually cannot use direct behavioral observation, they employ a variety of less direct data collection procedures.

The Clinical or Behavioral Interview

The clinical interview is the most common assessment procedure. Within the context of an interview, behavior therapists directly observe client behavior, inquire about behavioral antecedents and consequences, and operationalize the primary targets of therapy. For behaviorists, the *operational definition* or specific, measurable characteristics of client symptoms and goals are crucial behavioral assessment components.

Defining the client's problem(s) in precise behavioral terms is the first step in a behavioral assessment interview. Behavior therapists are not satisfied when clients describe themselves as "depressed" or "anxious" or "hyper." Instead, behaviorists seek concrete, specific behavioral information. Typical queries during a behavior therapy intake interview might include the following:

- "Tell me about everything that happens during the course of a day when you're depressed. Let's start with when you wake up in the morning and cover everything that happens until you go to bed at night . . . and I even want to know what happens throughout the night until the next morning."
- "Describe the physical sensations you experience in your body when you're feeling anxious."
- "You said you were acting 'hyper.' Tell me what that looks like . . . describe it to me so I can see it, as if I were a mouse in the corner watching it happen."

Behaviorists value information about both the internal (mood or physiology) and the external (behavior), as long as the information is clear, specific, and measurable.

Despite many practical advantages of behavioral interviews, this assessment procedure also has several disadvantages: (1) low interrater reliability, (2) lack of interviewer objectivity, and (3) frequent inconsistency between behavior within a clinical interview and behavior outside of therapy.

Behavior therapists compensate for the inconsistent and subjective nature of interviews through two strategies: First, they employ structured or diagnostic interviews such as the Structured Clinical Interview for the *Diagnostic and Statistical Manual of Mental Disorders,* fourth edition (*DSM-IV*), which helps improve interview reliability (First, Spitzer, Gibbon, & Williams, 1997). Second, they use additional assessment methods beyond interviewing procedures, to obtain client information (Sommers-Flanagan & Sommers-Flanagan, 1998).

Self-Monitoring

Although it's impractical for behavior therapists to directly observe client behavior outside therapy, it's perfectly acceptable for them to train clients to observe and monitor their own behavior. For example, clients can monitor food intake or keep track of the number of cigarettes they smoke. In cognitive-behavior therapy, clients frequently keep thought or emotion logs that include at least three components: (1) disturbing emotional states, (2) the exact behavior engaged in at the time of the emotional state, and (3) thoughts that occurred when the emotions emerged.

Client self-monitoring has advantages and disadvantages. On the positive side, self-monitoring is inexpensive, practical, and usually therapeutic. However, the client can easily collect inadequate or inaccurate information, or resist collecting any information at all.

Standardized Questionnaires

Behaviorists are famous for their preference for "objective" assessment measures over more "subjective" projective assessment procedures (Cormier & Nurius, 2003). Objective psychological measures include standardized administration and scoring. Additionally, behaviorists prefer instruments that have established reliability (i.e., internal consistency and consistency over time) and validity (i.e., the instrument measures what it purports to measure). Radical behaviorists, also called applied behavior analysts, emphasize that objective measurement must focus solely on overt or observable behaviors rather than internal mental processes.

Overall, behaviorists employ questionnaires as one way of determining whether a specific treatment is working. Objective measurement isn't perfect, but repeated measurement of client symptoms and behavior can help keep the therapist and client on the right track. This perspective is in direct contrast to the antiassessment attitude of most existential-humanistic therapists. Also, as discussed in this chapter's Practitioner Commentary, some behaviorists advocate repeated assessment and feedback as a means of enhancing therapy outcomes (see Practitioner Commentary 7.1).

Other Measures

Behavior therapists also use a variety of other measures to evaluate client symptoms and therapy progress (Truax, 2002). For example, behavior therapists may use intermittent or ongoing video or audiotape recordings or photographs to obtain direct samples of client behavior. Additionally, within research paradigms or in health psychology or behavioral medicine settings, physiological measures such as heart rate, blood pressure, and galvanic skin response are used to assess anxiety or anger levels (Gottman et al., 1995).

Specific Therapy Techniques

Behavior therapy encompasses a large array of therapeutic techniques. In order to identify necessary and sufficient ingredients for symptom reduction or alleviation, behavioral researchers have combined treatments, isolated specific treatment components, and compared treatment components. The following specific techniques constitute a standard regimen of primarily behavioral approaches, although many traditional and contemporary behavior therapies also employ cognitive procedures.

Operant Conditioning and Variants

In the tradition of Skinner and applied behavior analysis, perhaps the most straightforward application of behaviorism to therapy is direct operant conditioning. Skinner's emphasis is completely on environmental manipulation rather than processes of mind or cognition. In one of his more dramatic statements, he noted:

> I see no evidence of an inner world of mental life. . . . The appeal to cognitive states and processes is a diversion which could well be responsible for much of our failure to solve our problems. We need to change our behavior and we can do so only by changing our physical and social environments. (Skinner, 1977, p. 10)

The direct application of operant conditioning to human problems requires an analysis of the naturally occurring contingencies in the client's physical and social environment. To illustrate operant conditioning procedures, let's return to the parents who wanted their 15-year-old to stop speaking to them disrespectfully. If you recall, the parents' efforts to modify their teen's behavior by using positive reinforcement and punishment backfired. From the operant or applied behavior analysis perspective, the parents' efforts failed because they did not use operant conditioning in an appropriate manner. An appropriate use of operant conditioning involves several systematic steps.

First, the parents need to operationalize the target behaviors and identify behavioral objectives. This requires that behaviors of interest be precisely identified. It also requires determining whether they want to increase or decrease the frequency of each target behavior. In conjunction with their applied behavior analyst, the parents agreed on the following goals:

- Decrease profanity (use of traditional "cuss words") in the home or toward the parents.
- Decrease disrespectful gestures or nonverbal behaviors (e.g., giving "the finger," rolling her eyes, giving long heaving sighs).
- Decrease derogatory comments about the parents or their ideas, such as "You're stupid," "That sucks," or "This family is so lame."
- Increase their 15-year-old's smiling behavior, compliments toward the parents and younger sibling, and compliance with parental suggestions and advice.

Second, the therapist helped the parents develop a system for measuring the target behaviors. They were each given a pencil and notepad to track the exact frequency of their teen's behaviors. Additionally, they used a digital audiotape recorder to keep an ongoing record of the verbal interactions preceding and following their daughter's behaviors.

After analyzing the parents' notepads and audio-recorder data, the therapist helped the parents identify contingencies that were maintaining disrespectful speech and lack of respectful speech. During the 2-week baseline monitoring period, the parents recorded 16 incidents of undesirable behavior and 3 incidents of desirable behavior. Their home had become an aversive environment for all four family members.

It was determined that the parents' reaction to the disrespectful speech—giving in to demands, getting emotionally upset, or engaging in a protracted argument—were positively reinforcing problem behavior, whereas their relative lack of response to more pleasant behaviors was extinguishing the very behavior they wanted to increase. Furthermore, a variety of potential positive reinforcements were identified, including (1) taking their daughter out to dinner, (2) allowing her to rent DVDs, (3) taking her out for driving lessons, (4) allowing her to "instant message" friends on the family computer, and (5) spending money on her. This analysis led to the third stage of treatment: modification of existing environmental and social contingencies.

The parents were instructed in a very specific reinforcement and extinction procedure.

- The parents initiated a $10.00 weekly allowance program. This program provided their teen with money to spend as she wished. The only contingency for receiving the money was that whenever the 15-year-old used profanity, disrespectful gestures, or derogatory comments, she automatically lost $1.00 of the allowance, which she was scheduled to receive every Friday at 6:00 p.m.
- In response to the previously identified undesirable behaviors, the parents were to calmly and immediately state, "Okay, that's one dollar you've lost."
- The parents continued logging desirable behaviors. Using a variable-ratio reinforcement schedule, the parents provided one of the four reinforcers (a meal out, DVD rental, instant-messaging privileges, or practice driving) immediately after their teen displayed one of the aforementioned desirable target behaviors. To implement the variable ratio schedule, the parents were given a six-sided die. They were instructed to roll the die and then, depending upon the number they rolled, provide a positive reinforcer after that specific number of positive behaviors. Then, immediately after providing a reward, they once again rolled the die (privately, of course), and if the die came up "3," they planned to reward her again after three desirable behaviors. To reduce the number of positive reinforcements they provided, thereby fading her from the reinforcement program, the parents were given an additional die to use after every 2 weeks of increasing positive behaviors.

At the end of 8 weeks of using this operant conditioning program, the parents and therapist agreed that continued therapy was unnecessary. The parents said in their last session, "Thank you so much for your help. It's like we're getting acquainted with a new daughter."

Operant conditioning principles have also been widely applied to educational and institutional settings (Maag, 2001). Following Skinner's original work aimed at modifying the behavior of psychotic patients, operant conditioning within institutions has come to be known as a *token economy*. Within a token economy system, patients or students are provided with points or poker chips (symbolic rewards) for engaging in positive or desirable behaviors. These tokens then can be used as money, to obtain goods (e.g., food or toys) or privileges (e.g., computer time or recreational time).

Token economies have been criticized as coercive and as not having lasting effects that generalize to the world outside the institution (Glynn, 1990). In an ideal behavioral setting, reinforcements and punishments would be tightly controlled and then, after the desirable behavior patterns are well established, the behavioral contingencies would be slowly decreased (as in the case of the 15-year-old teen whose reinforcements were progressively decreased). This procedure is referred to as *fading* and is designed to maximize the likelihood of generalization of learning from one setting to another. The desired outcome occurs when a child, teen, or institutionalized adult eventually internalizes the contingency system; self-reinforcement and self-punishment are continued after institutionalization in the interest of self-control.

As an important side note, nearly 100 studies have shown that tangible positive reinforcement may undermine intrinsic motivation (Cameron & Pierce, 1994; Deci, 1971; Kohn, 1993). That is, if you reward people for doing something they are inclined to do anyway, you can actually reduce their motivation for doing the very behavior you are rewarding. There is also a body of literature rebutting this undermining hypothesis and claiming that positive reinforcement, when properly conceptualized and administered, can increase intrinsic motivation (Carton & Nowicki, 1998; Maag, 2001). Overall, although it is conceptually straightforward, operant conditioning carries with it many important subtleties in application. Consequently, further training is needed if you want to employ operant techniques in a consistently helpful fashion.

While positive reinforcement has had its share of criticism in recent years, the direct application of punishment, or *aversive conditioning,* as a therapeutic technique generates far more controversy. Historically, Thorndike (1932), Skinner (1953), and Estes (1944) all concluded that punishment led to the suppression of behavior but was not a permanent or very effective method for controlling behavior. At that time, punishment was generally viewed as insufficient to completely eliminate a learned response. Somewhat later, Solomon (1964) reopened the book on punishment by reporting that punishment alone was capable of generating new, learned behavior. Currently, although punishment is generally considered a powerful behavior modifier, it's also believed to have major drawbacks as a therapeutic or learning strategy. In particular, within the attachment and trauma literature, excessive punishment by caregivers is viewed as leading to what has been referred to as *trauma bonding.* A description of Harry Harlow's studies on attachment behaviors in monkeys (see Harlow, Harlow, Dodsworth, & Arling, 1966; Harlow, Harlow, & Suomi, 1971) provides a vivid example of the terrors of mixing love and punishment: "When Harlow presented baby macaques with mechanically devised spike-sprouting surrogates or mothers that suddenly puffed blasts of air, the infants gripped all the tighter to the only security they knew" (Hrdy, 1999, p. 398).

Punishment or aversive conditioning is usually used to reduce undesirable and maladaptive behavior. Specifically, it has been applied with some success to smoking cessation, repetitive self-injurious behavior, alcohol abuse or dependency, and sexual deviation. In their review of aversive conditioning procedures, Prochaska and Norcross (2003) outline an imposing set of guidelines for ethically and effectively using punishment as a behavior modifier. These guidelines are based on the scientific literature and illustrate why many behavior therapists are reluctant to employ punishment strategies. To be effective, punishment should be:

- Immediate (delay increases anxiety and decreases learning)
- Intense (punishment is more effective if it is more averse)
- Salient (it should be individually defined)
- Delivered early in the behavioral chain (before a problem intensifies)
- Delivered on a continuous schedule (because if the punishment does not always occur, the behavior you want to eliminate may be intermittently rewarded, which makes it much more difficult to eliminate)
- Provided across all stimulus situations (otherwise punishment is simply avoided)
- Delivered in a calm manner (so the recipient doesn't react to the punisher's anger instead of the punishment)
- Accompanied by teaching of alternative adaptive behaviors (so the recipient clearly learns what is desirable behavior)

In a recent meta-analysis of the effects of corporal punishment on children's behavior (Gershoff, 2002), punishment was associated with 1 desirable outcome (i.e., immediate behavioral compliance) and 10 undesirable outcomes, including less internalization of moral principles, potential abuse, delinquent behavior, and later abuse within an adult relationship. Despite this fairly clear indictment of corporal punishment, many parents and teachers, and some therapists, remain adamantly in favor of its use as a primary disciplinary technique (Baumrind, Larzelere, & Cowan, 2002). Some of this attachment to punishment as a learning tool by the nonscientific and nonbehaviorist population is directly linked to religious beliefs. It is also true that administering punishment provides the authority figure with negative reinforcement: Immediate compliance occurs, which reduces the authority figure's tension and discomfort (Maag, 2001); see section on imaginal or in vivo exposure and desensitization for more discussion of negative reinforcement).

Relaxation Training

Edmund Jacobson was the first modern scientist to write about relaxation training as a treatment procedure (Jacobson, 1924). In his book, *Progressive Relaxation,* he outlined principles and techniques of relaxation training that therapists still employ in the twenty-first century (Jacobson, 1938). Progressive muscle relaxation (PMR) was initially based on the assumption that muscular tension is an underlying cause of a variety of mental and emotional problems. In fact, Jacobson claimed that "nervous disturbance is at the same time mental disturbance. Neurosis and psychoneurosis are at the same time physiological disturbance; for they are forms of tension disorder" (Jacobson, 1978, p. viii). For Jacobson, individuals can cure neurosis through relaxation. More recently, among anxious clients, PMR is viewed as an extinction procedure. By pairing the muscle-tension conditioned stimulus with pleasurable relaxation, muscle tension as a stimulus or trigger for anxiety is extinguished.

Progressive muscle relaxation is still a common relaxation training approach, although others—such as breathing retraining, meditation, autogenic training, imagery, and hypnosis—are also popular (Benson, 1976; Bernstein & Borkovec, 1973; Hersen, 2002). Information on implementing relaxation procedures with clients is outlined in Putting It in Practice 7.1 and 7.2.

===== **Putting It in Practice 7.1** =====

Prepping Clients (and Yourself) for Progressive Muscle Relaxation

Before using relaxation training with clients, you should experience the procedure yourself. You can accomplish this either by going to a behavior therapist and asking to learn the procedure, using a PMR audiotape or CD (usually available at your public library or for purchase), or asking your professor to demonstrate the procedure in class.

We also recommend that you make your own audiotape or CD and use it for practicing. Getting comfortable with the right pace and voice tone for inducing a relaxed state is important. Don't be afraid to ask for feedback regarding your relaxation induction skills.

When working with clients, keep the following issues in mind:

- Have a quiet room and a comfortable chair available. Noise and discomfort are antithetical to relaxation. Reclining chairs are recommended. Lighting should be dim, but not dark.
- Give clients clear information as to why you're teaching PMR. If the rationale is not clear to them, they may not be motivated to participate fully.
- Explain the procedure. Say something like "I'll be instructing you to create tension and then let go of tension in specific muscle groups. Research shows that tensing your muscles first and then relaxing them helps you achieve a deeper relaxation than if you just tried to relax them without tensing them up first." You might demonstrate this by flexing and then relaxing your arm or shoulder muscles.
- Seat yourself in a position that doesn't distract clients. A face-to-face arrangement can make clients uncomfortable. Instead, place seats at a 90–120° angle.
- Emphasize that, like most skills, this skill—the ability to relax oneself—can be learned best through repeated practice. You might also mention that because people can learn to be tense and uptight they can also learn to be relaxed and peaceful.
- Tell your clients that they are in control of the relaxation process. To become relaxed, all they have to do is listen to you and follow along, but whether they listen and follow along is totally their choice.
- Warn clients that they may feel some unusual body sensations: "Some people feel tingling, others feel light and maybe a little dizzy, and still others feel heavy, like they're sinking into the chair. I don't know exactly how you'll feel, but we'll take a few minutes afterward to talk about how it felt to you."
- Let clients know they can keep their eyes open or shut. Some clients hate the idea of closing their eyes, and their discomfort should be respected. Usually, if clients want to keep their eyes open, it means that they're not yet feeling enough trust in you or the situation. However, it's fine to encourage clients to shut their eyes whenever they feel ready.
- Let clients know that they can move around if it helps them to be more comfortable. Similarly, if they wear glasses, they might want to remove them. The key is to facilitate physical comfort.

(continued)

=== **Putting It in Practice 7.1 (continued)** ===

- Check for physical pains or conditions (e.g., a knee or back problem) that might be inflamed by tensing muscles in that particular region. Omit any painful or injured body parts from the procedure.
- Let clients know that their minds may wander while you're talking and they're relaxing. That's okay. If they notice their minds wandering, all they need to do is gently bring attention back to whatever you're saying.
- Help clients have realistic, but optimistic, expectations: "Most people who do progressive relaxation find that it helps them relax a bit, but they don't find it amazing or dramatic. Some people find it extremely relaxing and wonderful. And a very small minority of people actually feel a little more tense after their first try. Whether you feel more tense, a little more relaxed, or a lot more relaxed isn't all that important, because with a little practice, everyone can learn to do this in a way that's beneficial."

Additional detailed information about using PMR is available from several sources (see Bernstein & Borkovec, 1973; Davis, McKay, & Eshelman, 2000; Goldfried & Davison, 1994).

Systematic Desensitization and Other Exposure-Based Behavioral Treatments

Joseph Wolpe formally introduced systematic desensitization as a treatment technique (Wolpe, 1958). In his original work, Wolpe reported a highly controversial treatment success rate of 80%, and therapists (especially psychoanalysts) criticized and challenged his procedures and results (Glover, 1959). To this day, Wolpe defends his claims of impressive success rates for systematic desensitization (Wolpe & Plaud, 1997).

Systematic desensitization is a combination of Jone's deconditioning approach and Jacobson's PMR procedure (M.C. Jones, 1924). Jacobson articulated the central place of relaxation in curing clients of anxious or disturbed conditions, stating that "to be relaxed is the direct physiological opposite of being excited or disturbed" (Jacobson, 1978, p. viii).

After clients are trained in PMR techniques, they build a *fear hierarchy* in collaboration with the therapist. Systematic desensitization usually proceeds in the following manner.

- The client identifies a range of various fear-inducing situations or objects.
- Typically, using a measuring system referred to as subjective units of distress (SUDs), the client, with the support of the therapist, rates each fear-inducing situation or object on a scale from 0 to 100 (0 = no distress; 100 = total distress).
- Early in the session the client engages in PMR.
- While deeply relaxed, the client is exposed, in vivo or through imagery, to the least feared item in the fear hierarchy.
- Subsequently, the client is exposed to each feared item, gradually progressing to the most feared item in the hierarchy.
- If the client experiences significant anxiety at any point during the imaginal or in vivo exposure process, the client reengages in PMR until relaxation overcomes anxiety.

Sample Progressive Muscle Relaxation Procedure

It's often beneficial to participate in this PMR procedure at the same time that you teach the client this procedure. However, as noted by Goldfried and Davison (1976), therapists should take care not to become so relaxed that they fall asleep during the procedure! A verbatim sample of PMR follows.

"Are you ready to start the progressive relaxation procedure? [Client responds affirmatively.] Okay. Just sit back and relax and breathe gently, deeply, and slowly. You can close your eyes now if that feels comfortable. All you have to do is listen and do your best to follow the instructions I give you.

"One interesting thing about progressive muscle relaxation is that it can make you aware of how different parts of your body are feeling. For a moment, just think about your left arm. It's like you can focus your attention on your left arm and be totally aware of it, much more aware than you usually are. Now focus your attention on your left hand and slowly clench it into a fist. That's it. Notice how that tension feels. Feel it in your hand and forearm just for a few moments. [Wait about 5 seconds.] Now let the tension go. Let your hand and forearm totally relax and be limp. Focus your attention on your hand and forearm now and notice the difference between how it felt when it was tense and how it feels now. Notice the difference."

Systematic tension and relaxation progressively continues into each of the following muscle groups:

- Right hand and arm: See preceding instructions.
- Back of both hands and forearms: "With your arms on the armrests, lift up your fingers and hands into the air so that the muscles in the back of your hands and arms are tense. That's it. Now feel that tension. Now let go of the tension and let your hands and arms drop back down and rest again. Feel the relaxation." (10 seconds)
- Arms, primarily biceps: "Now clench your fists again, but this time raise up your arms like a bodybuilder and flex your biceps. That's it, flex them both like you're in a body-building contest, and feel that tension in your muscles. Then, all at once, just relax your arms and let them come back down to their resting position. Good. Feel the limpness. Notice the difference between your muscles when they're tense and when they're relaxed." (10 seconds)
- Shoulders and neck: "Lots of people hold tension in their shoulders and neck, so now move your attention to your shoulders and neck. Good. Lift your shoulders up so that they almost touch your ears. Notice the tightness and tension growing in your shoulders, neck, and upper back. Feel it. Then let go of all the tension. Let your shoulders drop back to their normal position and just feel the difference. Now your shoulders, neck, and upper back muscles are limp and relaxed."

(continued)

Putting It in Practice 7.1 (continued)

- Face: "You can also relax the muscles in your face. To do this, close your eyes very tightly, clench your jaw, and grimace in such a way that your whole face is filled with tension. That's good. Your whole face, around your eyes, cheeks, and jaw, is tense and tight. Notice what that feels like, and now let go of the tension. Feel the relaxation replacing the tension. Your face now feels warm and relaxed. Just feel that warm and relaxed feeling all through your face."
- Chest and stomach: "As we've progressed through these muscle groups, you've been breathing comfortably and steadily. Now, as you pay attention to your breathing, take a deep breath and hold it and tighten up your stomach, so it's as solid and hard as you can get it. While you're holding your breath, pay attention to tension in your chest and stomach. Notice how they feel, and now just let go and release the air from your lungs and the tension from your chest and stomach. That's it. Let it all go away and notice the difference. It feels nice to let all that tension go away."
- Upper legs: "Now move your attention down to your legs, your upper legs. Notice how they feel. Stretch out your legs so that your thigh muscles are taut. Concentrate on how the muscles in your thighs feel. Concentrate on that tension. Let go of the tension and let your feet return to the floor. Notice how nice this new feeling of relaxation feels. Your thighs are just limp now, limp and calm."
- Lower legs and feet: "And now move your attention even lower, into your calves and feet. Lift your toes in the air until they're pointing upwards, lifted off the ground. You can feel your toes in your shoes straining and stretching upward, and you can feel the tension in your calves. Notice exactly how that tension feels. Then just let the tension go, and let it be replaced with relaxation. Let your feet return to a comfortable position on the floor."
- Ending: "Okay. Now we've gone through almost all of your major muscle groups. Before we stop, let's take a quick survey. If there's any tension left in one of your muscle groups, feel free to repeat the process and tense up that group and relax it again. That's it. Just say goodbye to all that tension. In just a moment, I'll count backward from five to one, as a signal that this muscle relaxation procedure is over. When I finish counting from five to one, you can just open your eyes and stretch, and we can talk about what the experience was like for you. Okay, coming up at the count of five to one, five—four—three—two—one. Wide awake. Good job."

Postrelaxation Guidelines

Different clients have different relaxation experiences. Most clients find the process at least mildly pleasant and relaxing. Nonetheless, check in with clients following the procedure so you know exactly how they felt. Then you can assign out-of-session homework for your clients to practice the procedure.

- Treatment continues systematically until the client achieves relaxation competence while simultaneously being exposed to the entire range of his or her fear hierarchy.

Systematic desensitization is both straightforward and potentially complex. Further reading and supervised practice are needed for you to master the skill. Detailed information on hierarchy development and other components of systematic desensitization are available elsewhere (Cormier & Nurius, 2003; Goldfried & Davison, 1994).

Imaginal or In Vivo Exposure and Desensitization

Systematic desensitization is a form of *exposure* treatment. Exposure treatments are based on the principle that clients are best treated by exposure to the very thing they want to avoid: the stimulus that evokes intense fear, anxiety, or other painful emotions. Mowrer (1947) used a two-factor theory of learning, based on animal studies, to explain how avoidance conditioning works. First, he explained that animals originally learn to fear a particular stimulus through classical conditioning. For example, a dog may learn to fear its owner's voice when it is raised due to the discovery of an unwelcome pile on the living room carpet. Then, if the dog remains in the room with its owner, fear continues to escalate.

Second, Mowrer explained that avoidance behavior is reinforced via operant conditioning. Specifically, if the dog manages to hide under the bed or dash out the front door of the house, it is likely to experience decreased fear and anxiety. Consequently, the avoidance behavior—running away and hiding—is negatively reinforced because it produces relief from fear, anxiety, and discomfort. *Negative reinforcement* is defined as the strengthening of a behavioral response by reducing or eliminating an aversive stimulus.

Note that exposure via systematic desensitization and the other procedures detailed hereafter are distinctively behavioral. However, the concept that psychological health is enhanced when clients face and embrace their fears is consistent with existential and Jungian theory.

Traditionally, there are two ways in which clients are exposed to their fears during systematic desensitization. The first approach involves exposure to fears through mental imagery. This approach allows clients to complete treatment without ever leaving their therapist's office. More recently, computer simulation (virtual reality) has been successfully used as an imaginal means of exposing clients to feared stimuli (Emmelkamp, et al., 2001).

Alternatively, clients may be treated with a combination of relaxation and in vivo exposure to feared stimuli. In vivo exposure involves direct exposure to real-life situations. For example, a client with a dental phobia is taken to the dentist's office for a series of treatment sessions. Overall, research suggests that in vivo exposure and desensitization procedures are more effective than imaginal procedures (Emmelkamp, 1994).

Massed (Intensive) or Spaced (Graduated) Exposure Sessions

Behavior therapists continue to tinker with the most optimal method for extinguishing fear responses in anxious or fearful clients. One question being examined empirically is this: Is desensitization more effective when clients are directly exposed to feared stimuli during a single session for a prolonged time period (such as one 3-hour session; a.k.a. *massed exposure*) or when they are slowly and incrementally exposed to feared stimuli during a series of shorter sessions (such as five 1-hour sessions; a.k.a. *spaced exposure*)? Initially, it was thought that massed exposure might result in higher dropout rates, greater likelihood of fear relapse, and a greater experience of stress by clients. However, early research suggests that massed and spaced exposure desensitization strategies yield no significant efficacy differences (Ost, Alm, Brandberg, & Breitholz, 2001).

Virtual Reality Exposure

Technological advancements have led to potential modifications in systematic desensitization procedures. Specifically, virtual reality exposure, a procedure wherein clients are immersed in a real-time computer-generated computer environment, has been empirically evaluated as an alternative to imaginal or in vivo exposure in cases of acrophobia (fear of heights), flight phobia, and spider phobia (Bornas, Fullana, Tortella-Feliu, Llabres, & de la Banda, 2001; Emmelkamp, Bruynzeel, Drost, & van der Mast, 2001; Garcia-Palacios, Hoffman, Carlin, Furness, & Botella, 2002). In a few initial studies, Emmelkamp and colleagues have reported that virtual reality exposure is as effective as in vivo exposure in reducing client anxiety and decreasing client avoidance of feared situations (Emmelkamp, Bruynzeel, et al., 2001; Emmelkamp, Krijn, et al., 2001).

Interoceptive Exposure

Research on Panic Disorder has revealed that some clients who experience intense fear are responding less to situational stimuli and more to internal physical sensations. Typical panic-prone individuals are highly sensitive to internal physical cues (e.g., increased heart rate, increased respiration, and dizziness) and interpret those sensations as signs of physical illness, impending death, or impending loss of consciousness (and associated humiliation). Although specific cognitive techniques have been developed to treat clients' tendencies to catastrophically overinterpret bodily sensations, a more behavioral technique, interoceptive exposure, has been developed to help clients learn, through exposure and practice, to deal more effectively with the physical aspects of intense anxiety or panic (Beck, Shipherd, & Zebb, 1997; Taylor, 2000).

Interoceptive exposure is identical to other exposure techniques except that the target exposure stimuli are internal physical cues. Commonly researched interoceptive exposure techniques involve hyperventilation, running in place, holding one's breath, breathing through a straw, and slowly spinning in circles to produce dizziness and increased heart rate. (Arntz, 2002; DeCola & Craske, 2002; Forsyth, Lejuez, & Finlay, 2000). Of course, before interoceptive exposure is initiated, the client has received education about bodily sensations, has learned relaxation techniques (e.g., breathing control or training), and has been taught cognitive restructuring skills. Then, through repeated successful exposure, the client becomes desensitized to previously feared physical cues (Bouton, Mineka, & Barlow, 2001; DeCola & Craske, 2002).

Response Prevention and Ritual Prevention

Mowrer's two-factor theory indicates that, when a client avoids or escapes a feared or distressing situation or stimulus, the maladaptive avoidance behavior is negatively reinforced (i.e., when the client feels relief from the negative anxiety, fear, or distress, the avoidance or escape behavior is reinforced or strengthened). Many examples of this negative reinforcement cycle are present across the spectrum of mental disorders. For example, clients with Bulimia Nervosa who purge after eating specific "forbidden" foods are relieving themselves from the anxiety and discomfort they experience upon ingesting the foods (Agras, Schneider, Arnow, Raeburn, & Telch, 1989). Therefore, purging behavior is negatively reinforced. Similarly, when a phobic client escapes from a phobic object or situation, or when a client with obsessive-compulsive symptoms engages in a repeated washing or checking behavior, negative reinforcement of maladaptive behavior occurs (Foa & Kozak, 1986; Franklin & Foa, 1998; March, Franklin, Nelson, & Foa, 2001).

It follows that, in order to be effective, exposure-based desensitization treatment must include response prevention. With the therapist's assistance, the client with bulimia is prevented from vomiting after ingesting a forbidden cookie, the agoraphobic client is prevented from fleeing a public place when anxiety begins to mount, and the client with Obsessive-Compulsive Disorder is prevented from washing his or her hands following exposure to a "contaminated" object. Without response or ritual prevention, the treatment may exacerbate the condition it is designed to treat.

Participant Modeling

In addition to operant principles, social learning principles have also been empirically evaluated for anxiety treatment (Bandura, Blanchard, & Ritter, 1969). Recall that, in her original work with Little Peter and other fearful children, Jones reported that social imitation was one of the two effective deconditioning strategies (M.C. Jones, 1924).

Like most behavioral techniques, in order to have a positive effect, participant modeling needs to be conducted in an appropriate and sensitive manner. For example, individuals with airplane or flight phobias generally don't find it helpful when they watch other passengers getting on a plane without experiencing distress. In fact, such observations can produce increased feelings of humiliation and hopelessness; seeing others easily confront fears that they find paralyzing is discouraging to phobic clients. The problem is that there is too large a gap in emotional state and skills between the model and the observer, so maximal vicarious learning does not occur. Instead of providing the client with general models of fear-free behavior, behavior therapists provide models of successful coping within the context of skill acquisition.

Group therapy provides an excellent opportunity for participant modeling and vicarious learning. This is why published treatment protocols for Panic Disorder often recommend using a group therapy format to take advantage of participant modeling effects (Craske, 1999).

Skills Training

Skills training techniques are primarily based on skill deficit models of psychopathology. Many clients suffering from behavioral disorders have not acquired the requisite skills for functioning across a broad range of domains. Consequently, behavior therapists evaluate their clients' functional skills during the assessment phase of therapy and then use specific skills training strategies to remediate the clients' skill deficits. Traditional skills training targets include assertiveness and other social behavior, and problem solving.

Assertiveness and Other Social Behavior

In the behavioral tradition, Wolpe, Lazarus, and others defined assertiveness as a learned behavior (Alberti & Emmons, 1970; Lazarus, 1973a; Wolpe, 1973). Generally, individuals are evaluated as having one of three possible social behavior styles: passive, aggressive, or assertive. *Passive* individuals behave in submissive ways; they say yes when they want to say no, avoid speaking up and asking for instructions or directions, and let others take advantage of them. *Aggressive* individuals dominate others, trying to get their way through coercive means. In contrast, the ideal or *assertive* individual speaks up, expresses feelings, and lets needs be known without dominating others.

In the 1970s, assertiveness training became popular as an individual, group, or self-help treatment for social difficulties. A number of self-help books on this treatment were published, including the highly acclaimed *Your Perfect Right: Assertiveness and Equality in Your Life and Relationships,* now in its eighth edition (Alberti & Emmons, 2001). The most common social behaviors targeted in assertiveness training are introducing oneself to strangers, giving and receiving compliments, saying no to requests from others, making requests of others, speaking up or voicing an opinion, and maintaining social conversations. Within a counseling context, assertive behavior is taught through the following strategies:

- Instruction: Clients are instructed in assertive eye contact, body posture, voice tone, and verbal delivery.
- Feedback: The therapist or group members give clients feedback regarding how their efforts at assertive behavior come across to others.
- Behavior rehearsal or role playing: Clients are given opportunities to practice specific assertive behaviors, such as asking for help or expressing disagreement without becoming angry or aggressive.
- Coaching: Therapists often whisper feedback and instructions in the client's ear as a role-play or practice scenario progresses.
- Modeling: The therapist or group members demonstrate appropriate assertive behavior for specific situations.
- Social reinforcement: The therapist or group members offer positive feedback and support for appropriate assertive behavior.
- Relaxation training: For some clients, relaxation training is needed to reduce anxiety in social situations.

Although assertiveness training remains a viable treatment option for many clients, its popularity has declined somewhat. However, the components of assertiveness training for individuals with specific social anxiety and social skills deficits are still of great interest. For example, Social Phobia—a condition characterized by an excessive, irrational fear of being scrutinized and evaluated by others—is frequently treated with a combination of relaxation and social skills training that includes almost all the components of traditional assertion training (e.g., instruction, feedback, behavior rehearsal, social reinforcement) and graduated or massed exposure to challenging social situations and interactions (McNeil, Sorrell, Vowles, & Billmeyer, 2002; Taylor, 1996). The standard behavioral treatment protocol for socially anxious individuals has been slightly refined, but it remains very closely related to generic assertion training procedures.

Problem Solving

Behaviorists frequently teach clients to follow a systematic, logical, and effective approach to solving problems, typically involving the following steps:

1. Define the problem.
2. Identify the goal.
3. Generate options.
4. Choose the best solution.
5. Evaluate the outcome.

Problem solving has been employed as a technique for working with children and adolescents. Kazdin reports that problem-solving training for youths with conduct disorder, in combination with parent training, consistently improves therapy outcomes (Kazdin, 1996; Kazdin, Siegel, & Bass, 1992). In addition to teaching some variant on the five-step approach previously listed, child and adolescent behavior therapists often focus specifically on a number of cognitive and behavioral concepts, such as means-ends thinking, generating behavioral alternatives, consequential thinking, and perspective taking (Shure, 1992; Sommers-Flanagan & Sommers-Flanagan, 1997; Spivack, Platt, & Shure, 1976). A brief verbatim therapy transcript excerpt illustrating the technique of generating behavioral alternatives is in Putting It in Practice 7.3.

Putting It in Practice 7.3

Generating Behavioral Alternatives with an Aggressive Adolescent

The 15-year-old male client in the following transcript reported that the night before the session, a male schoolmate had tried to "rape" the client's girlfriend. The client was angry and irritable and planning to "beat the shit out of [the fellow student]." During the session, I (John—here, JSF) am trying to help the boy identify behavioral alternatives to retributive violence. The transcript picks up about 10 minutes into the session.

Boy: He's gotta learn sometime.
JSF: I mean. I don't know for sure what the absolute best thing to do to this guy is . . . but I think before you act, it's important to think of all the different options you have.
Boy: I've been thinking a lot.
JSF: Well, tell me the other ones you've thought of.
Boy: Kick the shit out of him.
JSF: Okay, I know 2 things, actually maybe 3, that you said. One is kick the shit out of him, the other one is to do nothing . . .
Boy: The other is to shove something up his ass.
JSF: And, okay—shove—which is kinda like kicking the shit out of him. I mean to be violent toward him.
Boy: Yeah, Yeah.
JSF: So, what else?
Boy: I could nark on him.
JSF: Oh.
Boy: Tell the cops or something.
JSF: And I'm not saying that's the right thing to do either.
Boy: That's just stupid.

(continued)

=== **Putting It in Practice 7.3 (continued)** ===

JSF: I'm not saying that's the right thing to do . . . all I'm saying is that we should figure out, cause I know I think I have the same kind of impulse in your situation. Either, I wanna beat him up or kinda do the high and right-eous thing, which is to ignore him. And I'm not sure. Maybe one of those is the right thing, but I don't know. Now, we got three things—so you could nark on him.

Boy: It's not gonna happen though.

JSF: Yeah, but I don't care if that's gonna happen. So there's nark, there's ig-nore, there's beat the shit. What else?

Boy: Um. Just talk to him, would be okay. Just go up to him and yeah . . . I think we need to have a little chit-chat.

JSF: Okay. Talk to him.

Boy: But that's not gonna happen either. I don't think I could talk to him with-out, like, him pissing me off and me kicking the shit . . .

JSF: So, it might be so tempting when you talk to him that you just end up beating the shit out of him.

Boy: Yeah. Yeah.

JSF: But all we're doing is making a list. Okay. And you're doing great.

Boy: I could get someone to beat the shit out of him.

JSF: Get somebody to beat him up. So, kind of indirect violence—you kind of get him back physical—through physical pain. That's kind of the approach.

Boy: I could get some girl who's really fat to rape him . . . just like AHHHH—Shit.

JSF: So you could get a fat girl to rape him. Okay.

Boy: Someone like an unattractive looking bitch.

JSF: Okay. We're up to six options.

Boy: That's about it. . . .

JSF: So. So we got nark, we got ignore, we got beat the shit out of him, we got talk to him, we got get somebody else to beat the shit out of him, and get some fat girl to rape him.

Boy: Um . . . couple of those are pretty unrealistic, but.

JSF: We don't have to be realistic. I've got another unrealistic one. I got an-other one . . . Kinda to start some shameful rumor about him, you know.

Boy: That's a good idea.

JSF: I mean, it's a nonviolent way to get some revenge.

Boy: Like he has a little dick or something.

JSF: Yeah, good, exactly.

Boy: Maybe I'll do all these things.

JSF: Combination.

Boy: Yeah.

JSF: So we've got the shameful rumor option.

Boy: That's a good one. (excerpted from Sommers-Flanagan & Sommers-Flanagan, 1999)

This case illustrates what sometimes occurs when therapists generate behavioral alternatives with an angry adolescent. Initially, the boy appears to be blowing off steam and generating a spate of aggressive alternatives. This process, although not producing constructive alternatives, is important because the boy may be testing the therapist to see if he will react with judgment (during this brainstorming process it is very important for the therapist to remain positive and welcoming of all options, no matter how violent or absurd). As the boy produced the various aggressive ideas, he appeared to calm down somewhat. Also, the therapist repeatedly read the behavioral alternatives back to the client. This allows the boy to hear his ideas from a different perspective. Finally, toward the end, the therapist joins the boy in brainstorming and adds a marginally delinquent response. What the therapist is doing here (besides embarrassing himself) is modeling a less violent approach to revenge and hoping to get the boy to consider a non-physical alternative.

APPLICATION: CASE EXAMPLE

Discerning the difference between cognitive and behavioral therapies is difficult. Most behavior therapists use cognitive treatments, and most cognitive therapists use behavioral treatments. The following case illustrates a cognitive-behavioral approach. In this chapter, we focus on the behavior therapy techniques for Panic Disorder. In the next chapter (Chapter 8) we continue this case, adding cognitive components from a comprehensive cognitive-behavioral approach for Panic Disorder and Agoraphobia (Craske, 1999).

Case Description

Richard, a 56-year-old male, referred himself for therapy due to increasing anxiety and phobic and depressive symptoms. Richard was afraid to leave his home because of fears that he would have a panic attack. He reported experiencing "over ten" attacks in the past month. According to Richard, these attacks were increasing in intensity. During his intake session he indicated that panic attacks trigger fears that he's having a heart attack. Richard's father died of a massive heart attack at age 56.

Richard's health is excellent. He was rushed to the emergency room during his two most recent panic episodes. In both cases the physician determined that Richard's cardiac functioning was within normal limits. Nonetheless, his fear of panic attacks and heart attacks was escalating, and his increasing seclusion was adversely affecting his employment as a professor at a local vocational college. His wife, Linda, accompanied him to his intake session. At the time of the referral, Richard had stopped driving and was having his wife transport him.

Assessment Procedures

Richard was administered the Anxiety Disorders Interview Schedule for *DSM-IV*. This semistructured interview indicated that Richard's symptoms were consistent with Panic Disorder with Agoraphobia.

During the intake interview, Richard was instructed in self-monitoring procedures and given a packet of rating scales to further assess the quality and quantity of his panic and agoraphobic symptoms. He was asked to use the self-monitoring scales to rate the duration, intensity, situational context, and symptom profile of each panic attack that occurred during the 10 days between his intake interview and his first treatment session. Richard also kept a food and beverage log during this 10-day period to determine if there were any links between food and beverage consumption and his anxiety symptoms.

Richard was given a number of standardized assessment instruments to provide treatment planning information. These included the Body Sensations Questionnaire (Chambless, Caputo, Bright, & Gallagher, 1984), the Mobility Inventory Questionnaire (Chambless, Caputo, Gracely, Jasin, & Williams, 1985), and the Agoraphobia Cognitions Questionnaire (Chambless et al., 1984).

Medical Consultation

In Richard's case there were two primary reasons to seek a medical consultation. First, panic and agoraphobic symptoms can be caused or exacerbated by a variety of medical conditions. These conditions include heart disease, diabetes, hypoglycemia, hyperthyroidism, mitral valve prolapse, stroke, and more. Second, many clients who obtain behavioral treatment for panic and agoraphobia also simultaneously receive pharmacological treatment. However, currently it is difficult to ascertain whether adding medications—usually serotonin-specific reuptake inhibitors (e.g., Prozac, Paxil, or Zoloft)—will enhance or detract from behavioral treatment efficacy (Otto, Pollack, & Sabatino, 1996). Adding medications appears to help some clients while adversely affecting others due to physical side-effect sensitivity and motivation reduction. Consequently, it's best for the empirically oriented behavior therapist to consult with medical professionals to determine whether pharmacological treatment should be offered in each individual case.

Based on Richard's medical information, it was determined that he was suffering from primary rather than secondary panic symptoms (i.e., he did not have any medical conditions that were either causing or maintaining his anxiety symptoms). Additionally, after a conference with Richard and his physician regarding his physical sensitivity to medications, it was determined that behavioral treatment should proceed without adjunctive pharmacological treatment.

Treatment Excerpts and Commentary

The format of behavior therapy sessions is typically structured. In Richard's case, the therapist followed a specific five-component panic disorder protocol developed by Barlow and Craske (1989, 1994; DeCola & Craske, 2002). The five components are

1. Education about the nature of anxiety
2. Breathing retraining
3. Cognitive restructuring
4. Interoceptive exposure
5. Imaginal or in vivo exposure

Each session includes four parts: (1) general check-in and homework review, (2) educational information about panic and behavior therapy, (3) in-session behavioral or cognitive tasks, and (4) a new set of homework assignments. The main goal of this behavioral treatment protocol is to teach Richard to become his own therapist.

Sessions 1 and 2. Richard's homework was reviewed. During the 10 days since his intake interview, he left his home on eight separate occasions and had four panic attacks. His caffeine consumption appeared to be connected to his panic symptoms: Three of his four panic episodes were preceded by consumption of caffeinated sodas, coffee, or both. His primary panic symptoms included heart palpitations, dizziness, shortness of breath, tingling sensations in his extremities, and catastrophic thoughts of death and dying.

The first two sessions primarily focused on education and instruction regarding anxiety and panic physiology.

Therapist: Richard, excellent job on your homework. Looking this over gives us both a much better idea of how to get you back on track in your life.

Richard: Well, thanks.

Therapist: One of our main goals for today is to talk about what your panic symptoms mean. Let's start there.

Richard: Okay. Sounds good.

Therapist: The first thing is that even though the intense panic feelings you've been getting seem strange, they're completely natural. Humans are designed to experience panic just like you've been experiencing it. Why do you suppose that is?

Richard: Um. I've always figured that when my heart starts pounding and I get dizzy and all that, it must mean that something is terribly wrong.

Therapist: Exactly! The human internal panic response is an alarm system. Some people call it the fight-or-flight response. When it's working properly, the panic alarm is a great survival device. It increases blood pressure, tenses up muscles, and gets you ready to run or fight. It's supposed to go off exclusively during moments of extreme danger—like when you're crossing a street and a car is barreling straight at you, or when you're attacked by a mugger. Your main problem is that your alarm is misfiring. It's going off when you don't need it. You've been having a series of false alarms. Think about that. When you've had your panic attacks, have there been any extreme dangers you're facing?

Richard: Not exactly. But when I start to feel panicked, I'm sure I must be having a heart attack, just like my dad did when he was my age.

Therapist: What have the doctors said about that?

Richard: Well, they've told me my heart is fine. That it's in good shape.

Therapist: So the false alarm you're feeling has two main parts. There are the physical symptoms of heart pounding, dizziness, shortness of breath, and tingly hands—that's one part. And then there's the thought of "I'm going to die from a heart attack just like my dad" that grabs you. And both these signals, the physical sensations and the thought you're going to die, are false. There is no immediate big danger, and your heart is fine. Right?

Richard: That's what they say.

Therapist: Okay, I know it feels incredibly scary and it's a horrible feeling. I don't expect you to instantly believe what I'm saying or what your doctor is saying, because the feelings are real and you've been having them repeatedly. But let's take it a step further. What would happen if you were in a movie theater and a false alarm went off? What would happen if you just sat there, because you *knew* it was only a false alarm?

Richard: I—um, I think, uh, I'd get pretty freaked out sitting there if everybody else was rushing out.

Therapist: Perfect. So you'd feel some fear, but let's say you just sat there anyway and felt your fear, but you *recognize* that it's a false alarm and so you *know* that jumping up and running out isn't necessary. What would eventually happen?

Richard: I guess your point is that the fear would eventually go away. Is that it?

Therapist: That's right. Just like we talked about during your intake interview, eventually your heart stops pounding and returns to normal, and the tingling sensations go away, and your body's alarm shuts off and it returns to normal.

During this exchange the therapist is using an information-based approach to educate Richard regarding the natural role of panic and anxiety in humans. The therapist is also using a Socratic dialogue to engage Richard in this educational process. Richard is reluctant to completely believe his therapist and his doctor, but he's going along with the process. The content of the first two sessions is highly educational—principally because Richard needs a new and better explanation for his panic symptoms. During these sessions the following points are highlighted:

- Anxiety is composed of three parts: thoughts, feelings or sensations, and actions.
- With practice, Richard can become better at objectively observing his anxiety-related thoughts, feelings, and actions.
- His panic symptoms, although very disturbing and uncomfortable, are harmless.
- His panic symptoms are not caused by a "chemical imbalance." The chemical imbalance theory is a myth, because anxiety and panic are natural human responses to danger.
- When Richard feels intense physical sensations associated with panic but there is no clear external danger, his mind tries to find an explanation for his panic.
- Even though his father died from a heart attack when he was Richard's age, there's no evidence that the same thing will happen to Richard. (We explore this cognitive dimension to his panic more in Chapter 8.)
- The behavioral component of Richard's panic, his tendency to leave or avoid scary situations where he expects he might have a panic attack, results in his being rewarded for leaving and avoiding situations, because his symptoms decrease when he leaves or avoids a situation. Of course, this is a big part of the learning that contributes to Richard's panic. He's not getting a chance to learn that his symptoms will subside even when he stays in the situation.
- Therefore, one of the solutions to his growing panic is to face the panic symptoms, learn new skills for coping with the symptoms, and relearn that there's nothing to fear from his physical panic symptoms.

Even if Richard isn't completely convinced of the new explanation for his panic, the next step is to help him experience and face panic and deal with it effectively.

Therapist: Okay, Richard, we're about done for today, but of course I've got some homework for you again. You did such a great job with the first set, I'm guessing that doing homework comes naturally. This week I'd like you to slowly cut back on the caffeine intake. How do you think you might accomplish that?

Richard: I suppose I can get some of that caffeine-free soda. Well, actually my wife already picked some up.

Therapist: Excellent. So you've got an option waiting at home for you, and your wife is very supportive. And make that same switch to decaf coffee.

Richard: Okay.

Therapist: And keep up your self-monitoring panic log. The more we know about the patterns and symptoms, the better our work together will go.

Session 3. The main purpose of this session is to introduce breathing retraining as a method of relaxation and symptom control. It begins with a hyperventilation overbreathing demonstration. After a discussion of Richard's homework (he has managed to make it 2 weeks without caffeine, has had only two panic attacks in 2 weeks, and has completed his panic log very thoroughly) the therapist moves into a learning activity.

Therapist: Okay, Richard, remember last week we talked about your panic symptoms being a natural, but false, alarm?

Richard: Yeah, I remember.

Therapist: I got the impression that you weren't totally convinced of that idea, so if you want, we can discuss it a bit further, do a brief demonstration, and then focus on a new breathing technique that will help you calm yourself.

Richard: Yeah, I'm always a skeptic about everything. But I have to say I'm feeling a little better, and I think the no caffeine rule is helping.

Therapist: I'm sure it is, because like we've talked about, caffeine produces some of the physical sensations that trigger a panic attack. When the caffeine hits your system and your heart rate and breathing increase just a little bit, you can't help but notice it, and the false alarm can start that much easier.

Richard: Yeah. That seems right to me.

Therapist: What we want is for you to be able to turn off the false alarm. One of the best ways to do that is to practice a little controlled breathing. Watch me. [Therapist demonstrates diaphragmatic breathing, inhaling for about 3 seconds and exhaling for about 3–4 seconds.] Okay, now you try it. The point is to breathe in slowly for about 3 seconds and then breathe out slowly for 3 or 4 seconds. If you keep this up for a minute, you end up taking about 10 breaths in a minute. [Richard places one hand on his abdomen and begins the breathing process.]

Therapist: Okay, that's great. Now let's have you try it for one minute.

Richard: Okay. [Richard breathes slowly for 1 minute.]

Therapist: Nice job, Richard. You had a slow and steady pace. How did it feel?

Richard: It was fine. I felt a little uptight to start, but it got easier, smoother as I went along.

Therapist: Excellent. Now I'm going to show you something that's called over-breathing or hyperventilation. Watch. [Therapist stands up and breathes deeply and rapidly, as if trying to quickly blow up a balloon. After about 1 minute, he sits down and slows down his breathing again.] So, Richard, what did you see happening to me as I did the overbreathing?

Richard: I don't know what you felt like on the inside, but your face got red and when you sat down you looked a little unsteady.

Therapist: Right. I intentionally hyperventilated and felt some of what you feel during a panic attack. I got dizzy and light-headed, and my hands felt tingly. When I sat down and did the diaphragmatic breathing I could actually feel my heartbeat slowing back down.

Richard: That's pretty intense.

Therapist: You can probably guess what's next. I want you to try the same thing, and as soon as you start to feel any dizziness or heart pounding or any of the symptoms that bother you, I want you to sit down and do your diaphragmatic breathing until the feelings subside. Got it?

Richard: I'm not so sure. How do you know I won't have a full-blown attack?

Therapist: Actually, that's a big part of this activity. If you have a full-blown attack, I'll be here and guide you through the breathing and the symptoms will pass. Of course, our goal is for you to just feel a tiny bit of the symptoms and then sit down and relax and breathe. But even if it gets more extreme for you, we have plenty of time, so I'll be here and you'll get control back over your body. Ready?

Richard: Okay. [Richard rises from his chair and does the overbreathing for about 30 seconds, then sits down and, guided by his therapist, breathes steadily and slowly for about 90 seconds.]

Therapist: Now, Richard, tell me what you felt when overbreathing and what you're feeling now.

Richard: I'm okay now, but I did get dizzy. And my hands got tingly. It was amazingly similar to my attacks. But I'm okay now, maybe a little shaky, but okay.

Therapist: So you feel okay now. Actually, you look good too. And you gave your body an excellent lesson. Now your body is starting to know that the panic alarm can get turned on intentionally and that you can turn it back off yourself.

Richard and his therapist continue to debrief his overbreathing experience. The therapist explains the exact physiological mechanisms associated with hyperventilation. At the session's end Richard was asked to practice diaphragmatic breathing for 10 minutes, twice daily, until his next weekly session. He also was asked to continue abstaining from caffeine and keeping his panic logs.

At the beginning of session 4, Richard and his therapist begin working specifically on cognitive restructuring. Therefore, we'll wait until Chapter 8 to present the next phases of Richard's cognitive-behavioral therapy for Panic Disorder.

THERAPY OUTCOMES RESEARCH

Behavioral and cognitive therapists are far and away the largest producers and consumers of therapy outcomes research. Behaviorists probably produce more empirical research in 1 year than all other theoretical orientations combined produce in a decade (Grawe, Donati, & Bernauer, 1998). In the next section, we offer general historical comments, a brief articulation of specific therapies for specific disorders, and a few conceptual comments.

Historical Comments

Early meta-analyses of psychotherapy outcomes indicated that all therapy approaches are approximately equivalent in terms of general efficacy (Luborsky, Singer, &

Luborsky, 1975; Smith & Glass, 1977). Similarly, common factors research estimates that specific therapy techniques such as skills training or systematic desensitization account for about 15% of therapy efficacy on average (Ahn & Wampold, 2001; Asay & Lambert, 1999). Behaviorists take issue with these general conclusions and cite their own reviews and meta-analyses as evidence. For example, when Shapiro and Shapiro (1982) reanalyzed Smith, Glass, and Miller's (1980) meta-analysis with more tightly controlled experimental standards, they reported a superiority of behavioral and cognitive techniques over psychodynamic and humanistic approaches. Additionally, in a large, more recent meta-analysis, behavioral and cognitive-behavioral approaches were superior to psychodynamic and person-centered approaches (Grawe et al., 1998).

Behavioral researchers emphasize that therapies must be carefully defined, properly administered by adequately trained therapists, and evaluated with behaviorally specific measures. Behavior therapists sometimes criticize other therapists, even other behaviorists, when behavior therapy outcomes are not up to expected standards. For example, Wolpe claimed a remarkable 80–90% efficacy rate for behavior therapy, but he emphasized that this is the efficacy rate for true behavior therapy and not other forms of therapy inappropriately included in the behavior therapy category (Wolpe, 1958).

The tendency for therapists to believe in the superiority of their theoretically driven techniques is not unique to behavior therapy. Each theoretical perspective has adherents who consider their procedures to be inherently superior to all others. What *is* unique about behaviorists is that they base their belief in the superiority of behavior therapy primarily on scientific evidence. Rigorous empirical examination is an a priori behaviorist criterion of behavior therapy.

Specific Therapies for Specific Disorders

Different forms of behavior therapy have been empirically evaluated and determined to be effective for a wide range of life problems, psychiatric disorders, and medical conditions. Because we recognize that behavioral and cognitive-behavioral treatments often overlap, the following list includes the mostly or purely behavioral approaches that have been labeled "empirically validated" and "well-established" by the APA's Division 12 (Clinical Psychology) Task Force on Promotion and Dissemination of Psychological Procedures. Behavioral treatments represent 8 of the 16 "well-established" treatments, or 50% (Chambless et al., 1998).

- Exposure treatment for Agoraphobia
- Exposure or guided mastery for Specific Phobia
- Exposure and response prevention for Obsessive-Compulsive Disorder
- Behavior therapy for depression
- Behavior therapy for headache
- Behavior modification for Enuresis
- Parent training programs for children with oppositional behavior
- Behavioral marital therapy

Conceptual Commentary

Behavior therapy research has been criticized in a number of ways. First, traditionally behavior therapy research has focused on a narrow range of clinical problems that may not be entirely relevant to broader clinical practice. For example, behavior therapy is definitely the treatment of choice for clients whose chief complaint is "snake phobia." However, few therapists will encounter a client who is simply seeking snake phobia treatment.

Second, behavior therapy researchers are adept at designing and implementing treatment protocols and measurement techniques amenable to the scientific research paradigm. In particular, behaviorists focus on narrowly defined symptoms and then treat those very specific symptoms with specific behavioral interventions. Therefore, it should come as no surprise that behavior therapy research shows that behavior therapy effectively treats these symptoms. In contrast, other therapy approaches are often more interested in global life change, an increased sense of personal meaning, character change, or changes in interpersonal dynamics—all of which are harder to measure and probably harder to change than specific symptoms.

MULTICULTURAL PERSPECTIVES

Behavior therapy focuses directly on specific client problems and symptoms. Research generally indicates that racial and ethnic minority clients are more likely to prefer this active, directive, problem-focused form of therapy (Atkinson & Lowe, 1995; Sue & Sue, 2003).

Questions for Reflection

Why do you suppose racial and ethnic minority clients prefer active, directive therapists? What is it about active, directive therapy that might appeal to a minority client? What do you think might be uncomfortable about a therapist who is more nondirective and passive?

Sue and Sue (2003) provide the following answer to these questions:

> In multicultural counseling, the culturally diverse client is likely to approach the counselor with trepidation: "What makes you any different from all the Whites out there who have oppressed me?" "What makes you immune from inheriting the racial biases of your fore-bears?" "Before I open up to you [self-disclose], I want to know where you are coming from." . . . [W]e contend that the use of more directive, active, and influencing skills is more likely to provide personal information about where the therapist is coming from (self-disclosure). Giving advice or suggestions, interpreting, and telling the client how you, the counselor or therapist, feel are really acts of counselor self-disclosure . . . [and] . . . a culturally diverse client may not open up (self-disclose) until you, the helping professional self-disclose first. (p. 147)

The key point is that minority clients may hold off on trusting White therapists. Therefore, it's possible that behavioral therapists build trust by giving clients clear information about exactly where they're coming from. The racially or ethnically different client can then conclude: "I can pretty much tell what this therapist is all about. She's just trying to help me get rid of my symptoms." This conclusion on the client's part may help facilitate the therapeutic alliance or working relationship.

Although an active, directive style may be generally appealing to minority clients, specific behavioral interventions may or may not be multiculturally appropriate or acceptable. This means that behavior therapists need to be prepared to make more multicultural adjustments to the content of their interventions than to their overall style. Additionally, because a solid empirical research base that validates behavior therapy with minority clients is nonexistent (Chambless & Williams, 1995), therapy should proceed cautiously, with openness to the client's reaction to specific treatment approaches. For example, if Richard (from the case example discussed earlier) happened to be a Native American client, the therapist might state:

> "You have symptoms that fit with the diagnosis of Panic Disorder. There's a fairly standard treatment approach for panic disorder that has been well researched and has a good chance of being effective. However, I should also tell you that the research is mostly based on white clients, although there have been a few clients from other cultures involved in the research too. It's likely that the approach will be helpful to you, but I can't say that with complete scientific certainty. We can try this treatment approach for panic disorder because I think it still offers us the best chance of success. But also, as we proceed, let's keep our lines of communication totally open. Tell me if there's anything about this treatment for your panic symptoms that you find uncomfortable at all. Is that okay with you?"

Sue and Sue also reassure White counselors about providing minority clients with advice. They state: "As one minority client said to us, 'I'm not that weak, stupid, or fragile that what advice you give to me will be unquestioningly accepted'" (Sue & Sue, 2003, p. 148).

Questions for Reflection

With increasing numbers of minority students enrolling in counseling and psychology programs, minority therapists will increasingly be working with White clients. Do you think the trust issues articulated by Sue and Sue might affect a White client who's working with an African American, Latino, or Native American therapist? If so, how would they affect that relationship? If not, why not?

CONCLUDING COMMENTS

During their career's, B. F. Skinner, a strong proponent of behavioral determinism, and Carl Rogers, long an advocate of free will and human dignity, had numerous professional interactions. In the following excerpt, Rogers comments on an exchange they had while presenting their work together on a conference panel.

> Along with the development of technology has gone an underlying philosophy of rigid determinism in the psychological sciences which can perhaps best be illustrated by a brief exchange which I had with Prof. B. F. Skinner of Harvard at a recent conference. A paper given by Dr. Skinner led me to direct these remarks to him. "From what I understood Dr. Skinner to say, it is his understanding that though he might have thought he chose to come to this meeting, might have thought he had a purpose in giving his speech, such thoughts are really illusory. He actually made certain marks on paper and emitted certain sounds here simply because his genetic make-up and his past environment had operantly conditioned his behavior in such a way that it was rewarding to make these sounds, and that he

PRACTITIONER COMMENTARY 7.1

The Future (of Behavior Therapy) is Feedback!

The following discussion of using questionnaire feedback as a therapeutic tool was written by Scott T. Meier. Dr. Meier is professor and codirector of training of the program in counseling/school psychology in the Department of Counseling, School, and Educational Psychology, at the State University of New York at Buffalo.

One of the therapeutic strategies I suspect may become increasingly important in the future is the systematic use of feedback in counseling and psychotherapy. Most therapists now rely on informal or unstructured ways of knowing if and how their clients are making progress. That is, we infer from therapeutic conversations if the client is feeling better, or we might ask clients if they believe they are making progress. Although this is often all that is needed, there appear to be circumstances when a more systematic approach is useful.

I base this conclusion upon both my own therapeutic experiences (see Meier, 1999; Hoffman & Meier, 2001) and those in the professional literature. For example, Lambert and his colleagues (2001) have recently demonstrated the positive effects of feedback with clients who are failing to make progress in therapy. Using the Outcome Questionnaire (OQ) with university counseling center clients, they examined the effect of providing feedback to therapists with clients making and not making progress in therapy (based on OQ scores). Graphs and progress markers (colored dots that indicated whether the client was functioning in the normal range of OQ scores) were given to therapists to indicate which clients had an adequate rate of change, an inadequate rate of change, or failure to make any progress. Lambert and his colleagues found that OQ scores at termination were higher for clients who were initially not making progress but whose therapist was receiving feedback, compared to clients who were not making progress and whose therapist received no feedback. In fact, clients who were not progressing and whose therapist received no feedback worsened over time.

Basing their conclusions on this and similar studies, Gray and Lambert (2001) determined that

> Clinicians are not effective in gauging patient response to treatment, especially in early treatment sessions. However, when they are provided with feedback on poor treatment response, they develop a perspective on their patient's clinical progress that enables them to recalibrate treatment and make a substantial impact on improvement rates. . . . The major finding of the studies is that the use of feedback provides information that gives the clinician a perspective on change that cannot be derived from clinical intuition alone, and that this feedback enhances outcomes with at-risk clients. (p. 26)

Although therapists such as Gottman and Leiblum (1974) long ago recommended that clinicians obtain a "continuous monitoring of progress toward goals" with the data "used as feedback to make decisions about the effectiveness of intervention components of the treatment program" (p. v), a formal approach to this process is unusual among therapists. Yet some of the most successful psychotherapeutic approaches depend on feedback from comprehensive clinical assessments (e.g., Paul & Menditto, 1992), and innovative, well-thought-out approaches to obtaining feedback using nomothetic and idiographic methods have been developed (Clement, 1994; Meier, 1999). The future is feedback!

as a person doesn't enter into this. In fact if I get his thinking correctly, from his strictly scientific point of view, he, as a person, doesn't exist." In his reply Dr. Skinner said that he would not go into the question of whether he had any choice in the matter (presumably because the whole issue is illusory) but stated, "I do accept your characterization of my own presence here." I do not need to labor the point that for Dr. Skinner the concept of "learning to be free" would be quite meaningless. (Rogers, 1960, pp. 15–16)

Although Rogers offers an amusing critique of Skinner, it seems that contemporary behavior therapy has moved beyond rigid determinism. In fact, behavior therapy represents not only a flexible approach to therapy, but also one that is open to incorporating new techniques. The only rigidity inherent in the behavioral approach is its strict adherence to scientific validation of therapeutic techniques. Most of the behavior therapy perspective can be summed up in one sentence: If it can't be empirically validated, then it's not behavior therapy.

Overall, behavior therapists deserve credit for demonstrating that their particular approaches are effective—based on a quantitative scientific-medical model. Even more impressive is the fact that behavior therapy research has begun to identify which specific approaches are more and less likely to be effective with which specific problems. However, the question remains open regarding whether behavior therapy techniques are generally more effective than other techniques or whether behavior therapy researchers are simply better at demonstrating the efficacy of their techniques than adherents to other theoretical orientations. Either way, we close with Skinner's remarks as an apt summary of the behavioral scientist's credo: "Regard no practice as immutable. Change and be ready to change again. Accept no eternal verity. Experiment" (Skinner, 1970, p. viii).

STUDENT REVIEW ASSIGNMENTS

In this section you will review and further explore your understanding of behavior therapy.

Critical Corner

The following comments about behavior therapy represent both real and exaggerated criticisms. They are offered to stimulate your thoughts about behavior therapy. Please read the comments and then write your thoughts and reactions to the criticisms.

1. Some critics might claim that behavior therapy is fundamentally flawed because it involves one person (a designated expert) teaching another person (a vulnerable client) about what's normal and acceptable behavior. Although behaviorists may hide behind "symptom reduction" as their lofty goal, in reality they are simply teaching clients to ignore symptoms and the symptoms' important underlying messages to the client.
Response:

2. Despite the emphasis in this chapter on the flexible, clinically astute behavior therapist, most behavior therapists are just technicians. For the most part, they

aren't attuned to or very interested in clients' feelings, the dynamics of the therapy relationship, or life's meaning, and so they ignore these bigger issues, focusing instead on trivial matters.

Response:

3. Although there is ample scientific evidence attesting to the efficacy of behavior therapy, behavior therapists have generated most of this evidence. There is no doubt that behavior therapy researcher bias exists and that behavior therapist researchers construct outcome measures that rig the outcomes in their favor. Overall, the promotion of behavior therapies as "empirically validated therapies" smacks of a business-related scam designed to improve insurance reimbursement rates for behaviorally oriented therapy providers.

Response:

4. The length to which behavior therapists will go to dehumanize individuals is scary. Examples include aversive conditioning using electric shock; token economies, which curtail the freedom and dignity of patients; and the excessive punishment of children in our schools. The biggest problem with behavior therapy is that it treats clients more like rats or pigeons than humans.

Response:

5. Behavior therapy is currently governed by so many divergent learning theories that the entire field is not much more than a hodgepodge of different techniques. If you look hard, you'll see that it's difficult to find an underlying theory that guides the entire field. This lack of backbone will only get worse until behavior therapy begins to base itself on a coherent theory—rather than simply basing itself on scientific methodology.

Response:

Key Terms

- Behavior therapy
- Behaviorism
- Classical conditioning
- Operant conditioning
- Counter-conditioning
- Applied behavior analysis
- Stimulus-response (SR) theory
- Neobehavioristic mediational SR model
- Stimulus generalization

- Stimulus discrimination
- Extinction
- Spontaneous recovery
- Social learning theory
- Observational learning
- Positive reinforcement
- Punishment
- Negative reinforcement
- Systematic desensitization
- Self-efficacy

- Cognitive-behavioral therapy
- Behavioral ABCs
- Operational definition
- Self-monitoring
- Token economy
- Fading
- Aversive conditioning
- Progressive muscle relaxation
- Exposure treatment

- Imaginal and in vivo exposure
- Massed versus spaced exposure
- Virtual reality exposure
- Interoceptive exposure

- Response prevention
- Participant modeling
- Skills training
- Assertiveness training
- Problem solving

- Generating behavioral alternatives
- Breathing retraining
- Overbreathing
- Empirically validated treatments

Review Questions

1. Discuss the relative importance of John Watson and Mary Cover Jones in the development of applied behavior therapy techniques. Which of these researchers amassed a large amount of practical information about counter-conditioning?

2. Who is the historical figure to which applied behavior analysis can be traced? Do applied behavior analysts believe in using cognitive constructs to understand human behavior?

3. What is the difference between SR theory and neobehavioristic SR theory?

4. Explain how self-efficacy can be viewed as a cognitive variable in a therapy situation.

5. What is the difference between counter-conditioning and extinction? Which of these experimental procedures is more directly linked to response prevention? Which one is linked to systematic desensitization?

6. List and describe the behavioral ABCs.

7. What are the main methods that behavior therapists use to teach clients assertiveness skills?

8. What are the five steps of problem solving that behavior therapists teach clients as a part of skills training? Which of these steps was illustrated in the therapy excerpt with the aggressive adolescent?

9. In the case example involving Richard, it's clear that Richard does not initially believe all of the educational information that his therapist is providing him. Is the therapist concerned about Richard's disbelief? If so, what strategies does the therapist use to work on Richard's adherence to therapy?

10. Explain how overbreathing can be used in an interoceptive exposure model. Why is this approach especially appropriate for clients with Panic Disorder?

RECOMMENDED READINGS AND RESOURCES

The following resources provide additional information on behavior theory and therapy.

Lead Journals

Although there are dozens more behavior therapy journals available, we only list some of the main professional resources here.

- *Behavior Modification*
- *Behaviour Research and Therapy*
- *Behavior Therapy*
- *Child and Family Behavior Therapy*
- *Journal of Applied Behavior Analysis*
- *Journal of Behavior Therapy and Experimental Psychiatry*

Books and Articles

Arntz, A. (2002). Cognitive therapy versus interoceptive exposure as treatment of Panic Disorder without Agoraphobia. *Behaviour Research and Therapy, 40*, 325–341.

Bandura, A. (1977). Self-efficacy: Toward a unifying theory of behavioral change. *Psychological Review, 84*, 191–215.

Benson, H. (1976). *The relaxation response.* New York: Avon Books.

Bernstein, D. A., & Borkovec, T. D. (1973). *Progressive relaxation training: A manual for the helping professions.* Champaign, IL: Research Press.

Davis, M., McKay, M., & Eshelman, E. R. (2000). *The relaxation and stress reduction workbook.* Oakland, CA: New Harbinger.

Emmelkamp, P. M. G., Krijn, M., Hulsbosch, L., de Vries, S., Schuemie, M. J., & van der Mast, C. A. P. (2001). Virtual reality treatment versus exposure in vivo: A comparative evaluation in Acrophobia. *Behaviour Research and Therapy, 39*, 184–194.

Gershoff, E. T. (2002). Corporal punishment by parents and associated child behaviors and experiences: A meta-analytic and theoretical review. *Psychological Bulletin, 128*(4), 539–579.

Goldfried, M. R., & Davison, G. C. (1994). *Clinical behavior therapy* (2nd ed.). Oxford, England: Wiley.

Jones, M. C. (1924). The elimination of children's fear. *Journal of Experimental Psychology, 8*, 382–390.

Lazarus, A. A. (1971). *Behavior therapy and beyond.* New York: McGraw-Hill.

Mahoney, M. (1979). *Self-change: Strategies for solving personal problems.* New York: Norton.

Pavlov, I. P. (1972). *Conditioned reflexes* (G. V. Anrep, Trans.). London: Oxford University Press.

Skinner, B. F. (1953). *Science and human behavior.* New York: MacMillan.

Skinner, B. F. (1971). *Beyond freedom and dignity.* New York: Knopf.

Skinner, B. F. (1977). Why I am not a cognitive psychologist. *Behaviorism, 5*, 1–10.

Solomon, R. (1964). Punishment. *American Psychologist, 19*, 239–253.

Spivack, G., Platt, J. J., & Shure, M. B. (1976). *The problem-solving approach to adjustment.* San Francisco: Jossey-Bass.

Watson, J. B. (1924). *Behaviorism.* Chicago: University of Chicago Press.

Wolpe, J. (1958). *Psychotherapy by reciprocal inhibition.* Stanford, CA: Stanford University Press.

Videotapes

Carlson, J., & Kjos, D. (2000). *Behavior therapy with Dr. John Krumboltz* [Videotape]. Boston: Allyn & Bacon.

Goldfried, M. R. (1994). *Cognitive-affective behavior therapy* [Videotape]. Washington, DC: American Psychological Association.

Persons, J. B., Davidson, J., & Tompkins, M. A. (2000). *Activity scheduling* [Videotape]. Washington, DC: American Psychological Association.

Turner, S. M. (1998). *Behavior therapy for Obsessive-Compulsive Disorder* [Videotape]. Washington, DC: American Psychological Association.

Training Opportunities and Informational Web Sites

The Association for the Advancement of Behavior Therapy has over 4,500 members, an annual conference, and many resources on its web site (www.aabt.org).

The Association for Behavior Analysis exists to develop, enhance, and support the growth and vitality of behavior analysis through research, education, and practice. Its website is at www.abainternational.org.

Chapter 8

COGNITIVE THEORY AND THERAPY

True thoughts have duration in themselves. If the thoughts endure, the seed is enduring; if the seed endures, the energy endures; if the energy endures, then will the spirit endure. The spirit is thought; thought is the heart; the heart is the fire; the fire is the Elixir.

—Lu Yen

Whenever you experience an unpleasant feeling or sensation, try to recall what thoughts you had been having prior to this feeling.

—A. T. Beck, *Cognitive Therapy and the Emotional Disorders* (1976, p. 33)

IN THIS CHAPTER YOU WILL LEARN

- General forms and features of cognitive therapy approaches
- Theoretical principles underlying cognitive therapy
- The differences between Ellis's Rational-Emotive Behavior Therapy, Beck's cognitive therapy, and Meichenbaum's Stress Inoculation Training
- How cognitive theorists and therapists conceptualize client psychopathology
- How to prepare yourself and your clients for cognitive therapy
- Cognitive therapy assessment procedures
- Specific cognitive therapy techniques
- Ethical and multicultural issues facing cognitive therapists
- The empirical evidence supporting cognitive therapy

In the beginning, behaviorists didn't want to think about cognition, so it should come as no great surprise to find that a behaviorist did not discover cognitive therapy. On the other hand, as discussed in the previous chapter, some behaviorists included cognitions from the very beginning. One such behaviorist, Joseph Wolpe, opened Skinner's black box just enough to let in a little mental imagery. In his determination to be relevant and effective with real problems, he allowed clients to use imagery in the service of desensitization (Wolpe, 1958). Of course, in a basic sense, Wolpe was following the protocol of the neobehavioristic stimulus-response (S-R) theoretical model, but he allowed a form of cognition into his therapeutic work and thus may have started the behaviorists' tentative foray into cognition.

However, we suspect that Wolpe would find this observation ironic, at best. At the

1983 annual meeting of the Association for the Advancement of Behavior Therapy (the AABT), we listened to Joseph Wolpe condemn Michael Mahoney's use of a technique referred to as "mirror time" or "streaming" with a very disturbed young man. Streaming involved having the young man essentially free-associate while looking at himself in a mirror (Williams, Diehl, & Mahoney, 2002). Wolpe was clear and adamant: There were events happening at the conference that were far outside the realm of behavior therapy. Clearly, Mahoney and other "cognitive types" had gotten under Wolpe's skin. As Meichenbaum said years later, "Pressure was exerted by behaviorists to have cognitive behavioral researchers excluded from the AABT conferences, editorial boards, and even the organization" (Meichenbaum, 1992, p. 115). Of course, pressure from the behaviorists did not dampen the "cognitivists'" resolve but, instead, increased their motivation, and in 1977 a new journal, *Cognitive Therapy and Research,* was founded, with Michael Mahoney as editor.

In the following pages we explore the origins, nature, and practice of this fascinating form of therapy, which has one foot firmly planted in objective science, while the other foot is dancing around in the often amorphous field of human thought and consciousness.

One final note: The structure of this chapter is unique. Instead of including separate sections on biographical information, historical context, and theoretical principles, this chapter combines these sections to better address the plurality and unity of cognitive theory and therapy.

FORMS OF COGNITIVE THEORY AND THERAPY

The variety of histories associated with cognitive therapy undoubtedly reflects the fact that our understanding of the human mind is perpetually expanding. Also, it is clear that the so-called cognitive revolution in psychology and counseling was a function of many individuals, and consequently there is much less historical cohesion in cognitive theory than in theoretical approaches dominated by single individuals.

For purposes of clarity, we divide cognitive therapy into three separate, but related, therapeutic camps: the rational, empirical, and constructivist perspectives. We'll cover the first two in some depth, leaving most of the third perspective to be covered in Chapter 11.

Rational-Semantic Cognitive Therapies:

Albert Ellis is generally credited with the discovery and promotion of modern rational approaches to psychotherapy. Ellis formulated his approach after progressively discovering in his psychotherapy practice that traditional psychoanalysis was grossly ineffectual. Those of you familiar with Ellis's theory and interpersonal style can easily guess why it might be a good idea to quote him directly when describing his therapeutic approach. Ellis has a distinctive way of talking and writing about his Rational-Emotive Behavior Therapy, so his own words help the reader glimpse the theory. Further, Ellis is an imposing figure in psychology and counseling. Many have found that it is better to quote him directly than to misspeak and risk his ire. And so, in his own words, here is what Ellis discovered about psychotherapy in the mid-1950s:

> I realized more clearly that although people have remarkable differences and uniquenesses in their tastes, characteristics, goals, and enjoyments, they also have remarkable sameness

in the ways in which they disturb themselves "emotionally." People have, of course, thousands of specific irrational ideas and philosophies (not to mention superstitions and religiosities) which they creatively invent, dogmatically carry on, and stupidly upset themselves about. But we can easily put almost all these thousands of ideas into a few general categories. Once we do so, and then actively *look for* these categories, we can fairly quickly find them, show them to disturbed individuals, and also teach them how to give them up. (Ellis & Grieger, 1977, pp. 4–5)

In this statement Ellis efficiently summarizes five bedrock components of his theory of therapy:

1. People dogmatically adhere to irrational ideas and personal philosophies.
2. These irrational ideas cause people great distress and misery.
3. These ideas can be boiled down to a few basic categories.
4. Therapists can find these irrational categories rather easily in their clients' reasoning.
5. Therapists can successfully teach clients how to give up their misery-causing irrational beliefs.

Although Ellis began formulating and using rational psychotherapy in the 1950s, he acknowledges that many of his contemporaries were already heading the same direction—away from traditional psychoanalysis and toward more active-directive, cognitive-oriented therapy. In particular, he states:

Actually, they attributed to me more originality than I merited. By the late 1940s quite a few other therapists, most of them trained as I was in the field of psychoanalysis, had begun to see the severe limitations and myths of the analytic approach and had, whether they consciously acknowledged it or not, moved much closer to Adler than to Freud. (Ellis & Grieger, 1977, p. 4)

Not only does Ellis heartily credit Adler's pioneering acceptance of cognition; he also notes that his "rational psychotherapy" is based, in part, on the philosophical writings of ancient Greek and Roman stoics, particularly Epictetus. J. W. Bush (2002) describes Epictetus's history.

The first cognitive behavior therapist, so to speak, in the Western world was the philosopher Epictetus (c. 50–138 A.D.). He was born a slave in the Greek-speaking Roman province of Phrygia, in what is now central Turkey.

One day when Epictetus was working in the fields chained to an iron stake, his master approached him with the idea of tightening his leg shackle. Epictetus suggested that making the shackle tighter was not needed to keep him from running away, but would merely break his leg. The master was not persuaded, and sure enough Epictetus's leg was broken. But he did not protest or give any sign of distress. His master asked him why, and was told that since the leg was already irreversibly broken, there was really no point in getting upset about it. His master was so impressed by this demonstration of unflappability that he eventually set Epictetus free, and sent him away with money so he could become an itinerant philosopher. Epictetus considered this preferable to being a philosopher chained to a stake, and eventually came to Rome, then the capital of the Western world. Among the prominent Romans he influenced was the emperor Marcus Aurelius. (See Bush, 2002, for more information.)

Ellis initially referred to his therapy approach as *rational psychotherapy,* later changing the name to *Rational-Emotive Therapy.* In 1993, he inserted the word *behavior,* thus creating *Rational Emotive Behavior Therapy* (REBT), a phrase that better reflects the strong behavioral components of his therapeutic approach.

There is little argument about the fact that Ellis is one of the biggest "characters" in the history and practice of psychotherapy. His influence has been profound, from the publication and dissemination of many rational humor songs (including the infamous Albert Ellis Christmas Carols), to the direct training of thousands of REBT practitioners. Whenever we've heard him speak, there have been two consistent occurrences. First, he finds a reason to break into song (despite the fact that his voice quality and ability to carry a tune leave much to be desired). Second, he always manages to slip in the "f" word or other forms of profanity that draw adolescent snickers from even the most professional audiences.

Given Ellis's eccentric, direct, and abrasive characteristics, it's tempting to minimize his accomplishments. But in fact he has produced over 700 scholarly journal articles and 60 professional books. Additionally, he has probably provided therapy to more individuals than any other practitioner in the history of counseling and psychotherapy. In 1987, he wrote that he was working with 300 individual clients and five groups, while demonstrating his procedures at weekly "Five-Dollar Friday Night Workshops" (Ellis, 1987, p. 127). Moreover, he has continued his incredible work pace into the twenty-first century—amassing over 50 years of direct, applied clinical experience. For detailed information on Ellis's personal history, see Dryden (1989).

Most therapists identify Ellis's approach to therapy as rationalist, although he has publicly disagreed with this categorization (Ellis, 1992; Meichenbaum, 1992; Wessler, 1992). As a rationalist model, REBT encourages therapists to actively identify and label thoughts that cause clients distress and misery as *irrational thoughts.* In this model, therapists are thought to have the objectivity to examine clients' thoughts and accurately judge those thoughts as rational or irrational. In a professional exchange with Ellis, Meichenbaum criticized Ellis's rationalist position:

> As Mahoney (1991) and I have noted, it is both presumptuous and pejorative to characterize someone's beliefs as "irrational," as if one holds the axiomatic system of rationality. At times, I must confess, I feel Albert Ellis believes that he has been "chosen" to educate us all about what constitute "rational beliefs." (Meichenbaum, 1992, pp. 127–128)

In contrast, Ellis claims that REBT is a constructivist theory of therapy (Ellis, 1990, 1992, 1998).

Questions for Reflection

As you read this chapter, determine for yourself whether you believe REBT belongs more in the rationalist or the constructivist theoretical camp. Consider this question: Do you think REBT can be practiced in a manner that allows clients to co-construct new personal realities? Are the differences between REBT and the collaborative-empirical and constructivist-philosophical cognitive models mostly stylistic, or are there clear theoretical differences or incompatibilities?

Collaborative-Empirical Cognitive Therapies

In the following sections we examine the contributions of Aaron Beck and Donald Meichenbaum to cognitive theory and therapy.

Aaron Beck and Cognitive Therapy

Like Ellis, Aaron Beck was psychoanalytically trained. Early in his career he became interested in validating Freud's anger-turned-inward-upon-the-self theory of depression, but instead he ended up rejecting Freud's theory and articulating his own (Beck, 1961, 1963, 1970; D. A. Clark, Beck, & Alford, 1999). Many psychoanalytic colleagues ostracized Beck for questioning Freud (Weishaar, 1993). However, over time, Beck's groundbreaking work on depression was recognized as empirically valid, and his theory of depression and specific approaches to its treatment still represents one of the best-known and most scientifically supported discoveries in the field of counseling and psychotherapy. Here Beck describes how he discovered the centrality of cognition to human functioning:

> [T]he patient volunteered the information that while he had been expressing anger-laden criticisms of me, he had also had continual thoughts of a self-critical nature. He described two streams of thought occurring at about the same time; one stream having to do with his hostility and criticisms, which he had expressed in free association, and another that he had not expressed. He then reported the other stream of thoughts: "I said the wrong thing . . . I shouldn't have said that . . . I'm wrong to criticize him . . . I'm bad . . . He won't like me . . . I'm bad . . . I have no excuse for being so mean." (Beck, 1976, pp. 30–31)

This finding led Beck to eventually conclude that focusing on this *other* stream of consciousness was much more valuable to clients than the usual free association material targeted by traditional Freudian analysts.

Beck's approach to therapy has come to be known simply as *cognitive therapy*. He reasoned that

> psychological problems can be mastered by sharpening discriminations, correcting misconceptions and learning more adaptive attitudes. Since introspection, insight, reality testing, and learning are basically cognitive processes, this approach to the neuroses has been labeled cognitive therapy. (Beck, 1976, p. 20)

Similar to Ellis's REBT, cognitive therapy has taken on many of Beck's personal qualities. Beck is a soft-spoken, gentle man who works with clients in a collaborative and practical manner. His approach is as gentle as Ellis's approach is forceful. Beck is not interested in convincing clients of their irrational beliefs. Instead, he uses a style he refers to as *collaborative empiricism*, wherein he works together with clients to help them discover for themselves the maladaptive nature of their automatic thoughts. A key distinction between these two cognitively oriented therapists is that whereas Ellis emphasizes the forceful eradication of irrational thoughts, Beck emphasizes the collaborative modification of maladaptive thoughts (Beck et al., 1979; Clark, Beck, & Alford, 1999). Additional biographical information about Beck is available in Weishaar (1993).

Donald Meichenbaum and Self-Instructional Strategies

Donald Meichenbaum followed the path of behavior therapy into the field of cognitive therapy and beyond. In his early research he focused on impulsive schoolchildren and hospitalized adults diagnosed with schizophrenia. To his surprise, he discovered that both schizophrenics and children could improve their functioning after being taught to talk to themselves or to think aloud (Meichenbaum, 1969; Meichenbaum & Goodman, 1971).

A consummate observer and researcher, Meichenbaum's perspective has evolved over time. Initially, he integrated the work of Soviet psychologists Vygotsky (1962) and Luria (1961) with Bandura's (1965) vicarious learning model and the operant conditioning principle of fading to develop a systematic method for teaching children to use self-instructions to slow down and guide themselves through challenging problem-solving situations. His successful work with self-instruction led him to conclude that

> evidence has convincingly indicated that the therapist can and does significantly influence what the client says to [the therapist]. . . . Now it is time for the therapist to directly influence what the client says to himself. (Meichenbaum & Cameron, 1974, p. 117)

During this early period of his career, Meichenbaum's focus was on self-instructional training (SIT), which he—consistent with his behavioral roots—referred to as a form of cognitive behavior modification (Meichenbaum, 1977). At this time he emphasized that "behavior change occurs through a sequence of mediating processes involving the interaction of inner speech, cognitive structures, and behaviors and their resultant outcomes" (Meichenbaum, 1977, p. 218).

From this work, he later developed stress inoculation training, a specific approach for helping clients more effectively manage difficult stressors (Meichenbaum, 1985). Throughout this early and middle phase of his career, Meichenbaum focused primarily on empirical research and validation of highly practical approaches to helping clients. His style was similar to Beck's in that he was very collaborative and worked closely with clients to help them change their inner speech. In particular, Meichenbaum's model generally emphasized the development of self-instructional coping skills more than Ellis or Beck, and his style is much more openly empathic and emotionally oriented than most other cognitive therapists.

More recently, along with Michael Mahoney and other former behavioral and cognitive therapists, Meichenbaum has shifted somewhat toward the philosophical-constructivist model (Hoyt, 2000; Meichenbaum, 1992). Although he remains deeply interested in empiricism, his views are now strongly constructivist. In many ways, as his thinking evolves, he is also redefining cognitive therapy as an integrational approach. For example, at the Second Evolution of Psychotherapy Conference, he stated:

> [Cognitive behavior therapy,] which is phenomenologically oriented, attempts to explore by means of nondirective reflective procedures the client's world view. There is an intent to see the world through the client's eyes, rather than to challenge, confront, or interpret the client's thoughts. A major mode of achieving this objective is for the [cognitive behavior] therapist to "pluck" (pick out) key words and phrases that clients offer, and then to reflect them in an interrogative tone, but with the same affect (mirroring) in which they were expressed. The [cognitive behavior] therapist also may use the client's developmental accounts, as well as in-session client behavior, to help the client get in touch with his or her feelings. (Meichenbaum, 1992, pp. 117–118)

Meichenbaum's progression—from behavior therapy, to cognitive behavior modification, to cognitive-behavioral therapy, to constructivist cognitive-behavioral therapy—reflects a trend in the general direction of the entire field of counseling and psychotherapy away from distinct competing theories and toward integration (see

Chapter 13 for more on Meichenbaum's evolution as a therapist and for a review of specific integrational therapies).

Questions for Reflection

What do you see as the main differences between Ellis's more rationalist therapy approach and Beck's and Meichenbaum's approaches? Do you agree that REBT belongs in a separate category from the collaborative-empiricists? Is the proposed distinction between rational-semantic and collaborative-empirical cognitive therapies helpful, or is it just splitting hairs?

Philosophical-Constructivist Cognitive Therapies

Philosophical-constructivism is founded on the premise that humans actively construct their own reality. Previously we glimpsed this perspective in Individual Psychology (Chapter 3), and later we explore constructivism in much greater detail (Chapter 11). For the purposes of this chapter it is enough to note that several former collaborative-empirical cognitive therapists have shifted their thinking more toward the philosophical constructivist paradigm. Specifically, Michael Mahoney and Donald Meichenbaum, both of whom powerfully influenced the development of the empirical foundation for cognitive behavior therapy, now have moved away from more narrow, practical, and empirical cognitive behavior therapy and into wider, more philosophical, and less empirically driven constructivist philosophy (Mahoney, 1991; Meichenbaum, 1992). Mahoney refers to himself as an "inveterate conceptual pilgrim" (Mahoney, 1991, p. 113).

THEORETICAL PRINCIPLES

The essence of cognitive theory can be summarized in one sentence that Ellis attributes to Epictetus: "People are disturbed not by things, but by the view which they take of them" (Ellis & Dryden, 1997).

Cognitive theory and, in particular, cognitive behavioral theory are expansions of behavior therapy. Consider Watson's position that "[i]ntrospection forms no essential part of [behavior therapy] methods" (Watson, 1924, p. 158). Instead of systematically excluding introspection, cognitive theory includes introspection. For the cognitive theorist, discovering the client's subjective interpretation of reality is essential.

Similarly, if we look at Skinner's theoretical position, "Behavior is a function of its consequences" then cognitive theory transforms "consequences" from an objective to a subjective phenomenon. Now, behavior is a function of what the individual *thinks* about its consequences. The cognitive revision of behavioral stimulus-response (S-R) theory is the stimulus-organism-response (S-O-R) theory. In other words, as has been suggested above, cognitive theory emphasizes the individual organism's processing of environmental stimuli as the driving force determining his or her specific response. As a visual reminder of the meaning of S-O-R theory, imagine the "O" as representing the brain, or processing system, of the individual. For a response to occur, the individual's brain must process the incoming stimulus. Beck (1976) stated it this way: "[T]here is a conscious thought between an external event and a particular emotional response" (p. 27).

Rational Emotive Behavior Therapy

Rational Emotive Behavior Therapy theory views humans as neither inherently good nor inherently bad. Instead, Ellis considers humans to have the potential for thinking both rationally and irrationally. Unfortunately, humans have a strong tendency to think in crooked, mistaken, and irrational ways—and this is the primary source of human misery.

Ellis uses an A-B-C model to describe and discuss S-O-R theory. For Ellis, "A" represents the "activating event" that has occurred in an individual's life; the "B" refers to the individual's belief about the activating event; and "C" refers to the consequent emotion and behavior derived from the individual's belief.

The A-B-C model of REBT is best illustrated through an example: Jem comes to therapy feeling angry, depressed, hurt, and resentful. Last night his wife was not home at 6:00 p.m. for dinner as they had arranged. This event troubled him greatly. In REBT terms, the fact that Jem's wife was not home for dinner on time is identified as the *activating event*. Because his wife was late, he began mentally processing this event, thinking, "She doesn't care enough about me to be home for dinner on time." Further, he started imagining that she was late because she was with another man. Of course, there are a number of other specific beliefs he may adopt, but the main point is that he's thinking something like: "She doesn't really love me and prefers to spend time with other men."

Jem's wife finally arrived home at 7:45 p.m. She apologized, explaining that she was stuck in a meeting at work and couldn't call on her cell phone because the batteries had died. Unfortunately, this explanation did not convince Jem, and his feelings continued to escalate. He yelled at his wife for being so insensitive and then accused her of having an affair with a man at the office.

From Ellis's perspective, it's no wonder that Jem is feeling miserable. Dr. Ellis, never one to mince words, then explains to Jem that he is causing himself his own misery. He spells out the ABCs:

Jem's Activating Event:	His wife is late for dinner.
Jem's Belief:	His wife doesn't love or respect him any more. She's probably having an affair.
Jem's Consequent Feelings and Behavior:	Anger, sadness, hurt, resentment, and jealousy; yelling and accusing her of having an affair.

The main thrust of REBT is to demonstrate to Jem that his current belief about his wife's lateness is irrational. Ellis refers to this sort of belief as an irrational belief (iB). The purpose of rational emotive behavior therapy is to help substitute a rational belief (rB) for a current irrational belief (iB), which will result in more positive and more comfortable consequent feelings (C).

Ellis is well known for his direct and confrontive therapy style. Although it's easy to directly associate Ellis's style with REBT, not all Rational Emotive Behavior therapists are as direct, abrasive, and confrontive as Ellis.

Ellis's theory of therapy doesn't stop with the ABCs. The main purpose of confronting is to dispute (D) the irrational belief. He might choose to directly dispute Jem's belief by asking, "Is it true that your wife must always be home right on time to prove her love for you?" or "Isn't it true that sometimes your wife can be late and that it's really not all that awful—it doesn't mean she doesn't love you, but instead it's just an inconvenient behavior that sometimes happens to the best of couples?" As we will discuss later, REBT is a flexible form of therapy that allows therapists to use a wide range of techniques, all in the service of disputing, annihilating, or destroying the client's misery-causing irrational beliefs.

If all goes according to theory, Ellis's dispute of Jem's irrational belief (and Jem's own subsequent and ongoing disputations of his irrational belief) will have an effect (E) on Jem. Hopefully, this effect will be the development of a set of alternative, more effective beliefs. Finally, if the therapy is successful, Jem will experience a new feeling (F).

Questions for Reflection

In this example, Jem concludes that when his wife is late it represents evidence that she no longer loves him and is having an affair. As he waits home alone at the dinner table, what other interpretations or beliefs could Jem come up with to explain his wife's lateness? Given Jem's conclusion that his wife is having an affair, what do you suppose a psychoanalytic or object relations therapist might say about the cause of this irrational belief?

Theory of Psychopathology

In REBT psychopathology is a direct function of irrational beliefs. Ellis's theory of psychopathology is largely consistent with Horney's (1950) concept of the "tyranny of the shoulds." Ellis describes his views with his usual flair:

> [E]very single time my clients talk about their depression, obsession, or compulsion, I can quickly, when using RET, within a few minutes, zero in on one, or two, or three of their major musts: "I *must* do well; you *must* treat me beautifully; the world *must* be easy." I then show these clients that they have these *musts* and teach them to surrender them. Now, they have many subheadings and variations on their musts but they all seem to be variations on a major theme, which I call "musterbation, absolutistic thinking or dogma," which, I hypothesize, is at the core of human disturbance. (Ellis, 1987, p. 127)

Like Ellis, the REBT theory of psychopathology is direct, straightforward, and sometimes offensive. To further capture his perspective, another quotation is pertinent: "I said many years ago, that masturbation is good and delicious, but musterbation is evil and pernicious" (Ellis, 1987, p. 127).

Initially, Ellis had a list of 12 basic irrational beliefs that cause emotional suffering. He later added a 13th, and subsequently other REBT writers have added additional irrational beliefs. Ellis eventually decided that all irrational beliefs could be boiled down to the three very basic beliefs, all of which he connects to his concept of musterbation:

> One, I *must* do well and be approved by *significant* others, and if I don't do as well as I *should* or *must*, there's something really rotten about me. It's terrible that I am this way and I am a pretty worthless, rotten person. That irrational belief leads to feelings of depression, anxiety, despair and self-doubting. It's an ego *must*. I have to do well or *I'm* no good.

The second irrational belief is, "You other humans with whom I relate, my original family, my later family that I may have, my friends, my relatives, and people with whom I work, must, ought, and should treat me considerately and fairly and even specially, considering what a doll I am! Isn't it horrible that they don't and they had better roast in hell for eternity!" That's anger, that's rage, that's homicide, that's genocide.

Then the third irrational belief, "Conditions under which I live—my environment, social conditions, economic conditions, political conditions—must be arranged so that I easily and immediately, with no real effort, have a free lunch, get what I command. Isn't it horrible when those conditions are harsh and when they frustrate me? I can't stand it! I can't be happy at all under those awful conditions and I can only be miserable or kill myself!" That's low frustration tolerance. (Ellis, 1987, p. 126)

Beck and Cognitive Therapy

The theoretical principles of Beck's cognitive therapy are similar to Ellis's REBT. Key similarities include the premises that

- Cognition is at the core of human suffering.
- The therapist's job is to help clients modify distress-producing thoughts.

There are also several distinctions between cognitive therapy and REBT. Beck consistently criticizes Ellis's use of the term *irrational* to describe the rules by which people regulate their lives. For example, he stated:

Ellis (1962) refers to such rules as "irrational ideas." His term, while powerful, is not accurate. The ideas are generally not irrational but are too absolute, broad, and extreme; too highly personalized; and are used too arbitrarily to help the patient to handle the exigencies of his life. To be of greater use, the rules need to be remolded so that they are more precise and accurate, less egocentric, and more elastic. (Beck, 1976, p. 33)

Beck also uses a different procedure for helping clients modify their thoughts. Although both theorists emphasized teaching and learning, cognitive therapists use *collaborative empiricism* or scientific collaboration to help clients discover the inaccurate or maladaptive quality of their thoughts. Collaborative empiricism emphasizes joint work on a mutually defined problem. This joint work focuses on identification of the client's cognitive rules or hypotheses, testing of the validity of these hypotheses, and then possible modification of the hypotheses. This approach requires the therapist to work within the client's frame of reference, trying to see the world through the client's eyes (Shaw & Beck, 1977). It also emphasizes that clients are not defective but, instead, may need to adjust the lens through which they are viewing the world (Beck, Emery, & Greenberg, 1985).

Beck's theory of personality and psychotherapy includes the following characteristics:

1. In the process of living, individuals are exposed to a variety of specific life events or situations, some of which trigger automatic, maladaptive thoughts.
2. These *maladaptive thoughts* are characterized by their faultiness; they are too narrow, too broad, too extreme, or simply inaccurate.
3. An individual's maladaptive thoughts are usually derived from deeply held maladaptive *core beliefs* (a.k.a. *schemas* or dysfunctional attitudes).
4. Individuals generally acquire these core beliefs during childhood.

5. These automatic thoughts, core beliefs, and their associated emotional distur-
bances, can be modified via cognitive therapy—a procedure that does not require
exploration of a client's past.

Beck has succinctly described his particular cognitive model—emphasizing cognitions (automatic thoughts) and schemas:

> [C]ognitions (verbal and pictorial "events" in [the] stream of consciousness) are based on
> attitudes or assumptions (schemas), developed from previous experiences. For example, if
> a person interprets all his experiences in terms of whether he is competent and adequate,
> his thinking may be dominated by the schema, "Unless I do everything perfectly, I'm a
> failure." Consequently, he reacts to situations in terms of adequacy even when they are un-
> related to whether or not he is personally competent. (Beck et al., 1979, p. 3)

You may note that Beck's concept of core belief or schema is strikingly similar to Adler's lifestyle concept (Schulman, 1985).

Another feature of Beck's approach is the regular use of *Socratic questioning.* Therapists ask questions that help clients focus on (1) awareness of automatic thoughts and
core beliefs, (2) evaluation of the usefulness and accuracy of automatic thoughts and core
beliefs, and (3) possible strategies for modifying automatic thoughts and core beliefs.

Theory of Psychopathology

The general characteristics of Beck's theory of psychopathology are the same as those
of REBT. However, in contrast to Ellis, who focused on three basic irrational beliefs,
Beck emphasizes the client's *cognitive distortions* or faulty assumptions and misconceptions. These distortions, triggered by external events (Ellis's activating events) produce automatic thoughts, which are often linked to underlying core beliefs or schemas.
Beck has described several different types of cognitive distortions, some of which overlap somewhat with one another and are very similar to Ellis's irrational beliefs (Beck,
1976; Beck et al., 1979, 1985). Brief descriptions and examples of four of his most practical cognitive distortions are included in Table 8.1.

Questions for Reflection

What is the difference between a cognitive distortion and an irrational belief? Is
Beck's model, emphasizing (1) cognitive distortion, (2) automatic thoughts, and
(3) self-schemas or core beliefs significantly different than Ellis's ABC model?

Beck also theorized that specific automatic thoughts and core beliefs were indicative
of specific mental and emotional problems (Beck, 1976). As a consequence of his extensive research on depression, he concluded that a particular *cognitive triad* characterizes depressive conditions. Beck's cognitive triad consists of

- Negative evaluation of self: "I am unworthy."
- Negative evaluation of the world or specific events: "Everything is just more evi-
dence that the world is falling apart."
- Negative evaluation of the future: "Nothing will ever get better."

Table 8.1   Beck's Cognitive Distortions in Cognitive Therapy

Arbitrary Inference: This distortion is akin to jumping to conclusions and is similar to Ellis's (1962) catastrophizing, wherein clients conclude without any supporting or relevant evidence that the worst possible outcome will happen. For example, when a client with social anxiety heads out to a party, he or she might have the following automatic thoughts: "Oh no, I know I'm going to make a complete fool of myself. No one will like me. They'll probably laugh at me and make fun of me after I leave." This distortion may be connected to an underlying schema or core belief such as "I am socially disgusting and will always be rejected by others." In the case example later in this chapter, Richard makes an arbitrary inference that his therapist identifies as a catastrophizing thought.

Selective Abstraction: In this distortion, most relevant information about a situation is ignored while one minor detail provides the basis for a negative conclusion. For example, after completing an examination, you might focus solely on a test item you missed, concluding, "I know I missed that essential question. The professor will know how stupid I am. I might as well drop the class now. I'm such a loser. In fact, the world would probably be a better place if I was just dead." Of course, you may have gotten most other items on the test right. This distortion might reveal this underlying schema: "If I don't answer everything perfectly, then it proves I'm inadequate, undeserving, and worthless."

Personalization: This distortion is sometimes referred to as *self-referencing*. Victims of this distortion take everything personally. If someone doesn't say hello, they conclude that it's their fault. If the cashier gives them back incorrect change, they think the person is purposely taking advantage of them for some specific reason. This style of distortion can produce either anxiety or a paranoid state. In the case of paranoia, automatic thoughts might include, "I know she's out to get me; I could tell by the way she looked at me that she's been out to get me ever since I came in this store." This distortion may be connected to an underlying schema of "People are always untrustworthy. If I don't keep an eye on everybody all the time, someone's going to take advantage of me."

Dichotomous or Polarized Thinking: This distorted thinking style is common among clients with borderline or narcissistic personality traits. People and situations are usually evaluated as black or white, good or bad. When these clients come to counseling, they often either love or hate their therapist, with automatic thoughts like "This is the best therapist I've ever known. He's incredible. He's so insightful." The underlying schema may be "I must stay very close to good people and get away from the danger of bad people."

Labeling and Mislabeling: All humans use labels to describe themselves and others. Unfortunately, sometimes people hang onto inaccurate or maladaptive labels, despite their lack of utility. For example, when a client consistently labels himself a "loser" or a "wimp," the labels can have a powerful and negative effect on client behavior. Similarly, even an overly positive but inaccurate label can have maladaptive features (e.g., if a woman with narcissistic qualities labels herself "The Queen").

Magnification and Minimization: This distortion is also referred to as *overestimation and underestimation* and is illustrated in the case of Richard later in this chapter. It occurs when a client makes a mountain out of a molehill (and vice versa). For example, when clients exaggerate the likelihood that they will flunk a test, magnification has occurred. When clients minimize the extent of their hard work and its likelihood of paying off in the future, minimization has occurred.

Overgeneralization: This distortion occurs when an individual generalizes and comes to a strong conclusion on the basis of a single or small number of incidents. Obviously, when overgeneralization occurs, the conclusion may be unwarranted. For example, when a client concludes that he is destined to be rejected by all women simply because one or two women turned him down when he asked them out on a date, he is overgeneralizing.

There are several different renditions of cognitive distortions in the psychological literature. In his original work, Beck listed seven: Arbitrary Inference, Selective Abstraction, Personalization, Dichotomous or Polarized Thinking, Magnification and Minimization, and Labeling and Mislabeling (Beck, 1976). In his popular self-help books, Burns, a student of Beck, lists 10, somewhat more user-friendly, cognitive distortions (Burns, 1989). Table 8.1 describes Beck's original cognitive distortions.

Meichenbaum and Self-Instructional Training

Meichenbaum's self-instructional training and stress inoculation training is based on internal speech or verbal mediation. He stated that "behavior change occurs through a sequence of mediating processes involving the interaction of inner speech, cognitive structures, and behaviors and their resultant outcomes" (Meichenbaum, 1977, p. 218). His model, in the tradition of Bandura, is a reciprocal one, and therefore it emphasizes a moment-to-moment interactive relationship between the individual and the environment.

Stress inoculation training procedures have been used in the treatment of a wide variety of clinical problems (Meichenbaum, 1985, 1996; Novaco, 1979). These procedures involve three separate but interrelated treatment phases.

1. *Conceptualization.* This phase includes the development of a collaborative relationship, the use of Socratic questioning to educate clients about the nature and impact of stress, and conceptualization of stressful situations as "problems-to-be-solved" (Meichenbaum, 1996, p. 4). When stress is viewed as a challenge, the therapist can begin assisting the client in formulating personal or individualized methods for preparing for, confronting, and reflecting on stressful experiences.
2. *Skills acquisition and rehearsal.* During this phase specific coping skills are taught and practiced in the office setting and eventually in vivo. The particular skills taught are related to the individual problems. Examples include relaxation training, self-instructional training, emotional self-regulation, and communication skills training.
3. *Application and follow-through.* In this phase, clients apply their newly acquired coping skills to increasingly challenging stressors. Personal experiments are used to help inoculate clients from the effects of later stressful situations. Relapse prevention strategies, attribution procedures (in which clients are taught to take credit for their accomplishments), and booster sessions are built into this final phase of the stress inoculation training model.

The unique component of Meichenbaum's theory is his emphasis on immediate coping self-statements. For example, in the treatment of anger, Novaco coaches clients to prepare for provocations by saying the following things to themselves:

- This could be a rough situation, but I know how to deal with it.
- I can work out a plan to handle this. Easy does it.
- Remember, stick to the issues and don't take it personally. (Novaco, 1979, p. 269)

Somewhat later in the process, when potentially angry or aggressive individuals are coping with physical arousal, they are instructed to practice saying these things:

- My muscles are getting tight. Relax and slow things down.
- Time to take a deep breath. Let's take the issue point by point.
- He probably wants me to get angry, but I'm going to deal with it constructively. (Novaco, 1979, p. 269)

Similarly, Douglas and colleagues report using similar self-instructional coping strategies in the treatment of impulsive children. They taught children to make the following statements to themselves:

"I must stop and think before I begin." "What plans can I try?" "How would it work out if I did that?" "What shall I try next?" "Have I got it right so far?" "See I made a mistake there—I'll just erase it." "Now let's see, have I tried everything I can think of?" "I've done a pretty good job." (Douglas, Parry, Marton, & Garson, 1976, p. 408)

Stress inoculation training is now considered an empirically supported treatment for helping adults who are coping with stress (Saunders, Driskell, Hall, & Salas, 1996). The application of self-instructional procedures in the treatment of children with impulsive behavioral problems continues to profoundly influence current treatment and research, but outcomes in that area have been more mixed (see Kendall, 2000).

Questions for Reflection

Meichenbaum's model emphasizes inner speech. Is his model compatible with Ellis's and/or Beck's? Where would you place Meichenbaum's ongoing, coping-oriented inner speech in Ellis's ABC model? Does it fit well there? Where would you place it in Beck's model? Is Meichenbaum's inner speech an automatic thought? Or is it something else?

THE PRACTICE OF COGNITIVE THERAPY

Sometimes cognitive therapy seems very simple. It's as easy as 1, 2, 3:

1. Access clients' irrational or maladaptive thoughts.
2. Instruct clients in more adaptive or more rational thinking and/or teach internal verbal instructional coping strategies.
3. Support clients as they apply these new and developing skills in their lives.

Unfortunately, cognitive therapy isn't as easy as it appears. Whether you follow the model articulated by Ellis, Beck, Meichenbaum, or someone else, you'll need extensive training and supervision to achieve competence. For example, in the now classic text *Cognitive Therapy of Depression,* Beck and his colleagues include an 85-point checklist for measuring therapist competency (Beck et al., 1979).

Preparing Yourself to Do Therapy from a Cognitive Perspective

Whether following the REBT-rationalist model or the cognitive therapy–empirical model, cognitive therapists pay close attention to what clients think. Keep this in mind, because it will be your central focus.

Before working with clients from the cognitive perspective, it's a good idea to practice what you'll be preaching. There are a number of excellent books available for learning to practice cognitive therapy on yourself (or for using with clients). These include *The Feeling Good Handbook* (Burns, 1989), *How to Make Yourself Happy and Remarkably Less Disturbable* (Ellis, 1999a), and *Mind Over Mood* (Greenberger & Padesky, 1995). In addition, we recommend that, when reviewing the cognitive self-monitoring technique described in the assessment section of this chapter, you try it out on yourself.

Preparing your Client for Cognitive Therapy

It's possible for clients to incorrectly assume that cognitive therapy is exclusively an intellectually oriented therapy that excludes talk about emotional issues, or to have other misconceptions about the nature of cognitive therapy. As with all therapy orientations, it is a good idea to provide clients with specific information about cognitive therapy. An informational handout written by Judith S. Beck (daughter of Aaron Beck) is provided in Ethical Highlight 8.1.

In addition to using the straightforward descriptions of cognitive therapy that are included in informed consent materials, many cognitive therapists specifically use stories, demonstrations, and life examples to illustrate the powerful influence of cognitive processes on emotions. For example, we sometimes use a version of what we call the "bump in the night" scenario.

Therapist: I know it can be hard to believe that what and how you think can have such an amazing influence on your emotions, but it's true. Let me give you an example.

Client: Okay.

Therapist: Let's say you're lying in bed at night, trying to go to sleep, and suddenly, out of nowhere, you hear a thud somewhere in your house. What would you feel?

Client: I'd probably be scared.

Therapist: Okay, so the first thing that comes to mind is that you'd feel scared. How about if you were taking care of a very pesky dog for a friend of yours, how would you feel then?

Client: Well, if I knew it was the dog being pesky, then I'd feel annoyed, I guess. Probably I'd feel irritated that the dog was making noise while I'm trying to sleep.

Therapist: Perfect. So you've demonstrated that it's not the thud that produces your emotional reaction, but instead it's what you think about the thud. Tell me, when you first said you'd probably be scared in reaction to the thud, what thoughts went through your mind that would lead to that feeling?

Client: I thought you were suggesting that the thud meant that a burglar had broken into my house, and then of course I'd be scared.

Therapist: Exactly. In the absence of information about what caused the thud, you inserted the possibility of a burglar, and that would, of course, produce fear. But if you think it's a pesky dog, then you feel annoyed. And how about if your grandmother was staying at your house and you heard an unusual thud, what might come to mind then?

Client: I'd feel scared then too. Scared that she might have hurt herself. I'd get right up and go check on her.

Therapist: So now you're telling me that what you think not only directly affects your emotions, but also your behavior, because if you thought it was a burglar then you probably wouldn't jump up and check, you'd do something different, right?

Client: That's true.

Therapist: So, my point is that it's not the thud or what happens to you that produces your emotions and behavior, but instead, it's what you think about a situation. It's your assumption or belief about the situation that cause you to feel and act in particular ways.

Client: Yeah, I see what you mean.

In this example the therapist has effectively used a Socratic dialogue to educate his client about the cognitive theory of emotional disturbance. To view an alternative to this strategy, we recommend A. Freeman's videotape with adults (see Recommended Readings and Resources). A similar approach to providing a cognitive therapy orientation with young clients is included in Putting It in Practice 8.1.

Assessment Issues and Procedures

Similar to behavior therapists, cognitive therapists frequently use a wide variety of assessment strategies for evaluating, facilitating, and monitoring treatment progress. These assessment strategies include collaborative interviewing, self-rating scales, and cognitive self-monitoring.

Collaborative Interviewing

For most therapists who work within a cognitive therapy frame (with the possible exception of Albert Ellis), a collaborative assessment model is used. Persons and Tompkins (1997) articulate their approach to cognitive-behavioral case formulation:

> Whenever possible, the process of formulation is a collaborative one, with patient and therapist working together to make a Problem List, propose some core beliefs, set goals for treatment, choose interventions, and monitor progress. (p. 322)

The therapist is not the expert upon whom all therapy success depends. Instead, expertise is achieved when the client and therapist join together, using an empirical or investigation-oriented attitude.

A central task during an initial collaborative interview is to establish a clear and comprehensive problem list. Items on the problem list should be described in simple, descriptive, concrete terms. Persons and Tompkins (1997) recommend that about five to eight items be included on a problem list. For example, Susanna, a 25-year-old female, generated the following problem list during a collaborative interview:

1. *Depressive thoughts.* Susanna reports thoughts consistent with Beck's cognitive triad (Beck, 1970). She believes she is a worthless loser (negative evaluation of self), that the world is a rotten place (negative evaluation of the world), and that her life will continue to be miserable (negative evaluation of the future).

2. *Social isolation.* She is greatly dissatisfied with her social life. She has social contact outside of her workplace only once weekly or less.

3. *Procrastination and lack of self-discipline.* She struggles to keep her house clean, pay her bills on time, attend to personal hygiene, and organize her daily activities.

Putting It in Practice 8.1

Cognitive Storytelling With Young Clients

If you intend to do cognitive therapy with young clients, you need to prepare for the fact that often young clients are not highly interested in learning or applying cognitive techniques in their lives (Sommers-Flanagan & Sommers-Flanagan, 1997). This might be because of depression, lack of motivation, resistance to authority figures, or simply because young clients view talk therapy as boring.

To address the challenge of teaching cognitive therapy strategies to young clients, we developed a pre–cognitive therapy technique designed to illustrate cognitive therapy principles and to pique interest in applying these principles to life situations. This technique is called *cognitive storytelling*. We have collected stories from our own experiences, or from literature, that help illustrate the power of thought. To start the technique, we simply tell the young client that we have an interesting story to tell them and that we want them to try to figure out the moral of the story. Here's an example:

Road Rage

One time a man named Roger was driving down a two-lane road, when suddenly a red minivan, driving way too fast, passed him and rudely cut him off. Roger was furious. He started thinking about how stupid it was for whoever was driving that minivan to be driving so irresponsibly. He couldn't stop himself from calling that other driver a few cuss words under his breath. About 30 seconds later, Roger came to a railroad crossing, and sure enough there was a train holding up traffic. Roger was still steaming from having gotten passed and cut off by the minivan, who just happened to be stopped right in front of him. Since Roger had a few minutes and was extremely pissed off, he decided to teach that other driver a little lesson that would not soon be forgotten. So Roger hopped out of his car and approached the red minivan. He wasn't exactly sure what he was gonna say, but he knew he had a captive audience. When Roger stepped up to the driver's side window, he saw a man with a panicked expression on his face look up at him. Then he glanced at the back seat. There, sprawled across the seat, was a very pregnant woman lying with her knees up, breathing rapidly. Suddenly, Roger's road rage melted into a combination of embarrassment and pity. When the driver rolled down his window, Roger asked, "Is there anything I can do to help?"

After the story has ended, we talk about the implications of the story, using Socratic questioning. For example, we might ask questions such as these: "What do you think this story tells you about anger?" "Besides his anger, what else changes inside of Roger when he sees the pregnant woman in the back seat of the car?" "What do you think would happen inside of you if you were involved in a similar situation?" "What might Roger think the next time he sees someone driving recklessly on the road?" "How does this story apply to you in your life?"

ETHICAL HIGHLIGHT 8.1

Providing Clients with Information about Cognitive Therapy: A Question & Answer Session with Judith S. Beck

Q: What is cognitive therapy?

A: Cognitive therapy is one of the few forms of psychotherapy that has been scientifically tested and found to be effective in over three hundred clinical trials for many different disorders. In contrast to other forms of psychotherapy, cognitive therapy is usually more focused on the present, more time-limited, and more problem-solving oriented. Indeed, much of what the patient does is solve current problems. In addition, patients learn specific skills that they can use for the rest of their lives. These skills involve identifying distorted thinking, modifying beliefs, relating to others in different ways, and changing behaviors.

Q: What is the theory behind cognitive therapy?

A: Cognitive therapy is based on the cognitive model, which . . . simply [posits] that the way we perceive situations influences how we feel emotionally. For example, one person reading this [material] might think, "Wow! This sounds good, it's just what I've always been looking for!" and feels happy. Another person reading this information might think, "Well, this sounds good but I don't think I can do it." This person feels sad and discouraged. So it is not a situation which directly affects how a person feels emotionally, but rather [it affects] his or her thoughts in that situation. When people are in distress, they often do not think clearly and their thoughts are distorted in some way. Cognitive therapy helps people to identify their distressing thoughts and to evaluate how realistic the thoughts are. Then they learn to change their distorted thinking. When they think more realistically, they feel better. The emphasis is also consistently on solving problems and initiating behavioral change.

Q: What can I do to get ready for therapy?

A: An important first step is to set goals. Ask yourself, "How would I like to be different by the end of therapy?" Think specifically about changes you'd like to make at work, at home, [and] in your relationships with family, friends, co-workers, and others. Think about what symptoms have been bothering you and which you'd like to decrease or eliminate. Think about other areas that would improve your life: pursuing spiritual/intellectual/cultural interests, increasing exercise, decreasing bad habits, learning new interpersonal skills, improving management skills at work or at home. The therapist will help you evaluate and refine these goals and help you determine which goals you might be able to work at on your own and which ones you might want to work on in therapy.

Q: What happens during a typical therapy session?

A: Even before your therapy session begins, your therapist may have you fill out certain forms to assess your mood. Depression, Anxiety and Hopelessness Inventories help give you and the therapist an objective way of assessing your progress. One of the first things your therapist will do in the ther-

(continued)

ETHICAL HIGHLIGHT 8.1 (continued)

apy session is to determine how you've been feeling this week, compared to other weeks. This is what we call a mood check. The therapist will ask you what problem you'd like to put on the agenda for that session and what happened during the previous week that was important. Then the therapist will make a bridge between the previous therapy session and this week's therapy session by asking you what seemed important that you discussed during the past session, what self-help assignments you were able to do during the week, and whether there is anything about the therapy that you would like to see changed.

Next, you and the therapist will discuss the problem or problems you put on the agenda and do a combination of problem-solving and assessing the accuracy of your thoughts and beliefs in that problematic situation. You will also learn new skills. You and the therapist will discuss how you can make best use of what you've learned during the session in the coming week and the therapist will summarize the important points of the session and ask you for feedback: what was helpful about the session, what was not, anything that bothered you, anything the therapist didn't get right, anything you'd like to see changed. As you will see, both therapist and patient are quite active in this form of treatment.

Q: How long does therapy last?

A: Unless there are practical constraints, the decision about length of treatment is made cooperatively between therapist and patient. Often the therapist will have a rough idea after a session or two of how long it might take for you to reach the goals that you set at the first session. Some patients remain in therapy for just a brief time, six to eight sessions. Other patients who have had long-standing problems may choose to stay in therapy for many months. Initially, patients are seen once a week, unless they are in crisis. As soon as they are feeling better and seem ready to start tapering therapy, patient and therapist might agree to try therapy once every two weeks, then once every three weeks. This more gradual tapering of sessions allows you to practice the skills you've learned while [you are] still in therapy. Booster sessions are recommended three, six and twelve months after therapy has ended.

Q: What about medication?

A: Cognitive therapists, being both practical and collaborative, can discuss the advantages and disadvantages of medication with you. Many patients are treated without medication at all. Some disorders, however, respond better to a combination of medication and cognitive therapy. If you are on medication, or would like to be on medication, you might want to discuss with your therapist whether you should have a psychiatric consultation with a specialist (a psychopharmacologist) to ensure that you are on the right kind and dosage of medication. If you are not on medication and do not want to be on medication, you and your therapist might assess, after four to six weeks, how much you've progressed and determine whether you might

ETHICAL HIGHLIGHT 8.1 (continued)

want a psychiatric consultation at that time to obtain more information about medication.

Q: How can I make the best use of therapy?

A: One way is to ask your therapist how you might be able to supplement your psychotherapy with cognitive therapy readings, workbooks, client pamphlets, [and so on]. A second way is to prepare carefully for each session, thinking about what you learned in the previous session and jotting down what you want to discuss in the next session.

A third way to maximize therapy is to make sure that you try to bring the therapy session into your everyday life. A good way of doing this is by taking notes at the end of each session or recording the session or a summary of the session on audiotape. Make sure that you and the therapist leave enough time in the therapy session to discuss what would be helpful for you to do during the coming week and try to predict what difficulties you might have in doing these assignments so your therapist can help you before you leave the session.

Q: How will I know if therapy is working?

A: Most patients notice a decrease in their symptoms within three to four weeks of therapy if they have been faithfully attending sessions and doing the suggested assignments between sessions on a daily basis. They also see the scores on their objective tests begin to drop within several weeks.

This information is reproduced with permission from Judith S. Beck, Ph.D., director of the Beck Institute for Cognitive Therapy and Research. You can find this information and more at the Institute's web site: www.geocities.com/spiroll2/cbtexplained.html.

4. *Internet preoccupation.* She spends many hours a day surfing the Internet. Although she reports enjoying this, she also reports that her Internet activity increases markedly when she needs to pay bills, has a social opportunity, or is facing deadlines.

5. *Lack of academic progress.* She would like to finish her bachelor's degree, but she frequently drops out of class after enrolling and either obtains an incomplete or withdraws from the class.

6. *Disrupted sleep patterns.* She reports difficulty sleeping, which she sees as being related to her problems with procrastination.

The process of generating a problem list helps the client and therapist begin to develop hypotheses about the client's core beliefs. Greenberger and Padesky (1995) provide specific examples of questions to use when exploring client problems. These questions help elucidate the client's inner, cognitive world. They recommend asking questions like these:

- What was going through your mind just before you started to feel this way?
- What does this say about you?

- What does this mean about you . . . your life . . . your future?
- What are you afraid might happen?
- What is the worst thing that could happen if this were true?
- What does this mean about the other person(s) or people in general?
- Do you have images or memories in this situation? If so, what are they? (Greenberger & Padesky, 1995, p. 36).

In Susanna's case it was discovered that she basically considered herself "a loser" who had "no willpower" and who had always "been a miserable failure at initiating social relationships." Furthermore, she thought others were consistently critiquing her and noticing her inadequacies. These core beliefs became the main target for change in her therapy experience.

Self-Rating Scales

At the beginning of therapy and throughout the therapy process, cognitive therapists make liberal use of self-rating scales. For example, Beck developed the Beck Depression Inventory (BDI) to evaluate and monitor depression during treatment (Beck, Ward, Mendelson, Mock, & Erbaugh, 1961). Empirically minded cognitive therapists often have their clients complete the BDI at the very beginning of each therapy session. Similar rating scales that cognitive therapists frequently use include the Beck Anxiety Inventory (Beck, Epstein, Brown, & Steer, 1988), the Penn State Worry Questionnaire (Meyer, Miller, Metzger, & Borkevec, 1990), and the Children's Depression Inventory (Kovacs, 1992).

Cognitive Self-Monitoring

To practice cognitive therapy, it is crucial to teach clients to pay attention to their automatic thoughts. Cognitive self-monitoring is one of the most effective ways to help clients increase awareness of automatic thoughts. Although cognitive self-monitoring and the exploration of maladaptive or irrational thoughts begin within therapy sessions, it's very important for clients to continue monitoring their thoughts outside therapy sessions.

Although there are several versions of cognitive self-monitoring procedures available, Persons (1989) recommends the use of a generic "Thought Record." To use a Thought Record, clients are instructed to jot down the following basic information immediately after experiencing a strong emotional response: (1) date and time of the emotional response, (2) the situation that elicited the emotional response, (3) the behaviors the client engaged in, (4) the emotions that were elicited, (5) the associated thoughts that occurred during the situation, and (6) any other related responses.

The client's Thought Record provides a foundation for cognitive interventions. Beck and his colleagues (Beck et al., 1979), as well as other cognitive authors (Burns, 1989), recommend transforming a generic Thought Record into a more specific theory-based therapeutic tool by having clients use the language of automatic thoughts, cognitive distortions, and rational responses. Clients are instructed to create 3 columns with these terms as labels and to record their experiences accordingly. This is called the three-column-technique. Table 8.2 provides a sample of a more expanded Thought Record. Developing either a Thought Record or a record using the three columns is a common homework assignment.

Table 8.2   Thought Record Sample

Situation	Emotion	Automatic Thoughts	Cognitive Distortion	Rational Response	Outcome/ New Feeling
Briefly describe the situation linked to the unpleasant feelings.	Specify and rate the emotion (Sad, Anxious, Angry) on a 0-100 scale.	State the automatic thought that accompanied the emotion.	Classify the cognitive distortion present within the automatic thought.	Replace the automatic thought with a more rational (or adaptive) response.	Rate the feelings again to see if the rational response modified them.
Home alone on Saturday night	Sad: 85	"I'm always alone. No one will ever love me. No one will ever want to be with me."	Dichotomous thinking and catastrophizing.	Being home on Saturday night is better than being with someone I don't like. Just because I'm not in a relationship now doesn't mean I'll never be in one.	Sad: 45

> ### Questions for Reflection
>
> If you were a client, can you imagine using a three-column cognitive self-monitoring log or Thought Record on a regular basis? What do you suppose would stop you from using this sort of assessment procedure on yourself? What would help motivate you to use a Thought Record?

Specific Therapy Techniques

There are numerous, highly accessible, and highly practical cognitive therapy techniques that practitioners can employ. The following techniques are derived from several main sources (Burns, 1989; Ellis, 1999; McMillin, 1986).

Generating Alternative Interpretations

In Chapter 8 we gave an example of the technique of generating behavioral alternatives. The technique of generating alternative interpretations is based on the same model, with the specific focus being on thoughts or interpretations rather than behaviors.

Generating alternative interpretations is a useful technique with clients who hold onto maladaptive or irrational automatic thoughts despite the fact that other, more reasonable, interpretations or explanations exist. As McMillin (1986) notes, the first interpretation of a scene is often the worst, the most negative, or the most catastrophic. Unfortunately, first interpretations can be difficult to counter. This technique teaches clients to immediately counter first interpretations with at least four other reasonable alternatives, using the following guidelines:

1. The client keeps a written log of the very worst emotions experienced during a 1-week period. This log includes a brief description of the activating event (A) and a brief description of the first interpretation (iB).
2. At the next session this homework is reviewed and the client is given an additional assignment: "After logging your initial interpretation, add four different but equally plausible interpretations." McMillin (1986) uses the following example:

   Situation: A single 25-year-old woman just broke up with her boyfriend.
   First interpretation: There is something wrong with me. I am inadequate, and I'll probably never develop a lasting relationship with a man.
   Alternative interpretations:
   - I haven't met the right man.
   - I don't want to give up my freedom right now.
   - My boyfriend and I didn't have the right chemistry together.
   - My boyfriend was afraid to commit to me or to the relationship. (McMillin, 1986, p. 12)
3. At the next session, the therapist helps the client determine which of the four interpretations has the most supporting evidence. It is important to help the client use an objective review of the data rather than subjective impressions or hunches.
4. The client continues using this four alternative procedure when an emotionally distressing event occurs. Additionally, the client is coached to write down the alternative interpretations, but then to wait and decide which interpretation is best only after adequate time has passed to distance her from the event. Then the client is asked to practice this procedure with every upsetting event for the next month until it becomes an automatic response (McMillin, 1986).

Like the generation of behavioral alternatives, this technique is especially useful with adolescents. In a series of studies, Kenneth Dodge and his colleagues have demonstrated that youths who consistently display aggressive behavior often do so, in part, because they have quickly and incorrectly interpreted the behavior of other youths as hostile (Dodge, 1980; Dodge & Frame, 1982; Dodge & Somberg, 1987). This phenomenon is called *misattribution of hostility*. For example, if a youth disposed toward aggression is walking through the hall at school and another student inadvertently bumps him, the youth is likely to attribute the bump to an intentional hostile act. Consequently, the potential for retaliation is increased.

In our work with aggressive youths, we have used the technique of generating alternative interpretations with two minor modifications. First, we sometimes use a timing device to add a real-world pressure to the interpretation generation process: "Okay, now you've got 60 seconds to come up with as many alternative explanations as possible. I'll time you." Second, we sometimes add a concrete reward (stickers, money, baseball cards) as an incentive for youths to come up with alternative interpretations: "I'll give you one baseball card for every alternative you can come up with" (see Sommers-Flanagan & Sommers-Flanagan, 1997).

Vigorous and Forceful Disputing: A Favorite Technique from Albert Ellis

In the book *Favorite Counseling and Therapy Techniques* (Rosenthal, 1999), Albert Ellis shared his approach for vigorously disputing irrational beliefs. This technique stems from Ellis's view that an individual can begin to lightly adopt a rational belief (e.g., "I want people to like me, but I can live happily if they don't") while at the same time strongly holding onto an opposing irrational belief with more intensity (e.g., "But I really absolutely need their approval and have nothing to live for if I don't get it!").

To help clients who have this problem, Ellis suggests that you first explain to them that "vigorous, forceful, and persistent" disputing of irrational beliefs is often needed to "actually replace them with rational beliefs" (Ellis, 1999b, p. 76). Next, provide your clients with the following written instructions, encouraging them to partake in this homework assignment to vigorously dispute their irrational beliefs.

> One way to do highly powerful, vigorous disputing is to use a tape recorder and to record one of your strong Irrational Beliefs into it, such as, "If I fail this job interview I am about to have, that will prove that I'll never get a good job and that I might as well apply only for low-level positions!" Figure out several Disputes to the Irrational Belief and strongly present them on this same tape. For example: "Even if I do poorly on this interview, that only will show that I failed this time, but never will show that I'll always fail and can never do well in other interviews. Maybe they'll still hire me for the job. But if they don't, I can learn by my mistakes, can do better in other interviews, and likely can get the kind of job I want."
>
> Listen to your Disputing. Let other people, including your therapist or members of your therapy group, listen to it. Do it over in a more forceful and vigorous manner and let them listen to it again, to see if you do it better and more forcefully, until they agree that you are getting more powerful at doing it. Keep listening to it until you see that you are able to convince yourself and others that your Disputing is becoming more and more powerful and more convincing. (Ellis, 1999b, pp. 76–77)

As you can see, Ellis's prescribed homework assignment essentially amounts to repeated practice at more and more forceful cognitive disputing procedures. This homework assignment flows directly from his therapeutic style: That is, if clients can mount a forceful and rational counterattack against their irrational beliefs, they'll be able to minimize and hopefully eliminate their irrational thinking.

Thinking in Shades of Grey

This technique is derived from Burns (1989). It involves taking a client's automatic thoughts, assumptions, or conclusions about a specific performance and placing them on a concrete, measurable scale.

In the following case, Jackson, a 35-year-old engineer, was referred to therapy because his perfectionistic standards were resulting in extremely slow performance. Additionally, he was suffering from several depressive symptoms that seemed to be associated with his perfectionism and work performance. After focusing on his automatic thoughts, he produced the following written description of himself and his core beliefs or self-schema:

"I am basically defective. Therefore, to prove I'm not defective, I have to do a better, higher quality job on my work than anyone else. Every task I do must be performed flawlessly, or there is just more proof that I'm defective. But accomplishing one or two tasks perfectly is not sufficient proof of my adequacy. Therefore, I've got to keep working . . . or I've failed, period. Also, my basic assumption is that to fail at one task is to fail altogether."

Obviously, Jackson was suffering from a terrible case of the "tyranny of the shoulds" (Horney, 1950), and several cognitive and behavioral procedures are employed in his overall treatment. However, as one entry point for questioning his rigid self-schema, we used the technique of thinking in shades of grey.

Jackson's therapist worked with him to develop a 100-point performance rating scale. Initially, Jackson confided that a normal scale might include ratings from zero to 100, but for him the meaning of each rating from zero to 95 would be "failure." To illustrate, he drew the scale shown in Table 8.3.

Table 8.3

96–100	Complete success
75–95	Complete failure
50–74	Complete failure
25–49	Complete failure
0–24	Complete failure

In Jackson's cognitive world, the only way he could achieve complete success was to have a performance that he rated as 96–100.

Collaborating with his therapist, Jackson developed a new rating scale that he could experiment with when evaluating his work-related performance. His new scale is shown in Table 8.4.

Table 8.4

96–100	Complete success
85–95	Partial success
75–84	Marginally acceptable
0–74	Complete failure

Jackson's new scale represented a compromise between him and his therapist. To continue the technique of thinking in shades of grey, Jackson took his new scale for a "test drive" by using it for a week at work. His assignment was to rate himself using this new scale and to occasionally double-check his ratings with his supervisor's ratings of his performance. To Jackson's surprise, his supervisor always rated the quality of his performance in the top two categories, and Jackson himself discovered that all of his self-ratings were also in the top two categories.

Exploring the Consequences of Giving up the "Should" Rule

This technique is a variation of response prevention discussed by Beck and colleagues (Beck et al., 1979; Shaw & Beck, 1977). It was employed in Jackson's case because much more work was needed to help him change his self-schema. Specifically, Jackson was instructed to clearly verbalize his "should" rule, to predict what would happen if the should was not followed, to carry out an experiment to test the prediction, and to revise his should rule according to the outcome of the experiment (Beck et al., 1979, p. 255).

As in the example in Beck's work, Jackson was given a series of activities designed to test his should statement: "Every task I do must (should) be performed flawlessly or there is just more proof that I'm defective." He predicted that he might receive a reprimand from his boss if he ignored this should and turned in poor-quality work. Consequently, he was asked to perform several work tasks as quickly as he could, but still keeping his overall work quality within the 75–84 "marginally acceptable" range. Jackson successfully completed this test of his should rule and discovered that instead of receiving a reprimand from his boss, he received a pat on the back for a job well done.

Other Cognitive Techniques

There are many more cognitive techniques available to the cognitive therapist. Most of these techniques focus on using mental strategies—usually verbal, linguistic, or based on visual imagery—to manage or eliminate problematic symptoms. Several key resources are listed at the end of this chapter (see Recommended Readings and Resources).

APPLICATION: CASE EXAMPLE

In Chapter 7, we described the first three sessions of the case of Richard, a 56-year-old professor at a vocational college who had referred himself for cognitive-behavior therapy due to recurring panic attacks. Sessions 4–12 follow here.

Session 4. Richard's homework was reviewed. Between sessions he had one full-blown panic attack and two minor incidents that he managed to cope with by using diaphragmatic breathing. He reported no use of caffeine or other stimulants. He also reported practicing diaphragmatic breathing 12 times over the course of 7 days. During his major panic episode, Richard was out with his wife shopping, became separated from her, and then began worrying about her because she never leaves him alone when they're out together. The entries in his panic log included several references to catastrophic thoughts and overestimations. (Remember, many authors have offered different renditions of common cognitive dysfunctions or distortions. In this case we emphasize two: catastrophic thoughts and overestimations. Both are commonly linked to panic and anxiety states. It is important for the therapist to teach clients how to identify and distinguish unhelpful cognitive distortions. It is far less important that the therapist use Beck's or Ellis's specific language for describing the distortions.)

Session 4 begins with direct education about maladaptive thoughts.

Therapist: I see here on your panic logs that when you got separated from your wife, Linda, your mind started running a hundred miles an hour. Tell me about what you were thinking and feeling when you couldn't find her.

Richard: She said she was just going to the restroom, and so I was browsing around by the restrooms, and I never saw her come out. I kept waiting and waiting, and it felt like forever. I got all worked up. Ever since this panic stuff started, she's been like my shadow. When she didn't come out I kept thinking that she must be hurt or sick or, my God, that maybe she was passed out or even dead. I finally got a woman to go in and check on her, and she wasn't in there, and then my mind really started racing. I thought she'd left me. I was sure that she'd finally gotten sick and tired of dealing with me and had snuck away.

Therapist: So where was she?

Richard: Oh, I guess there was an elderly woman in the bathroom who had gotten confused, and Linda took her to the help desk and they asked a bunch of questions. She said she felt terrible about being gone so long, but she had to help this woman, and then the woman got frightened and didn't want her to leave. I guess I must have wandered away a little ways when Linda came out with the woman, 'cause I never saw them at all.

Therapist: So then how did you and Linda get back together, and then what happened?

Richard: Linda found me in a cold sweat by the restrooms. I was trying to figure out why she would leave me and I was imagining life without her, and she came dashing up and started to explain everything, but I was in such a panic state I just had to go home. I couldn't get myself to focus and breathe and calm down. I just had to go home to settle myself down. I'm sorry.

Therapist: It sounds like that was terribly frightening for you. There's no need to apologize. Like we've talked about before, those false alarms you've been having aren't going to go away all at once. You've been making great progress. What's important is that we take a good hard look at what happened and learn from it so you can keep getting the upper hand on the panic.

Richard: Yeah, I know. But I can't help feeling like I disappointed myself, and you too.

Therapist: Well, actually, I have to say you had what looks like an excellent week. You practiced the diaphragmatic breathing and used it to calm yourself. And the incident that happened with Linda is perfect for us to use to understand even more about what's causing the panic.

Richard: You think so?

Therapist: Absolutely. The next item on today's agenda is for us to talk about this thing we call "automatic thoughts." As most people go through the day, they have things happen and then their minds quickly produce automatic thoughts about what just happened to them. When you were waiting for Linda and she didn't come out, you immediately started thinking that something terrible was wrong. You said you thought she was hurt or sick or dead in the bathroom. Those are terribly stressful thoughts. And then, as soon as the woman went in there and told you the bathroom was empty, it sounds like your first thought was that Linda was so sick of you that she had up and left you. Is that right?

Richard: Yeah. That's right.

Therapist: Okay, now that you're calm, I want to ask you some questions about what you were thinking in the store. Ready?

Richard: Yeah.

Therapist: Has Linda ever gotten hurt or injured in a public restroom before?

Richard: No. I know. That's a crazy thing for me to think.

Therapist: Actually, it's not totally crazy, it's just a big overestimation. Based on the fact that she's in good health and the fact that this has never happened before in your history of being together makes the odds that she would get hurt in the bathroom very unlikely. You see what I'm saying, it's possible, but very unlikely.

Richard: Okay.

Therapist: And here are some more questions. Does Linda love you?

Richard: Yes. I'm sure of that.

Therapist: And has she ever said that she's tired of being with you?

Richard: Nope.

Therapist: And were the two of you in a fight or having a bad time at the store?

Richard: Oh no. We like to shop together. We always have fun going out shopping. We don't always buy all that much, but we have a good time looking around.

Therapist: Okay, so the thought that she'd up and left you is not really overestimating. It's more like a catastrophic thought. Your automatic thought was of the worst possible relationship catastrophe—even though there was absolutely no evidence to support it. You and Linda have been together for thirty years. She says she loves you and is happy to be with you and you were having a good time, but somehow you assumed that she must be tired of you and therefore she had left you permanently.

Richard: Man. That does sound pretty crazy. You're right. When we talk about this it's like that thought came out of left field. Maybe I'm a little tired of myself, but Linda hasn't ever complained. But you know, at the time, for about four or five horrible minutes, I had myself convinced it was true.

Therapist: So you had a catastrophic thought that came out of the blue, but it might be kind of related to your own weariness with yourself. Your brain grabbed onto a convenient explanation. You've been tired of yourself, and so the best, ready-made explanation for Linda's absence was the same, that she was tired of you, too.

At this point, the therapist continues with an educational approach. He more thoroughly explains to Richard the difference between a maladaptive overestimation thought and a maladaptive catastrophic thought. An overestimation is the inflation of the likelihood of a negative outcome. Since it was possible that Linda was sick or hurt in the bathroom, Richard's automatic thought is classified as an overestimation. However, his quick assumption that Linda has left him has no support whatsoever, so it's categorized as a catastrophic thought. The therapist helps Richard see that he has a pattern of overestimation and catastrophizing in reaction to his physical symptoms. When he feels his heart rate increase he immediately thinks he's having a heart attack (overestimation), and he also has accompanying catastrophic thoughts ("this is terribly embarrassing. I'm such a weak person that Linda might leave me for this").

Richard's homework at the end of the fourth session is somewhat different. He is asked to keep a Thought Record whenever he begins feeling anxious. This record includes a column for the situation (e.g., standing in line at a movie theater), behaviors engaged in (e.g., fidgeting and shallow breathing), emotions or feelings (e.g., anxiety and worry), and automatic thoughts (e.g., oh no, we won't get into the movie and it's my fault, and if we don't get in Linda will be disappointed, and she'll get so sick of me that she'll want a divorce). Richard is also asked to categorize his automatic thoughts as mostly overestimating or mostly catastrophizing.

Session 5. Richard didn't have any full-blown panic attacks between sessions 4 and 5. He had several near misses, but he managed to use his breathing skills to cope effectively. He continued to work hard on his homework. The bulk of session 5 was spent on developing and practicing methods for countering or logically disputing the typical automatic thoughts that he experiences. The purpose of sticking with this focus is to prepare Richard for session 6, which involves a significant amount of intense interoceptive exposure.

Session 6. Richard had one panic attack between sessions 5 and 6. He arrived at the session quite discouraged and expressed disappointment in himself. The therapist provided Richard with empathy and reassurance, primarily focusing on the fact that he's in the process of teaching his body how to turn off a false alarm system that's been functioning for years. After using empathy, reassurance, and educational information, the therapist begins several interoceptive exposure trials.

> **Therapist:** Okay, Richard, I think you're ready for some more antipanic practice. Is that okay with you?
>
> **Richard:** Well, uh, okay. If you think I'm ready.
>
> **Therapist:** I'm sure you're ready. Our first activity is called the chair spin. It's designed to get you feeling dizzy, which is one of the symptoms you have when your panic alarm goes off. You spin yourself till you're dizzy, and then you can use both of the coping skills we've been working on to calm your body back down. So, once you're dizzy, do the breathing and the rational thinking exercise.
>
> **Richard:** Okay. What should I say to myself for the rational thinking?
>
> **Therapist:** Remember what we talked about last week? You had some great rebuttals for your overestimations and catastrophizing. For today, the main thing is to quickly identify whatever automatic thought comes into your mind and replace it with one of those two rebuttals.
>
> **Richard:** I can't remember them very clearly.
>
> **Therapist:** Okay, good. I'm glad you mentioned that. I've got them here in my notes. [Therapist pages through file for about 15 seconds.] Okay. Here they are. When you feel your body's alarm going off, you suggested saying to yourself, "This is my false alarm. I can get my body back to normal with some deep breathing." And for the thoughts about having a heart attack, you suggested, "I have proof from my doctor that my heart is in great shape." Remember?
>
> **Richard:** Yeah. Right. I've got it.
>
> **Therapist:** For today, let's write those thoughts out on a piece of paper and you can say them out loud while you do your breathing, okay?
>
> **Richard:** Yeah. Good idea. That way I don't have to suffer from brain lock like I do sometimes.

The therapist led Richard through three separate interoceptive exposure activities. These included chair spinning, breathing through a straw until some panic feelings emerged, and jogging in place. Richard was able to calm himself down each time. During the third activity, he chose to think his automatic thought-counters internally instead of saying them out loud. Richard left the session much more optimistic than when he arrived.

Questions for Reflection

As a therapist, what problems or worries do you imagine facing as you lead a client through interoceptive exposure activities? Do you think you might feel some anxiety about using these activities? If so, what would you need to do in preparation to help yourself implement these empirically justified strategies?

Sessions 7 and 8. Richard did not have any panic episodes during these weeks. His optimism continued to rise, and he and his therapist began talking about termination. During these sessions he continued interoceptive exposure practice and diaphragmatic breathing.

Session 9. Richard had two panic attacks between sessions 8 and 9 and came into therapy very discouraged. Much of this session focused on Richard's "explanation" for his relapse.

> **Richard:** I don't know why. I went backwards this week. I'm just a basket case. I guess this stuff works fine for most people, but it's looking like I'm weaker than most people.
>
> **Therapist:** Okay, Richard, you had a relapse. That's the reality. But I also hear you coming up with a fictional explanation for your relapse. I know we've been working hard on the breathing and dealing with your automatic overestimations and catastrophizing, and so I'm pretty sure you can figure this out. What type of thought is this explanation—that you're too weak a person to be successful—you have for your relapse?
>
> **Richard:** Geeze. You mean this is just another one of those crazy thoughts?
>
> **Therapist:** Right. So you had a relapse. Now you need an explanation. Unfortunately, your explanation doesn't hold water. You're not a weak person. You've been dealing with this stuff like a hero. You've kept going to work; you've shown me more self-discipline than most people who walk through this door. Let's toss your weakness theory and come up with a better explanation.
>
> **Richard:** I, uh. I don't know what else could it be.
>
> **Therapist:** What did we talk about for about 15 minutes last week?
>
> **Richard:** [20 seconds of silence.] Um. Yeah, I think we talked about me stopping therapy in a few weeks.
>
> **Therapist:** Right. That's a much better explanation. So what you're telling me with these two panic attacks is that we need to deal with the end of your counseling slowly and carefully because your *thoughts* of ending counseling are serving as a *trigger* for your false alarm system. The other thing it reminds me of is your tendency to quickly think that Linda will abandon you forever for one reason or another. Let's take a look at another trigger for your panics that we haven't really focused on much yet. Those automatic thoughts you have about Linda and the ones you just had about being weak seem to be what we call weakness or "defect thoughts." Somewhere inside, you think you're weak and defective, and so when something goes wrong, you've got this instant explanation. Unfortunately, your explanation makes things worse.
>
> **Richard:** Do you really think it's possible for me to overcome this?
>
> **Therapist:** I'll answer that, but first, how about if you look at the evidence and tell me what you think? What do you think your chances of recovery are?

Richard's response to this question revealed significant optimism, and the therapist let him take the lead in a discussion of what he needed for counseling to end on a smooth note. Richard suggested that they revise their plan and continue counseling for 15 sessions. He said he wanted to do two more weekly sessions and then cut back to every other week for two sessions and then possibly do monthly sessions. The therapist added that even after therapy was over, Richard could still do telephone check-ins or even schedule a booster session. These possibilities seemed to greatly relieve Richard, which helped initiate a further discussion about his abandonment anxiety. Of course, when discussing this issue the therapist stuck with the cognitive-behavioral model and recommended that Richard begin some imaginal exposure to losing Linda in their next session.

Sessions 10–15. Richard was virtually panic-free between sessions 9 and 10.

Richard: It's been a great week. I'm feeling more like the old me all the time.

Therapist: What do you think is helping the most?

Richard: I think it's mostly two things. The breathing and the no caffeine rule. Oh yeah, those new thoughts work pretty well too. If I can just get myself to check my automatic thoughts at the door, then I've got a much better chance of staying calm.

The therapist wanted Richard to reflect on what's working for him and continued some Socratic questioning with that end in mind. However, eventually he returned to the agenda item of imaginal exposure of losing Linda.

Therapist: Remember last week we talked about how your automatic thoughts about losing Linda and about feeling defective might be related to the panic you had after we talked about ending therapy?

Richard: Yeah. That was interesting.

Therapist: Okay. Well, today I think we should take the bull by the horns and face the possibility of your losing Linda. We can do this in your imagination, with mental imagery.

Richard: I don't even like to think about that.

Therapist: Remember when we talked about avoidance when we first started counseling together? What do you think avoiding the thought of losing Linda does for you?

Richard: Yeah, yeah, I know. You can't conquer your fears without facing them. How many times have you told me that?

Therapist: Hmm. Obviously, enough that you remember, which demonstrates the fact that you're smart and tough and willing to face things that are very hard.

Here the therapist is loosening up a bit and using strength-based factual statements to help Richard increase his motivation to face thoughts that he'd prefer not to face.

Therapist: Okay, before we do this imagination activity, let's talk about the automatic thoughts that pop into your head along with thoughts that Linda might leave. What else do you think at the same time?

Richard: Well, typically it's something about me being too much of a burden and so she's tired of me and wants to get away.

Therapist: How long have you had these thoughts?

Richard: Well, we've been married thirty years.

Therapist: So, for thirty years you've been thinking she'll get tired of you, but she still hasn't.

Richard: But then I think if she spends time away from me, then she'll realize what a big hassle I am to be married to.

Therapist: So if you're with her too much, she'll get tired of you, but if you're away from her, she'll probably realize that being around you is a pain. Have I got that right?

Richard: Sounds pretty crazy, huh?

Therapist: Oh, it's not crazy, it's just not helpful. It's sort of like your panic false alarms. It's natural to feel insecure, everybody does sometimes, but when you get insecure, you compound it by thinking about how worthless you are to be around. What else could you think instead?

Richard: I could remind myself that I'm really a pretty good-looking chap!

Therapist: Great. Very nice, and what else makes you a good relationship partner?

Richard: I've got a steady job. I'm pretty thoughtful—I've never forgotten our anniversary or her birthday.

Therapist: Excellent.

During sessions 11–13, Richard began spending short periods of time away from Linda to practice dealing with abandonment anxiety. He continued practicing his breathing, and he worked hard on cognitive restructuring by inserting new and better explanations for situations that previously caused him excessive anxiety and panic. In the end, Richard was seen for a total of 15 sessions and one additional follow-up at 6 months after treatment.

Richard had only one more panic attack over the course of treatment. This occurred between sessions 12 and 13, immediately after he "downed a double latte" to "test" to see if he would be able to drink caffeine again. On the basis of this experiment, he concluded he was better off without caffeine.

THERAPY OUTCOMES RESEARCH

As is the case with behavior therapy, the efficacy of cognitive and cognitive-behavior therapies is well documented. Seven of the 16 empirically validated therapies have strong or primary cognitive treatment components (Chambless et al., 1998). If you recall from Chapter 7, eight of these validated therapies are behavioral, and several of these are primarily exposure-based treatments with cognitive components (Foa, Rothbaum, & Furr, 2003), meaning that, overall, 15 of the 16 well-established therapies are essentially cognitive-behavioral (93.7%). Given this overwhelming scientific nod to cognitive and behavioral treatments, it's no wonder that the APA's Division 12 (Clinical Psychology) Task Force faced strong criticism from adherents to other theoretical perspectives (Bohart, O'Hara, & Leitner, 1998; Chambless, 2002; Garfield, 1998).

Validated therapies that have a particularly strong cognitive emphasis include the following:

- Cognitive-behavior therapy for Panic Disorder with and without Agoraphobia
- Cognitive-behavior therapy for Generalized Anxiety Disorder
- Stress inoculation training for coping with stressors
- Cognitive therapy for depression
- Cognitive-behavior therapy for Bulimia Nervosa
- Multicomponent cognitive-behavior therapy for pain associated with rheumatic disease
- Multicomponent cognitive-behavior therapy with relapse prevention for smoking cessation

When it comes to evaluating the efficacy of cognitive therapy, Ellis brings an additional interesting issue to the forefront. Specifically, he has claimed throughout his career that the therapeutic relationship is often minimally important to therapeutic success. Of course, this flies in the face of common factors research, as well as the empirically supported therapy relationship project (Norcross, 2002). Nevertheless, Ellis takes on this issue with his usual direct style:

> [S]everal recent studies have shown that during the therapy sessions . . . clients tend to feel better when their therapists are warm and accepting.
>
> Of course! What client would not feel better when the therapist kisses his/her ass in the office? Damned few! Many such clients, however, actually become more needy of approval and hence become unhealthier, if the therapeutic alliance becomes too damned close. (Ellis, 1996, p. 151)

Questions for Reflection

What are your thoughts on Ellis's criticism of therapy relationships that are "too damned close"? Do you think some therapy relationships are too close? Are some too distant? Do you think there is an ideal degree of closeness that might be associated with optimal outcomes? Might that closeness vary with different clients and different forms of therapy?

Despite Ellis's criticisms, most research shows that cognitive and behavioral therapies are more effective when a positive therapeutic relationship is part of the treatment package; when cognitive-behavioral therapy is implemented without a therapist (via bibliotherapy), its effectiveness is very limited or nonexistent (Meichenbaum & Turk, 1987).

MULTICULTURAL PERSPECTIVES

As discussed in Chapter 7, individuals from different cultural groups may prefer different therapy approaches. In this chapter, we explore a related question: Are some therapy approaches differentially effective, depending upon the client's cultural or ethnic background?

Overall, there's very little empirical data on which we can base our answer to this question. Chambless and associates articulated this problem in their review and update of empirically validated treatments:

> Examining the citations for empirically validated treatments identified in the 1995 task force report, we find not a single study included tests of the efficacy of the treatment for ethnic minority populations. Most investigators did not specify ethnicity of subjects or used only white subjects. Out of about 41 studies cited, only 6–7 made any reference to race or ethnicity of subjects. . . . Not one used ethnicity as a variable of interest. (Chambless et al., 1998, p. 5)

Lacking relevant controlled studies on therapy effectiveness, we turn to anecdotal, analogue, and quasi-experimental data to guide our exploration of the differential effectiveness of various therapy approaches with diverse cultural groups.

As reviewed by Meichenbaum in an interview with Michael Hoyt (Hoyt, 2000), there are some reports of recommendations for different cognitive-behavioral procedures for trauma victims of different cultures. For example, Agger and Jensen (1990) reported that torture victims from several South American countries experienced great benefit from writing about and reliving their traumas. In contrast, therapists who work with torture victims from Southeast Asia report just the opposite—that their clients do not benefit from trauma memory work and instead seem to gain the most from concrete, here-and-now interventions designed to facilitate their coping and functioning at home and at work (Kinzie, 1994; Mollica, 1988).

These reports suggest that client ethnicity may play a strong role in determining the appropriate treatment approach for diverse clients. They also indicate that it's unlikely that any specific technique for a specific problem will be universally effective for different cultural groups. A recent study demonstrated that an empirically validated treatment—exposure for Agoraphobia—was less effective for African American clients (Chambless & Williams, 1995). This should cause further questions about the generalizability of effective treatments from Caucasian clients to nonCaucasian clients.

Questions for Reflection

How will you determine what particular approach to use with clients from different cultural backgrounds? What can you do besides consulting the empirical literature?

A recent study provides another important perspective on how practitioners should choose specific treatments for clients of color. In this study, 136 Asian American college students were asked to rate the credibility of cognitive therapy versus time-limited dynamic therapy for depression (Wong, Kim, Zane, Kim, & Huang, 2003). Results from this study indicated that the students' cultural identity and attitude toward self moderated the credibility ratings they gave to the two therapy approaches. These findings suggest that each individual client of color may, depending upon personal internal factors, differentially view the acceptability or credibility of various treatments.

CONCLUDING COMMENTS

There's little doubt about the efficacy of cognitive therapy. Both philosophically and empirically it has demonstrated itself to be a logical and effective form of treatment. Cognitive theory and therapy also provide us with an excellent general metaphor representing the many paradoxes of counseling and psychotherapy theory.

As a theory and technique the cognitive approach is both new and old. It is empirical and philosophical. Its roots come from the behavioral, psychoanalytic, and constructivist philosophical traditions. In addition, the study of cognitive approaches raises crucial questions about the nature of the relationship between therapist and client. Should the therapist be a judgmental expert or an empirically oriented collaborator? How much faith should we place in the client's mentalistic processes? Do we rely on objective scientific facts or subjective client experiences?

In a relatively short time period, cognitive approaches have performed exceptionally well under the experimental microscope, with precisely defined symptoms and carefully measured outcomes. Within this set of definitions, cognitive therapy can claim significant scientific support. So have we arrived? Do cognitive-behavioral techniques

---

PRACTITIONER COMMENTARY 8.1

Why Do I Practice Cognitive Therapy?

The following commentary was written by Judith S. Beck, Ph.D., director of the Beck Institute for Cognitive Therapy and Research at the University of Pennsylvania.

Why do I practice cognitive therapy? Aside from the familial connection (my father, Aaron T. Beck, M.D., is the "father" of cognitive therapy), it is the most widely researched form of psychotherapy; it has been shown in over 350 research studies to be effective. If I had an ear infection, I would first seek the treatment that has been demonstrated most efficacious. Why should it be different for psychiatric disorders or psychological problems?

Other than research efficacy, it is the one form of psychotherapy that makes sense to me. Take a typical depressed patient. Nancy, a 32-year-old married sales clerk with a young child, has been clinically depressed for almost a year. She has quit her job, spends much of the day in bed, has given over most of her child-rearing responsibilities to her mother and husband, goes out only infrequently, and has withdrawn from family and friends. She is very sad, hopeless, weighted down, self-critical; she gets little if any pleasure from activities or interactions with others and little sense of achievement from anything she does.

It just makes sense to me to work directly on the problems Nancy has today, teaching her cognitive and behavioral skills to get her life in order and decrease her depression. Behaviorally, I help Nancy plan a schedule: getting out of bed at a reasonable time each morning, getting bathed and dressed immediately, and preparing breakfast for herself and her daughter. We include calling friends, doing small household tasks, taking walks, and doing one errand. Cognitively I help her identify and respond to her negative thinking. Some of her dysfunctional thoughts are related to the behavioral tasks I have suggested: "I'll be too tired to get out of bed. I won't know what to make for breakfast. [My friend] Jean won't want to hear from me. It won't help to take a walk." Other dysfunctional thoughts are about herself ("I'm worthless"), her world ("Life is too hard"), and the future ("I'll never get better").

We tackle Nancy's problems one by one. In the context of discussing and solving problems, I teach her the skills she needs. Cognitive skills include identifying her depressed thoughts, evaluating her thinking, and developing more realistic, adaptive views. I also help her respond to her deeper-level ideas, her beliefs or basic understandings that shape her perception of her experience, ideas that, left unmodified, might contribute to a relapse sometime in the future.

While doing cognitive therapy, I need to use all my basic counseling skills to establish and maintain a strong therapeutic alliance. I am highly collaborative with the patient, working with her as a "team" to help her get better; I provide rationales for the strategies I use; I use active listening and empathy, and I provide support. And I ask for feedback at every session to make sure that I have understood the patient correctly and that the process of therapy is amenable to her. But perhaps most importantly, I am quite active in the session—providing direction, offering suggestions, teaching her skills. Doing all of these things helps the patient recover most quickly.

Why do I specialize in cognitive therapy? Because it is humane, it is effective, and it is the quickest way to alleviate suffering.

provide the ultimate answer to human suffering? Is cognitive therapy the way forward for human growth and actualization? Wherever there is certainty, there is always room for doubt, and Mahoney provides us with some. He states:

> I do not believe that the simple cueing, recitation, or reinforcement of positive self-statements or the rationalistic "reconstruction" of explicit beliefs are optimal or sufficient approaches for facilitating significant and enduring personal development. (Mahoney, 1985, p. 14)

Even further, in his magnum opus, *Human Change Processes* (Mahoney, 1991), he quotes Hayek (1979), suggesting there may even be a superstitious quality to scientific validation:

> An age of superstitions is a time when people imagine that they know more than they do. In this sense the twentieth century was certainly an outstanding age of superstition, and the cause of this is an overestimation of what science has achieved—not in the field of comparatively simple phenomena, where it has, of course, been extraordinarily successful, but in the field of complex phenomena, where the application of the techniques which prove so helpful with essentially simple phenomena has proved to be very misleading. (Hayek, 1979, p. 176)

Hayek's comments suggest that it might be possible to ask larger, more complex questions than "does this technique make this symptom go away?" Cognitive and cognitive-behavioral approaches are very effective and, in many ways, very satisfying. Failing to at least think about using cognitive and behavioral techniques in certain situations and with certain diagnoses might almost be considered malpractice, due to their proven efficacy. But the question always remains: Shall we continue our search for even more optimal approaches for facilitating enduring personal development?

STUDENT REVIEW ASSIGNMENTS

The following exercises will allow you to further explore your understanding of cognitive therapy.

Critical Corner

The following comments about cognitive therapy represent both real and exaggerated criticisms. They're offered to stimulate your thoughts about cognitive therapy. Please read the comments and then write your thoughts and reactions to the criticisms.

1. Some critics, especially humanistic and existential therapists, contend that cognitive therapy is too intellectual. They emphasize that most clients actually need to more deeply feel, experience, and understand their emotions, rather than using cognitive tactics to talk themselves out of important emotional states. What are your thoughts on this criticism? Do clients need to be more intellectual or more emotional?

Response:

2. The foundation of all cognitive therapies is the same: As an expert, the therapist first demonstrates to the client that the latter is thinking in a way that is either irrational or maladaptive, and then the therapist teaches the client new and better ways to think. When you consider this fact, isn't it true that all cognitive therapies are a bit presumptuous? Then, when you consider this presumptuous assumption even further, doesn't it make you want to become a more sensitive cognitive therapist—perhaps a constructivist who honors clients' experiences and helps them rewrite their personal narratives in a more positive and strength-based manner? It's no wonder that Mahoney and Meichenbaum have moved on.

Response:

3. The fact is that when therapists need therapy, most of them—even cognitive and behavioral therapists—go to psychodynamic or experientially oriented therapists. Why would that be? One possibility is that engaging in rigid cognitive and behavioral approaches is both demanding and tiresome. How many clients really want to keep detailed cognitive monitoring logs and tediously dispute their maladaptive cognitive distortions? Don't you think it's true that insight-oriented therapies are intrinsically more exciting than cognitive and behavioral approaches? Even worse, isn't it true that insight-oriented therapy is, in contrast to cognitive therapy, much more likely to produce the motivation for new learning?

Response:

4. Despite the fact that cognitive therapists pride themselves on their empirical foundation, relatively little data are available on the application of cognitive therapy with various cultural groups. Given the complete absence of empirical data on cognitive methods with diverse clients, in order to stay consistent with their orientation, cognitive therapists should either label their treatment approaches as "experimental" with non-White clients or refrain from using their treatment methods with non-White clients. What are your thoughts on this issue? Because of their criticism of humanistic-existential therapists, aren't cognitive therapists being hypocritical when they apply their techniques on non-White clients?

Response:

Reviewing Key Terms

- Rational-semantic cognitive therapy
- Collaborative-empirical cognitive therapy
- Philosophical-constructivist therapy
- Stimulus-organism response (S-O-R) theory
- The REBT ABCs

- Collaborative empiricism
- Automatic thoughts
- Self-schemas or core beliefs
- Socratic questioning
- Cognitive distortions
- Arbitrary inference
- Selective abstraction
- Personalization

- Dichotomous/ polarized thinking
- Stress inoculation training
- Self-instructional training
- Collaborative interviewing
- Problem list

- Thought Record or cognitive self-monitoring
- Generating alternative interpretations

- Misattribution of hostility
- Vigorous and forceful disputation
- Thinking in shades of grey

- Exploring the consequences of giving up the should rule
- Empirically validated treatments

Review Questions

1. What are the main differences between Ellis's REBT and Beck's cognitive therapy?
2. What are the five bedrock assumptions of Ellis's REBT?
3. Meichenbaum's approach is based on verbal mediational processes. In practical terms, what does he mean by verbal mediational processes?
4. List and describe four of Beck's cognitive distortions.
5. Provide examples of what sorts of self-talk Meichenbaum might teach anxious or angry clients when using stress inoculation training approaches.
6. List and describe the REBT ABCs (including D, E, and F).
7. Describe what Beck means by a self-schema.
8. What are the three steps of stress inoculation training?
9. What information would you put into a Thought Record?
10. What is cognitive storytelling, and what is the purpose of using it with young clients?

RECOMMENDED READINGS AND RESOURCES

The following resources offer additional information on cognitive therapy.

Lead Journals

- *Behavioural and Cognitive Psychotherapy*
- *Cognitive and Behavioral Practice*
- *Cognitive Therapy and Research*
- *Journal of Cognitive Psychotherapy*
- *Journal of Rational-Emotive and Cognitive-Behavior Therapy*

Books and Articles

Beck, A. T. (1976). *Cognitive therapy and the emotional disorders.* New York: New American Library.

Beck, A. T., Emery, G., & Greenberg, R. L. (1985). *Anxiety disorders and phobias: A cognitive perspective.* New York: Basic Books.

Beck, A. T., Rush, A., Shaw, B., & Emery, G. (1979). *Cognitive therapy of depression.* New York: Guilford Press.

Beck, J. S. (1995). *Cognitive therapy: Basics and beyond.* New York: Guilford Press.

Burns, D. (1989). *The feeling good handbook.* New York: Morrow.

Clark, D. A., Beck, A. T., & Alford, B. A. (1999). *Scientific foundation of cognitive theory and therapy of depression.* New York: Wiley.

Dryden, W. (1989). Albert Ellis: An efficient and passionate life. *Journal of Counseling and Development, 67,* 539–546.

Ellis, A. (1999). *How to make yourself happy and remarkably less disturbable.* San Luis Obispo, CA: Impact Publishers.

Ellis, A., & Harper, R. (1997). *A guide to rational living.* North Hollywood, CA: Wilshire.

Greenberger, D., & Padesky, C. A. (1995). *Mind over mood: Change how you feel by changing the way you think.* New York: Guilford Press.

Kendall, P. C. (Ed.). (2000). *Child and adolescent therapy: Cognitive-behavioral procedures* (2nd ed.). New York: Guilford Press.

Mahoney, M. (1991). *Human change processes.* New York: Basic Books.

Meichenbaum, D. (1977). *Cognitive behavior modification: An integrative approach.* New York: Plenum.

Meichenbaum, D. (1985). *Stress inoculation training.* New York: Pergamon Press.

Novaco, R. W. (1979). The cognitive regulation of anger. In P. C. Kendall & S. D. Hollon (Eds.), *Cognitive behavioral interventions: Theory, research, and procedures* (pp. 241–285). New York: Academic Press.

Persons, J. B. (1989). *Cognitive therapy in practice: A case formulation approach.* New York: Norton.

Vygotsky, L. (1962). *Thought and language.* New York: Wiley.

Weishaar, M. E. (1993). *Aaron T. Beck.* London: Sage.

Videotapes

Clark, D. M. (1998). *Cognitive therapy for panic disorder* [Videotape]. Washington, DC: American Psychological Association.

Davidson, J., Persons, J. B., & Tompkins, M. A. (2000). *Structure of the therapy session* [Videotape]. Washington, DC: American Psychological Association.

Davidson, J., Persons, J. B., & Tompkins, M. A. (2000). *Using the Thought Record* [Videotape]. Washington, DC: American Psychological Association.

Layden, M. A. (1998). *Cognitive therapy for borderline personality disorder* [Videotape]. Washington, DC: American Psychological Association.

Marlatt, G. A. (1998). *Cognitive-behavioral relapse prevention for addictions* [Videotape]. Washington, DC: American Psychological Association.

Persons, J. B. (1994). *Cognitive-behavior therapy* [Videotape]. Washington, DC: American Psychological Association.

Persons, J. B., Tompkins, M. A., & Davidson, J. (2000). *Individualized case formulation and treatment planning* [Videotape]. Washington, DC: American Psychological Association.

Tompkins, M. A., Persons, J. B., & Davidson, J. (2000). *Schema change methods* [Videotape]. Washington, DC: American Psychological Association.

Organizations and Web Sites

Albert Ellis Institute (web site: www.irebt.org)

The Beck Institute for Cognitive Therapy and Research; Judith S. Beck, director (web site: www.geocities.com/spiroll2/cbtexplained.html)

American Institute for Cognitive Therapy (web site: www.CognitiveTherapyNYC.com)

International Association for Cognitive Therapy (web site: http://iacp.asu.edu)

The Center for Cognitive Therapy (web site: www.padesky.com)

Chapter 9

CHOICE THEORY AND THE NEW REALITY THERAPY

> *The seeds of almost all unhappiness are planted early in our lives when we begin to encounter people who have discovered not only what is right for them—but also, unfortunately, what is right for us.*
>
> —William Glasser, *Choice Theory* (1998, p. 4)

Reality therapy officially came into being in the mid-1960s, around the time *Reality Therapy: A New Approach to Psychiatry* (Glasser, 1965) was published. As is true of a number of the theories covered in this book, reality therapy was initially the product of a single man, in this case William Glasser. Glasser speaks of the inspiration he got from mentors and colleagues, and the guidance his students and patients offered. He also consistently expresses gratitude for the support he receives from his wife, Carleen, a constant companion in Glasser's life and work. Although Glasser remains a much revered figure in the desemination and application of reality therapy, many other certified reality therapists now provide training in reality therapy (Wubbolding, 2003).

BIOGRAPHICAL INFORMATION: WILLIAM GLASSER

William Glasser was born May 11, 1925, in Cleveland, Ohio. Parrot (1997) described Glasser's childhood as relatively "uneventful and happy" (p. 356). Perhaps because he does not consider exploration of the past to be a valuable part of therapy, little has been written about Glasser's childhood. However, in one of his more recent books, Glasser (1998) described his parents in some detail:

> If the Olympics had an event in controlling, my mother could have gone for the gold medal. My father was totally choice theory. Never in the more than sixty years that I knew him did I ever see him try to control another person except when he was being goaded by my mother. And even then, his heart was not in it. (p. 90)

Despite his parents' "incompatibility," Glasser indicated that they "were always loving" toward him (1998, p. 89).

As a young adult, Glasser chose to become a chemical engineer, but he then changed his focus and began a Ph.D. program in clinical psychology. He obtained his master's degree in clinical psychology in 1948, but his advisors apparently rejected his dissertation. Subsequently, he was admitted to medical school at Western Reserve University and obtained his M.D. at the very young age of 28 (in case you're keeping track, Glasser finished three challenging degrees—a B.S. in chemical engineering, an M.A. in clinical psychology, and an M.D.—by age 28). By 1957, Glasser had completed his psychiatric residency at the Veterans Administration and UCLA. He became board certified in psychiatry in 1961.

During his psychiatric residency at UCLA, Glasser began questioning "the basic tenets of conventional psychiatry" (Glasser, 1965, p. xxv). In the acknowledgments of *Reality Therapy* (1965), he writes about how he told his mentor, psychiatrist G. L. Harrington, M.D., of his doubts about traditional psychiatry: "When I hesitatingly expressed my own concern, he reached across the desk, shook my hand and said join the club'" (p. xxv). Glasser goes on to convey a deep gratitude to Harrington, whom he later referred to as "my mentor . . . [and] the most skillful psychiatrist I've ever known" (1998, p. 5). Even further, he wrote, "Nothing that I can say briefly or in many pages could express how grateful I am for the time he generously spent to make this [reality therapy] possible" (p. xxv).

HISTORICAL CONTEXT

It's always difficult to determine, in retrospect, the inspiration and roots of a particular individual's thinking. There are clearly historical and theoretical predecessors to Glasser, but it's unclear when and how earlier thinkers influenced him.

At first glance, because reality therapy essentially involves teaching clients how to think, plan, and behave more effectively, you might be tempted to think of it as a particular form of cognitive-behavioral counseling or psychotherapy. In fact, some modern textbooks classify reality therapy in such a way: "Glasser's reality therapy can be considered a cognitive-behavioral therapy, but one that focuses very much on realism and how to treat difficult clients" (Ivey, D'Andrea, Ivey, & Simek-Morgan, 2002, p. 218). However, basing our conclusions on Glasser's recent work and conversations with Glasser himself, we believe that classifying reality therapy as a cognitive or behavioral therapy is inaccurate (Wubbolding, 2000). This is partly because, as you will read below, Glasser is adamantly opposed to behavior modification approaches to human change.

In many ways, Glasser's conceptual beliefs about how individuals and groups change reflect humanistic-existential theory. Gerald Corey stated, in his review of one of Glasser's books, "I particularly like the existential emphasis on the roles of choice and responsibility" (Glasser, 2000, p. i). Clearly, Glasser's emphasis on the personal choice of an individual—the individual's inherent freedom—has an existential feel. His orientation toward personal responsibility is in the tradition of great existentialists such as Viktor Frankl and Irvin Yalom (Frankl, 1967; Yalom, 1980; see Chapter 5). Additionally, Glasser places immense value on the authentic encounter between therapist and client. He views the therapy relationship as a key factor in treatment success. For Glasser, the relationship between therapist and client is characterized primarily by kindness, connection, and a genuine desire to help the client, and secondarily by a teaching or educational process. The following statement illustrates his emphasis on authenticity and connection:

> [T]herapy is not perfect. Psychiatrists make mistakes like everyone else. I handled that mistake by admitting it and learning something from it. When I admit a mistake, it makes me more human and increases the connection. If I don't admit it, I risk harming our connection or looking stupid. (Glasser, 2000, p. 91)

Besides the clear link between existential-humanistic philosophy and reality therapy, other writers have speculated on the roots of Glasser's thinking. Croll (1992) described how reality therapy's emphasis on personal responsibility can be traced to Ralph Waldo Emerson's concept of self-reliance. In contrast, both Rozsnafsky (1974) and Whitehouse (1984) link Glasser's theory to Alfred Adler's individual psychology. Additionally, Wubbolding—whose name, after Glasser's is most strongly linked to reality therapy—considers reality therapy to have similarities with many different theoretical approaches, but he emphasizes that reality therapy is a unique approach (2000).

As you can see, choice theory and reality therapy, despite an emphasis on behavior and thinking processes, are philosophically different from traditional behavioral or cognitive therapy approaches.

Questions for Reflection

Have you encountered choice theory and reality therapy previously? If so, what has been your impression of where they fit as theoretical perspectives? As you read this chapter be sure to consider Glasser's ideas within the context of previous theoretical contributions. Speculate on the historical factors and bodies of knowledge that may have influenced Glasser.

THEORETICAL PRINCIPLES

Choice theory holds that humans are internally motivated. If you compare this basic assumption of choice theory to the primary theoretical assumption of behaviorism, you can begin to appreciate the fundamental contradiction between choice theory and behaviorism. As you probably recall, B. F. Skinner believed that behavior is a function of its consequences (see Chapter 7). Skinner's theoretical position implies that humans have little internal choice over their behavior, because behavior is controlled by environmental factors. In contrast, according to choice theory, environmental factors only provide humans with information; after obtaining and processing external information, we then choose exactly how we want to behave.

Glasser (1998) claims that behaviorism—which he unaffectionately refers to as *external control psychology*—currently dominates human thinking and reasoning. He states:

> The simple operational premise of the external control psychology the world uses is: Punish the people who are doing wrong, so they will do what we say is right; then reward them, so they keep doing what we want them to do. This premise dominates the thinking of most people on Earth. (pp. 5–6)

Further, Glasser considers the domination of our thinking by external control psychology to be an unfortunate reality with many negative consequences. He blames much of our current social and psychological distress on external control psychology. In his words,

> [T]his psychology is a terrible plague that invades every part of our lives. It destroys our happiness, our health, our marriages, our families, our ability to get an education, and our

willingness to do high-quality work. It is the cause of most of the violence, crime, drug abuse, and unloving sex that are pervasive in our society. (1998, p. 7)

Not surprisingly, Glasser would like the world to discard external control psychology and replace it with his approach to human psychology: choice theory. Glasser views choice theory as the road to human happiness. In contrast, Wubbolding notes that it is not choice theory, per se, that leads to human happiness, but learning and utilization of an internal control psychology system (R. E. Wubbolding, personal communication, May 6, 2003). The reason internal control psychology can make us happy is this: If we understand the principles of internal control, we will stop trying to control the behavior of others and recognize that we can only control our own behavior. This shift in thinking will help people begin meeting their basic human needs in a more direct, healthy, and adaptive manner.

From the behavioral perspective, if you're reading this book, you're doing so to avoid potential punishments, to gain potential reinforcement, or both. You might be reading to avoid failing an upcoming test or to gain rewards associated with knowledge acquisition—perhaps your professor or a fellow student will smile at you or compliment you if you make an informed comment in class. In contrast, from the choice theory perspective, you're reading this book only because you're choosing to read this book. You might, at any time, regardless of potential environmental and external consequences, decide to put this book down and stop reading. For the choice theorist, decisions are made not on the basis of external contingencies, but on the basis of internal factors.

If choice theory posits that humans make decisions based on internal factors, the next reasonable question is one that philosophers and psychologists have struggled with for centuries. What internal forces or factors guide human decision making? Or, as Glasser (1998) has put it, what is the "underlying motivation for all our behavior" (p. 25)?

The Five Basic Human Needs

According to choice theory, all of us are motivated to satisfy one or more of five basic, genetically encoded, human needs. These needs are survival, love and belonging, power (or achievement), freedom (or independence), and fun (or enjoyment).

Glasser likes to say that choice theory may be simple, but it's not simplistic. Choice theory's straightforward list of human needs can be mistaken as being overly simplistic, but such is not the case. As we explore the needs in greater detail, you'll discover that humans are not directly acted upon by each independent need. Instead, sometimes survival needs are linked with needs for love or power, and each individual experiences a unique blend of human need states. It's as if the human needs derived from choice theory are five separate primary colors on an artist's palette. Consider the unlimited number of colors you could generate by mixing these five primary colors. If you can imagine the skilled artist noticing the unique hue or texture in an original painting, then you can probably also imagine the skilled reality therapist noticing the unique blend of human needs being articulated by the behavior, thoughts, feelings, and physical condition of an individual undergoing therapy.

In contrast to the other four needs, the first human need, survival, is a physical need. Glasser (1998) writes extensively about the five basic human needs in *Choice Theory*. In the following sections, we summarize each.

Survival

For most of us, in our daily lives, the need to survive and the concept of survival is rather distant. Directly confronting life-threatening conditions on a regular basis is rare; even during times of war and terror, typically only a minority of the world's citizens directly experience life-threatening conditions.

There's a big difference between survival as an intellectual concept and survival as a personal experience. Glasser (1998) provides an example of conceptual survival, the kind of survival we all can talk about from an intellectual distance:

> All living creatures are genetically programmed to struggle to survive. The Spanish word *ganas* describes the strong desire to engage in this struggle better than any word I know. It means the desire to work hard, carry on, do whatever it takes to ensure survival, and go beyond survival to security. . . . If you are looking for a mate you can count on to help build a family and a life with you, find one with *ganas* and treat him or her well. Try not to criticize this motivated mate; you don't want the *ganas* turned against you. (p. 31)

Conceptual survival is intellectually intriguing. Often, abstract theoretical discussions about survival take people to the related topic of species survival and evolutionary biology. Glasser addresses this issue in choice theory, noting that sexual pleasure, a genetically wired-in human response, is a very effective means of insuring species survival. For Glasser, individual survival needs are expressed through total behavior (including our thoughts, behaviors, feelings, and physiology).

Love and Belonging

Glasser believes the need to love and belong is the primary human need, because we need other people in our lives to meet most of the rest of our needs most of the time.

In support of Glasser's emphasis on the primacy of the human need to love and belong, you can easily notice that the influence of love and belonging is everywhere. If you doubt this statement, just turn on the television or the radio, or look at a few popular magazine covers. There are more songs, jokes, books, and other materials about love, sex, and friendship than any other topic, including survival. William Shakespeare's play, *Romeo and Juliet,* articulates the power of love. When faced with a choice between love and survival, Romeo and Juliet poignantly express their preference. They choose to give up survival rather than giving up love.

From the perspective of choice theory, suicide is usually a choice that arises out of a conflict between survival and another basic need. Recall Patrick Henry, who spoke eloquently of his choice between survival and freedom when he said, "Give me liberty, or give me death." Similarly, young children, in their uniquely direct manner, articulate their preference for power and fun over survival when they threaten to hold their breath unless they get what they want.

Glasser has made many interesting statements about the need for love and belonging that can help individuals address their needs in this very important area. One bit of advice he provides for anyone who's looking for romantic love is this: "Especially ask yourself, 'If I were not hormonally attracted to this person, would he or she be someone I would enjoy as a friend?' If the answer is no, there is little chance for that love to succeed" (1998, p. 36).

The need for love and belonging in humans runs strong and deep. It includes sexual love, friendship love, and romantic love. Be sure to watch for it in yourself and your clients. Unfortunately, needs for love and belonging are often confounded by our human need for power. In this regard, Glasser (1998) states:

> To keep any love, sexual or not, going, we need to go back to . . . friendship. . . . Unlike lovers or even many family members, good friends can keep their friendship going for a lifetime because they do not indulge in the fantasies of ownership. (pp. 35–36)

In other words, according to choice theory, love relationships are often derailed by the human need for power.

Questions for Reflection

Think about your history of love relationships. Think also of the love relationships you've seen in close friends and family. Based on these observations, do you think Glasser's claim that power needs interfere with love relationships is true? Can you think of examples when one or both persons' power needs damaged or destroyed a previously loving relationship?

Power

Wubbolding has emphasized that power needs are often viewed in a negative manner. He prefers the use of more positive descriptors of this basic human need, such as *achievement, inner control,* or *accomplishment* (Wubbolding, 2000).

Most humans enjoy having at least a little power. This is true partly because being completely powerless is often aversive and partly because having power and influence is intrinsically gratifying. Imagine that you're very hungry, so you walk into a restaurant, but no one greets you or offers to serve you. Out of desperation, you call out for help, but still there's no response. Finally, in even greater desperation, you pull cash out of your purse or wallet and wave it around, but still no one looks at you or offers to help you. Although this example may seem silly, if you think about the conditions faced by African Americans in the southern United States in the early 1960s, you get a small taste of what it may have been like to experience the powerlessness associated with racial discrimination.

In contrast to the preceding example, some individuals in the world, due to wealth or status, wield immense power. For example, the queen of England or the crown prince of Saudi Arabia will probably never experience the sort of powerlessness and helplessness frequently experienced by individuals living in poverty or those who happened to be born female or of a nondominant or persecuted race within certain geographic regions. From the perspective of choice theory, either extreme, excessive striving for power or experiencing oneself as powerless may result in unhappiness and a need for counseling. In contrast to some reality therapy practitioners (R. E. Wubbolding, personal communication, May 6, 2003), Glasser (1998) considers an excess need for power to be a deeply destructive force within our Western culture:

> Driven by power, we have created a pecking order in almost everything we do; social position, neighborhoods, dwellings, clothing, grades, winning, wealth, beauty, race, strength, physique, the size of our breasts or biceps, cars, food, furniture, television ratings, and almost anything else you can think of has been turned into a power struggle. (p. 38)

Freud might have considered our culture's problems with power as stemming from a fixation in the phallic stage of psychosexual development. Interestingly, like Freud, Glasser discusses early childhood as a time when our human needs for power, and the gratification associated with meeting those needs, become recognized. He states:

> As infants, once we get a taste of power through seeing our parents or others jump to attention to give us what we want, our need for more power starts to take over. By the time we are teenagers, power pushes us far beyond what we would do if our only motivation was to survive and get loving attention. (p. 38)

Often, when we teach or counsel parents of young children, the parents bitterly complain about having a "manipulative" child. Based on choice theory, it's perfectly natural for all children to try to manipulate, or gain power over, parents and their family situation. However, as Glasser (2002) points out in his recent book, *Unhappy Teens,* children usually get too focused on power and freedom only when their needs for love and belonging are unmet (this is, of course, a basic concept in individual psychology; see Chapter 3). Unfortunately, many parents have difficulty setting very basic limits with their young children and therefore base their relationship on the exchange of goods and services from the external control perspective. Consequently, the children's primary means of having needs fulfilled gets channeled into power and freedom. Glasser describes part of this process in the case of Jackie, a teenager featured in *Unhappy Teens:*

> If she's unable to satisfy her need for love and belonging, she turns to the two needs, power and freedom, that may seem easier to satisfy but which will further disconnect her if she succeeds in satisfying them. She uses all that violent language for gaining both power and freedom. If she can't find a way to get connected again, she'll stay the same or get worse. (2002, p. 85)

It's tempting to cast a negative light on the human need for power. After all, it's been said that "power corrupts, and absolute power corrupts absolutely." But from the choice theory perspective, power is just another human need: "By itself, power is neither good nor bad. It is how it is defined, acquired, and used that makes the difference" (Glasser, 1998, p. 38). As with all other human needs, individuals can become preoccupied with needs for power, and they can go about obtaining their power needs in cruel, insensitive, or overly selfish ways.

People get preoccupied with power, freedom, or fun for two main reasons. First, their preoccupation is caused by their inability to be involved in a satisfying relationship. The need for love and belonging is primary, so when it is unfulfilled, efforts to fulfill the other needs may get out of control. Second, some people have incorrectly turned to external control theory as a means for getting their love and belonging needs met. This causes them to pursue needs for power or fun because, somewhere inside, they really think that having more property, more power, more toys, and more fun will get them what they really want: a loving and fulfilling relationship.

People who use power as a substitute for intimacy often seem addicted to power. They want to get ahead, to dominate the competition, to greedily acquire money and property, to win at all costs, or to control the lives and livelihoods of others. Without the concept of power needs, it's hard to explain why very wealthy people continue to accumulate material possessions. Clearly, many wealthy people have already accumulated a number of possessions that extends far beyond addressing their basic needs for survival, love, freedom, and fun. Why do some people keep purchasing more and more material objects in what appears to be a desperate effort to meet their needs for power, freedom, or fun? Who really needs 20 cars, 10 boats, a 40,000-square-foot house, and a large staff of servants and maids?

Consistent with the writings of Carl Rogers (*On Personal Power,* 1977) and Alfred Adler's concept of social interest, Glasser claims that power can be used for positive or prosocial purposes. He even admits to his own power needs: "[M]any people gain power working for the common good. . . . I have written this book to try to help people, and if I succeed, I will feel very good and very powerful" (1998, p. 38). In addition, Wubbolding emphasizes that having an internal sense of achievement or accomplishment is a strong, positive, and constructive basic need that individuals experience (2000). He also pointed out, in his review of this chapter, that the preceding discussion about power needs was overly negative because the word *power* brings with it so much definitional baggage.

Questions for Reflection

What do you think of Wubbolding's point about using *achievement* as a synonym, perhaps even a preferred synonym, for *power*? Do you feel more positive about having achievement needs or power needs? In a different vein, Glasser's position that children who do not experience love and belonging often turn to power as a substitute for their interpersonal intimacy needs should ring a distant bell. In Chapter 3, we discussed Rudolf Dreikurs's formulation that children who don't feel they belong or don't feel useful will often try to have their needs met through attention, power and control, revenge, and despair. What do you think of the striking similarity between these two theoretical perspectives? Have you observed children whose needs for power seem to dominate their interactions with others? Do you think strong-willed or power-needy children are that way because of psychological needs or because of a biological temperament?

Freedom

Many teenagers long for the day they will receive their driver's license; they yearn for their very own car. When they get behind the wheel and independently drive away from their family home for the first time, they sometimes want to shout out in joy at their new-found freedom. Not surprisingly, this need is sometimes referred to as *independence* (R. E. Wubbolding, personal communication, May 6, 2003).

As Glasser (1998) states, "freedom concerns us mainly when we perceive that it is threatened" (p. 39). Examples of how human concern for freedom is increased in the presence of threats abound. Think of the increasing concerns for civil liberties in the United States following the passing of the Patriot Act and the strong (and often violent) efforts of oppressed people throughout the world to obtain and maintain their liberty.

The fact that many teenagers respond to the clarion call for freedom suggests, from the perspective of choice theory, that teenagers are often being denied freedom by their parents. Many parents throughout the world use the psychology of external control with their children. Consequently, it should be no surprise to discover teenagers striving hard to meet their basic human needs for freedom. In the words of Glasser (1998), "I believe that the need for freedom is evolution's attempt to provide the correct balance between your need to try to force me to live my life the way you want and my need to be free of that force" (p. 40).

Choice theory postulates that creativity in humans is directly connected to freedom. For example, if you're unable to express yourself or if no one listens to you when you do express yourself, you may channel your creative impulses into a destructive behavior pattern or an illness. In a case of a college-age woman who was experiencing auditory hallucinations, Glasser (2000) writes:

> Rebecca is fearful that the life she is choosing to lead . . . will alienate her from her mother and family. This fear, coupled with all the pressure she is putting on herself to give up that satisfying life, is triggering her creativity to produce the voices [auditory hallucinations]. My task is to create a good-enough relationship with her so that I can encourage her to live the life she wants. (p. 123)

This case illustrates how a problem related to limited freedom—or at least the perception of limited freedom—can cause a client to produce a particularly creative symptom. From the choice theory perspective, many women of Freud's era who were experiencing hysteria symptoms were probably creatively expressing their pain and frustration at the limits and abuses imposed upon them by society.

Glasser also notes that creativity, when unburdened from control or freedom limitations, is often much less focused on the self and can be used more naturally to benefit others.

Fun

When we teach graduate courses in psychology and counseling, many students are pleased that Glasser places *fun* on his short list of human needs. Of course, we remind them that Glasser was not the first psychological theorist to emphasize the importance of fun to psychological development. As far as we know, Leon Saul (1973), a respected psychoanalyst, originally proposed that *play* be added to Freud's very short psychoanalytic list of the basic human activities, *love* and *work.*

Glasser (1998) believes that "the need for fun became built into our genes" (p. 41). He directly links the need for fun to play, and, even further, he links playing to learning, asserting that "[t]he day we stop playing is the day we stop learning."

Glasser has also stated that fun "is the easiest need to satisfy" and "is best defined by laughter" (p. 41). Having your need for fun met is commonly linked to or blended with having other needs met. In particular, for many people, fun is deeply intertwined with the most primary human need, the need for love and belonging.

Your Quality World

There is an old story, perhaps a myth, about a man named Lawrence P. Berra, better known to most of us as the great New York Yankee baseball player Yogi Berra. One day, when a player on his team was called out on a close play at second base in a crucial game, Yogi went charging onto the field to protest the call. The umpire explained that he, unlike Yogi, was an objective observer and that he, unlike Yogi, had been only about 5 feet from the play, while Yogi had been over 100 feet away, seated in the dugout. When Yogi heard the umpire's logic, he became more angry than ever and snapped back, "Listen ump, *I wouldn't have seen it, if I hadn't believed it*" (adapted from Leber, 1991).

In this story, Yogi has the integrity to admit that it's his belief about the world that affects his perception of whether his player was safe or out at second base. He's saying that, even though there's an objective reality out there, everyone sees the world from his or her own unique personal perspective. Most of us are strongly influenced by what we personally want and believe in. Yogi Berra wants his team to win, and so he sees everything in that light. His team and its success have become big parts of his quality world.

According to choice theory, your quality world consists of a small group of memories or mental pictures that you associate with obtaining one or more of your basic needs. For example, if someone helped you survive, experience love, or have fun, you're likely to put that person into your quality world. Glasser posits that your quality world includes three categories:

1. People
2. Things or experiences
3. Ideas or systems of belief

He states that

the overwhelming reason we chose to put these particular pictures into our quality worlds is that when we were with these people; when we owned, used, or experienced these things; and when we put these beliefs into action, they felt much better than did other people, things, or beliefs. (1998, p. 45)

Choice theory holds that everyone's quality world is different. For example, if you're an avid baseball fan, you probably very much enjoyed the preceding story about Yogi Berra because, somehow and some way, baseball got into your quality world and stayed there. However, if, for whatever reason, you hate baseball, you probably enjoyed the story somewhat less than your baseball-loving classmate, because baseball, as a thing or activity, never found a permanent place in your quality world.

People, things and activities, and ideas or systems of belief move in and out of our quality worlds. For most people, their quality world is a relatively stable place; with the possible exception of romantic love interests, highly valued people, things or experiences, and ideas or systems of belief ordinarily come and go from your quality world rather slowly. In fact, it can be very difficult for some people to let someone get out of their quality world—which, as you can imagine, may result in some serious problems, including stalking and even murder.

The main point is that therapists need to do two things with respect to a client's quality world. First, you need to do your best to understand what's in your client's quality world. Second, to have a chance at helping your client begin to use choice theory to improve his or her life, you need to get into your client's quality world.

Glasser and other reality therapists use different strategies to get into a client's quality world. All of these strategies are founded on this underlying principle: Act with clients in a way that gives them both hope for, and an experience of, having their basic human needs met. For example, when a reality therapist establishes a positive, genuine, and respectful relationship with clients, an experience of love and belonging ensues. Therapists can address client power or internal control needs by emphasizing how much choice they have in their lives and within their sessions (see Practitioner Commentary 9.1 for Wubbolding's application of reality therapy as an empowering experience). Finally, reality therapists don't exert external control over clients by insisting that they give up people, things and activities, and ideas and beliefs that are already deeply imbedded in the clients' quality world.

Total Behavior

According to choice theory, all we do from birth to death is behave. It may be the strength of this belief or the focus of this concept that often causes people to incorrectly categorize reality therapy as a behavioral or cognitive-behavior therapy (Ivey et al., 2002).

Choice theory includes a concept referred to as *total behavior*. Total behavior includes four distinct, but inseparable, components that are always occurring simultaneously:

1. Acting
2. Thinking
3. Feeling
4. Physiology

Total behavior is often described using an automobile analogy (Corey, 2001). Imagine you're sitting in the driver's seat of a front-wheel-drive vehicle. You place the keys in the ignition and turn on the engine. According to choice theory, the engine represents your basic needs, because it's your desire to have those needs fulfilled that powers your overall system. As you put the car into gear and step on the accelerator, you keep a firm grip on the steering wheel, because you want to guide yourself toward your destination. Of course, because you want your needs met as efficiently as possible, when you get up in the morning and hop in your choice theory car, you almost always steer toward the same exciting destination—you steer in the direction of your quality world. That's because you learned early in your life that doing so gives you the best possible chance of getting your five basic needs met. If you're interested in love and belonging, you may steer your car in that direction by making breakfast for your family or for your romantic interest. If you want power, you may down a triple latte from the drive-through espresso stand on your way to work. If your first thoughts focus on survival, you may move as quickly as possible to a place that affords you food, shelter, and clothing. If you have a strong need for freedom or fun, well, you can imagine where those needs might take you.

In the car analogy, the two front wheels represent acting and thinking. These parts of our total behavior are under our direct control. We steer them in one direction or another to get what we want. Although sometimes it might feel like we have little control over our thoughts, Glasser believes that thoughts, like behaviors, are chosen. In contrast, the back wheels of the car represent our feelings and physiology. According to the total behavior concept of choice theory, our feelings and physiology are also a product of choice, albeit indirect choice. As Glasser (2000) states, "This concept explains that we can only directly choose our actions and thoughts. But we have indirect control over most of our feelings and some of our physiology" (p. 226).

Choice Theory and Psychopathology

Glasser has a particular view of client psychopathology that some reality therapists share but that others strongly oppose. As you read about Glasser's perspective, it's important to keep in mind that it is entirely possible to practice reality therapy while completely disagreeing with Glasser's stance on psychopathology (R. E. Wubbolding, personal communication, May 6, 2003).

In 1965, while working as a psychiatrist at a school for delinquent girls, Glasser succinctly expressed his view of psychopathology. He wrote: "[t]he philosophy which underlies all treatment at the Ventura School is that mental illness does not exist" (Glasser, 1965, p. 85). Glasser's position on psychopathology and mental illness is similar to that of Thomas Szasz (1970) and Peter Breggin (1991). He believes deeply in human problems and human suffering, but he does not believe that mental illness exists (except for extreme forms in which brain pathology is clearly present, such as Alzheimer's disease, brain trauma, or brain injury). Despite his medical background, he does not prescribe or recommend medications for clients. In his most recent book, *Unhappy Teens,* he states:

> Even though I am a well-known psychiatrist, since I've developed choice theory, I have given up thinking of human unhappiness as some sort of mental illness caused by something mysterious going on in the brain. (Glasser, 2002, p. 2)

Glasser's extreme position—that we choose our behavior and are completely responsible for all our emotional, behavioral, and even physical problems—often makes students, clients, and even practicing reality therapists uncomfortable. In particular, when Glasser uses verbs like *headaching, depressing,* and *angering* to describe human problems, you might start to think that he's being insensitive to challenges faced by deeply distressed or disturbed clients. In contrast, if you watch him in action, Glasser doesn't act, write, or talk about clients in ways that reflect insensitivity. Instead, his conceptualization of choice theory as an explanation for human behavior is so complete that he believes the most compassionate approach he can take is to set clients free and empower them by helping them see their mental, emotional, and physical pain in terms of personal choice. The point is that insensitivity, in practice, lies in the practitioner and not the theory (R. E. Wubbolding, personal communication, May 6, 2003).

As you might imagine, many individuals and many clients who come for counseling are not the least bit interested—at least initially—in using a choice theory model to explain their problems. That's because it's often more appealing to use an external control theory model and thereby abdicate personal responsibility. Unfortunately, from the choice theory perspective, hanging onto external explanations for problems may initially feel better, but, in the end, believing you do not have personal choice over your condition will increase your suffering and decrease your chances of recovery. In the extended case example later in this chapter, we show how Glasser approaches situations in which clients are resistant to the idea that they're choosing their own behavior and associated problems.

Glasser contends that choice theory applies to virtually all cases of human suffering, including situations in which a client is experiencing psychotic symptoms or schizophrenia. As he explains here, much of his approach to counseling psychotic clients is consistent with how he counsels all other clients:

> Contrary to much current thinking, there is no problem doing psychotherapy with a person who hears voices or suffers from delusions. Although I accept that the symptoms are there, I rarely refer to them in therapy. Most psychotic people can be reached if you concentrate on what they do that is sane. . . . I focus on these sane behaviors and work hard to try to create what I know every client I have ever seen, psychotic or not, wants: *good relationships that start with me.* (2000, p. 122)

The formation of a positive and constructive relationship is the foundation of client success in reality therapy. As Wubbolding and Brickell state, "The practice of reality therapy embraces what Rogers referred to as *the necessary and sufficient conditions for change*" (1998, p. 47). Consistent with the view that love and belonging is the primary human need, in reality therapy the relationship is the primary factor underlying client change. However, in reality therapy, unlike person-centered theory, the positive relationship between therapist and client is not sufficient for therapeutic change to take place. Instead, a second essential factor is emphasized. In the following excerpt, Glasser is discussing a young man who has come for counseling due to symptoms of depression.

> The need for psychotherapy, or at least for extensive psychotherapy, would be reduced if capable people such as this young man knew and used choice theory in their lives. But he doesn't know it, so my job is to teach it to him as part of the counseling. What I will teach him is that he is not satisfied with a present relationship, the problem that always brings people to counseling. His past could have contributed to the problem, but even though most current psychotherapies initially focus on it, the past is never the problem. (1998, pp. 62–63)

For Glasser and reality therapy, then, your ability to relieve clients of problems and suffering hinges on two main factors: how well you can establish a positive therapy relationship (and thereby enter into your client's quality world) and how effectively you can teach your client to use choice theory in his or her life. Teaching clients to use choice theory involves the distinct process of teaching clients to use Wubbolding's Wanting Doing Evaluating and Planning (or WDEP) model (see Practitioner Commentary 9.1).

If there is no such thing as mental illness, then how does choice theory explain why otherwise perfectly intelligent people would act and think in ways that cause them physical and emotional misery? What causes pathological or maladaptive behavior? Glasser (1998) states that there are three logical reasons why so many people choose . . . the whole gamut of what is commonly called mental illness, such as depressing, anxietying, or phobicking. Even sicknesses like adult rheumatoid arthritis may be explained by these same three reasons" (p. 79). As before, we should emphasize that the following views of psychopathology are somewhat distinct to Glasser; many reality therapists do not agree with Glasser's theories of psychopathology.

Glasser's three logical explanations for pathological behavior might be better described as *purposes.* In other words, the purpose of pathological behavior is to accomplish the following goals: (1) restraining anger, (2) getting help, and (3) avoiding things we don't want to face.

Restraining Anger

For Glasser, *depressing* is the most common solution to the problem of anger. Similar to—but not the same as—the psychoanalytic conceptualization of depression as anger turned inward, depressing is viewed by reality therapists as a means by which anger is restrained or managed. Using the language of choice theory, here's how the process works.

Something in your life doesn't go just the way you want it to go. For example, you wanted your boyfriend to meet you at the movies, and he doesn't show up. When this happens, you probably feel upset, frustrated, and out of control. Then, just like most people, on the heels of your frustration, you're likely to have an immediate impulse to anger. Anger is a normal survival-related response built into our genes. As Glasser says, "Angering is the first total behavior most of us think of when someone in our quality worlds does something that is very much out of sync with what we want the person to do" (1998, p. 80). Although Wubbolding also presents anger as a natural reaction, he emphasizes that "[h]urt and fear are the primary feelings—then comes anger" (personal communication, May 6, 2003).

To return to Glasser's perspective, you probably learned that angering is not a very effective or acceptable choice for getting your love and acceptance needs met, so you may choose instead to depress. Depressing is, for the most part, much safer than angering, but it also has many drawbacks, not the least of which is that it feels absolutely miserable. While discussing the case of "Todd," Glasser describes the immediate benefits of depressing over angering:

> Depressing prevented Todd from going after his wife, harming her, and even killing her, a common behavior in this country where weapons are so available. It also might have prevented him from killing himself. Suicide is another total behavior that people choose when they have given up on the idea that they will ever be able to get their lives back into effective control. (1998, p. 81)

If, like Todd, you're restraining your anger by depressing, reality therapy can relieve the problem by helping you find a better way (a better choice) to regain more direct control over fulfilling your need for love and acceptance. Part of this better way will undoubtedly include understanding one of the basic axioms of choice theory: You can only control yourself!

Getting Help

Depressing and other forms of misery are often ways for us to get the love, power, or freedom we crave. Unfortunately for everyone involved, depressing can be a very effective method of controlling important people in your life. It can also be an effective method for gaining sympathy, support, and medications from mental health professionals. This is one reason why Glasser firmly believes that professional counselors and psychologists should not pay much attention to their clients' symptoms. However, he also emphasizes that professionals should not be cold or uncaring. He states, "If it is coupled with compassion, not allowing anyone to control us with depressing helps them to see that there are much better choices than to depress" (1998, p. 82).

In a practical sense, reality therapists must sometimes pay attention to their clients' symptoms, because to ignore them is incompatible with being compassionate. The challenge is to gently and empathically help clients critically evaluate whether their symptoms are helping them fulfill their basic needs (Wubbolding, Brickell, Loi, & Al-Rashidi, 2001).

Avoiding Things

Sometimes we all would like to avoid doing things that we're afraid of or that we just don't want to do. For example, you may need to talk to your advisor or department chair about a thesis or dissertation topic, but you're a bit nervous about what he or she might think about your idea. In that case, it would be quite easy to avoid scheduling an advising session. Or maybe you've had some conflicts with your parents (probably because they're trying to control or advise you in one way or another), and therefore you're reluctant to call them or visit them on your semester break. As it turns out, depressing, panicking, obsessing, and many other behaviors commonly considered to be mental illness are excellent ways to avoid dealing with a life situation—a reality—that simply needs to be addressed. As Glasser would say, in these situations, you have two choices: "[C]hange what you want or change your behavior" (1998, p. 83).

Choice Theory in a Nutshell

As a review of the theoretical material covered so far and a preview of upcoming sections focusing on reality therapy, Glasser's (1998) Ten Axioms of Choice Theory are listed below.

1. The only person whose behavior we can control is our own.
2. All we can give another person is information.
3. All long-lasting psychological problems are relationship problems.
4. The problem relationship is always part of our present life.
5. What happened in the past has everything to do with what we are today, but we can only satisfy our basic needs right now and plan to continue satisfying them in the future.
6. We can only satisfy our needs by satisfying the pictures in our quality world.
7. All we do is behave.
8. All behavior is total behavior and is made up of four components: acting, thinking, feeling, and physiology.
9. All total behavior is chosen, but we only have direct control over the acting and thinking components. We can only control our feeling and physiology indirectly through how we choose to act and think.
10. All total behavior is designated by verbs and named by the part that is the most recognizable.

THE PRACTICE OF REALITY THERAPY

To do reality therapy you must—at the very least—spend time absorbing the concepts of choice theory. Even better, you can obtain a reality therapy certification through the Willam Glasser Institute (see Recommended Readings and Resources for more information).

Preparing Yourself To Do Reality Therapy

As with most therapies, reality therapy works best if you understand the underlying theory not merely intellectually, but also emotionally. Therefore, we recommend that you try living your life, for at least a week, based completely on choice theory, before you seriously consider using it to help others. Putting It in Practice 9.1 and 9.2 provide you with guidelines for deepening your personal and daily understanding of choice theory.

Assessment Issues and Procedures

Typically, Glasser doesn't use standardized assessment procedures with clients. Instead, he relies exclusively on choice theory to provide him with information about what clients are struggling with when they come to therapy. In contrast, reality therapists

---

Putting It in Practice 9.1

Living Choice Theory: The Four Big Questions

Four questions have been developed to help students and clients live the choice theory lifestyle (Wubbolding, 1988). These questions are derived from Wubbolding's WDEP formula. During one full week, do your best to keep these four reality therapy questions on your mind:

1. What do you want? (Wants)
2. What are you doing? (Doing)
3. Is it working? (Evaluation)
4. Should you make a new plan? (Planning)

   In reality therapy, every day we're operating on the basis of a personal plan. The plan may or may not be a good one, and it may or may not be well articulated. The point is this: You're doing something to get your basic needs met. Therefore, consistently ask yourself the four preceding questions. This will help make your choices and your plan more explicit.

   These four questions are incredibly powerful and practical. Think about how you might apply them when doing therapy with a teenager. Now think about how you might apply them as a consultant for a local business. The fact is, whether you're consulting with a teenager or a business leader, there are hardly any other four questions that are more relevant and practical.

   In the space that follows each question, answer the four questions for yourself today.

What do you want?

What are you doing?

Is it working?

Should you make a new plan?

   After you've answered the questions, go back and think about what you've written as your answer for question 1. Can you link your answer to the basic human needs as outlined in choice theory and in Putting It in Practice 9.2?

====== **Putting It in Practice 9.2** ======

Living a Choice Theory Lifestyle

We hope you recall the concept of lifestyle from the Adlerian perspective. However, for this activity, we're referring to lifestyle from a generic and non-Adlerian perspective. The goal of this activity is to help you think, act, and feel like a choice theorist, a prerequisite for becoming a reality therapist.

Even before you start, get clear on this: You don't have to participate in this activity. Based on choice theory, you will only participate in this activity if you want to. Of course, we want you to and Bill Glasser wants you to, but really, to practice the theory, what matters most is for you to feel and embrace the power of your personal choice. Are you willing to choose to participate in this activity? If so, proceed. If not, we accept your decision.

Recall the concept of total behavior. We have direct control over the front two wheels—our thoughts and behavior. Keep that basic fact in the forefront of your mind. Every thought and behavior you engage in is yours; you are responsible for everything you think and do. The following advice from Glasser may help you begin meditating and reflecting on the power and responsibility associated with your choices:

> [T]he next time you are a little "depressed," don't say to yourself or to anyone else: "I'm depressed." Instead, say, "I'm choosing to depress because a relationship in my life is not working for me right now. I'm going to try to figure out a better choice." If you take this suggestion, you will immediately begin to see how correct grammar may lead you to conclude, If I choose all I do, maybe I can choose to do something better. (Glasser, 2000, p. 26)

Now, please take about 5–10 minutes to meditate and reflect on choice. Again, remember, you're choosing everything. If you meditate on the concept of personal choice, you're the one choosing that behavior. If you avoid meditating, you're choosing that as well. As you meditate on personal choice, try not to argue with the concept, but if you do, you're simply choosing that too. Try to accept and let the complete and total power of your personal choice flow over you.

After you've meditated on choice, think about your personal needs. We list the basic human needs. Your job is to write next to each need a sentence or two about what you're currently doing in your life to meet that particular need. A list with sample statements follows.

Survival: "I choose to work to make money to pay my rent and feed myself."

Love and belonging: "My needs for love and belonging are met by choosing to keep in contact with my parents and sisters. I also often choose to spend time with other graduate students in psychology and counseling. I choose to belong to that peer group."

Power: "What am I doing to gain a sense of achievement or inner control? I feel powerful when I get attention from other people. I used to choose to get that attention by depressing myself. Now I'm choosing to be in group therapy and to be on a recreational soccer team."

(continued)

Putting It in Practice 9.2 (continued)

Freedom: "I keep my sense of freedom by choosing to live alone in a small apartment. By not living with someone else, I am able to choose everything I do when at home, without experiencing any interpersonal conflict."

Fun: "Right now I'm choosing to have fun by going to movies, playing the guitar at my apartment, and being on a soccer team. I used to go out drinking with some friends for fun and for a sense of belonging, but I'm choosing to do that less often."

Now it's your turn. List what you're doing to meet your five basic needs:

Survival:

Love and belonging:

Power:

Freedom:

Fun:

Are any of your needs currently unmet? If so, choice theory predicts that you might be feeling bad, sad, angry, or dissatisfied. Make a plan for how you can get your needs met in the most direct way possible . . . but make sure that your plan doesn't involve getting your needs met by trying to control another person. Trying to control someone else is always outside the philosophy of choice theory. Instead, if you want someone to do something, simply ask him or her, but follow up your request with the acknowledgment "it's your choice."

---

may or may not use traditional assessment procedures. This distinction is a good example of why it's important to separate the theorist from the therapeutic practice. Glasser is generally against testing, medications, and diagnostic procedures, but many reality therapists find choice theory and reality therapy completely compatible with these standard mental health practices. In other words, just because Glasser has a particular philosophy about diagnosis doesn't mean that you can't consider choice theory explanations and use reality therapy procedures.

Glasser has repeatedly stated the rather extreme view that there is one primary underlying reason why clients come for therapy. He believes they come because they're experiencing a present, unsatisfying relationship. Variations on this primary reason for seeking therapy include clients who have a conflict between a relationship and another

---

┌─────────────────────────────────┐
│ **PRACTITIONER COMMENTARY 9.1** │
└─────────────────────────────────┘

The Interface Between Choice Theory and Reality Therapy

Robert E. Wubbolding, Ed.D., director of training for the William Glasser Institute, provided the following commentary.

Reality therapy, based on choice theory, has long been criticized as a short-term, symptom-oriented problem-solving method. Now that brief, outcome-based counseling has become fashionable, reality therapy is gaining prominence and acceptance. To gain its rightful place in academia, however, will require more extensive research-based studies. Nevertheless, contrary to common belief, there are studies validating its effectiveness.

I have found that when students learn the theory accurately they see it as a comprehensive explanation of human behavior. To enhance its practicality, I have summarized the delivery system WDEP. *W* means exploring clients' wants and perceptions (i.e., what they want from the world around them and how hard they are willing to work to satisfy their wants). They also examine how they perceive themselves in the world as well as what they can control and not control. In the *D* component, the counselor helps clients describe their choices, their self-talk (e.g., "even though my choices are ineffective, I'll continue to do the same thing"), and their feelings—such as hurt, fear, anger, depression, and many others. The cornerstone in the practice of reality therapy is *E,* self-evaluation. No one changes a behavior without first determining that current choices are ineffective. In *Reality Therapy for the 21st Century,* I describe 22 types of reality therapy self-evaluation based on choice theory. A few of the self-evaluation questions follow: "Is what you're doing helping or hurting?" "Is what you want realistically attainable?" "Does your self-talk help or impede need satisfying choices?" I have found this component to be increasingly necessary with clients, many of whom come from substance abusing, attention-deficit/hyperactivity disordered or simply tumultuous families in which expectations are, to say the least, inconsistent. In such an environment children grow up lacking the ability to self-evaluate; hence the need for a mentor to teach this skill.

In counseling any client my goal is to become part of his or her inner discourse. I cannot do this by communicating a lack of interest in the presenting issue—depression, blaming others, external perceived locus of control. I *always* deal directly with these issues and *then* proceed to discuss his or her relationships and choices by listening carefully for wants. For me, anything less demeans clients, worsens their frustration, and communicates that my agenda is more important than their pain.

The WDEP system is clearly based on an environment that avoids the toxic ABCs: arguing, blaming, criticizing, demanding, and getting lost in excuses. The helpful components of the environment include being determined, courteous, and enthusiastic; using paradoxical techniques; using informed consent; respecting boundaries; creating a sense of anticipation; discussing problems not as problems but as client solutions that have not helped; suspending judgment; using reflective listening; and many others.

One of my missions as a counselor, psychologist, and university professor is to make reality therapy academically both respected and respectable. A second goal is to promote it as a usable system, not as a cult. So I urge you, as students hoping to be respected therapists and helpers, to realize that reality therapy is a system practical *for you.* You need not imitate the style of anyone else. Adapt it to your own personality: assertive, laid-back, action-centered, or more cognitive. Select one, two, or three ideas from this excellent chapter that you will use!

basic need and clients who are experiencing distress because they have no satisfying relationships at all. Once again, reality therapy practitioners may or may not adopt Glasser's perspective on the reason why clients come for therapy.

Many times and in many ways Glasser has defined his perspective of why humans become unhappy and seek therapy. Recently, he clearly articulated his view once again (1998):

> From the perspective of forty years of psychiatric practice, it has become apparent to me that all unhappy people have the same problem: They are unable to get along well with the people they want to get along well with. (p. 5)

This theoretical stance—that there must be a relationship problem underlying all client problems—makes the therapist's assessment task straightforward, although not always simple.

As they interview clients, reality therapists reflect on the following assessment issues or questions. Keep in mind that these are not necessarily questions that the reality therapist asks the client directly; instead, these are questions the reality therapist is trying to evaluate and address when providing counseling (for hundreds of additional questions, see Wubbolding, 2000).

- What is the nature of the client's unsatisfying relationship or relationship-related conflict?
- Will the client be able to understand and use choice theory to improve his or her ability to meet the basic needs? If so, the therapist can move quickly into explaining choice theory. If not, the therapist will need to use various strategies, such as in-session demonstration, rational persuasion, reframing, and so on, to help the client understand how choice theory works.
- Who and what is within the client's quality world?
- How is the client going about meeting his or her needs for survival, love and belonging, power, freedom, and fun?
- Is the client overemphasizing any of the basic human needs?
- What's going wrong as the client tries to get his or her basic human needs met?
- Have there been past successes that can show the client that he or she can use choice theory to meet these needs now and in the future?

Overall, when it comes to assessment, reality therapists keep their eyes and ears focused on their view of the primary therapy goals for nearly every therapy client. These goals include

1. *Human connection.* Reality therapists continuously ask themselves this outcome-related question: Is my client becoming less disconnected and more connected with people in his or her quality world?
2. *Using choice theory.* Is my client able to let go of his or her efforts to control others and use choice theory in his or her life?
3. *Understanding total behavior.* Does my client understand that his or her actions and thoughts are directly chosen and that his or her feelings and physiology fall in line with these chosen actions and thoughts?

4. *Developing effective plans.* Is my client developing and implementing practical and useful plans for getting the basic human needs met?

5. *Counseling.* Is my client getting from the counseling what he or she came for?

APPLICATION: CASE EXAMPLE

The case of Teresa is adapted from Glasser's *Counseling with Choice Theory* (2000).

Preparing Teresa to Use Choice Theory and Reality Therapy

A significant part of reality therapy involves teaching clients to use choice theory in their lives. Of course, it's not appropriate or effective to simply tell clients that they are choosing their misery, because clients usually respond to being directly informed that they are "depressing" or "headaching" with defensiveness and resistance. Therefore, the strategies for teaching clients about choice theory are smooth, empathic, and gradual.

In some cases, Glasser recommends that clients buy and read his book *Choice Theory* (1998) so they will understand the theory from which he is operating. However, from a therapist's perspective, we consider his more recent book, *Counseling with Choice Theory* (2000), to be a better illustration of his theory in action. In *Counseling with Choice Theory* Glasser illustrates how to teach choice theory to clients early in counseling.

For example, when working with Teresa, a very depressed woman (i.e., a woman who is choosing to depress), Glasser articulates the thinking that guides his work:

> I was determined not to ask Teresa to tell me her story and, especially, not to ask her how she felt. I had to try to convince her that she was making ineffective choices in her life, knowing full well that my claim that she was making choices, especially choosing to depress, would be the furthest thing from her mind. If I couldn't begin to convince her on the first visit, there was little chance of any measurable progress. (2000, p. 129)

Glasser is illustrating several reality therapy concepts. First, he mentally prepares himself to focus on the positive. His plan is to steadfastly avoid asking his client to describe her misery. Second, his goal is to "try to convince her" that she's making poor choices. As you can see from Glasser's language here, he understands that she will not be coming to therapy expecting to be held personally responsible for her depressive symptoms. Third, Glasser is set on working quickly. He wants to convince her of the merits of choice theory before she leaves his office.

Although reality therapy is predominantly an educational approach to client change, it is not simply didactic; it is also broadly experiential. Note, in this case, Glasser's next move:

> I started by rising briskly, greeting her warmly, and offering my hand. Teresa was surprised by my energy and enthusiasm to see her. I was not the first therapist she had seen, and she was used to using her depressing to take over the interview. (p. 129)

As you can see, Glasser—although he does not believe in it—is actively resisting the countertransference. He anticipates, because the client is making choices to depress, that she will also try to use her depressing style to disempower the therapy and to depress the therapist. This illustrates an early assessment and educational or role-induction rule for reality therapists: Do your best to determine how clients use people to confirm their external control view of the world, and then do your best to behave in a way that does not validate their style. Instead of succumbing to his client's depressing style, Glasser models choice theory: He chooses to be upbeat and positive, despite the client's interpersonal cues for depressing and hopelessness.

As in most therapies, Glasser uses formal role induction procedures. He uses "explanation" to educate his client on what to expect from him and from therapy (see Sommers-Flanagan & Sommers-Flanagan, 2003):

> Teresa, therapy is not easy. I have to ask you some hard questions that may even confuse you a little, but I'm doing it because I want very much to help you. But please, if I say anything that you don't think is right, ask me why, and I'll explain as well as I can. This isn't really a hard question, but I'd like you to try to do your best to answer it. What do you think a psychiatrist can do for you? (pp. 130–131)

Therapy Techniques and Therapy Process

With this statement, Glasser is not only using explanation to help the client know what to expect from him, he's also genuinely enacting his theory. Specifically, when he says, "I want very much to help you" and "I'd like you to try to do your best" he's directly expressing what he wants and then leaving the rest to her, a strategy perfectly in line with choice theory axiom 2: All we can give another person is information.

When Teresa responds to Glasser's question about what a psychiatrist can do with a fairly predictable "Help me to feel better," he is then able to use a positive cognitive frame to help Teresa stay with the positive and possibly experience hope. He responds, "Fine, that's the answer I was hoping for: You think you can use some help; you haven't given up."

If a client has preconceived ideas about how therapy should proceed, working with a reality therapist may feel quite different or even confusing, a point that Glasser addressed in his direct explanation about his approach to therapy and his desire to be helpful. In Teresa's case, she has preconceived notions about therapy and about mental illness stemming from her previous experiences with mental health professionals. Unfortunately from the reality therapy perspective, Teresa has learned external control concepts that are incompatible with choice theory. In particular, Teresa expects to talk about her past and believes she is suffering from clinical depression and may need medication. The pertinent question at this point is this: How can Glasser introduce his particular brand of theory and his beliefs about the nonexistence of mental illness without offending the client? The answer to this question, at least in the case of Teresa, is *politely and indirectly.* Glasser proceeds:

> **Glasser:** Now I'm going to ask you a question that may not make much sense. Are you willing to try to answer it?
> **Teresa:** You're the doctor, ask me, and I'll try to answer.
> **Glasser:** Is it okay if we don't talk at all about how you feel or about your life? You said it was a disaster; I'd just as [soon] not talk about it. (p. 131)

Teresa is naturally taken aback by Glasser's question. She can't help but wonder what's up with this therapist who doesn't want to talk about her troubles. After all, from her point of view, if he doesn't want to talk about her troubles and misery, then what on earth could he want to talk about?

It may even seem strange to you, the educated reader of this book, that Glasser doesn't want to listen to Teresa talk about her problems. However, like the solution-oriented therapists whom we'll talk about more in Chapter 11, Glasser has his reasons for avoiding depressing talk. Perhaps the central reason is that, as suggested by choice theory, Teresa has been habitually meeting her basic human needs through various maladaptive strategies. From the choice theory perspective, Teresa may be getting her power needs met, at least indirectly, by depressing. It may be that people take care of her, listen to her, and think about her when she acts depressed. Or it may be that somewhere inside she feels better, because if she's depressed, then she has a good, legitimate reason for not having her needs for love and belonging met. Of course, just as the psychoanalytic therapist can't directly tell clients, "Hey, you've got some unresolved anal issues that are interfering with your adult attachments," reality therapists can't blurt out, "You're meeting your power needs and explaining away your unmet love and belonging needs by choosing to act depressed." As in psychoanalytic therapy, a practical issue that reality therapists must address is the issue of timing and client readiness. In other words, unlike Glasser in this case, reality therapists sometimes talk with clients about their symptoms and their misery. As Wubbolding states, "Avoiding a discussion of the presenting problem is a sure way to lose the client!" (personal communication, May 6, 2003).

At some point in his first session with clients, Glasser introduces the concept of choice. Sometimes he does so directly and early on, and at other times, apparently according to his sense of how resistant the client may be to choice theory concepts, he waits longer. At still other times he introduces the concept indirectly. In Teresa's case, Glasser waits a while before introducing choice theory because, it appears, he first wants to reduce her resistance to choice theory by helping her feel at least a tiny bit better—a goal he tries to accomplish by being upbeat, positive, genuinely interested in helping, and strongly opposed to talking about anything in her past that is related to her current misery.

In this next exchange, Glasser introduces choice theory, but Teresa misses the point, instead returning to the importance of her talking about her feelings in therapy.

> **Glasser:** Please, Teresa, tell me. Has it done any good to talk about your misery to anyone? Like, do you choose to feel better after telling someone how miserable you are?" [I'm tangentially introducing the idea that she can choose to feel better. I wonder if she'll pick up on it? She didn't.]
>
> **Teresa:** Wait a second, you're getting me confused. I've got to tell you how I feel. How can you help me if you don't know how I feel?

A little later, Glasser formally and directly introduces the concept of choice into counseling.

> **Glasser:** Everyone who comes in here is choosing to feel bad. No one who chooses to feel good ever comes in. At least they've never come to see me. I don't think it's [feeling bad] a very good choice. That's why I don't want to talk about it.
>
> **Teresa:** I don't know what you're talking about. I don't choose to feel bad. (p. 132)

No one ever said educating clients (or the general populace) on choice theory was going to be easy, and in the preceding exchange Teresa makes it clear that she's not giving up her external control theory without a fight. When practicing reality therapy, you must be prepared to use a variety of skills and strategies to teach your clients choice theory. You must be—like Glasser—kindly, but doggedly, persistent in convincing clients of the validity of choice theory. However, unlike Glasser, many reality therapists are less direct, more empathic, and more patient in helping clients begin to understand the power of their choices. In many ways, Glasser's version of reality therapy is similar to Ellis's version of cognitive therapy. And, as is the case with cognitive therapy, there is more than one way to help clients take responsibility for their total behavior.

Eventually, teaching your client choice theory stops being a role induction activity and becomes a major part of the therapy itself. Rarely do clients grasp the complete implication of choice theory immediately. This is probably partly because most individuals are steeped in external control psychology. They come to therapy believing they have a chemical imbalance, or believing they have a thing called Schizophrenia, and they've often been treated by mental health professionals who make a living teaching external control psychology. In addition, clients often cling to the tenets of external control psychology because of unmet or out-of-control power needs. These clients are usually working hard to control others, and it's very challenging for them to break out of their pattern of meddling with other people's lives instead of their own.

Additional Therapy Techniques

Common techniques used by Glasser for teaching choice theory to clients include in-session demonstration, rational argument or persuasion, and out-of-session experiments or homework. In his session with Teresa, he frequently uses rational argument.

> **Glasser:** Well, if you don't choose to feel bad, then how come you feel bad?
> **Teresa:** I feel bad because my life is a disaster. What else could I feel?
> **Glasser:** But does choosing to feel bad help you in any way to feel better? I realize I'm confusing you, but I'm trying to help you. How you feel is a part of the way you choose to live your life. You chose what you did all day yesterday. Did you feel good or bad yesterday? (p. 132)

He then moves quickly to an in-session demonstration:

> **Glasser:** Think about how you feel now and how you felt a few minutes ago when you walked in the door. Let's say hello again. Here, give my hand a good shake. [I reach out my hand, and she gives it a much more vigorous shake than she did when she came in.]
> **Teresa:** Okay, you're right. I feel a little better. I do.
> **Glasser:** Aren't you choosing to feel better? You could have chosen to continue to feel the way you did when you came in.

And then he moves back to rational argument or persuasion:

> **Glasser:** If you were suffering from clinical depression, how could you feel better all of a sudden?

As you can see, Glasser is persistent (perhaps even relentless) in his efforts to teach his client that her "depression" is a function not of a chemical imbalance or a diagnostic label, but of her choice to depress. Even further, he eventually emphasizes to every client that their problems are a direct result of their best—albeit unsuccessful—efforts to deal with either an unsatisfying relationship or the lack of any relationships at all. In his session with Teresa, he used the following question to get her to focus on her loss of and lack of a relationship:

> **Glasser:** When you give up on your life, what is it that you really give up on? Think a minute. If you can answer that question, I think you can really get some help. (p. 134)

For Teresa, of course, giving up on her life had coincided with her husband's walking out on her. Like many people who respond well to choice theory, she had previously felt better and functioned better because she was previously making more positive choices in her life. Consequently, for Glasser, at least one avenue for helping Teresa make good choices was to have her reflect, even if only briefly, on the fact that she had made some positive choices in the past. This is the exception to the general rule that reality therapy does not focus on the past. The exception is that reality therapy focuses on the past only when the focus includes something positive or successful. Consistent with his theory, Glasser asked Teresa the following question:

> **Glasser:** When you felt good, what did you choose to do that you've totally stopped doing now? (p. 134)

Notice now that, when Teresa answers, Glasser molds her response into something that better fits with choice theory.

> **Teresa:** I did things, I saw people, I took care of my children, I wasn't broke all the time. I had a life.
> **Glasser:** That's a perfect answer except for one little detail. You chose all those good things; you chose to have a life.
> **Teresa:** Okay, okay, but that's all gone. In your words, tell me how I can choose to have a life now. (p. 134)

Teresa is signaling to Glasser that she's willing to give his theory a try. It appears that Glasser has gotten into her quality world. Once a client has accepted some basic parts of choice theory, it's time to move on toward application. Not surprisingly, Glasser is directive when assigning homework or home experiments. For the most part, these assignments are characterized by two overarching themes. First, the assignments help the client experience the fact that front-wheel behavior or thinking directly affects rear-wheel feelings and physiology. In our work using reality therapy with teens, we often sketch out the reality therapy car to illustrate total behavior concepts. Second, reality therapy homework includes active and effective planning. In the following excerpt, both forms of homework are illustrated.

> **Glasser:** That's right, you can't separate choosing how you feel from choosing what you do. They go together. But you can go home and spend the rest of the

day saying to yourself: *Teresa, face it. Good or bad, happy or sad, you're choosing everything you do all day long.* (p. 135; italics in original)

Then, a bit later, Glasser uses a homework assignment to help Teresa establish a short-term plan.

> **Glasser:** All right, let's start. . . . What could you choose to do tomorrow that would be better than today?
>
> **Teresa:** I could choose not to sit around all day.

From a reality therapy perspective, a bad plan may be no better than no plan at all (Wubbolding, 2000). Although Teresa generated a plan, she generated a negative plan and a vague plan. As a result, Glasser intervenes to help her establish a more specific and attainable plan. Again, he is direct and clear in his reasoning:

> **Glasser:** No, that won't work. It'd be like trying to choose not to eat so much. I'm not looking for you to choose not to do anything. I'm looking for you to start to choose to do something better than you're doing now. Something active, so that you have to get up and get going. [Then she said something that made us both smile. She was getting it.]
>
> **Teresa:** I could choose to clean the house. It's a mess. (p. 135)

In many ways, Glasser has already reached the beginning of the end stage of therapy with Teresa. After only a few more comments, Teresa is ready to go home and choose a different, more positive, and more constructive behavior. But the next thing Glasser does in this case is somewhat surprising. After a brief period of praising Teresa for "getting it," he makes a special, spontaneous-sounding contractual agreement with her. He asks her to call and leave him a message every time she chooses to do something all week. He also asks her to leave her number on his answering machine and tells her he'll find time to call her back.

At the end of Teresa's therapy, Glasser takes another step that's somewhat unusual. He asks Teresa if she's read *The Divine Secrets of the Ya-Ya Sisterhood.* And then he offers to help her start her very own "Ya Ya group" (p. 138). He concludes with this charge:

> **Glasser:** For thousands of years, women have supported women. It may even be why the human species has survived. I say, take advantage of your genetic good fortune. Care for each other. (p. 138)

Questions for Reflection

After reading this case, what do you think you might be able to incorporate into your own counseling practice? Are there any behaviors that Glasser engages in that you think would be an especially poor fit for you? Is there anything he does that you really want to try out?

ETHICAL HIGHLIGHT 9.1

The Risks of Insensitivity

To begin with, consider this: Glasser's approach to psychiatry, psychology, and counseling is radical. His beliefs that mental disorders don't exist and that anxiety, depression, and schizophrenia are the responsibility of the client run counter to most contemporary approaches to therapy and mental illness. Consequently, if you choose to blindly imitate Glasser rather than integrating reality therapy principles into your practice, you may end up offending clients or even other mental health professionals because of your unorthodox views and approach.

In addition, reality therapy is sometimes viewed as a directive and insensitive form of therapy that permits therapists to simply confront clients with the reality of the consequences of their choices. For example, in the case of Teresa, at one point Glasser tells her, "you don't have to tell me how you feel. I know how you feel" (p. 132). Obviously, this statement can be considered blatantly insensitive and in direct violation of existential-humanistic principles of empathy and an I-Thou relationship (see Chapters 5 and 6).

From our perspective, Glasser's work with Teresa is neither insensitive nor unethical. However, taken out of context, Glasser's words are insensitive and blunt. And this is where the main ethical danger lies.

Unfortunately, in our experience, reality therapy often appeals to students and professionals who are somewhat bossy and directive in their personality styles. Reality therapy becomes most offensive and potentially unethical when employed in a confrontive manner by naturally bossy therapists who don't understand choice theory.

We have especially seen this tendency in poorly trained professionals who work with juvenile delinquents. The end result is that the professional becomes directive, bossy, confrontive, and insensitive—all in the name of "reality therapy." Of course, in our opinion, directive, bossy, confrontive, and insensitive therapist behavior is not reality therapy; it's just bad behavior and may well be unethical. In fact, when practiced in this manner, reality therapy is transformed into just another effort to apply external control tactics to difficult youths (who are already reacting to adult efforts at external control).

In conclusion, this is our advice: If you choose to practice reality therapy, we strongly recommend that you do so skillfully. It's not a good idea to simply read a couple of Glasser's books and try to imitate him. Instead, the best way to ensure that your reality therapy skills are adequate is by becoming a certified reality therapist and integrating what you learn into your practice (see Recommended Readings and Resources). On the other hand, if you choose to inappropriately twist reality therapy approaches into another form of external control psychology because you haven't obtained adequate training on how to really conduct reality therapy, then you run the risk of behaving unethically—or simply of doing poor therapy.

MORE REALITY THERAPY TECHNIQUES

Consistent with other existentially oriented therapists, Glasser doesn't write extensively about specific therapy techniques. Generally speaking, reality therapists are free to be themselves within the context of establishing a positive therapy relationship and teaching clients choice theory. Despite the fact that Glasser doesn't write much about specific techniques, he uses and advocates the use of a number of more or less technical interventions.

Building The Therapy Relationship

In recent years, Glasser has written in greater detail about relationship-building and relationship-destroying behaviors or habits. He considers these habits to be consistently positive or negative for all relationships, both within and outside of therapy. That being the case, his "seven caring habits" and "seven deadly habits" provide excellent guidelines for how reality therapists should and shouldn't behave toward clients. Glasser's seven caring habits are listed here along with brief descriptions and examples.

1. *Supporting.* Reality therapists help clients focus on what they want from life. By doing so, and by helping them obtain it in a direct and constructive way, reality therapists communicate support. Another way Glasser communicates support to clients is by working with them on specific tasks. For example, to a client who wanted to write a letter to an important person, Glasser suggests, "Write the letter and bring it in to me. We'll look it over together before you send it. Is that OK?" (1998, p. 68).

2. *Encouraging.* Reality therapists are positive and encouraging with clients. Technically, this emerges in several forms: When focusing on the person or, in rare cases, on the person's past, the reality therapist emphasizes successes and positive identity; also, there is an emphasis on connection between therapist and client. For example, with a client who was struggling with a reluctance to talk, Glasser used an encouraging statement in a direct manner that has come to be associated with reality therapy: "Well, say it anyway. This is the place to say hard-to-say things" (1998, p. 65).

3. *Listening.* Many non–reality therapists view reality therapy as a wholly directive and confrontive therapy. In truth, reality therapists emphasize listening. Their listening is less in the mold of nondirective Carl Rogers listening and more in the mold of a friend's listening to another friend. Additionally, reality therapists intentionally choose to listen to clients' successes, plans, and efforts to connect with others, and they minimize listening to clients' talk about symptoms or negative past experiences. Consistent with the WDEP model, reality therapists listen for wants and perceptions (W); actions, self-talk, and feelings (D); self-evaluations (E); and plans (P).

4. *Accepting.* Reality therapists accept the fact that all clients want to fulfill their five basic human needs. This provides an excellent foundation for empathy and connecting within the therapy session. However, reality therapists never accept client statements that externalize responsibility. This is probably why many students and professionals inaccurately view reality therapy as being harshly confrontational. In truth, reality therapists use teaching techniques—not harsh con-

frontation—when clients externalize responsibility. Put simply, reality therapists accept client needs and then teach them choice theory.

5. *Trusting.* Reality therapists communicate trust in many ways. For example, when Glasser tells Teresa to call him and leave messages and that he'll call her back, he's building a trust relationship.

6. *Respecting.* Again, the point is that reality therapists respect what people want. The following excerpt from a case in which Glasser is working with a married man who wants to become a woman illustrates his emphasis on both connecting with clients and respecting them:

   > I could turn him over to someone else, but we've made a good connection. He may think I am afraid to deal with his problem, and we'll lose the connection. It's that connection that's all important. Even his wife will look for that connection—that I really want to help him; that I respect him even though he wants to be a woman. (2000, pp. 90–91)

7. *Negotiating differences.* Reality therapy is all about negotiating differences. A basic assumption of choice theory is that although all individuals have the same five basic needs, all will have unique ways in which they want those needs fulfilled. The reality therapist helps clients negotiate the differences between what they want from life and what they're getting from life. In couples therapy, Glasser emphasizes a concept called "the solving circle" to help clients constructively negotiate their differences. With regard to the solving circle, he tells couples: "Unless both of you are in the circle, you cannot negotiate; all you can do is argue" (1998, p. 95).

Reality Therapy And Confrontation

Because reality therapy has been misconstrued as a harshly confrontive therapeutic approach, once again we want to emphasize the fact that reality therapy is a gently confrontive therapy. It helps clients learn and deeply understand the power, control, and choice they have in their lives (Wubbolding & Brickell, 2000). To further articulate reality therapy's stance against harsh confrontation, we list the seven deadly habits of choice theory:

1. Criticizing
2. Blaming
3. Complaining
4. Nagging
5. Threatening
6. Punishing
7. Bribing or rewarding to control

In his usual style, Glasser is direct and clear about the negative consequences of using the seven deadly habits. He states: "There is nothing intangible about any of them; they are clear and explicit. Exhibiting them in any relationship will damage that relationship. If you keep doing so, the relationship will be destroyed" (2002, p. 13).

The following is an example of the type of confrontive technique that is often inaccurately associated with reality therapy. The counselor is confronting a teenage client on his efforts to find a job.

Counselor: Where else did you go?

Client: I tried a couple other [gas] stations too. Nobody wants to look at me. They don't pay too good anyway. Nuts to them!

Counselor: So you haven't really done too much looking. Sounds like you want it served on a silver plate, Joe. Do you think looking at a couple of gas stations is really going to get you a job? (Ivey et al., 2002, p. 219)

As you can see, although the counselor is supposedly doing reality therapy, his statements are inconsistent with the principles of reality therapy. A reality therapist wouldn't use the judgmental criticism offered up by the counselor. Instead, a more constructive approach that brings the counselor and client together to work on the problem would be used. Specifically, a reality therapy response would focus on practical ways the client can get what he wants—a job that provides money (a form of power that enhances freedom), as well as a certain amount of human connection (love and acceptance). In a word, the reality therapist's focus in the preceding situation would be on *planning* (see Practitioner Commentary 9.1 for alternative wording for questioning and confronting clients from a reality therapy perspective).

Helping Clients Develop Effective Plans

Wubbolding has written extensively about how reality therapists help clients develop plans for making positive life changes (1988, 1991, 2000). As in Teresa's case, reality therapists help clients make positive and constructive plans. Wubbolding (1988) uses the acronym SAMIC³ to outline the essential ingredients of an effective plan:

S = Simple: Effective plans are simple. If a plan generated in reality therapy is too complex, the client may become confused or overwhelmed and therefore not follow through.

A = Attainable: Effective plans are attainable or realistic. If the plan is unattainable, the client will probably become discouraged. As Glasser did in the case of Teresa, you should help your client adopt a small and realistic plan.

M = Measurable: Effective plans are measurable. Clients need to know if the plan is working and if they're making progress.

I = Immediate: Effective plans can be enacted immediately, or at least very soon. If clients have to wait too long to implement a plan, the immediate motivation and/or the memory of exactly what to do may be compromised.

C = Controlled: Effective plans are controlled exclusively by the planner. Be sure to avoid having clients develop plans that are contingent on someone else's behavior.

C = Committed: Clients need to commit to their plans. Obviously, if a client is only half-heartedly invested in the plan, then the plan is less likely to succeed.

C = Continuous: Effective plans are continuously implemented. This is where the practice of choice theory and reality therapy is similar to Eastern or mindfulness approaches to mental health. When functioning well, reality therapy clients have continuous awareness of what they want and of their plan for getting what they want. This high level of awareness reminds us of mindfulness or conscious-raising therapeutic techniques.

Wubbolding (1988) also recommends that individuals learning to conduct reality therapy develop a plan for themselves. In particular, he notes that to be effective reality therapists, it's very important for practitioners to plan to obtain consultation and/or supervision from certified reality therapists (see Recommended Readings and Resources).

Putting It in Practice 9.3

Helping Clients with Self-Evaluation

Robert Wubbolding is one of the leading reality therapists in the world. His approach to therapy is supportive and somewhat in contrast to the Glasser case excerpt included earlier. One of the techniques he encourages therapists to use with their clients is called *client inner self-evaluation.* Wubbolding considers self-evaluation for clients to be a crucial "prelude to change" (1999, p. 196).

The goal of this technique is to help clients evaluate how well their total behaviors are helping them obtain what they want from life. Wubbolding recommends that therapists adapt the following eight questions to fit their particular client:

1. "Is the overall direction of your life a plus or a minus? Are you heading in the direction you would like to go?"
2. "Are your specific actions effective in getting what you want? When you did such and such yesterday, did it help or hurt you? Did it help or hurt the people around you?"
3. "Did such and such a behavior violate the rules?" (This question is useful for students who believe that antisocial actions help them.)
4. "Is what you did or are doing acceptable? Is it in line with or against any unwritten rules?"
5. "Is what you want from others, from yourself, from school, from work, and from society realistically attainable?"
6. "Is what you want genuinely good for you? Will it help you or hurt you in the long run and in the short run if you have what you want?"
7. "Does it help you to view the world—parents, students, friends, employees, and so on—in the manner you have chosen?"
8. "Are the plans you have made for change genuinely satisfying to you, and are they helpful in attaining your wants (goals that have been evaluated previously)? Does your plan fulfill the characteristics of an effective plan? Is it simple, attainable, measurable, immediate, and controlled (SAMIC) by you, the planner?" (Wubbolding, 1999, p. 197)

Because they ask the client to look at himself or herself and self-evaluate, each of these questions posed by Wubbolding is inherently confrontive. However, be sure to notice the tone of the questions posed by Wubbolding and compare them to the judgmental confrontations used in the Ivey example. The key point is that reality therapists question their clients and help them align their wants with their behaviors and their plans, but they do so in a gentle and collaborative manner. (Many additional questions generated by Wubbolding are in his book *Reality Therapy for the 21st Century,* 2000.)

THERAPY OUTCOMES RESEARCH

In some ways, there is a puzzling lack of empirical research on reality therapy. In other ways, the absence of controlled studies on reality therapy efficacy is not at all surprising. Historically, existential therapists have eschewed systematic evaluation of therapy outcome (see Chapter 5). Although reality therapy is not a purely existential approach, its existential roots may be related to the absence of outcome research. On the other hand, reality therapy is a short-term, directive form of therapy that would be relatively easy to evaluate.

The few published studies on reality therapy efficacy indicate positive results. For example, in a study of a reality therapy–based group therapy for chronic pain management, 22 veterans reported increased coping skills, greater need satisfaction, and overall satisfaction with the treatment (Sherman, 2000). Unfortunately, this study, like most empirical research on reality therapy, had a small sample and didn't include a control or comparison group. The best review of reality therapy research is in a chapter of Wubbolding's recent book (2000).

Glasser and reality therapists frequently report successful case studies (Glasser, 2000). However, these case studies do not employ systematic single-subject research designs. To date, it's impossible to say whether reality therapy will stand up to more rigorous scientific scrutiny.

Although we appreciate and believe in the importance of scientific research, there are also other measures of the effectiveness of a specific therapy approach. In particular, reality therapy, like the Energizer Bunny, just keeps going and going. As noted hereafter, Glasser is currently using his theory with a community of 20,000, and his approach is arguably one of the more prominent and popular theoretical approaches used to teach responsibility to schoolchildren. Many practitioners report using reality therapy principles and procedures in their work with young people, especially delinquent or predelinquent youth (Richardson & Wubbolding, 2001).

MULTICULTURAL PERSPECTIVES

As an approach to therapy, choice theory has been practiced with a wide range of ethnic groups and has been promoted in many countries (Cheong, 2001; Kim, 2002; Mickel & Liddie-Hamilton, 2002; Tham, 2001). Recently, Wubbolding and associates published an article promoting reality therapy and choice theory as a viable approach that can be modified and adapted to many cultures (Wubbolding et al., 1998). This article was prepared by 11 signatories from 10 different countries.

Reality therapy may be an especially good fit for working with clients with diverse ethnocultural backgrounds. In *Theories of Counseling and Psychotherapy: A Multicultural Perspective,* A. Ivey and associates assert that "[r]eality therapy has much to offer multicultural counseling and therapy, for the emphasis on responsibility to others and society is in accord with Native American Indian and Asian and Asian-American value systems" (Ivey et al., 2002, pp. 220–221).

Glasser, in a recent interview with Wubbolding, emphasized his perspective on the multicultural applicability of choice theory:

> [C]hoice theory is strongly based on the idea that built into our genetic structure are five basic human needs, and that all people on earth today, regardless of their size, shape, color,

or anything else, have exactly the same genetic structure. We are all one race. (Wubbolding, 2000, p. 61)

From a multicultural perspective, Glasser's comment captures only one of two important realities. Although he emphasizes the culturally universal, he completely neglects the culturally specific (Sue & Sue, 2003). For the most part, in his writings he does not address the potential genetic differences and nonshared environmental experiences common to ethnically diverse populations.

In contrast, Wubbolding (2000) has written with more sensitivity about the application of choice theory and reality therapy to non-Western individuals and groups. His book *Reality Therapy for the 21st Century* devotes a chapter to his experiences applying choice theory to multicultural groups. As an example of his pioneering efforts to apply reality therapy to Japanese individuals, he notes: "There is no exact Japanese translation for the word 'plan,' just as there is no exact word for 'accountability'" (2000, p. 181).

Wubbolding's message is that reality therapists must respect specific language and cultural differences when applying choice theory to individuals from different cultures. He emphasizes that asking questions like "What do you want?" or "Would that help?" may be far too direct and possibly difficult for Asian clients to interpret. Instead, he suggests modifications such as "What are you looking for?" and "Would that be a minus or a plus?" Asian students with whom we have worked concur with Wubbolding's ideas for modifying choice theory for Asian clients. For more information on the application of reality therapy to diverse populations, we recommend Wubbolding's recent book (Wubbolding, 2000; see Recommended Readings and Resources).

CONCLUDING COMMENTS

Because this chapter has been so focused on Glasser, his theory, and his approach to therapy, by now you may already feel that you know Bill Glasser fairly well. Nonetheless, in this section we will provide more direct information and observations into who he is as a person.

Bill Glasser is still a very active professional, often presenting his theory and therapy approach to state and national counseling and psychology associations. Most recently, I (John) ran into him after watching him and his wife present an extended role play at the 2002 annual meeting of the American Counseling Association. Dr. Glasser was sitting in the exhibit hall selling his books to virtually everyone who happened by. He was kind, friendly, and engaging.

If you happen to attend a conference where Dr. Glasser is present, I recommend that you seize the opportunity and meet him. At the very least, he is one of our few remaining living legends. Further, if you approach him, I think you'll find him very accessible, he seems to enjoy talking with people after presentations, possibly because he has so much to teach. Conceptually, at this point in his life, Dr. Glasser is traversing Erik Erikson's (1963) generativity stage, meaning that he is working very hard on what he can pass on to individuals and society. In fact, if you do choose to approach him, don't be surprised if Dr. Glasser tries to convince you to buy one (or more) of his books. At the 2002 conference, he managed to sell me two books and a videotape . . . despite the fact that I didn't have a means of payment with me. He simply said, "You look like an honest person, so I'll trust you to send me a check." I chose to comply with his request. I should add that, consistent with his theoretical perspective, Dr. Glasser does not use high pressure or controlling sales tactics. Instead, he simply is unabashedly enthusiastic about the value of his work. As Wubbolding states, "One of his most admirable traits is that at age 78, 20 years after he could have retired, his is as idealistic as a 25 year-old. He still believes that each book he writes will change the world" (R. E. Wubbolding, personal communication, May 6, 2003).

Despite his entrepreneurial spirit, I'm convinced that Dr. Glasser's salesmanship is not aimed toward financial gain. His efforts to spread the word about choice theory are less about the Adlerian concept of self-interest and personal gain and more about Adlerian social interest. Clearly, Dr. Glasser is deeply involved in an effort aimed at helping individuals to be less interested in controlling each other and more interested in making healthy choices. As an example, in 1997, he began a project with the city of Corning, New York, to teach its 20,000 residents how to use choice theory in their lives and in their community. Overall, this seems to be a laudable choice.

> *It is my vision to teach choice theory to the world.*
> *I invite you to join me in this effort.*
> —William Glasser, *Unhappy Teenagers:*
> *A Way for Parents and Teachers to Reach Them* (2002, p. 190)

STUDENT REVIEW ASSIGNMENTS

The following exercises will encourage you to think further about choice theory and reality therapy.

Critical Corner

Before you complete the following critique assignment for choice theory and reality therapy, we should acknowledge that even though Glasser considers personal criticism to be a deadly habit, we're certain that he would support an intellectual critical analysis of his psychological theory and therapeutic approach.

Below, to provoke your reactions, six extreme criticisms of reality therapy are listed and briefly described. As you read these criticisms, write out your response to the criticism. Remember, you can write in defense of the theory and its application, or you can continue the critique in your writing assignment.

1. Choice theory and reality therapy refuse to acknowledge the power and relevance of unconscious processes in human functioning and in the therapeutic process. For example, Glasser considers transference and dreams to be irrelevant to counseling. Given the rich and unique human interactions associated with dreams and transference, do you think reality therapists are missing an opportunity by considering them irrelevant to counseling? On the other hand, do you think excluding dreams and transference might make therapy more efficient?
Response:

2. If reality therapists reject transference, they probably also reject the concept of countertransference. Do you think that ignoring these basic relationship dynamics might blind therapists to their own issues, impulses, and other countertrans-

ference reactions? How would ignorance of your countertransference reactions have a detrimental effect on therapy process and outcome?

Response:

3. Glasser espouses the radical view that mental illness does not exist. This position might cause clients to feel blamed for their symptoms and might even cause them to think the reality therapist believes their distress is imaginary or "in their heads." What do you think of Glasser's disbelief in the existence of mental illness? Can you be a reality therapist and disagree with Glasser?

Response:

4. Although there is some research indicating that reality therapy is effective, there are no rigorously controlled outcome studies, and reality therapy is not considered an empirically validated therapy. Without extensive empirical evidence, how can a professional therapist place faith in reality therapy procedures?

Response:

5. Choice theory includes several intangible and immeasurable concepts like the five basic human needs, the quality world, and total behavior. These constructs, like the id, ego, and superego, are imaginary or conceptual and lack empirical support to validate their existence. Do you think that reality therapy is based on a theoretical fiction, or do you think we will eventually accumulate evidence to support choice theory?

Response:

6. Glasser ignores or rejects ethical boundaries typical of most usual and customary therapeutic procedures. For example, he tells clients, "We can talk as long as you want" and sometimes meets with clients who are old friends of the family (Glasser, 2000). What do you think of his unconventionally friendly approach to therapy? What might be the ethical dangers linked to his approach?

Response:

Reviewing Key Terms

- External Control Psychology
- Choice theory's five basic human needs (list and define)
- The three types of information in your quality world (list and define)
- The four components of total behavior (list and define)
- WDEP system and four questions of choice theory
- The 10 axioms of choice theory
- The seven deadly habits
- SAMIC[3]

Key Theory Questions

1. How do reality therapists define mental illness?
2. Why do reality therapists use the terms *depressing* and *headaching*?
3. Would a reality therapist work with a psychotic patient? If so, how?
4. Do you think transference and countertransference have a place in reality therapy? If so, how do they fit?
5. What are the three logical explanations of pathological behavior?
6. What are the four main goals of therapy, from the reality therapist's perspective?
7. Why do reality therapists mostly ignore clients' complaints and their clients' pasts?
8. How do reality therapists use rational argument in counseling?
9. How do they use in-session demonstrations?
10. For reality therapists, what constitutes a good homework assignment and a good plan?
11. Come up with a client homework assignment that emphasizes front-wheel behaviors and thoughts.

RECOMMENDED READINGS AND RESOURCES

The following resources provide more information about choice theory and reality therapy.

Lead Journal

- *International Journal of Reality Therapy*

Books and Articles

Glasser, W. (1965). *Reality therapy: A new approach to psychiatry.* New York: Harper & Row.

Glasser, W. (1998). *Choice theory: A new psychology of personal freedom.* New York: HarperCollins.

Glasser, W. (2000). *Reality therapy in action.* New York: HarperCollins.

Glasser, W. (2002). *Unhappy teenagers: A way for parents and teachers to reach them.* New York: HarperCollins.

Glasser, W. (2003). *Warning: Psychiatry can be hazardous to your health.* New York: HarperCollins.

Wubbolding, R. E. (1991). *Understanding reality therapy.* New York: Harper & Row.

Wubbolding, R. E. (1999). Client inner self-evaluation: A necessary prelude to change. In H. G. Rosenthal (Ed.), *Favorite counseling and therapy techniques* (pp. 196–197). Washington, DC: Accelerated Development.

Wubbolding, R. E. (2000). *Reality therapy for the 21st century.* Muncie, IN: Accelerated Development.

Wubbolding, R. E., Al-Rashidi, B., Brickell, J., Kakitani, M., Kim, R. I., Lennon, B., Lojk, L., Ong, K. H., Honey, I., Stijacic, D., & Tham, E. (1998). Multicultural awareness: Implications for reality therapy and choice theory. *International Journal of Reality Therapy, 17,* 4–6.

Videotapes

Carlson, J., & Kjos, D. (2000). *Reality therapy with Dr. Robert Wubbolding* [Videotape]. Boston: Allyn & Bacon.

Many other reality therapy and choice theory audio and videotapes are listed at www.wglasser.com/SOTAG.htm.

Training Organizations and Web Sites

The William Glasser Institute (web site: www.wglasserinst.com)

Center for Reality Therapy (e-mail: wubsrt@fuse.net)

The Austin Center for Reality Therapy and Quality School Support (web site: www.acrtqss.home.texas.net)

Chapter 10 ———————————————————————

FEMINIST THEORY AND THERAPY

For years, psychiatric journals have touted the salutary effects of antidepressants by printing "before" and "after" pictures showing a woman leaning on a mop looking despondently at her kitchen floor, and then happily mopping it after taking her medication.

—E. Kaschak, *Engendered Lives* (1992, p. 22)

IN THIS CHAPTER YOU WILL LEARN

- The history and context of feminist psychological theory
- The relationship between feminism and feminist therapy
- Central theoretical principles of feminist mental health work
- Ways in which feminist therapy principles apply to counseling
- Ways to seek feminist supervision
- Strategies for developing a written and verbal informed consent process
- The ethical framework surrounding feminist therapy

The title of this chapter could be misleading if you take it to mean a monolithic entity that can be easily described and put into practice. Feminist therapy—or more aptly, therapies—share a common problem with existential therapies: Various forms and renditions of feminist therapy spring from a common set of beliefs, but they have evolved in many directions, depending on the thoughts, values, experiences, and philosophies of each individual practitioner or writer. This chapter provides you with our view of the essence of feminist therapy and the psychological theory behind it. There are many exciting variations on the theme to explore as you develop your own philosophies and practices.

KEY FIGURES AND HISTORICAL CONTEXT IN FEMINIST THERAPY

No single theorist can be identified as the founder or originator of feminist psychological theory or feminist therapy. Most feminists have their favorite heroes who they would argue deserve this honor. Certainly, Jean Baker Miller was a central figure, with her books *Psychoanalysis and Women,* published in 1973, and *Toward a New Psychol-*

ogy of Women, first published in 1976. Phyllis Chesler wrote *Women and Madness,* first published in 1972, and in 1966 Juliet Mitchell published *Women: The Longest Revolution.* Later, in 1976, she published *Psychoanalysis and Feminism.* This list is a small representation of one era in the history of feminism. In truth, many, many women and men contributed to this evolving theory of human functioning and human distress. Even the origins of feminism are inclusive, mutual, and a shared human experience.

Centuries before the term *feminism* was coined, there were those who protested the systematic exclusion of women from the functions of adult civic life. Plato's (c. 440 B.C.) vision for identifying and training the best and brightest to serve as the ruling class included the possibility of women being trained. In the late 1800s John Stuart Mill, influenced in part by his friendship and marriage to feminist Harriett Taylor, wrote against the oppression of women and of the great costs to society resulting from this oppression (Mill, 1912). Although Sigmund Freud ultimately failed to remain forthright about his exposure to the suffering of women due to their subordinate position in society, his associate Alfred Adler did not. As discussed in Chapter 3, Adler was first among psychoanalysts openly to point to the terrible damage done by society to women. He strongly condemned the subjugation of women, claiming that this treatment of the female sex was in fact a root cause of the psychological problems not only of women but of men and children as well. In *Psychoanalysis and Women,* Miller (1973) quotes Adler as he discusses women and society (Adler, 1927):

> All our institutions, our traditional attitudes, our laws, our morals, our customs, give evidence of the fact that they are determined and maintained by privileged males for the glory of male domination. These institutions reach out into the very nurseries and have a great influence upon the child's soul. (p. 40)

Although it is difficult to identify an exact date, from the early twentieth century forward, in psychiatry, as in many fields, women slowly, against great odds, began joining the ranks of educated male professionals. In a paper addressing the genesis of the castration complex in women in 1922, Karen Horney (1967) said,

> In this formulation we have assumed as an axiomatic fact that females feel at a disadvantage because of their genital organs, without this being regarded as constituting a problem in itself—possibly because to masculine narcissism this has seemed too self-evident to need explanation. Nevertheless, the conclusion so far drawn from the investigations—amounting as it does to an assertion that one half of the human race is discontented with the sex assigned to it and can overcome this discontent only in favorable circumstance—is decidedly unsatisfying, not only to feminine narcissism but also to biological science. (p. 38)

Thus, though painstakingly slow and with many setbacks, we begin to see cracks in the all-male foundational thinking. Among others, Clara Thompson, Helene Deutsch, Anna Freud, Margaret Mahler, and Karen Horney chipped away at dominant male views of human development and pathology presented by thinkers and writers in psychoanalysis. These women offered compelling alternative arguments for concepts such as penis envy, female masochism, and feminine inferiority.

A Working Definition

Feminist theory has at its core a belief in equality between the sexes. It embodies the belief that women should be fully included in economic, social, and political opportunities and decision making. Funkerburk and Fukuyama (2001) define feminism as "the belief that human beings are of equal worth and that the pervading patriarchal social structures which perpetuate a hierarchy of dominance, based upon gender, must be resisted and transformed toward a more equitable system" (p. 4).

Since the 1960s, feminist mental health theorists, researchers, and therapists have exercised ever-increasing influence in the field. For our purposes, a feminist is simply someone who believes in basic equality for women, and a feminist therapist is one who believes in and acts on principles of feminist theory in psychotherapy. Feminist theory in general and feminist theories of mental health particularly have sought to identify and address cultural forces and practices that are inherently psychologically damaging to women.

Questions for Reflection

This last sentence provides ample food for thought. What cultural forces and practices do you think are inherently psychologically damaging to women? In contrast, what cultural forces and practices do you think are inherently psychologically damaging to men? Are the same forces and practices damaging to both men and women? Or are the forces and practices that damage women different from those that damage men?

THEORETICAL PRINCIPLES OF FEMINIST THEORY AND THERAPY

Feminist theory is at once complex and simple, innocent and insidious, common sensical and profound. What can be more obvious (at least to the Western European mind) than the notion that every baby born deserves to pursue her or his calling to the fullest, with no obstacles arbitrarily put in place due to its sex, race, or culture? On the other hand, what can be more challenging to most status quos than the notion that one's sex should not in any way determine one's role in culture or excuse one from culturally identified adult obligations, such as serving in the military or providing adequate nurturing and income to raise healthy offspring? The principles underlying feminist therapy are directly linked to the basic premise that females deserve the same opportunities for development provided to males in any given culture *and* that males, in turn, deserve similar rights.

Nearly 15 years ago, in a psychology of women class at a small, private college, we asked the members (all female) if they believed they should have the option of staying home with their children or working and hiring child care. The response was unanimous. All fourteen were adamant: The choice to stay home or enter the workplace should be theirs! We then asked if their children's father should have the same option. The response was mixed and made for great discussion. Men's rights and women's rights are inextricably bound together. A change in one has a direct impact on the other.

Questions for Reflection

In your opinion, what are the costs of equality between the sexes? What are the gains?

For instance, one of our colleagues likes to say, "When we allow ourselves to say 'women and children' we leave out a third of the equation. Until men provide equal care for babies, we will have war" (Clark, personal communication, March 20, 1991).

An Overarching, Long-Lived Problem: Male as Normative

Although male and female babies are born at roughly the same rate throughout the world, most cultures place greater value on male babies and regard maleness as normative (Gilbert & Scher, 1999). As far as we know, this has been true throughout recorded history (Lips, 1999). But what does "male as normative" mean?

Essentially, male as normative means that maleness sets the standard for whatever is considered normal, average, or representative. Conversely, it means that anything deviating from male has the potential to be seen as abnormal and inferior (e.g., Beauvoir, 1952). It also has meaning and implications at many other levels. For example, male as normative means that

- Males will be overrepresented in research, decision making, politics, literature, entertainment, and descriptions of what it means to be human, healthy, fulfilled, and successful. In the arena of mental health this implies that because women become depressed at higher rates than men do, there must be something inherently weak or defective about being female. Even further, we have had participants in suicide prevention workshops comment that the best explanation for why women attempt suicide three times more often than men and that men complete suicide four times more often than women is that "at least men can do the job right." This radical, male-as-normative perspective defends even the potential pathology of successful suicide as normal or better because it occurs more often in men.

- If an entity has an unknown gender and has no stereotypically identifying features, it will be referred to as male until proven otherwise. Think of Bugs Bunny, Daffy Duck, Big Bird, Grover, and other animated figures who could be female but are portrayed automatically as male.

- For the most part, adjectives traditionally used to describe males will be used as compliments for males, and often for females (i.e., s/he is so active, dominant, strong!); in contrast, adjectives traditionally used to describe females will have less positive valence overall and may be viewed as insulting when applied to a male (i.e., soft, demure, yielding): "while males may be ridiculed and humiliated for behaving or sounding or looking like females, so may females. Women are subject to censure not only for behaving too much like men, but for behaving too much like women" (Kaschak, 1992, p. 40). The consistent meaning of "throwing like a girl" is always to throw poorly, weakly, or ineptly.

- The male carries the familial identity, so if children are given only one family name, it is the father's family name. If children carry more than one family name and one is dropped in marriage or adulthood, the maternal name is dropped and the identity of maternal lineage may be lost.

- Women's activities are named as such, whereas male activities are simply activities. Women's tennis, versus tennis. Women's work, versus work. Women's ways of knowing, versus ways of knowing. If a college history class focuses on reform workers in a given era and most or all of the workers happen to be male, the class will most likely be called "Nineteenth-Century Reform Workers." However, if the

---

======   **Putting It in Practice 10.1**   ======

Male as Normative . . . Still the Norm?

Do you find it hard to believe that maleness is still the norm in our progressive, egalitarian society? Although it is true that things are changing, change is slow, and sometimes we regress. As an everyday example, count the created characters on *Sesame Street.* Use one hand for the guys and one for the gals. No, Miss Piggy doesn't count. She's a muppet. Sit down and watch your fill of popular TV shows. The latest statistics indicate that you'll see almost two males for every female. Check the statistics on women in politics. Did you know that many of the drugs tested for human dosage and consumption were, until quite recently, tested almost exclusively on males? Until very, very recently, the needs and experiences of women and girls in warfare were completely ignored (Mazurana, McKay, Carlson, & Kasper, 2002). On the lighter side, how many sports teams comprised of women have some sort of added prefix or suffix indicating that the team is female? There are the Grizzlies, and there are the Lady Grizzlies. In one particular college, near and dear to our hearts, the men's Grizzly basketball team has slightly fewer wins most years, with the Lady Griz often outperforming them. Because of this status, the Lady Griz team is sometimes the one meant when a speaker says, "Wow, those Griz are having a tremendous season." Sometimes you hear people actually explain, "I'm talking about the Men Griz here," in order to clarify which team they are discussing. Further, the soccer coach has raised a few eyebrows by insisting that her team be called the Grizzlies soccer team. Many feel these women should be called the Lady Griz even though there is no male soccer team at the university. Even worse is the tendency inappropriately to feminize already inappropriate team names, such as the Bravettes.

---

workers were women, it wouldn't be unusual for the class to be called "Women Reform Workers in the Nineteenth Century."

You may disagree with some of the examples just given, or perhaps you can think of even better examples yourself. Cumulatively they illustrate the point that maleness has been and still is the primary normative definition of being human. This leads us to a core tenet of feminist (and multicultural) therapy: When a culture treats certain members as exemplary, or normal, and other members as both different from normal and generally inferior, it takes a psychological toll (Sparks & Park, 2002). The problem resides in the culture, not in the individual. Therefore, in coping with the distress and damage they are experiencing, women need to recognize that the main sources of the problems are not within them but within their culture. Against this backdrop of male as normative, three main theoretical principles emerge that inform feminist therapy.

Principle I: Femaleness and Maleness are Central, Powerful Aspects of Our Identity

The first principle of feminist psychological theory is that both biologically determined sexual characteristics and socially constructed gender-role expectations play a central role in understanding client problems.

There are a few biological distinctions that cause humans to be classified as male or female. These include the sex chromosomes and sex-determining genes, the H-Y antigen, gonads, certain hormones, and internal reproductive organs (Zucker, 2001). Thus, the majority of those classified as female are born with clitorises, labia, vaginas, and uteruses and at puberty will develop breasts and begin a menstrual cycle that will last until late midlife. The majority of those classified as male will have testicles and penises and at puberty will experience a hormonally driven change in their vocal cords that lowers their voices. While well over 90% of human biology is the same for both sexes, there are some important physical and hormonal differences. It should be noted that the differences vary greatly within any group of males or females and that a significant number of babies are born with less pronounced sexual determination. Given culture's adamant insistence on *male* and *female* as dichotomous categories, these individuals often struggle to find their sense of identity (Dreger, 1997).

Beyond these few biological differences—differences that theorists identify as sexual differences—humans add many layers to the notions of maleness and femaleness. Much of the behavior we classify as male or female is a cultural construction and is not biologically determined. These socially constructed attributes of maleness or femaleness are often referred to as *gender* (Worell & Remer, 2003). In some cultures, it is considered feminine to be emotionally needy and unstable. In others, it is considered feminine to be stoic, centered, and the source of stability for the family. Some cultures prefer their males to be physically aggressive. Others may value intellectual skills as indicators of maleness. Determining just what is biological and what is socially constructed has been the goal of many research projects and the source of much controversy (Unger, 2001). In fact, biologist Ruth Bleir (1984, 1988), after years of examining this issue, has concluded that there is "no firm evidence for a biological basis of behavioral differences between females and males" (Worell & Remer, 2003, p. 14). Regardless of exactly where the division might lie, feminist theory rejects the notion that biology is destiny and holds suspect most claims of innate male-female behavioral differences, especially when such differences are used to exclude or devalue individuals on the basis of sex or gender.

Questions for Reflection

What do you think of Bleir's claim that there are no clear biologically based behavioral differences between males and females? Can you think of any differences that you would clearly attribute to biology rather than to psychosocial influences? If you dare, discuss these possible differences with your classmates.

Feminist theorists realize the enormous power of this biological and cultural division between humans. "Difference is the velvet glove on the iron fist of domination. This is as true when differences are affirmed as when they are denied" (MacKinnon, 1987, p. 8). As Mitchell (1966) explained,

> The situation of women is different from that of any other social group. This is because they are not one of a number of isolable units, but half a totality: the human species. Women are essential and irreplaceable: they cannot therefore be exploited in the same way as other groups can. They are fundamental to the human condition, yet in their economic, social and political roles, they are marginal. It is precisely this combination—fundamental and marginal at one and the same time—that has been fatal to them. (p. 18)

Human development theorists believe that the first self-defining division we make as a developing infant is between that of ourselves and our primary caretaker. At some point in early infancy, the baby determines that she and mommy are *not* one entity (Mahler & Pine, 1975). The second, equally informative and identity-delineating division is that of our sexual designation. Researchers believe that as early as 18 months, many toddlers have absorbed their sexual identity—whether they are regarded as boys or girls—and have begun selectively processing information accordingly. Psychoanalytically oriented theorists have explored the effects of this early self-identification from Freud forward, with feminists adding important dimensions to consider, such as the effects of children raised almost exclusively by one parent (e.g., Chodorow, 1978).

This drive to fit with one's sexually identified group opens the door for culture to step in and offer the developing human all sorts of potentially useful and potentially harmful guidance. From religious instruction to Saturday morning cartoons, from the lyrics of popular music to the examples that parents offer, young people are shaped toward expressing their gender according to cultural rules (Powlishta, Sen, Serbin, Poulin-Dubois, & Eichstedt, 2001). For example, advertising aimed at children takes advantage of this avid seeking of identity. "Girl" ads are soft, pastel, nurturing, and relationship-oriented. "Boy" ads are loud and active and often feature competition or cleverness as a main theme (Gilbert & Scher, 1999).

No matter what you believe about the relative contributions of biology and environment, sexual identity is a powerful defining feature of our overall human identity. Some argue that feminist work must deconstruct these cultural concepts of male and female because of the blinders they create, the limits they set, and the damage they do (Cosgrove, 2002). These theorists argue that we need to focus more on the ways men and women are in fact similar and also to allow the diversity *among* women to be respected and emphasized, rather than allowing the concept of gender to define what it means to be male or female. This is in keeping with what Gilbert and Scher (1999) dubbed the *iron rule,* which states that "for any psychological or cognitive variable studied by psychologists, the differences within each sex are always greater than the differences between the two sexes" (p. 37).

Questions for Reflection

Do you think the saying "Boys will be boys" provides an excuse for certain behaviors? Perpetuates myths? Is simply explanatory?

Principle II: The Dominant Culture is Damaging to Those Who Don't Fit the Mold

The second principle guiding feminist therapists is this: A great deal of human suffering and distress is directly attributable to inequities suffered by women and others who were not born into the White, male, privileged class in North America and Western Europe. Because male has been considered normative, anything not male is in danger of being considered abnormal. The pioneering work of Sandra Bem (1974) and others has given us a glimpse into this phenomenon. Adjectives seen as describing males are also adjectives used to describe psychologically healthy adults. Feminine adjectives are far more often labeled as deviant or troublesome. Broverman, Broverman, Clarkson, Rosenkrantz, and Vogel (1970) conducted a pivotal study that asked counselors and therapists to identify healthy males, healthy females, and healthy adults. The healthy adult (no sex specified) and the healthy male were described almost exactly the same. The healthy female was described as more childlike, less independent, and less rational.

In the *Diagnostic and Statistical Manual of Mental Disorders–Fourth Edition* (*DSM-IV*), character disorders listed in Axis II are descriptions of human personality tendencies taken to the extreme. Many stereotypically feminine tendencies can be identified in these so-called disorders such as dependent personality disorder, histrionic personality disorder, and borderline personality disorder. Stereotypically masculine attributes, even if taken to the extreme, are not pathologized to the same extent. If you think about it, you probably know people who might qualify for labels (if they existed) such as independent personality disorder, empathy-deficiency disorder, or thrill-seeking disorder. Narcissistic Personality Disorder *is* diagnosed more often in men, as is, unfortunately for all of us, Antisocial Personality Disorder. People diagnosed with most Axis II personality disorders end up in counseling or even inpatient psychiatric treatment. However, having an Antisocial Personality Disorder, especially when paired with bad luck, often results in prison terms. Some argue that absent the bad luck and with a little added intellect, these same symptoms lead to great monetary or political success in many contemporary cultures.

Whereas it is clear that society damages those who do not fit the mold, it is also true that those stuck in the mold pay a price as well. Many problems faced by men, such as homophobia, aggression, workaholism, and the inability to relate to women, children, or even their own emotional selves, are by-products of male socialization (Levant & Pollack, 1995). The painful costs of the devaluation of all things feminine and the strict rules for being male are evidenced in William Pollack's (2000) book, *Real Boys' Voices.* Scotty, a 13-year-old boy from a small town in the Northeast, said, "Boys are supposed to shut up and take it, to keep it all in. It's harder for them to release or vent without feeling girly. And that can drive them to shoot themselves" (p. ix).

Most of us have at least one experience of being teased or limited because of behaviors that those around us judged as wrong for our gender. Gender definitions are rigid and constraining. Because of the strong emphasis in our culture on the individual, any individual who is unable to conform to these constraints is likely to think something is wrong with her rather that something being wrong with the constraints (Kaschak, 1992).

Questions for Reflection

Think about ways you personally have not fit your "gender" mold. Is it hard to admit? Something you feel proud of? Puzzled by? Have you gained or lost by not fitting? Have you been harassed or valued for being gender-diverse?

Principle III: Consciousness Is Part of Healing and Change

The third principle feminist therapists incorporate into their work is the belief that clients must recognize the culturally inflicted damage they are carrying to begin to heal and change. Similar to the psychoanalytic belief in the power of insight, feminist therapists believe that becoming conscious of all the ways the culture uses, hurts, and limits women simply because they are women is central to healing and empowerment. Changing oneself to be happy by accommodating to one's inferior status is anathema to feminist therapy, although this goal is still subtly present in many other forms of therapy.

The familiar feminist saying that the personal is political is fundamental to feminist therapy. Social transformation is as important as personal transformation (Funkerburk & Fukuyama, 2001), and the authentic experience of the latter should lead to the former. One measure of success in feminist therapy might be increased social interest and awareness—an optimistic desire to change the world for the better—an outcome with which Adlerians would certainly agree. As stated by Worell and Remer (2003),

> Overall, our feminist psychological practice approach seeks a dual outcome: assisting women toward empowerment in their own lives and seeking change in whatever social power structures form the basis of many of their problems. (p. 18)

The first logical place for such consciousness raising to occur is in the therapy relationship itself. Therefore, the therapy relationship must not reenact the damaging hierarchical practices present in the dominant culture. Clients must be respected as equal partners in the exploring and healing processes entailed in counseling (Brody, 1984; Bruns & Trimble, 2001). Their backgrounds, cultural practices, beliefs, and specific needs must be taken into account, and their pace and needs respected. The counselor must be a skilled listener and helper, exercising authority while at the same time encouraging and welcoming the client to exercise her own authority as well. In the case example described in the section titled "Feminist Therapy in Action," you will see the counselor attempting to strike this delicate balance.

To give you an example of how consciousness raising might manifest in therapy, imagine a woman coming for counseling because she feels chronically tired, sad, and frustrated in her attempts to balance her career and family demands. A feminist therapist will gently explore the various demands, the self-imposed and other-imposed messages of what matters and how to prioritize. In addition, assuming that there is evidence suggesting a need for education in this area, the feminist therapist may provide her client with research information about dual-career couples in our culture.

Research shows that male partners still report feeling entitled to do less at home than their spouse does, no matter who works more hours or earns more money outside the home. Further, many women agree with their spouses in this assessment (Gilbert & Rader, 2001). This personal entitlement that men feel is situated in the culture—it is a social norm. Further, when women try to understand their frustrations, they often compare themselves to other women, rather than comparing themselves to their own spouses. Therefore, women might decide that even though they're doing more work at home than their husbands are, this is fair because men's jobs are more important (Steil, 1997) or because other women have even less cooperative spouses, so they should count themselves lucky. If this were the case with a given client, research findings such as these may cast a whole new light on the burdens she is carrying and on how society has contributed to these burdens.

From there, the client may feel empowered to initiate a constructive dialogue with her spouse about their respective family duties. Further, she may speak with other women in similar situations, providing them with information and support to ask for a fairer distribution of family and housework. Feminist therapists would see such an outcome as therapeutic for both the woman in question and for our evolving culture.

THE PRACTICE OF FEMINIST THERAPY

Claiming that you practice feminist therapy can be a daunting task. Understanding that feminist theory and therapy are inclusive and compatible with other approaches can make it easier to claim your feminist perspective. In Practitioner Commentary 10.1, Susan Simonds, PhD, discusses how she came to develop her own eclectic, feminist approach.

PRACTITIONER COMMENTARY 10.1

Finding My Own Eclectic Feminist Theory

The following commentary articulates Susan Simonds's personal evolution as an eclectically oriented feminist.

I became a psychotherapist 20 years ago. My first graduate program was based in a medical school and was very psychoanalytically oriented. I was already a feminist, yet I found nothing women-sensitive in that program, although my entire class was made up of women. During a lecture about penis envy as the source of women's identity, I got so angry that I disrupted the class and was reprimanded by my professor (a man). At that time (1979), there was only one book about the psychology of women (Jean Baker Miller's *New Psychology of Women*). I spent years searching for a theory that fit me. When I worked with sexual trauma survivors, I discovered constructivist self-development theory (CSDT; McCann & Pearlman, 1990; Pearlman & Saakvitne, 1995), which is an integrative model developed for working with trauma survivors. Other important influences were Judith Herman's (1992) three-phase model of trauma treatment, Lillian Comaz-Diaz's (1994) integrative approach, and the Stone Center's relational model, which is a feminist theory of development and of therapy (Jordan et al., 1991). As I grew as a therapist, I incorporated pieces of CSDT, relational theory, and feminist theory. I am a very practical person as well as a rather intense person, and in my own life I found that mindfulness in meditation and mindfulness in daily life were incredibly helpful. I began to use mindfulness with my clients along with the other theories I mentioned. Then I decided that I had created my own integrative model of therapy, which I called integrative relational therapy (Simonds, 2001), or IRT. I developed this model in my work with depressed women. I had not found any treatment models for depression that incorporated the same level of complexity, flexibility, and compassion that I had found in CSDT and the Stone Center's relational model. I developed a model that is simple, yet complex, and integrates all of the above theories as well as practical strategies that are grounded in the research in depression treatment. When I first started to talk about my own model in professional seminars, I found it hard to say "integrative relational therapy" out loud. My mouth stumbled over the words. I was having a hard time feeling smart or important enough to have my own theory. Who was I to have a theory? It was a several-year process of owning my own power and being able to grow into being a psychologist who has her own theory. One of the things that helped me was giving lots of seminars and saying the words out loud over and over to a room full of people. Another thing that helped move me along was reading several journal articles in which psychologists named their own theories. When I read the credentials of these authors (all men, by the way), I realized that my credentials were just as solid. So now I am a psychologist who can proudly and comfortably say, "I have my own theoretical model, integrative relational therapy."

Preparing Yourself to Do Therapy from a Feminist Perspective

Authentically living and practicing what you believe is a lifelong challenge—and a goal that most of us only approximate. Living consciously as a feminist in our culture isn't easy. To do so flies in the face of thousands of years of overt subjugation of women. Admittedly, it is rare to find anyone in our dominant culture who would claim that someone should have life choices limited simply due to the sex she was born. Most would agree that all humans deserve equal opportunities to develop, achieve, and express themselves. By our loose and inclusive definition, most people would thus be feminists, although it is likely that many would eschew the label or at least feel very uncomfortable being called a feminist. This is because the term *feminism* has taken on significant baggage over the years and suffered a fair amount of derogation and, as Faludi (1991) calls it, backlash by those resistant to a change in the existing power structure. In the extreme, feminists are seen as man haters who are destroying the fabric of family life and society itself.

Questions for Reflection

Why is change that results in equal opportunities for people resisted? Who benefits from the status quo, and who gains from derogating a more equal role for women in the fabric of society?

Practicing as a feminist therapist is different from using portions of feminist theory to inform your work. Even an avowed nonfeminist might use certain strategies or seek certain outcomes associated with feminist therapy. However, if you believe the following three statements, then being a feminist therapist is an option for you.

- Gender stereotypes and limits are responsible for psychological damage and human suffering for both men and women.
- Gender stereotypes and limits must be changed at the societal level and must be constantly questioned at the personal level.
- Clients benefit when they recognize the damage and limits they've endured from cultural sexism, begin healing through conscious awareness, and become involved in changing things for themselves and other women in whatever measure is realistic.

Another way to glimpse, in a more operational sense, what it might mean to be a feminist therapist is apparent in the following eight tenets of feminist psychology from Worell and Remer's (2003) text, *Feminist Perspectives in Therapy: Empowering Diverse Women:*

1. *We advocate inclusiveness.* We acknowledge that the social impact of gender is experienced unequally and unfairly for women with diverse personal and social identities, including ethnicity and culture, sexual and affectional orientation, socioeconomic status, nationality, age, and physical characteristics.
2. *We advocate equality.* We recognize that the politics of gender are reflected in lower social status and unequal access to valued resources for a majority of women in most societies.

3. *We seek new knowledge.* We value and advocate increased understanding about the diversity of women's experience as it is framed by multiple personal and social identities.

4. *We attend to context.* Women's lives are embedded in the social, economic, and political contexts of their lives and should not be studied in isolation.

5. *We acknowledge values.* Personal and social values enter into all human enterprises; education, science, practice, and social advocacy are never value-free.

6. *We advocate change.* We are committed to action to accomplish social, economic, and political change toward establishing equal justice for all persons.

7. *We attend to process.* Decision-making processes that affect personal and group outcomes should be consensual and consistent with feminist principles of mutual respect and honoring all voices.

8. *We expand psychological practice.* We recognize that feminist principles can be applied to all professional activities in which we engage: theory building, prevention, counseling and therapy, assessment, pedagogy, curriculum development, research, supervision, leadership, and professional training (p. 18).

Becoming a feminist therapist is a developmental process (Bruns & Trimble, 2001). There are few if any specific techniques to master, but rather philosophical and relational principals and concepts to embody and enact. One crucial ingredient for beginning therapists is finding a feminist supervisor and mentor (see Putting It in Practice 10.2). There are important ethical aspects that most feminists believe are important as well (see Ethical Highlight 10.1).

Putting It in Practice 10.2

How in the World Do You Find a Real Live Feminist Supervisor?

Getting exciting, growth-producing supervision is an important part of becoming a mature professional. But can you just go around asking people if they are feminist to get the supervision you want? Of course you can.

Feminism means different things to different people, and being a feminist is a developmental process. You may or may not find a supervisor in your local area who has developed her (or his) feminism enough to have what you want. You may want to join organizations with national and international membership, or at least to attend their professional meetings. The American Psychological Association's (APA) Divisions 35, (Psychology of Women) and 17 (Counseling Psychology's section on women) are devoted to the specific needs and concerns of women, and since 1978 the APA has published guidelines for working with women that are in keeping with the provision of professional, ethical feminist therapy. There are other national and international collectives and professional organizations such as the Feminist Therapy Institute (www.feministtherapyinstitute.org) and the Association for Women in Psychology (www.theworks.baka.com/awp). You might want to do further reading about how feminist supervision varies from other forms of supervision. We provide reading suggestions at the end of this chapter.

Preparing Your Client for Feminist Therapy

As stressed in the first chapter, we firmly believe that clients have the right to know their counselors' educational background, theoretical orientations, and other important policies and practices. Informed consent is an essential component of a healthy therapeutic relationship. A feminist therapy orientation is easily the most politically charged of all the theoretical orientations covered in this text. Can feminist therapists work successfully with those who find feminism offensive, wrong-headed, or even evil? Believe it or not, our answer is a firm "sometimes." How can this be?

A sample explanation of a feminist orientation is provided in Putting It in Practice 10.3.

The process of informed consent goes beyond a written document. It is an important part of your interactions with clients. Because they believe the therapy relationship is a partnership, feminist therapists engage in ongoing informed consent. They let clients know why they suggest certain activities, homework, or topic areas. They check

---

=== **Putting It in Practice 10.3** ===

Aspects of a Feminist Informed Consent

Mental health professionals work from different theoretical perspectives. That is, they have different beliefs about what hurts, limits, or damages people and what it takes to heal or change. My own perspectives will influence the ways I will work with you. . . .

As a feminist, I believe that both women and men deserve equal chances for jobs, recreation, and other things that make life meaningful. I believe that our gender matters a great deal to us and can sometimes get in the way of our development. I also believe our culture can make things tough on men or women because of how narrowly we've defined these terms. Often, people find that exploring gender issues makes a big difference in the ways they feel about themselves. What does this mean in my work with you?

First, it is important for you to know this: I will not try to change your beliefs. I will respect our differences.

Second, we will be partners in our work together. You are the expert on you, and I hope that I can offer my education and experiences as you work on the issues that are bringing you to counseling.

Third, sometimes as we explore the distress you're feeling in your life, we may talk about social and cultural forces outside of yourself that are increasing your distress. We may also talk about how you've come to believe unhelpful messages given to you by our culture.

Fourth, because therapy is about you and your life, we will focus on what you can do, what you can think or believe, and how you can act to help you feel better about yourself and your life situation. Sometimes this will involve changing the way you think or other things inside yourself. Other times it will involve changing your life situation or learning to deal with your life situation more assertively.

Fifth, the overarching goal of therapy is to empower you as a person.

in on the therapy relationship frequently to ensure that they respect client questions and wishes. Consider the following exchange:

C: It says here in your paperwork that you're a feminist. I didn't know that when I made the appointment.

T: Yes, it is important for us to consider that part of my professional identity. Probably some other parts too.

C: Well, I don't know if I would have come in if I'd known this.

T: Sounds like you're pretty unsure about working with someone like me who says she's a feminist.

C: Yes, I am. And I only have six visits total with my managed care.

T: Yeah, I can see why this would feel bad. How about this? Let's explore what I mean in my paperwork, and let's explore what brought you in, and if you feel it would be better to work with someone else, I won't turn this session in to your company.

C: Wow, really? I mean, yes. I guess that would be okay. Thanks.

T: What happened inside you when you read that informed consent?

C: Well, I'm not comfortable with gays and I think women need to raise their children at home, and I know it isn't good for animal testing and all, but I like wearing make-up and I respect my husband, at least when he's sober [client gets a little emotional].

T: You know, I can tell you've got a lot on your mind, both from what you filled out and the way you just said that. I want to assure you about a couple things and then hear more about what's troubling you. Would that be okay?

C: Yeah. Sorry. I'm pretty strung out.

T: That's okay. You've made a good choice to get some help. I just want you to know that my counseling work is all about you, not all about me. I don't need to change you at all. I just want to help you change in the ways you think are best for you. We don't need to talk about gays. I don't have any hard and fast rules about the ways women should dress or raise kids or anything. I just believe women deserve a fair shake, on their own terms. But I don't push it. I mostly listen and reflect things back to you.

C: But I like men, and I think they deserve our support working and all. My dad worked himself to death, basically. [Client gets teary again.]

T: So far, I don't think we really disagree in ways that will matter in our work together, but I'm sure open to talking about it some more. And I can see that your dad meant a lot to you. [Therapist makes two statements, giving her client the choice to respond to further concerns about the feminist orientation or to move into some of what is troubling her.]

C: He was my savior. That's why I got together with my husband. They seemed so much alike. Boy, was I ever wrong. That's why I have to get some help. I need some perspective or something. I guess I want to just get on with talking about it. It's okay what you believe as long as you're not going to push it or judge me. I've got to talk about it, or I'm going to just up and leave him.

T: Okay. Seems really important to let you get some things talked through today. But anytime you feel worried about what I'm thinking, or if you feel like I'm pushing some kind of agenda, will you tell me?

C: Yeah. I think so.

From this interaction, it's possible to see how a solidly feminist therapist might hold real appeal for clients who may not ever envision becoming feminists themselves. The fact is that, for clients, feeling empowered and respected is an appealing experience. However, an honest, careful exchange is both necessary and in keeping with ethical client preparation.

Assessment Issues and Procedures

Understanding personal and social power is an overarching concern in feminist therapy. For an eloquent statement to this effect, take a look at the code of ethics from the Feminist Therapy Institute in Ethical Highlight 10.1. During intake, feminists pay close attention to context and listen carefully for evidence of oppression, abuse, and under-developed sense of self. Feminist therapists minimize the use of terms such as mental disease and disorder and focus instead on conceptualizing what they hear as problems or difficulties faced by the client. This is not to say that feminist therapists don't ever diagnose; when they do, however, they are likely to see the causative factors for the diagnosis as being an interaction between culturally imposed damage and (possibly uninformed) choices made by the client.

Issues that most feminist therapists will assess, either directly or indirectly, are described next. It is important to note that feminist therapists are careful to balance their assessment and goal setting in ways that allow clients to recognize strengths and past coping successes as well as areas needing change (Santos de Barona, 1997).

Self-Esteem of the Client

Feminists are aware that women have been and continue to be socialized to measure their worth by the desirability of the men they're with or by the number of people they nurture (Rodman Aronson & Schaler Bucholz, 2001). Mating and nurturing are important to all human beings. However, these two human accomplishments are not necessarily enough for adult fulfillment. Further, a woman might have gone on and found other means to bolster her self-esteem, but she may have done so at great cost. In 1986 Jean Baker Miller wrote,

> Some women have managed to create other roles for themselves to contribute to their self-esteem. But a woman who has done so has violated a dominant system of values that says she is not worthy: indeed, it implies there must be something wrong with her for even wanting alternatives. (p. 45)

It would be nice to believe that things had changed significantly since Miller wrote those words, but the clinical experience of many feminist therapists would argue otherwise (Wright, 2002).

Gender-Role Comfort and Level of Development

Women have been encouraged to limit their personal development. They've been encouraged, instead, to seek a male to provide income and identity and see themselves as adjunct to male needs, careers, and achievements. Many women seek counseling and support when the marriage explodes, the Cinderella story goes bad, the children don't need them anymore, or, for whatever reasons, they've outgrown their worlds and don't know what's making life seem so meaningless. Feminist therapists are alert for signs of these gender-role constraints and developmental arrests.

Gender-Based Communication Difficulties

Did you know that the average woman says "I'm sorry" significantly more often than does the average man in our culture (Tannen, 1990)? Further, when women use that phrase, they often mean something different from what a man might mean when he says it. There are many other documented gender-based differences in communication styles. Many women are socialized to be submissive, indirect, and other-oriented (Lips, 1999). For many years, assertiveness training has been a significant educational aspect of feminist therapy. Women are helped to find their voice, speak up, and make sure they are understood. On the other hand, Tannen (1990) notes, "if women's and men's styles are shown to be different, it is usually women who are told to change" (p. 15).

It may be that assertiveness is not the only answer to gender-based communication problems. Certainly, the inability to communicate comfortably, directly, and assertively can leave people feeling frustrated and ineffective in the dominant culture of the United States. However, many cultures do not share our preference for direct, assertive communication. In Japanese culture, being indirect is considered appropriate, and the Japanese have refined the skill to a fine art. Perhaps the real need is for men to take a few less-assertiveness classes. The need for education and enlightenment in this area is especially easy to observe. For instance, speakers of either sex are rated as more likable and influential if they adopt a competent style as opposed to a dominant style. However, men tended to rate women who were speaking in a competent style as less likable, more threatening, and less influential than men using the same style (Carli, LaFleur, & Loeber, 1995).

Questions for Reflection

What gender differences have you noticed in communication style and content? Can you think of mental health implications for these differences? Can you imagine changes that would involve joint, or shared, responsibility between the sexes?

Issues in Intimacy and Body

Female sexuality is still, amazingly, less well-understood than male sexuality. As noted in a recent article titled "Female Sexual Disorders: Psychiatric Aspects," the author says simply and without apology, "Knowledge of female sexuality has consistently lagged behind our knowledge of male sexuality" (Segraves, 2002, p. 420). Many women do not understand their own bodies well and feel guilty and confused, unable to express their sexual needs in their intimate relationships. The female orgasm has been the subject of many books and much lively debate, from at least Sigmund Freud forward. Part of the women's movement in the 1960s focused on women's reclaiming their bodies. Unfortunately, the reclamation doesn't yet appear to be complete. In fact, eating disorders (e.g., Fallon, Katzman, & Wooley, 1994), obesity, sexual dysfunctions, and other body-related distresses are quite common among women (Tavris, 1998). Many women who come to counseling have experienced sexual abuse or rape. They may or may not focus on this trauma, but such experiences are quite likely to have negative effects on overall psychological well-being and current attempts at satisfying intimate relationships.

Further, feminist therapists will be aware of the damages done by homophobia in our culture. Celia Kitzinger (2001) writes,

The classic models of lifespan development, interpersonal attraction, relationship formation and dissolution, parenting, personality, stress and coping, and so on are based on an
unacknowledged assumption of heterosexuality just as surely as they are based on sexist
assumptions of masculinity and femininity. (p. 275)

Concluding Comments about Feminist Assessment

Feminist therapists are familiar with most standard assessment procedures and de-
vices. However, if used, standardized assessment results are interpreted carefully;
women and persons from other cultures might score in patterns that could be interpreted as disorders or pathology but in fact could also be seen as deviating from the
dominant cultural norms in ways that reflect the cost of differing, rather than true
pathology. Feminist therapists are careful to include cultural and contextual information in their case formulation; more important, they include the client herself in active
self-assessment (Worell & Remer, 2003).

APPLICATION: CASE EXAMPLE

Feminist therapy is technically eclectic. This means that feminist therapists use strategies and techniques originating in many other theories—techniques that have been
shown to be generally effective in the counseling process. However, the underlying goals
of feminist therapy are not eclectic. They include

- Helping clients see the patterns and social forces that have diminished their sense
  of power and control
- Encouraging clients to reclaim power and authority in the direction of their lives
- Allowing clients to experience this shared power in the therapy relationship

There are many practicing and publishing feminist therapists. In this section we
summarize the highlights of an unscripted demonstration videotape featuring Laura S.
Brown, PhD, working in her third session with a client named Ellen (Brown, 1994). The
client-therapist interactions below are paraphrased rather than verbatim.

Ellen is a 34-year-old client mandated to engage in counseling because of her drug
problem. Four important themes show themselves throughout the session:

1. Defining the therapy relationship and allowing it to grow
2. Encouraging emotional awareness
3. Gently exploring a past trauma
4. Highlighting the role Ellen's gender has played in her life situation and problem

Dr. Brown begins by asking a general question about how Ellen's week was, and
Ellen responds in a very upbeat fashion. Paraphrased excerpts follow:

Dr. Brown: What's been happening emotionally?
Ellen: Um, well, I've been excited and nervous. Lots of job interviews. I want to
find something because I don't like to not be busy.
Dr. Brown: And when you're not busy?
Ellen: I'm just happier when I'm busy. My family isn't much for, you know, just

sitting around. I'm not big on introspection, really. We just didn't just ask each other how we felt and stuff in my family.

Dr. Brown: So what's it like to be starting this process with me?

Ellen: Well, it's not like I had a big choice. I mean you're okay, good listener and all, but my family just doesn't do this. We weren't processors, so it isn't natural for me.

In this short exchange, we can see Dr. Brown focusing on Ellen's emotions, carefully asking about the busyness and what is under that. Ellen responds by hedging some, assuring Dr. Brown that she finds Dr. Brown to be a nice enough person but indicating that this really isn't natural, nor is it her (Ellen's) choice to be here. Dr. Brown doesn't challenge Ellen, but instead the session moves on in an accepting, conversational way.

Ellen explains that she went to a Narcotics Anonymous (NA) meeting in Baltimore, and Dr. Brown lifts her eyebrows, saying "Baltimore?" in a surprised tone. Ellen acknowledges that it is quite a distance from her home, but she doesn't want to be seen by anyone who might know her locally. This leads to a gentle inquiry: "Ellen, what will people see if they see the real Ellen?"

Ellen defends herself against this question, talking for a while about clothes, jewelry, and the desire she believes everyone shares to stay hidden. Dr. Brown stays on the theme, asking about what dark secrets Ellen fears that people might see, and Ellen talks about her drug use and her feelings that the use is her own business, not something people need to know about or judge her on. She makes the claim that it really hasn't interfered with her life, but catches herself, just as Dr. Brown says, with warmth, "Wait a minute. What's wrong with this picture?"

Ellen admits that her drug use did cause a slight problem, in that she lost her job and has to go to counseling, but she denies most of the problem. Rather than going after the denial, Dr. Brown comments gently:

Dr. Brown: How things look is very important to you, and it is very hard for you to keep it up. It's very tiring.

Ellen: Yes, I work hard at how I look. And I'm not saying it isn't tiring.

Dr. Brown: Let yourself notice the tiredness. Don't talk about it. Just notice your body and how tired it is in there. Feel how hard it is to keep that pretty picture in place.

Ellen complies, with Dr. Brown's guiding encouragement. She relaxes her body and is quiet, while Dr. Brown encourages her to keep relaxing. Ellen actually lets herself tear up a little bit. She is able to talk about how hard she tries and how much she wishes her father would be proud of her. She spontaneously explores her father's gender messages—either be a lawyer like him or a wife and mother. Ellen explains that she can't do either. She faces how alone that makes her feel. Dr. Brown asks a strategic question: "Ellen, when did you get yourself to be at peace that you're father will never, ever say he's proud of you, no matter what you do?" Ellen admits that though her father will never say that, she *isn't* at peace about it and at 34 is still letting that wish drive her life. Together, for a short time, Dr. Brown and Ellen explore how alone she is and how no one has ever really taken care of her much. At this point, Dr. Brown tells Ellen she would like to revisit something Ellen mentioned last session—the fact that when Ellen was in college, someone she knew broke into her apartment and raped her.

Ellen: Yeah, I don't think there's that much to talk about. It was college. I was trying things out, you know. Freedom. Being an adult. Lots of sex and stuff. I was giving it away for free anyway, so I didn't think there was much to do. I told my brother later. He said I should tell the police and see a psychologist, but I didn't. I mean I sort of chose that life. I thought, hey, if guys can sow their wild oats, so can I. So I was pretty out there. I tried it all. No inhibitions. I guess the drugs aided that. I can say that back then, I really was a drug addict.

Dr. Brown: So, you felt like, I can do this. It's my choice, and if it hurts or feels bad, it's my own fault?

Ellen: Yeah, I chose it. That's how I feel about the rape, I guess. I don't know.

Dr. Brown: Ellen, what's your body saying as you say, "I don't know"?

Ellen: It's tired . . . I didn't stand up for my own body. It's a little sad. But I can't go back now and change it.

Dr. Brown: No, but we can explore how that experience might be affecting things now—how being an adult, sexual woman is for you now. What do you wish would have happened?

Ellen tearfully admits her wish that someone might have helped her, been there for her. She condemns herself as well, claiming that she should have handled it, wishing she had fought her assailant but noting that her drug-induced state made that unlikely. She ends with a sort of wistful statement: "I wish someone would have been there, but there wasn't anyone. So I dealt with it."

Dr. Brown: Ain't that the story of life?

Ellen: [In a surprised tone] Yeah, that's true. I guess I could have told Aunt Alisha, but I didn't want to burden her.

Dr. Brown: Is it gonna be okay to burden me? How scared are you that I'll bail out on you?

Ellen: Well, you can't do that, can you? And ultimately this will end anyway. You're not always gonna be there.

Dr. Brown: That's true. This will end when you want it to.

Ellen: That's not what I understood from the court.

Dr. Brown: Yeah, but after the court thing is taken care of, it'll be up to you.

As the session ends, Dr. Brown asks Ellen to consider doing two things during the week: going to one more NA meeting and using her art, either in writing or painting, to explore the question: What does Ellen want? Ellen agrees, saying that she has neglected her painting. Smiling, Ellen also says that the painting will have to be a Monet, because she only has impressions, but no clarity. Dr. Brown counters with support and the observation that even a Monet, from the right position, is clear. Ellen acts surprised and pleased. Dr. Brown ends the session focusing on scheduling for next week, indicating that she expects Ellen to come but making it clear that the schedule has flexibility.

Commentary. The importance of the therapy relationships is woven throughout these vignettes. Dr. Brown uses a number of opportunities to explore how Ellen feels about being there, about sharing herself openly, about fears of being a burden or being dumped. She also affirms the fact that Ellen does have some choice about this process, even if the beginning of therapy is court-ordered. She works with Ellen on the rape she disclosed in passing last session and certainly will work further with this traumatic experience.

At the conclusion of the tape, Dr. Brown reflects on the session. Her goals for Ellen were to help the relationship develop and encourage Ellen to listen to her emotional self, which Dr. Brown explains to be especially important with women who have used substances to numb emotions after traumatic experiences. She also notes her intention to begin exploring gender issues and how Ellen constructs herself as an adult woman. Dr. Brown notes, however, that she never "hits clients over the head with it." Rather, she pairs it with what matters to them, helping them see their lives with new lenses.

Dr. Brown explained that she would be attentive to what it means to be a woman in a care-taking role in Ellen's life. There is a real need to find balance between helping Ellen respect herself as an adult decision maker and not leaving her hanging out there, as she's been hung out alone all her life. In Ellen's case, as in many, it is important for the client to know that she will not be abandoned, judged, or overpowered as she begins to explore her pain and seek ways to make changes (adapted from Brown, 1994).

THERAPY OUTCOMES RESEARCH

Does feminist therapy accomplish what it intends to accomplish? How would that be measured? Traditional measures of therapy efficacy focus on the elimination or reduction of the symptoms or problems that brought the client to counseling. Feminist therapists believe that the root causes of many difficulties lie within the patriarchal, oppressive culture of the client, and they work to help raise their clients' consciousness in this important area. Unfortunately, becoming conscious of the damaging aspects of our external world may not change the world or make the difficulties go away. However, as a result of feminist therapy, clients may gradually (or sometimes rapidly)

- Change the ways they view their world
- Reclaim and use their personal power
- Grow and develop in ways that had been stymied
- Relate to others in more productive, fulfilling ways

In an effort to establish a relevant measure of feminist therapy outcomes, J. Worell and Chandler (1996) developed a scale to measure client empowerment. Based on early research with this instrument, it appears that clients who experience feminist therapy tend to report a greater sense of empowerment or resilience—possibly as a function of the therapy (Chandler, Worell, Johnson, Blount, & Lusk, 1999).

Although there has been little systematic research focusing directly on the efficacy of feminist therapy, J. Worell and Johnson (2003) are optimistic in their summary of the existing research:

> These preliminary studies on measuring process and outcomes in feminist therapy are suggestive and encouraging. They suggest that feminist therapy, when articulated in a structured and clearly defined model, is a unique and measurable form of intervention that provides positive outcomes for women in personal distress. (p. 327)

Prochaska and Norcross (2003) come to a similar conclusion in their brief review of the efficacy of feminist therapy. Although they report that no significant changes are typically found on standardized measures of symptom reduction when feminist therapy is investigated, they also note this important finding:

A Code of Ethics for Feminists

A well-written code of ethics provides the essential definition of a given endeavor or profession (R. Sommers-Flanagan, 2001). We include the entire Feminist Therapy Code of Ethics because it serves as an eloquent summary of this chapter. We have little doubt that many ethical questions are raised for you as you read about and contemplate feminist theory and therapy, and we hope that you'll take time to consider each in some depth.

FEMINIST THERAPY INSTITUTE'S CODE OF ETHICS*
REVISED, 1999

Preamble

Feminist therapy evolved from feminist philosophy, psychological theory and practice, and political theory. In particular feminists recognize the impact of society in creating and maintaining the problems and issues brought into therapy. Briefly, feminists believe the personal is political. Basic tenets of feminism include a belief in the equal worth of all human beings, a recognition that each individual's personal experiences and situations are reflective of and an influence on society's institutionalized attitudes and values, and a commitment to political and social change that equalizes power among people. Feminists are committed to recognizing and reducing the pervasive influences and insidious effects of oppressive societal attitudes and society. Thus, a feminist analysis addresses the understanding of power and its interconnections among gender, race, culture, class, physical ability, sexual orientation, age, and antisemitism as well as all forms of oppression based on religion, ethnicity, and heritage. Feminist therapists also live in and are subject to those same influences and effects and consistently monitor their beliefs and behaviors as a result of those influences. Feminist therapists adhere to and integrate feminist analyses in all spheres of their work as therapists, educators, consultants, administrators, writers, editors, and/or researchers. Feminist therapists are accountable for the management of the power differential within these roles and accept responsibility for that power. Because of the limitations of a purely intrapsychic model of human functioning, feminist therapists facilitate the understanding of the interactive effects of the client's internal and external worlds. Feminist therapists possess knowledge about the psychology of women and girls and utilize feminist scholarship to revise theories and practices, incorporating new knowledge as it is generated.

Feminist therapists are trained in a variety of disciplines, theoretical orientations, and degrees of structure. They come from different cultural, economic, ethnic, and racial backgrounds. They work in many types of settings with a diversity of clients and practice different modalities of therapy, training, and research. Feminist therapy theory integrates feminist principles into other theories of human development and change.

The ethical guidelines that follow are additive to, rather than a replacement for, the ethical principles of the profession in which a feminist therapist practices. Amid this diversity, feminist therapists are joined together by their feminist analyses and perspectives. Additionally, they work toward incorporating feminist principles into existing professional standards when appropriate.

Feminist therapists live with and practice in competing forces and complex controlling interests. When mental health care involves third-party payers, it is feminist therapists' responsibility to advocate for the best possible therapeutic process for the client, including short or long term therapy. Care and compassion for clients include protection of confidentiality and awareness of the impacts of economic and political considerations, including the increasing disparity between the quality of therapeutic care available for those with or without third-party payers.

Feminist therapists assume a proactive stance toward the eradication of oppression in their lives and work toward empowering women and girls. They are respectful of individual differences, examining oppressive aspects of both their own and clients' value systems. Feminist therapists engage in social change activities, broadly defined, outside of and apart from their work in their professions. Such activities may vary in scope and content but are an essential aspect of a feminist perspective.

This code is a series of positive statements which provide guidelines for feminist therapy practice, training, and research. Feminist therapists who are members of other professional organizations adhere to the ethical codes of those organizations. Feminist therapists who are not members of such organizations are guided by the ethical standards of the organization closest to their mode of practice. These statements provide more specific guidelines within the context of and as an extension of most ethical codes. When ethical guidelines are in conflict, the feminist therapist is accountable for how she prioritizes her choices.

These ethical guidelines, then, are focused on the issues feminist therapists, educators, and researchers have found especially important in their professional settings. As with any code of therapy ethics, the well-being of clients is the guiding principle underlying this code. The feminist therapy issues which relate directly to the client's well-being include cultural diversities and oppressions, power differentials, overlapping relationships, therapist accountability, and social change.

Even though the principles are stated separately, each interfaces with the others to form an interdependent whole. In addition, the code is a living document and thus is continually in the process of change. The Feminist Therapy Institute's Code of Ethics is shaped by economic and cultural forces in North America and by the experiences of its members. Members encourage an ongoing international dialogue about feminist and ethical issues. It recognizes that ethical codes are aspirational and ethical behaviors are on a continuum rather than reflecting dichotomies. Additionally, ethical guidelines and legal requirements may differ. The Feminist Therapy Institute provides educational interventions for its members rather than disciplinary activity.

Ethical Guidelines for Feminist Therapists

I. Cultural Diversities and Oppressions
   A. A feminist therapist increases her accessibility to and for a wide range of clients from her own and other identified groups through flexible delivery of services. When appropriate, the feminist therapist assists clients in accessing other services and intervenes when a client's rights are violated.
   B. A feminist therapist is aware of the meaning and impact of her own ethnic and cultural background, gender, class, age, and sexual orientation, and actively attempts to become knowledgeable about alternatives from sources other than her clients. She is actively engaged in broadening her knowledge of ethnic and cultural experiences, non-dominant and dominant.
   C. Recognizing that the dominant culture determines the norm, the therapist's goal is to uncover and respect cultural and experiential differences, including those based on long term or recent immigration and/or refugee status.

(continued)

    D. A feminist therapist evaluates her ongoing interactions with her clientele for any evidence of her biases or discriminatory attitudes and practices. She also monitors her other interactions, including service delivery, teaching, writing, and all professional activities. The feminist therapist accepts responsibility for taking action to confront and change any interfering, oppressing, or devaluing biases she has.

II. Power Differentials

    A. A feminist therapist acknowledges the inherent power differentials between client and therapist and models effective use of personal, structural, or institutional power. In using the power differential to the benefit of the client, she does not take control or power which rightfully belongs to her client.

    B. A feminist therapist discloses information to the client which facilitates the therapeutic process, including information communicated to others. The therapist is responsible for using self-disclosure only with purpose and discretion and in the interest of the client.

    C. A feminist therapist negotiates and renegotiates formal and/or informal contacts with clients in an ongoing mutual process. As part of the decision-making process, she makes explicit the therapeutic issues involved.

    D. A feminist therapist educates her clients regarding power relationships. She informs clients of their rights as consumers of therapy, including procedures for resolving differences and filing grievances. She clarifies power in its various forms as it exists within other areas of her life, including professional roles, social/governmental structures, and interpersonal relationships. She assists her clients in finding ways to protect themselves and, if requested, to seek redness.

III. Overlapping Relationships

    A. A feminist therapist recognizes the complexity and conflicting priorities inherent in multiple or overlapping relationships. The therapist accepts responsibility for monitoring such relationships to prevent potential abuse of or harm to the client.

    B. A feminist therapist is actively involved in her community. As a result, she is aware of the need for confidentiality in all settings. Recognizing that her client's concerns and general well-being are primary, she self-monitors both public and private statements and comments. Situations may develop through community involvement where power dynamics shift, including a client having equal or more authority than the therapist. In all such situations a feminist therapist maintains accountability.

    C. When accepting third party payments, a feminist therapist is especially cognizant of and clearly communicates to her client the multiple obligations, roles, and responsibilities of the therapist. When working in institutional settings, she clarifies to all involved parties where her allegiances lie. She also monitors multiple and conflicting expectations between clients and caregivers, especially when working with children and elders.

    D. A feminist therapist does not engage in sexual intimacies nor any overtly or covertly sexualized behaviors with a client or former client.

IV. Therapist Accountability

    A. A feminist therapist is accountable to herself, to colleagues, and especially to her clients.

    B. A feminist therapist will contract to work with clients and issues within the realm of her competencies. If problems beyond her competencies surface, the feminist therapist utilizes consultation and available resources. She respects the integrity of the relationship by stating the limits of her training and providing the client with the possibilities of continuing with her or changing therapists.

C. A feminist therapist recognizes her personal and professional needs and utilizes ongoing self-evaluation, peer support, consultation, supervision, continuing education, and/or personal therapy. She evaluates, maintains, and seeks to improve her competencies, as well as her emotional, physical, mental, and spiritual well-being. When the feminist therapist has experienced a similar stressful or damaging event as her client, she seeks consultation.

D. A feminist therapist continually re-evaluates her training, theoretical background, and research to include developments in feminist knowledge. She integrates feminism into psychological theory, receives ongoing therapy training, and acknowledges the limits of her competencies.

E. A feminist therapist engages in self-care activities in an ongoing manner outside the work setting. She recognizes her own needs and vulnerabilities as well as the unique stresses inherent in this work. She demonstrates an ability to establish boundaries with the client that are healthy for both of them. She also is willing to self-nurture in appropriate and self-empowering ways.

V. Social Change

A. A feminist therapist seeks multiple avenues for impacting change, including public education and advocacy within professional organizations, lobbying for legislative actions, and other appropriate activities.

B. A feminist therapist actively questions practices in her community that appear harmful to clients or therapists. She assists clients in intervening on their own behalf. As appropriate, the feminist therapist herself intervenes, especially when other practitioners appear to be engaging in harmful, unethical, or illegal behaviors.

C. When appropriate, a feminist therapist encourages a client's recognition of criminal behaviors and also facilitates the client's navigation of the criminal justice system.

D. A feminist therapist, teacher, or researcher is alert to the control of information dissemination and questions pressures to conform to and use dominant mainstream standards. As technological methods of communication change and increase, the feminist therapist recognizes the socioeconomic aspects of these developments and communicates according to clients' access to technology.

E. A feminist therapist, teacher, or researcher recognizes the political is personal in a world where social change is a constant.

The Feminist Therapy Institute, Inc.
Corporate Office:
50 South Steele, #850
Denver, CO 80209
Administrator: Polly Taylor
128 Moffitt Street
San Francisco, CA 94131

Researchers who ask women to report experiences, or who have participated themselves, using self-reports and participant observation, have found significant changes in social/political awareness, vocational interests, attitudes, self-perception, sex roles, and ego strength. (p. 436)

Overall, as with other less symptom-oriented therapies, it is difficult to evaluate fairly the efficacy of feminist therapy based on traditional and existing outcome assessment procedures. Therefore, at present, feminist therapy is not listed as an empirically validated treatment approach (Chambless et al., 1998).

MULTICULTURAL PERSPECTIVES

Some cynics might argue that feminist therapy is limited to special populations or to just one special population—discontented White women with a feminist bent. Historically, feminist theorists have admitted that feminist theory lacked diversity and complexity. A panel with four women of color we put together for a psychology of women class in 1989 stated unanimously that they didn't feel sexism was as devastating in their lives as racism, and they were hesitant to identify with the feminist movement for this reason. In 1992 Brown and Brodsky published an article titled "The Future of Feminist Therapy," in which they stated, "Currently, feminist therapy theory is neither diverse nor complex in the reality it reflects. It has been deficient from the start in its inclusiveness of the lives and realities of women of color, poor or working class women, non–North American women, women over sixty-five, or women with disabilities" (p. 52).

Many feminist therapists and writers have worked and are working to change this perceived narrowness. We would also argue that this narrowness was no worse than the cultural encapsulation present in other theories; in fact, feminists have been among the first and most vocal of those advocating for diverse and multicultural perspectives in the practice of counseling and psychotherapy. For example, in a testament to their sensitivity to persons with disabilities, years before other professional conferences had signers for the deaf, feminist conferences made a point of having signers and of meeting only in fully accessible conference centers.

At the core of feminist thinking is the notion that subjugation of any segment of the human species based on race, ethnicity, religious beliefs, sex, disability, or sexual orientation is wrong. Therefore, feminist theory is extremely applicable to other populations suffering from externally imposed limits, stereotypes, abuse, and exploitation. Of course, a certain creative tension arises when feminist therapists find themselves wanting to honor the cultures and beliefs of clients when those same cultures and beliefs include definitions of women's roles that feminists find to be limiting, oppressive, or even abusive of women.

CONCLUDING COMMENTS

There are two reasons that feminist theory and therapy might cease to exist, one utopian, the other Orwellian. In the best of worlds, feminism would seem a quaint fact of history because women and men would exist in egalitarian societies in which one's sex did not limit or define one's development. In the worst of scenarios, feminism would be known as an evil that was eradicated just in time to save the family, and men, from

The Personal Is Political

Suzanne Comingo Griffith, PhD, is a professor in the Counseling and Psychological Professions Department at the University of Wisconsin–Superior (UWS). Griffith has been coordinator of the women's studies minor and cochair of the Women's Studies Consortium in the state-wide system.

She reports,

Interestingly, we have more males than females involved in teaching women's studies courses and serving on these change-agency committees. Given that women are only 30% of the faculty, this may not be surprising (the number of faculty of color is only 5%). The men who are involved with us see the need for change and understand how such changes will benefit all of us. We are "comrades-in-arms" in moving forward and preventing roll-back.

For me, the personal is political; if I am not part of the solution then I am part of the problem. Right now we are concerned about how budget cuts (national, state, university) will affect vulnerable and protected groups.

Griffith has published in the area of race-gender-class issues, especially on how to teach about this intersection of sensitive issues. Recently, her work on campus environment change was published as a case study by National Women's Studies Association. With a male colleague at UWS, she has been working on ways of including issues of poverty and class, especially the impact of poverty on women, in undergraduate psychology courses. Off campus, Griffith is on the Board for the Duluth, Minnesota–based Program to Aid Victims of Sexual Assault and serves on the Douglas County/Superior Wisconsin Council on Child Protection. Griffith says of these many involvements,

Yes, I am busy and, what's more, I love the work I do in all of these areas. Yet the most meaningful area of my work is with counseling students—knowing that they will be working with children and adults who are often in vulnerable states. I am keen to bring the feminist perspective into their awareness: issues of power and power analysis, empowerment, demystifying the process, awareness of the impact of the sociocultural and economic context, and the instrumental role of diversity of gender, age, ability, sexuality, religion, race, and class in the forming of their own and their clients' perspectives. I thoroughly enjoy watching the graduate counseling students grow while in graduate school. At the same time I feel it is necessary to warn them that this program can be hazardous to their relationships: They will grow and be excited by their increased understanding of themselves and potentially of others, but this growth may create or increase a tension. By enrolling and investing in this professional development, they have voted to change. I warn that others around them may not be excited by their growth and change. Therefore, they can address this tension from early on by being aware of their own tension over change and that of significant others. Since the entire process of counseling is about change (in thought, word, deed, emotion) *and* one's resistance to it, exploring this tension early on gives them the tools to proceed with these challenges. Certainly, if change or adjustment to it was easy, people would not need counseling. So, being aware of the competing forces within themselves (which benefits from a deconstruction based on race, sex, class, and culture) helps them understand the process their clients must engage with. I also think that they need to be aware of the power the client gives to them, as counselors (quite similar to the power students give instructors), and the ethical choices they have for using this powerful position. So the personal is political—and the political is personal in a very real sense—in counselor training. I believe feminism provides me with additional and exceptional tools for facilitating student learning and for my critique of that process. However, it is getting harder and harder for me to separate this view from a multicultural/social justice critique that requires for us, as part of the White majority, that same understanding of competing perspectives nationally and internationally.

certain destruction. Each possibility is unlikely, so for the foreseeable future, feminist theorists and practitioners will have an important role.

STUDENT REVIEW ASSIGNMENTS

The following exercises will encourage you to think further about choice theory and reality therapy.

Critical Corner

Read and consider the following critical statements about feminist theory and therapy. Write your response to the criticisms in the space provided.

1. Feminist therapists readily admit that one outcome they hope for, client by client, is a change in the way society functions. Is this a political agenda, or just a rather ambitious therapeutic goal for society? If it is a political agenda, is therapy really the place to promote it?
Response:

2. Feminism is in direct contradiction to some of the teachings regarding women's roles of many of the world's largest religions, although feminists can be found within each of these religions as well. Can a feminist therapist work ethically and effectively with clients who believe many feminist tenets are wrong? If so, how?
Response:

3. A pillar of feminist theory is that humans must learn to live in ways that share power. Egalitarian relationships, rather than hierarchical, are the goal. Yet the therapist has the benefit of title, being paid, setting boundaries, and being the authority. Are these power differentials paradoxical to feminist therapy? Can they be overcome?
Response:

Reviewing Key Terms

Look back through the chapter and create your own explanations of the following terms:

- The personal is political
- Consciousness raising
- Gender roles
- Power
- Egalitarian relationships
- Feminist
- Biology is destiny
- Subjugation
- Hierarchy
- Exploitation
- Diversity

Review Questions

1. If you have read the chapters in order, you are approaching the end of this text. You should be able to identify aspects of earlier theorists evidenced in the tech-

niques and goals of feminist therapy. See if you can list ways the following theoretical orientations are compatible with feminist work:

- Adlerian
- Jungian
- Person-centered
- Reality Therapy
- Cognitive-behavioral

2. How does philosophical feminism inform and shape feminist therapy?
3. What would you say are the most important of the eight tenets of feminist psychology from Worell and Remer?
4. What distinguishes the ethics code for feminist therapists from other general ethical guidelines?
5. Freud supposedly believed that biology is destiny. How would a feminist therapist argue this statement?

RECOMMENDED READINGS AND RESOURCES

The following resources may help you deepen your understanding of feminist theory and therapy.

Lead Journals

- *Gender and Psychoanalysis*
- *Journal of Gay and Lesbian Psychotherapy*
- *Men and Masculinities*
- *Psychology of Men and Masculinity*
- *Psychology Women Quarterly*
- *Sex Roles*
- *Women and Therapy*

Books and Articles

Beauvoir, S. de. (1952). *The second sex.* New York: Knopf.

Chesler, P. (1972). *Women and madness.* New York: Doubleday.

Chodorow, N. J. (1989). *Feminism and psychoanalytic theory.* New Haven: Yale University Press.

Faludi, S. (1991). *Backlash: The undeclared war against American women.* New York: Craun.

Freidan, B. (1963). *The feminine mystique.* New York: Norton.

Freud, A. (1966). *The ego and the mechanisms of defense* (Vol. 2). New York: International Universities Press.

Gilbert, L. A., & Scher, M. (1999). *Gender and sex in counseling and psychotherapy.* Boston: Allyn & Bacon.

Gilligan, C. (1977). *In a different voice.* Cambridge, MA: Harvard University Press.

Horney, K. (1967). *Feminine psychology.* New York: Norton.

Hrdy, S. B. (1999). *Mother nature.* New York: Pantheon Books.

Hyde, J. S. (1996). *Half the human experience: The psychology of women* (2nd ed.). Lexington, MA: DC Heath.

Miller, J. B. (Ed.). (1973). *Psychoanalysis and women.* New York: Brunner/Mazel.

Mitchell, J. (1966). *Women: The longest revolution.* New York: Pantheon Books.

Mitchell, J. (1976). *Psychoanalysis and feminism: Freud, Reich, Laing, and women.* New York: Random House.

Porter, N., & Vasquez, M. (1997). Covision: Feminist supervision, process, and collaboration. In J. W. a. N. G. Johnson (Ed.), *Shaping the future of feminist psychology: Education, research, and practice* (pp. 155–172). Washington, DC: American Psychological Association.

Tavris, C. (1998). *The mismeasure of woman.* New York: Smith, Peter.

Thompson, C. (1971). *On women.* New York: New American Library.

Unger, R. K. (Ed.). (2001). *Handbook of the psychology of women and gender.* New York: Wiley.

Worell, J. R., & Remer, P. (2003). *Feminist perspectives in therapy: Empowering diverse women* (2nd ed.). New York: Wiley.

Videotapes

Brown, L. (1994). *Feminist therapy* [Videotape]. Washington, DC: American Psychological Association.

Jhally, S. (1995). *Dreamworlds II* [Videotape]. Northampton, MA: Media Education Association.

Kilbourne, J. (2000). *Killing us softly III* [Videotape]. Northampton, MA: Media Education Association.

Training Organizations and Web Sites

The Feminist Therapy Institute (web site: www.feministtherapyinstitute.org)

Jean Baker Miller Training Institute (web site: www.wellesley.edu/JBMTI)

Association for Women in Psychology (web site: www.theworks.baka.com/awp)

National Organization for Women (NOW) (web site: www.now.org)

Newcomb College Center for Research on Women (web site: www.tulane.edu/wc)

Wellesley Centers for Women (web site: www.wcwonline.org)

For biographical information on many of the women discussed in this chapter, visit www.webster.edu\~woolflm\women.html.

Chapter 11

CONSTRUCTIVIST THEORY AND THERAPY

Constructive therapies are approaches that begin with the recognition that humans are meaning makers who construct, not simply uncover, their psychological realities. They are based on "the construction that we are constructive."

—Michael F. Hoyt, *The Handbook of Constructive Therapies* (1998, p. 3)

We are what we think. All that we are arises with our thoughts. With our thoughts, we make the world.

—Buddha (quoted in Boldt, 1999, p. 91)

IN THIS CHAPTER YOU WILL LEARN

- Key historical figures who contributed to the development of constructive therapy
- Basic theoretical concepts associated with constructivism
- The differences between solution-focused brief therapy, solution-oriented therapy, and narrative therapy
- A wide range of techniques used by constructive therapists
- Multicultural applications and implications of constructive therapy
- The efficacy of solution-based and narrative therapies
- Foundational ethical assumptions of constructive therapies

Without question, the best way to begin a chapter on constructive theory and therapy is with a story.

Once upon a time, there was a boy who kept breaking school rules and was mandated to counseling. When asked what kind of guy he was, he answered, "I'm the kind of guy who doesn't get caught," even though there was strong evidence to the contrary. His counselor asked him to add a new description of himself. In response to the question, "What kind of guy are you?" the boy was supposed to say, "I'm the kind of guy who thinks things through." The boy thought this was very funny, but he complied. Each week, in addition to their other interactions, the counselor would say, "What kind of guy are you?" and the boy, with a big grin, would answer, "I'm the kind of guy who thinks things through." The counselor would agree. "Yes, you are. I can see it." The counselor even had the boy's mother step into the office to hear her son describe himself this new way. Everyone laughed as the boy used his best John Wayne voice to drawl the words.

A few weeks went by. Believe it or not, the boy's rule breaking declined, and he was able to terminate therapy. Sometime later, he told his mom that those words echoed in his head every time he started to screw up and break a rule. He told her that even when he wanted to think, "I won't get caught," those other words were there, lurking in the background, which somehow made him think about the fact that he often *did* get caught, and it wasn't worth it. The boy had become the kind of guy who thought things through.

As we enter the field of theoretical constructivism, reality seems less easily defined than ever. Is the boy in the preceding story a budding antisocial, convincing his mother that counseling worked so he wouldn't need to go anymore? Or is he a disarmingly frank kid who complied with a silly saying that actually changed the way he thought about himself and his actions? Can a simple shift in perspective—the boy parroting (and perhaps beginning to believe) a different internal description—really produce a sudden and lasting change in human behavior?

Constructive theories and therapies place a strong emphasis on helping clients reconstruct or restory their lives in more adaptive and satisfying ways. This emphasis requires that therapy interactions focus primarily on the present and future. In some ways, to explore constructive theories is to dive more deeply into the abyss of "as if" as introduced to philosophers (and Alfred Adler) in the early twentieth century by Hans Vaihinger (1911). Perhaps constructivist theory is just a revisitation of Adler's idiographic fictional finalism writ large (Watts, 2003).

Constructivism is philosophically and psychologically compelling, especially within our contemporary multivariate, multidimensional, and multicultural society. It places itself squarely in the domain of postmodernism. As a consequence of this philosophical position, we humans can no longer stake any claim to objectivity. Everything is perspective, and perspective is everything. Hierarchical structures of expert and nonexpert are challenged. Each of us views reality through our own particular set of lenses. A powerful conceptualization of constructivist approaches to therapy comes from Michael White (1993), who describes the therapist as not just "taking history," but "making history." Certainly, in their own particular and sometimes peculiar way, constructive theorists and therapists are currently making history in counseling and psychotherapy.

BIOGRAPHICAL INFORMATION AND HISTORICAL CONTEXT

It is difficult to examine the historical context of a theoretical approach that is being formulated, implemented, and evaluated even as we write. To make matters worse, some constructive theorists have what appears to be a theory-based tendency to speak with an individual voice—elaborating on their personal views rather than citing references, historical roots, or empirical data (de Shazer, 1985; Walter & Peller, 1996). In addition, there is a clear split in the constructivist field. Specifically, some writers include solution-based and strategic approaches within the constructive domain, whereas others exclude these approaches from their reviews of constructivist literature (Hoyt, 1998; Neimeyer & Mahoney, 1995).

Despite these obstacles, we can say with confidence that constructivist approaches to counseling and psychotherapy have roots in traditional talk therapy. As an example,

Steve Shazer, a co-originator of solution-focused therapy, used a phrase from Sigmund Freud (Words were originally magic) as a title for one of his solution-focused books (de Shazer, 1994). In the 1915 writings from which Shazer was quoting, Freud wrote,

> Nothing takes place in a psycho-analytic treatment but an exchange of words. . . . The patient talks. . . . The doctor listens. . . . Words were originally magic and to this day words have retained much of their ancient magical power. By words one person can make another blissfully happy or drive him to despair. . . . Words provoke affects and are in general the means of mutual influence among men. (Freud, 1961, p. 17)

As Freud notes, the magical power of words began long before psychoanalysis. Ancient healers, storytellers, and religious evangelists clearly knew of the power of words. Regardless of your particular religious or spiritual beliefs, it is difficult to argue over the indisputable word and story power included in the I Ching, the Bible, the Koran, the Talmud, the sayings of Confucius, the Book of Mormon, and other religious documents. The same is true for many indigenous cultures. Simon Ortiz (1993) writes,

> What would I be without language? My existence has been determined by language, not only spoken but the unspoken, the language of speech and the language of motion. I can't remember a world without memory. Memory, immediate and far away in the past, something in the sinew, blood, ageless cell. Although I don't recall the exact moment I spoke or tried to speak, I know the feeling of something tugging at the core of the mind, something unutterable uttered into existence. It is language that brings us into being in order to know life. (p. 29)

Early philosophers who contributed to the development of constructive theory and therapy include Immanuel Kant and Hans Vaihinger. Kant's view that reality is unknowable and Vaihinger's conception of many individual fictional realities both are at the root of contemporary constructive theory. Constructivism is in opposition to modernism or objectivism. Constructivism holds that individuals perceive and construct reality based on their own experiences, whereas objectivism holds that individuals know reality by passively receiving sensory information directly from the environment.

With the publication of *The Psychology of Personal Constructs,* George Kelly (1955) developed the first unarguably constructive approach to psychotherapy. He wrote,

> Life provides man with no scientific footholds on reality, suggests to him no narrative plots, offers no rhythmic metaphor to confirm the moving resonance of a human theme. If he chooses to write tragedy, then tragedy it will be; if comedy, then that is what will come of it; and if burlesque, he, the sole reader, must learn to laugh at his misanthropic caricatures of the only person he knows—himself. (Kelly, 1969, p. 24)

Kelly outlined many foundational constructivist psychological concepts. Although Vaihinger and other philosophers influenced him, his theoretical work is based primarily on clinical observations. For example, early in his theoretical transformation from Freudian analysis to personal constructs, Kelly began "deliberately" offering clients "preposterous interpretations." His only criteria were that the interpretative statements (1) integrate his clients' current perspective and (2) have ramifications "for approaching the future in a different way" (Kelly, 1969, p. 52). Somewhat to his surprise, Kelly discovered that his preposterous interpretations often worked very well in moving clients toward more positive future behavior and emotions.

Milton Erickson, Strategic Hypnotherapy, and Solution-Based Approaches

De Shazer and others trace the modern origin of solution-focused constructivist thinking to the late, great hypnotherapist Milton Erickson (de Shazer, 1985; Haley, 1973; O'Hanlon & Bertolino, 1998). Erickson is also considered the innovative inspiration for the strategic therapy approach with individuals and families (Goldenberg & Goldenberg, 2000). In his therapeutic work, Erickson made no effort to correct "causative underlying maladjustments" lurking in his clients' unconscious, self, past, or environment (Haley, 1967, p. 393). Instead, his focus was on how to deconstruct and reconstruct the skills and strengths his clients brought with them to therapy. The following case, adapted from Rossi (1980) and later summarized in O'Hanlon and Bertolino (1998), illustrates Erickson's strength-based approach.

> A 70-year-old woman named Ma met with Erickson. She was unable to read despite many years of sincere effort. She had resolved to learn how to read at age 16 but had subsequently become frightened and blanked out whenever someone tried to teach her. Erickson promised her that she would be reading and writing within three weeks.
>
> Erickson's approach to teaching Ma to read was innovative. He told her that she wouldn't have to learn anything that she didn't already know. The core of his message was that she already had within her all of the skills and strengths needed to learn to read and write.
>
> He asked her to pick up a pencil in any old way she wanted. Then, he had her make some marks with the pencil on paper, just scribbling, like any baby might do. Progressively, he had her make straight lines at various angles, donut holes, donut halves, and two sides of a gabled roof. As a way to decrease her anxiety about writing, Erickson did not have the woman learn to copy letters but instead had her draw objects that she had been familiar with during her lifetime. He had her practice making these familiar marks on paper between sessions.
>
> During their next meeting, Erickson explained to Ma that the only difference between a pile of lumber and a house was that the house was put together in a particular way. Ma agreed but didn't see the relevance between building a house from lumber and turning pencil marks on a page into letters. Then, Erickson helped Ma make a series of 26 new marks, based on the marks she had previously produced. Of course, these marks were the 26 letters of the English alphabet.
>
> Erickson's work with Ma continued along the same lines. He coaxed her into naming the different letters and words she produced. After all, just as farm animals needed names, so did the marks she produced on a piece of paper. Eventually, he had her write a sentence: "Get going Ma and put some grub on the table." This was a statement she had frequently heard from her late husband, which helped Ma realize that reading was just like talking. In the end, without causing Ma any anxiety whatsoever, Erickson taught her to read and write in less than three weeks.

Erickson was a powerful and creative individual whose work is generally highly regarded (Erickson, 1954; Erickson, Rossi, & Rossi, 1976). He made many contributions to what we know about psychotherapy today. He is best known for brief hypnotherapeutic techniques and innovative approaches to working with individual cases. One of his most significant contributions to therapy is the intervention referred to as *utilization* (Erickson, 1954).

Utilization is both an intervention and a theoretical concept. Erickson believed it was crucial for clients to utilize whatever strengths they brought with them to therapy. These strengths included their humor, work experiences, language style, personal resources, and nonverbal behaviors. As with Ma, Erickson incorporated or utilized the personal qualities his clients possessed into their therapeutic work.

Erickson's legacy is characterized by three of his personal attributes. We believe these qualities continue to shine through and shape the contemporary practice of many constructive therapies and therapists. Erickson was many things, but in particular he was

- Optimistic (and confident)
- Clever (and intelligent)
- Indirect (and collaborative)

Erickson was so positive and creative with clients that, before long, often without even realizing what had happened, clients would experience a doubling or trebling of their previously undernoticed and underutilized personal strengths and resources.

Questions for Reflection

As you read through this chapter, ponder the following questions: How much of Erickson's personality (or personal attributes) are reflected in the development and evolving nature of constructive theory and therapy? Also, as you think back to previous chapters, do you recognize how the personalities of Freud, Adler, Jung, Rogers, Ellis, and other major theorists shape how their therapies are practiced?

The Palo Alto Projects and Brief Therapy in Italy

In 1952 Gregory Bateson began the Double-Bind Communications Project (DBCP) with Jay Haley, John Weakland, and Donald Jackson (as consultant) in Palo Alto, California. This project focused on communication patterns in schizophrenic families. Shortly after this project started, Haley and Weakland became interested in communication patterns that occur between hypnotherapist and client. With Bateson's encouragement, Haley and Weakland began attending some of Milton Erickson's hypnosis workshops and visited him regularly in Phoenix.

In 1958 Jackson established the Mental Research Institute (MRI) along with Virginia Satir and Paul Watzlawick, also in Palo Alto. This project and the DBCP both focused on the power of verbal and nonverbal communication in influencing human behavior. The project boundaries were somewhat blurred because Jackson was heavily involved in both. Together, the projects resulted in over 200 professional publications, including numerous books (Bateson, Jackson, Haley, & Weakland, 1963; G. Greenberg, 1977; Watzlawick, 1963; J. Weakland, 1962).

In 1968 the Brief Therapy Center was established at MRI. By that time the DBCP had ended and Haley and Weakland had joined MRI. Around the same time, four Italian psychiatrists led by Mara Selvini-Palazzoli broke away from their more psychoanalytically trained colleagues and formed the Milan Center for the Study of the Family. Their goal was to work more specifically with family systems using briefer therapy models. The Milan group was strongly influenced by the Palo Alto group and, in particular, by the publication *Pragmatics of Human Communication* (Watzlawick, Beavin,

& Jackson, 1967). In an interesting development, Watzlawick became the main consultant for the Milan group.

Haley and Cloe Madanes (who was trained at MRI) later married and developed the strategic approach to family and individual therapy (Madanes & Haley, 1977). The essence of strategic therapy is to devise a unique strategy for each particular client or family problem. There are numerous strategic therapy techniques, but the most relevant to our discussion is positive relabeling or reframing. In one famous case, Haley informed a woman whose husband had recently chased her around the house with an ax that her husband "was simply trying to get close to her" (Goldenberg & Goldenberg, 2000, p. 235). Obviously Haley's positive relabeling in that case was a bit over the top. However, the point is that strategic therapy approaches were boldly positive. Similarly, in her work at the Milan Center, Selvini-Palazzoli and her group (Selvini-Palazzoli, Boscolo, Cecchin, & Prata, 1974) developed an active-directive family therapy technique called *positive connotation,* in which negative symptoms or behaviors are recast in a positive light (e.g., "Your child is setting fires in order to get your attention and some emotional warmth in his life").

Questions for Reflection

Some writers have strongly criticized the extremely positive reframing approaches that Haley and Selvini-Palazzoli popularized. What are your thoughts on this issue? Are the provocatively positive reframes mentioned in the preceding paragraph too unrealistic? Is it possible that positive reformulations of blatantly negative behavior can be useful to clients?

Efran and Fauber (1995) offer the following criticism of overly positive therapy interventions based on "verbal magic":

> In our view, some workers have stretched the meaning of such terms as reframing and positive connotation . . . to the breaking point. They underestimate the solidity of a constructed reality and assume that because something is language dependent, it is insubstantial and can be easily modified by relabeling problems willy-nilly. They feel free to portray faults as virtues, failures as successes, and selfishness as altruism. Some therapists will say almost anything for strategic effect. Critics have attacked such ad hoc conceptualizations as superficial and manipulative—an uncomfortable melding of the roles of therapist and con artist. . . . We tend to agree. (p. 291)

Discovering Solutions and Narratives

The work of Kelly, Erickson, Bateson, MRI, the Milan Group, and Haley and Madanes are the most direct ancestors of contemporary constructivist theory and therapy. Within the constructivist paradigm, this chapter focuses primarily on two distinct approaches: solution-focused brief therapy and narrative therapy.

Solution-Focused Brief Therapy

Steve de Shazer and Insoo Kim Berg cofounded the Brief Family Therapy Center (BFTC) in Milwaukee in 1978 and developed solution-focused brief therapy. Their approach emphasizes that clients don't need to know anything about why or how their problem originated. Even further, therapists also don't need to know anything about how clients' problems developed—and they need to know very little about the problem itself. Instead, solution-focused brief therapy primarily (and often exclusively) focuses on helping clients generate solutions. De Shazer refers to standard therapy interventions as "formula tasks" and "skeleton keys" (de Shazer, 1985, p. 119). In the following, he describes the similarity of his approach to that of the Milan group:

> [The Milan group's] prescription (which follows a formula) and our "formula tasks" (each of which are standardized) suggest something about the nature of therapeutic intervention and change which has not been clearly described before: Interventions can initiate change without the therapist's first understanding, in any detail, what has been going on. (de Shazer, 1985, p. 119)

More recently, de Shazer has been inspired by Ludwig Wittgenstein's concepts of language games as interpersonal determinants of reality (Wittgenstein, 1968). Berg and de Shazer (1993) articulate this linguistic development:

> As the client and therapist talk more and more about the solution they want to construct together, they come to believe in the truth or reality of what they are talking about. This is the way language works, naturally. (p. 6)

Not long after solution-focused brief therapy began growing in popularity, William O'Hanlon and Michele Weiner-Davis developed solution-oriented therapy. The solution-oriented approach is derived from three main theoretical-practical precursors: (1) Milton Erickson's work; (2) strategic intervention and problem-solving techniques developed at MRI; and (3) de Shazer and Berg's solution-focused brief therapy. O'Hanlon (1998) describes the evolution of his approach:

> In the early 1980's I began a correspondence with Steve de Shazer. . . . [H]e and some colleagues had begun what came to be called the Brief Family Therapy Center. . . . De Shazer and I shared a common view that mainstream therapies that saw clients as pathological and resistant were all wrong. People were naturally cooperative if approached in the right way and treated as resourceful and competent. De Shazer's work began to take shape and has turned into "solution-focused therapy." . . . My work took shape and I began to call it "solution-oriented therapy." . . . Because the two were often confused and I have some major differences with the Milwaukee approach, I began to speak of my approach as "possibility therapy." (p. 139)

The differences between these two solution-based approaches are small but important. Essentially, O'Hanlon and Weiner-Davis's approach focuses more on acknowledging and validating clients' emotions and experience and is somewhat less directive and less formulaic, more collaborative, and more open to considering political, gender, and historical factors as important in problem development. O'Hanlon also believes that therapists must take responsibility for pursuing issues that clients do not bring up—especially if the issues lead to violent, dangerous, or painful life outcomes. In contrast, de Shazer (Hoyt, 1994) has gone on record to say that therapists should avoid reading "between the lines" and instead simply stick with what the client is saying is the problem and whatever is working (e.g., "[if] he says he doesn't drink too much and it's not a problem. Leave it alone. Take it seriously"; pp. 29–30).

Narrative Therapy

Michael White of Australia and David Epston of New Zealand met in 1981 at an Australian–New Zealander family therapy conference and subsequently developed a therapeutic approach based on *narrative metaphor.* The personal narrative metaphor is the story that defines and organizes each individual's life and relationship with the world. As we live and accumulate experiences, we each develop a personal story or narrative that gives our lives meaning and continuity. Much like a well-written story, our personal narrative includes an organized plot, characters, points of tension and climax, and a beginning, middle, and end.

White was strongly influenced by Michel Foucault, a French intellectual and social critic (Foucault, 1965). Foucault accused dominant culture of oppressively maintaining power and control over minority groups by eliminating alternative historical perspectives. Eventually, the dominant culture turns its historical stories into objective truth, and alternative ways of being are pathologized. White's application of Foucault's thinking to the therapy process allows individuals who have oppressed themselves through personal narratives to deconstruct and reconstruct their life stories into more complete, more adaptive, and personally meaningful storylines (White & Epston, 1990). Narrative therapy as formulated by White and Epston also helps individuals break free from internalized social, cultural, and political oppression and rewrite their life stories from a perspective of personal freedom.

David Epston introduced narrative metaphor concepts to White (Goldenberg & Goldenberg, 2000). He also has pioneered the use of letters to clients as an extension of therapy (Epston, 1994). In collaboration with Stephan Madigan of Canada, Epston co-founded the Anti-anorexia/Anti-bulimia League, an organization that turns so-called eating disordered patients into empowered community and political activists. According to Madigan, narrative approaches spring from diverse sources, including Foucault, Bateson, feminism, anthropology, geography, and postmodernism (Carlson & Kjos, 2000a). These approaches also carry the distinct flavor of George Kelly's (1955) psychology of personal constructs.

THEORETICAL PRINCIPLES OF CONSTRUCTIVE THERAPY

Constructivist theory is firmly grounded in postmodern thought.

Postmodernism

The most basic position that postmodernists' hold is antirealism. Postmodernists firmly believe in the fact that there is no such thing as objective fact. This position is, of course, at once illogical, subjective, nonlinear, and essentially unprovable, but from the postmodernist's perspective, such is the inherent nature of all things. de Shazer articulates the subjective or antirealist nature of client symptoms when he writes, "There are no wet beds, no voices without people, no depressions. There is only *talk* about wet beds, *talk* about voices without people, and *talk* about depression" (de Shazer, 1993, p. 93).

Let's take a moment to deconstruct postmodernism. As a term, *postmodernism* derives from art and literature. It originally referred to a movement or perspective that was in opposition to or in reaction against modern art or literature. Of course, this means that to define postmodernism adequately, we must first define modernism. Technically, modernism is associated with the scientific, objective, and deterministic paradigm of an external reality. In some ways, however, defining modernism is like trying to catch a snowflake because all things modern melt away very quickly with the passage of time. It is possible to define the modern art and modern science period and style, but when doing so, we are struck that using the word *modern* in that context is a misnomer. Modern art is no longer modern art in the sense that it is no longer contemporary but instead representative of a static period in time. In the end, we are left with the conclusion that postmodernism is something opposed to or against something that was once—but is no longer—modern. We are also left with the problem of naming the next movement or perspective or paradigm. Will we soon be entering the period of postpostmodernism or postmodernism II? However that issue gets resolved, postmodernism is extremely subjective—and perhaps is designed to emphasize subjectivity.

If you are feeling confused, that's exactly the point. Milton Erickson sometimes based his therapeutic interventions on what he referred to as *confusion techniques* (Erickson, 1964). In an effort to produce positive change, he would speak to clients in ways that were circular, nonlinear, and confusing.

Questions for Reflection

Think about what it is like to experience confusion. What might be the purpose of Erickson's confusion tactics? Recall back in Chapter 9 that William Glasser, just before introducing choice theory to a new client, tells her that he may be confusing her but that he's not trying to confuse her. As you read on, consider the possibility that Glasser may have been intentionally or unintentionally using a confusion technique to help ready his client to accept choice theory.

For Erickson, before helping clients develop more adaptive and healthy beliefs, it was sometimes necessary to help them deconstruct and temporarily let go of old beliefs. One method he employed to facilitate belief deconstruction was confusion. Once confusion set in, client responsiveness to hearing and accepting alternative ways of thinking were increased. As discussed in Chapter 8, Albert Ellis helped clients deconstruct irrational beliefs through vigorous disputation. In contrast, similar to Erickson, constructive therapists help clients deconstruct and reconstruct specific beliefs as well as personal narratives through a careful and subtle use of words and language.

Language and Languaging

Constructive therapists focus on how language builds, maintains, and changes each individual's worldview. As Hoyt (1998, p. 4) states, "Language and languaging are the ways we make meaning and exchange information." Essentially, language determines reality. As Efran and Fauber (1995) described,

> Language is where people live. . . . It allows people to have names, to "know" who they are, and to carve separable things out of the interconnected flux that they take to be the universe. One can manage to play baseball without a shortstop, but not without the words

and symbols that differentiate first base from home plate. Without language, it would not be possible for a person to engage in self-conscious thought, to keep an appointment book, or to have problems. (p. 279)

Given their focus on language, constructivists are open to an entire domain of potential therapeutic interventions including relabeling, reframing, solution-focused questioning, restorying, and problem externalization. We review these approaches in the practice of constructive therapy section.

Many other language-based interventions are based in the cognitive psychological models. Specifically, Ellis's rational-emotive behavior therapy and Beck's cognitive therapy both rely on Epictetus's 2000-year-old philosophy that people "are disturbed not by the things that happen to them, but by their views of these things" (Ellis, 1998). As we look through the constructivist lens, it appears that when cognitive therapists use cognitive restructuring techniques to help clients modify their core schemas or beliefs about themselves, they are using a constructivist-oriented language technique. In fact, Ellis has recently indicated that REBT *is* a constructive therapy approach (Ellis, 1998, p. 83).

Change is Both Constant and Inevitable

For the human infant and constructive theorist, change is a constant. Adaptation is a requirement. Every day the infant and constructivist make new discoveries about their worlds. Most psychology and counseling students are aware of Jean Piaget's cognitive developmental concepts of assimilation and accommodation. To review, Piaget postulated that assimilation and accommodation drive cognitive adaptation. In other words, humans assimilate and accommodate information from their environment to learn what they need to know about surviving and thriving in the world.

Assimilation is the process of fitting reality and personal experience into one's current cognitive organization. For example, when a 2-year-old child sees a butterfly floating by and points into the sky and says, "Look, Daddy. A birdie!" she is assimilating new information into her old cognitive organization. For her, things that fly or float through the air are birdies. Unless her father or another available person tells her the differences between birdies and butterflies, the little girl will not cognitively adapt and essentially will learn nothing new, despite her new perceptual experience.

However, if the 2-year-old's father happens to be paying attention and says, "No honey, that's a butterfly" and then the child learns to distinguish between birds and butterflies, accommodation has occurred. Accommodation is the modification or adjustment of one's cognitive organization that comes as a result of the demands of reality and personal experience.

Like infants, adults also consistently have opportunities to make new discoveries based on new experiences. Narrative therapists, in particular, help clients focus on their lived experiences and integrate them into their personal narratives. This process is very similar to Piaget's accommodation. In essence, change is always happening, and small changes are all that is needed to begin a ripple effect toward larger changes.

As described in more detail later, therapy conversations are opportunities to reconstruct, restory, or accommodate experiences from the past. You may recall the concept of introjection or "swallowing whole" from Chapter 5 (existential and Gestalt). In constructive therapy, particularly its narrative therapy format, the therapist helps clients cough up their old life stories and chew them up in a new and different way before trying to swallow and digest them again.

Therapy Is a Collaborative, Cooperative, Co-constructive Conversation

The constructivist theoretical position with respect to therapy relationships is egalitarian. The therapist is viewed as collaborating and cooperating with the client. Consequently, therapists are considered accountable when clients resist therapy. As we've stated elsewhere, "the responsibility for making the connection and doing therapeutic work falls on the professional, not on the client" (J. Sommers-Flanagan & Sommers-Flanagan, 1997, p. 6).

Moving the responsibility for cooperation and resistance from the client to the therapist is a major contribution of constructive theory. It is not surprising that many involuntary clients are relieved when an appointed therapist focuses on strengths and possibilities, rather than trying to break down denial and get them to admit to owning the problem. The gentle, collaborative, and positive approach that constructive therapists advocate may be why many therapists and agencies that work with involuntary or mandated clients find constructive approaches so useful (see Tohn & Oshlag, 1996). Various constructive therapists have made similar statements about resistance and problem ownership:

- "Resistance is not a useful concept" (de Shazer, 1984; Selekman, 1993, p. 25).
- "The person is not the problem. The problem is the problem" (Monk, 1997).
- "Allowing resistance [and] externalizing of the problem [is encouraged]" (Neimeyer, 1995, p. 17).

A major goal of constructive therapy is to coconstruct a new and better reality with clients. Epston and White (1995) conceptualize this process as "consulting your consultants":

> When people are established as consultants to themselves, to others, and to the therapist, they experience themselves as more of an authority on their own lives, their problems, and the solutions to these problems. (p. 345)

Therapy Focuses on Positive Qualities, Strengths, and Solutions

With the preceding emphasis on collaboration and cooperation and co-construction of new stories, you might think that constructive therapists strive for an absolutely equal sharing of power in their relationship with clients. After all, egalitarianism is a basic constructive theoretical position. Even further, the client is respected and viewed as her own best expert. Not long ago, a student in one of our theories classes queried us about this egalitarian theoretical position. As we lectured on solution-focused methods for leading clients toward solutions, she exclaimed, "But just a few minutes ago you said constructive theory embraces equality between therapist and client and views the client as the best expert on her own reality. I thought that meant constructive therapists don't lead their clients?"

Well, the truth is, although constructive therapists respect and accept their client's perspectives, they also direct and lead clients specifically in a preplanned direction—toward their personal strengths and positive problem-solving abilities. As J. H. Weakland (1993) states, "Just as one cannot not communicate, one cannot not influence" (p. 143). Weiner-Davis (1993) asks, "Since we cannot avoid leading, the question becomes, 'Where shall we lead our clients?'" (p. 156).

The answer to this question is simple: Constructive therapists direct clients toward (1) solutions, (2) exceptions to their problem-centered viewpoint, (3) optimism and self-efficacy, and (4) new versions of personal stories that promote greater psychological health (Monk, 1997). In this way, constructive theory and therapy are clearly laden with the values of Erickson's utilization concept.

Theory of Psychopathology

Constructive theory does not support or utilize traditional models of psychopathology. Diagnosing clients is viewed as an unhelpful procedure. Client symptoms such as anxiety and depression are not really objective entities but part of an individual's personal emotional experience cast within an overall personal life narrative. Instead of using diagnostic categories, constructive therapists meet clients where they are, emphasizing unique strengths that each client brings to therapy.

On the other hand, constructive therapists are practical and in touch with contemporary needs for diagnostic assessment and categorization. As most of us recognize, diagnosis and labeling constitute a means of professional communication, and constructivists respect this form of communication (while at the same time questioning its usefulness). Consequently, solution-focused, possibility, and narrative approaches are routinely applied to the treatment of many different traditional problems. These applications include alcoholic narratives, grief therapy, eating disorders, domestic violence, dissociative disorders, and more (see Hoyt, 1998; S. D. Miller, Hubble, & Duncan, 1996; Monk, Winslade, Crocket, & Epston, 1997).

Broadly speaking, there are two main determinants of client problems, regardless of whether the client is an individual, couple, or family:

The client has gotten stuck using ineffective solutions. This view, derived from Erickson's work and the Mental Research Institute approach, emphasizes that individuals become stuck repeating maladaptive behavior patterns even though they possess many personal strengths and resources. For the most part, clients become stuck because they construct their experiences, using language and other meaning-making procedures, in a manner leading to stuckness. Constructive therapists examine client symptoms, problems, and psychopathology for the sole purpose of deconstruction. As noted previously, many solution-focused therapists almost completely ignore client statements about problems and reorient therapy conversations toward solutions.

The client believes in an unhealthy, pathology-based self-, couple, or family narrative. Narrative therapists believe that human problems develop when clients write themselves into their self-narratives as inadequate, problem-plagued losers. Clients often show up in therapy because they have constructed a narrative in which the dominant theme of "personal problem" is obscuring a nondominant theme of "personal strength and resourcefulness."

THE PRACTICE OF CONSTRUCTIVE THERAPY

As is the case with all distinct therapy approaches, practicing effective constructive therapy requires that you feel comfortable with the basic tenets of constructive theory.

| Questions for Reflection |

The following questions are adapted from Friedman's summary of the belief system of a constructive therapist. Read and respond to the questions to see if constructive theory and therapy are compatible with your growing personal theory of therapy:

- Do you believe in a socially constructed reality?
- Do you want to engage in a therapeutic relationship in which you and your client co-construct meanings in dialogue or conversation?
- Are you comfortable moving away from a hierarchical distinction in therapy and toward a more egalitarian offering of ideas and respect for differences?
- Are you willing to maintain empathy and respect for your client's predicament and believe in the power of the therapeutic conversation to liberate suppressed, ignored, or previously unacknowledged voices or stories?
- Will you coconstruct goals and negotiate the therapy direction, placing the client back in the driver's seat, as an expert on her own predicaments and dilemmas?
- Are you willing to search for and amplify client competencies, strengths, and resources and avoid being a detective of pathology or reifying rigid diagnostic distinctions?
- Will you avoid a vocabulary of deficit and dysfunction, replacing the jargon of pathology (and distance) with the language of the everyday?
- Can you maintain a futuristic and optimistic attitude toward client change? (adapted from Friedman, 1996, pp. 450–451)

Preparing Yourself to Do Therapy from a Constructivist Perspective

In the spirit of what narrative therapists often refer to as *lived experience,* we encourage you to examine your personal repetitive tendencies by participating in the activity described in Putting It in Practice 11.1.

Preparing Your Client for Constructive Therapy

Little has been written about preparing clients for constructive therapy. There may be several reasons for this.

- Constructive therapies are relatively new, so little has been written on role induction.
- The historical roots of constructive therapy, including the work of Erickson and the MRI group, were often characterized by indirectness. Consequently, a direct message about what to expect from therapy may be considered counterproductive.
- Constructivist approaches generally emphasize meeting clients where they are, which may lead to less need for presession or early-session information sharing.
- Solution-based approaches capitalize on the fact that their strength-based, accepting, and respecting style is a pleasant but unexpected surprise for clients.

===== **Putting It in Practice 11.1** =====

Applying Strategic-Constructive Techniques to Yourself: Recommendations from Giorgi Nardone

The strategic-constructivist approach is not only a therapeutic model, but also a school of thought regarding how human beings relate to reality, or how each of us relates to self, others, and the world, and how, by this process, we "construct" the reality in which we live.

According to this perspective, we construct and maintain our problems. This human ability works in both directions; we are able to construct dysfunctional realities as well as functional ones. Since we are the builders of our reality, we can also, within limits, give reality a positive direction.

I offer the following suggestions, derived from the strategic problem-solving model, that you can use to aid your personal development.

1. My first strategic recommendation is this: Observe your tendency to repeat reactions and attitudes that you've applied to problems in the past. Obviously, you need to observe both the attempted solutions that worked and those that did not; but the most important thing is to discover which of them you have repeated. The branch of psychology that studies problem-solving processes emphasizes that the human mind tends to construct scripts of strategies and that these scripts repeat themselves even when we are facing a new or different problem.

2. It should not be too difficult for each of us to notice our redundant applications of habitual problem-solving strategies. This tendency, as such, is not pathogenic. Pathologies emerge when the scenarios become inflexible and we are unable to change them, even when their failure is obvious. Thus, the first step is to become aware of our usual "attempted solutions."

3. Once we have recognized our habitual attempted solutions, the next step is to examine one of our problems and try to find at least five possible strategies for solving it, apart from the solution that spontaneously comes to mind. This may sound like a simple procedure, but I invite you to try the experiment. It is not at all easy to find five different ways to deal with the same problem. In my students' experience, it is rather easy to find three solutions, but to reach the minimum of five that I require of them usually turns out to be a difficult enterprise.

4. The most effective suggestion is to ask ourselves, when no further alternatives come to mind, how another person that we know might look at the situation and react to it. We should try to imagine being in that person's position. Most times, this simple stratagem unblocks our ability to think of alternatives.

5. Once we have identified at least five possible strategies, we should start applying the first one and observe its effects. If it produces no effects within a short time, or the effects are undesirable, we replace it with the second strategy and proceed the same way. This apparently simple but laborious mental

game safeguards us from the mental trap of adhering rigidly to the same strategy, a trap to which, as I have already discussed, we are naturally predisposed. Moreover, this procedure makes our imagination more creative and flexible.

6. The last technique I like to describe is often the first step we need to take in order to produce a change in our current reactions. It consists of spending a few days repeatedly asking ourselves: "What could I do to make the situation worse? If I really wanted to increase the problem, how could I achieve that? What should I think or not think in order to make things even worse?" By asking ourselves these questions when we are in a difficult, apparently insoluble situation, we force ourselves to aim our strategic constructions at making the situation worse, not better. The effects are usually twofold:

   (a) We identify several ways of thinking and acting that would worsen the situation. This shows us what we must avoid doing or thinking. That, in itself, is a way to block any attempted solutions that maintain or complicate the problem.

   (b) When we prod our imagination to complicate our problems, alternative solutions that we had never contemplated before come to mind, as a reaction. This is a well-known effect of using paradoxical logic in communications between the mind and itself.

About four thousand years ago, Lao Tsu said, "If you want to make a thing straight, try first to bend it even more" (personal communication, 2002).

Both solution-based and narrative therapy approaches use questions as their primary therapeutic technique. As an interviewing strategy, questions are not without problems. Person-centered theorists have written about negative patterns associated with asking too many questions (e.g., I am the expert with all the right questions and you are the client who needs to answer my questions in such a way to allow me to provide you with help). Additionally, questioning is an inherently controlling technique that allows interviewers to direct interviewees toward preplanned destinations (J. Sommers-Flanagan & Sommers-Flanagan, 2003).

To help address potential negative outcomes associated with excessive questioning, Monk (1997) describes using a role induction statement in narrative therapy with a young client:

A therapy of questions can easily make the client feel like the subject of an interrogation. To avoid the power imbalance that might follow from this kind of conversation, I sought permission from Peter to ask him some more questions, saying that if I asked too many questions, he could either not answer them or tell me he was "questioned out." (p. 9)

At its core, constructive therapy is a collaborative endeavor. This may be the biggest reason why constructive therapists haven't emphasized role induction procedures. Instead of formally introducing clients to the therapy process, the constructive therapist continuously collaborates with clients to identify goals, strategies, and the overall therapy direction.

Assessment Issues and Procedures

Constructive therapy approaches use minimal formal assessment procedures. In keeping with de Shazer's (1985) emphasis on keys to solution and White and Epston's (1990) emphasis on client narratives, the primary focus of therapy is either on identifying and implementing solutions or on deconstructing problem narratives and constructing more satisfying narratives. Narrative therapists and possibility therapists spend a bit more time assessing and exploring client problems than does solution-focused brief therapies. Overall, from the constructive perspective, too much time spent discussing problems might only strengthen, build, and further deepen the problem-focused worldviews of clients. In contrast, a main therapy goal is to help clients develop solution- and strength-focused worldviews and adaptive personal narratives.

Even though solution-focused brief therapists want clients to shift from problem talk to solution talk, it's still important to begin therapy by allowing clients to tell their stories. If therapists ignore the client's problem from the outset of therapy, rapport is damaged and the therapist may adopt erroneous assumptions about the client. The general rule for solution-focused brief therapists at the beginning of therapy is to follow the client's lead. This rule flows from Erickson's indirect hypnotic approach with clients, in which therapists begin by pacing the client and later take the lead and make indirect and direct suggestions (Haley, 1967). Insoo Kim Berg also articulates this philosophy when she talks about leading from behind (Berg & Miller, 1992).

Opening the Session

Discovering the client's view of the problem is the primary initial focus for constructive therapists. The solution-focused brief therapist usually begins therapy with a query like, "What brings you here?" This standard opening allows clients to discuss their conceptualization of the problem and take the lead in the ensuing therapeutic conversation.

In keeping with their optimistic orientation, solution-based therapists ask questions that stimulate clients to begin moving up a positive path. For example, a therapist might ask a reluctant client, "What could happen during our time today that will make your visit with me worthwhile?" Other typical beginning questions include "If this session goes very well, what will we accomplish together?" and "How did you decide to come to counseling?" Usually, when these sorts of questions are asked, clients are prompted to identify specific goals that they hopes for and want from treatment. Identifying or constructing reasonable goals is an important assessment component of solution-based therapies.

Narrative therapists want to know the original construction of the problem; this involves gathering information about how the problem first started and how it initially affected the client's view of herself (Monk, 1997). Additional initial narrative-based assessment questions include "How will your life go forward if [the problem] continues into the future?" and "How will your life go forward if [the problem] gets smaller or goes away completely?"

A key concept to keep in mind when constructing assessment questions from the narrative perspective is to work on externalizing the problem from the person or the family. This is accomplished by consistently referring to the problem as a separate entity and not something owned by an individual.

Scaling Questions

Solution-focused therapists use scaling questions as their main assessment technique (Skidmore, 1993; in Skidmore, 1996, p. 259). Scaling questions ask clients to rate problems, progress, or virtually any therapy-related issue on a scale of 1 to 10. Typically, 1 is considered the lowest or worst possible rating and 10 the highest or best possible rating.

The following therapy excerpt illustrates how a solution-focused therapist might use scaling questions to (1) obtain an initial rating of the size of the client's problem from the client's perspective, (2) monitor client progress, (3) identify intermediate therapy goals, and (4) make specific plans for improvement.

> **(1) Therapist:** Tell me, on a scale from one to ten, with one being completely and totally depressed and ten being feeling the best a person can possibly feel, how would you rate your feelings today?
>
> **Client:** Oh, I'd say I'm at about a three today.
>
> **(2) Therapist:** Last week you gave yourself a rating of three. What rating would you give yourself today?
>
> **Client:** Hmm. I guess I think I'm still at about a three.
>
> **(3) Therapist:** So if you're still at a three right now, exactly what would need to be different to bump your rating up to a four?
>
> **Client:** I don't know. Maybe if I could get up in the morning without feeling so damn tired. Or if I could make it through the workday without thinking about how stupid and meaningless my job is.
>
> **(3) Therapist:** So if you weren't tired in the morning that would make it a four? Or would you need to have both those changes happen, both waking up refreshed and thinking that your job is meaningful?
>
> **Client:** Either waking up feeling good or feeling better about my job would make it a four. Both of those would make it a five or maybe even a six.
>
> **(4) Therapist:** Let's look at your job first. What exactly do you need to do to make it feel just a little more meaningful? What would make your job meaningful enough to bump your daily rating up to a four for tomorrow?

Percentage Questions

Percentage questions are very similar to scaling questions in that they give therapists a simple method for measuring exactly what change would look like. Typical percentage questions include: "How would your life be different if you were 1% less depressed?" "How about if you were 10% less depressed?" and "How about if you were 100% less depressed?"

Assessing Client Motivation

The primary goal of therapy is change. Because change is constant, sometimes therapy is just a matter of helping clients notice changes that are already happening. Other times, producing specific change and movement directly related to the client's stated problem is critical.

All clients are not equally interested in personal change. Some are strongly interested in change, and therefore they're considered *customers for change.* Others appear in therapy only because a significant other has insisted on their participation. These clients are commonly referred to as *complainants.* Still others, especially court-mandated clients, are not the least bit interested in change; these clients are referred to as *visitors to treatment.* Ideally, the constructive therapist can indirectly convince clients who are complainants or visitors to become customers for change (de Shazer, 1988).

To assess motivation and obtain a commitment for working on change, a narrative therapist might ask the following question at the end of a first session: "Are you more interested in finding a way to move beyond your depression and lead a normal life, or are you more interested in accepting that your depressed state is permanent and therefore you just need ways of coping with depression?" Of course, the motivated and committed client will voice a greater interest in the former option as opposed to the latter.

The Credulous Approach to Assessment

In his usual common-sense manner, Kelly pioneered the credulous approach to assessment. He summarizes this approach by stating, "If you don't know what is wrong with a person, ask him [sic]; he may tell you" (Kelly, 1955, p. 322). Kelly's approach—and every approach associated with constructive therapy—emphasizes that clients are the best expert on their own lives and should be treated as such.

Is Formal Assessment Really Required for a Constructive Therapist?

The radical solution-focused view of assessment holds that traditional assessment is unnecessary. De Shazer (1985) articulates this position:

> For an intervention to successfully fit, it is not necessary to have detailed knowledge of the complaint. It is not necessary even to be able to construct with any rigor how the trouble is maintained in order to prompt solution. . . . All that is necessary is that the person involved in a troublesome situation does something different, even if that behavior is seemingly irrational, certainly irrelevant, obviously bizarre, or humorous. (p. 7)

Despite his irreverent position regarding assessment of client problems, De Shazer has a straightforward but complex method for evaluating client complaints and quickly providing potential solutions. His approach doesn't involve traditional or formal assessment, but it does offer therapists a menu of potential formula solutions linked to client complaints. De Shazer's system is described in Putting It in Practice 11.2.

Specific Therapy Techniques

In this section we include specific therapy techniques derived from solution-focused brief therapy, solution-oriented therapy, and narrative therapy. We make theoretical distinctions regarding each technique as much as possible, but practically speaking, these constructive therapies use many overlapping technical procedures.

The Pretreatment Change Question

Research indicates that clients often begin improving between the time they call for an appointment and the first session (Beyebach, Morejon, Palenzuela, & Rodriguez-Arias, 1996). To help clients focus on how they're already using their strengths and resources effectively, a version of the following question is asked at the beginning of the first session: "What improvements in your situation have you noticed between the time when you called the clinic for your appointment and right now?" Solution-focused brief therapists report that a large percentage of clients have begun making changes prior to their first session (Weiner-Davis, de Shazer, & Gingerich, 1987).

Unique Account and Redescription Questions

As a specific therapy tool, Michael White (1988) developed unique account and redescription questions. These questions, which we like to refer to as "How did you man-

De Shazer's Complaint-Solution Assessment System

In his complaint-solution assessment system, de Shazer (1985) identifies 12 typical complaints that he views as doors leading to various solutions. Table 11.1 describes each complaint-door and corresponding solution. Some constructive theorists and therapists consider de Shazer's complaint-prescription system too formulaic (Efran & Fauber, 1995; O'Hanlon, 1998).

Client complaint	Formula solution prescription
The client complains about a bit or sequence of behavior: "When I'm depressed, I can't get myself out of bed in the morning."	Assign a specific task: "On the days when you do get out of bed in the morning, what's the first thing you do? Go ahead and do that each morning."
The client complains about the meanings ascribed to a situation: "My wife won't stop nagging me about getting a better job. She thinks I'm a lazy good-for-nothing husband."	Use reframing: "It's clear your wife loves you very much and is concerned about your happiness."
The client complains about the frequency of a problem behavior or experience: "I'm always worrying about everything—my husband's health, my daughter's marriage, our financial situation."	Assign a specific task: "You're worrying is important. I'd like you to schedule a half hour every day to just focus on worrying. What time would work best for you?"
The client complains about the physical location where the problem occurs: "I only drink when I'm out with my buddies on Friday's after work."	Suggest a new location: "Where could you and your buddies go after work and not drink?"
The client complains that the problem is involuntary: "I can't stop myself from pulling out hair from my eyebrows."	Prescribe the symptom, ask for exceptions to the rule, or suggest a new location: "I notice you still have plenty of eyebrow hairs left; would you get to work on that this week?" or "What's happening during those times when you don't pull out your eyebrow hairs?" or "Where are you when you don't pull out your eyebrow hairs?"
The client complains about significant others involved in the problem: "And then my wife totally sabotages my diet by baking all these cakes and cookies."	Ask when guilt will be resolved or what difference it will make to them: "When will your wife be free from guilt over contributing to your weight problem?" or "What difference will it make to your wife if you choose not to eat her cakes and cookies?"
The client complains about who or what is to blame for the problem: "This whole situation is my brother's fault. He is totally insensitive and selfish."	Ask when guilt will be resolved: "When is it likely for your brother's guilt in this matter to be resolved?"
The client complains about an environmental factor or situation such as job, economic status, living space, etc.: "My job sucks. My boss rides me constantly and I don't like any of my coworkers."	Suggest a new location: "You could either quit your job or spend time with your boss and coworkers at some place where you might actually enjoy them."
The client complains about a physiological state or feeling: "I weigh about 190 pounds and have tried everything to lose weight. I'd like to weigh 125 to 130 pounds."	Use symptom prescription: "The first thing you need to do is go home and start eating. When you get up to 220 pounds, come back and I can help you" (adapted from Haley, 1973, pp. 115–119).

(continued)

Putting It in Practice 11.2 (continued)

Client complaint	Formula solution prescription
The client complains about the past: "My parents were abusive and critical of me when I was young. They favored my sister."	Talk about a past success: "You were able to graduate from high school with high honors."
The client complains about likely future situations that are catastrophic or dire: "I know I'm gonna flunk my history test."	Talk about a past success or focus on new expectations: "How did you pass your last one?" or "What would you have to do to get a D on your exam?"
The client has excessively idealistic or utopian expectations: "I know I'll be able to get a job this summer, no problem."	Focus on new expectations or focus on a minimal change: "What if it was hard to get a job this summer? How would you cope with that?" or "Tell me what it would look like if you just put 10% more effort into getting a job."

Source. Adapted from de Shazer (1985).

age that?" questions, constitute the mainstay of many solution-based and narrative therapy approaches. These questions, phrased in many different ways and accompanied by genuine interest, are used whenever clients say anything that might be construed as progress. Narrative therapists typically refer to these glimmers of hope as a *unique outcome* or *sparkling moment* (Monk et al., 1997; White & Epston, 1990). Examples include

- How did you beat the fear and go out shopping?
- How did you manage to get yourself out of bed and in here for this appointment despite the depression?
- You just stopped drinking last week cold turkey! How did you accomplish that?
- What were you telling yourself when you were feeling a little better last month?

From the narrative perspective, the client's personal narrative can never match the depth and richness of the client's lived experiences. Unfortunately, what usually gets dismissed or pruned away from the client's story are the moments of strength, the instant of courage in the face of adversity, and experiences of positive decision making. Consequently, it's crucial for therapists not only to highlight these sparkling moments but also to help the client articulate and repeat their occurrences using words, images, and even movements. The key is to acknowledge, not ignore, these positive, lived moments. Monk (1997) compares the therapist's nurturance for sparkling moments to the process of building a fire:

> These sparkling moments, or new developments in relation to the problem-saturated story, need to be historicized so that they do not hang lifeless and disconnected. I like to describe this stage of the narrative interview as similar to the task of building a fire. To keep the first flickering flame alive, you place tiny twigs very carefully and strategically over the flame. If the twig is too large, the flame could be suffocated. If there is only one twig, it will quickly be spent and the flame will be extinguished. The fire needs to be gently nurtured by the

placing of twigs in such a way that oxygen can feed the flames. Larger sticks are then placed on the fire, and soon the fire has a life of its own. (pp. 16–17)

Monk's analogy is an excellent warning. Therapists need to pay attention to sparkling moments but not to jump in too enthusiastically when they first emerge. If therapists are too excited about client progress, the client may quickly retreat back into his or her safe and unsatisfactory life story.

Externalizing Conversations

Virtually everyone recognizes the tendency for clients (and other humans) to blame either themselves or others when things go awry. Blaming is a natural, unhelpful human phenomenon.

Externalizing conversations are designed to help clients, couples, and families stop blaming themselves and one another. Through problem externalization, clients can dissociate from the problem, look at it from a greater distance, and develop strategies for eliminating it. Externalizing conversation examples include "How long have you been working against this marijuana problem?" and "I notice you two occasionally get in a pattern where Franco is afraid to speak for fear of Maria's criticism, while Maria gets more and more angry whenever Franco retreats and doesn't speak his mind. What have the two of you been doing to fight against that pattern?"

When individual clients, couples, or families engage in therapeutic externalizing conversations, they usually experience considerable relief. This is because clients typically come to counseling worrying that the therapist's all-seeing and all-knowing eye will pierce their defenses and hold them 100% responsible for their problems. Instead, externalizing conversations take away clients' sense of accountability and reduce defensiveness, thereby allowing clients to work constructively against their presenting problems.

Questions for Reflection

Can you imagine using externalizing questions with clients? Consider how you might initiate an externalizing conversation in the following situations: (1) A client comes in complaining of "biological" depression; (2) a client has a long history of panic attacks and agoraphobia; (3) referred by a probation officer, a parent and teenager come in to work on the teen's pattern of delinquent behavior.

Carl Rogers with a Twist

O'Hanlon credits Carl Rogers with teaching him the importance of showing empathy and compassion for clients. He also describes a unique technique for showing empathy and compassion while at the same time helping clients move beyond their negative or traumatic feelings from the past. Examples of this technique, entitled "Carl Rogers with a Twist," include the following:

Client: I feel like cutting myself.
Therapist: You've felt like cutting yourself (O'Hanlon & Bertolino, 1998, p. 47).
[In this example the therapist is validating the client but shifting to past tense.]
Client: I have flashbacks all the time.

Therapist: So you have flashbacks a lot of the time.

[In this example the therapist transforms the client's verbal disclosure from a global to a partial perception.]

Client: I'm a bad person because I was sexually abused.

Therapist: So you've really gotten the idea that you are bad because you were sexually abused.

[In this last example the therapist shifts the client's words from factual to perceptual.]

Relabeling

From the constructive perspective, relabeling and reframing are at the core of therapy. Specifically, clients are customers for change, and therapy is a conversation. Some therapists are not therapists at all; instead they are coaches and consultants. Constructivists systematically relabel and reframe each of these aspects of therapy to make the process more user-friendly and egalitarian.

In our experience, we have seen therapy-resistant teens quickly become cooperative when we relabel the therapy process. For example, teens who boldly claim, "I think therapy is stupid" and "You can't make me talk in here" suddenly calm down and talk openly when we respond to their complaints with, "Yeah, okay, so let's not do therapy today. How about if we have a consultation meeting instead? I won't be your therapist today; I'll just be you're consultant" (see J. Sommers-Flanagan & Sommers-Flanagan, 1997)

Language use is a foundation for reframing or, as Haley (1976) discussed, positive relabeling. In his solution-focused book on working with adolescents, Selekman (1993) recommends using a forced-teaming reframe with an adolescent who was referred by a probation officer. Selekman suggests that he and the client team together to surprise and prove to the probation officer that the boy can avoid trouble and be successful. This approach captures the boy's attention, intriguing him and motivating him to work harder with the counselor.

Similarly, many parents resist using positive reinforcement approaches with their children because they view such strategies as bribery. In our work with difficult adolescents, it has been very helpful when parents redefine rewards as *positive incentives* rather than bribery, which helps them become more open to using positive approaches to influencing their children (J. Sommers-Flanagan & Sommers-Flanagan, 1997).

Presuppositional Questions

In and of itself, goal setting is a powerful force for change. Surprisingly, it wasn't until 1970 that goal setting was conceptualized as a direct way in which individual and group behavior could be modified (Ryan, 1970). Locke and Latham (1990, 2002) and others have demonstrated that individuals perform better when they have specific, difficult goals.

Constructive therapists use presuppositional questions to cocreate therapeutic and life goals with clients (DeJong & Berg, 2002). These questions presuppose that a positive change has already been made and ask for specific descriptions of these changes. O'Hanlon and Bertolino (1998) illustrate a presuppositional question using an approach they refer to as *videotalk:*

Let's say that a few weeks, months, or more time has elapsed and your problem has been resolved. If you and I were to watch a videotape of your life in the future, what would you be doing on that tape that would show that things were better? (p. 90)

There are many creative versions of presupposition questions using language ranging from crystal balls to letters (or postcards) from the future. The main point is to construct a question that helps clients hear, feel, and clearly picture themselves functioning in the future without their problems. Some therapists believe that the longer clients
can focus on positive, problem-free, goal-attained futures within a session, the greater
likelihood they have of making the solution-focused future happen (Staton, personal
communication, November 19, 2002).

Formula Tasks

In addition to the formula pretreatment change question discussed previously, there are
several other solution-based formula tasks. De Shazer (1984, 1985; de Shazer & Molnar, 1984) originally developed these tasks. Three of his most popular and useful tasks
are described next. For information on de Shazer's other formula tasks (e.g., "read
write and burn" and "the structured fight task") readers are referred to *Keys to Solution in Brief Therapy* (de Shazer, 1985).

The *first session formula task* is designed to help clients shift from a focus on the past
and negative expectations to a present-future focus and positive expectations. This task
is based on the assumption that, in general, there are many positive qualities already existing within most families who come for treatment.

> Between now and the next time we meet, I would like you to notice what is happening in
> your family that you would like to continue to happen. (original version, de Shazer, 1985,
> p. 137; quoted in Selekman, 1993, p. 8)

Selekman (1993) reports that clients he works with usually return to their second session with two or three specific descriptions of positive interactions they would like to
have continue.

The *miracle question* is probably the most well-known solution-focused therapy technique. De Shazer's (1988) original version of the miracle question follows:

> Suppose you were to go home tonight, and while you were asleep, a miracle happened and
> this problem was solved. How will you know the miracle happened? What will be differ-
> ent? (p. 5)

The miracle question is simply another presuppositional question that helps clients
focus on a positive future. When clients respond to the question, it is important for therapists to obtain clear, concrete, and behaviorally specific descriptions of what would be
different. In some ways, this question helps clients develop and hopefully maintain a
positive future vision. The question also builds rapport with clients; when therapists
validate and nurture each answer the client provides, the therapy alliance is deepened.

The miracle question is a flexible intervention that can be modified for use with various populations. For example, Bertolino (1999) suggests an alternative wording when
using the miracle question with young clients:

> Suppose that when you went home tonight and went to sleep, something strange happened
> to you and your life changed for the better. You may or may not know what actually hap-
> pened, but you knew that your problem had gone away. What will be different? (p. 75)

Bertolino recommends substituting the word *strange* for *miracle*. He also suggests
that therapists working with youth might use *weird* or an alternative word the client has

previously used in therapy. He advises therapists to modify their language style when working with young clients.

Tohn and Oshlag (1996) describe a slightly different version of the miracle question for use with mandated clients:

> **Suppose** that tonight, after our session, you go home and fall asleep, and while you are sleeping a miracle happens. The miracle is that **the problems that brought you here today** are solved, but you don't know that the miracle has happened because you are asleep. When you wake up in the morning, what will be some of the first things you will **notice** that will be different that will tell you this miracle has happened? (pp. 170–171, bold in original)

Tohn and Oslag include critical words and wording in boldface type. They explain that beginning with the word suppose is crucial because it leads clients toward pretending that the miracle has already happened, rather than speculating on whether it will or will not happen. They also note that saying "the problems that brought you here" focuses the question on the reality of the situation. In contrast, they note that when therapists use "your problem is solved," clients are likely to respond with a more grandiose disappearance of the problem. Finally, they use the word *notice* toward the end of the intervention to help clients respond using a wide range of sensory experiences.

Exception questions are also a standard formula solution-based intervention (DeJong & Berg, 2002). In keeping with the theoretical position that only small changes are needed to instigate larger changes, exception questions seek minor evidence that the client's problem is not always huge and overbearing. Bertolino (1999) provides several examples of exception questions for use with teenage clients:

- It seems that when this problem is happening, things are pretty difficult. When does the problem seem less noticeable to you? What is everyone doing when it's less noticeable?
- When does the problem appear to happen less?
- What is your son/daughter doing when he/she is not in trouble?
- Tell me what it's like when the problem is a little less dominating.

Exception question are designed to build hope and to identify small behavioral patterns or sequences when the problem is either occurring less or not occurring at all. Constructive therapists use exception sequences to build a case for preexisting client strengths and resources. These sequences can be helpful in building up or feeding the client's adaptive storyline in contrast to the problem-saturated storyline.

The *do something different task* is a direct but nonspecific intervention that is especially well suited to repeating, dissatisfying behavior sequences. For example, if a parent comes to therapy complaining about her son's recurrent tantrums, the therapist might tell the parent to do something totally different the next time a tantrum occurs.

As is the case with very direct but nonspecific interventions, the therapist cannot know in advance what different behavior the client may select to engage in. This unknown and unknowable component of the intervention fuels both creativity and danger. It releases clients from previously stuck behavior patterns but may also implicitly give them permission to act out inappropriately or even violently. In one case reported by de Shazer (1985), the father of a young boy with a pattern of lying came up with the idea of rubbing his son's face in "bullshit" whenever a lie was suspected. Fortunately, the boy's mother wouldn't allow such an intervention, so the father chose a less violent option of buying a can of "bullshit repellent" from a local novelty shop and spraying his son with it on the next occasion of a lie. Although de Shazer reports success in this case, it clearly illustrates the fact that clients are more than capable of coming up with bad and even abusive ideas for doing something different when left completely to their own design.

Letter Writing

In an effort to deepen the therapeutic process and further stimulate the development of alternative storylines, Epston, (1994; White & Epston, 1990) pioneered the use of letter writing as a narrative therapeutic technique. Epston uses and recommends several letter formats. Next, we describe some of these formats and provide brief examples. For more detailed examples, you should consult *Narrative Means to Therapeutic Ends* (White & Epston, 1990)

In the *summary* letter, narrative therapists write to clients immediately following a therapeutic conversation. Summary letters typically are written from the therapist's perspective but highlight sparkling moments and use the client's words to produce a more strength- and hope-based storyline.

Letters of invitation are typically written to family members who are reluctant to attend therapy sessions. These letters gently highlight the individual's important status in the family, focusing on the positive reasons for attending a session, rather than on the negative consequences or implications associated with nonattendance. The following letter of invitation, written by Mary Underwood and David Epston, illustrates a primary narrative strategy of telling a storyline with more than one possible outcome and then allowing the client to choose her direction (White & Epston, 1990, pp. 89–90):

> Dear Jane,
>
> I'm writing because we didn't get to meet each other last Wednesday at 5 P.M.
>
> My name is Mary. I've worked at Leslie Centre for four years. I have a daughter just a little younger than you.
>
> When your mother phoned to say your family wouldn't be coming in, she said you were feeling badly with acne that had flared up. I can understand how you felt—I sometimes get a rash on my face and neck myself.
>
> It's hard writing to you when I don't even know what you look like. If you send me a photo, I'll send you one.
>
> Well it's pretty clear that things are going wrong in your family. Growing up is very hard these days—I'm sure it's harder than it used to be. It sounds like you're failing to get to school sometimes and failing to get on with your life. That would sure make anyone feel miserable.
>
> When I meet with your mother and father next time, I would think that you'll probably have another attack of acne—and I know what it's like to face people when you're not at your best—I do it quite often.
>
> So I'll understand if you don't feel up to coming and facing into your future.
>
> But, on the other hand, I'd feel really badly talking behind your back with your mother and father.
>
> I've been thinking of this dilemma quite a bit and I've come up with some ideas. I wonder what you think about them:
>
> 1. Could you get a friend to represent you at the session—a bit like a lawyer—who could come in your place and speak for you?
> 2. If that's not a good idea, what about you let your mother or father choose a friend of theirs to represent you?
> 3. If that's not a good idea, what about you go on "stand by" at the telephone while your parents are here? Then I can call you if I get the impression that your parents

have forgotten what it's like to be your age. I can ask for a few ideas about how it
feels for you.

Sounds like you've got your parents pretty worried about you.

If you really want to show your parents this letter it doesn't really matter. But I'd prefer
you didn't.

I'm planning to meet with your mother and father on Wednesday, April 3rd, at 5:30 P.M.
I suppose you might come or you might not or you might try one of those other ideas. It's
up to you, I guess.

Well, bye for now,

    Yours sincerely,

      Mary

Redundancy letters articulate observations and client reports of overlapping or enmeshed family roles. For example, a daughter in a family system may be overly identified with her mother and therefore enacting a parental role with younger siblings.
Along with the observation of this family dynamic, the redundancy letter outlines the
client's impulse, using her own words, to move forward and establish a more unique
identity of her own. Redundancy letters are often accompanied by a discharge letter;
in a discharge letter one family member formally discharges another family member
from performing a redundant duty (e.g., the mother and therapist work together to
write a kind and compassionate letter to the daughter releasing her from parental duties).

At the end of therapy, *letters of prediction* are written to help clients continue
strength-based storylines into the future. Epston asks clients permission to make predictions for the future and then mails the letters—usually with a "private and confidential" label and an instruction "not to be viewed until [six months after the final ses-
sion]" (White & Epston, 1990, p. 94). He cites two reasons for using prediction letters.
First, he notes that the letters serve as a 6-month follow-up or review that is both interesting and potentially helpful (White & Epston, 1990, p. 94). Second, he suspects that
most clients will not wait six months to open the letter and that it therefore serves as a
possible positive prophesy.

Both Epston and White discuss writing many other types of letters, letters that
spring from the issues and concerns expressed to them during sessions. Some of these
additional letter variations include letters of reference, counterreferral letters, and letters for special occasions. White, in particular, includes several examples of what he
refers to as brief letters designed to strengthen the positive therapeutic narrative. An example follows in which White maps a client's personal influence in her own life:

Dear Molly,

    Anorexia nervosa had claimed 99% of your life. You only held 1% of your own terri-
tory. You have said that you now hold 25% of your own territory. This means that you have
reclaimed 24% of yourself from anorexia nervosa, and you achieved this over the last eight
months. And yet, you despair for all those lost years, for the two-thirds of your life under
its influence.

    Tell me, if you were to pick up another 24% over the next eight months, and then 24%
over the next eight months and so on, how long would it take you to reach 200% and be experiencing double value in your life? And should you keep on in this way, how old would
you be at the point when you have regained all the time that was lost? And what will it mean
that your life is accelerating right at the time that other are slowing down in their lives?

    Just curious,

    M.W. (White & Epston, 1990, p. 116)

White's letter is a potent example of problem externalization using scaling information for feedback and personal influence mapping.

Clearly, writing letters to clients has great potential for influencing clients. In our work with young clients we have experimented with in-session note-passing. We've noticed that clients are often surprised and touched at receiving a written communiqué from a concerned and interested therapist (J. Sommers-Flanagan & Sommers-Flanagan, 1997). Commenting on the therapeutic power of letter writing to clients, White (1995) estimates that a single letter may contain within it the significance of four to five therapy sessions.

Reflecting Teams or Therapeutic Breaks

The contemporary concept of a reflecting team stems from Norwegian psychiatrist Tom Andersen's approach to family therapy (Andersen, 1987, 1991, 1995). Following his lead, many therapists have integrated reflecting teams or therapeutic breaks into individual, couple, and family therapy. This approach, which emphasizes multiple perspectives or realities, is highly consistent with constructivist thinking.

Andersen's reflective team is a feedback procedure that is much different from the traditional one-way mirror in family therapy training (Andersen, 1987). In the one-way mirror paradigm, a supervisor and fellow students sit behind a one-way mirror and observe family therapy sessions. Sometimes the supervisor communicates with the therapist about appropriate therapeutic interventions via a bug-in-the-ear device. Overall, the standard procedure emphasizes supervisory input and a rich discussion of "the case" either midway during the session or immediately afterwards.

Consistent with postmodern constructivist thinking, Andersen's reflecting team breaks down hierarchical boundaries of traditional one-way mirror supervision by introducing a two-way mirror reflecting team. Originally, his reflecting team procedures consisted of the following:

1. During an impasse when the therapist is unsure how to proceed, or at a pre-planned time, a reflecting team meeting is initiated.
2. The therapy session stops as the therapist and family turn to the mirror and the lights and sound system are reversed.
3. The therapist and family watch and listen as the reflecting team spontaneously provide tentative hypotheses about the family's problem issues.
4. During the reflecting team meeting, care is taken to talk about the family in a respectful, nonpathologizing manner.
5. When the reflecting team meeting ends, the lights and sound system are again reversed and family members and therapist have a conversation about the reflecting team's conversation.

Reflecting teams seek to honor the family, while at the same time providing fresh new perspectives. This procedure helps the family feel important, listened to, and accepted. After using the reflecting team approach for a number of years, Andersen (1995) described some of his discoveries:

When we finally began to use this mode we were surprised at how easy it was to talk without using nasty or hurtful words. Later it became evident that how we talk depends on the context in which we talk. If we choose to speak about the family without them present, we easily speak "professionally," in a detached manner. If we choose to speak about them in their presence, we naturally use everyday language and speak in a friendly manner. (p. 16)

The reflecting team approach as articulated by Andersen is a gentle and collaborative experience. He emphasizes that the reflecting team speak with uncertainty, with inclusive both-and language ("*both* this could be true *and* this other thing could be true, too"), and without negative connotations (Andersen, 1991, p. 61).

Andersen's approach is in contrast to the more provocative, hierarchical, and sometimes double-binding approaches derived from Erickson's work and the MRI group. For example, de Shazer (1985) reports using the following feedback intervention with a couple whose drug use was, in the eyes of the woman, adversely affecting their marriage.

You've got a problem.
It seems to us, Ralph, that your marital problems are being exacerbated by the drugs, or fogged over by the drugs, or perhaps even created by the drugs. Perhaps you need to stop the drugs, just to see what is going on. But, on the other hand, we agree with you Jane, that if you two were to stop the drugs, then there might be nothing there. And, you might not have time to create anything before the marriage broke up. In short, we don't know what the fuck you are going to do.
I suggest you think about what I just said, and decide what actions you are going to take . . . first. (p. 52)

De Shazer reported that the clients cut down on their drug use immediately after the intervention. Within weeks, both clients stopped using drugs and managed to stay married and to develop healthier common interests.

Questions for Reflection

As you contrast Andersen's and de Shazer's styles, what major differences do you notice? Which approach are you more comfortable with and why?

APPLICATION: CASE EXAMPLE

The constructive therapy literature is filled with brief case examples and vignettes. Ordinarily, these cases are reported as anecdotes or stories, rather than as verbatim therapy transcripts or single-case research. To give you a sense of how a possibility therapist approaches therapy with a difficult teen, we include a brief verbatim exchange published by Bob Bertolino.

In the following case, Bertolino illustrates the brief, persistently hopeful, language-based approach often characteristic of solution-oriented or possibility therapy. We do not include an example from the solution-focused brief therapy or narrative models because anecdotes and examples of those approaches were well represented throughout the chapter.

The Case of a Resistant Teenager

The following excerpt from a case of an angry 14-year-old boy is from Bob Bertolino's 1999 book, *Therapy with Troubled Teenagers.* This is the case of a Caucasian boy who was referred for counseling by his juvenile probation officer. The boy had a history of curfew violation, running away, truancy, and assaultive behavior. Bertolino's comments on the case are in brackets.

Bob: So where would you like to start?

Richard: I had to come. My DJO (Deputy Juvenile Officer) told me if I didn't, she'd put me back in juvy. I didn't have a choice.

Laura (mom): It was a condition of his probation.

Bob: Do you think that was her way of getting you to come, or would you have come on your own if she would have just recommended it?

Richard: If I didn't have to, I wouldn't be here.

Laura: She had to make him come . . . 'cause he wouldn't have come.

Bob: I can understand that you wouldn't have come without her telling you to . . . but I'm glad you're here. Did she say to you what she thinks needs to happen here?

Richard: I don't remember.

Laura: Yes you do . . . she said you need to find some ways to handle your anger better.

Bob: Can you be more specific about that? What does he do when he's angry?

[I'm looking for an action description here.]

Laura: He gets mad then there's hell to pay 'cause he won't listen. He just takes off and does what he pleases.

Bob: Takes off and leaves?

Laura: Yeah, he goes wherever he wants and comes home when he feels like it.

Bob (to Richard): What about that? Would you add or change anything about that?

Richard: I don't know.

Bob: OK, he gets angry and takes off sometimes . . . what else might have led your juvenile officer to send you here?

[I said "sometimes" he takes off, suggesting that he doesn't do it every time.]

Richard: 'Cause I was with some friends and we got caught after curfew. It wasn't any big deal . . . she's just always on my case about something.

Bob: So, because sometimes she's had to lay down the law with you, it's felt like she's hassling you. How many times were you out after curfew?

[When people use statements that are generalized and closed down, we want to find small, subtle ways of opening up possibilities. There are several ways to do this. In this instance, I slightly modified Richard's statement in three ways. First, I used "sometimes" instead of "always." Next, I changed the tense to the past. Thus, she is not currently on his case, but has done so previously. Last, I translated his statement of what was happening into a perception by saying, "You feel like." It is important to acknowledge and validate without closing down the possibilities for change; however, the therapist must balance the two because too much of either can also close down avenues of change.]

(Bertolino, 1999, pp. 189–191)

We include this case to emphasize the language details associated with the possibility approach. The entire case is available in Bertolina's book (1999).

PRACTITIONER COMMENTARY 11.1

Therapy is Research and Research is Therapy: The Evolution of a Strategic Constructivist

This commentary is written by Giorgio Nardone.

I was still a young epistemologist with a planned academic career, when I first arrived at MRI to study at the so-called Palo Alto School of Thinking. This experience made me shift from the pure philosophy of science to psychotherapy. So from then onwards, I began to dedicate my studies and works to human problems and their possible solutions. Moreover, Paul Watzlawick and John Weakland were the encouraging and stimulating supervisors of my first research project on phobic-obsessive disorders treatment, still today my most popular topic.

Thanks to this successful project, many colleagues approached me to ask for training, as well as a lot of patients ask for therapy for the so-called untreatable phobias or obsessions. All this pushed me to work more and more, both in therapy and in research. This is the way in which, every time a research project finishes another takes off, in a sort of virtual spiral.

I still have in my mind the encouraging image of John saying "no" while nodding "yes". Paul is for me much more than a master colleague, and a friend; we have shared till now 15 years of working together, three coauthored books, and more then 100 workshops and conferences, held all around the world.

Thanks both to their initial help and the further work together with my collaborator, I have successfully tried to evolve the MRI traditional brief strategic therapy beyond its limits, particularly through long-term empirical-experimental research. I set up specific protocols of the treatments for phobic-obsessive pathologies as well as for eating disorders, which revealed elevated results both in terms of efficacy (87% solved cases) and efficiency (mean duration of therapy 7 sessions) in their application on more than five hundred cases during 10 years of work at the Strategic Therapy Center in Arezzo.

My current objectives rely mostly on the fact that I am constantly faced by the challenge of devising effective strategies for the solution of further complicated pathologies. I actually do not place my trust in any strong theory but only in operative knowledge, because even the best theory, if rigid, becomes a deterministic trap. If the work is driven by the goal to be reached, this helps to keep our mind elastic and free and our strategies concrete and effective. From my point of view, therapy is research and research is therapy. We can really get to how a problem works only by means of its solution.

THERAPY OUTCOMES RESEARCH

The two different constructivist approaches to therapy reviewed in this chapter (solution-based and narrative) take two distinctly different approaches to outcomes research.

Solution-based therapists enthusiastically point to a variety of data indicating that their therapy approach is at least equivalent to traditional therapies. They claim (1) that research has already convincingly shown that all therapy approaches are essentially equivalent (Duncan, Hubble, Miller, & Coleman, 1998), (2) that there is a "large body of research" indicating that brief therapy is effective (Koss & Shiang, 1994), and (3) that solution-based therapies are brief (de Shazer, 1991). Using this reasoning in combination with numerous case reports, testimonials, client surveys, and a single, uncontrolled outcome study conducted at the BFTC, solution-based therapists stake their claim to therapeutic effectiveness (DeJong & Hopwood, 1996; McKeel, 1996). In many ways, the solution-based approach to evaluating empirical literature is consistent with their dogmatically positive framing of client problem situations as being saturated with solutions. Of course, the possibility remains that they may be correct in their claims, but as S. D. Miller et al. (1996) summarize in the introduction to their edited volume, *Handbook of Solution-Focused Brief Therapy,* the scientific evidence is absent:

> Not only does no single collection of studies exist, but for the most part there simply are no research studies to report! In fact, in spite of having been around for ten years, no well-controlled, scientifically sound outcome studies on solution-focused therapy have every been conducted or published in any peer-reviewed professional journal. (p. 2)

Narrative theorists and therapists take a more philosophical view of treatment outcomes research. From their perspective, narrow, symptom-based evaluations consistent with outcomes research are inadequate to address the qualitative changes that may or may not occur within clients as a function of therapy. This perspective is similar to existential, feminist, and multicultural theorists who are deeply dissatisfied with reductionistic scientific evaluation methods.

MULTICULTURAL PERSPECTIVES

> *Oh sun, moon, stars, our other relatives peering at us from the inside of god's house walk with us as we climb into the next century naked but for the stories we have of each other. Keep us from giving up in this land of nightmares which is also the land of miracles.*
>
> *We sing our song which we've been promised has no beginning or end.*
>
> —Joy Harjo (from Reconciliation—A Prayer)

In theory, constructive therapies are deeply multicultural. This is because constructive theory emphasizes respect for the individual; respect for personal language, languaging, and narrative; and respect for each individual's construction of reality. In practice, constructive therapies may not always live up to their theoretical ideals.

Overall, multicultural sensitivity among constructive therapies seems to fall along a continuum. On the far left of the continuum lies narrative therapy, the most multiculturally oriented of all constructive approaches. The extreme sensitivity to human diversity articulated among narrative therapists may attain because White and Epston were strongly influenced by a wide diversity of thought and have worked directly with aboriginal tribal populations in Australia and New Zealand.

O'Hanlon's possibility therapy (previously solution-oriented therapy) also values and honors human diversity. However, his approaches are somewhat more formulaic and therefore could be practiced in ways reflecting a less-than-ideal multicultural orientation.

At the other end of the continuum lies solution-focused brief therapy. With its em-

ETHICAL HIGHLIGHT 11.1

Constructive Ethical Principles

In this ethical highlight, Giorgio Nardone discusses the ethical issues that emerge for him as he teaches his students strategic-constructivist therapy.

The theoretically related ethical position guiding both my practice and my personal life is based on the constructivistic nonnormative concept, defining all pathologies as a dysfunctional interaction of the subject with himself, the others, and the world.

From this perspective, the first stance requires the therapist to be respectful with every human being. Furthermore, being a psychotherapist requires the ability to understand how human systems work dysfunctionally, as well as the knowledge and the know-how in making them work functionally.

In a really practical way I have listed for my students a series of ethical principles to follow in their practice:

- Formulate together with the patient an agreement on the objectives of the therapy; both parties should recognize their respective responsibilities.
- Avoid labeling the patient pathologically.
- Keep in mind that we, as therapists, are at the service of the patient, not the other way around.
- We should be able to give an estimate (obviously a probabilistic one) of the duration of therapy. This will give the patient a parameter of reliability of what he or she is doing.
- Beware of excessive compliments as well as of continuous denigration. Compliments are pleasurable but will not cure the patient; denigrating comments can at times be useful; but when they are constant, they will only make the patient worse.
- Evaluate the changes the patient has obtained concretely, in terms of patient's state, and put forward the evaluation to the patient. This would oblige the patient to do the same. Furthermore, this will keep you from becoming too absorbed in the therapy and losing sight of concrete facts.
- Whenever giving therapeutic advice or prescription, evaluate the expected costs and benefits critically together with your patient to avoid using a cannon to shoot a fly and because it will be the patient who will be shouldering the costs.
- If the patient's state does not show any improvement after a period of 3 or 4 months, first opt to change strategies. If concrete results remain unseen, terminate the therapy at once and refer the patient to another colleague more adequate for the case. If a therapy that does not work is continued, it becomes harmful.
- The patient's problems should be treated primarily with therapies that expose him or her to the smallest possible risks or dangers at the lowest existential cost. Change to higher-impact methods only if the low-impact methods have produced no results. Remember the therapeutic maxim is obtaining much with a little.

phasis on brevity, formulaic interventions, and disinterest in each individual's unique problem, solution-focused brief therapy has the greatest likelihood among constructive theories of being multiculturally insensitive. However, it should be emphasized that his approach is not inherently insensitive and that it has attracted a strong international appeal. In particular, the cofounder of the approach, Insoo Kim Berg, is Korean.

To articulate the multicultural potential of constructive therapy, we provide an excerpt of an essay written by New Zealand psychiatrist Glen Simblett. This essay illustrates the rich, egalitarian, multicultural, and nontraditional nature of narrative therapy. It focuses on an unsuccessful traditional psychiatric case with a native woman in New Zealand.

Leila and the Tiger

Leila was Maori [a New Zealand native]. Twenty-four years old. A woman. A patient. She stood in my office and handed me a drawing. Neither of us sat down. I was puzzled. This was meant to be a routine outpatient follow-up to Leila's recent discharge from a psychiatric unit. Pictures are not normally a part of that. Ten minutes earlier, I had been uncertain if she was even going to keep the appointment. We had only met a couple times. The last time had been particularly difficult and unpleasant. She had been so troubled by hallucinatory voices commanding her to hurt herself and her family that I had coerced her into accepting admission to the hospital for further assessment and treatment. I had later heard that while there she had stopped talking, eating, and drinking. Her physical health had deteriorated rapidly. Against the advice of her doctors, she had stopped treatment and persuaded her family to discharge her from the hospital to see a tohunga [a Maori healer]. Some incredulity had been expressed about that by the white mental health workers. They asked if potatoes in her shoes were going to stop a depressive psychosis or schizophrenia.

I was about to find out.

The drawing was an incomplete profile of the head of a tiger.

"It's a tiger," I said lamely.

She waited silently. There had been some words written beside the tiger. I could still see the erasure marks.

"Was something written there?"

Leila nodded—the slightest tilt of her head. "There was a story to go with it. I changed my mind about writing it."

I knew that I was holding something significant in my hands but did not have the faintest idea how to respond. I was outside my psychiatric training. Outside the country I was born in. Outside my culture. I knew enough to register that, but not enough to know how to proceed.

I clutched at straws.

"I really like this picture, but I don't know what it means," I said.

"Do you want to hear the story?"

We still hovered uncertainly. I noticed that she was nearer the door than I was, and the door was still open. She avoided my gaze.

"Yes, I would like to."

Leila took a deep breath. "This is a tiger. A tiger has nine lives. This tiger only has five lives left. Do you want to know what happened to the other lives?"

I did, but I didn't. Part of me knew what was coming next, and I didn't want to hear it.

"Yes I do," I lied.

"It lost its first life in the family it was born in because of their abuse and punishment. It lost its second life to drugs and alcohol. She [sic] lost her third life in a marriage where there was no room for her hopes and ideas." She paused, for the first time catching my gaze with culturally surprising boldness. "She lost her last life when she was admitted to a psychiatric unit."

Another pause.

"She hasn't got many lives left now," Leila added.

She waited silently. Patiently. It was not an accusation. Just a statement. The way it was for her.

Where do you go from here? You begin again, maybe. I invited her to sit down. We closed the door and we talked. We tried to understand each other's point of view. We tried not to blame.

I still find it hard to understand why she gave me another chance like that, why she did not just give up on yet another Pakeha [white] doctor who did not understand. I often wonder if I would have been so generous if the roles had been reversed. The tiger drawing still hangs on the wall of my office. It acts as a gentle caution and constant reminder to me of the dangers of dominant discourse. (Simblett, 1997, pp. 121–122)

Simblett's experience with Leila and his exposure to White and Epston's narrative approach transformed the way he practices psychiatry. He now reads referral letters from other physicians aloud to his patients and asks for their comments. He also now formulates client problems differently. For example, rather than viewing clients with anorexia symptoms as having family relationship problems and internal psychological problems, he provides them information about the Auckland Anti-Anorexia/Anti-Bulimia Leagues to help empower them to fight against anorexia. The story of Leila and the tiger is about the personal and psychiatric transformation that occurs when professionals stop to really listen to their client's stories.

Applications Beyond Individual Therapy

Constructive approaches are considered part and parcel of an individual's personal philosophy and, as such, have been applied within a wide variety of therapeutic settings. In particular, both narrative and solution-based approaches are especially popular among family therapists and within school counseling situations. Consistent with its roots in feminist theory and Foucault's social critique of dominant power systems, narrative approaches and their philosophical foundations are used to promote larger social change movements. Narrative approaches are used to make social commentaries about poverty, homelessness, and other adverse social conditions:

Families of poverty have been stripped of much of the power to write their own stories. Their narratives of hopelessness, helplessness and dependency have been cowritten, if not dictated, by social institutions. When the institutional and societal coauthors of these stories are made invisible, when the family narratives are presented as if constructed by the families alone, family members become even more depressed, potential helpers are confused, and everybody becomes less effectual. (Minuchin, 1991, p. 49)

Based on this perspective, solutions to individual client problems require not only a reauthoring process initiated and maintained by clients but also social consciousness raising and a broader and deeper social-cultural reauthoring. As Coale (1992) has suggested, rapid reconstruction of an individual client's or family's socially imbedded problems is not recommended as an adequate approach. In a statement that clearly articulates the need for deeper social change, she notes, "Reframing hunger has no usefulness for poor families" (p. 19).

CONCLUDING COMMENTS

There is probably no single existing theoretical orientation containing the breadth of diversity associated with constructive theory. On the one hand, solution-based approaches emphasize formulaic, brief, and surface-oriented techniques designed to produce relatively small changes. These small changes are then viewed as having a potential ripple effect in producing bigger and more profound changes over time. It is not surprising that solution-based approaches are sometimes criticized for ignoring client problems and denying the significance of human emotional pain and suffering.

On the other hand, narrative approaches emphasize using language to produce profound, transformative client changes. Although there is some overlap in technique, in contrast to solution-based therapists, narrative therapists are not in a hurry to fix clients and send them out the door in a minimum amount of time and with a minimum of human intimacy. Instead, narrative therapists listen to the depths of clients' personal stories, searching for tiny sparkling moments in the rubble of difficult lives. Narrative therapists join with clients in attacking maladaptive personal narratives. This joining is not merely surface or superficial. It is deep and abiding, sometimes even including personal letters from therapist to the client.

STUDENT REVIEW ASSIGNMENTS

The following exercises will allow you to further explore your understanding of cognitive therapy.

Critical Corner

The following extremely critical statements are designed to provoke your critical analysis (and defense) of constructivist theory and therapy. Read the statements and write down your response in the space following.

1. De Shazer and others contend that because therapy usually only lasts 6 to 10 sessions, it is the therapist's responsibility to work within that framework. Although this statement makes sense on the surface, it is so absurdly general and nomothetic that it constitutes gross neglect of the individual and the ideal. To assume that every new client is just another average 6 to 10-session client is completely counter to narrative, constructive principles. It succumbs to external socio-scientific-cultural-political forces currently operating in the world, rather than legitimately constructing a unique therapy designed to meet the needs of distressed individuals. In this way, de Shazer advocates a therapy of what *tends to be* rather than a therapy of exciting new possibilities.
    Response:

2. Many constructive therapy books and resources (especially those emphasizing solution-based approaches) repeatedly proclaim the nearly magical power of solution-focused interventions. Typically, numerous cases are presented in which the astute and clever therapist almost tricks the clients into focusing on their positive attributes. In the end, thanks to the solution-focused approach, the clients

quickly succeed in meeting their treatment goals and leave happily ever after. The truth is that solution-based approaches are briefer than traditional approaches and result in goal attainment principally because the criteria for success are set so low and the therapist gives many indirect and some direct messages to clients that they're really not particularly interested in discussing deeper emotional issues. Its no wonder why there aren't any controlled outcome studies because solution-focused therapists are in such a hurry to get clients out of their offices that they would never take the time needed to conduct a systematic and depth-oriented evaluation of therapy efficacy.

Response:

3. Constructive theory claims to be an egalitarian approach to therapy. However, the approach is extremely value-based and invalidating of clients' experience of their personal problems. How can constructive theory be egalitarian when it blatantly leads clients toward focusing on positive solutions and sparkling moments?

Response:

4. Narrative and constructive approaches often sound more like philosophy than psychology. Constructive writers emphasize lived experience, discourse, contemporary hermeneutics, and the value of not knowing (Anderson & Levin, 1998). Isn't it likely that all this philosophizing about the human condition moves the therapist away from establishing the deep human connection necessary for therapy to work?

Response:

Reviewing Key Terms

- Constructivism
- Postmodern philosophy
- Utilization
- Solution-focused brief therapy
- Solution-oriented (possibility) therapy
- Narrative therapy
- Ripple effect
- Assimilation

- Accommodation
- Lived experience
- Problem externalization
- Credulous assessment
- Formula task
- Pretreatment change question
- Unique account or sparkling moment
- Externalizing conversation

- Carl Rogers with a twist
- Relabeling or reframing
- Presuppositional questions
- Miracle question
- Exception questions
- The do something different task
- Letter writing formats
- Reflecting team

Review Questions

1. Who was the first contemporary constructive therapist?
2. What is Milton Erickson's utilization technique?

3. What is positive connotation, and what research group developed positive connotation as a technique?

4. What is a sparkling moment or unique outcome?

5. What are the key differences between solution-focused brief therapy and solution-oriented (or possibility) therapy?

6. What is the constructivist view of resistance? When resistance occurs, whose responsibility is it?

7. What is the purpose of Erickson's confusion technique?

8. What is the purpose of Giorgio Nardone's recommendation that clients or students identify several ways of thinking and acting that would worsen the situation?

9. To what do the terms *customer, complainants,* and *visitors* refer?

10. What is the constructivist view of assessment? How much formal psychological assessment is recommended?

11. What is a scaling question?

12. Which therapy approach explores the client's original problem construction?

13. According to Nardone, what is the first ethical stance of the constructive therapist?

14. What does the treatment outcome research say about the efficacy of solution-based and narrative therapies?

RECOMMENDED READINGS AND RESOURCES

The following resources are available to help deepen your understanding of constructive theory and practice.

Lead Journals

- *Constructive Change*
- *Constructivism in the Human Sciences*
- *Journal of Strategic and Systemic Therapies*
- *Journal of Constructivist Psychology*

Books and Articles

Berg, I. K., & Miller, S. D. (1992). *Working with the problem drinker: A solution-focused approach.* New York: Norton.

Bertolino, B. (1999). *Therapy with troubled teenagers: Rewriting young lives in progress.* New York: Wiley.

Coale, H. W. (1992). The constructivist emphasis on language: A critical conversation. *Journal of Strategic and Systemic Therapies, 11*(1), 12–26.

de Shazer, S. (1985). *Keys to solution in brief therapy.* New York: Norton.

de Shazer, S. (1994). *Words were originally magic.* New York: Norton.

DeJong, P., & Berg, I. K. (2002). *Interviewing for solutions* (2nd ed.). Belmont, CA: Brooks/Cole.

Efran, J. S., & Fauber, R. L. (1995). Radical constructivism: Questions and answers. In R. A. Neimeyer & M. Mahoney (Eds.), *Constructivism in psychotherapy* (pp. 275–304). Washington, DC: American Psychological Association.

Epston, D., Morris, F., & Maisel, R. (1995). A narrative approach to so-called anorexia/bulimia. In K. Weingarten (Ed.), *Cultural resistance: Challenging beliefs about men, women, and therapy* (pp. 69–96). London: Haworth Press.

Erickson, M. H. (1964). The confusion technique in hypnosis. *American Journal of Clinical Hypnosis, 6,* 183–207.

Foucault, M. (1965). *Madness and civilization: A history of insanity in the age of reason.* New York: Random House.

Haley, J. (1973). *Uncommon therapy: The psychiatric techniques of Milton H. Erickson.* New York: Norton.

Hoyt, M. F. (2002). How I embody a narrative constructive approach. *Journal of Constructivist Psychology, 15*(4), 279–289.

Hoyt, M. F. (Ed.). (1998). *The handbook of constructive therapies: Innovative approaches from leading practitioners.* San Francisco, CA: Jossey-Bass.

Hoyt, M. F. (2000). Cognitive-behavioural treatment of post-traumatic stress disorder from a narrative constructivist perspective: A conversation with Donald Meichenbaum. In M. Scott & S. Palmer (Eds.), *Trauma and post-traumatic stress disorder* (pp. 49–69). London: Cassell.

Mahoney, M. J. (Ed.). (1995). *Cognitive and constructive psychotherapies: Theory, research, and practice.* New York: Springer.

Miller, S. D., Hubble, M. A., & Duncan, B. L. (1996). *Handbook of solution-focused brief therapy.* San Francisco: Jossey-Bass.

Nardone, G. (1996). *Brief strategic solution-oriented therapy of phobic and obsessive disorders.* Northvale, NJ: Aronson.

Neimeyer, R. A., & Mahoney, M. (Eds.). (1995). *Constructivism in psychotherapy.* Washington, DC: American Psychological Association.

O'Hanlon, W. H., & Weiner-Davis, M. (1989). *In search of solutions: A new direction in psychotherapy.* New York: Norton.

Selvini-Palazzoli, M., Boscolo, L., Cecchin, G., & Prata, G. (1974). The treatment of children through brief therapy of their parents. *Family Process, 13,* 429–442.

Watzlawick, P., Beavin, J. H., & Jackson, D. D. (1967). *Pragmatics of human communication.* New York: Norton.

White, M., & Epston, D. (1990). *Narrative means to therapeutic ends.* New York: Norton.

Videotapes

Carlson, J., & Kjos, D. (2000). *Narrative therapy with Stephen Madigan* [Videotape]. Boston: Allyn & Bacon.

Eleven different solution-focused videotapes are listed on the Brief Family Therapy Center web site (see next section).

Training Organizations and Web Sites

Milton Erickson Foundation, (web site: www.ericksonfoundation.org)

Brief Family Therapy Center, (web site: www.brief-therapy.org)

Narrative Training Associates, (web site: www.narrativetherapy.org)

Narrative therapy workshops with Epston and White are listed on (web site: www.narrativeapproaches.com)

Chapter 12 ———————————————————

MULTICULTURAL AND NON-WESTERN THEORIES

Man is much more simply human than otherwise.
——Harry Stack Sullivan, *The Interpersonal Theory of Psychiatry* (1953, p. 4)

You can't understand people until you've walked a mile in their moccasins.
——Seen on a sign in a café in Absarokee, Montana

IN THIS CHAPTER YOU WILL LEARN

- The concept of multicultural theory as the fourth force in counseling and psychotherapy
- Key figures in the history of multicultural theory
- The historical context that led to multicultural counseling
- Various definitions of culture, multiculturalism, and multicultural counseling
- General theoretical principles of multicultural counseling
- Personality and psychopathology from a multicultural perspective
- Assessment issues in multicultural mental health work
- Efficacy with culture in mind
- Alternatives to Western approaches to psychological healing and growth
- Ethical concerns in multicultural counseling

For a moment, bathe your psyche in the following words and the images they bring:

Culture. Many cultures. Multicultural. Mixed culture.
Texture. Richly textured. Many colored. Multidimensional.
Black. White. Red. Brown. Yellow.
Religion. Faith. Spirit. Soul. Spiritual. Transcendent. Communal.

We learned in Chapter 11 that language shapes thought. If so, what happens when our language is inadequate for describing what we know and what we want to know? What if it's impossible to use words to articulate our perceptions and experiences?

In this chapter we discuss a perspective that stretches our linguistic abilities to the breaking point. On a technical level, we discuss the foundation of multicultural theories of counseling and psychotherapy. On a deeper level, we discuss what makes us different and what makes us the same. For many of us, both sides of this dialectic ring true. We are all different and we are all the same. For others, emphasizing only the differences or only the similarities has become standard procedure.

Theories of multiculturalism are considered the fourth force in the family of theories. The first three forces are

- Psychodynamic, process-oriented theories that deal with the unconscious in one way or another
- Behavioral and learning theories that emphasize how human learning is at the foundation of human experience, psychopathology, and change
- Humanistic, relationship-oriented theories that believe in the human potential for change, healing, and growth—if the right circumstances and understandings are present

Multiculturalism argues that people are a product of their culture and deserve to be understood foremost as such. Many theories texts, for many good reasons, place feminist theories and multicultural theories in the same chapter. We are sure you can imagine why.

Considering counseling and psychotherapy from a multicultural view is challenging in that these are professional endeavors conceived of and developed within a very Western cultural frame. Given the right angle, the notions of the 50-minute hour and the talking cure can seem small, quaint, and terribly culture-bound. We hope this chapter provides you with insights and alternative ways of thinking about mental health and psychological distress across cultures.

HISTORICAL CONTEXT AND IMPORTANT CONTRIBUTORS

Many writers, practitioners, and researchers have contributed to current multicultural theories. The following list will undoubtedly omit key figures we should have included, but because our choice is to provide an incomplete list or no list at all, we've chosen to offer the following list as a starting point. The professionals named are courageous thinkers, writers, theorists, and practitioners whose work has been of great value in advancing multicultural thinking and application in mental health. If you review their work and check the people they have worked with and the authors they cite, it will be a good beginning to your exposure to the many dimensions of multicultural theory and practice.

Contributors

Second-generation Chinese brothers (all of whom are trained in psychology) Derald Wing Sue, Stanley Sue, and David Sue have been strong voices in general multicultural theory for well over 30 years. The husband and wife team Allen and Mary Bradford Ivey, along with many coauthors and researchers, have also contributed to multiculturalism, as has Paul Pederson, Joseph Trimble, Pat Arredondo, and Teresa LaFromboise. Freddy Paniagua has worked steadily on the issues of diagnosis and assessment in a multicultural society.

Authors Sari Dworkin and Fernando Gutierrez (1992) were among the first to address the diverse needs of gay, lesbian, bisexual, and transgendered people, and Carolyn Vash, Beatrice Wright, and Irving Goffmann were early voices that pointed to the specific needs of persons with disabilities.

Historical Context

Similar to feminist theory, multicultural theory did not spring to life as a result of abstract armchair speculation about the nature of humans and human need. It came into being—or, more accurately, was driven into being—by the painful recognition that the worldview of the privileged White male was not the only viable worldview on the face of the planet. Such recognition usually included firsthand experience of the damaging application of this narrow worldview to the psychological functioning and needs of people other than middle- and upper-class White males.

There are many appalling historic examples of the misapplication of Western psychological theory and technique to non-White and nonmale populations. In the worst scenarios, White, upper-class males made sweeping statements about what was good or bad for individuals from other cultures. Further, they made sweeping indictments about the so-called abnormal functioning or limited intellectual and functional potential of persons of color, as well as of women. When viewed from a multicultural perspective, these sweeping judgments are clearly and remarkably racist. At the time, however, these judgments were framed as multiculturally sensitive. Take, for example, the following statement from the highly regarded *Southern Literary Messenger* in 1843. This statement claims that the White race suffers terribly from slavery, while African Americans thrive as slaves:

> We are not friendly to slavery. We lament and deplore it as the greatest evil that could be inflicted on our country. We lament it not for the sake of the black race but of the white. The former, who are slaves, are not only far happier in a state of slavery than of freedom, but we believe the happiest class on this continent. (quoted in Kutchins & Kirk, 1997, p. 204)

This example of considering slavery as a benefit to African Americans would be more stunning if it were simply an isolated example of multicultural insensitivity and racism. Unfortunately, there are many other examples where dominant White American-European physicians, psychologists, counselors, and social workers displayed profound insensitivity toward diverse cultures. A few powerful examples are included in Putting It in Practice 12.1.

For one group to claim that another group is benefiting from systematic oppression is a foundation for stereotyping, prejudice, and all forms of racism, classism, ageism, and sexism. In her powerful book *For Your Own Good,* Alice Miller (1984) points out this same dynamic from the perspective of children who are hit, kicked, slapped, and physically abused all for the sake of helping them develop properly.

From the multicultural perspective, the dominant culture's tendency to identify what's good for nondominant groups includes a series of amazing oversights. That is, the dominant culture forgot to (and still forgets to)

Historical Examples of Multicultural Insensitivity

In 1851 physician S. A. Cartwright claimed to have discovered two mental diseases peculiar to Africans. The first, *drapetomania,* caused slaves to have uncontrollable urges to run away from their masters. The cure? Whipping the devil out of them. The second disease, *dysaethesia,* affected mind and body, causing disobedience and disrespect. The cure? Extra hard labor, causing blood to finally reach the brain and give liberty to the mind (see Szasz, 1970).

Among his many conclusions about the biological, psychological, and moral inferiority of women, Freud claimed that women suffered from an underdeveloped superego, the result being that

> they show less sense of justice than men, that they are less ready to submit to the great necessities of life, that they are more often influenced in their judgments by feelings of affection or hostility—all these would be amply accounted for by the modification in the formation of their superego which we have already inferred. (Freud, 1948, pp. 196–197)

Unfortunately, from Freud's perspective, there is no treatment or cure available for being born a woman.

Baca and Cervantes (1984) quote Lewis Terman (1916), the original author of the Stanford-Binet Intelligence Scale, as having written the following:

> A low level of intelligence is very, very common among Spanish-Indians and Mexican families of the Southwest and also among Negroes. Their dullness seems to be racial, or at least inherent in the family stocks from which they come. The fact that one meets this type with such extraordinary frequency among Indians, Mexican, and Negroes suggests quite forcibly that the whole question of racial differences in mental traits will have to be taken up anew and by experimental methods. The writer predicts that when this is done there will be discovered enormously significant racial differences in general intelligence, differences which cannot be wiped out by any scheme of mental culture.
>
> Children of this group should be segregated into special classes and be given instruction which is concrete and practical. They cannot master abstractions but they often can be made efficient workers, able to look out for themselves. There is no possibility at the present in convincing society that they should not be allowed to reproduce, although from a eugenic point of view they constitute a grave problem because of their unusually prolific breeding. (p. 147)

Until all too recently, ego-dystonic homosexuality was listed in the *Diagnostic and Statistical Manual of Mental Disorders (DSM)* as a diagnosable mental disorder (American Psychiatric Association, 1980; Marmor, 1980). In a discussion of the course of ego-dystonic homosexuality, the *DSM* III clearly acknowledges the powerful influence of culture on an individual's acceptance of homosexuality:

> There is some evidence that in time many individuals with this disorder give up the yearning to become heterosexual and accept themselves as homosexuals. This process is apparently facilitated by the presence of a supportive homosexual subculture. (American Psychiatric Association, 1980, p. 281)

As these examples amply illustrate, human tolerance for differences is often quite limited, and the tendency of those in power or in the majority is to define differences not simply as differences, but as inferiorities or mental disorders. This is especially true if these differences irritate or frighten those in power because, as Thomas Szasz (1970) notes, categorizing someone as inferior or as being mentally ill is a subjective process: "Which kinds of social deviance are regarded as mental illnesses? The answer is, those that entail personal conduct not conforming to psychiatrically defined and enforced rules of mental health" (p. xxvi).

- Try systematically to understand the perspective of the nondominant group by simply asking them for their opinion on the subject—and listening to their answers!
- Step into the alternative culture in an effort to deepen mutual understanding and respect.
- Consider that the nondominant group might not speak up on its own behalf for fear of reprisal.

What Is Culture?

Defining what we mean by *culture* is a task that itself has cultural and political overtones. Christopher (1996) states,

> Culture permeates our lives much more thoroughly or pervasively than we tend to consider. Because of Western culture's individualistic orientation, we tend to think of the individual first and of culture second. . . . What this tendency to give primacy to the self overlooks is the manner in which culture precedes us. (p. 17)

Christopher helps us understand that cultural development often precedes individual development. Using the influential anthropologist Geertz's (1973) definition of culture as webs of significance that give coherence and meaning to our lives, Christopher states, "Our social practices, institutions, family structures, and daily life make sense and 'hang together' because of these webs of significance" (p. 17). Further, he points out that culture shapes us, gives us views of human nature, and provides our moral framework. Culture tells us both what should be considered a good life and what should be considered deviant.

We will discuss other definitions of culture later in the chapter. However, it is important to note that self-identification with one's groups and cultures is an important area of psychological research. Humans are group-seeking creatures. Even as scholars have tried to understand the irrational social forces behind the rise of racism, fascism, or other fundamentalist movements, they recognize that "the striving for self-worth by belonging to a strong and glorious 'we' is an important force even in the development of 'normal' ethnic, religious, and national movements" (Suleiman, 2002, p. 33).

In our work and writing about young people, we've made the claim that children belong to a different culture than adults (J. Sommers-Flanagan & Sommers-Flanagan, 1997). This concept illustrates the constantly changing nature of culture because even though you were a member of a group once upon a time, you do not necessarily know what it means to be a member now. Parents and young people alike can easily attest to the enormous group and cultural pressures brought to bear on young people—pressures that adults may or may not fully understand. Failing to look, speak, act, and dress within defined youth-cultural bounds can be punished in most painful ways. Counselors working with young people can find the application of multicultural counseling principles most helpful.

In summary, providing a definition of the term *culture* is neither easy nor without controversy. This may be an indication of how very important the concept is. Culture plays a central role in defining what it means to be human.

What Is Multiculturalism?

The term *multicultural* is relatively new and is not without political baggage. Webster's Dictionary offers this definition: "Of, relating to, or designed for a combination of several distinct cultures." Terms like *cross-cultural* and *intercultural* tend to insinuate the same set of values and concerns, but most writers have settled on a preference for the term *multicultural*. The term *transcultural*, however, has a different meaning. Transculturalists are more focused on the commonalities between cultures and are more oriented toward universals that might be applicable to all humankind (Rouchy, 2002). At the core, the term *multicultural* acknowledges the idea of culture, and by acknowledging that there is more than one viable culture, it might be said to insinuate *value* in the existence of more than one. The mere act of attempting to accommodate more than one culture is a political act. In her book *Imagining Literacy*, Ramona Fernandez (2001) discusses the watering down or institutionalizing of the term *multiculturalism:*

> What does it name? Often, it seems to be used mindlessly as a mild concession to the many differences around us. While the term seems to challenge established attitudes, it has often been used to depoliticize any effective resistance to those attitudes. Like the melting pot allusions of an earlier era, multiculturalism (spelled with or without the hyphen) can mean almost anything, or nothing, depending on who deploys the term. Wahneema Lubiano, Peter Erickson, and the Chicago Cultural Studies Group have published interesting essays demonstrating that this term is being used in ways that ensure that it will not contest established injustices and cultural norms. On the contrary, administrative agencies have invented self-serving theories of multiculturalism that only reinstitute historical divisions and oppressions. Lubiano advocates a radical or "strong" multiculturalism that reconceptualizes education and its relation to power instead of deploying it as a rhetorical device to "manage" diverse student populations and curricula. (p. iv)

The cultures represented in the term *multicultural* are often dependent on the speaker. Many argue that the worst discrimination and abuse has occurred across racial divides. Others argue that history provides many horrifying examples of religious discrimination. Gender, disability, sexual orientation, and class also represent cultures within the meaning of multicultural. Citizens of the United States may resist the idea of class as a source of cultural discrimination, but as columnist Ellen Goodman (2003) writes,

> Through thick and thin, boom and bust, we tenaciously hold on to the belief that we are, fundamentally, a classless society. This self-image survives even though we have the most unequal distribution of wealth in the Western world. It survives even though 1 percent of us owns 40 percent of the wealth. And even though there's less income mobility between generations in our country than in any other but South Africa and Great Britain. (p. 4)

We believe that the term *multicultural* should indeed include class, as well as the other categories named, and perhaps others as well. Although there are problems with the term and struggles within the dominant culture for both definition and sincere expression, the idea of multiculturalism is profound and will be pivotal in the coming decades.

What Is Multicultural Counseling?

Given the controversies and ambiguities in the definitions of both culture and multiculturalism, you might guess that defining multicultural counseling would also be challenging. Derald Wing Sue offers the following definition of multicultural counseling:

> Multicultural counseling and therapy can be defined as both a helping role and a process that uses modalities and defines goals consistent with the life experiences and cultural val-

ues of clients, recognizes client identities to include individual, group, and universal dimensions, advocates the use of universal and culture-specific strategies and roles in the healing process, and balances the importance of individualism and collectivism in the assessment, diagnosis, and treatment of client and client systems. (Sue, in press)

This definition, and the attempts to define and offer culturally sensitive or multicultural counseling have a very short history. Until quite recently, mental health theorists and practitioners have underestimated the power of culture in defining the individual, health, morality, and worldviews of other cultural groups. In fact, most psychological theories can be accused of having serious, if not fatal, monocultural biases. The American Psychological Association and the American Counseling Association both now have divisions devoted to minority-ethnic issues; diversity issues; gay, lesbian, and bisexual issues; and social justice concerns. In addition, the American Psychiatric Association's *DSM* now has (since 1994) sections titled "Specific Culture and Gender Features" for each psychiatric diagnosis (Mezzich et al., 1999). However, most or all of the serious thinking, research, and scholarship in these areas has occurred only very recently (in the last 20 years or so) and is still fraught with theoretical and ideological infighting and vagueness. Further, as suggested earlier by Fernandez (2001), many institutions deftly pay brief homage to multicultural and gender issues (as in the *DSM*) while continuing forward with most of their status quo theories and approaches unmodified.

THEORETICAL PRINCIPLES

At the theoretical level, multiculturalism as applied to mental health elevates and centralizes the role of culture in defining psychological functioning, psychological distress, and psychological well-being (D. W. Sue, Bingham, Porche-Burke, & Vasquez, 1999). Culture is understood as a set of learnings one obtains from the environment into which one has been born or the environment in which one is functioning (Axelson, 1999). There are many dimensions to culture, and specific definitions of culture are often based on whether or not certain of these dimensions are included. As we noted earlier, some of these dimensions include race (or ethnicity), sex, religion, socioeconomic circumstances, sexual orientation, and abilities or disabilities. There is no definitive, agreed-upon set of principles for multicultural theories because of diversity of opinion in the finer points of what it means to be multiculturally oriented. However, there is significant common ground as well. We offer the following principles as guides to understanding general multicultural theory.

Principle I. We were born and raised in a culture (or set of cultures) that influence our ways of being (or cosmologies; Duran & Duran, 1995). Politically, these memberships can either enhance or limit our life opportunities.

In a chapter titled "White Privilege: Unpacking the Invisible Knapsack," Peggy McIntosh (1998) helps readers understand the invisible nature of privileges accorded to the dominant culture. She points out that in the United States, middle- and upper-class White people carry with them a set of unearned assets available to them at any time. One of the effects of membership in the dominant culture is unconsciousness of the trappings of that very culture. Often, students from the dominant culture have trouble talking about their cultural values and practices because, to them, these values seem universal rather than culturally determined. These practices and values come sharply into view only when contrasted with practices and values that are markedly different.

One obvious problem facing multicultural theorists and practitioners is that "[w]e are all of us as individuals already mixed ethnically and culturally; our roots are historically constructed out of subtly mediated cultural strands" (Fernandez, 2001, p. ix). We share attributes and learnings with many groups, and the salience of our membership varies for each of us and across the life span. Being from Montana seemed quite unremarkable to us until we lived for a time in upstate New York, Belize City, and the United Kingdom, where our identity as Montanans took on a much more defined and sometimes shifting set of attributes. Regardless of how many cultures we are part of, each shapes us whether or not we recognize it. Consistent with constructivist theory, multiculturalism suggests that we construct our worldviews based on our cultural experiences and memberships, and consciously or not, we are often privileged or disadvantaged by these memberships as well.

As is true with the definition of multicultural, there is controversy within the domain of multicultural counseling about what groups to include when one considers diversity (D. W. Sue & Sue, 2003). In one sense, all counseling is multicultural in that the counselor and the client are always from different families and have different life experiences, possibly different sexes, different socioeconomic experiences, and so on (Axelson, 1999). Most multicultural thinkers acknowledge these differences but believe that to call all counseling multicultural misses the point of the power of culture in our lives. D. W. Sue and Sue (2003) believe in an inclusive model of diversity that includes race, religion, sex, disability, and socioeconomic class. Others argue that even this inclusivity waters down the power of certain cultural domains, most notably race (Helms, 1994).

In the late 1980s a panel we organized with four women of color addressed this issue in a psychology of women class. When asked, each claimed that her experience of racial identity was stronger than her gender identity and that their experience of racial prejudice was far greater and more damaging than the experience of sexism as women. For them, race trumped sex in terms of cultural definition, power, and oppression.

Questions for Reflection

With what group of others do you most closely identify? Those from your home town? Those of your same sex? Religion? Race? Income level? IQ level? Who are the people with whom you feel most relaxed? Most known? How do you think your particular identity might influence your approach to counseling others? Do you think it's possible, as suggested by McIntosh (1998), that if you are in the dominant cultural group you are likely to be unconscious to many aspects of your privileged status?

Principle II. We make distinctions between groups of people based on race, religion, sex, sexual orientation, ethnicity, physical and mental disabilities, and socioeconomic status.

Implicit in the theoretical underpinnings of multiculturalism is the notion of group differences. If you met a young woman who grew up in an Amish community in Pennsylvania, you would probably assume that you are quite different from her in many ways. If you met five of her friends and relatives, you would probably assume there to be many commonly held beliefs, experiences, and ways of being between them. As you well know, humans make meaning by noticing similarities and differences around them. Our brains are always busy sorting out the salient attributes of a given set of stimuli. If something has four legs and a flat surface, we most likely call it a table. When we use this same strategy with "types" of people, difficulties immediately present themselves. Which are the appropriate attributes to use when grouping people into cultures or subcultures? As noted earlier, we are not just members of one group. No human being has exactly the same life experiences, so members of a given group often seem more different than alike. We can learn all about a given group and still meet many members who violate several of the norms we learned about the group.

Further complicating these grouping questions, humans have a tendency to use mental short-cuts that can easily become stereotypes. A *stereotype* is "a standardized mental picture that is held in common by members of a group and that represents an oversimplified opinion, affective attitude, or uncritical judgment" (Webster's Dictionary). Distinctions that allow for cultural recognition as a group are quite different from oversimplified opinions about the group, made from the outside, with limited exposure to group members.

Principle III. A multiculturalist stance is intended to foster greater understanding between members of different cultural groups and to strive toward egalitarian treatment of all humans, inclusive of their cultural identities.

D. W. Sue et al. (1999) write,

> Multiculturalism is not only about understanding different perspectives and worldviews but also about social justice. As such it is not value neutral. Multiculturalism stands against beliefs and behaviors that oppress other groups and deny them equal access and opportunity. (p. 1064)

It seems that humans do not easily live in culturally inclusive ways. The values and beliefs we were raised with or have found to be true for us in our cultural experiences do not easily move aside so that we can examine and accept someone else's values and beliefs as valid in their own right. Although Principle III articulates an important ideal, the following quotations indicate the difficulties and the distance we still have to go. The first is by Lucy Lippard (1990) from her book *Mixed Blessings: New Art in a Multicultural America:*

> The terminology in which an issue is expressed is indicative of the quality of the discourse, and the fact that there are no euphonious ways to describe today's cross-cultural exchange reflects the deep social and historical awkwardness underlying that exchange. Much has been tried and found wanting. Writing about intercultural art, looking for satisfying ways to describe the groups involved, many of whom are living between cultures, I find myself caught in a web of ungainly, pompous, condescending, even ugly language. (p. 10)

This next quotation is from a talk given by Stefan Auer (2000) that focused on minority rights in Central Europe:

> To strike the right balance between unity and diversity, and between individual and collective rights, requires careful consideration of intricate and often ultimately insoluble problems. When demands for social justice are incommensurable with demands for cultural recognition, a choice has to be made that excludes other options. (p. 2)

This final quotation is by Carlos Alberto Torres (1998) from his book *Democracy, Education, and Multiculturalism: Dilemmas of Citizenship in a Global World* (1998):

> The challenge for educators, parents, students, and policymakers is to think critically about the failures of the past and about the myriad exclusionary practices that still pervade the process of schooling—hence bringing to the forefront issues of power and domination, class, race, and gender. (p. 87)

Clearly, counseling and psychotherapy are not the only domains struggling to become more culturally aware and inclusive. Ignorance, arrogance, fear, and intolerance have taken their tolls for too long. A multicultural worldview and multicultural practices are essential to development on both individual and global levels.

Theory of Personality

From a multicultural perspective, individual personality is heavily influenced by cultural experience. In fact, multicultural counselors note that even the idea of personality is an essentialist way of approaching human beings and is therefore a culture-bound concept (Markus & Kitayama, 1998). There are many dimensions of intra- and interpersonal functioning that vary by culture. What is considered normal, acceptable, or abnormal and troublesome varies widely among cultures. Examples of such differences are offered in Putting It in Practice 12.2.

Individualistic versus Collectivist Orientation

One of the most common dialectical discussions in the multicultural literature is that of individualistic versus collectivist cultures. Individualistic cultures, like the dominant culture in the United States, place enormous value on the personal liberty of the individual and the supremacy of self-interests over those of the group. Autonomy is a highly

---

Putting It in Practice 12.2

Dimensions That Vary Across Cultures

Cultural beliefs and practices vary on an infinite number of subtle dimensions. This list includes some of the more obvious and more researched of these dimensions. Rather than list cultures and their take on each dimension, we challenge you to articulate the practices or beliefs of your own culture on each of these. Then either in person, or through readings, explore how other cultures vary along these dimensions. While doing this, you may think of obvious dimensions we omitted. Add them in and share them with your classmates.

- Eye contact
- Conception of time and timeliness
- Signs of respect
- Language
- Spirituality and Religion
- Kinship systems
- Directness in communication style

- Collectivist versus individual orientation
- Aging
- Dress
- Gender roles
- Definitions of the good life
- Educational practices
- Family definitions and duties

regarded goal and virtue, and personality is often viewed as separate from family and culture.

In collectivist cultures, values and norms are more shared. The self and the personality are defined in terms of group memberships, and the group needs and values are more central than those of the individual. Collectivists tend to evaluate themselves based on the attainment of commonly held group goals, whereas individualists are more likely to orient toward individual responsibility and to establish personal goals (Earley & Gibson, 1998; Triandis, 1994 #654).

Although this individualistic orientation is still predominant, theorists within Western culture point to problems with this value orientation. In 1975 Robert Hogan wrote in the *American Psychologist,*

> A central theme in Western European history for about 800 years has been the decline of the medieval synthesis or, alternatively, the emergence of individualism. Two hundred years ago individualism was a moral and religious ideal capable of legitimizing revolutions and inspiriting sober and thoughtful minds. Sometimes in the last century, however, social thinkers began to regard individualism in more ambivalent terms, even in some cases as a possible indicator of social decay. (p. 533)

Further, in agreement with the alarm sounded by the existentialists, and in agreement with Jung's theory of the costs of repression, William Donohue (1990) writes,

> The defining mark of contemporary American culture is the celebrated idea of liberty without limits. Freedom is cost in purely individualistic terms, there being no notion of, nor respect for, the common good. The individual is entitled to do exactly as he pleases, short of the most blatant and egregious violation of another person's rights. There is endless talk of the rights of the individual, but nary a word spoken of any concomitant responsibilities. Right and wrong are relative, having no discernible objective reference or content. That which burdens the individual is seen as unfair, and anything that restricts choices is condemned. This is the heart and soul of the new freedom. It is also the heart and soul of our psychological and social disorders. (p. 221)

Collectivist cultural values and personality traits are difficult for a counselor raised in an individualistic culture to understand and honor in the counseling process. Consider this quotation from the ancient Hindu holy text, the Bhagavad Gita, as quoted by Michael Brannigan (2000):

> The man who has given up all desire
> and moves without wanting anything
> Who says neither mine nor I
> wins peace. (p. 44)

Quite often, clients who are second-generation citizens of the United States arrive in therapy, struggling with individualistic desires to attain certain levels of education in areas of interest while at the same time honoring the family's wishes and original cultural practices. You can see that by trying to balance these two divergent values, clients can experience a unique, personal conflict.

Acculturation and the Infamous Melting Pot

On an individual level, acculturation (or ethnocultural orientation) refers to "a process of giving up one's traditional cultural values and behaviors while taking on the values and behaviors of the dominant social structure" (Atkinson, Lowe, & Mathews, 1995, p. 131). For example, Garrett and Pichette (2000) identified five cultural orientation types within American Indian populations that were previously discussed in the literature (Herring, 1996; LaFromboise, Trimble, & Mohatt, 1990):

1. *Traditional.* The individual thinks in the native tongue and practices traditional tribal customs and tribal worship methods.
2. *Marginal.* The individual is not fully connected with traditional Indian culture or mainstream society. Both languages may be spoken.
3. *Bicultural.* The individual is relatively comfortable and conversant in both sets of cultural values.
4. *Assimilated.* The individual is oriented toward the mainstream social culture and has little interest in traditional tribal practices.
5. *Pantraditional.* The individual has been exposed to and perhaps adopted mainstream values but has made an intentional effort to return to traditional values.

What about acculturation and its role in personality development? Once upon a time, many in the dominant culture in the United States believed in a concept called *the melting pot,* in which, over time, many cultures would melt down, adding their own flavor and color to the soup but losing their distinguishing features in the process. Many believe that this was a thinly disguised way of asserting that minority groups would shed their inferior ways of being and in a matter of a generation or two simply "become White" (Axelson, 1999). More recent metaphors for ways in which many cultures live side by side, mixing and marrying, include the ideas of salad or stew. Cultures remain identifiable, each uniquely contributing to the whole. No metaphor is perfect, neither at the societal level nor at the individual level. Cultural identity and even racial identity, at the individual level, can be unique mixtures and expressions. Take, for example, the famous golfer Tiger Woods, who is African-Indonesian-Caucasian American, or Thomas Jefferson's descendants from his wife's half-sister and slave, Sally Hemings, who was half-African, half-Caucasian. One branch of her lineage developed a Black identity, and the other developed a White identity.

Multicultural counselors realize that cultural identity isn't static and that racial identity and affiliation cannot be assumed by glancing at the color of one's skin or the shape of one's eyes. However, culturally sensitive counselors also realize that a client's personality can be greatly influenced by the experience of being a minority within a dominant culture. Family functioning and identity also can be challenged and severely stressed by second-generation members assuming the values and practices of the dominant culture (McGoldrick, 1998). Swartz-Kulstad and Martin (1999) identified five separate contextual factors serving as building blocks for human behavior:

1. Ethnocultural orientation or acculturation
2. Family environment
3. Community environment
4. Communication style
5. Language usage (see also J. Sommers-Flanagan & Sommers-Flanagan, 2003)

Theory of Psychopathology

Like feminist theory, multicultural theory acknowledges the role of social forces in the understanding and causation of suffering and pathology. Multicultural practitioners are extremely cautious in using standardized assessment instruments and diagnoses and take care to explore any concerns within the beliefs and practices of the client's culture (Paniagua, 2001). Multicultural counselors do not quickly impose pathological labels on troubling behaviors but instead seek to understand the meaning of the behaviors from within the cultural context of each individual or family.

Within different cultures, the names of disorders, the beliefs about causation, and the types of symptoms that are manifest vary greatly. In fact, human distress may not be seen primarily through a psychological lens. It may be viewed religiously or philosophically instead. This has led some to argue for the development of indigenous psychologies (Ho, 1998). From the University of Hong Kong, David Ho writes,

> In particular, much of Western psychology may be irrelevant or inapplicable in Asia. Western ideological presuppositions, such as individualism, are alien to the Asian ethos. Thus, a reliance on Western psychology can only lead to an incomplete, even distorted, understanding of Asia or of Asians. Moreover, the wholesale importation of Western psychology into Asia represents a form of cultural imperialism that perpetuates the colonialization of the mind. To an alarming degree, Asians are now confronted by stereotypes about themselves generated not only by Western researchers but also by Asian researchers relying on imported, mainly American, psychology. (p. 89)

THE PRACTICE OF MULTICULTURAL COUNSELING

In an article titled "Rethinking Multicultural Counseling: Implications for Counselor Education," Das (1995) offers the following reminders for practitioners:

- Culture shapes the behavior, values, and beliefs of all humans. Both client and counselor are products of their cultures.
- Problems that minority cultures face in accessing mental health services stem both from different worldviews and cultural values *and* from narrow attitudes and ignorance on the part of service providers.
- All counseling can be regarded as multicultural when culture is defined as including not only race, ethnicity, and nationality but also gender, age, social class, sexual orientation, and disability.
- People in minority groups experience life stress due to sociocultural pressures and stressors and often seek counseling due to these difficulties.
- Traditional counseling still mirrors the overdeveloped Western value of individualism.

Practicing multicultural counseling means including client's cultures and their cultural values and experiences centrally and directly in the counseling process. However, this requires sensitivity and flexibility in application. For instance, we knew someone who worked with Jake, a young man from the Crow Indian Reservation in Montana. Jake was a very busy physician who was having trouble relating to his son. His counselor asked about his tribal affiliation, and Jake readily stated that he was 75% Crow but that he "wasn't traditional." Further, Jake stated adamantly that being Crow was unrelated to his current difficulties. A careful inquiry into what Jake meant by these statements revealed the deeply conflicted feelings Jake was having about the many cultures (Crow, medical professional, and father) to which he belonged and the pressures he experienced because of this.

Even when clients insist that their particular cultural background isn't relevant to the counseling process, multiculturally aware mental health counselors realize the power of one's cultural background and membership. It isn't necessary to work directly with cultural material or conflicts, but this awareness informs the counselor's understanding nonetheless.

It is also important to note that cultures themselves have enormously varied views of what constitutes pathology and deviance and what causes these troubles. In our text *Clinical Interviewing* (J. Sommers-Flanagan & Sommers-Flanagan, 2003), we provide readers with examples of this variation. You can also find similar lists in Cuellar and Paniagua (2000) and Paniagua (1998).

Preparing Yourself to Do Therapy from a Multicultural Perspective

We hope that all students in the mental health professions will strive to work within a multicultural frame. At this stage in our development as humans, it seems unethical to do otherwise. As Corey, Corey, and Callanan (2003) state unequivocally in their ethics text, "Cultural diversity is a fact of life in today's world, and counselors can no longer afford to ignore the issues involved in counseling culturally diverse populations." Does this mean you must become an expert in all the cultures you might encounter in your work? No. Does it mean you have a responsibility to become as culturally aware as you possibly can and to continue to do so throughout your professional career? Yes.

If you're reading this text, you probably aren't intentionally racist in your worldview, but you're probably racist nonetheless (see Ethical Highlight 12.1). As noted, racism can be unintentional and unconscious (McIntosh, 1998; Ridley, 1995). People who believe they're free of all racist beliefs are most likely drastically underestimating the power of subtle racist attitudes and beliefs still present in most cultures, especially the dominant U.S. culture. How does one get rid of, or at least bring to consciousness, deeply buried racist attitudes and damaging cultural stereotypes? Pederson (2000) advocates adopting a lifelong willingness to examine and reexamine our beliefs and assumptions about any group of people. Exposure and education are also essential. As early as 1962, Wrenn noted the phenomenon he called *cultural encapsulation*. Culturally encapsulated people are unaccepting, insensitive, or completely ignorant of cultural practices other than their own. This reminds us of an anonymous saying we take hope in: "Monoculturalism is a disability that can be cured."

Questions for Reflection

Identifying one's own stereotypes, racism, and cultural judgments is difficult work. Can you imagine yourself admitting to and dealing with your own personal racist assumptions? What do you believe might be effective ways for you to do this work for yourself and for your future clients?

=== **ETHICAL HIGHLIGHT 12.1** ===

Pay Attention To What You Pay Attention To: Focusing on Individual, Family, Community, and Cultural Strengths

Brent G. Richardson, PhD, of Xavier University contributed the following essay (adapted from Richardson, 2001).

In my graduate counseling classes, I sometimes ask for volunteers to try the following experiment:

I ask them to close their eyes. I tell them that when they open their eyes, they will have fifteen seconds to try to memorize everything in the room that is gray. After fifteen seconds, I have them close their eyes again. Now, I ask them to tell the class everything around them that is green. They will probably have difficulty remembering many green items.

Lessons learned long ago from Pavlov's dog and Skinner's box about the potency of positive reinforcement sometimes get lost in the shuffle with counselors and other helping professionals. It is easy to become so focused on what is gray and drab; we neglect what is green and alive. We become so focused on problem behaviors and perceived weaknesses that we neglect to recognize and build on strengths.

In my cross-cultural counseling classes, students complete two Interaction Plans in which they conduct personal interviews, attend community meetings, and attend social or political functions with persons who are culturally different from themselves. One semester, several students chose to interview Reverend Damon Lynch III, a prominent African American community leader in Over the Rhine (a community in Cincinnati). During their interview, the students learned that this valuable lesson should also be applied to communities and cultures as well as individuals. What follows are excerpts from one of those student's paper eloquently processing her experience.

> We discussed many times what we were going to ask Reverend Lynch. We wrote out questions we had thought of and felt we were pretty prepared for our interview. We each introduced ourselves and discussed our multicultural counseling class and the nature of our assignment. . . . We indicated that we hoped he would be able to give us a better understanding of the basic needs and concerns of this community. . . .

> Reverend Lynch paused reflectively, then slowly began to explain that he did not want to talk about needs and concerns of the community; neither did he think it was a good place for us to start. He said he did not want to "label the community as deficient, and that's what has happened too long in communities like this. We would be labeling if we started there."

> He explained, "This is a rich community. It is rich with the resources, assets, people with gifts, institutions, and businesses. As a matter of fact, this is one of the richest communities in Cincinnati. There is no other community in the city that holds the promise that this community holds. When we talk about our children, we talk about the resource and the assets that they are, and the gifts they have. We need to spend some time on the focus that if the community is going to change, it is going to start with the strengths that we have."

(continued)

=== **ETHICAL HIGHLIGHT 12.1** ===

He used the analogy of the glass that is half filled with water. "Is it half full or half empty?" he asked. In our attempt to show our optimism we answered that the glass was half full. He replied, "No actually, it is both, but if you are going to rebuild the community with this cup, it is obvious that you need to start with what is half full. Traditionally, in communities like this, people start with the part that is half empty. I am just saying this to caution you two that when you go somewhere else to speak, instead of asking about their deficiencies, it would be better to ask about their strengths."

Needless to say, I felt I had just been to church, and learned a good lesson. I then felt that all of the questions we had prepared were totally useless and inappropriate. We had a few minutes of silence. Then we rephrased our questions. "Reverend Lynch, could you please tell us about the strengths of the community?" (Reverend Lynch then talked at length about specific strengths of the community.)

. . . I started this experience thinking that I was empathic enough to the needs of the Over the Rhine community. I ended it with the realization that I have a lot to learn. I started the interview with the need to have someone confirm my concerns and beliefs about the community. Instead I was left exposed and ashamed by how stereotypical I was. I was embarrassed by my inability to perceive the positive aspects of the community. It is as if those of us who are privileged majority cannot perceive the possibility of positive life outside our mode. We have a lot to learn.

This student should be commended for her willingness to entertain new ways of being and seeing. She should also be applauded for learning from her experiences. Too often, we opt for defending our own perceptions of the world at the expense of personal and professional growth. I know I do. Reverend Lynch identified a common trap that many of us fall into, particularly when working with racial minority groups: rushing in and focusing on perceived individual, family, or community weaknesses rather than recognizing and building on existing strengths and potential. This is a difficult paradigm shift to make because many theoretical models are deficit-oriented, focusing on what is supposedly wrong with clients, students, families, or systems. Regardless of your theoretical orientation, counseling students should periodically assess their own thoughts, feelings, and behaviors regarding the populations they serve. What are you paying attention to?

The American Counseling Association has established a set of multicultural competencies, based on an article by D. W. Sue, Arredondo, and McDavis (1992). These competencies are expanded upon in D. W. Sue and Sue's (2003) book *Counseling the Culturally Diverse*. We've provided an abbreviated form of these competencies in Table 12.1. Please read through these competencies carefully; they provide a very challenging and succinct picture of what it means to be a multicultural counselor.

Being a multicultural counselor doesn't mean you'll never judge another culture negatively. Occasionally, you will be shocked, alarmed, or offended by another culture's beliefs and practices. You will feel the urge to try and change the members of that culture, or at least to retreat as far from them as possible. You will feel a surge of identification with your own culture and a sense of relief about the comfort and rightness of your culture's practices. These are not constructive reactions; they are, as Sullivan sug-

Table 12.1   Multicultural Competencies

Awareness and Acceptance

Culturally competent mental health professionals are aware of their own cultural background and experiences. They can articulate what it means to be a member of their culture. Further, they have begun the process of accepting other cultural practices and beliefs as equally valid and worthy. They work to increase their awareness of their own biases and fears with regard to race, gender, sexual orientation, poverty, and/or religious beliefs.

Knowledge

Culturally competent mental health professionals realize that they must seek specific knowledge about the cultures they are most likely to encounter in their work. This knowledge should include sociopolitical history, current challenges faced by the culture, and basic cultural beliefs, values, and practices. This may necessitate talking with willing members of the culture who can serve as educators and informants because written literature in these areas may not exist. Such information must be handled with deference and respect.

Skills

Culturally competent mental health professionals realize that techniques and strategies for change must be tailored to meet the needs of clients from diverse cultures. They realize that sometimes they may need to step outside the institutionalized procedures in order to maximize their chances for effective connection and intervention. Culturally competent mental health professionals have developed both verbal and nonverbal responses and styles to enhance effective communication. In addition, they have developed the skills necessary to recognize their own shortcomings with regard to being of help to certain cultures and, when necessary, have the skills to transfer clients or find other ways to have the client's needs met.

---

gests in the opening quote to this chapter, simply human reactions. Luckily, humans have choices about their reactions and can work to obtain insight into why they react the ways they do. Learning to understand, modulate, and alter your reactions with increased knowledge, patience, and maturity is part of the multicultural journey. Trappist monk Thomas Merton (1974) wrote about his deep regrets for the ways religious missionaries have contributed to cultural genocide. He asked the thought provoking question, What would the world be like if different cultures had encountered each other with questions instead of answers? What if the questions went something like these?

- What can you tell me about yourselves?
- What would you like to know about us?
- What can you teach me about the Creator?

Similarly, as mental health professionals, we must learn to listen first and provide information later, if necessary. We cannot assume that we know what psychologically maladaptive functioning looks like or what psychological health would be in the context of another culture. Further, we cannot decide which cultural practices should remain central to a client traversing many cultures and which the client might wish to leave behind. Even further, at the global level, we cannot improve, cure, or fix other cultures (Christopher, 1999). That is the job of the members of the culture themselves. We have enough work to do with the maintenance and repair of our own cultures.

Preparing Your Client for Multicultural Therapy

Often, clients from cultures other than yours will appreciate a brief acknowledgment of your differing cultural backgrounds. Other times, however, they will not. It depends on their culture! For example, in their helpful guidelines for counseling clients from different cultures, D. W. Sue and Sue (2003) suggest considering an immediate and direct discussion of ethnic-racial differences with African American clients but not with American Indian, Latino, or Asian clients.

Acknowledgment of cultural differences might be experienced as too direct by some cultures; it may even be seen as a means by which you are establishing your superiority. Obviously, this requires a tentative, caring attitude. In addition, if not done carefully, direct discussion of culture might lead clients to believe that you are attributing their distress to their cultural identity. One counselor we knew was seeing a Chinese American woman for the first time. He asked about her family and her Asian heritage shortly after she complained that everyone seemed to treat her like a child. She responded energetically with, "I know you think Chinese women act quiet, like black-eyed Barbie dolls, but not me. It's not about being Chinese at all. It's about my coworkers and my stupid husband. I have something to say once in a while, and I say it. But they get all bent out of shape."

In the early stages of establishing a therapeutic relationship, multiculturally oriented counselors might say something like,

> In my work, I've come to believe that our culture is very important in our lives. By culture, I mean things like race, religion, sex and sexual orientation, and other things we think of as identifying features. You and I are probably different in some ways, and alike in some ways. When we bump into the ways we are different, I hope we can explore them in ways that matter to you. I'll try to be as open and nonjudgmental as I can be. If you think I'm missing the boat, I hope you'll let me know.

We've had the experience of seeing clients from very different cultural experiences than our own. Sometimes, they're eager to provide background and education for us as we go along in therapy. Other times, they tell us they're tired of explaining their culture to everyone and believe that it is our job to become more familiar with Cherokees, Serbians, or whatever group is in question.

This can be true simply for members of a given minority as well. A gay student of ours became weary trying to answer student and faculty queries about his gay culture. He cleverly gave us the hint by purchasing three books he believed to be useful and donating them to the clinic library. Then, when asked a question, he would only answer if the person asking had bothered to at least skim through these books.

If you are a member of a minority culture and are training to be a mental health professional in the dominant culture, you face unique challenges in preparing your clients from a multicultural perspective. A counselor we know who was born and raised in Malawi has worked out a very gracious introduction that includes acknowledging her accent and cultural differences in a way that allows the client to feel understood in the first session. During the informed consent portion of the first interview, she finds different ways to say the following:

> I imagine you might be a little surprised to find a counselor like me here in Montana. I grew up in Malawi, Africa, and my education is both from there and from here in the United States. Sometimes, people find my accent a little hard at first, so I have to ask you if you feel comfortable asking me to repeat myself. I mean, really. Can you imagine doing counseling if you can't understand each other?

Using the obvious fact of her accent, this counselor wisely opens the door to the important questions that clients feel when encountering a therapist from a culture different from their own: Can this person really understand me enough to help? Exploring that question can have rich therapeutic value. For many if not most clients from minority cultures attempting to exist and thrive in the dominant culture, the question of being understood and cared for looms very large.

Assessment Issues and Procedures

As you might imagine, this area is very compelling for multiculturally oriented mental health professionals. Earlier in the chapter, we offered some horrifying examples of misused assessment procedures. Any assessment done with culturally different clients must be done with extreme caution to avoid being unethical and inaccurate. Both the American Counseling Association and the American Psychological Association have specific ethical guidelines for multicultural assessment. Mezzich et al. (1999) report,

> The cultural effort for DSM-IV resulted in significant innovations including an introductory cultural statement, cultural considerations for the use of diagnostic categories and criteria, a glossary of culture-bound syndromes and idioms of distress, and an outline for a cultural formulation. However, proposals that challenged universalistic nosological assumptions and argued for the contextualization of illness, diagnosis, and care were minimally incorporated and marginally placed. Further culturally informed research is needed to ensure that future diagnostic systems incorporate a genuinely comprehensive framework, responsive to the complexity of health problems in increasingly multicultural societies. (p. 457)

Multicultural therapists look first to their clients' cultures for clues about how best to assess the nature of the presenting problems. Further, they look to culture to define appropriate treatment goals. Too often we forget that our ideas about health and the good life are as culturally bound as are our visions of problems and troubles. As Christopher (1999) states,

> Theories and measures of psychological well-being may be best thought of as different "takes" on the good or ideal person. Understandings of psychological well-being necessarily rely upon moral visions that are culturally embedded and frequently culture specific. If we forget this point and believe that we are discovering universal and ahistorical psychological truths rather than reinterpreting and extending our society's or community's moral visions, then we run the high risk of casting non-Western people, ethnic minorities, and women as inherently less psychologically healthy. (p 149)

Historically, psychological and intellectual assessment has been used in biased and prejudicial ways with ethnic minorities and women. Multicultural assessment requires significant training and experience. Lopez and Carillo (2001) writes, "Multicultural assessment requires a solid foundation in traditional assessment theory and methods" (p. 226). Further, he explains that multiculturally competent assessors must be able to discern how the given culture relates to the behaviors or sets of behaviors in question; finally, they must be able to formulate and test both culture-specific and more general dysfunction-impairment hypotheses. Obviously, conducting skilled assessments of people from other cultures requires a great deal of training, supervision, and experience. Overdiagnosing, underdiagnosing, and misdiagnosing psychopathology in clients from diverse cultures has been a critical problem for many years (Paniagua, 2001). D. W. Sue et al. (1999) sound this cautionary note:

The invisibility of Whiteness makes those who enjoy the advantages it confers oblivious and unaware. Euro-American psychologists are likely to perceive their worldview as normative, and as a result these biases may be reflected in criteria used to judge normality-abnormality, standards of practice, and the code of ethics. (p. 1065)

To provide culturally competent assessment, therapists should use a culture-specific service delivery, possibly including test administration in the client's native language; evaluate the client as a cultural being prior to testing; observe for culture-specific syndromes; select culture-specific tests; and critically examine the standardization procedures and norms used in testing procedures (Dana, 1996).

APPLICATION: CASE EXAMPLE

Shonda was a 19-year-old American Indian athlete whose father was half-Latino. She came to college on a full-ride basketball scholarship. In high school Shonda was a local legend, leading her team to three state titles. She was the pride of her tribe and her small town. College was a different story. Almost on arrival, she got involved with a young man from another tribe and began a regular pattern of partying. Her grades slipped; she missed practices or arrived late; and although still occasionally spectacular on the court, she was becoming progressively more inconsistent. Her coach finally contacted Dr. N., a counselor in town known to work successfully with both athletes and with American Indian families. Shonda's coach insisted that she try some counseling and made the call himself, even offering to accompany Shonda to the first session. Over the telephone he told Dr. N. that Shonda seemed down, unresponsive to guidance, and generally difficult to relate to. On the rare occasions when she really engaged and asserted herself on the court, it wasn't unusual for her to blow up and get into a shoving match with a teammate. Shonda's coach was also very worried about her alcohol use.

Comment: Shonda embodies a number of cultures. She identifies herself as American Indian, but her father's heritage includes being half-Latino, and Shonda spoke a little Spanish as well as a little Blackfeet. Besides these racial-ethnic identities, Shonda has a strong identity as an athlete. Athletes, as a cultural group, do not easily admit weakness and do not easily seek counseling (Maniar, Curry, Sommers-Flanagan, & Walsh, 2001). Dr. N., having worked with reluctant athletes before, is well aware of this attribute.

Shonda arrived for her first session alone. She immediately told Dr. N. that she didn't want to come but that she'd rather come herself than have her coach drag her in. After the usual informed consent discussions and after Dr. N. told Shonda what the coach had said, she asked the traditional, "But I'm interested in what brings *you* in to see me, Shonda. From your perspective."

Shonda responded with an attempt at humor: "My feet brought me, I guess."

Dr. N. laughed and smiled and finally said, "Good answer. Sometimes I ask questions in a weird way. I guess my feet brought me here today, too. I'm guessing from what you said before that your feet just *barely* brought you here today."

Shonda smiled, apparently pleased that Dr. N. liked her joke.

Comment: Dr. N. knew that many American Indians enjoy laughter and joking. Rather than interpreting Shonda's joke as sarcastic hostility or feeling put off by the joke, she felt included and trusted with a bit of humor.

Encouraged, Dr. N. decided that it was time to get a few cultural cards on the table. She asked, with genuine interest, "I know you played ball for Benton. Are you a member of the tribe there?"

Shonda nodded, averting her gaze, but smiling. "Yeah. My mom's from there, and all my folks. But I have cousins who are White and cousins who are very dark. Strange, huh? And my boyfriend's only half, so if we had kids, they wouldn't even meet the quota."

Comment: Shonda's response to Dr. N's entry into the cultural arena produced a variety of cultural and personal information and illustrates how a brief disclosure presents a huge range of alternatives to the multicultural counselor. Consider these options:

- Shonda's mentioning of the blood quota may be a test for Dr. N. because blood quota is not a well-known issue outside Indian country. How should Dr. N. respond? Should she ignore the blood quota issue? Should she act more informed or less informed than she actually is?

- Shonda shares her multiracial identity. Should Dr. N. pursue this area in order to gather more specific information about Shonda's racial identity?

- When Shonda mention's having "kids" with her boyfriend it might indicate a pregnancy, hope of a pregnancy, and all that becoming pregnant means symbolically and literally. Should Dr. N. directly ask about whether Shonda is pregnant or thinking about getting pregnant?

- American Indian girls and young women often get overt messages about achievement and covert messages about getting pregnant and having babies. Should Dr. N. explore these issues?

- Overall, Shonda's initial responsiveness is relatively open and therefore gives Dr. N. hope for a connection. Shonda's averted gaze also may indicate a sign of respect. Should Dr. N. notice this openness and appreciate it?

Dr. N. nodded sympathetically. Her mind was filled with the preceding options. Dr. N. knew that she and Shonda did not have enough of a relationship for her to ask directly about underlying issues—yet. So she resolved to continue listening very carefully and to stay with the central content of what Shonda was saying instead of trying to interpret deeper possibilities.

"Wow. That blood quantum controversy is really something. I've been following the news on it a little bit. What do you think about it?"

"It sucks. You know I learned more about it at college than I knew before about how it was genocide, really. A planned way to make sure there were no Indians at all after a while."

"Yeah, it's pretty awful. Lots of those policies seem to hurt Indians more than being helpful. And some of the policies are so complicated that you have to come to college to learn more about them. How did you learn about it in class?"

"I'm taking Native American studies. I like it. But English sucks and so does my math class."

"Yeah," Dr. N. smiled. "It must be quite an adjustment, coming away to college, taking classes you don't like and keeping up your basketball, all at the same time."

"Nah. My cousin Sidney is here. He introduced me to Derrick. It's been pretty fun. But the coach. He's the one having a problem. I can play ball, if he'll just get off my case."

Comment: Dr. N. is working at connecting with Shonda on a comfortable level. During these interactions Shonda is responsive. But then, as soon as she mentions "adjustment" and "basketball," Shonda disagrees with Dr. N., asserting that the adjustment is no problem and that her coach is her problem. At this point Dr. N. could directly ask about what the coach does that's a problem, but instead she chooses a person-centered reflection because she wants Shonda to know that she will not force a viewpoint onto Shonda that Shonda doesn't agree with.

"So you've been having fun and the adjustment hasn't been too hard and it sounds like you still want to play ball. It's just the coaching and practice that aren't going well?"

Shonda looked around the office, not immediately responding to Dr. N. She yawned. Then she offered an engaging smile and asked, "How many times do I need to come in here?"

Comment: It's hard to say whether Dr. N.'s paraphrase fell flat or whether it made Shonda consider the implications of a longer-term relationship because it was accurate. Either way, what's important is for Dr. N. to acknowledge openly that engaging in therapy is a choice.

"I don't know. I don't even know if you need to come in here. I'm interested in what you think. Most of the people I see tell me counseling is very helpful. But it's not the right thing for everybody. How about we talk about counseling and whether it might be helpful for you before we make any decisions either way about how many times you should come, or even if you need to come at all. Is that okay with you?"

Comment: Dr. N. is staying open to the possibility that Shonda may not engage in counseling, while at the same time trying to evaluate her expectations about counseling before any firm decisions are made.

Shonda paused a long time, looking down. Dr. N. sat quietly. Finally, Shonda said, "I don't know. I don't even know if I can stick around here for that long. College isn't what I thought it would be."

Comment: Shonda indirectly answered the question by opening up a new area of discussion. It's not unusual for Indian clients to be subtle and indirect in their verbal responses.

Dr. N. glanced at Shonda and looked downward herself for a few seconds before cautiously asking, "What is it about college that's making it hard to want to stick around?"

Shonda fidgeted in the silence that followed. Dr. N. reminded herself to breathe and to wait patiently. Shonda was deciding what to say and what not to say, and it was important that her choice in that process be respected. Finally, she said, "It's really sorta stupid. College is okay. It just feels weird. I've been on the res for 18 years. I know everybody and everybody knows me. It's home. This isn't home. It's that simple. I like my cousin and I like Derrick, but God I miss my mom and my family back home."

Comment: Therapy has now started. It would be inappropriate for Dr. N. to go back to her question about Shonda's expectations for counseling. Now is a time to gently and somewhat indirectly explore Shonda's feelings. In other words, Dr. N. should avoid using stock questions like, "How do you feel about that?"

"When you put it that way," Dr. N. began, "I get an image of you with a big, weird, and sorta bad feeling inside. What about being on the reservation would help make the weird feelings get better?"

"I'd be around my family. I'd know everybody on the res and everybody would know me. There's no strangers there. Around here, aside from my cousin and Derrick, everybody is a stranger. Especially my God-damn coach. Man he's strange."

Comment: In clinical and diagnostic terms, Dr. N. might categorize Shonda's description of her experience at college as indicative of separation anxiety. If Dr. N. was behaviorally oriented, she might systematically evaluate Shonda's anxiety symptoms and then educate her about options for anxiety reduction. In psychodynamic terms, Shonda is recapitulating her dilemma right within the counseling session. The issue is, "Shall I stay here where I feel uncomfortable and anxious, or shall I go away to some place where I'm comfortable and not anxious? As the session progressed, Dr. N. engaged Shonda in a brief brainstorming activity focusing on what might make being at college "feel better" if she decided to stay. During the activity, Dr. N. used a bit of humor on occasion (at one point asking Shonda about the possibility of having her mom come live in her dorm room). Overall, the session proceeded smoothly, and toward the end Dr. N. asked Shonda if she would come for three more sessions just to sort out whether to stay in college or go home to the reservation. Shonda agreed, and they scheduled an appointment.

Dr. N. did not assign Shonda homework to complete between sessions. Instead, because the therapy connection was fragile, she did some homework herself. She went online and tried to find out a little more information about the reservation where Shonda grew up.

Shonda showed up about 15 minutes late for her second session. Neither she nor Dr. N. commented on the lateness. Among some American Indians there is a concept referred to as Indian time. In essence, this concept emphasizes the fact that things happen when they happen. Although Shonda's lateness might reflect Indian time, it also might reflect her ambivalence about coming back. However, interpreting lateness is generally a bad idea early in therapy with an Indian client. The therapist needs to relax the time-bound orientation associated with the dominant White culture. Dr. N. also chose to open the session with two gifts, one metaphorical and the other edible.

After greeting and as soon as they sat down, Dr. N. opened with, "Hey, Shonda. I picked up a chocolate chip cookie for you from the bakery down the street. They're pretty good." Dr. N. handed a small bakery bag to Shonda and pulled an identical bag for herself out of her purse. "I figured with all that basketball practice you have that you probably get pretty hungry."

"Thanks," Shonda replied. "I love chocolate chip cookies."

"You know, after our talk last time I thought I should find out a little more about what life is like up on your reservation, so I got on the Internet and found a couple of Web sites that had some information."

"Really? I didn't know my res had a Web site. What'd you find out?"

"Well, of course there was some info about the Indian Health Services. And I found a little café or bar or something that had a Web site."

"Yeah. That musta been the Brown Horse Bar and Grill. That's where the drunks hang out."

"Right. Okay, so I've got a quiz for you. The Indian Health Services Web site had a staff directory, and since you said you know everyone on the res, I thought I'd throw a couple names out and see if you recognize them."

Comment: Socializing and gift giving are very important in most Indian cultures. Dr. N. wants her therapy office to be a comfortable place for Shonda, so she's making clear efforts to behave almost like a member of Shonda's extended family from the reservation. Typically, if Shonda was on the reservation and feeling distress, she might go and talk with an aunt or grandmother, and some sort of food might be included in the interaction. In the ensuing conversation, Shonda clearly proves that she knows just about everybody who works at Tribal Health. After about 8 to 10 minutes of munching cookies and checking on Shonda's knowledge of the Tribal Health staff, Dr. N. moves toward a more serious topic.

"So, Shonda, last time we talked about how it feels pretty weird for you to be here, away from the res. Have you had any thoughts or reactions to our conversation from last time?"

"Well yeah," Shonda began, "I kept thinking about the one thing you said about having my mom come live in my dorm room. It just sorta made me feel good. I thought about what it would be like having my mom in my dorm room making me fry bread and waking me up in the morning."

"That sounds like a nice scene. Do you think she'd come down and do the same for me?"

Shonda giggled. "You know, I bet she would. And you'd love her fry bread. Everybody loves her fry bread. You know, that's probably why I know everybody on the res, cause every one of them's had my mom's fry bread."

"How often have you been talking to your mom?" Dr. N. asked.

"About twice a week. Just enough to make me miss her crazy like. It's long distance and I can't afford much more and she can't afford it either."

"Well, I guess the best thing to say about that is that it totally sucks," Dr. N. offered.

Final Comment: From a traditional psychodynamic, person-centered, or behavioral therapy perspective, the preceding interactions may not seem either professional or much like therapy. However, this case is provided to illustrate a culturally sensitive therapy approach.

Based on a contemporary diagnostic system, Shonda might qualify for separation anxiety disorder, and the most empirically reasonable approach would likely be some form of systematic desensitization. From a psychoanalytic perspective, Shonda probably needs to further internalize a loving mother-object so that she can nurture herself in the absence of her mother. In our view, the culture-sensitive approach is accomplishing both of these objectives at the same time. Dr. N. has begun the desensitization process and the discussions of Shonda's mother are resulting in an increased cognitive presence of her mother.

As therapy proceeded, Dr. N. continued to work with Shonda using a culture-sensitive frame. She also helped Shonda begin to notice and then change the ways in which she was coping with her separation anxiety. Sometimes through humor and sometimes through more serious but somewhat indirect communication, Dr. N. was able to guide Shonda to the creation of a home away from home. This involved joining the campus Native American Club, learning some calming and soothing techniques to use instead of alcohol, and developing a support system both on and off campus. As it turns out, Shonda's relationship with Derrick continued, and Dr. N. and Shonda were

---

Questions for Reflection

What are your thoughts and reactions to the informal and somewhat social approach to therapy that Dr. N. employed in this case? We did not include the formal introduction between Dr. N. and Shonda at the beginning of therapy. How do you suppose Dr. N. introduced herself? Do you think that Dr. N. insisted that Shonda call her Dr. N. or that she encouraged communication on a first-name basis?

able to talk directly about using birth control rather than risking a pregnancy that would almost certainly land her back on the reservation. Shonda was able to see that returning to the reservation was always an option for her, but that if she decided to return, she would prefer doing so on her own terms and not because she had a growing fetus in her womb.

Specific Therapy Techniques

Multicultural counseling is not an approach that emphasizes techniques. Instead, as illustrated in the preceding case example, multicultural counseling emphasizes a relationship that respects the client's cultural identity and affiliation. It is also inappropriate to outline specific techniques for multicultural counseling because clients with different ethnocultural backgrounds will prefer different therapy approaches. For example, whereas African American and Latino clients tend to prefer more directive styles that include feedback and advice, American Indian clients tend to prefer more nondirective approaches (see D. W. Sue & Sue, 2003).

S. Sue (1998) identified three specific skills that he considers indicative of cross-cultural therapeutic competency. These skills include

- *Scientific mindedness.* Therapists who use scientific mindedness form hypotheses about their clients rather than coming to firm and premature conclusions. These therapists also develop creative ways to test their initial hypotheses about minority clients and then act on the basis of the data they obtain and not their prejudices or prejudgments.
- *Dynamic sizing.* Therapists with this skill know when to generalize and be inclusive and when to individualize and be exclusive. This means knowing when to apply general knowledge about a culture to an individual and when to focus more on the individual than the culture.
- *Culture-specific expertise.* This involves acquiring knowledge about one's own culture and about the client's culture. It also involves the application of that knowledge in a culturally sensitive and effective manner.

S. Sue (1998) emphasizes that effective multicultural therapy requires more than just familiarity with the client's culture and intercultural sensitivity. In addition, the therapist needs to acquire and practice scientific mindedness and dynamic sizing.

Therapy Outcomes Research

The rational foundation for establishing multicultural or culturally sensitive therapy approaches is unarguable. Taking each client's individual cultural background into consideration is the rational and logical thing to do.

In contrast, the empirical foundation for multicultural therapy is much more controversial (G. C. N. Hall, 2001). Problems associated with empirical validation of culturally sensitive treatments are legion. In fact, it is hard to imagine how researchers could collect data to support the efficacy of multicultural treatment. Think about cases involving American Indians, Laotian refugees, Asian Americans, or Latino immigrants. How could researchers accurately measure the concerns of all these clients as they enter treatment? In many cases, the client's conception of the problem may be dramatically different from a traditional Western diagnostic label. Further, can you imagine using a manualized treatment approach with a young Latino immigrant suffering from susto? (Susto can occur when a frightening incident causes a person's soul to leave his or her body. The result is depression and physical malady. The customary treatment in Mexico and Central America includes ritual healings in which the person's soul is called back to the body.) Then, even if a manualized treatment were acceptable, is it possible for researchers to administer standardized questionnaires to determine the efficacy of treatment?

A more practical and perhaps answerable question is this: What therapy situations and therapist skills produce positive outcomes among culturally diverse populations?

Early research indicated that about 50% of ethnic clients dropped out of treatment after an initial therapy session (S. Sue, 1977). To determine whether ethnic-minority clients stay in treatment longer if they work with ethnically-matched therapists, S. Sue and colleagues evaluated records of thousands of African American, Asian American, Mexican American, and White clients seen in the Los Angeles County mental health system (S. Sue, Fujino, Takeuchi, & Zane, 1991). The results indicated that Asian American and Mexican Americans clearly benefited from seeing an ethnically (and linguistically) matched therapist. The findings for African American and White clients were mixed; matching resulted in greater therapy attendance, but no clear effects on outcomes were found.

Sue and colleagues also evaluated the relationship of ethnic-specific services on treatment outcomes (Takeuchi, Sue, & Yeh, 1995). Ethnic-specific services are defined as treatments that try to respond to the cultural needs of clients (e.g., culturally sensitive greetings are used, Chinese clients are served tea instead of coffee, etc.). Overall, the research showed that ethnic clients stay in treatment longer when offered ethnic-specific services. Additional research also indicated that clients benefit from what is termed a *cognitive match,* in which the therapist and client use similar ways of identifying goals and resolving problems and have similar degrees of acculturation (S. Sue, 1998).

Research on the effects of multicultural training on therapy outcome are similarly positive. Specifically, therapists with greater multicultural competence report higher levels of self-efficacy, and treatment outcomes are generally better (Atkinson & Lowe, 1995; Constantine, 2001; Tomlinson-Clarke, 2000).

Overall, the research consistently points to the conclusion that culture and cultural competence do matter.

There has been a limited amount of generic therapy outcomes research with ethnic-minority clients. The general conclusions follow:

- Outcomes with African American clients are generally equal to or somewhat less positive than outcomes with White Americans.
- There is not enough published research with American Indian clients to make even tentative statements.
- Conclusions about Asian Americans are also premature, although there have been four outcome studies with this population (S. Sue & Lam, 2002)
- A meta-analysis on treatment effectiveness with Latino clients produced results similar to treatment outcomes with White Americans. However, 57% of the therapy was conducted in Spanish, once again suggesting that ethnic and linguistic sensitivity is important (Navarro, 1993).

In conclusion, at present there is such meager evidence that contemporary empirically supported treatments are effective with minority populations that Atkinson and colleagues queried in the title of a recent article "Multiculturally Sensitive Empirically Supported Treatments—An Oxymoron?" (Atkinson, Bui, & Mori, 2001).

Questions for Reflection

Outcome research with multicultural populations is sorely lacking in the empirical literature. As a budding researcher and practitioner, how would you address this issue? If you decided to do your thesis or dissertation on this topic, how would you proceed?

NON-WESTERN THEORIES AND TECHNIQUES

The preceding section and case example focused on multicultural theory and therapy. But what about non-Western theories of counseling and psychotherapy? How do they differ from multicultural approaches?

In a technical sense, there is no such thing as non-Western counseling theory and therapy. This is because all counseling and psychotherapy are concepts and procedures that specifically arose within the confines of Western thinking (D. W. Sue & Sue, 2003).

Nevertheless, other cultures have developed sophisticated means of describing, understanding, and addressing human mental distress and disease, as well as the human striving for wholeness and actualization, even though they do not have formal theories of counseling and psychotherapy. The title of this chapter, therefore, is actually a misnomer.

Questions for Reflection

If counseling and psychotherapy are Western inventions designed to help people who are members of the culture from which the concepts sprang, why try to understand other cultural approaches to psychological well-being and distress? Why not let cultures address their own problems internally?

Of course, there are many answers to the questions you just considered. An intriguing one is offered by James Harbeck (2001), who wrote an article titled "The Transcendent Function of Interculturalism." In this article Harbeck notes that Jung believed that we achieve transcendence in finding the union of opposites. As we discussed in the Jungian chapter, and in others, "What we humans take to be ourselves is only a rather narrow area of focus on the surface of a much larger Self" (p. 14). Harbeck argues that we need to encounter other cultures and other ways of thinking and doing things to free up repressed parts of ourselves. He quotes Kathy Foley (1992):

> Are cross-cultural drama, dance, and music the ultimate in cultural tourism? Club Med experiences of "the real thing" without any substantive connection to the internal stuff that codes a performance? Or is it the very reality of the arts to allow us to test the boundaries of self and other where the experience stretches us toward realizing the other is only a possibility of self that for cultural reasons is suppressed? (p. 13)

PRACTITIONER COMMENTARY 12.1

Reflections of a Process-Oriented Contextualist

The following comments were contributed by Luis Vargas, associate professor and director of the clinical psychology predoctoral internship program in the Department of Psychiatry at the University of New Mexico School of Medicine.

I have always considered myself a scientist-practitioner. I am a strong believer in evidence-based practice. I have always strived to be culturally responsive in my work. However, I have been bothered by psychology's increasing emphasis on empirically supported treatments and on the current focus on cultural competence. I don't say this to be provocative or iconoclastic. I say this out of concern about what we are endeavoring to do as psychologists involved in carrying out interventions.

The emphasis on "empirical support" troubles me for three major reasons. One, it seems to assume that support of an intervention must come from one epistemology, empiricism, and, I believe, epistemologies are, to use Hallowell's term from anthropology, culturally constituted. Second, the term excludes other forms of evidence, which, I believe are potential sources of important contributions to the area of mental health (e.g., contextualist, social constructionist, and narrative perspectives), particularly in working with culturally diverse groups. Third, empiricists' efforts to "manualize" treatment has, I believe, unintentionally de-emphasized the critical aspect of the interaction between therapist and client. Over the years, my focus in the process of conducting culturally responsive psychotherapeutic interventions has been much more on who the psychologist is and less on who the clients are. You see, as psychologists involved in intervention, we inevitably transmit culture—for example, sometimes imperialistically (as in, "let me teach these African American parents proper parenting skills or practices") or sometimes in a dominant-culture-centric way (as in, "this Mexican mother and son are enmeshed and they need to learn to relate appropriately" or "this American Indian father needs to assume a more appropriately paternal role in the limit-setting with his children"). What is proper or appropriate is determined by cultural context. When we, as psychologists, interact with our clients, we become part of that context. The effects of these interactions are multidirectional—we are changed as much as we may facilitate change. Because of this, we must appreciate how we ourselves are culturally constituted before we embark in an endeavor to intervene with others.

The focus on cultural competence also worries me. I very much try to be culturally responsive to my clients. But can I say that I am "culturally competent?" Absolutely not! I am still, despite my many and genuine efforts, "a toro (bull) in a China shop" with all the cultural implications of this altered adage intended. I do not believe that "cultural competence" is the best way to think about what we want to do or teach. I believe that thinking in terms of "cultural competence" often leads to an emphasis on teaching to cultural content and, therefore, running the risk of teaching to stereotypes or of making static overgeneralizations about local cultures. It can lead to a patronizing sense of complacency and a misguided sense of expertise that may further alienate us from those with whom we intend

---

PRACTITIONER COMMENTARY 12.1 (continued)

to work. Culture is not about outcome. Culture is an ever-changing process. One cannot get a firm grip of it just as one cannot get a good grasp of water. As an educator, what I try to do is to teach about the process of culture—how we will never obtain enough cultural content, how important it is to understand the cultural context in which we are working, and how crucial it is to understand our role in the interactions with the people with whom we want to work or the communities in which we seek to intervene. I try to emphasize the need to appreciate our values, beliefs, and attitudes in interaction with those of our clients, the need to appreciate issues of power and privilege, the need to understand and appreciate our clients' world views, and the need to work in collaboration with our clients. I do not want to enter the intervention arena (whether in family therapy or in implementing a community-based intervention) as an "expert" who has the answers and knows what needs to be done. I am not a conquistador, intent on supplanting my culture on others. I have a certain expertise that, when connected with the knowledge and experience of my clients, can be helpful and meaningful to my clients.

There is no question that Western ideas are rapidly permeating the world. Many have noted that the Western cultural view is biased toward masculinist, individualistic, essentialist, and rationalist worldviews. The result of the Western bias, from a Jungian view, is an imbalance at the individual level, as well as the cultural level: Certain tendencies that are natural to the Self are repressed into the unconscious and thereby subject to devaluation and derogation.

One rather self-serving answer to the preceding question for reflection is that we need other cultures to reveal our own repressions to ourselves. We need other ways of seeing to open our own eyes.

Another answer is that, unfortunately, psychological inquiry has not seen itself as culturally determined. Until quite recently, and even now in many ways, psychology claimed and claims to be an objective science seeking transferable, universal truths and, by extension, offering universally effective interventions in the face of human distress or disease. We have not confined ourselves, in the dominant culture, to an application of judgments, diagnoses, and healing practices to only those within the culture. We have freely and naively acted as though our pain, our desires, and our cures were applicable to all people. Further, other cultures are directly importing U.S.-style psychology.

As an example, to our great surprise one day, twelve copies of our clinical interviewing text arrived at our door looking very, very different from the copies to which we had become accustomed. They were copies of our text published in *Chinese*! Not only did we not know that this had occurred, but our inability to read Chinese made it impossible for us to comprehend the translation quality. It had never entered our minds that someday our words (or their translation) might be read by Chinese students in their own language.

Time went by, and by chance we met a Chinese journalist who was bilingual and who was interested in studying psychology in China. We showed her a copy of the book, and she read through a few pages, chuckling to herself. Apparently, the translator had chosen to represent the word *client* with the Chinese character for *visitor.* As we talked it over, she explained that there is no Chinese word for client as we used it in the book. There is the word *patient,* and there is the word *client* as in a business transaction. So, coping with this problem, the translator decided on the word *visitor.* Our friend wasn't sure the translator had made the best choice, but there it was. We have no idea what ramifications might result from that seemingly simple translation decision, and at a larger level, we have no idea how many of the concepts we discussed in our book will be understood in China. It's an intimidating thought.

You might have noticed that we included commentary about multicultural applications and concerns in each chapter describing the various theories covered in this book. However, that might be said to be a Band-Aid approach to a hemorrhage, especially in the case where the ideas of Western-style wholeness, pathology, and healing and Western-based assessments of other cultures are exported directly into the center of other cultures. A little multicultural thinking and inclusion are better than none, but such inclusion by and large ignores the deeply imbedded beliefs and values of other cultures. Michael Brannigan (2000) writes,

> In order to participate in global dialogue, we need to construct secure bridges of cultural awareness, sensitivity, and understanding that run deeper than a merely superficial interest in Asian imports, such as martial arts, Chinese acupuncture, yoga, Japanese acupressure, Tai Chi, and Korean gingsen. (p. v)

Diverse cultural approaches to human psychological distress include viewing both the concept of mind and ideas about human functioning through different lenses. Far more than in Western theories, these lenses include philosophical-ethical, religious-spiritual, ancestral-familial, and even political considerations.

Signs of the Buddha Here and There

In his book *Talking Cures,* Peter Bankart (1997) uses his extensive exposure to Japanese culture to help the reader understand some of the core differences between Japanese culture and the dominant culture in the United States. He includes chapters on two contemporary treatments in Japan, Morita and Naikan, as well as one chapter on Yoga and one on Zen Buddhism. Bankart also offers lucid summaries of the central contributions of both Confucianism and the Tao to the psychological functioning of many Asian people.

Although we cannot explore these areas as Bankart did, it seems worth noting the many ways in which Buddhism and one of Buddhism's central tenets, mindfulness, have become part of some Western treatment modalities. Buddhism has been said to be the most psychological of the world's religions and the most spiritual of the world's psychologies (Epstein, 1998, p. 16). However, attempting to classify Buddhism is controversial. With all its beliefs, rituals, and religious-sounding components, such as monks and temples, it can be said to resemble a religion. However, Buddhists do not believe in a creator, higher power, or godlike entity, so Buddhism can therefore perhaps more accurately be called an applied philosophy. *Buddhism* is a very broad, general term applying to practices that are quite diverse (Kumar, 2002). However, some central tenets are present across this diversity.

After achieving enlightenment, the Buddha taught Four Noble Truths:

1. All is suffering (or suffering is everywhere).
2. The cause of suffering is craving, desiring, or having greed.

3. Suffering can be stopped or eliminated.

4. To eliminate suffering, one must follow the Eightfold path.

Morgan (1996, pp. 57–58) explains the Eightfold path as containing guidance for attaining wisdom, for being moral, and for meditation. She names these as follows:

Wisdom

- Right understanding is the perception of the world as it really is, without delusions. This involves particularly understanding suffering, the law of cause and effect, and impermanence.
- Right thought involves the purification of the mind and heart and the growth of thoughts of unselfishness and compassion, which will then be the roots of action.

Morality

- Right speech means the discipline of not lying and not gossiping or talking in any way that will encourage malice or hatred.
- Right action is usually expanded into the five precepts: avoid taking life, stealing, committing sexual misconduct, and taking stimulants and intoxicants.
- Right livelihood is a worthwhile job or way of life that avoids causing harm or injustice to other beings.

Meditation

- Right effort is the mental discipline that prevents evil arising, tries to stop evil that has arisen, and encourages what is good.
- Right mindfulness involves total attention to the activities of the body, speech, and mind.
- Right concentration is the training of the mind in meditation stages.

Some mental health professionals have integrated Buddhist perspectives into their work with clients (see Chapter 13). Mark Epstein (1998), an American psychiatrist, tells of his deepening understanding and appreciation of Buddhism's contributions to mental health in his book *Going to Pieces without Falling Apart.* He writes,

> I knew that the emptiness (or sunyata) from a Buddhist perspective, was an understanding of one's true nature, an intuition of the absence of inherent identity in people or in things. It was the one core psychological truth of Buddhism. Emptiness from a Western perspective, seemed to me to be a tortured feeling of distress, and absence of vitality, a sense of being not quite real enough, of disconnection. (p. 13)

Meditation, or seeking mindfulness through emptying one's mind, is a core value of Buddhism, and meditation practices have been increasingly used in various combinations with other treatment modalities and mixed in with other theoretical orientations. G. Alan Marlatt (2002), noted researcher and psychologist in the area of addiction, writes of his own exploration of Buddhist practice, with his interest in its clinical applications beginning with himself. In his 2002 article "Buddhist Philosophy and the Treatment of Addictive Behavior," he explores the important contributions that meditation and mindfulness can make to understanding and treating addictions.

Mindfulness has also been used in treating pain (Kabat-Zinn, 1990), in promoting holistic health in persons with HIV and AIDS (Logsdon-Conradsen, 2002), and, perhaps most notably, in Marsha Linehan's (1993) dialectical behavior therapy for persons diagnosed with borderline personality disorder (see Chapter 13 and A. L. Miller & Rathus, 2000).

Spirituality Invited Back In

In cultures other than Western European, the title of this section would be seen as ludicrous. Spirituality would not be invited back in because it would never have left. For most indigenous people and for most people born and raised in Asia, Africa, or Latin America, "spirituality is a life force that undergirds our existence in the universe" (Sue et al., 1999, p. 1064). However, those of us reared and educated in the logical positivist view of psychology find spiritual transcendence and centrality a bit challenging to include. But such inclusion is not optional for multiculturalists, as evidenced in the following quotation:

> [A] psychology based solely on the separation of science and spirituality and that uses primarily the segmented and reductionistic tenets of the natural sciences is one that may not be shared by three quarters of the world nor by the emerging culturally diverse groups in the United States. (D. W. Sue et al., 1999, p. 1065)

From Thomas Moore (1994), in his best-selling book, *Care of the Soul,* we hear,

> In the modern world, we separate religion and psychology, spiritual practice and therapy. There is considerable interest in healing this split, but if it is going to be bridged, our very idea of what we are doing in our psychology has to be radically re-imagined. Psychology and spirituality need to be seen as one. (p. xv)

If spirituality and psychology are to be reunited, serious implications for therapists and therapy follow. A psychotherapy that focuses on caring not only for the client's psyche and symptoms but also for his or her soul and spirit is a very different psychotherapy indeed.

Karasu (1999) contends that counseling and psychotherapy stemming from the traditional—psychoanalytic, behavioral, and humanistic—approaches leave clients spiritually bereft. He states that even if

> psychological conflicts are relatively resolved, deficits filled, and defects corrected, ultimately patients still experience posttherapeutic dysphoria, a loss of meaning or sense of emptiness, a nonluminous hollow. These diverse strategies have shed limited light and left patients bereft, because in the process of treatment (if not the psychopathology itself) the person's soul has been neglected and spiritual connections severed. (p. 144)

Questions for Reflection

Is it possible to integrate religious and spiritual concepts into counseling and psychotherapy while still honoring the theories and techniques we've studied thus far in this book? How would you answer the question, where is the soul and where is the spirit in modern counseling and psychotherapy?

Putting It in Practice 12.3

This homework assignment is from the book Favorite Counseling and Therapy Homework Assignments (Breggin, 2001, pp. 58–59).

A Dangerous Assignment

Based on the therapy principle, "Do unto others as you would have others do unto you," I rarely assign homework to my clients. . . .

There is, however, one exception: a homework assignment that I guarantee will improve my clients' lives and the lives of almost everyone they touch. If only as an experiment for a week or two, I suggest that they try being nice to everyone they meet. I explain, "Before we get together again, try being courteous and kind to everyone you deal with, even people you find unworthy or aggravating."

Some religions speak of greeting the God within each person we meet; the Quakers talk about addressing "that of God," which is in other people with respect and even reverence.

Naturally, like most of us, my clients are tempted to dismiss "being nice" as utopian, unmanly, embarrassing, and even dangerous. Rarely does anyone gratefully declare, "That's a great idea, Peter. An application of universal truths to my personal life. I can't wait to put it into action."

For many clients and therapists there is more to life than behavior change and more to their symptoms than cognitive restructuring might address. Although secular humanists such as Carl Rogers sometimes approach human relationships in a manner that seems intrinsically spiritual or divine, even his approach can be seen as missing something essential that many people seek. See Putting It in Practice 12.3 for an example of a spiritually oriented therapy technique.

THERAPY OUTCOMES RESEARCH

There has been no systematic effort to empirically evaluate spiritual approaches to counseling and psychotherapy. In this regard, Karasu (1999) clearly states that the effectiveness of spiritual psychotherapy is immeasurable:

> *Spiritual psychotherapy is not like academic psychotherapies.* Spiritual psychotherapy cannot be standardized in operational manuals that homogenize all treatment. It is not based on large-scale bureaucratic research requirements, efficacy, efficiency, or cost-effectiveness. It does not steer in shallow water, is not superficial or strictly short-term; it does not prescribe and predict. Rather, it is highly improvisational and fully accepts (if not promotes) heterogeneity. Its N equals one and is by definition immeasurable. It is not a matter of science and proof, but belief and faith. It steers in deep waters. (p. 160)

CONCLUDING COMMENTS

Conceptually, multicultural theory is simple. What could be simpler than a theoretical stance pointing out that culture is central in human development and human perception? However, as D. W. Sue et al. (1999) stated unequivocally, multicultural theory is not value neutral. In fact, the theory itself entails a belief in social justice. Harvard philosopher John Rawls (1971) proposed that social justice could be achieved only if we chose our social policies from behind a veil of ignorance so that we could not know where or who we might be in the society for which we were making the rules. We might be White, Black, poor, rich, prematurely disabled, male, female, old, young, and so on. If we had absolutely no way of knowing where we would step into life, what would we consider the best social policy?

Many argue that even Rawls gets it wrong because his system insinuates humans achieving a consensus will fail to take into account minority views (Tjeltveit, 1999). And of course, such a veil is impossible. We can only approximate understanding the experiences of other people, and we can never rid ourselves of our cultural identities. The best we can hope for is a rich understanding of ourselves as members in our various cultures and a constantly evolving appreciation and understanding of other cultures, other values, and other people.

STUDENT REVIEW ASSIGNMENTS

These assignments are designed to help you review and reflect on the content of this chapter.

Critical Corner

The following comments about multicultural therapy represent both real and exaggerated criticisms. They are offered only to stimulate your thinking about this important approach to counseling and psychotherapy. Please read the comments and then write your thoughts and reactions to the criticisms.

1. A true multicultural theory is impossible. Just as has been emphasized in this chapter, every individual is different—even individuals who come from the same cultural background and even individuals who come from the same family within the same culture. Therefore, although cultural awareness and sensitivity are a nice idea, in reality every counseling situation is a counseling situation with a unique individual.
Response:

2. Generally speaking, multicultural theory places the responsibility for psychopathology and human suffering on the culture rather than on the individual. Even within the context of therapy, most multicultural approaches emphasize how the therapist must become culturally sensitive to a wide range of different ways of thinking, being, and living. Doesn't this emphasis seem out of proportion sometimes? In the end, isn't the client responsible for his or her problems? Isn't it the client's responsibility to communicate his or her situation to the counselor rather than the counselor's responsibility to speak the language of all cultures?
Response:

3. Cultural relativism aside, there are some basic truths. If a client comes for therapy and reports symptoms of anxiety or depression, an empirically validated treatment should be provided regardless of the client's culture. It may be helpful to explain the therapy to the client, but the fact remains that all clients should receive the most promising treatments available. When it comes to effective therapy, science is blind to racial and ethnic differences.
Response:

4. Respecting your client's cultural perspective is one thing, but what if that perspective is destructive, oppressive, or simply wrong? If an Afghan couple comes to see you and the husband insists that the woman needs to keep her head covered and that their female children should receive no formal education, do you just accept these cultural differences? Is it acceptable for parents to beat their children or for women's genitalia to be mutilated all in the name of cultural diversity?
Response:

5. Working with spiritual and soulful issues in therapy is not only impossible, it's generally ill advised. After all, the most tragic and horrendous acts in the history of the world were usually fueled by one of two factors: religion or money. How can scientifically oriented therapists who are dedicated to the well-being of humans focus on intangible and potentially misleading and destructive intangible concepts such as soul and spirit? To do so is inherently unethical.
Response:

Key Terms

- Fourth force
- Drapetomania
- Dysaethesia
- Ego-dystonic homo-sexuality
- Culture
- Multiculturalism
- Transcultural
- Multicultural counseling

- Stereotype
- Individualistic
- Collectivist
- Acculturation or ethno-cultural orientation
- Monoculturalism
- Scientific mindedness
- Dynamic sizing
- Culture-specific expertise

- Ethnic match
- Ethnic-specific services
- Cognitive match
- Buddhism
- Four Noble Truths
- Eightfold path
- Mindfulness

Review Questions

1. Why is multicultural theory referred to as the fourth force in counseling and psychotherapy?
2. Discuss how the lack of consideration of divergent cultural perspectives might result in therapists' assigning damaging diagnoses and labels to clients.

3. What does Christopher (1996) mean when he says that the culture precedes the individual? Are there any traditional theories of counseling and psychotherapy that include similar concepts?

4. Identify several ways a client with a collectivist orientation might affect you. Then identify how a client with a strong individualistic orientation might affect you.

5. Summarize the three main multicultural competencies.

6. Identify and describe several principles of multicultural competence in assessment.

7. What is the status of multicultural outcomes research? Which ethnic group has the most evidence of responding positively to counseling and psychotherapy?

8. Explain how there could be no such thing as non-Western counseling theory and therapy.

9. In the treatment of which mental disorders or client problems has mindfulness meditation shown promise?

10. What is the status of spiritual psychotherapy outcomes research?

RECOMMENDED READINGS AND RESOURCES

The following resources may help you explore multicultural theory and therapy in greater depth.

Lead Journals

- *Cultural Diversity and Ethnic Minority Psychology*
- *Journal of Cross Cultural Psychology*
- *Journal of Multicultural Counseling*

Books and Articles

Adler, L. L., & Mukherji, B. R. (1995). *Spirit versus scalpel: Traditional healing and modern psychotherapy.* Westport, CT: Bergin & Garvey.

Axelson, J. A. (1999). *Counseling and development in a multicultural society* (3rd ed.). Belmont, CA: Wadsworth.

Barnett-Friel, P. (Ed.). (2000). *Aspects of personal faith: Personality and religion in Western and Eastern traditions.* Lanham, MD: International Scholars.

Gopaul-McNicol, S., & Thomas-Presswood, T. (1998). *Working with linguistically and culturally different children: Innovative clinical and educational approaches.* Boston: Allyn & Bacon.

Ivey, A. E., D'Andrea, M., Ivey, M. B., & Simek-Morgan, L. (2002). *Theories of counseling and psychotherapy: A multicultural perspective* (5th ed.). Boston: Allyn & Bacon.

Kabat-Zinn, J. (1994). *Wherever you go there you are.* New York: Hyperion.

Karasu, T. B. (1999). Spiritual psychotherapy. *American Journal of Psychotherapy, 53,* 143–162.

Paniagua, F. (2001). *Diagnosis in a multicultural context: A casebook for mental health professionals.* London: Sage.

Pedersen, P. (2000). *A handbook for developing multicultural awareness.* Alexandria, VA: American Counseling Association.

Pedersen, P., & Ivey, A. E. (1993). *Culture-centered counseling and interviewing skills: A practical guide.* Westport, CN: Praeger.

Richards, P. S., & Bergin, A. E. (2000). *Handbook of psychotherapy and religious diversity.* Washington, DC: American Psychological Association.

Sommers-Flanagan, J., & Sommers-Flanagan, R. (2003). *Clinical interviewing.* New York: Wiley.

Sparks, E. E., & Park, A. H. (Eds.). (2002). *The integration of feminism and multiculturalism: Ethical dilemmas at the border.* Washington, DC: American Psychological Association.

Sue, D. W., Bingham, R., Porche-Burke, L., & Vasquez, M. J. T. (1999). The diversification of psychology: A multicultural revolution. *American Psychologist, 54,* 1061–1069.

Sue, D. W., & Sue, D. (2003). *Counseling the cuturally diverse: Theory and practice* (3rd ed.). New York: Wiley.

Sue, S. (1999). Science, ethnicity, and bias: Where have we gone wrong? *American Psychologist, 54,* 1070–1077.

Swartz-Kulstad, J. L., & Martin, W. E. J. (1999). Impact of culture and context on psychosocial adaptation: The cultural and contextual guide process. *Journal of Counseling and Development, 77,* 281–293.

Tjeltveit, A. D. (1999). *Ethics and values in psychotherapy.* New York: Routledge

Vontress, C. E., Johnson, J. A., & Epp, L. R. (1999). *Cross-cultural counseling: A casebook.* Alexandria, VA: American Counseling Association.

Videotapes

Comas-Diaz, L. (1994). *Ethnocultural psychotherapy* [Videotape]. Washington, DC: American Psychological Association.

Training Organizations and Web Sites

Association for Multicultural Counseling and Development, (web site: www.amcd-aca.org)

Chapter 13

INTEGRATIVE THEORIES OF COUNSELING AND PSYCHOTHERAPY

[M]any clinicians have realized that one true path to formulating and treating human problems does not exist—no single orientation has all the answers.

—A. A. Lazarus, L. E. Beutler, and J. C. Norcross,
"The Future of Technical Eclecticism" (1992, p. 11)

We are drowning in information, while starving for wisdom. The world henceforth will be run by synthesizers, people able to put together the right information at the right time, think critically about it, and make important choices wisely.

—E. O. Wilson, *Conscilience* (1999, p. 269)

IN THIS CHAPTER YOU WILL LEARN

- Reasons why there are so many approaches to conducting counseling and psychotherapy
- Benefits and drawbacks of theoretical loyalties and conflicts
- Foundational aspects of integration and eclecticism
- Historical and contemporary trends in psychotherapy integration
- Four main options for theoretical choice and application
- Definitions of ideological purism, theoretical integration, common factors, and technical eclecticism as they relate to the following:
  - Multimodal therapy
  - Eye movement desensitization and reprocessing
  - Dialectical behavioral therapy
  - Interpersonal psychotherapy
  - Process-experiential therapy
  - Acceptance and commitment therapy
  - Cognitive-constructivist model
  - Transtheoretical change model

If you've made it through the first 12 chapters of this book, then you know firsthand that the history and practice of counseling and psychotherapy encompass a wide range of diverse ideas. In that sense, the history and practice of counseling and psychotherapy reflect significant diversity in thought and action.

But why this diversity? How did all those incredibly insightful and able minds come up with so many different ways of practicing therapy? If people are, as Harry Stack Sullivan (1953) contended over 50 years ago, simply more human than anything else, why then is there not greater uniformity of thought when it comes to practicing psychotherapy? Aren't there some basic truths and consistencies in how humans suffer and how they can move toward recovery, or at least in how humans develop and how they can become more actualized and fulfilled?

These questions lead us toward both contradiction and integration. It is likely that all therapy approaches could benefit from a deeper understanding of the primary inconsistencies within our profession.

Arkowitz (1997) identified two major contradictions in psychotherapy and counseling:

> On the one hand, a large number of psychotherapists have a strong commitment to a particular psychotherapy approach. On the other hand, there is little evidence that any of the . . . psychotherapy approaches . . . is more effective than another. . . . On the one hand, societies, institutes, centers, and journals devoted to particular therapy approaches dominate the field of psychotherapy. On the other hand, the majority of practicing therapists do not identify themselves as adhering to one particular approach, but instead refer to themselves as "eclectic" or "integrative." (p. 227)

The purpose of this chapter is to explore contradictions and integrations central to the theory and practice of counseling and psychotherapy.

FOUNDATIONS OF THEORETICAL DIVERSITY AND INTEGRATION

We believe that there are at least three main sources of theoretical and practical diversity in psychotherapy: individuality, cultural specificity, and human conflict.

Individuality

Perhaps Adler captured this concept best when he used the term *Individual Psychology* to label his particular brand of psychological theory and therapy. Adler emphasized that every child born into the same family is at the same time born into a different family.

This is a fundamental aspect of the psychology of individual differences. Every perspective is unique. Like snowflakes, no two individuals are alike; even identical twins experience the world differently. As a consequence, how could we possibly expect uniformity of theoretical thought and practice in counseling and psychotherapy? Although many theorists, like Sullivan (1953) and Glasser (1998), emphasize the universality of all humanity, there is no way to completely reconcile universality with individuality. Integrational and eclectic approaches to therapy may allow greater latitude in addressing each client as a unique individual being.

Cultural Specificity

As contemporary feminists and multiculturalists emphasize, some individuals and groups are systematically treated differently—often discriminated against—throughout the world. Sex, race, ethnicity, social class, sexual orientation, religion, and many other factors distinguish individuals from one another. Each of these factors might determine not only whether someone seeks therapy but also whether they even have access to therapy.

The choice to seek mental health counseling of any type carries vastly different meanings depending on cultural values and practices. Imagine the ways you might explain the potential benefits of psychotherapy to a Wyoming cattle rancher. Then imagine doing the same for Laotian refugees or American Indians. The values imbedded within cultures influence whether contemporary therapy is viewed as a valuable service, witchcraft, hocus-pocus, a waste of time, a growth opportunity, or a choice only the desperate would make. Certainly, integrational and eclectic therapy approaches must address cultural backgrounds values, and needs.

Human Conflict

Thus far in this book, we have reviewed 11 relatively distinct theoretical approaches to counseling and psychotherapy. Adherents to the various theoretical perspectives frequently debate and criticize one another. There are often strong feelings of loyalty to one's perspectives and equally strong doubt about others. Such conflicting views arise out of abiding personal and professional attachments to particular theoretical ideas and therapeutic techniques.

Our friends in the field of conflict mediation and resolution are quick to point out that conflict should not be avoided because it can potentially lead to positive transformations. Certainly, when it comes to the history, evolution, and diversity of our field, human conflict has probably been a good thing for counseling and psychotherapy. Consider the following:

- In 1896 Freud was ostracized by his colleagues for suggesting that sexual abuse was at the roots of hysteria. Freud later recanted his seduction hypothesis, but in the process he invented a remarkable theory of human personality and psychotherapy.
- In 1911 Adler had the audacity to suggest that women's so-called psychopathology was at least partially generated and maintained by social factors—including systematic discrimination. For that tremendous insight, Sigmund Freud and his psychoanalytic cronies essentially sent Adler packing from the Vienna Psychoanalytic Society. Fortunately for everyone, Adler never recanted his view.
- In 1913 Jung and Freud finalized their theoretical divorce. Despite conflicts (and perhaps because of them), Jung individuated from Freud and was highly motivated to continue developing his unique approach to understanding the human psyche. Just think about the richness of theory we would have lost had Jung suppressed his unique thoughts about symbol, archetype, and the collective unconscious.
- In the late 1920s Adler dismissed Frankl from his study group. One would have hoped that Adler, so empathic toward the oppressed and working-class citizens, would not have stooped so low as to place alternative viewpoints on an extinction

schedule, but history and humans often disappoint. Frankl emerged like a phoenix after World War II championing *meaning* as central in psychotherapy and human development.

- In the 1920s and 1930s Karen Horney wrote forcefully about the neglected feminine perspective in psychoanalysis. Instead of submitting to proper authority, she voiced her views and entered into conflict with her colleagues.

- When, in 1936, he was rebuffed by Freud, Fritz Perls did not slip away into obscurity. Instead, he emerged with the attitude, "I'll show you—you can't do this to me" and became remarkably influential and productive (F. Perls, 1969b, p. 57).

- In the 1950s and 1960s there were the great discussions and debates between Carl Rogers and B. F. Skinner. These powerful clashes of divergent views stimulated many ensuing debates and publications.

- In the late 1960s and continuing into the present, feminist therapists have reshaped theories and techniques that would have otherwise continued to reinforce a male-as-normative status quo in psychotherapy.

- In the 1970s some staunch behaviorists, including Joseph Wolpe, threatened to exile cognitivists such as Beck, Goldfried, Meichenbaum, and Mahoney from the ranks of behaviorism. Instead, part of the outcome was the birth of a new journal, *Cognitive Therapy and Research.*

- In the 1990s Francine Shapiro's approach to treating traumatized clients, Eye Movement Desensitization Reprocessing (EMDR), received sharp criticism from many quarters (Blake, Abueg, Woodward, & Keane, 1993; Lohr, Kleinknecht, Tolin, & Barrett, 1995). Fortunately, instead of shying away from empirical scrutiny, Shapiro has continued to work toward evaluating and validating her treatment approach.

- Over the course of 20-plus years, Michael Mahoney and others have developed from avid behaviorists to leading constructivist thinkers.

There have been many other examples of productive conflict within the counseling and psychotherapy field. This conflict has undoubtedly contributed to the depth and breadth of theories and approaches available today. We take solace in the fact that the creative behaviors of Adler, Jung, Frankl, Horney, Perls, Mahoney, Meichenbaum, Shapiro, and many others did not extinguish; they did not go quietly into the night or lose their voices. Instead, the history of psychotherapeutic theory is peppered with examples of how rejection is often a form of positive reinforcement and a great source of

---

Questions for Reflection

Because diversity of perspective and culture is always present, is conflict inevitable? Would we have attained the theoretical diversity and sophistication we now have in counseling and psychotherapy without intense arguments, debates, division, and conflict? What if Freud had welcomed Adler's ideas into the psychoanalytic theoretical fold? Would that have reduced Adler's motivation to express himself? In a general sense, is it better to begin with one big inclusive theory and explain all apparent contradictions through the lens of the theory, or is it better to begin with a narrow theory, with an open attitude toward adding new dimensions? Assimilate, accommodate, or start over? Which is better?

motivation. We hope the outcomes of these conflicts will cause you to think positively of the many arguments about the best way to approach therapy that you have had—and will have—with your classmates and professors and eventual colleagues.

HISTORICAL AND THEORETICAL TRENDS IN COUNSELING AND PSYCHOTHERAPY INTEGRATION

Overall, there are four major options open to ethical, theory-based counseling and psychotherapy:

1. Ideological purity
2. Theoretical integration
3. Focus on common factors
4. Technical eclecticism

Faced with ambiguity and contradiction, humans tend to seek clarity, consistency, and security. How do you respond to Arkowitz's (1997) contradictions introduced at the beginning of this chapter? Even more specifically, how do you answer the following question: With so many different theories and therapies to choose from, how will you choose which approach to use with your clients? This is a question that only an existentialist could love.

It's no wonder that when dealing with this huge range of theoretical and therapeutic alternatives, theorists, therapists, and researchers have quite naturally scattered into different groups, seeking the security of an adequate, overarching explanation to hang on to. Perhaps what we all long for is a set of principles that will tell us exactly how to be most effective for most of the clients most of the time. In response to a large array of choices and client needs, combined with inadequate empirical guidance, most therapists have tended to take one of the four paths listed previously.

Ideological Purity

Historically, most therapists were ideological purists. There is a great advantage in studying and learning one theoretical approach to therapy and applying it ethically and competently (see Ethical Highlight 13.1). Ideological purity emphasizes depth over breadth. It is very appealing in a practical sense; it allows you to become a master of one approach, rather than a mediocre jack-of-all-trades. Focusing on one main approach can ease the ambiguity inherent in practicing therapy.

On the negative side, when taken to an extreme, ideological purity can turn into ideological dogmatism. As Freud's behaviors so aptly illustrated, one can have a remarkably, and ultimately damaging, lack of openness toward alternative explanations of human nature and human healing. The underlying message of the ideological dogmatist is this: I have found my theoretical orientation, and I see and explain the world through it. I live by its tenets and treat it as sacred and unalterably true.

Even in today's diverse world, many professionals continue to be ideological purists—they practice one form of therapy, and they practice it well. Judith Beck's description of why she is a cognitive therapist (see Chapter 8) is an excellent example of ideological purity (but not dogmatism).

Theoretical Integration

Theoretical integration involves the combining of two or more theoretical approaches to maximize therapeutic effectiveness. This perspective is generally based on the idea that two heads are better than one. Historically, most theoretical integrations have involved the integration of psychoanalytic practice and learning theory (or behavior therapy).

In 1950 Dollard and Miller published *Personality and Psychotherapy: An Analysis in Terms of Learning, Thinking, and Culture.* This book was an early and impressive effort at integrating psychoanalytic and behavioral principles. Dollard and Miller were far ahead of their time; their work actually preceded the development of specific, applied behavior therapy techniques.

During the ensuing 20 to 25 years, only a few select theorists discussed potential theoretical integration (Alexander, 1963; London, 1964). The next major effort at integration was Wachtel's (1977) publication of *Psychoanalysis and Behavior Therapy: Toward an Integration.*

Overall, Wachtel's intent was to develop an open and evolving theoretical framework. His goal was not designed to be a specific hybrid theory. He wanted to develop a system that might change as learning theory and psychoanalytic theory continued to change and develop.

Contemporary approaches to theoretical integration differ from Dollard and Miller's and Wachtel's earlier efforts in that the focus is not exclusively on integrating behavioral and psychoanalytic theory and therapy. Instead, as described later, theorist-therapist-researchers such as Marsha Linehan and Leslie Greenberg have integrated two or more nonpsychoanalytic approaches in an effort to facilitate treatment process and outcome (L. S. Greenberg et al., 1993; Linehan, 1993). See Practitioner Commentary 13.1 for a contemporary view on integrationism versus eclecticism.

Common Factors

In Chapter 1 we discussed the common factors approach to counseling and psychotherapy. This approach springs from the search for central methods and principles of human change that exist across many diverse theoretical perspectives and therapeutic practices.

Early writings on common factors began to appear in the literature in the 1930s (Rosenzweig, 1936). Somewhat later, Alexander and French (1946) articulated the concept of *corrective emotional experience.* Their definition of corrective emotional experience is stated in a way that is potentially inclusive of alternative theoretical perspectives:

> In all forms of . . . psychotherapy, the basic therapeutic principle is the same: To re-expose the patient, under more favorable circumstances, to emotional situations which he could

---

Questions for Reflection

Can you recast Alexander and French's definition of corrective emotional experience in other theoretical language? For example, could you describe Mary Cover Jones's work with Little Peter and other fearful children as corrective emotional experiences? How about Fritz Perls's concept of unfinished business in Gestalt therapy? What other diverse theories of therapy might be compatible with the concept of corrective emotional experience?

PRACTITIONER COMMENTARY 13.1

Integrational, Not Eclectic

The following commentary was provided by David Scherer, associate professor of counseling at the University of New Mexico.

As an undergraduate, 30 years ago, I was inundated with behaviorism. In my first jobs, prior to going to graduate school, I was immersed in psychoanalytic ideas. In graduate school, I was introduced to socioecological models, in general, and ultimately endorsed systems theory and structural family therapy, in particular, as my theory and therapy of choice.

I abide by my theoretical beliefs, but I'm not particularly chauvinistic about them. One of the virtues of the diversity of theories I have been exposed to is the respect I have for others' theoretical perspectives. While I suspect I will always use and profess socioecological and systems tenets as the foundation for my academic and therapeutic work, I do work at developing an "integrative" theoretical orientation. For example, my assessment of an individual's or family's issues may be systemic, although my intervention may include a fair amount of cognitive-behavioral techniques. However, I am deeply skeptical of "eclecticism," which in my view often blends philosophically incompatible ideas resulting in confused and ill-conceived therapeutic technique.

I prefer to ground my work on empiricism, and I strongly encourage the young counselors and psychotherapists that I teach and supervise to devote themselves to understanding the science of human nature. My therapeutic conceptualizations and interventions are always informed by my knowledge of development, physiology, cognition, and social processes. I frequently use theory and research about temperament, attachment, cognitive development, socioemotional development, the physiological bases of behavior, attribution theory, and group and family interaction in the work that I do with my clients and the explanations I give them.

---

not handle in the past. The patient, in order to be helped, must undergo a corrective emotional experience suitable to repair the traumatic influence of previous experiences. (Alexander & French, 1946, p. 66)

Over the years many other therapists have conceptualized and articulated specific therapeutic principles that are now accepted as common factors. Central among these common therapeutic principles is Rogers's *certain type of relationship* as discussed in Chapter 6. Currently, many theorists integrate Rogers's concepts of unconditional positive regard, congruence, and accurate empathy into their therapeutic approaches, although some do it more formally and systematically than others (L. S. Greenberg, 2002a; Linehan, 1993; Schofield, 1964).

Jerome Frank (1961, 1973; Frank & Frank, 1991) developed a comprehensive common factors model of psychotherapy. He states:

All psychotherapeutic methods are elaborations and variations of age-old procedures of psychological healing. These include confession, atonement and absolutions, encouragement, positive and negative reinforcements, modeling, and promulgation of a particular set of values. These methods become embedded in theories as to the causes and cures of various conditions which often become highly elaborated. (Frank, 1985, pp. 49–50)

Frank's common factors model was developed from his study of a variety of historical and intercultural sources (Frank, 1961). It includes several components that continue to be relevant to practicing therapists.

The Demoralization Hypothesis

Frank emphasizes in his writings that not only are there common factors or components of effective therapy, but people who come for therapy are also experiencing a common form of distress. He refers to this common distress as the demoralization hypothesis:

> Demoralization occurs when, because of lack of certain skills or confusion of goals, an individual becomes persistently unable to master situations which both the individual and others expect him or her to handle or when the individual experiences continued distress which he or she cannot adequately explain or alleviate. Demoralization may be summed up as a feeling of subjective incompetence, coupled with distress. (Frank, 1985, p. 56)

There is evidence supporting the existence of demoralization among many therapy clients (Dohrenwend, Shrout, & Egri, 1980; Frank, 1974). Frank identifies a range of demoralization symptoms, such as low self-esteem, anxiety, sadness, and hopelessness. These are often the initial target of effective therapy.

Shared Therapeutic Components

Frank has defined the following shared components of effective therapy.

- *An emotionally charged, confiding relationship with a helping person.* This therapeutic component has been articulated by many theorists and is clearly supported by empirical research (Lambert, 1992; Norcross, 2002; C. R. Rogers, 1957).
- *A healing setting.* Frank emphasizes that a healing setting includes two functional parts. First, the setting elevates the therapist's prestige as a healer or helper. Second, the setting provides a sense of safety.
- *A rationale, conceptual scheme, or myth.* Clients need a plausible explanation for their symptoms and for the treatment approach to be used.
- *A ritual.* Clients (and therapists) need to participate in a process or ritual that they both believe will bring about a cure or improved functioning.

Frank uses the terms *myth* and *ritual* intentionally to convey universal aspects of all psychotherapeutic approaches across cultures. The content of specific myths and rituals do not necessarily have any inherent healing properties. Instead, myths and rituals function specifically to combat demoralization:

Questions for Reflection

Turn back to Chapter 1 and review Lambert's common psychotherapeutic factors based on his analysis of empirical outcomes research. Do you think that Lambert's empirical analysis is a contemporary confirmation of Frank's common factors theory? How do Lambert's common factors of (1) extratherapeutic change, (2) therapeutic relationship, (3) expectancy, and (4) techniques match up with Frank's formulations?

====== ETHICAL HIGHLIGHT 13.1 ======

Eclecticism Requires Expertise in Multiple Domains

A colleague of ours who worked for years as a rehabilitation counselor told us that in her first rehab job interview, she was asked if she had a single theoretical orientation or if she was eclectic. Clearly, the expected answer was eclectic. In fact, she later discovered that her new boss believed that adherence to a single theory was a sign of intellectual weakness and applied laziness. He insisted that his counselors display person-centered attributes, be comfortable with cognitive-behavioral strategies, be aware of and sensitive to feminist and multicultural theory, and be well versed in the application of many career and human development theories and assessment strategies. He also insisted on a well-articulated rationale for the treatment plan and encouraged counselors to pay attention to what worked and why. Obviously, this wasn't an office for the theoretically faint of heart. In this setting, eclectic meant "know quite a bit about quite a lot and pay attention to what works."

All therapeutic myths and rituals, irrespective of differences in specific content, have in common functions that combat demoralization by strengthening the therapeutic relationship, inspiring expectations of help, providing new learning experiences, arousing the patient emotionally, enhancing the sense of mastery or self-efficacy, and affording opportunities for rehearsal and practice. (Frank, 1985, p. 61)

Technical Eclecticism

In direct opposition to ideological purism, some professionals, like the boss described in Ethical Highlight 13.1, avoid singular theoretical commitments. These therapists readily choose one technique or another for individual clients without much concern for theoretical compatibility among the techniques they might choose. Their selection of a particular therapy technique is usually based on one of three factors: (1) relevant empirical outcomes research, (2) the pragmatics of the situation, or (3) clinical intuition. In common parlance, this has been referred to as an eclectic orientation. In a more disparaging description, one of our own supervisors referred to it as "flying by the seat of your pants" (Bornstein, personal communication, October 1987).

Eclecticism has been both lauded and criticized over the years. In several recent studies of therapists' theoretical orientations, for every category of mental health therapist (clinical and counseling psychologists, counselors, social workers, and psychiatrists), identification with an eclectic or integrative orientation was found to be most common (Bechtoldt, Norcross, Wyckoff, Pokrywa, & Campbell, 2001; Norcross, Karg, & Prochaska, 1997; Norcross, Strausser, & Missar, 1988).

This finding is somewhat surprising to those trained during a time when singular choice of theoretical orientations was common. In the past, being eclectic was often considered bad form. For example, in 1970 Esyenck referred to eclecticism as a "mishmash of theories, a hugger-mugger of procedures, a gallimaufry of therapies" with no systematic rationale for treatment application (p. 145). Of course, it is especially ironic that this derogatory view of eclectic therapists was put forth by Eysenck because in his famous 1952 review of psychotherapy efficacy he identified 7,293 cases treated by eclectic means with a 64% "cure" or recovery rate. Perhaps what's most interesting in Eysenck's original review is that eclectic psychotherapy treatment was evaluated nearly 10 times as often as were other approaches. This suggests that this "hugger-mugger of procedures" may have been remarkably common long before it was overtly fashionable.

More recently, there has been a distinction made between "bad" (seat-of-the-pants) eclecticism and "good" (empirical and/or planful) eclecticism. Similar to Eysenck's criticisms, Lazarus et al. (1992) commented on therapy approaches blended together in "an arbitrary, subjective, if not capricious manner" (p. 11). When one chooses what to do with a client in a whimsical, unreasoned, or even impulsive manner, one is engaging in *syncretism* (Lazarus et al., 1992, p. 12). As one of our colleagues says, "Sometimes counselors mix up the words eclectic and electric—they think they can just do whatever turns them on" (Richardson, personal communication, November 2002). In contrast, eclecticism is positively defined as "[s]electing what appears to be best in various doctrines, methods, or styles" (Lazarus et al., 1992, p. 11).

As described in Chapter 7, in many ways, behavioral theory and therapy are the most flexible of all theoretical orientations. Essentially, behaviorists contend that they practice a form of therapy based on scientific research and observable processes. Their interest is not in a static theory but in what has been tested in the laboratory and in what has been demonstrated as effective. In that sense, behaviorists are, to some extent, naturally eclectic. Consequently, it is not surprising that the first movements toward technical eclecticism came from the behavioral camp.

In 1969 Gordon Paul posed the following question to his behavioral colleagues: "What treatment, by whom, is most effective for this individual with that specific problem, under which set of circumstances, and how does it come about?" (p. 44). This question, sometimes referred to as the *who-how-whom question,* provides a strong rationale for technical eclecticism. It is consistent with the overall goal of matching specific therapy approaches with specific clients (and specific client problems)—a goal that is openly endorsed by eclectic therapists. This approach is also consistent in principle with the medical model and the proliferation of psychiatric diagnosis and empirically validated treatments. In essence, a primary purpose of the diagnostic system of the *Diagnostic and Statistical Manual of Mental Disorders* (*DSM*) is to identify specific disease entities that are best ameliorated through the application of specific (often pharmacological) treatments.

Eclectic approaches to therapy have been popular since at least 1970. Despite Eysenck's admonitions, in 1970 approximately 50% of clinical psychologists identified themselves as eclectic (Garfield & Kurtz, 1975). About 5 years later, 64% of clinical psychologists claimed to be eclectic (Garfield & Kurtz, 1977). More recent surveys conducted with a broader range of mental health professionals indicate that between 30% and 70% of all professionals label themselves as eclectic (Bechtoldt et al., 2001; Norcross et al., 1997).

THE PRACTICE OF SPECIFIC ECLECTIC OR INTEGRATIVE THERAPIES

This section provides a brief sampling of some of the main eclectic or integrative forms of therapy. We chose these because they have been developed, named, and promoted in terms of problems areas, assessment strategies, or appropriate range of techniques. Typically, these approaches incorporate therapy principles derived from a variety of counseling and psychotherapy systems. The treatment approaches we include in this section have both integrational and empirical roots.

The terms *technical eclecticism, therapy integration,* and *common factors* are useful, but they do not provide perfectly distinct categories for the following therapy approaches. In this section we occasionally refer to these categories because they represent the current state of the science. As we review these applications, you may find yourself questioning how (and even if) the approaches fit into one category or another. If so, you're not alone; we frequently second-guessed ourselves in the process of deciding which terminology to use for the approaches we describe next.

A current trend in psychotherapy is the formulation of therapeutic approaches designed for treating specific disorders, or even the direct pairing of specific techniques with specific symptoms. Due to the time and financial pressures present in mental health provision today, treatment manuals have been developed that delineate recommended techniques for common client symptoms. Many of the treatments described next are partially a product of the manualization movement in counseling and psychotherapy.

Preparing Yourself to Do Therapy from an Eclectic or Integrational Perspective

In contrast to historical syncretism and the hugger-mugger approach to eclecticism, learning contemporary eclectic and integrative models of therapy can be quite demanding. Many of the therapy approaches derived from empirical research require close adherence to manualized treatment procedures. As Beutler (2000) aptly noted, learning "contemporary lists of empirically supported treatments [is] . . . ill-advised as well as unreasonable and infeasible."

The practical problem is how one therapist can learn the many distinctive approaches to therapy described in the manualized, empirical literature. Beutler notes that there are nearly 70 empirically recognized treatments, and it is impossible to be skilled in so many different approaches. Our advice for this dilemma is to learn the basics about the different approaches and then focus on learning just a few procedures very well.

Preparing Your Client for Eclectic or Integrative Therapy

As we've stressed throughout the book, informed consent is important even if you aren't giving your clients a thumbnail sketch of a particular theory. Informed consent statements for eclectic mental health professionals might be the most challenging of all. Here's a list of the issues related to theory that might be important to consider.

1. Avoid the word *eclectic* or define it simply.
2. Indicate your reasons for not adhering to a certain theory or set of techniques.
3. Explain how you will choose the kinds of techniques you will use.
4. Discuss your overall theory of human change and why you think your services might be of help.
5. Mention the theoretical origins of any techniques you might commonly use.
6. Indicate a willingness to discuss the reasons for choices you might make during the course of the client's work with you.

Remember, informed consent is a process. The eclectic or integrational mental health professional is responsible for continually ensuring that clients are aware of and consent to the use of various techniques. Clients have a right to know your rationale, your expectations, and a reasonable sense of possible outcomes.

Multimodal Therapy: The Technical Eclecticism of Arnold Lazarus

Lazarus has been a prolific and controversial clinician and writer for just over 50 years. He coined the term *technical eclecticism* in 1967, noting the following:

> To attempt a theoretical rapprochement is as futile as trying to picture the edge of the universe. But to read through the vast amount of literature on psychotherapy, *in search of techniques,* can be clinically enriching and therapeutically rewarding. (Lazarus, 1967, p. 416)

Currently, his position on theoretical integration remains essentially the same. He is not the least bit interested in blending theories; as a self-identified behaviorist, he is interested only in the practical application of approaches that are helpful to the client.

It is not surprising that Lazarus also has an opinion about why technical eclecticism is preferable to theoretical purity. In 1971, he claimed that

> the most essential ingredients for an effective psychotherapist are *flexibility* and *versatility.* This implies an ability to play many roles and to use many techniques in order to fit the therapy to the needs and idiosyncrasies of each patient. By contrast, therapists with pet theories or specially favored techniques usually manage, in their own minds at least, to fit their patients' problems within the confines of their particular brand of treatment. (p. 33)

Lazarus's therapy approach is indeed characterized by flexibility and diversity. It is widely known as Multimodal Therapy (Lazarus, 1973b, 1989, 1997).

Multimodal therapists apply specific techniques and adopt specific interpersonal styles in an effort to help clients obtain their goals. There are primary foci of multimodal therapy: assessment, technical applications, and therapist interpersonal style.

Assessment

Lazarus describes the underlying assumption for his therapeutic and assessment system:

> The multimodal orientation (Lazarus, 1997) is predicated on the assumption that most psychological problems are multifaceted, multidetermined, and multilayered, and that comprehensive therapy calls for a careful assessment of seven parameters or "modalities." (Lazarus, 2000, p. 93)

The seven modalities are behavior, affect, sensation, imagery, cognition, interpersonal relationships, and drugs (including all biological processes). The modalities are listed and described in Table 13.1. At the end of each description there is a specific question suggested by Lazarus to guide the clinician's thinking about the category (Lazarus, 2000). To facilitate recall, Lazarus uses the acronym BASIC I.D. to represent the seven parameters of human functioning.

For multimodal therapists, assessment and diagnosis involve a thorough evaluation of the BASIC I.D. Subsequently, treatment focuses on alleviating the problematic patterns occurring within these seven areas of functioning.

Table 13.1   The BASIC I.D.

Area of Functioning	Description
Behavior	This category includes observable and measurable behaviors. Therapists gather information about (a) frequent actions, (b) habits, and (c) frequent behavioral reactions. Examples: smoking, regular aerobic exercise (or lack thereof), hair pulling, nail biting, yelling. Question: What behaviors does he or she want to increase or decrease?
Affective responses	This category includes emotions and moods. Therapists gather information about emotions that the client finds either problematic or helpful. Examples: anger, sadness, anxiety, guilt. This is the only category that is addressed indirectly—because like William Glasser (1998), Lazarus believes that emotions cannot be elicited or changed directly. Question: What affective reactions are proving disturbing?
Sensations	This category includes the five senses: taste, touch, smell, vision, and hearing. The therapist is especially interested in the client's pleasant or unpleasant sensations. Examples: pain, dizziness, palpitations, depersonalization. Question: What are the client's precise sensory pains and pleasures?
Imagery	This category includes mental pictures or visualization. Therapists ask clients about the images they see and experience during times of stress or distress and during functional or dysfunctional moments. Examples: helpful or success images that occur before and during a stressful event and unhelpful, disturbing, or failure images. Question: What intrusive images need to be replaced by positive visualizations?
Cognition	This category includes the nonvisual or semantic influences or symptoms. Therapists gather information about what clients think to themselves or say to themselves when functioning well and when functioning poorly. Examples: personal values, rational and irrational thoughts, cognitive distortions, maladaptive automatic thoughts. Question: What dysfunctional beliefs and faulty cognitions are in need of restructuring?
Interpersonal relationships	This category includes all human interactions. Therapists gather information about the nature, quality, and quantity of satisfying and dissatisfying interpersonal relationships. Examples: friendships, romantic relationships, primary family relationships, family of origin relationships, and work relationships. Question: Who are the client's significant others and what essential processes are at play vis-à-vis his or her interpersonal network?
Drugs and biology	This category includes all physical or biological areas, including substance use. Therapists gather information about the client's eating, sleeping, and exercise or activity levels as well as medications and licit and illicit drug use. Examples: physical exam information, specific amount of alcohol and drug use. Question: What are the important facts about the client's drug use (recreational or prescribed) and his or her general medical-biological well-being?

Source. Questions are from Lazarus (2000, pp. 93–94).

Technical Applications

Multimodal therapists consider using any therapy technique that seems appropriate based on empirical research or a logical or practical rationale. Sometimes multimodal therapists also use their intuition when determining what therapy approach to use (Lazarus, 1971, 1997).

To conduct multimodal therapy requires skill in a wide variety of therapeutic interventions. For example, in the glossary of his 1989 book, Lazarus lists 39 principal techniques. Learning these techniques, which range from focusing to behavior rehearsal, is a challenge inherent in being a multimodal therapist.

Therapist Style

Multimodal therapy emphasizes individual differences. Because every client is different, it is essential for therapists to change their style based on each new client. Lazarus (1971) states that "a flexible therapist has no fixed pattern of approaching new patients. He usually perceives what his patient needs and then tries to fit the role" (p. 50). For example, Lazarus criticizes person-centered therapists for not shifting their interpersonal styles based on different client traits: "These person-centered counselors do not ask if individual differences may warrant a confrontational style for some, or point to an austere business-like atmosphere for others . . . or when a sphinx-like guru might be made to order" (Lazarus, 1993, pp. 404–405).

Lazarus refers to shifting one's therapeutic style as becoming an *authentic chameleon.* Some of the interpersonal variables therapists should consider varying depending on clients' needs, preferences, or expectations include

- Level of formality or informality
- Amount of personal disclosure
- How much or how often a new topic of conversation is initiated
- Level of directiveness
- Level of supportiveness
- Level of reflectiveness (Lazarus, 1993)

Questions for Reflection

What other interpersonal style variables might you vary depending on the client you're seeing? Assuming that client response varies with different therapist styles, how will you decide how to approach a given client? Can you assume that most elderly clients will respond better to respectful communication and that most teens will respond better to humor and irreverence? What other factors, besides age, might you want to consider when trying to decide what sort of interpersonal style to use when approaching a new client?

One method for determining what interpersonal style to adopt with new clients is to obtain specific assessment data prior to the initial meeting. Lazarus recommends using the Multimodal Life History Inventory, which includes questions pertaining to clients' expectations for therapy (Lazarus & Lazarus, 1991). For example, if a client writes, "I hope therapy is like a mirror so I can start understanding myself better," a more person-centered approach may be desirable.

Determining the best therapeutic style is often a judgment call the therapist has to make on the spot. Lazarus (1993) shares a story in which he sensed that a particular client (a 39-year-old woman) would respond well to humor and sarcasm:

> When she first entered my office, she looked me up and down and asked, "Why do you have graves outside your office?" In perfect Rogerian style I said, "I have graves outside my office?" "Look out the window dummy!" she replied. I went to my office window and looked out. Two new flower beds had been installed alongside the front walk on the grass. It was early spring and the shoots had yet to emerge from the soil. "Well, since you ask," I said, "I have just buried one of my clinical failures in the one grave and the other is earmarked for you . . . if you turn out to be an uncooperative client." The twinkle in her eye told me that my response was an appropriate one. (p. 406)

By including Lazarus's humorous example, we are not advocating the regular use of sarcasm with 39-year-old female clients. Obviously, if used with the wrong client at the wrong time (you can imagine the situation), Lazarus's joke might have produced a strong adverse reaction. Using humor and sarcasm and acting like an authentic chameleon in therapy can be risky business. However, as Lazarus suggests, learning to modify your interpersonal style with clients is a skill that may well be worth cultivating, though with caution.

Eye Movement Desensitization Reprocessing

Some therapy approaches are more difficult to categorize than others. Eye Movement Desensitization and Reprocessing (EMDR), a specific treatment approach developed by Francine Shapiro (1989), is difficult to place in a particular pigeonhole. Some reviewers classify it as a form of behavior therapy (Corey, 2001), whereas others refer to it as a more circumscribed exposure-based treatment modality (Prochaska & Norcross, 2003). After debating the issue ourselves, we think it probably best fits as a technically eclectic treatment, although it might also be cast as an integrative treatment approach. F. Shapiro herself (1995, 1999) has alternatively referred to it as an integrative and syncletic approach. Another reason why we review it in this chapter is that it represents the current tendency among therapeutic innovators to develop treatments that do not fit clearly into a single theoretical model.

EMDR was originally designed to address trauma symptoms in general and to alleviate disturbing traumatic memories in particular. Shapiro discovered EMDR as a consequence of her own personal trauma experience and disturbing memories. In 1979, while working on her doctorate in English literature at New York University, she was diagnosed with cancer. Rather than continuing with her doctoral work in English literature, she left New York to study clinical psychology.

Years later, in 1987, as Shapiro was walking through a park, she felt distress stemming from memories associated with her cancer experience. After focusing on these memories for a few minutes she suddenly noticed that her disturbing thoughts were gone. When she managed to bring them back into her mind, she found that her previously disturbing thoughts had lost much of their disturbing quality. She then tried to recreate what she had just experienced and discovered that her eyes were moving very rapidly in a back and forth or horizontal manner. Later, she found that when she intentionally focused on a trauma-related memory and simultaneously moved her eyes back and forth, the memory was quickly desensitized.

Initially, Shapiro labeled her treatment approach Eye Movement Desensitization

(F. Shapiro, 1989), emphasizing the importance of specific eye movements in alleviating trauma symptoms. However, she later renamed her approach EMDR, primarily to capture the more complex psychological processes that she believes underlie its efficacy (F. Shapiro, 1995). She considers EMDR to be an integrative treatment because it includes principles from the following theoretical perspectives:

- *Psychodynamic.* There is a focus on past events and traumas that form the foundation for dysfunction.
- *Behavioral.* There is a focus on present stimuli, with specific behaviors expected of the client.
- *Cognitive.* There is a focus on negative and positive beliefs, as well as utilization of an information-processing model.
- *Person-centered.* EMDR therapists follow the client's lead rather than always dictating the course or direction of therapy.
- *Physiological or body-centered.* There is a focus on physical-affective links associated with trauma experiences.

In contrast to Shapiro's classification of EMDR as integrative, we place it in the technically eclectic camp because it seems empirically driven, pragmatic, and less dependent on traditional theoretical foundations than most other integrative approaches are.

For many reasons, EMDR has been—and continues to be—a controversial therapeutic approach. Partly due to claims that EMDR can quickly and efficiently (often after three 90-minutes sessions or fewer) reduce or eliminate chronic trauma symptoms, Shapiro's therapy has sometimes been sharply criticized as a simplistic fad or power therapy (Figley, 1997). The fact that EMDR training is tightly controlled by Shapiro, is shrouded in some mystery, and requires the payment of a fee (along with an agreement not to share details of the procedures with the "uncertified") has undoubtedly added fuel to the critics' claims. Finally, Prochaska and Norcross (2003) suggest that gender bias may also contribute to some of the strong resistance Shapiro has faced from the male-dominated professions of psychology and psychiatry. A brief sample of a critique of EMDR follows:

> The most widely known and studied of the Power Therapies is EMDR. This technique involves the waving of fingers in front of a patient's face, or alternative maneuvers such as finger snapping, to alter neural connections between affect, cognition and memory. Although the face validity of this technique is questionable and its theoretical explanation approaches the limits of neurobabble . . . EMDR has been taught to over 23,000 clinicians worldwide in the short span of eight years. Training in EMDR now requires a "Level II" workshop for certification in the eye movement method . . . despite several studies finding that eye movements add nothing to treatment outcome (see Lohr, Tolin, & Lilienfeld, 1998). Studies on EMDR (see Lohr et al., 1995; and Lohr et al., 1998) further show that effects of the technique are largely limited to verbal report indices, and are no greater than those achieved by already established exposure-based therapies. (Rosen, Lohr, McNally, & Herbert, 2000, pp. 134–135)

Shapiro counters her critics with strong arguments in defense of EMDR. She even takes the unusual step of admitting responsibility for some misconceptions surrounding EMDR:

> Contrary to a common misconception, EMDR, as it is currently practiced, is not a simple, by-the-book procedure dominated by the use of repeated eye movements (despite its name), but rather an integrated form of therapy incorporating aspects of many traditional psychological orientations . . . and one that makes use of a variety of bilateral stimuli besides eye movements. The inaugural study . . . did indeed stress directed eye movements as the primary component of the therapy. This incorrect and unfortunate interpretation of the method can be explained by the author's concentration on the concrete actions in which she was engaging during therapy, rather than on the attendant complexity of the methodology actually employed and the underlying processes thought to be engendered by it. (F. Shapiro, 1999, p. 37)

Shapiro has taken another important step in defense of EMDR: She has given her cognitive-behavioral and scientifically oriented critics a taste of their own medicine. That is, in a remarkably short period, she has accumulated a significant series of empirical studies supporting the efficacy of EMDR with traumatized clients. Overall, the research (including two meta-analyses) points to the general effectiveness of EMDR (Boudewyns & Hyer, 1996; P. R. Davidson & Parker, 2001; Rothbaum, 1997; Van Etten & Taylor, 1998). These studies, focusing on rape victims, single-trauma victims, and multiple-trauma victims, often show that EMDR produces results similar to more traditional exposure treatments in less time. Even more impressive is the fact that the APA Division of Clinical Psychology's Task Force on Promotion and Dissemination of Psychological Procedures includes EMDR as a "probably efficacious" treatment for civilian Post-Traumatic Stress Disorder (PTSD; Chambless et al., 1998). The only other treatments that have attained this status in the treatment of PTSD are standard cognitive-behavioral fare: stress inoculation training and exposure treatment.

The standard EMDR procedure includes eight basic phases:

1. History
2. Preparation
3. Assessment
4. Desensitization
5. Installation
6. Body scan
7. Closure
8. Reevaluation

Detailed information regarding EMDR practice is available in any of Shapiro's many works in the area (F. Shapiro, 1995, 1997, 2001). Additionally, as noted earlier, EMDR certification requires completion of a Level II EMDR workshop (see Recommended Readings and Resources).

At this point, an explanation for why EMDR works is only partially developed. Shapiro believes that trauma produces an overwhelming amount of disturbing information that must be processed neurologically. This information processing is halted by a particular brain region, causing neural pathology. The application of EMDR helps clients resume normal processing of their traumatic experiences. Shapiro believes that EMDR may access mechanisms present in normal learning and in REM sleep to facilitate information processing (F. Shapiro, 1995, 1997, 2001). At this point, the research indicates that the rhythmic eye movements that the therapy was originally based on may not be necessary for EMDR's effectiveness (Feske & Goldstein, 1995; Lohr et al.,

1998). Admittedly, much of the evidence and many of the explanations for using EMDR are alternatively compelling and mysterious.

In recent years EMDR treatment has expanded into problem areas other than PTSD. Specifically, there are treatment protocols available for addictions, anxiety, grief and loss, illness and somatic disorders, pain, performance enhancement, phobias, general stress reduction, and others (F. Shapiro, 2001). Additionally, despite accusations that EMDR is a treatment approach designed for profit, Shapiro and many EMDR practitioners have generously offered pro bono services to trauma victims through the EMDR Humanitarian Assistance Program. Specifically, EMDR has been offered to many victims of natural and human-caused trauma victims in the Balkans, Bosnia, Northern Ireland, Oklahoma City, New York City, San Salvador, and many other locales.

Interpersonal Psychotherapy

Interpersonal psychotherapy (IPT) was briefly described in Chapter 2 as a relatively new therapeutic approach that integrates principles of traditional psychodynamic therapy—especially the interpersonal psychiatry of Harry Stack Sullivan (1953)—with more pragmatic, empirical formulations of depression. In that sense, IPT can be considered an integrational-empirical approach.

IPT was originally developed by psychiatrist Gerald L. Klerman as a research-based treatment for depression. More recently, IPT has been adapted and applied to a number of disorders other than depression. The main characteristics of IPT are that

- It is time-limited.
- It focuses on one or two interpersonal problem areas.
- It focuses on current, rather than past, interpersonal relationships.
- It has an interpersonal, rather than intrapsychic, emphasis.
- It addresses cognitive-behavioral issues but emphasizes these factors only in terms of how they affect important social relationships.
- It recognizes, but does not focus on, personality variables.
- It is based on a medical model in which the client is viewed as having clinical depression, a specific medical disorder for which a specific treatment is most appropriate.

Weissman, Markowitz, and Klerman (2000) describe the underlying conceptual foundation of IPT:

> The idea underlying IPT is simple: psychiatric syndromes such as depression, however multidetermined their causes, usually occur in a social and interpersonal context. A marriage breaks up; a friendship dissolves; children leave home; a job is lost; a loved one dies; a person moves, is promoted, or retires. (p. xi)

The main foci of IPT are to help clients (1) recognize the relationship between depressive symptoms and interpersonal problems and (2) find ways to deal more effectively with interpersonal problems, thereby alleviating depressive symptoms.

IPT includes three treatment phases. In the first three sessions, a diagnostic evaluation and psychiatric history are conducted and a framework for treatment is established. Within the context of the psychiatric history, an interpersonal inventory is also obtained. This inventory reviews the client's current social functioning and interpersonal relationships. It also examines any changes in relationships that may have occurred near the time when the depressive symptoms increased.

Consistent with the medical model, during this first phase of treatment the client is assigned the sick role. This strategy may seem foreign to those of us trained in providing psychosocial treatments. Assignment of the sick role includes the giving of a diagnosis (clinical depression) and carries with it two implications: (1) Clients may be relieved of overwhelming social obligations, and (2) clients are expected to work in treatment to recover their full functioning.

Also during the first phase of treatment, clients are evaluated for possible simultaneous antidepressant medication treatment, educated about the nature of depression, and offered an interpersonal formulation.

The interpersonal formulation involves linking the client's depressive symptoms to one of four possible specific interpersonal situations:

1. *Grief.* Complicated bereavement following the death of a loved one
2. *Interpersonal role dispute.* Conflicts in an important social relationship (spouse, family member, coworker, or close friend)
3. *Role transition.* A change in life status, including the beginning or end of a relationship, retirement, graduation, medical diagnosis, and so on
4. *Interpersonal deficit.* When a client lacks specific social skills that contribute to relationship problems

During the middle (second) phase of treatment, the therapist applies strategies to address the client's interpersonal problems, as articulated in the interpersonal formulation. Specific strategies of IPT are reviewed and described in the interpersonal treatment manual (see Klerman et al., 1984; Weissman et al., 2000). IPT sessions typically begin with the query, "How have things been since we last met?" (Weissman et al., 2000, p. 21). The purpose of this question is to help clients focus on recent interpersonal events and recent mood. The therapist's job is to link these two issues and help the client make plans to address the interpersonal problems that are fueling the depressive symptoms.

The final phase of treatment focuses on the recognition and consolidation of treatment gains. Additionally, strategies for facing and coping with future depressive episodes are reviewed.

IPT has been adapted for treating problems and mental disorders other than depression. It also has been validated as a treatment for adolescent depression (Mufson et al., 1993). Information on IPT training programs and certification is included at the end of this chapter.

Process-Experiential Psychotherapy

Process-Experiential Psychotherapy is a relatively new approach to psychotherapy with deep roots in person-centered theory (L. S. Greenberg, 2002a). The therapy emphasizes the formation of a relationship based on Rogers's core conditions and then, from the trusting relationship foundation, seeks to explore and resolve the client's affective problems. However, this treatment is much more active than traditional person-centered therapy and relies heavily on Gestalt techniques to help clients experience and address their emotional issues.

As Goldman and Greenberg (1997) state, the resolution of affective problems is based on the following person-centered theoretical principles:

> Clients are consistently encouraged to identify and symbolize internal experience and bodily felt referents in order to create new meaning. Therapy is seen as facilitating conscious choice and reasoned action based on increased access to and awareness of inner experience and feeling. (pp. 402–403)

In contrast to traditional person-centered therapy, after the client-therapist relationship is adequately established (usually this takes at least two sessions), process-experiential therapists take a much more active and directive role in helping identify areas where clients are suffering from emotional and behavioral problems. Again, it is important to note that although therapists are more active and directive in this treatment, they do not take the lead in determining what content the client should focus on or what needs to be fixed. Instead, therapists provide process direction, and "[a]t all times, the therapist tries to make psychological *contact* with and convey a *genuine* understanding of the client's internal experience" (Goldman & Greenberg, 1997, p. 403).

Much of the assessment and case formulation process in Greenberg's therapy involves simultaneously experiencing and observing for a wide range of global and specific indicators of the client's affective problem markers. Usually, when these markers are identified, they lead directly to a particular form or style of intervention—some of which are derived from person-centered therapy and others that are derived from Gestalt therapy (two-chair and empty-chair dialogues are commonly used to heighten client affect and increase the client's felt experience). The affective markers, therapeutic tasks, and desired resolution states for process-experiential therapy are summarized in Table 13.2.

Overall, as noted, process-experiential therapy employs a focused, active, and directive therapeutic style with a special emphasis on empty-chair dialogues and two-chair enactment. However, its main process-oriented goal is virtually the same as that of person-centered therapy. Specifically, process-experiential therapy is designed to help "clients to explore and re-integrate previously disallowed or muted self-information" (Goldman & Greenberg, 1997, p. 409).

Process-experiential therapy is not considered an empirically validated or supported treatment (Chambless et al., 1998). However, research continues to accumulate on the importance of integrating emotional focusing, understanding, and expression into therapeutic procedures (L. S. Greenberg, 2002b; L. S. Greenberg et al., 1994; L. S. Greenberg & Foerster, 1996; L. S. Greenberg & Malcolm, 2002). Obviously, the emotional side of life constitutes a powerful experience for both clients and nonclients. Process-experiential therapy offers clinicians and clients a systematic strategy for examining and experiencing emotions in therapy. It appears that this strategy may be either considered a coherent approach in its own right or integrated into other treatment approaches as a powerful and facilitating therapeutic process (L. S. Greenberg, 2002b).

Dialectical Behavior Therapy

Marsha Linehan and her colleagues at the University of Washington Suicidal Behaviors Research Clinic developed dialectical behavior therapy (DBT) as a specific treat-

Table 13.2   Affective Markers, Therapeutic Tasks, and Desired Resolution States in Process Experiential Therapy

Affective marker	Therapeutic task	Desired resolution state
The client expresses a problematic reaction through puzzlement about appropriate emotional and behavioral responses to a specific situation.	The therapist uses reflection of content, feeling, and walking within to help the client's primary feelings systematically unfold.	The client obtains a new view of self-in-the-world functioning.
The client has an absent or unclear felt sense of his or her experience.	The therapist uses an experiential focusing technique to help the client obtain a clearer sense of his or her felt experience.	The client is able to symbolize a felt sense and productively process an experience.
The client experiences a self-evaluative split: One aspect of the self is critical toward another aspect of self.	The therapist gently prompts the client toward using a two-chair dialogue.	The client experiences self-acceptance and integration of previously split components of the self.
There is a self-interruptive split in which a part of the client interrupts or constricts an emotional experience.	The therapist gently prompts the client toward using a two-chair enactment.	The client is able to experience self-expression and empowerment.
A lingering unresolved feeling toward a significant other or unfinished business emerges.	The therapist gently prompts the client toward dialoguing with a significant other using an empty-chair technique.	The client is able to either forgive the other or hold the other accountable. The self is affirmed or separated from the other.
The client experiences a heightened sense of vulnerability, shame, or insecurity.	The therapist empathically affirms the client.	The client experiences self-affirmation and feels understood and stronger.

Source. Adapted from Goldman and Greenberg (1997).

ment for women who were exhibiting parasuicidal behavior and suffering from Borderline Personality Disorder (BPD). Parasuicidal behavior includes all intentional self-injurious behavior, some of which is also characterized by suicidal intent. DBT is an integrative treatment approach in that it blends cognitive-behavioral and Eastern meditation practices with elements of psychodynamic, person-centered, Gestalt, strategic, and paradoxical approaches (Heard & Linehan, 1994).

DBT is a comprehensive and promising approach directed toward a very difficult clinical population. Typically, therapists who work with clients who are chronically suicidal and self-destructive and who experience emotional dysregulation quickly become discouraged, cynical, and burned out. This has often led therapists to strongly criticize their clients, sometimes disparagingly referring to them as *borderlines*. In contrast, DBT maintains a positive perspective, and the model weaves in support for the therapist in coping with this difficult client population. This balance approach, with both optimistic and realistic components, combined with its growing empirical status, has led to some rave reviews:

Not since Beck's cognitive therapy has a treatment in the cognitive-behavioral tradition sparked the interest of clinicians throughout the U.S. and Europe and ignited a quiet revolution in their approach to therapy. (A. L. Miller & Rathus, 2000, p. 420)

DBT is based on a biosocial theoretical model of BPD. Specifically, the primary deficit associated with BPD is identified as emotional dysregulation. On the biological side, BPD clients are viewed as being biologically predisposed to emotional dysregulation. Linehan believes that "individuals with BPD have emotional responses to environmental stimuli that occur more quickly, are more intense, and have a slower return to baseline than the responses of non-BPD individuals" (Linehan & Schmidt, 1995, p. 562).

On the social side, BPD clients are viewed as being within an environment that provides a poor fit for emotionally dysregulated behavior. Over time, this social environment often becomes "chronically and pervasively" emotionally invalidating—the BPD client consistently receives communications indicating that her emotional and behavioral responses are "incorrect, faulty, inappropriate" (A. L. Miller & Rathus, 2000, p. 421).

DBT is also founded on dialectical philosophy. An extensive discussion of dialectical philosophy is in Wells (1972), and a description of Hegelian philosophy is in Weiss (1974). Simply put, this philosophy emphasizes that reality includes opposing forces that are constantly shifting and changing. The three-stage process through which change occurs is referred to as the dialectic. For example, as applied to a suicidal client, the dialectic transformation occurs in the following stages:

- *First.* An initial proposition, "Life has meaning and positive possibilities," is experienced.
- *Second.* The initial proposition is negated through a contradictory experience: "Life has no relevance, meaning, or positive possibilities."
- *Third.* The contradiction is resolved through the negation of the negation: "Life can be both inherently meaningful and completely irrelevant."

Through DBT, the client is encouraged to grapple with both sides of this contradiction, with the eventual result being greater acceptance of transitory meaning and irrelevance in life and resultant improved emotional regulation skills.

DBT also embraces another dialectic within the therapy process. That is, clients and their emotional condition are completely embraced and accepted (as in Eastern philosophy and person-centered theory). However, at the same time, the client is engaged in a purposeful change process designed to help with emotional dysregulation and environmental invalidation (Linehan, 1993). Essentially, the therapist is saying to the client: "I accept you as you are, and I am helping you to change."

The practice of DBT is comprehensive and includes five functions delivered in various modalities. The functions include

1. Enhancing the client's skills and capabilities
2. Improving the client's motivation
3. Generalizing the client's skills and capabilities from therapy to the client's life outside therapy

4. Improving the therapist's capabilities and motivation to treat BPD patients
5. Structuring the client's environment to support and validate the client's and therapist's capabilities (Linehan, 1993)

To address these functions, the therapist and client engage in the following activities and modalities: (1) The client commits to 12 months of psychoeducational skills training in a group-therapy setting; (2) the client works individually with a therapist to increase motivation, address barriers to skill acquisition and application, and generalize specific skills to the real world; (3) when therapists commit to providing weekly therapy for the client, they also commit to participating in a weekly professional consultation group to get technical assistance and emotional support; (4) family sessions or consultations with the client's personal environment are conducted to facilitate client emotional validation and skill development.

As you can see, DBT is not a therapy for the meek. It requires that both therapist and client make considerable commitments to training and ongoing skill development.

Thus far, empirical support for DBT is relatively strong. The American Psychological Association's Division 12 Task Force listed DBT as a probably efficacious treatment for borderline personality disorder (Chambless et al., 1998). Currently, DBT is being adapted for use with adolescents, substance abusers, domestic violence cases, violent male inmates, and elderly clients with depression and personality disorders (Dimeff, Rizvi, Brown, & Linehan, 2000; Fruzzetti & Levensky, 2000; Linehan, 2000; McCann, Ball, & Ivanoff, 2000; A. L. Miller & Rathus, 2000; Rathus & Miller, 2000).

Acceptance and Commitment Therapy

Another behaviorally oriented therapy with a strong emphasis on the person-centered concept of acceptance has gained popularity in recent years. This therapy is called acceptance and commitment therapy (ACT, pronounced as a word and not as a set of initials). The developers of ACT clearly identify their approach as integrational:

> Is ACT a behavior therapy, a cognitive-behavioral therapy, a type of clinical behavior analysis, a contextual therapy, or a humanistic/existential/Gestalt therapy? It is all of these. . . .
> We do not view the distinctions between these streams of thought to be important to the ACT work, and relish the fact that it spans several seemingly distinct traditions. (Hayes, Strosahl, & Wilson, 1999, p. 79)

ACT is a new kind of radical behaviorism. In perhaps its most unique contribution to the literature, ACT authors are extremely critical of existing diagnostic and medical models. They emphasize that current medically based therapy systems are operating on the wrong paradigm. Specifically, they reason that the assumption of healthy normality and the assumption that abnormality is a disease are both flawed and that the disease, disorder, or psychopathology model has fared quite poorly over the years:

> Considering how much attention has been afforded the medical model within psychology and psychiatry, it is a bit shocking to note how little progress has been made in establishing syndromes as disease entities. . . . The "comorbidity" rates in the current diagnostic system are so high as to challenge the basic credibility of the nosology. . . . Even if clients can be given a label such as panic disorder with agoraphobia, or obsessive-compulsive disorder, many of the issues within therapy will still have to do with other problems: jobs, chil-

dren, relationships, sexual identity, careers, anger, sadness, drinking problems, or the meaning of life. (Hayes et al., 1999, p. 5)

The main point emphasized forth by Hayes and his colleagues is that clinical researchers have been seeking support for an invalid model. They offer an alternative or supplemental view:

ACT supplements the traditional view by bringing a different assumption to the study of psychological distress. It is based on the assumption of destructive normality: The idea that ordinary human psychological processes can themselves lead to extremely destructive and dysfunctional results and can amplify or exacerbate unusual pathological processes. (Hayes et al., 1999, p. 6)

In other words, based on the ACT model, human suffering is normal, and normal human processes can produce suffering. Should you be interested in obtaining more information about this radical new perspective on therapy and the nature of psychopathology, we recommend the most recent book by Hayes et al. (1999).

Cognitive-Constructivist Psychotherapy

Many therapy approaches identified and described in the previous chapters might well fit into this eclectic and integrational chapter. Specifically, Adlerian therapy, choice theory and therapy, and feminist therapy all have strong eclectic or integrational qualities (Watts, 2003). However, none of these approaches are as inclusive and cutting-edge as modern cognitive-constructivist theory and therapy (in terms of the more philosophical form of constructivism, rather than solution-based approaches). Mahoney (1991) describes the integrative quality of constructivism thus:

[D]espite the apparent novelty of some of its assertions, constructive metatheory incorporates aspects of the wisdom embedded in many major theoretical perspectives in psychology. Psychoanalysts, behaviorists, cognitivists, existentialists, and humanists can all find many threads of their respective traditions in the conceptual tapestry woven by psychological constructivism. While this was not an explicit intention of constructivist theorists, it reflects their openness to valuable contributions from a diversity of sources. Given this conceptual richness and diversity, constructive metatheory may be a particularly promising candidate for the continuing exploration of "integrations" and convergence among the major psychological theories. (p 113)

As you may recall from Chapter 8, Donald Meichenbaum has progressively evolved from a behavior therapist to a cognitive-behavioral therapist to a constructivist cognitive-behavioral therapist. In the following statement he made during a 1994 interview, he clearly integrates psychoanalytic and person-centered concepts into his therapeutic mix while still remaining sensitive to basic cognitive and behavioral issues. This statement is an elegant representation of the integrative thinking and therapeutic approach utilized by a sophisticated and seasoned therapist:

[F]or meaningful change to occur, it has to be "affectively charged." I am referring to the time-honoured concept of "corrective emotional experience" (Alexander & French, 1946). People can readily dismiss, discount, dissuade themselves of the "data." They don't really accept data as "evidence," and it is critical therapeutically to work with clients in order to ensure that they take the data they have collected as evidence to unfreeze their beliefs—to get into the nature of the clients' belief system and to nurture an internal dialogue that they would find most adaptive, as compared to being "stuck" in maladaptive patterns of thinking and behaving. . . . I think the therapeutic relationship is the glue that makes the various therapeutic procedures work. (Hoyt, 2000, pp. 53–54)

Overall, as we look to the future of psychological theory and counseling and psychotherapy practice, it may be that cognitive constructivism will become the most prominent and pervasive theoretical perspective (Watts, 2003). On the other hand, another competing overarching theoretical model is the transtheoretical change model.

A Higher-Order Integrational and Common Factors Model: The Transtheoretical Change Model

In the late 1970s James Prochaska began looking at theories of psychotherapy in a new way. While reviewing traditional psychotherapy systems, he discovered that most theories emphasize personality and psychopathology, both of which orient therapists toward why people don't change rather than why people do change (Prochaska, 1979). Consequently, he and his colleagues began their groundbreaking work on developing a new theory of therapy—a transtheoretical model focusing on how people change (Prochaska & DiClemente, 1982; Prochaska, DiClemente, & Norcross, 1993; Prochaska, Norcross, & DiClemente, 1994).

The transtheoretical model is a higher-order integrational theory of psychotherapy, emphasizing both common factors and theoretical integration. The model seeks to

- Respect the fundamental diversity and essential unity of therapy systems
- Emphasize empiricism
- Account for how people change inside and outside of therapy
- Address physical and mental health problems
- Encourage therapists to be innovators and not simply borrowers from various systems (Prochaska & Norcross, 2003)

When the transtheoretical model was developed, counseling and psychotherapy were ripe for creative, integrative ideas. In the 1970s, eclecticism was very popular, but it was also associated with soft thinking, fragmentation, and superficiality, as described earlier in this chapter (Eysenck, 1970; D. S. Smith, 1982).

Prochaska (1995) considers his development of the transtheoretical model to be a product of increasing divergence in the field. Based on Guilford's (1956) model of intelligence he notes that periods of divergence need to be followed by higher levels of convergent thinking. Consequently, because therapy approaches had become so fragmented in the 1970s, the time was right for greater rapprochement or convergence in counseling and psychotherapy, as Goldfried (1980, 1982) had called for.

The transtheoretical model focuses on three different dimensions of change:

1. Change processes
2. Stages of change
3. Levels of change

Table 13.3   Common Change Processes and Theoretical Origins

Consciousness raising	Processes of personal insight and awareness that stem from feedback and education	Psychodynamic theory Feminist theory
Dramatic relief	Catharsis and expressive procedures	Gestalt theory
Self-re-evaluation	An examination of self, self-schema, and other variables	Cognitive therapy, constructivist, and Adlerian
Environmental re-evaluation	Information processing with an environmental focus	Cognitive and constructivist theory
Self-liberation	A focus on personal freedom	Existential and choice theory
Social-liberation	A focus on freedom from social oppression	Feminist, existential, and constructivist
Counterconditioning	New learning that overcomes old learning	Behavioral
Stimulus control	Management of environmental stimuli	Behavioral
Reinforcement management	Management of environmental contingencies	Behavioral
Helping relationship	The healing potential of a helping relationship	Person-centered

Change Processes

Beginning with research focused on addictive behaviors, Prochaska and his colleagues sought to identify common change processes occurring across divergent theoretical orientations. Most recently, they identified 10 primary change processes (Prochaska, 1995; Prochaska & Norcross, 2003). These processes, along with their likely theoretical roots, are listed in Table 13.3.

Stages of Change

Some clients come to therapy ready to change for the better. Other clients end up in therapy with little or no motivation for change. Recognizing these basic differences, as well as more subtle change levels, Prochaska and his colleagues identified six stages of change:

1. *Precontemplation.* During this stage, the individual has little or no interest in changing his behavior.
2. *Contemplation.* During this stage, the individual is aware that a problem exists, but she has not yet made a clear commitment to making a personal change.
3. *Preparation.* During preparation, there may be some intention and effort made toward change. For example, a sedentary individual may go out and buy running shoes or join a fitness club. There may be occasional ventures forth into action, but mostly these individuals are so deep into contemplation that they're beginning some minimal action toward change but are not yet into the action stage.
4. *Action.* During action, people are plunging into the change process. These are the clients whom most therapists love to see because their motivation is so high that

they quickly engage in the therapy process and often make considerable and immediate progress. Prochaska (1995, p. 410) defines this stage as the "successful alteration of a problem behavior for a period from 1 day to 6 months."

5. *Maintenance.* During maintenance, people continue with their action and deepen their commitment toward permanent change. There is continual work or action toward relapse prevention. This stage continues from 6 months to infinity, but relapse often occurs at some point during maintenance. For example, many alcohol- or drug-addicted individuals reach the maintenance stage only to experience relapse. Then, they generally cycle back through the stages of change again in an effort to obtain mastery over their problem. This recycling tendency is apparent in many nonclients as many individuals repeatedly make the same New Year's resolutions (for five or more years) until finally maintaining their goal for over 6 months (Norcross & Vangarelli, 1989).

6. *Termination.* During termination, people have 100% confidence (or self-efficacy) that they will not engage in the problem behavior again. They also report having no urges to engage in the problem behavior again. Prochaska uses a 5-year criterion of symptom liberation, plus 100% confidence, for classification into this stage. In a study of recovering alcoholics and smokers, 17% and 16% of former drinkers and smokers were classified as being in the termination stage of change (Snow, Prochaska, & Rossi, 1992).

Levels of Change

Prochaska identified five different levels of change:

1. Symptom/situational problems
2. Maladaptive cognitions
3. Current interpersonal conflicts
4. Family-systems conflicts
5. Intrapersonal conflicts

Based on the transtheoretical model, change efforts are initially directed toward the symptom-situation level because most clients come to therapy seeking relief from a particular distressing symptom or situation. However, as Prochaska points out, rarely does therapy proceed in a simple and straightforward manner that focuses solely on symptom elimination (Prochaska, 1995). Instead, as clients participate in therapy for longer periods, they delve deeper into cognitive, interpersonal, familial, and intrapsychic issues.

One of the advantages of the transtheoretical model is its emphasis on the interactive and integrative nature of therapeutic processes, stages, and levels. For example, when clients are in the precontemplative stage, it is most likely that if they respond at all, they will respond intermittently to the educational and feedback processes associated with consciousness raising. Alternatively, when clients are in the contemplative or preparation stages, they may be ready to experience a sudden and dramatic relief, followed by regression or relapse. Additionally, it is best to focus on symptom and situational issues with clients in these early stages of change, as they are unlikely to be motivated enough to explore deeper, more personal issues (i.e., interpersonal, familial, or intrapsychic conflicts).

PRACTITIONER COMMENTARY 13.2

A Winding (and Serendipitous) Road to Eclecticism

In the following commentary, Kurt D. Michael, of Appalachian State University in North Carolina, describes his own unique journey to being a cognitive-behavioral therapist who is strongly influenced by interpersonal theory.

I developed my theoretical perspective through some misfortune and plain luck! As a first-year graduate student taking personality and psychotherapy, I and three colleagues were assigned the task of teaching the rest of the students in class about the interpersonal approach (seminar method). As part of the project, we produced a slide presentation (via Lotus), and we were not very savvy about the recently developed technology. As a group, we made almost 50 slides with incredibly detailed information about Harry Stack Sullivan's approach. Well, it was my job to put the finishing touches on the presentation, and I proceeded to erase the entire thing by inadvertently saving the wrong copy! So, needless to say, my colleagues were not altogether happy with me, given that the presentation was a mere three days away! So, after staying up several nights reproducing the entire talk, I became well acquainted with Harry's approach. It was actually a miracle I didn't rebel altogether and refuse to cast my eyes upon his name again! But I persisted and soon realized that my in-depth (and arduous) reproduction of the product afforded me the opportunity to learn and eventually love this particular theoretical approach. Since this "accident" I have only become more impressed with the richness and utility of the interpersonal approach. The more I work with children and families, the more I come to believe that the key to any psychotherapeutic approach is based on relationships—therapist-client, family of origin, work relationships, intimate relationships, and so on. If I can understand a person's core relationship dynamics, then I have gone a long way in helping to facilitate the development of myriad conceptualization and treatment possibilities. Further, the interpersonal approach is entirely consistent with cognitive, behavioral, and systems-based approaches. Indeed, it has been suggested that some of the basic tenets of the interpersonal approach were bona fide predecessors to the cognitive movement (e.g., dichotomous conceptualization: "good mother, bad mother"). So, in sum, I conceptualize my cases from an interpersonal standpoint, which then allows me to formulate specific treatment goals grounded in the cognitive and behavioral paradigms. I have the richness of a dynamic approach with the practicality of empirically supported therapeutic technologies. (February 1, 2003)

The Last Best Therapy Dialectic

In this text we have made the journey from psychoanalysis to psychotherapy integration. We have covered diverse and sometimes abstract theoretical viewpoints as well as a wide array of concrete therapy techniques. And now we have reached our last best dialectic.

In Chapter 1 we made a case for the importance of theory—despite its apparent empirical unimportance with respect to therapeutic outcome. Consequently, in each chapter we highlighted and emphasized specific therapy techniques. We hope that we've provided enough depth that you feel conversant with the ideas behind the theories, as well as enough practical exposure to put a few of these theories and techniques into practice in your first supervised clinical experiences.

After reading this far, you now understand that doing therapy is far more than the simple application of specific techniques. The last best therapy dialectic is the relationship between theory and technique. To dive deeply into theory and wrestle with the intellectual and elemental truths of the human condition is necessary, but insufficient. Alternatively, to dive directly into specific therapy techniques—to talk, act, emote, monitor cognitions, and join with clients in the discovery process—is also necessary, but insufficient. Theory requires the experimental and experiential action of technique, and technique needs theoretical grounding. Theory and technique are the yin and yang of counseling and psychotherapy.

CONCLUDING COMMENTS

At the beginning of this chapter, we quote E. O. Wilson, Harvard professor and thinker. The message is clear. In every domain of human endeavor, we have more information than we can possibly sort out and use effectively. Wisdom consists of knowing both *what* to know and *how* to use what you know. A careful analysis and synthesis of the material in this book will go a long ways toward helping you know what you need to know—at least to begin your journey as a mental health professional.

There are some dangerous truths about theories that tempt students to walk away from the intellectual work involved and just try to help people the best they can. Very few mental health professionals are in a position simply to adhere to one theoretical orientation and use only the techniques related to that orientation. In the real world, with its diverse demands and needs, no theory is a perfect fit. Further, taken at face value, many of the theories covered in this book might be waved aside as irrelevant to the tasks faced by a counselor at a youth home, a psychologist in an inpatient setting, a school counselor, a psychotherapist in private practice, and so on. The temptation is to lose patience and throw out the notion of theories altogether: Theories are for academics or people with more time and money than the average counselor has.

But we very much hope you won't take these theories at face value or treat them narrowly as historical artifacts—the musings of narcissistic or slightly addled forefathers and mothers. Instead, regard each perspective as a product of time, place, deep contemplation, and a sincere desire to understand and alleviate human suffering. At the very least, ethical mental health professionals should be able to do three things: First, they should be able to articulate their own theories of why humans develop mental distress and what helps bring relief and healing. Second, they should be able to compare and contrast their theories with those in this book. Finally, they should be able to explain their choices of techniques in the context of both theory and outcome.

===== **Putting It in Practice 13.1** =====

A Concluding Image: Group Therapy with Some Exceptionally Difficult Clients

There are indeed many ways to practice counseling and psychotherapy. There are also many ways to end a book. Because this is a textbook, we are tempted to end it with a logical and rational analysis of future trends in counseling and psychotherapy. However, because humans have difficulty predicting tomorrow's weather, we chose a different, more irreverent ending for this book. Instead of embracing the rational and logical conclusion, we leave you with a fantasy.

After reading and writing about so many great therapy minds, one of us (you can guess which one) had the following daydream: Imagine many of the historical and contemporary therapy masters gathered together in one location. They form a circle and begin a discussion. Old friends and rivals are reunited. Freud appears and shakes hands with Jean Miller Baker, who has brought quite a number of impressive-looking women with her. Fritz Perls tries to kiss some of their hands. Adler brings his wife. Carl Rogers signs a book for Prochaska. New friends are made, old rivalries rejuvenated. Insoo Kim Berg smiles quietly off to one side. Jung notes to himself that she must be an introvert. What might happen in this circumstance? What might happen in *An Encounter Group for the Major Players*?

After some initial mingling, the group process begins:

Rogers: I wonder where we might want to start.

Raissa Adler: Here's where I'm starting. I'm not taking the minutes for this meeting. I did that back in 1912 for the Free Psychoanalytic Society, so I've put in my time. It's someone else's turn, and I nominate a male, any male. Women have been taking notes in meetings for so long it's ridiculous. The problem with women's psyches has more to do with oppression than repression.

Feminists: You go woman! We're with you.

Freud: That's it. Say whatever comes to mind.

Ellis: If you want to think that taking notes is oppression, that's up to you, but as far as I can tell, you're oppressing yourself with a bunch of damn crazy, irrational thinking.

Beck: You know Al, we've been through this before, but what I think you mean is that Raissa's thinking that taking notes is oppression could be maladaptive, but not irrational.

Glasser: Raissa can choose to take notes or choose not to take notes. She can also choose to think she's oppressed or choose not to think she's oppressed. Personally, Raissa, I recommend that you read my book, *Choice Theory.* I want you to read it, and I think it will help you, but of course, whether you read it or not, that's completely your choice.

F. Perls: Be here now, Raissa. Act out those feelings. Be the pen. Talk to the paper.

L. Perls: Fritz, she can be the pen without your assistance. If by chance she finds herself, that's beautiful.

(continued)

=== **Putting It in Practice 13.1 (continued)** ===

Ellis: She won't find a goddamn thing in this group of love-slobs without a flashlight.

Skinner: Uh. Albert. I've been wanting to mention to you that if you could just keep quiet when people in here say inappropriate things, we might have a chance at extinguishing that particular behavior.

Ellis: Well, Burris, did you have an irrational thought that someone might actually care about your opinion before you engaged in that speaking behavior, or was it just a function of its consequences?

Rollo May: Freedom and dignity are the essence of being. There's far too much freedom, with very little dignity in this room.

Jung: Could we pause a moment and embrace our shadows?

I. K. Berg: If a miracle happened and we all got out of this group without anyone being murdered, what would that look like?

A. Adler: My God, I just remembered an earlier memory. No wonder I felt so inferior.

Freud: I hate that word. I just want to be recognized for my contributions. It would make my mother proud.

Rogers: It's like if only I can make my mother happy. And getting recognized, being remembered, that's one big way you can have that experience.

Ellis: Siggy, my man. Let me just say this. That crap about being recognized and making your mother proud is the most f—ing ridiculous thing I've ever heard in my life. What's the big deal if everybody forgets you? What's the terrible, awful, very bad thing that will happen? I mean, think logically about this. You'll be dead and it won't make a white rat's ass difference if people remember you or not.

Feminists: That's right. I can't believe we're agreeing with Albert Ellis. White males can afford to play with such big ideas. Immortality. Do you have a clue about the legacy you've actually left? There have been decades of girls and women with destroyed self-esteems. Do you recognize that they litter your road to "greatness"?

Mahoney: I can see Freud as great and I can see feminism as great. Even this lived moment in our genetic epistemology exudes the potential for greatness. We are not a passive repository of sensory experience, but instead, we co-construct this reality.

Prochaska: This entire group seems to me to be in the precontemplation stage.

D. W. Sue: Yeah, well, I might consider change if we could construct in a minority voice or two? Most of what I've heard thus far is the construction of a very narrow, White reality. Culture is primary, and we need to include color if we're to meet the needs of everyone, including Raissa, who happens to have a strong Russian ethnocultural identity.

Raissa Adler: [Slowly stands and walks over and embraces D. W. Sue.]

Rogers: What I'm seeing and what I'm hearing, if I'm getting this right, is affection and appreciation. Two people who have, now and again, felt marginalized are able to connect more deeply with each other than with anyone else.

M. White: Actually, Carl, I think I'd just call that a sparkling moment.

STUDENT REVIEW ASSIGNMENTS

These assignments are designed to help you review and reflect on the content of this chapter.

Critical Corner

1. The most anyone should expect of practicing mental health professionals is that they try to listen and help people with problems. Theory is like philosophy: nice but irrelevant in the day-to-day world. What would help is more guidance on what to do when, not on explaining how people get into the messes they get into.
Response:

2. People who come for help don't really care about your theoretical orientation. In fact, they are unlikely even to get the gist of what you are talking about. After all, they haven't been to graduate school and suffered through a theories class, and they are in some kind of pain. It is unethical to take up their time trying to explain yourself to them.
Response:

3. This emphasis on empirical outcomes and scientifically matching techniques with problems is just a good way to get grant money. Humans are too complex to ever respond the same way enough to guarantee that a given technique is the right one to use with a certain problem. Problems are unique to each individual; therefore, what helps one person might make another person worse.
Response:

4. Choose one of the following:
   - The safest thing to do is just pick a theory and stick with it. There's no way to know enough otherwise. The simpler the theory, the better.
   - The safest thing to do is forget theories and just do techniques that you believe in yourself. If all else fails, just listen and nod.
   - The safest thing to do is just work with one kind of problem and refer everyone who doesn't have that problem to someone else.
   - The safest thing to do is give good advice and have a generous supply of self-help books.
Response:

Reviewing Key Terms

- Individuality
- Cultural specificity
- Human conflict
- Technical eclecticism
- Syncretism
- Ideological purism
- Theoretical integration
- Common factors

- Multimodal therapy
- Eye Movement Desensitization and Reprocessing
- Dialectical Behavioral Therapy
- Interpersonal Psychotherapy

- Process-Experiential Therapy
- Acceptance and Commitment Therapy
- Cognitive-Constructivist
- Transtheoretical Change Model

Review Questions

1. What are the three proposed sources of theoretical and practical diversity noted in this chapter?
2. What are the four paths often taken by therapists to try to deal with the inconsistency and ambiguity inherent in psychological theory and therapy?
3. Describe the basic concept of corrective emotional experience.
4. What are J. Frank's ingredients that are common to all forms of therapy?
5. What are some of the problems or pitfalls of manualized therapies?
6. Discuss A. Lazarus's view of the authentic chameleon.
7. What is the general explanation for the effectiveness of EMDR? How would you explain its apparent effectiveness?
8. Which form of treatment described in this chapter is derived from a medical model, and which completely rejects the medical-disease model of psychopathology?
9. What two theoretical perspectives underlie process-experiential psychotherapy?
10. Explain the main dialectics in dialectic behavior therapy.

RECOMMENDED READINGS AND RESOURCES

The following readings and resources may help you in furthering your understanding of the integrative theories of counseling and psychotherapy.

Lead Journals

- *Evidence-Based Mental Health*
- *Integrative Psychiatry*
- *Journal of Psychotherapy Integration*

Books and Articles

Ahn, H.-N., & Wampold, B. E. (2001). Where oh where are the specific ingredients? A meta-analysis of component studies in counseling and psychotherapy. *Journal of Counseling Psychology, 48*(3), 251–257.

Alexander, F. (1963). The dynamics of psychotherapy in light of learning theory. *American Journal of Psychiatry, 120,* 440–448.

Frank, J. D., & Frank, J. B. (1991). *Persuasion and healing* (3rd ed.). Baltimore: Johns Hopkins University Press.

French, T. M. (1958). *The integrations of behavior.* (Vol. 3). Chicago: University of Chicago Press.

Garfield, S. L., & Kurtz, R. (1977). A study of eclectic views. *Journal of Consulting and Clinical Psychology, 45,* 78–83.

Gaston, L. (1990). The concept of the alliance and its role in psychotherapy: Theoretical and empirical considerations. *Psychotherapy, 27,* 143–153.

Goldfried, M. R. (1982). *Converging themes in psychotherapy.* New York: Springer.

Greenberg, L. S. (2002). *Emotion-focused therapy: Coaching clients to work through their feelings.* Washington, DC: American Psychological Association.

Greenberg, L. S., & Malcolm, W. (2002). Resolving unfinished business: Relating process to outcome. *Journal of Consulting and Clinical Psychology, 70*(2), 406–416.

Heard, H. L., & Linehan, M. (1994). Dialectical behavior therapy: An integrative approach to the treatment of borderline personality disorder. *Journal of Psychotherapy Integration, 4,* 55–82.

Kabat-Zinn, J. (1994). Wherever you go there you are. New York: Hyperion.

Klerman, G. L. E., Weissman, M. M., & Ed (Eds.). (1993). *New applications of interpersonal psychotherapy.* Washington, DC: American Psychiatric Association.

Lazarus, A. A. (1997). *Brief but comprehensive psychotherapy: The multimodal way.* New York: Springer.

Lazarus, A. A., & Lazarus, C. N. (1991). *Multimodal life history inventory.* Champaign, IL: Research Press.

Linehan, M. M. (1993). *Cognitive behavioral therapy of borderline personality disorder.* New York: Guilford Press.

Linehan, M. M. (1993). *Skills training manual for treating borderline personality disorder.* New York: Guilford Press.

Linehan, M. M. (2000). The empirical basis of dialectical behavior therapy: Development of new treatments versus evaluation of existing treatments. *Clinical Psychology: Science and Practice, 7*(1), 113–119.

Messer, S. B., & Wampold, B. E. (2002). Let's face facts: Common factors are more potent than specific therapy ingredients. *Clinical Psychology: Science and Practice, 9*(1), 21–25.

Prochaska, J. O., DiClemente, C. C., & Norcross, J. C. (1993). In search of how people change. *American Psychologist, 47,* 1102–1114.

Shapiro, F. (2001). *Eye Movement Desensitization and Reprocessing: Basic principles, protocols, and procedures* (2nd ed.). New York: Guilford Press.

Wachtel, P. L. (1977). *Psychoanalysis and behavior therapy: Toward an integration.* New York: Basic Books.

Videotapes

Greenberg, L. S. (1994). *Process-experiential psychotherapy* [Videotape]. Washington, DC: American Psychological Association.

Lazarus, A. A. (1994). *Multimodal therapy* [Videotape]. Washington, DC: American Psychological Association.

Norcross, J. C. (1994). *Prescriptive eclectic therapy* [Videotape]. Washington, DC: American Psychological Association.

Shapiro, F. (1998). *EMDR (eye movement desensitization reprocessing) for trauma* [Videotape]. Washington, DC: American Psychological Association.

Training Organizations and Web Sites

Society for the Exploration of Psychotherapy Integration (web site: www.cyberpsych.org/sepi/sepi.html)

References

Adler, A. (1898) *Gesundheitsbuch für die Schneidergewerbe [Healthbook for the tailors' trade].* Berlin: Heymanns.

Adler, A. (1927). *Understanding human nature.* Garden City, NY: Garden City.

Adler, A. (1935). Introduction. *International Journal of Individual Psychology, 1*(1), 5–8.

Adler, A. (1936). On the interpretation of dreams. *International Journal of Individual Psychology, 2*(1), 3–16.

Adler, A. (1937). Position in the family constellation influence life-style. *International Journal of Individual Psychology, 3*(3), 211–227.

Adler, A. (1956a). *The individual psychology of Alfred Adler.* New York: Basic Books.

Adler, A. (1956b). The meaning of life. In H. L. Ansbacher & R. R. Ansbacher (Eds.), *The individual psychology of Alfred Adler.* New York: Harper.

Adler, A. (1958). *What life should mean to you.* New York: Capricorn.

Adler, A. (1964). *Problems of neurosis: A book of case histories.* New York: Harper Torchbooks.

Adler, A. (1964). *Social interest: A challenge to mankind* (J. Linton & R. Vaughan, Trans.). New York: Capricorn.

Adler, A. (1983). *The practice and theory of individual psychology* (P. Radin, Trans.). Totowa, NJ: Littlefield, Adams. (Original work published 1912)

Agger, L., & Jensen, S. B. (1990). Testimony as ritual and evidence in psychotherapy for political refugees. *Journal of Traumatic Stress, 3,* 115–130.

Agras, W. S., Schneider, J. A., Arnow, B., Raeburn, S. D., & Telch, C. F. (1989). Cognitive-behavioral and response-prevention treatments for bulimia nervosa. *Journal of Consulting and Clinical Psychology, 57,* 215–221.

Ahn, H.-N., & Wampold, B. E. (2001). Where oh where are the specific ingredients? A meta-analysis of component studies in counseling and psychotherapy. *Journal of Counseling Psychology, 48*(3), 251–257.

Ainsworth, M. D. (1969). Object relations, dependency, and attachment: A theoretical review of the infant-mother relationship. *Child Development, 40*(4), 969–1025.

Alberti, R. E., & Emmons, M. L. (1970). *Your perfect right: A guide to assertive behavior.* Atascadero, CA: Impact Publishers.

Alberti, R. E., & Emmons, M. L. (2001). *Your perfect right: Assertiveness and equality in your life and relationships* (8th ed.). Atascadero, CA: Impact Publishers.

Alexander, F. (1963). The dynamics of psychotherapy in light of learning theory. *American Journal of Psychiatry, 120,* 440–448.

Alexander, F., & French, T. M. (1946). *Psychoanalytic psychotherapy.* New York: Ronald.

American Counseling Association. (1995). *Code of ethics and standards of practice.* Alexandria, VA: Author.

American Psychiatric Association. (1980). *Diagnostic and statistical manual of mental disorders* (3rd ed.). Washington, DC: Author.

American Psychiatric Association. (1993). *Principles of medical ethics with annotions especially applicable to psychiatry.* Washington, DC: Author.

American Psychiatric Association. (2000). *Diagnostic and statistical manual of mental disorders* (4th ed., Text Revision). Washington, DC: Author.

American Psychological Association. (2002). Ethical principles of psychologists and code of conduct. *American Psychologist, 57,* 1060–1073.

Andersen, T. (1987). The reflecting team: Dialogue and metadialogue in clinical work. *Family Process, 26,* 415–426.

Andersen, T. (1991). *The reflecting team: Dialogues and dialogues about dialogues.* New York: Norton.

Andersen, T. (1995). Reflecting processes: Acts of informing and forming: You can borrow my eyes, but you must not take them away from me! In S. Friedman (Ed.), *The reflecting team in action: Collaborative practices in psychotherapy* (pp. 11–37) New York: Guilford Press.

Anderson, H., & Levin, S. (1998). Generative conversations. In M. F. Hoyt (Ed.), *The handbook of constructivist therapies* (pp. 46–67). San Francisco: Jossey-Bass.

Arkowitz, H. (1997). Integrative theories of therapy. In P. L. Wachtel & S. B. Messer (Eds.), *Theories of psychotherapy: Origins and evolution* (pp. 227–288). Washington DC: American Psychological Association.

Arntz, A. (2002). Cognitive therapy versus interoceptive exposure as treatment of panic disorder without agoraphobia. *Behaviour Research and Therapy, 40,* 325–341.

Asay, T. P., & Lambert, M. J. (1999). The empirical case for the common factors in therapy: Quantitative findings. In M. A. Hubble, B. L. Duncan, & S. D. Miller (Eds.), *The heart and soul of change* (pp. 33–56). Washington, DC: American Psychological Association.

Atkinson, D. R., Bui, U., & Mori, S. (2001). Multiculturally sensitive empirically supported treatments—an oxymoron? In J. G. Ponterotto, J. M. Casas, L. A. Suzuki, & C. M. Alexander (Eds.), *Handbook of multicultural counseling* (pp. 542–574). Thousand Oaks, CA: Sage.

Atkinson, D. R., & Lowe, S. M. (1995). The role of ethnicity, cultural knowledge, and conventional techniques in counseling and psychotherapy. In J. G. Ponterotto, J. M. Casas, L. A. Suzuki, & C. M. Alexander (Eds.), *Handbook of multicultural counseling* (pp. 387–414). Thousand Oaks, CA: Sage.

Atkinson, D. R., Lowe, S. M., & Mathews, L. (1995). Asian-American acculturation, gender and willingness to seek counseling. *Journal of Multicultural Counseling and Development, 23,* 130–138.

Atkinson, D. R., Maruyama, M., & Matsui, S. (1978). The effects of conselor race and counseling approach on Asian Americans' perceptions of counselor credibility. *Journal of Counseling Psychology, 25,* 76–83.

Auer, S. (2000). Reflections on minority rights in Central Europe. In C. O'Brien & L. Hancock (Eds.), *Re-writing rights in Europe* (pp. 124–148). Aldershot, Australia: Ashgate.

Axelson, J. A. (1999). *Counseling and development in a multicultural society* (3rd ed.). Belmont, CA: Wadsworth.

Axline, V. M. (1964). *Dibs in search of self.* New York: Ballentine Books.

Baca, L., & Cervantes, H. T. (1984). *The bilingual special education interface* (1st ed.). St. Louis, MO: Times Mirror/Mosby College.

Balint, E. (1950). Changing therapeutic aims and techniques in psychoanalysis. *International Journal of Psychoanalytic Psychology, 31,* 117–124.

Balint, M., Ornstein, P. H., & Balint, E. (1972). *Focal psychotherapy.* Philadelphia: Lippincott.

Bandura, A. (1965). Vicarious processes: A case of no-trial learning. In L. Berkowitz (Ed.), *Advances in experimental social psychology* (Vol. 2, pp. 49–91). New York: Academic Press.

Bandura, A. (1971). Psychotherapy based on modeling procedures. In A. E. Bergin & S. L. Garfield (Eds.), *Handbook of psychotherapy and behavior change: An empirical analysis* (pp. 653–708). New York: Wiley.

Bandura, A. (1977). Self-efficacy: Toward a unifying theory of behavioral change. *Psychological Review, 84,* 191–215.

Bandura, A. (1978). The self system in reciprocal determinism. *American Psychologist, 33,* 344–358.

Bandura, A., & Adams, N. E. (1977). Analysis of self-efficacy theory of behavioral change. *Cognitive Therapy and Research, 1,* 287–310.

Bandura, A., Blanchard, E. B., & Ritter, B. (1969). Relative efficacy of desensitization and modeling approaches for inducing behavioral, affective, and attitudinal changes. *Journal of Personality and Social Psychology, 13,* 173–199.

Bandura, A., Ross, D., & Ross, S. A. (1963). Imitation of film-mediated aggressive models. *Journal of Abnormal and Social Psychology, 66,* 3–11.

Bandura, A., & Walters, R. H. (1963). *Social learning and personality development.* New York: Holt, Rinehart, and Winston.

Bankart, C. P. (1997). *Talking cures: A history of Western and Eastern psychotherapies.* Pacific Grove, CA: Brooks/Cole.

Barlow, D., & Craske, M. G. (1989). *Mastery of your anxiety and panic.* New York: Guilford Press.

Barlow, D., & Craske, M. G. (1994). *Mastery of your anxiety and panic* (Vol. 2). San Antonio, TX: Harcourt Brace.

Barrett-Lennard, G. T. (1981). The empathy cycle: Refinement of a nuclear concept. *Journal of Counseling Psychology, 28,* 91–100.

Bateson, G., Jackson, D. D., Haley, J., & Weakland, J. H. (1963). A note on the double bind: 1962. *Family Process, 2*(1), 154–161.

Baumgardner, P. (1975). *Legacy from Fritz.* Palo Alto, CA: Science and Behavior Books.

Baumrind, D., Larzelere, R. E., & Cowan, P. A. (2002). Ordinary physical punishment: Is it harmful? Comment on Gershoff (2002). *Psychological Bulletin, 128*(4), 580–589.

Beauvoir, S. de. (1952). *The second sex.* New York: Knopf.

Bechtoldt, H., Norcross, J. C., Wyckoff, L. A., Pokrywa, M. L., & Campbell, L. F. (2001). Theoretical orientations and employment settings of clinical and counseling psychologists: A comparative study. *Clinical Psychologist, 54,* 3–6.

Beck, A. T. (1961). A systematic investigation of depression. *Comprehensive Psychiatry, 2,* 163-170.

Beck, A. T. (1963). Thinking and depression. *Archives of General Psychiatry, 9,* 324–333.

Beck, A. T. (1970). The core problem in depression: The cognitive triad. In J. Masserman (Ed.), *Depression: Theories and therapies* (pp. 47–55). New York: Grune & Stratton.

Beck, A. T. (1976). *Cognitive therapy and the emotional disorders.* New York: New American Library.

Beck, A. T., Emery, G., & Greenberg, R. L. (1985). *Anxiety disorders and phobias: A cognitive perspective.* New York: Basic Books.

Beck, A. T., Epstein, N., Brown, G., & Steer, R. (1988). An inventory for measuring clinical anxiety: Psychometric properties. *Journal of Consulting and Clinical Psychology, 56,* 893–897.

Beck, A. T., Rush, A., Shaw, B., & Emery, G. (1979). *Cognitive therapy of depression.* New York: Guilford Press.

Beck, A. T., Ward, C. H., Mendelson, M., Mock, J., & Erbaugh, J. (1961). An inventory for measuring depression. *Archives of General Psychiatry, 4,* 561–571.

Beck, J. G., Shipherd, J. C., & Zebb, B. J. (1997). How does interoceptive exposure for panic disorder work? An uncontrolled case study. *Journal of Anxiety Disorders, 11,* 541–556.

Beitman, B. D. (1987). *The structure of individual psychotherapy.* New York: Guilford Press.

Bem, S. L. (1974). The measurement of psychological androgyny. *Journal of Consulting and Clinical Psychology, 42,* 155–162.

Benjamin, J. (1990). An outline of intersubjectivity: The development of recognition. *Psychoanalytic Psychology, 7,* 33–46.

Benson, H. (1976). *The relaxation response.* New York: Avon Books.

Berg, I. K., & de Shazer, S. (1993). Making numbers talk: Language in therapy. In S. Friedman (Ed.), *The new language of change: Constructive collaboration in psychotherapy* (pp. 5–24). New York: Guilford Press.

Berg, I. K., & Miller, S. D. (1992). *Working with the problem drinker: A solution-focused approach.* New York: Norton.

Bernstein, D. A., & Borkovec, T. D. (1973). *Progressive relaxation training: A manual for the helping professions.* Champaign, IL: Research Press.

Bertolino, B. (1999). *Therapy with troubled teenagers: Rewriting young lives in progress.* New York: Wiley.

Beutler, L. E. (2000). Empirically based decision making in clinical practice. *Prevention and Treatment.* Retrieved December 17, 2002 from http://journals.apa.org/prevention/volume3/pre0030027a.html

Beyebach, M., Morejon, A. R., Palenzuela, D. L., & Rodriguez-Arias, J. L. (1996). Research on the process of solution-focused therapy. In S. D. Miller, M. A. Hubble, & B. L. Duncan (Eds.), *Handbook of solution-focused brief therapy* (pp. 299–334). San Francisco: Jossey-Bass.

Bion, W. R. (1988). A theory of thinking Melanie Klein today: Developments in theory and practice. In E. B. Spillius (Ed.) *Mainly theory* (Vol. 1, pp. 178–186). Florence, KY: US Taylor & Francis/Routledge (1988 vii, 1358 Series New library of psychoanalysis, 1987).

Bitter, J. R., & Nicoll, W. G. (2000). Adlerian brief therapy with individuals: Process and practice. *Journal of Individual Psychology, 56*(1), 31–44.

Blake, D. D., Abueg, F. R., Woodward, S. H., & Keane, T. M. (1993). Treatment efficacy in posttraumatic stress disorder. In T. R. Giles (Ed.), *Handbook of effective psychotherapy.* New York: Plenum.

Bleier, R. (1984). *Science and gender: A critique of biology and its theories on women.* Elmsford, NE: Pergamon Press.

Bleier, R. (1988). Sex differences research: Science or belief. In R. Bleier (Ed.), *Feminist approaches to science* (pp. 147–164). New York: Pergamon Press.

Bly, R. (1988). *A little book on the human shadow.* San Francisco: Harper.

Boesky, D. (1990). The psychoanalytic process and its components. *Psychoanalytic Quarterly, 59,* 550–584.

Bohart, A. C. (1995). The person-centered psychotherapies. In A. S. Gurman & S. B. Messer (Eds.), *Essential psychotherapies* (pp. 85–127). New York: Guilford Press.

Bohart, A. C., & Greenberg, L. S. (1997). *Empathy reconsidered.* Washington, DC: American Psychological Association.

Bohart, A. C., O'Hara, M., & Leitner, L. M. (1998). Empirically violated treatments: Disenfranchisement of humanistic and other psychotherapies. *Psychotherapy Research, 8*(2), 141–157.

Boldt, L. G. (1999). *Zen and the art of making a living.* New York: Penguin Putnam.

Bollas, C., & Sundelson, D. (1995). *The new informants: The betrayal of confidentiality in psychoanalysis and psychotherapy.* Northvale, NJ: Aronson.

Bornas, X., Fullana, M. A., Tortella-Feliu, M., Llabres, J., & de la Banda, G. G. (2001). Computer-assisted therapy in the treatment of flight phobia. *Cognitive and Behavioral Practice, 8,* 234–240.

Bottome, P. (1936). Limits to a human being—if any. *International Journal of Individual Psychology, 2*(4), 37–48.

Bottome, P. (1939). *Alfred Adler, apostle of freedom.* London: Faber and Faber.

Boudewyns, P. A., & Hyer, L. A. (1996). Eye movement desensitization and reprocessing as treatment for post-traumatic stress disorder. *Clinical Psychology and Psychotherapy, 3,* 185–195.

Bouton, M. E., Mineka, S., & Barlow, D. (2001). A modern learning theory perspective on the etiology of panic disorder. *Psychological Review, 108,* 4–32.

Bozarth, J. (1999). Person-Centered Therapy: A revolutionary paradigm. In T. Merry (Ed.), *Person-Centered Approach and Client-Centred Therapy essential readers series* (pp. 59–87). Ross-on-Wye: PCCS Books.

Bowers, K. S., & Meichenbaum, D. (1984). *The unconscious reconsidered.* New York: Wiley.

Bowlby, J. (1977). The making and breaking of affectional bonds: II. Some principles of psychotherapy. *British Journal of Psychiatry, 130,* 421–431.

Bowlby, J. (1978). Attachment theory and its therapeutic implications. *Adolescent Psychiatry, 6,* 5–33.

Bowlby, J. (1988). *A secure base: Parent-child attachment and healthy human development.* New York: Basic Books.

Bradway, K., & Detloff, W. (1996). Psychological type: A 32-year follow-up. *Journal of Analytical Psychology, 41,* 553–574.

Brannigan, M. C. (2000). *Striking a balance: A primer in traditional Asian values.* New York: Seven Bridges Press.

Breggin, P. R. (1991). *Toxic psychiatry: Why therapy, empathy and love must replace the drugs, electroshock and biochemical theories of the "new psychiatry."* New York: St. Martins.

Breggin, P. R. (2001). A dangerous assignment. In H. G. Rosenthal (Ed.), *Favorite counseling and therapy homework assignments* (pp. 58–59). Washington, DC: Accelerated Development.

Brenner, C. (1973). *An elementary textbook of psychoanalysis* (Rev. ed.). Madison, CT: International Universities Press.

Breuer, J., & Freud, S. (1957). *Studies on hysteria.* Oxford: Basic Books.

Brody, C. M. (Ed.). (1984). *Women therapists working with women: New theory and process of feminist therapy.* New York: Springer.

Broverman, I. K., Broverman, D. M., Clarkson, F. E., Rosenkrantz, P. S., & Vogel, S. R. (1970). Sex-role stereotypes and clinical judgement of mental health. *Journal of Consulting and Clinical Psychology, 34,* 1–7.

Brown, L. S. (1994). *Feminist therapy* [Videotape]. Washington, DC: American Psychological Association.

Brown, L. S., & Brodsky, A. M. (1992). The future of feminist therapy. *Psychotherapy, 29,* 51–57.

Browne, E. G. (1921). *Arabian medicine.* New York: Macmillan.

Bruch, H. (1981). Teaching and learning of psychotherapy. *Canadian Journal of Psychiatry, 26,* 86–92.

Bruns, C. M., & Trimble, C. (2001). Rising tide: Taking our place as young feminist psychologists. *Women and Therapy special issue: The next generation: Third wave feminist psychotherapy, 23*(2), 19–36.

Buber, M. (1970). *I and thou.* New York: Scribner.

Buie, D. H. (1981). Empathy: Its nature and limitations. *Journal of the American Psychoanalytic Association, 29,* 281–307.

Burke, J. F. (1989). *Contemporary approaches to psychotherapy and counseling: The self-regulation model.* Pacific Grove, CA: Brooks/Cole.

Burns, D. (1989). *The feeling good handbook.* New York: Morrow.

Bush, J. W. (2002). *Epictetus, the fundamentals.* Retrieved October 28, 2002, from cognitivetherapy.com/epictetus.html

Cameron, J., & Pierce, D. (1994). Reinforcement, reward, and intrinsic motivation: A meta-analysis. *Review of Educational Research, 64,* 363–423.

Campbell, J. (Ed.). (1971). *The portable Jung.* New York: Viking Press.

Carkuff, R. R. (1987). *The art of helping* (6th ed.). Amherst, MA: Human Resource Development Press.

Carli, L. L., LaFleur, S. J., & Loeber, C. C. (1995). Nonverbal behavior, gender and influence. *Journal of Personality and Social Psychology, 68,* 1030–1041.

Carlson, J., & Kjos, D. (2000a). *Narrative therapy with Stephen Madigan* [Videotape]. Boston: Allyn & Bacon.

Carlson, J., & Kjos, D. (2000b). *Person centered therapy with Dr. Natalie Rogers* [Videotape]. Boston: Allyn & Bacon.

Carton, J. S., & Nowicki, S. J. (1998). Should behavior therapists stop using reinforcement? A reexamination of the undermining effect of reinforcement on intrinsic motivation. *Behavior Therapy, 29,* 65–86.

Chambless, D. L. (2002). Identification of empirically supported counseling psychology interventions: Commentary. *Counseling Psychologist, 30*(2), 302–308.

Chambless, D. L., Baker, M. J., Baucom, D. H., Beutler, L. E., Calhoun, K. S., Crits-Christoph, P., Daiuto, A., DeRubeis, R., Detweiler, J., Haaga, D. A. F., Bennett-Johnson, S., McCurry, S., Mueser, K. T., Pope, K. S., Sanderson, W. C., Shoham, V., Stickle, T., Williams, D. A., & Woody, S. R. (1998). Update on empirically validated therapies: II. *Clinical Psychologist, 51,* 3–16.

Chambless, D. L., Caputo, G., Bright, P., & Gallagher, R. (1984). Assessment of fear in agoraphobia: The Body Sensations Questionnaire and the Agoraphobia Cognitions Questionnaire. *Journal of Consulting and Clinical Psychology, 52,* 1090–1097.

Chambless, D. L., Caputo, G., Gracely, S., Jasin, E., & Williams, C. (1985). Assessment of fear in agoraphobics: The Mobility Inventory for Agoraphobia. *Behaviour Research and Therapy, 23,* 35–44.

Chambless, D. L., & Williams, K. E. (1995). A preliminary study of the effects of exposure in vivo for African Americans with agoraphobia. *Behavior Therapy, 26,* 501–515.

Chandler, R., Worell, J., Johnson, D., Blount, A., & Lusk, M. (1999). *Measuring long-term outcomes of feminist counseling and psychotherapy.* Paper presented at the Annual Convention of the American Psychological Association, Boston, MA.

Cheong, E. S. (2001). A theoretical study on the application of choice theory and reality therapy in Korea. *International Journal of Reality Therapy, 20*(2), 8–11.

Chesler, P. (1972). *Women and madness.* New York: Doubleday.

Chodorow, N. J. (1978). *The reproduction of mothering.* Berkeley: University of California Press.

Christopher, J. C. (1996). Counseling's inescapable moral visions. *Journal of Counseling and Development, 75,* 17–25.

Christopher, J. C. (1999). Situating psychological well-being: Exploring the cultural roots of its theory and research. *Journal of Counseling and Development, 77,* 141–152.

Clark, D. A., Beck, A. T., & Alford, B. A. (1999). *Scientific foundation of cognitive theory and therapy of depression.* New York: Wiley.

Clement, P. W. (1994). Quantitative evaluation of 26 years of private practice. *Professional Psychology: Research and Practice, 25,* 173–176.

Coale, H. W. (1992). The constructivist emphasis on language: A critical conversation. *Journal of Strategic and Systemic Therapies, 11*(1), 12–26.

Constantine, M. G. (2001). The relationship between general counseling self-efficacy and self-perceived multicultural counseling competence in supervisees. *Clinical Supervisor, 20,* 81–90.

Corey, G. (2001). *Theory and practice of counseling and psychotherapy.* Belmont, CA: Brooks/Cole.

Corey, G., Corey, M. S., & Callanan, P. (2003). *Issues and ethics in the helping professions* (6th ed.). Belmont, CA: Brooks/Cole.

Cormier, L. S., & Hackney, H. (1987). *The professional counselor: A process guide to helping.* Englewood Cliffs, NJ: Prentice Hall.

Cormier, L. S., & Nurius, P. (2003). *Interviewing strategies for helpers* (5th ed.). Monterey, CA: Brooks/Cole.

Corsini, R. (1998). Turning the tables on the client: Making the client the counselor. In H. G. Rosenthal (Ed.), *Favorite counseling techniques: 51 therapists share their most creative strategies* (pp. 54–57). Washington, DC: Accelerated Development.

Corsini, R., & Wedding, D. (Eds.). (2000). *Current psychotherapies* (6th ed.). Itasca, IL: Peacock.

Cosgrove, L. (2002). Resisting essentialism in feminist therapy theory: Some epistemological considerations. *Women and Therapy, 25*(1), 89–112.

Craske, M. G. (1999). *Anxiety disorders: Psychological approaches to theory and treatment.* Boulder, CO: Westview Press.

Croll, M. (1992). The individualist roots of reality therapy: A textual analysis of Emerson's "self-reliance" and Glasser's reality therapy. *Journal of Reality Therapy, 11,* 22–26.

Cuellar, I., & Paniagua, F. A. (Eds.). (2000). *Handbook of multicultural mental health: Assessment and treatment of diverse populations.* New York: Academic Press.

Daldrup, R. J., Beutler, L. E., Engle, D., & Greenberg, L. S. (1988). *Focused expressive psychotherapy: Freeing the overcontrolled patient.* New York: Guilford Press.

Dana, R. H. (1996). Culturally competent assessment practice in the United States. *Journal of Personality Assessment, 66,* 472–487.

Das, A. K. (1995). Rethinking multicultural counseling: Implications for counselor education. *Journal of Counseling and Development, 74*(1), 45–52.

Davidson, F. (1995). *Old age I: A conversation with Joan Erikson* [Videotape]. San Luis Obispo, CA: Davidson Films.

Davidson, P. R., & Parker, K. C. (2001). Eye Movement Desensitization and Reprocessing (EMDR): A meta-analysis. *Journal of Consulting and Clinical Psychology, 69,* 305–316.

Davis, M., McKay, M., & Eshelman, E. R. (2000). *The relaxation and stress reduction workbook.* Oakland, CA: New Harbinger.

Dawes, R. M. (1994). *House of cards: Psychology and psychotherapy built on myth.* New York: Free Press.

DeCarvalho, R. J. (1996). Rollo R. May (1909–1994): A biographical sketch. *Journal of Humanistic Psychology, 36*(2), 8–16.

Deci, E. L. (1971). Effects of externally mediated rewards on intrinsic motivation. *Journal of Personality and Social Psychology, 18,* 105–115.

DeCola, J. P., & Craske, M. G. (2002). Panic and agoraphobia. In M. Hersen (Ed.), *Clinical behavior therapy: Adults and children* (pp. 52–74). New York: Wiley.

DeJong, P., & Berg, I. K. (2002). *Interviewing for solutions* (2nd ed.). Belmont, CA: Brooks/Cole.

DeJong, P., & Hopwood, L. E. (1996). Outcome research on treatment conducted at the Brief Family Therapy Center, 1992–1993. In S. D. Miller, M. A. Hubble, & B. L. Duncan (Eds.), *Handbook of solution-focused brief therapy.* San Francisco: Jossey-Bass.

de Shazer, S. (1984). The death of resistance. *Family Process, 23,* 79–93.

de Shazer, S. (1985). *Keys to solution in brief therapy.* New York: Norton.

de Shazer, S. (1988). *Clues: Investigating solutions in brief therapy.* New York: Norton.

de Shazer, S. (1991). *Putting differences to work.* New York: Norton.

de Shazer, S. (1993). Creative misunderstanding: There is no escape from language. In S. G. Gilligan & R. Price (Eds.), *Therapeutic conversations* (pp. 81–90). New York: Norton.

de Shazer, S. (1994). *Words were originally magic.* New York: Norton.

de Shazer, S., & Molnar, A. (1984). Four useful interventions in brief family therapy. *Journal of Marital and Family Therapy, 10*(3), 297–304.

Dewey, J. (1920). *Reconstruction in philosophy.* Boston: Beacon.

DiMascio, A., Weissman, M. M., Prusoff, B. A., Neu, C., Zwilling, M., & Klerman, G. L. (1979). Differential symptom reduction by drugs and psychotherapy in acute depression. *Archives of General Psychiatry, 36,* 1450–1456.

Dimeff, L., Rizvi, S. L., Brown, M., & Linehan, M. M. (2000). Dialectical behavior therapy for substance abuse: A pilot application to methamphetamine-dependent women with borderline personality disorder. *Cognitive and Behavioral Practice, 7*(4), 457–468.

Dinkmeyer, D. C., Dinkmeyer, D. C., Jr., & Sperry, L. (1987). *Adlerian counseling and psychotherapy* (2nd ed.). Columbus, OH: Merrill.

Dinkmeyer, D. C., & Eckstein, D. (1996). *Leadership by encouragement.* Boca Raton, FL: CRC Press.

Dodge, K. A. (1980). Social cognition and children's aggressive behavior. *Child Development, 51,* 162–170.

Dodge, K. A., & Frame, C. L. (1982). Social cognitive biases and deficits in aggressive boys. *Child Development, 53,* 620–635.

Dodge, K. A., & Somberg, D. R. (1987). Hostile attributional biases among aggressive boys are exacerbated under conditions of threat to the self. *Child Development, 58,* 213–224.

Dohrenwend, B. P., Shrout, P. E., Egri, G., & S., M. F. (1980). Nonspecific psychological distress and other dimensions of psychopathology: Measures for use in the general population. *Archives of General Psychiatry, 37,* 1229–1236.

Dollard, J., & Miller, N. E. (1950). *Personality and psychotherapy: An analysis in terms of learning, thinking, and culture.* New York: McGraw-Hill.

Donohue, W. A. (1990). *The new freedom: Individualism and collectivism in the social lives of Americans.* New Brunswick, NJ: Transaction.

Douglas, B., Parry, P., Marton, P., & Garson, C. (1976). Assessment of a cognitive training program for hyperactive children. *Journal of Abnormal Child Psychology, 4,* 389–410.

Dreger, A. D. (1997). *Hermophrodites and the medical invention of sex.* Boston: Harvard University Press.

Dreikurs, R. (1948). *The challenge of parenthood.* New York: Hawthorne.

Dreikurs, R. (1950). *Fundamentals of Adlerian psychology.* New York: Greenberg.

Dreikurs, R. (1969). *Psychodynamics, psychotherapy, and counseling.* Chicago: Alfred Adler Institute.

Dreikurs, R., & Mosak, H. H. (1966). The tasks of life: I. Adler's three tasks. *Individual Psychology, 4,* 18–22.

Dreikurs, R., & Mosak, H. H. (1967). The tasks of life: II. The fourth life task. *Individual Psychology, 4,* 51–55.

Dryden, W. (1989). Albert Ellis: An efficient and passionate life. *Journal of Counseling and Development, 67,* 539–546.

Duan, C., Rose, T. B., & Kraatz, R. A. (2002). Empathy. In G. S. Tryon (Ed.), *Counseling based on process research: Applying what we know* (pp. 197–231). Boston: Allyn & Bacon.

Dubelle, S. (1997, September). Part two: Excerpts from an interview with Heinz Ansbacher, Ph.D. *Quarterly: Publication of the Adlerian Psychology Association of British Columbia,* 5–7.

Duncan, B. L., Hubble, M. A., Miller, S. D., & Coleman, S. T. (1998). Escaping the lost world of impossibility. In M. F. Hoyt (Ed.), *The handbook of constructive therapies* (pp. 293–313). San Francisco: Jossey-Bass.

Duran, E., & Duran, B. (1995). *Native American postcolonial psychology*. Albany: State University of New York Press.

Dworkin, S. H., & Gutierrez, F. J. (1992). *Counseling gay men and lesbians: Journey to the end of the rainbow*. Alexandria, VA: American Counseling Association.

Earley, P. C., & Gibson, C. B. (1998). Taking stock in our progress on individualism-collectivism: 100 years of solidarity and community. *Journal of Management, 24,* 265–304.

Efran, J. S., & Fauber, R. L. (1995). Radical constructivism: Questions and answers. In R. A. Neimeyer & M. Mahoney (Eds.), *Constructivism in psychotherapy* (pp. 275–304). Washington, DC: American Psychological Association.

Egan, G. (2002). *The skilled helper* (7th ed.). Pacific Grove, CA: Brooks/Cole.

Elkin, I. E., Shea, T., Watkins, J. T., Imber, S. D., Stotsky, S. M., Collins, J. F., Glass, D. R., Pilkonis, P. A., Leber, W. R., Docherty, J. P., Fiester, S. J., & Parloff, M. B. (1989). National Institute of Mental Health Treatment of Depression Collaborative Research Program: General effectiveness of treatment. *Archives of General Psychiatry, 46,* 974–982.

Ellenberger, H. F. (1970). *The discovery of the unconscious: The history and evolution of dynamic psychiatry*. New York: Basic Books.

Elliott, D. (1986). A conceptual analysis of codes of ethics. *Journal of Mass Media Ethics, 1,* 12–20.

Elliot, R., Greenberg, L. S., & Lietaer, G. (2002). Research on experiential psychotherapies. In M. Lambert (Ed.), *Handbook of psychotherapy and behavior change* (5th ed.). New York: Wiley.

Ellis, A. (1962). *Reason and emotion in psychotherapy*. New York: Stuart.

Ellis, A. (1970). Tribute to Alfred Adler. *Journal of Individual Psychology, 26,* 11–12.

Ellis, A. (1987). The evolution of rational-emotive therapy (RET) and cognitive behavior therapy (CBT). In J. K. Zeig (Ed.), *The evolution of psychotherapy* (pp. 107–132). New York: Brunner/Mazel.

Ellis, A. (1990). Is rational-emotive therapy (RET) "rationalist" or "constructivist"? In A. Ellis & W. Dryden (Eds.), *The essential Albert Ellis*. New York: Springer.

Ellis, A. (1992). Discussion by Albert Ellis, Ph.D. In J. K. Zeig (Ed.), *The evolution of psychotherapy: The second conference* (pp. 122–127). New York: Brunner/Mazel.

Ellis, A. (1996). How I learned to help clients feel better and get better. *Psychotherapy, 33,* 149–151.

Ellis, A. (1998). How rational emotive behavior therapy belongs in the constructivist camp. In M. F. Hoyt (Ed.), *The handbook of constructive therapies* (pp. 83–99). San Francisco: Jossey-Bass.

Ellis, A. (1999a). *How to make yourself happy and remarkably less disturbable*. San Luis Obispo, CA: Impact Publishers.

Ellis, A. (1999b). Vigorous disputing of irrational beliefs in rational-emotive behavior therapy (REBT). In H. G. Rosenthal (Ed.), *Favorite counseling and therapy techniques* (pp. 76–77). Washington, DC: Accelerated Development.

Ellis, A., & Dryden, W. (1997). *The practice of rational-emotive therapy* (Rev. ed.). New York: Springer.

Ellis, A., & Grieger, R. (1977). *Handbook of rational-emotive therapy.* New York: Springer.

Emmelkamp, P. M. G. (1994). Behavior therapy with adults. In A. E. Bergin & S. L. Garfield (Eds.), *Handbook of psychotherapy and behavior change* (pp. 379–427). New York: Wiley.

Emmelkamp, P. M. G., Bruynzeel, M., Drost, L., & van der Mast, C. A. P. (2001). Virtual reality treatment in acrophobia: A comparison with exposure in vivo. *Cyber Psychology and Behavior, 4,* 335–339.

Emmelkamp, P. M. G., Krijn, M., Hulsbosch, L., de Vries, S., Schuemie, M. J., & van der Mast, C. A. P. (2001). Virtual reality treatment versus exposure in vivo: A comparative evaluation in acrophobia. *Behaviour Research and Therapy, 40,* 509–516.

Epstein, M. (1998). *Going to pieces without falling apart.* New York: Broadway Books.

Epston, D. (1994). Extending the conversation. *Family Networker, 18*(6), 30–37, 62–63.

Epston, D., & White, M. (1995). Termination as a rite of passage: Questioning strategies for a therapy of inclusion. In R. A. Neimeyer & M. Mahoney (Eds.), *Constructivism in psychotherapy* (pp. 339–356). Washington, DC: American Psychological Association.

Erickson, M. H. (1954). Special techniques of brief hypnotherapy. *Journal of Clinical and Experimental Hypnosis, 2,* 109–129.

Erickson, M. H. (1964). The confusion technique in hypnosis. *American Journal of Clinical Hypnosis, 6,* 183–207.

Erickson, M. H., Rossi, E. L., & Rossi, S. (1976). *Hypnotic realities.* New York: Irvington.

Erikson, E. H. (1963). *Childhood and society* (2nd ed.). New York: Norton.

Estes, W. (1944). An experimental study of punishment. *Psychological Monographs, 57*(Whole No. 263).

Eysenck, H. J. (1952). The effects of psychotherapy: An evaluation. *Journal of Consulting Psychology, 16,* 319–324.

Eysenck, H. J. (1959). Learning theory and behaviour therapy. *Journal of Mental Science, 105,* 61–75.

Eysenck, H. J. (Ed.). (1960). *Behaviour therapy and the neuroses.* New York: Pergamon.

Eysenck, H. J. (Ed.). (1964). *Experiments in behavior therapy.* New York: Pergamon.

Eysenck, H. J. (1970). A mish-mash of theories. *International Journal of Psychiatry, 9,* 140–146.

Fairbairn, W. R. D. (1952). *Psychoanalytic studies of the personality.* London: Tavistock.

Fairburn, C. G., Jones, R., Peveler, R. C., Hope, R. A., & O'Conner, M. (1993). Psychotherapy and bulimia nervosa: Longer-term effects of interpersonal psychotherapy, behavior therapy, and cognitive behavior therapy. *Archives of General Psychiatry, 50,* 419–428.

Fallon, P., Katzman, M. A., & Wooley, S. C. (Eds.). (1994). *Feminist perspectives on eating disorders.* New York: Guilford Press.

Faludi, S. (1991). *Backlash: The undeclared war against American women.* New York: Craun.

Faraday, A. (1981). *Dream power.* New York: Berkley Books.

Fenichel, O. (1945). *The psychoanalytic theory of neurosis.* New York: Norton.

Ferenczi, S. (1920). The further development of an active therapy in psychoanalysis. In J. Rickman (Ed.), *Further contributions to the theory and techniques of psychoanalysis.* London: Hogarth Press.

Ferenczi, S. (1950). *The selected papers of Sandor Ferenczi.* New York: Basic Books.

Fernandez, R. (2001). *Imagining literacy.* Austin: University of Texas Press.

Feske, U., & Goldstein, A. (1995, November). *Does rapid eye movement induce relaxation?* Paper presented at the 29th annual Convention of the Association for the Advancement of Behavior Therapy, Washington, DC.

Figley, C. (1997, December). *The active ingredients of the Power Therapies.* Paper presented at the The Power Therapies: A conference for the integrative and innovative use of EMDR, TFT, EFT, advanced NLP, and TIR, Lakewood, CO.

First, M. B., Spitzer, R. L., Gibbon, M., & Williams, J. B. W. (1997). *User's guide for the Structured Clinical Interview for DSM-IV Axis I Disorders: Clinician version.* Washington, DC: American Psychiatric Press.

Fishman, D. B., & Franks, C. M. (1997). The conceptual evolution of behavior therapy. In P. L. Wachtel & S. B. Messer (Eds.), *Theories of psychotherapy: Origins and evolution* (pp. 131–180). Washington, DC: American Psychological Association.

Foa, E. B., & Kozak, M. J. (1986). Emotional processing of fear: Exposure to corrective information. *Psychological Bulletin, 99,* 20–35.

Foa, E. B., Rothbaum, B. O., & Furr, J. M. (2003). Augmenting exposure therapy with other CBT procedures. *Psychiatric Annals, 33*(1), 47–53.

Foley, K. (1992). *Essays on Southeast Asian performing arts: Local manifestations and cross-cultural implications.* Los Angeles: UC Regents.

Fonagy, P. (1999, April 16). *The process of change and the change of processes: What can change in a "good analysis."* Paper presented at the spring meeting of Division 39 of the American Psychological Association, New York.

Fonagy, P., Kachele, H., Krause, R., Jones, E., Perron, R., & Lopez, L. (1999). *An open door review of outcome studies in psychoanalysis.* London: International Psychoanalytic Association.

Fonagy, P., & Target, M. (1996). Predictors of outcomes in child psychoanalysis: A retrospective study of 763 cases at the Anna Freud Centre. *Journal of the American Psychoanalytic Association, 44,* 27–77.

Forsyth, J. P., Lejuez, C. W., & Finlay, C. (2000). Anxiogenic effects of repeated administrations of 20% CO_2-enriched air: Stability within sessions and habituation across time. *Journal of Behavior Therapy and Experimental Psychiatry, 31,* 103–121.

Foucault, M. (1965). *Madness and civilization: A history of insanity in the age of reason.* New York: Random House.

Frank, J. D. (1961). *Persuasion and healing.* Baltimore: Johns Hopkins University Press.

Frank, J. D. (1973). *Persuasion and healing: A comparative study of psychotherapy* (Rev. ed.). Baltimore: Johns Hopkins University Press.

Frank, J. D. (1974). Psychotherapy: The restoration of morale. *American Journal of Psychiatry, 131,* 271–274.

Frank, J. D. (1985). Therapeutic components shared by all psychotherapies. In M. Mahoney & A. Freeman (Eds.), *Cognition and psychotherapy* (pp. 39–80). New York: Plenum.

Frank, J. D., & Frank, J. B. (1991). *Persuasion and healing* (3rd ed.). Baltimore: Johns Hopkins University Press.

Frankl, V. (1967). *Psychotherapy and existentialism: Selected papers on logotherapy.* New York: Clarion.

Franklin, M. E., & Foa, E. (1998). Cognitive-behavioral treatment of obsessive compulsive disorder. In P. E. Nathan & J. M. Gorman (Eds.), *A guide to treatments that work* (pp. 339–357). Oxford, England: Oxford University Press.

Franks, C. M., & Barbrack, C. R. (1983). Behavior therapy with adults: An integrative perspective. In M. Hersen, A. E. Kazdin, & A. S. Bellack (Eds.), *The clinical psychology handbook* (pp. 507–523). New York: Pergamon.

French, T. M. (1958). *The integrations of behavior.* (Vol. 3). Chicago: University of Chicago Press.

Freud, S. (1896, April 21). *The aetiology of hysteria.* Paper presented at the the Society for Psychiatry and Neurology, Vienna.

Freud, S. (1923). *Group psychology and the analysis of the ego.* London: Hogarth Press.

Freud, S. (1948). Some psychical consequences of the anatomical distinction between the sexes (J. Strachey, Trans.). In J. Strachey (Ed.), *The standard edition of the complete works of Sigmund Freud* (Vol. 5, pp. 186–197). London: Hogarth.

Freud, S. (1955). Analysis of a phobia in a five-year-old boy. In J. Strachey (Ed.), *Standard edition of the complete psychological works of Sigmund Freud.* (Vol. 10, pp. 3–149). London: Hogarth Press.

Freud, S. (1957). The future prospects of psycho-analytic therapy (J. Strachey, Trans.). In J. Strachey (Ed.), *The standard edition of the complete works of Sigmund Freud* (Vol. 11, pp. 139–152.). London: Hogarth Press.

Freud, S. (1958). On the beginning of treatment: Further recommendations on the technique of psychoanalysis (J. Strachey, Trans.). In J. Strachey (Ed.), *Standard edition of the complete psychological works of Sigmund Freud* (Vol. 12, pp. 122–144). London: Hogarth Press.

Freud, S. (1961). Introductory lectures on psycho-analysis (Parts 1 & 2) (J. Strachey, Trans.). In J. Strachey (Ed.), *The standard edition of the complete psychological works of Sigmund Freud* (Vol. 15, pp. 15–239). London: Hogarth Press.

Freud, S. (1963). *Introductory lectures on psycho-analysis* (Part 3) (J. Strachey, Trans.). Standard edition of the complete psychological works of Sigmund Freud (Vol. 16, pp. 243–476). London: Hogarth Press.

Freud, S. (1964). *New introductory lectures on psychoanalysis* (Vol. 22, J. Strachey, Trans.). London: Hogarth Press.

Freud, S. (1966). The dynamics of transference (J. Strachey, Trans.). In J. Strachey (Ed.), *Standard edition of the complete psychological works of Sigmund Freud* (Vol. 12, pp. 97–108). London: Hogarth Press.

Friedman, S. (1996). Couples therapy: Changing conversations. In H. Rosen & K. T. Kuehlwein (Eds.), *Constructing realities: Meaning-making perspectives for psychotherapists* (pp. 413–453). San Francisco: Jossey-Bass.

Fruzzetti, A. E., & Levensky, E. R. (2000). Dialectical behavior therapy for domestic violence: Rationale and procedures. *Cognitive and Behavioral Practice, 7,* 435–447.

Funkerburk, J. R., & Fukuyama, M. A. (2001). Feminism, multiculturalism, and spirituality: Convergent and divergent forces in psychotherapy. *Women and Therapy, 24*(3/4), 1–18.

Gallagher-Thompson, D., & Steffen, A. M. (1994). Comparative effects of cognitive-behavioral and brief dynamic therapy for depressed family caregivers. *Journal of Consulting and Clinical Psychology, 62,* 543–549.

Garcia-Palacios, A., Hoffman, H., Carlin, A., Furness, T. A. I., & Botella, C. (2002). Virtual reality in the treatment of spider phobia: A controlled study. *Behaviour Research and Therapy, 40,* 983–993.

Garfield, S. L. (1998). Some comments on empirically supported treatments. *Journal of Consulting and Clinical Psychology, 66*(1), 121–125.

Garfield, S. L., & Kurtz, R. (1975). Clinical psychologists: A survey of selected attitudes and views. *Clinical Psychologist, 28,* 4–7.

Garfield, S. L., & Kurtz, R. (1977). A study of eclectic views. *Journal of Consulting and Clinical Psychology, 45,* 78–83.

Garrett, M. T., & Pichette, E. F. (2000). Red as an apple: Native American acculturation and counseling with or without reservation. *Journal of Counseling and Development, 78,* 3–13.

Gaston, L. (1990). The concept of the alliance and its role in psychotherapy: Theoretical and empirical considerations. *Psychotherapy, 27,* 143–153.

Gedo, J. E. (1979). *Beyond interpretation.* New York: International Universities Press.

Geertz, C. (1973). *The interpretation of cultures.* New York: Basic Books.

Gelso, C. J., & Hayes, J. A. (1998). *The psychotherapy relationship: Theory, research, and practice.* New York: Wiley.

Gendlin, E. T. (1981). *Focusing* (2nd ed.). New York: Bantam.

Gendlin, E. T. (1996). *Focusing-oriented psychotherapy: A manual of the experiential method.* New York: Guilford Press.

Gershoff, E. T. (2002). Corporal punishment by parents and associated child behaviors and experiences: A meta-analytic and theoretical review. *Psychological Bulletin, 128*(4), 539–579.

Ghent, E. (1989). Credo: The dialectics of one-person and two-person psychologies. *Contemporary Psychoanalysis, 25,* 169–209.

Gilbert, L. A., & Rader, J. (2001). Current perspectives on women's adult roles: Work, family, and life. In R. K. Unger (Ed.), *Handbook of the psychology of women and gender* (pp. 156–169). New York: Wiley.

Gilbert, L. A., & Scher, M. (1999). *Gender and sex in counseling and psychotherapy.* Boston: Allyn & Bacon.

Gill, M. M. (1994). *Psychoanalysis in transition: A personal view.* Hillsdale, NJ: Analytic Press.

Glasser, W. (1965). *Reality therapy: A new approach to psychiatry.* New York: Harper and Row.

Glasser, W. (1998). *Choice theory: A new psychology of personal freedom.* New York: HarperCollins.

Glasser, W. (2000). *Reality therapy in action.* New York: HarperCollins.

Glasser, W. (2002). *Unhappy teenagers: A way for parents and teachers to reach them.* New York: HarperCollins.

Glover, E. (1959). Critical notice. *British Journal of Medical Psychology, 32,* 68–74.

Glynn, S. M. (1990). Token economy approaches for psychiatric patients: Progress and pitfalls over 25 years. *Behavior Modification Special Issue: Recent developments in the behavioral treatment of chronic psychiatric illness, 14*(4), 383–407.

Goldenberg, I., & Goldenberg, H. (2000). *Family therapy: An overview* (5th ed.). Belmont, CA: Brooks/Cole.

Goldfried, M. R. (1980). Toward the delineation of therapeutic change principles. *American Psychologist, 35,* 991–999.

Goldfried, M. R. (1982). *Converging themes in psychotherapy.* New York: Springer.

Goldfried, M. R., & Davison, G. C. (1976). *Clinical behavior therapy.* New York: Holt, Rinehart and Winston.

Goldfried, M. R., & Davison, G. C. (1994). *Clinical behavior therapy* (2nd ed.). Oxford, England: Wiley.

Goldman, R., & Greenberg, L. S. (1997). Case formulation in process-experiential therapy. In T. D. Eells (Ed.), *Handbook of psychotherapy case formulation* (pp. 402–429). New York: Guilford Press.

Goldstein, E. G. (1994). Self-disclosure in treatment: What therapists do and don't talk about. *Clinical Social Work Journal, 22,* 417–433.

Goodman, E. (2003, January 12). Bush takes sides with the powerful. *Missoulian,* p. 4.

Gordon, T. (1975). *Parent effectiveness training.* Pittsburgh, PA: Three Rivers Press.

Gottman, J. M., Jacobson, N. S., Rushe, R. H., Hortt, J. W., Babcock, J., & La Taillade, J. J. (1995). The relationship between heart rate reactivity, emotionally aggressive behavior, and general violence in batterers. *Journal of Family Psychology, 9,* 227–248.

Gottman, J. M., & Leiblum, S. R. (1974). *How to do psychotherapy and how to evaluate it.* New York: Holt, Rinehart and Winston.

Gould, W. B. (1993). *Viktor E. Frankl: Life with meaning.* Pacific Grove, CA: Brooks/Cole.

Grawe, K., Donati, R., & Bernauer, F. (1998). *Psychotherapy in transition.* Seattle: Hogrefe & Huber.

Gray, G. V., & Lambert, M. J. (2001). Feedback: A key to improving therapy outcomes. *Behavioral Healthcare Tomorrow, 10,* 25–45.

Greenberg, G. (1977). The family interactional perspective: A study and examination of the work of Don D. Jackson. *Family Process, 16,* 385–412.

Greenberg, L. S. (2002a). *Emotion-focused therapy: Coaching clients to work through their feelings.* Washington, DC: American Psychological Association.

Greenberg, L. S. (2002b). Integrating an emotion-focused approach to treatment into psychotherapy integration. *Journal of Psychotherapy Integration, 12*(2), 154–189.

Greenberg, L. S., Elliott, R., & Lietaer, G. (1994). Research on experiential psychotherapy. In A. E. Bergin & S. L. Garfield (Eds.), *Handbook of psychotherapy and behavior change* (4th ed., pp. 509–539). New York: Wiley.

Greenberg, L. S., & Foerster, F. S. (1996). Task analysis exemplified: The process of resolving unfinished business. *Journal of Consulting and Clinical Psychology, 64*(3), 439–446.

Greenberg, L. S., & Malcolm, W. (2002). Resolving unfinished business: Relating process to outcome. *Journal of Consulting and Clinical Psychology, 70*(2), 406–416.

Greenberg, L. S., Rice, L. N., & Elliot, R. (1993). *Facilitating emotional change: The moment-by-moment process.* New York: Guilford Press.

Greenberger, D., & Padesky, C. A. (1995). *Mind over mood: Change how you feel by changing the way you think.* New York: Guilford Press.

Guerney, B. (1977). *Relationship enhancement therapy.* San Francisco: Jossey-Bass.

Guerney, L. (2001). Child-centered play therapy. *International Journal of Play Therapy, 10*(2), 13–31.

Guerney, L., & Guerney, B. (1989). Child relationship enhancement: Family therapy and parent education. *Person-Centered Review Special Issue: Person-centered approaches with families, 4*(3), 344–357.

Guilford, J. (1956). The structure of intellect. *Psychological Bulletin, 53,* 267–293.

Haley, J. (Ed.). (1967). *Advanced techniques of hypnosis and therapy: Selected papers of Milton H. Erickson, M.D.* New York: Grune & Stratton.

Haley, J. (1973). *Uncommon therapy: The psychiatric techniques of Milton H. Erickson.* New York: Norton.

Haley, J. (1976). *Problem solving therapy.* San Francisco: Jossey-Bass.

Haley, J. (1977). A quiz for young therapists. *Psychotherapy, 14*(2), 165–168.

Hall, C. S., & Lindzey, G. (1970). *Theories of personality* (2nd ed.). New York: Wiley.

Hall, G. C. N. (2001). Psychotherapy research with ethnic minorities: Empirical ethical, and conceptual issues. *Journal of Consulting and Clinical Psychology, 69,* 502–510.

Hamilton, J. W. (1995). Some comments on Kohut's "The two analyses of Mr. Z." *Psychoanalytic Psychology, 11,* 525–536.

Harbeck, J. (2001). The transcendent function of interculturalism. *Studies in the Literary Imagination, 34*(2), 13–27.

Harlow, H. K., Harlow, M. K., Dodsworth, R. O., & Arling, G. L. (1966). Maternal behavior of rhesus monkeys deprived of mothering and peer association in infancy. *Proceedings of the American Philosophical Society, 110,* 58–66.

Harlow, H. K., Harlow, M. K., & Suomi, S. J. (1971). From thought to therapy: Lessons from a private laboratory. *American Scientist, 659,* 538–549.

Hartmann, H. (1958). *Ego psychology and the problem of adaptation.* Madison, CT: International Universities Press.

Hayek, F. A. (1979). *Law, legislation, and liberty: The political order of a free people* (Vol. 3). Chicago: University of Chicago Press.

Hayes, S. C., Strosahl, K. D., & Wilson, K. G. (1999). *Acceptance and commitment therapy: An experiential approach to behavior change.* New York: Guilford Press.

Heard, H. L., & Linehan, M. (1994). Dialectical behavior therapy: An integrative approach to the treatment of borderline personality disorder. *Journal of Psychotherapy Integration, 4,* 55–82.

Helms, J. E. (1994). How multiculturalism obscures racial factors in the therapy process: Comment on Ridley et al. (1994), Sadowski et al. (1994), Ottavi et al. (1994), and Thompson et al. (1994). *Journal of Counseling Psychology, 41,* 162–165.

Hepburn, R. (1965). Questions about the meaning of life. *Religious Studies, 1,* 125–140.

Herring, R. D. (1996). Synergetic counseling and Native American Indian students. *Journal of Counseling and Development, 74,* 542–547.

Hersen, M. (2002). *Clinical behavior therapy: Adults and children.* New York: Wiley.

Hill, K. A. (1987). Meta-analysis of paradoxical interventions. *Psychotherapy, 24,* 266–270.

Ho, D. Y. F. (1998). Indigenous psychologies. *Journal of Cross-Cultural Psychology, 290*(1), 88–103.

Hoffman, B., & Meier, S. T. (2001). An individualized approach to managed mental health care in colleges and universities: A case study. *Journal of College Student Psychotherapy, 15,* 49–64.

Hoffman, E. (1994). *The drive for self: Alfred Adler and the founding of individual psychology.* Reading, MA: Addison-Wesley.

Hogan, R. (1975). Theoretical egocentrism and the problem of compliance. *American Psychologist, 30,* 533–540.

Horner, A. J. (1998). *Working with the core relationship problem in psychotherapy: A handbook for clinicians.* San Francisco: Jossey-Bass.

Horney, K. (1932). The dread of women: Observations on a specific difference in the dread felt by men and by women respectively for the opposite sex. *International Journal of Psycho-Analysis, 13,* 348–360.

Horney, K. (1942). *Self-analysis.* New York: Norton.

Horney, K. (1950). *Neurosis and human growth: The struggle toward self-realization.* New York: Norton.

Horney, K. (1967). *Feminine psychology.* New York: Norton.

Horowitz, M. J., Marmar, C., Krupnick, J., Wilner, N., Kaltreider, N., & Wallerstein, R. (1984). *Personality styles and brief psychotherapy.* New York: Basic Books.

Hoyt, M. F. (1994). On the importance of keeping it simple and taking the patient seriously: A conversation with Steve de Shazer and John Weakland. In M. F. Hoyt (Ed.), *Constructive therapies* (pp. 11–40). New York: Guilford Press.

Hoyt, M. F. (Ed.). (1998). *The handbook of constructive therapies: Innovative approaches from leading practitioners.* San Francisco: Jossey-Bass/Pfeiffer.

Hoyt, M. F. (2000). Cognitive-behavioural treatment of post-traumatic stress disorder from a narrative constructivist perspective: A conversation with Donald Meichenbaum. In M. Scott & S. Palmer (Eds.), *Trauma and post-traumatic stress disorder* (pp. 49–69). London: Cassell.

Hrdy, S. B. (1999). *Mother nature.* New York: Pantheon.

Hubble, M. A., Duncan, B. L., & Miller, S. D. (Eds.). (1999). *The heart and soul of change.* Washington, DC: American Psychological Association.

Hughes, D. (1998). *Building the bonds of attachment: Awakening love in deeply troubled children.* Northvale, NJ: Aronson.

Ivey, A. E., D'Andrea, M., Ivey, M. B., & Simek-Morgan, L. (2002). *Theories of counseling and psychotherapy: A multicultural perspective* (5th ed.). Boston: Allyn & Bacon.

Jacobson, E. (1924). The technic of progressive relaxation. *Journal of Nervous and Mental Disease, 60*(6), 568–578.

Jacobson, E. (1938). *Progressive relaxation.* Chicago: University of Chicago Press.

Jacobson, E. (1978). *You must relax* (5th ed.). New York: McGraw-Hill.

James, W. (1992). *William James, writings 1878–1899.* New York: Library of America.

Jenkins, A. H. (1997). The empathic context in psychotherapy with people of color. In A. C. Bohart & L. S. Greenberg (Eds.), *Empathy reconsidered: New directions in psychology* (pp. 321–342). Washington, DC: American Psychological Association.

Jones, E. E. (1961). The life and work of Sigmund Freud (L. Trilling & S. Marcus, Trans.). In L. Trilling & S. Marcus (Eds.) (Vol. Abridged). New York: Basic Books.

Jones, E. E. (2000). *Therapeutic action: A guide to psychoanalytic therapy.* Northvale, NJ: Aronson.

Jones, M. C. (1924). The elimination of children's fear. *Journal of Experimental Psychology, 8,* 382–390.

Jung, C. G. (1938). *Psychology and religion.* New Haven, CT: Yale University Press.

Jung, C. G. (1946). On the nature of the psyche. In H. Read, M. Fordham, & G. Adler (Eds.), *Collected works, Bollingen series XX* (Vol. 8, pp. 159–234). Princeton, NJ: Princeton University Press.

Jung, C. G. (1950). Concerning rebirth. In H. Read, M. Fordham, & G. Adler (Eds.), *Collected works, Bollingen series XX* (Vol. 9, Pt. 1, pp. 111–149). Princeton, NJ: Princeton University Press.

Jung, C. G. (1954a). The development of personality. In H. Read, M. Fordham, & G. Adler (Eds.), *Collected works, Bollingen series XX* (Vol. 17, pp. 160–165). New York: Pantheon.

Jung, C. G. (1954b). Marriage as a psychological relationship. In H. Read, M. Fordham, & G. Adler (Eds.), *Collected works, Bollingen series XX* (Vol. 17, pp. 189–201). Princeton, NJ: Princeton University Press.

Jung, C. G. (1965). *Memories, dreams, reflections.* New York: Vintage Books.

Jung, C. G. (1966a). The problem of the attitude-type. In H. Read, M. Fordham, & G. Adler (Eds.), *Collected works, Bollingen series XX* (Vol. 7, pp. 41–63). New York: Pantheon.

Jung, C. G. (1966b). The psychology of the transference. In H. Read, M. Fordham, & G. Adler (Eds.), *Collected works, Bollingen series XX* (Vol. 16, pp. 164–235). Princeton, NJ: Princeton University Press.

Kabat-Zinn, J. (1990). *Full catastrophe living: Using the wisdom of your body and mind to face stress, pain, and illness.* New York: Delta.

Kahler, E. (1989). *The tower and the abyss.* Princeton, NJ: Transaction.

Karasu, T. B. (1999). Spiritual psychotherapy. *American Journal of Psychotherapy, 53,* 143–162.

Kaschak, E. (1992). *Engendered lives.* New York: HarperCollins.

Kaufmann, Y. (1989). Analytical psychotherapy. In R. Corsini & D. Wedding (Eds.), *Current psychotherapies* (pp. 119–152). Itasca, IL: Peacock.

Kazdin, A. E. (1996). Problem solving and parent management in treating aggressive and antisocial behavior. In E. D. Hibbs & P. S. Jensen (Eds.), *Psychosocial treatments for child and adolescent disorders: Empirically based strategies for clinical practice* (pp. 377–408). Washington, DC: American Psychological Association.

Kazdin, A. E., Siegel, T., & Bass, D. (1992). Cognitive problem-solving skills training and parent management training in the treatment of antisocial behavior in children. *Journal of Consulting and Clinical Psychology, 60,* 733–747.

Keillor, G. (2002). *The Writer's Almanac.* Minneapolis: Minnesota Public Radio.

Kelleher, K. (1992). The afternoon of life: Jung's view of the tasks of the second half of life. *Perspectives in Psychiatric Care, 28*(2), 25–28.

Kelly, G. A. (1955). *The psychology of personal constructs.* New York: Norton.

Kelly, G. A. (1969). Ontological acceleration. In B. Maher (Ed.), *Clinical psychology and personality: The selected papers of George Kelly* (pp. 7–45). New York: Wiley.

Kendall, P. C. (Ed.). (2000). *Child and adolescent therapy: Cognitive-behavioral procedures* (2nd ed.). New York: Guilford Press.

Kim, K.-H. (2002). The effect of a reality therapy program on the responsibility for elementary school children in Korea. *International Journal of Reality Therapy, 22*(1), 30–33.

Kinzie, J. D. (1994). Countertransference in the treatment of Southeast Asian refugees. In J. P. Wilson & J. D. Lindy (Eds.), *Countertransference in the treatment of PTSD* (pp. 249–262). New York: Guilford Press.

Kirschenbaum, H., & Henderson, V. L. (Eds.). (1989). *Carl Rogers: Dialogues.* Boston: Houghton Mifflin.

Kitzinger, C. (2001). Sexualities. In R. K. Unger (Ed.), *Handbook of the psychology of women and gender* (pp. 272–285). New York: Wiley.

Kivlighan, D. M. J. (2002). Transference, interpretation, and insight: A research-practice model. In G. S. Tryon (Ed.), *Counseling based on process research: Applying what we know* (pp. 166–196). Boston: Allyn & Bacon.

Klerman, G. L., Weissman, M. M., Rounsaville, B. J., & Chevron, E. S. (1984). *Interpersonal psychotherapy of depression.* New York: Basic Books.

Klerman, G. L., Weissman, M. M., Rounsaville, B. J., & Chevron, E. S. (1995). Interpersonal psychotherapy for depression. *Journal of Psychotherapy Practice and Research, 4*(4), 342–351.

Knight, R. P. (1941). Evaluation of the results of psychoanalytic therapy. *American Journal of Psychiatry, 98,* 434–436.

Kohn, A. (1993). *Punished by rewards: The trouble with gold stars, incentive plans, A's, praise, and other bribes.* Boston: Houghton-Mifflin.

Kohut, H. H. (1959). Introspection, empathy, and psychoanalysis. *Journal of American Psycholanalysis Association, 7,* 459–483.

Kohut, H. H. (1971). *The analysis of self.* New York: International Universities Press.

Kohut, H. H. (1977). *Restoration of the self.* New York: International Universities Press.

Kohut, H. H. (1984). *How does analysis cure?* Chicago: University of Chicago Press.

Korchin, S. J. (1976). *Modern clinical psychology: Principles of intervention in the clinic and community.* Oxford: Basic Books.

Koss, M., & Shiang, J. (1994). Research on brief psychotherapy. In A. E. Bergin & S. L. Garfield (Eds.), *Handbook of psychotherapy and behavior change* (4th ed., pp. 664–700). New York: Wiley.

Kottler, J. A., & Brown, R. W. (1996). *Introduction to therapeutic counseling.* Pacific Grove, CA: Brooks/Cole.

Kovacs, M. (1992). *Childrens Depression Inventory.* Toronto, Ontario: Multi-Health Systems.

Krumboltz, J. D. (1965). Behavioral counseling: Rationale and research. *Personnel and Guidance Journal, 44,* 383–387.

Kumar, S. (2002). An introduction to Buddhism for the cognitive behavioral therapist. *Cognitive and Behavioral Practice, 9,* 40–43.

Kutchins, H., & Kirk, S. A. (1997). *Making us crazy.* New York: Free Press.

Lacan, J. (1988). *The seminar of Jacques Lacan, Book I* (J. Forrester, Trans.). Cambridge: Cambridge University Press.

LaFromboise, T. D., Trimble, J. E., & Mohatt, G. V. (1990). Counseling intervention and American Indian tradition: An integrative approach. *Counseling Psychologist, 18,* 628–654.

Lambert, M. J. (1992). Implications of outcome research for psychotherapy integration. In J. C. Norcross & M. R. Goldstein (Eds.), *Handbook of psychotherapy integration* (pp. 94–129). New York: Basic Books.

Lambert, M. J., & Bergin, A. E. (1994). The effectiveness of psychotherapy. In A. E. Bergin & S. L. Garfield (Eds.), *Handbook of psychotherapy and behavior change* (4th ed., pp. 143–189). New York: Wiley.

Lambert, M. J., Whipple, J. L., Smart, D. W., Vermeesch, D. A., Nielsen, S. L., & Hawkins, E. J. (2001). The effects of providing therapists with feedback on patient progress during psychotherapy: Are outcomes enhanced? *Psychotherapy Research, 11,* 49–68.

Lazarus, A. A. (1958). New methods in psychotherapy: A case study. *South African Medical Journal, 32,* 660–664.

Lazarus, A. A. (1967). In support of technical eclecticism. *Psychological Reports, 21,* 415–416.

Lazarus, A. A. (1971). *Behavior therapy and beyond.* New York: McGraw-Hill.

Lazarus, A. A. (1973a). *Clinical behavior therapy.* Oxford: Branna/Mazel.

Lazarus, A. A. (1973b). Multimodal behavior therapy: Treating the "BASIC ID." *Journal of Nervous and Mental Disease, 156*(6), 404–411.

Lazarus, A. A. (1989). *The practice of multimodal therapy: Systematic, comprehensive, and effective psychotherapy.* Baltimore: Johns Hopkins University Press.

Lazarus, A. A. (1991). A plague on Little Hans and Little Albert. *Psychotherapy: Theory, Research, Practice, Training, 28*(3), 444–447.

Lazarus, A. A. (1993). Tailoring the therapeutic relationship, or being an authentic chameleon. *Psychotherapy, 30,* 404–407.

Lazarus, A. A. (1997). *Brief but comprehensive psychotherapy: The multimodal way.* New York: Springer.

Lazarus, A. A. (2000). Multimodal replenishment. *Professional Psychology: Research and Practice, 31*(1), 93–94.

Lazarus, A. A., Beutler, L. E., & Norcross, J. C. (1992). The future of technical eclecticism. *Psychotherapy, 29,* 11–20.

Lazarus, A. A., & Lazarus, C. N. (1991). *Multimodal life history inventory.* Champaign, IL: Research Press.

Leber, P. (1991). Is there an alternative to the randomized controlled trial? *Psychopharmacology Bulletin, 27,* 3–8.

Levant, R. F., & Pollack, W. S. (1995). *A new psychology of men.* New York: Basic Books.

Levy, S. T. (1984). *Principles of interpretation.* New York: Aronson.

Lewis, R. W. B. (1991). *The Jameses: A family narrative.* New York: Farrar, Straus and Giroux.

Linehan, M. M. (1993). *Cognitive behavioral therapy of borderline personality disorder.* New York: Guilford Press.

Linehan, M. M. (2000). Commentary on innovations in dialectal behavior therapy. *Cognitive and Behavioral Practice, 7*(4), 478–481.

Linehan, M. M., & Schmidt, H. I. (1995). The dialectics of effective treatment of borderline personality disorder. In W. O'Donohue & L. Krasner (Eds.), *Theories of behavior therapy* (pp. 553–584). Washington, DC: American Psychological Association.

Lippard, L. (1990). *Mixed blessings: New art in a multicultural America.* New York: Pantheon.

Lips, H. (1999). *A new psychology of women: Gender, culture, and ethnicity.* Mountain View, CA: Mayfield.

Locke, E. A., & Latham, G. P. (1990). *A theory of goal setting and task performance.* Englewood Cliffs, NJ: Prentice Hall.

Locke, E. A., & Latham, G. P. (2002). Building a practically useful theory of goal setting and task motivation: A 35-year odyssey. *American Psychologist, 57,* 705–717.

Logsdon-Conradsen, S. (2002). Using mindfulness meditation to promote holistic health in individuals with HIV/AIDS. *Cognitive and Behavioral Practice, 9,* 67–72.

Lohr, J. M., Kleinknecht, R. A., Tolin, D. F., & Barrett, R. H. (1995). The empirical status of the clinical application of eye movement desensitization and reprocessing. *Journal of Behavior Therapy and Experimental Psychiatry, 26,* 285–302.

Lohr, J. M., Tolin, D. F., & Lilienfeld, S. O. (1998). Efficacy of eye movement desensitization and reprocessing: Implications for behavior therapy. *Behavior Therapy, 29,* 123–156.

London, P. (1964). *The modes and morals of psychotherapy.* New York: Holt, Rinehart, and Winston.

Lopez, A. G., & Carillo, E. (2001). *The Latino psychiatric patient: Assessment and treatment.* Washington, DC: American Psychiatric Press.

Luborsky, L. (1984). *Principles of psychoanalytic psychotherapy: A manual for supportive-expressive treatment.* New York: Basic Books.

Luborsky, L., Diguer, L., Seligman, D. A., Rosenthal, R., Krause, E. D., Johnson, S., Halperin, G., Bishop, M., Berman, J. S., & Schweizer, E. (1999). The researcher's own therapy allegiances: A "wild card" in comparisons of treatment efficacy. *Clinical Psychology: Science and Practice, 6*(1), 95–106.

Luborsky, L., & et al. (1985). A verification of Freud's grandest clinical hypothesis: The transference. *Clinical Psychology Review Special Issue: Current thinking in psychoanalysis, 5*(3), 231–246.

Luborsky, L., Singer, B., & Luborsky, L. (1975). Comparative studies of psychotherapies: Is it true that "everybody has won so all shall have prizes?" *Archives of General Psychiatry, 32,* 995–1008.

Luria, A. (1961). *The role of speech in the regulation of normal and abnormal behavior.* New York: Liveright.

Maag, J. W. (2001). Rewarded by punishment: Reflections on the disuse of positive reinforcement in the schools. *Exceptional Children, 67,* 173–186.

MacKinnon, C. A. (1987). *Feminism unmodified: Discourses on life and law.* Cambridge, MA: Harvard University Press.

Madanes, C., & Haley, J. (1977). Dimensions of family therapy. *Journal of Nervous and Mental Disease, 165,* 88–98.

Mahler, M. S., & Pine, F. (1975). *The psychological birth of the human infant: Symbiosis and individuation.* New York: Basic Books.

Mahoney, M., (1984). Psychoanalysis and behaviorism: The yin and yang of determinism. In H. Arkowitz & S. B. Messer (Eds.), *Psychoanalysis and behavior therapy: Is integration possible?* (pp. 303–325). New York: Plenum.

Mahoney, M. (1985). Psychotherapy and human change processes. In M. Mahoney & A. Freeman (Eds.), *Cognition and psychotherapy* (pp. 3–48). New York: Plenum.

Mahoney, M. J. (1991). *Human change processes.* New York: Basic Books.

Mahoney, M. J. (1988). Constructive metatheory: II. Implications for psychotherapy. *International Journal of Personal Construct Psychology, 1*(4), 299–315.

Maniar, S. D., Curry, L. A., Sommers-Flanagan, J., & Walsh, J. A. (2001). Student athlete preferences in seeking help when confronted with sport performance problems. *Sport Psychologist, 15*(2), 205–223.

March, J. S., Franklin, M., Nelson, A., & Foa, E. (2001). Cognitive-behavioral psychotherapy for pediatric obsessive-compulsive disorder. *Journal of Clinical Child Psychology, 30,* 8–18.

Markus, H. R., & Kitayama, S. (1998). The cultural psychology of personality. *Journal of Cross-Cultural Psychology, 29*(1), 63–87.

Marlatt, G. A. (2002). Buddhist philosophy and the treatment of addictive behavior. *Cognitive and Behavioral Practice, 9,* 44–50.

Marlo, H., & Kline, J. S. (1998). Synchronicity and psychotherapy: Unconscious communication in the psychotherapeutic relationship. *Psychotherapy: Theory, Research, Practice, Training, 35*(1), 13–22.

Marmor, J. (1980). Homosexuality and the issue of mental illness. In J. Marmor (Ed.), *Homosexual behavior: A modern reappraisal* (pp. 33–49). New York: Basic Books.

Masson, J. M. (1984). *The assault on truth: Freud's suppression of the seduction theory.* New York: Farrar, Straus and Giroux.

Masson, J. M. (1988). *Against therapy: Emotional tyranny and the myth of psychological healing.* New York: Atheneum.

May, R. (1962). Introduction (H. E. Barnes, Trans.). In *Existential psychoanalysis* (pp. 1–17). Chicago: Regnery.

May, R. (1969). *Love and will.* New York: Norton.

May, R. (1977). *The meaning of anxiety* (Rev. ed.). New York: Norton.

May, R. (1982). The problem of evil: An open letter to Carl Rogers. *Journal of Humanistic Psychology, 22*(3), 10–21.

May, R. (1983). *The discovery of being: Writings in existential psychology.* New York: Norton.

May, R., Angel, E., & Ellenberger, H. F. (Eds.). (1958). *Existence: A new dimension in psychiatry and psychology.* New York: Basic Books.

Mazurana, D. E., McKay, S. A., Carlson, K. C., & Kasper, J. C. (2002). Girls in fighting forces and groups: Their recruitment, participation, demobilization, and reintegration. *Peace and Conflict: Journal of Peace Psychology, 8*(2), 97–123.

McCann, R. A., Ball, E. M., & Ivanoff, A. (2000). DBT with an inpatient forensic population: The CMHIP forensic model. *Cognitive and Behavioral Practice, 7,* 447–456.

McCartney, J. (1966). Overt transference. *Journal of Sex Research, 2,* 227–237.

McCleary, R. A., & Lazarus, R. S. (1949). Autonomic discrimination without awareness. *Journal of Personality, 18,* 171–179.

McGoldrick, M. (Ed.). (1998). *Re-visioning family therapy: Race, gender, and culture in clinical practice.* New York: Guilford Press.

McIntosh, P. (1998). White privilege: Unpacking the invisible knapsack. In M. McGoldrick (Ed.), *Re-visioning family therapy: Race, gender and culture in clinical practice* (pp. 147–152). New York: Guilford Press.

McKeel, A. J. (1996). A clinician's guide to research on solution-focused brief therapy. In S. D. Miller, M. A. Hubble, & B. L. Duncan (Eds.), *Handbook of solution-focused brief therapy* (pp. 251–271). San Francisco: Jossey-Bass.

McMillin, R. (1986). *Handbook of cognitive therapy techniques.* New York: Norton.

McNeil, D. W., Sorrell, J. T., Vowles, K. E., & Billmeyer, T. W. (2002). Social phobia. In M. Hersen (Ed.), *Clinical behavior therapy: Adults and children* (pp. 90–105). New York: Wiley.

Meichenbaum, D. (1969). The effects of instructions and reinforcement on thinking and language behaviors of schizophrenics. *Behaviour Research and Therapy, 7,* 101–114.

Meichenbaum, D. (1977). *Cognitive behavior modification: An integrative approach.* New York: Plenum.

Meichenbaum, D. (1985). *Stress inoculation training.* New York: Pergamon Press.

Meichenbaum, D. (1992). Evolution of cognitive behavior therapy: Origins, tenets, and clinical examples. In J. K. Zeig (Ed.), *The evolution of psychotherapy: The second conference* (pp. 114–128). New York: Brunner/Mazel.

Meichenbaum, D. (1996). Stress inoculation training for coping with stressors. *Clinical Psychologist, 49,* 4–7.

Meichenbaum, D., & Cameron, R. (1974). The clinical potential of modifying what clients say to themselves. *Psychotherapy, 11,* 103–117.

Meichenbaum, D., & Goodman, J. (1971). Training impulsive children to talk to themselves. *Journal of Abnormal Psychology, 77,* 115–126.

Meichenbaum, D., & Turk, D. (1987). *Facilitating treatment adherence: A practitioner's guidebook.* New York: Plenum.

Meier, S. T. (1999). Training the practitioner-scientist: Bridging case conceptualization, assessment, and intervention. *The Counseling Psychologist, 29,* 589–613.

Merton, T. (1974). *A Thomas Merton reader.* New York: Doubleday.

Messer, S. B., & Wachtel, P. L. (1997). The contemporary psychotherapeutic landscape: Issues and prospects. In P. L. Wachtel & S. B. Messer (Eds.), *Theories of psychotherapy: Origins and evolution* (pp. 1–38). Washington, DC: American Psychological Association.

Meyer, T. J., Miller, M. L., Metzger, R. L., & Borkovec, T. D. (1990). Development and validation of the Penn State Worry Questionnaire. *Behaviour Research & Therapy, 28*(6), 487–495.

Mezzich, J. E., Kirmayer, L. J., Kleinman, A., Frabrega, H. J., Paron, D. L., Good, B., Lin, K.-M., & Manson, S. M. (1999). The place of culture in DSM-IV. *Journal of Nervous and Mental Disease, 187*(18), 457–464.

Mickel, E., & Liddie-Hamilton, B. (2002). Family therapy in transition: African centered family healing. *International Journal of Reality Therapy, 22*(1), 34–36.

Mill, J. S. (1912). *"The subjection of women" in three essays.* London: Oxford University Press.

Miller, A. (1984). *For your own good: Hidden cruelty in child-rearing and the roots of violence* (2nd ed.). New York: Farrar, Straus, Giroux.

Miller, A. L., & Rathus, J. H. (2000). Special series dialectical behavioral therapy: Adaptations and new applications. *Cognitive and Behavioral Practice, 7,* 420–425.

Miller, J. B. (1976). *Toward a new psychology of women.* Boston: Beacon Press.

Miller, J. B. (1986). *Toward a new psychology of women* (2nd ed.). Boston: Beacon Press.

Miller, J. B. (Ed.). (1973). *Psychoanalysis and women.* New York: Brunner/Mazel.

Miller, P. (1983). *Theories of developmental psychology.* San Francisco: W. H. Freeman.

Miller, S. D., Hubble, M. A., & Duncan, B. L. (1996). *Handbook of solution-focused brief therapy.* San Francisco: Jossey-Bass.

Miller, W. R. (1978). Behavioral treatment of problem drinkers: A comparative outcome study of three controlled drinking therapies. *Journal of Consulting and Clinical Psychology, 46*(1), 74–86.

Miller, W. R., & Rollnick, S. (1998). *Motivational interviewing (Vols. 1–7)* [Video]. Albuquerque, NM: Horizon West Productions.

Miller, W. R., & Rollnick, S. (2002). *Motivational interviewing: Preparing people for change* (2nd ed.). New York: Guilford Press.

Miller, W. R., & Taylor, C. A. (1980). Relative effectiveness of bibliotherapy, individual and group self-control training in the treatment of problem drinkers. *Addictive Behaviors, 5*(1), 13–24.

Minuchin, S. (1991). The seductions of constructivism. *Family Therapy Networker, 9*(5), 47–50.

Mitchell, J. (1966). *Women: The longest revolution.* New York: Pantheon.

Mitchell, J. (1976). *Psychoanalysis and feminism: Freud, Reich, Laing, and women.* New York: Random House.

Mollica, R. F. (1988). The trauma story: The psychiatric case of refugee survivors of violence and torture. In R. Ochberg (Ed.), *Post-traumatic therapy and victims of violence* (pp. 295–314). New York: Brunner/Mazel.

Monk, G. (1997). How narrative therapy works. In G. Monk, J. Winslade, K. Crocket, & D. Epston (Eds.), *Narrative therapy in practice: The archaeology of hope* (pp. 3–31). San Francisco: Jossey-Bass.

Monk, G., Winslade, J., Crocket, K., & Epston, D. (Eds.). (1997). *Narrative therapy in practice: The archaeology of hope.* San Francisco: Jossey-Bass.

Moore, T. (1994). *Care of the soul.* New York: Perennial.

Moreau, D., Mufson, L., Weissman, M. M., & Klerman, G. L. (1991). Interpersonal psychotherapy for adolescent depression: Description of modification and preliminary application. *Journal of the American Academy of Child and Adolescent Psychiatry, 30*(4), 642–651.

Morgan, P. (1996). Buddhism. In P. Morgan & C. Lawton (Eds.), *Ethical issues in six religious traditions* (pp. 62–94). Edinburgh, Scotland: Edinburgh University Press.

Mosak, H. H. (1972). Life style assessment: A demonstration focused on family constellation. *Journal of Individual Psychology, 28,* 232–247.

Mosak, H. H. (1985). Interrupting a depression: The pushbutton technique. *Individual Psychology, 41,* 210–214.

Mosak, H. H. (1987). Guilt, guilt feelings, regret and repentance. *Individual Psychology, 43,* 288–295.

Mosak, H. H. (1989). Adlerian psychotherapy. In R. Corsini & D. Weddings (Eds.), *Current psychotherapies* (4th ed., pp. 65–116). Itasca, IL: Peacock.

Mosak, H. H. (1995). Adlerian psychotherapy. In R. Corsini & D. Wedding (Eds.), *Current psychotherapies* (5th ed., pp. 51–94). Itasca, IL: Peacock.

Mosak, H. H., & Dreikurs, R. (1967). The life tasks: III. The fifth life task. *Individual Psychology, 5,* 16–22.

Mosak, H. H., & Kopp, R. R. (1973). The early recollections of Adler, Freud, and Jung. *Journal of Individual Psychology, 29,* 157–166.

Mosak, H. H., & Maniacci, M. P. (1999). *A primer of Adlerian psychology: The analytic-behavioral-cognitive psychology of Alfred Adler.* Philadelphia: Taylor & Francis.

Mowrer, O. H. (1947). On the dual nature of learning: A reinterpretation of "conditioning" and "problem-solving." *Harvard Education Review, 17,* 102–148.

Mufson, L., Moreau, D., Weissman, M. M., & Klerman, G. L. (1993). *Interpersonal psychotherapy for depressed adolescents.* New York: Guilford Press.

Myers, I. B. (1955). *Gifts differing: Understanding personality types.* Palo Alto, CA: Davies-Black.

Myers, I. B., & Myers, P. (1997). *Gifts differing: Understanding personality types.* Palo Alto, CA: Consulting Psychologists Press.

Navarro, A. M. (1993). Effectividad de las psicoterapias con Latinos en los estados unidos: Una revisión meta-analytica. *Interamerican Journal of Psychology, 27,* 131–146.

Neimeyer, R. A. (1995). Constructivist psychotherapies: Features, foundations, and future directions. In R. A. Neimeyer & M. Mahoney (Eds.), *Constructivism in psychotherapy* (pp. 11–38). Washington, DC: American Psychological Association.

Neimeyer, R. A., & Mahoney, M. (Eds.). (1995). *Constructivism in psychotherapy.* Washington, DC: American Psychological Association.

Norcross, J. C. (Ed.). (2002). *Psychotherapy relationships that work.* New York: Oxford University Press.

Norcross, J. C., Karg, R. S., & Prochaska, J. O. (1997). Clinical psychologists in the 1990s. *Clinical Psychologist, 50,* 4–9.

Norcross, J. C., Strausser, D. J., & Missar, C. D. (1988). The process and outcomes of psychotherapists' personal treatment experiences. *Psychotherapy, 25,* 36–43.

Norcross, J. C., & Vangarelli, D. J. (1989). The resolution solution: Longitudinal examination of New Year's change attempts. *Journal of Substance Abuse, 1,* 127–134.

Novaco, R. W. (1979). The cognitive regulation of anger. In P. C. Kendall & S. D. Hollon (Eds.), *Cognitive behavioral interventions: Theory, research, and procedures* (pp. 241–285). New York: Academic Press.

Oaklander, V. (1978). *Windows to our children.* Moab, UT: Real People Press.

O'Hanlon, W. H. (1998). Possibility therapy: An inclusive, collaborative, solution-based model of psychotherapy. In M. F. Hoyt (Ed.), *The handbook of constructive therapies* (pp. 137–158). San Francisco: Jossey-Bass.

O'Hanlon, W. H., & Bertolino, B. (1998). *Even from a broken web: Brief, respectful, solution-oriented therapy for sexual abuse and trauma.* New York: Wiley.

Orgler, H. (1963). *Alfred Adler: The man and his work.* New York: Mentor Books.

Orne, M., & Wender, P. (1968). Anticipatory socialization for psychotherapy: Method and rationale. *American Journal of Psychiatry, 124,* 1209–1211.

Ortiz, S. (1993). The language we know. In P. Riley (Ed.), *Growing up Native American* (pp. 29–38). New York: Morrow.

Ost, L.-G., Alm, T., Brandberg, M., & Breitholz, E. (2001). One vs five sessions of exposure and five sessions of cognitive therapy in the treatment of claustrophobia. *Behaviour Research and Therapy, 39,* 167–183.

Otto, M. W., Pollack, M. H., & Sabatino, S. A. (1996). Maintenance of remission following cognitive behavior therapy for panic disorder. *Behavior Therapy, 27,* 472–482.

Paivio, S. C., & Greenberg, L. S. (1995). Resolving "unfinished business": Efficacy of experiential therapy using empty-chair dialogue. *Journal of Consulting and Clinical Psychology, 63*(3), 419–425.

Pajak, E. (2002). Clinical supervision and psychological functions: A new direction for theory and practice. *Journal of Curriculum and Supervision, 17*(3), 189–205.

Paniagua, F. A. (1998). *Assessing and treating culturally diverse clients: A practical guide* (2nd ed.). London: Sage.

Paniagua, F. A. (2001). *Diagnosis in a multicultural context.* Thousand Oaks, CA: Sage.

Parloff, M. B., Waskow, I. E., & Wolfe, B. E. (1978). Research on therapist variables in relation to process and outcome. In S. L. Garfield & A. E. Bergin (Eds.), *Handbook of psychotherapy and behavior change: An empirical analysis.* New York: Wiley.

Parrott, L. I. (1997). *Counseling and psychotherapy.* New York: McGraw-Hill.

Patterson, C. H., & Hidore, S. (1997). *Successful psychotherapy: A caring, loving relationship.* Northvale, NJ: Jason Aronson.

Paul, G. L. (1969). Behavior modification research: Design and tactics. In C. M. Franks (Ed.), *Behavior therapy: Appraisal and status* (pp. 29–62). New York: McGraw-Hill.

Paul, G. L., & Menditto, A. A. (1992). Effectiveness of inpatient treatment programs for mentally ill adults in public psychiatric facilities. *Applied & Preventive Psychology, 1,* 41–63.

Pavlov, L. P. (1906). The scientific investigation of the psychical faculties or processes in the higher animals. *Science, 24,* 613–619.

Pavlov, L. P. (1927). *Conditioned reflexes* (G. V. Anrep, Trans.). London: Oxford University Press.

Pearson, C. S. (1989). *The hero within: Six archetypes we live with.* San Francisco: Harper & Row.

Peck, M. S. (1978). *The road less traveled.* New York: Simon & Schuster.

Pedersen, P. (2000). *A handbook for developing multicultural awareness.* Alexandria, VA: American Counseling Association.

Perls, F. (1969a). *Gestalt therapy verbatim.* Moab, UT: Real People Press.

Perls, F. (1969b): *In and out the garbage pail.* Moab, UT: Real People Press.

Perls, F. (1973). *The Gestalt approach and eye witness to therapy.* New York: Bantam Books.

Perls, F., Hefferline, R. F., & Goodman, P. (1951). *Gestalt therapy.* New York: Bantam Books.

Perls, L. (1990). A talk for the 25th anniversary. *Gestalt Journal, 13*(2), 15–22.

Persons, J. B. (1989). *Cognitive therapy in practice: A case formulation approach.* New York: Norton.

Persons, J. B., & Tompkins, M. A. (1997). Cognitive-behavioral case formulation. In T. D. Eells (Ed.), *Handbook of psychotherapy case formulation* (pp. 314–339). New York: Guilford Press.

Petroff, E. A. E. (1986). *Medieval women's visionary literature.* New York: Oxford University Press.

Pietikainen, P. (2001). Dynamic psychology, utopia, and escape from history: The case of C. G. Jung. *Utopian Studies, 12*(1), 41–55.

Pine, F. (1990). *Drive, ego, object, and self: A synthesis for clinical work.* New York: Basic Books.

Pipes, R. B., & Davenport, D. S. (1999). *Introduction to psychotherapy: Common clinical wisdom.* Englewood Cliffs, NJ: Prentice Hall.

Pollack, W. S. (2000). *Real boys' voices.* New York: Penguin Books.

Pope, K. S. (1988). How clients are harmed by sexual contact with mental health professionals. *Journal of Counseling and Development, 67,* 222–226.

Pope, K. S. (1990a). Therapist-patient sex as sex abuse: Six scientific, professional and practical dilemmas in addressing victimization and rehabilitation. *Professional Psychology: Research and Practice, 21,* 227–239.

Pope, K. S. (1990b). Therapist-patient sexual involvement: A review of the research. *Clinical Psychology Review, 10,* 477–490.

Pope, K. S., & Vasquez, M. J. T. (1998). *Ethics in psychotherapy and counseling: A practical guide* (2nd ed.). San Francisco, CA: Jossey-Bass/Pfeiffer.

Popp, C. A., Diguer, L., Luborsky, L., Faude, J., Johnson, S., Morris, M., Schaffler, N., Schaffer, P., Schmidt, K. (1996). Repetitive relationship themes in waking narratives and dreams. *Journal of Consulting and Clinical Psychology, 64*(5), 1073–1078.

Powlishta, K. K., Sen, M. G., Serbin, L. A., Poulin-Dubois, D., & Eichstedt, J. A. (2001). From infancy through middle childhood: The role of cognitive and social factors in becoming gendered. In R. K. Unger (Ed.), *Handbook of the psychology of women and gender.* New York: Wiley.

Prochaska, J. O. (1979). *Systems of psychotherapy: A transtheoretical analysis.* Chicago: Dorsey.

Prochaska, J. O. (1995). An eclectic and integrative approach: Transtheoretical therapy. In A. S. Gurman & S. B. Messer (Eds.), *Essential psychotherapies* (pp. 403–440). New York: Guilford Press.

Prochaska, J. O., & DiClemente, C. C. (1982). Transtheoretical therapy: Toward a more integrative model of change. *Psychotherapy, 19,* 276–278.

Prochaska, J. O., DiClemente, C. C., & Norcross, J. C. (1993). In search of how people change. *American Psychologist, 47,* 1102–1114.

Prochaska, J. O., & Norcross, J. C. (2003). *Systems of psychotherapy: A transtheoretical analysis* (5th ed.). Pacific Grove, CA: Brooks/Cole.

Prochaska, J. O., Norcross, J. C., & DiClemente, C. C. (1994). *Changing for good.* New York: William Morrow.

Quenk, N. L. (2000). *Essentials of Myers-Briggs Type Indicator.* New York: Wiley.

Quinn, S. (1987). *A mind of her own: The life of Karen Horney.* New York: Summit Books.

Rachman, S. (1965). Aversion therapy: Chemical or electrical? *Behaviour Research and Therapy, 2,* 289–300.

Rachman, S. (Ed.). (1997). *The best of Behaviour Research and Therapy.* New York: Pergamon.

Rapaport, D. (1951). *Organization and pathology of thought.* New York: Columbia University Press.

Raskin, N. J. (1992, August). *Not necessary, perhaps sufficient, definitely facilitative.* Paper presented at the American Psychological Association, Washington, DC.

Raskin, N. J., & Rogers, C. R. (1989). Person-centered therapy. In R. Corsini & D. Wedding (Eds.), *Current psychotherapies* (pp. 154–194). Itasca, IL: Peacock.

Rathus, J. H., & Miller, A. L. (2000). DBT for adolescents: Dialectical dilemmas and secondary treatment targets. *Cognitive and Behavioral Practice, 7,* 425–434.

Rawls, J. (1971). *A theory of justice.* Cambridge: Harvard University Press.

Renik, O. (1993). Analytic interaction: Conceptualizing technique in light of the analyst's irreducible subjectivity. *Psychoanalytic Quarterly, 62,* 553–571.

Richardson, B. G. (2001). *Working with challenging youth: Lessons learned along the way.* Philadelphia: Brunner-Routledge.

Richardson, B. G., & Wubbolding, R. E. (2001). Five interrelated challenges for using reality therapy with challenging students. *International Journal of Reality Therapy, 20*(2), 35–39.

Ridley, C. R. (1995). *Overcoming unintentional racism in counseling and therapy: A practitioners guide to intentional intervention.* Thousand Oaks, CA: Sage.

Ringstrom, P. A. (2001). Cultivating the improvisational in psychoanalytic treatment. *Psychoanalytic Dialogues, 11,* 727–754.

Rodman Aronson, K. M., & Schaler Bucholz, E. (2001). The post-feminist era: Still striving for equality in relationships. *American Journal of Family Therapy, 29*(2), 109–124.

Rogers, C. R. (1939). *The clinical treatment of the problem child.* Boston: Houghton Mifflin.

Rogers, C. R. (1942a). *Counseling and psychotherapy.* Boston: Houghton Mifflin.

Rogers, C. R. (1942b). The use of electrically recorded interviews in improving psychotherapeutic techniques. *American Journal of Orthopsychiatry, 12,* 429–434.

Rogers, C. R. (1951). *Client-centered therapy.* Boston: Houghton Mifflin.

Rogers, C. R. (1957). The necessary and sufficient conditions of therapeutic personality change. *Journal of Consulting Psychology, 21,* 95–103.

Rogers, C. R. (1958). The characteristics of a helping relationship. *Personnel and Guidance Journal, 37,* 6–16.

Rogers, C. R. (1959). A theory of therapy, personality, and interpersonal relationships, as developed in the client-centered framework. In S. Koch (Ed.), *Psychology: A study of a science* (pp. 184–256). New York: McGraw-Hill.

Rogers, C. R. (1960, December 2–4). *The individual and the design of culture.* Paper presented at the Conference on Evolutionary Theory and Human Progress, New York.

Rogers, C. R. (1961). *On becoming a person.* Boston: Houghton Mifflin.

Rogers, C. R. (1963). *Mrs. P. S.* [Audiotape]. Orlando, FL: American Academy of Psychotherapists.

Rogers, C. R., & Russell, D. E. (2002). *Carl Rogers the quiet revolutionary: A post-humous autobiography.* Roseville, CA: Penmarin Books.

Rogers, C. R. (1967a). Autobiography. In E. G. Boring & G. Lindzey (Eds.), *A history of psychology in autobiography* (Vol. 5, pp. 341–384). New York: Appleton.

Rogers, C. R. (Ed.). (1967b). *The therapeutic relationship and its impact: A study of psychotherapy with schizophrenics.* Madison: University of Wisconsin Press.

Rogers, C. R. (1969). *Freedom to learn: A view of what education might become.* Columbus, OH: Merrill.

Rogers, C. R. (1970). *Carl Rogers on encounter groups.* New York: Harper & Row.

Rogers, C. R. (1975). Empathy: An unappreciated way of being. *Counseling Psychologist, 21,* 95–103.

Rogers, C. R. (1977). *Carl Rogers on personal power.* New York: Delacorte Press.

Rogers, C. R. (1980). *A way of being.* Boston: Houghton Mifflin.

Rogers, C. R. (1986). Carl Rogers on the development of the person-centered approach. *Person-Centered Review, 1,* 257–259.

Rogers, C. R., & Haigh, G. (1983). I walk softly through life. *Voices: The Art and Science of Psychotherapy, 18,* 6–14.

Rogers, C. R. (1965). *Three approaches to psychotherapy* [Videotape]. Corona del Mar, CA: Psychological and Educational Films.

Rogers, N. (1996). *The creative connection.* New York: Science and Behavior Books.

Rollnick, S., & Miller, W. R. (1995). What is motivational interviewing? *Behavioural and Cognitive Psychotherapy, 23*(4), 325–334.

Rosen, G. M., Lohr, J. M., McNally, R. J., & Herbert, J. D. (2000). Power therapies, miraculous claims and the cures that fail. In M. J. Scott & S. Palmer (Eds.), *Trauma and post-traumatic stress disorder* (pp. 134–136). London: Cassell.

Rosenthal, H. G. (Ed.). (1999). *Favorite counseling and therapy techniques.* Washington, DC: Accelerated Development.

Rosenzweig, S. (1936). Some implicit common factors in diverse methods in psychotherapy. *American Journal of Orthopsychiatry, 6,* 412–415.

Rossi, E. L. (1980). *The nature of hypnosis and suggestion: The collected papers of Milton H. Erickson on hypnosis* (Vol. 1). New York: Irvington.

Rothbaum, B. O. (1997). A controlled study of eye movement desensitization and reprocessing for posttraumatic stress disordered sexual assault victims. *Bulletin of the Menninger Clinic, 61,* 317–334.

Rouchy, J. C. (2002). Cultural identity and groups of belonging. *Group Special Issue, 26,* 205–217.

Rowling, J. K. (1997). *Harry Potter and the Sorcerer's Stone.* New York: Scholastic Press.

Roy v. Hartogs, 366 (New York 1975).

Rozsnafsky, J. (1974). The impact of Alfred Adler on three "free-will" therapies of the 1960's. *Journal of Individual Psychology, 30,* 65–80.

Ryan, T. A. (1970). *Intentional behavior.* New York: Ronald Press.

Rybak, C. J., Russell-Chapin, L. A., & Moser, M. E. (2000). Jung and the theories of gender development. *Journal of Humanistic Counseling, Education and Development, 38*(3), 152–161.

Santos de Barona, M., & Dutton, M. (1997). Feminist perspectives on assessment. In J. W. N. G. Johnson (Ed.), *Shaping the future of feminist psychology: Education, research, and practice* (pp. 37–56). Washington, DC: American Psychological Association.

Sartre, J.-P. (1953). *Existential psychoanalysis* (H. E. Barnes, Trans.). Chicago: Regnery.

Sartre, J.-P. (1971). *Being and nothingness.* New York: Bantam Books.

Saul, L. (1973). *Psychodynamically-based psychotherapy.* New York: Jason Aronson.

Saunders, T., Driskell, J. E., Hall, J., & Salas, E. (1996). The effect of stress inoculation training on anxiety and performance. *Journal of Occupational Health Psychology, 1,* 170–186.

Schofield, W. (1964). *Psychotherapy: The purchase of friendship.* Englewood Cliffs, NJ: Prentice Hall.

Schulman, B. H. (1965). A comparison of Allport's and the Adlerian concepts of life style. *Individual Psychology, 3,* 14–21.

Schulman, B. H. (1985). Cognitive therapy and the individual psychology of Alfred Adler. In M. Mahoney & A. Freeman (Eds.), *Cognition and psychotherapy* (pp. 243–258). New York: Plenum.

Schur, M. (1972). *Freud: Living and dying.* New York: International Universities Press.

Segraves, R. T. (2002). Female sexual disorders: Psychiatric aspects. *Canadian Journal of Psychiatry, 47*(5), 419–425.

Selekman, M. D. (1993). *Pathways to change: Brief therapy solutions with difficult adolescents.* New York: Guilford Press.

Seligman, M. E. P. (1975). *Helplessness: On depression, development, and death.* San Francisco: W. H. Freeman.

Seligman, M. E. P. (1995). The effectiveness of psychotherapy: The Consumer Reports study. *American Psychologist, 50,* 965–974.

Selling, L. S. (1943). *Men against madness.* New York: Garden City Books.

Selvini-Palazzoli, M., Boscolo, L., Cecchin, G., & Prata, G. (1974). The treatment of children through brief therapy of their parents. *Family Process, 13,* 429–442.

Serlin, I. (1999). An interview with Irvin Yalom. *Review of Existential Psychology and Psychiatry, 24*(1, 2, & 3), 142–146.

Shah, I. (1966). *The exploits of the incomparable Mulla Nasrudin.* New York: Simon & Schuster.

Shapiro, D. A., & Shapiro, D. (1982). Meta-analysis of comparative therapy outcome studies: A replication and refinement. *Psychological Bulletin, 92,* 581–604.

Shapiro, F. (1989). Eye movement desensitization: A new treatment for post-traumatic stress disorder. *Journal of Behavior Therapy and Experimental Psychiatry, 20,* 211–217.

Shapiro, F. (1995). *Eye movement desensitization and reprocessing: Basic principles, protocols, and procedures.* New York: Guilford Press.

Shapiro, F. (1997). *EMDR: The breakthrough therapy for overcoming anxiety, stress and trauma.* New York: Basic Books.

Shapiro, F. (1999). Eye movement desensitization and reprocessing (EMDR) and the anxiety disorders: Clinical and research implications of an integrated psychotherapy treatment. *Journal of Anxiety Disorders, 13,* 35–67.

Shapiro, F. (2001). *Eye movement desensitization and reprocessing: Basic principles, protocols, and procedures* (2nd ed.). New York: Guilford Press.

Shaw, B., & Beck, A. T. (1977). The treatment of depression with cognitive therapy. In A. Ellis & R. Grieger (Eds.), *Handbook of rational-emotive therapy* (pp. 309–326). New York: Springer.

Shepard, M. (1972). *The love treatment.* New York: Paperback Library.

Sherman, K. C. (2000). CT/RT in chronic pain management: Using choice theory/reality therapy as a cognitive-behavioral intervention for chronic pain management: A pilot study. *International Journal of Reality Therapy, 19*(2), 10–14.

Shoham-Salomon, V., & Rosenthal, R. (1987). Paradoxical interventions: A meta-analysis. *Journal of Consulting and Clinical Psychology, 55,* 22–28.

Shure, M. B. (1992). *I can problem solve: An interpersonal cognitive problem-solving program.* Champaign, IL: Research Press.

Sicher, L. (1935). A case of manic-depressive insanity. *International Journal of Individual Psychology, 1*(1), 40–56.

Sicher, L. (1991). A declaration of interdependence. *Individual Psychology, 47*(1), 10–16.

Silverman, W. H. (1996). Cookbooks, manuals, and paint-by-numbers: Psychotherapy in the 90's. *Psychotherapy, 33,* 207–215.

Simblett, G. J. (1997). Leila and the tiger: Narrative approaches to psychiatry. In G. Monk, J. Winslade, K. Crocket, & D. Epston (Eds.), *Narrative therapy in practice: The archaeology of hope* (pp. 121–157). San Francisco: Jossey-Bass.

Simi, N. L., & Mahalik, J. R. (1997). Comparison of feminist versus psychoanalytic/dynamic and other therapists on self-disclosure. *Psychology of Women Quarterly, 21,* 465–483.

Singer, J. (1973). *Boundaries of the soul: The practice of Jung's psychology.* Garden City, NY: Doubleday.

Skinner, B. F. (1938). *The behavior of organisms.* New York: Appleton-Century-Crofts.

Skinner, B. F. (1948). *Walden II.* New York: MacMillan.

Skinner, B. F. (1953). *Science and human behavior.* New York: MacMillan.

Skinner, B. F. (1970). *Walden two* (Rev. ed.). London: MacMillan.

Skinner, B. F. (1971). *Beyond freedom and dignity.* New York: Knopf.

Skinner, B. F. (1977). Why I am not a cognitive psychologist. *Behaviorism, 5,* 1–10.

Skinner, B. F., Solomon, H. C., & Lindsley, O. R. (1953). *Studies in behavior therapy: Status report I.* Unpublished paper. Metropolitan State Hospital, Waltham, MA.

Smail, D. (1984). *Illusion and reality: The meaning of anxiety.* London, England: Constable.

Smith, D. S. (1982). Trends in counseling and psychotherapy. *American Psychologist, 37,* 802–809.

Smith, M. L., & Glass, G. V. (1977). Meta-analysis of psychotherapy outcome. *American Psychologist, 32,* 752–760.

Smith, M. L., Glass, G. V., & Miller, T. I. (1980). *The benefits of psychotherapy.* Baltimore: Johns Hopkins University Press.

Snow, M. G., Prochaska, J. O., & Rossi, J. S. (1992). Stages of change for smoking cessation among former problem drinkers. *Journal of Substance Abuse, 4,* 107–116.

Snyder, D. K., & Wills, R. M. (1989). Behavioral versus insight-oriented marital therapy: Effects on individual and interspousal functioning. *Journal of Consulting and Clinical Psychology, 57,* 39–46.

Snyder, D. K., Wills, R. M., & Grady-Fletcher, A. (1991). Long-term effectiveness of behavioral versus insight-oriented marital therapy: A 4-year follow-up study. *Journal of Consulting and Clinical Psychology, 59,* 138–141.

Solomon, R. (1964). Punishment. *American Psychologist, 19,* 239–253.

Sommers-Flanagan, J., & Sommers-Flanagan, R. (1997). *Tough kids, cool counseling: User-friendly approaches with challenging youth.* Alexandria, VA: American Counseling Association.

Sommers-Flanagan, J., & Sommers-Flanagan, R. (1998). Assessment and diagnosis of conduct disorder. *Journal of Counseling and Development, 76*(2), 189–197.

Sommers-Flanagan, J., & Sommers-Flanagan, R. (1999, August 23). *Psychotherapy with treatment-resistant youth: User-friendly approaches.* Paper presented at the 107th annual meeting of the American Psychological Association, Boston.

Sommers-Flanagan, J., & Sommers-Flanagan, R. (2001). The three-step emotional change trick. In H. G. Kaduson & C. E. Schaefer (Eds.), *101 more favorite play therapy techniques* (pp. 439–444). New York: Jason Aronson.

Sommers-Flanagan, J., & Sommers-Flanagan, R. (2003). *Clinical interviewing* (3rd ed.). New York: Wiley.

Sommers-Flanagan, R. (2001). Ethics: Philosophical roots-practical applications. In F. Flach (Ed.), *Ethics in psychotherapy* (Vol. 4, pp. 21–27). New York: Hatherleigh.

Sommers-Flanagan, R., Elliott, D., & Sommers-Flanagan, J. (1998). Exploring the edges: Boundaries and breaks. *Ethics and Behavior, 8*(1), 37–48.

Sparks, E. E., & Park, A. H. (Eds.). (2002). *The integration of feminism and multiculturalism: Ethical dilemmas at the border.* Washington, DC: American Psychological Association.

Spezzano, C. (1996). The three faces of two-person psychology: Development, ontology, and epistemology. *Psychoanalytic Dialogues, 6,* 599–622.

Spivack, G., Platt, J. J., & Shure, M. B. (1976). *The problem-solving approach to adjustment.* San Francisco: Jossey-Bass.

St. Clair, M. (2000). *Object relations and self psychology: An introduction.* Pacific Grove, CA: Brooks/Cole.

Steil, J. M. (1997). *Marital equality: Its relationship to the well-being of husbands and wives.* Thousand Oaks, CA: Sage.

Stein, H. T. (2002). *A questionnaire to save interview time in Adlerian brief therapy.* Retrieved December 21, 2000, from http://ourworld.compuserve.com/homepages/hstein/quest-br.htm

Stern, D. N. (1985). *The interpersonal world of the infant.* New York: Basic Books.

Storm, L. (1999). Synchronicity, causality, and acausality. *Journal of Parapsychology, 63*(3), 247–269.

Strupp, H. H., & Binder, J. L. (1984). *Psychotherapy in a new key.* New York: Basic Books.

Sue, D. W. (in press). Racial-cultural competence: Awareness, knowledge, and skills. In R. T. Carter (Ed.), *Handbook of multicultural psychology and education.* New York: Wiley.

Sue, D. W., Arredondo, P., & McDavis, R. J. (1992). Multicultural Counseling Competencies and Standards: A call to the profession. *Journal of Multicultural Counseling & Development, 20,* 64–88.

Sue, D. W., Bingham, R., Porche-Burke, L., & Vasquez, M. J. T. (1999). The diversification of psychology: A multicultural revolution. *American Psychologist, 54,* 1061–1069.

Sue, D. W., & Sue, D. (2003). *Counseling the culturally diverse: Theory and practice* (3rd ed.). New York: Wiley.

Sue, S. (1977). Community mental health services to minority groups: Some optimism, some pessimism. *American Psychologist, 32,* 616–624.

Sue, S. (1998). In search of cultural competence in psychotherapy and counseling. *American Psychologist, 53,* 440–448.

Sue, S., Fujino, D., Takeuchi, D., & Zane, N. (1991). Community mental health services for ethnic minority groups: A test of the cultural responsiveness hypothesis. *Journal of Consulting and Clinical Psychology, 59,* 533–540.

Sue, S., & Lam, A. G. (2002). Cultural and demographic diversity. In J. C. Norcross (Ed.), *Psychotherapy relationships that work* (pp. 401–421). New York: Oxford University.

Suleiman, R. (2002). Minority self-categorization: The case of the Palestinians in Israel. *Peace and Conflict: Journal of Peace Psychology, 8*(1), 31–46.

Sullivan, H. S. (1953). *The interpersonal theory of psychiatry.* New York: Norton.

Swartz-Kulstad, J. L., & Martin, W. E. J. (1999). Impact of culture and context on psychosocial adaptation: The cultural and contextual guide process. *Journal of Counseling and Development, 77,* 281–293.

Sweeney, T. J. (1989). *Adlerian counseling* (3rd ed.). Muncie, IN: Accelerated Development.

Szasz, T. S. (1970). *The manufacture of madness.* New York: McGraw-Hill.

Takeuchi, D., Sue, S., & Yeh, M. (1995). Return rates and outcomes from ethnicity-specific mental health programs in Los Angeles. *American Journal of Public Health, 85,* 638–643.

Tallman, K., & Bohart, A. C. (1999). The client as a common factor: Clients as self-healers. In M. A. Hubble, B. L. Duncan, & S. D. Miller (Eds.), *The heart and soul of change* (pp. 91–131). Washington, DC: American Psychological Association.

Tannen, D. (1990). *You just don't understand me: Women and men in conversation.* New York: Ballantine Books.

Tavris, C. (1998). *The mismeasure of woman.* New York: Smith, Peter.

Taylor, S. (1996). Meta-analysis of cognitive-behavioral treatments for social phobia. *Journal of Behavior Therapy and Experimental Psychiatry, 27,* 1–9.

Taylor, S. (2000). *Understanding and treating panic disorder: Cognitive-behavioural approaches.* New York: Wiley.

Terman, L. (1916). *The measurement of intelligence.* Boston: Houghton Mifflin.

Tham, S. E. (2001). The meaning of choice theory for the women of Albania. *International Journal of Reality Therapy, 21*(1), 4–6.

Thorndike, E. L. (1911). *Animal intelligence.* New York: MacMillan.

Thorndike, E. L. (1932). *The fundamentals of learning.* New York: Teachers College, Columbia University.

Thorne, B. (2002). *The mystical power of Person-Centred Therapy: Hope beyond despair.* London: Whurr Publishers.

Tillich, P. (1961). Existentialism and psychotherapy. *Review of Existential Psychology and Psychiatry, 1*(1), 9.

Tjeltveit, A. C. (1999). *Ethics and values in psychotherapy.* Florence, KY: Taylor & Francis/Routledge.

Tohn, S. L., & Oshlag, J. A. (1996). Solution-focused therapy with mandated clients: Cooperating with the uncooperative. In M. F. Hoyt (Ed.), *Handbook of solution-focused brief therapy* (pp. 152–183). San Francisco: Jossey-Bass.

Tolstoy, L. (1929). *My confession, my religion, the gospel in brief.* New York: Scribner.

Tomlinson-Clarke, S. (2000). Assessing outcomes in a multicultural training course: A qualitative study. *Counselling Psychology Quarterly, 13,* 221–231.

Torres, C. A. (1998). *Democracy, education, and multiculturalism: Dilemmas of citizenship in a global world.* New York: Rowman and Littlefield.

Triandis, H. C. (1994). *Culture and social behavior.* New York: McGraw-Hill.

Truax, P. (2002). Behavioral case conceptualization for adults. In M. Hersen (Ed.), *Clinical behavior therapy: Adults and children* (pp. 3–36). New York: Wiley.

Ulanov, A. (1997). Jung and religion: The opposing Self. In P. Young-Eisendrath & T. Dawson (Eds.), *The Cambridge companion to Jung.* Cambridge, UK: Cambridge University Press.

Unger, R. K. (Ed.). (2001). *Handbook of the psychology of women and gender.* New York: Wiley.

Vaihinger, H. (1911). *The psychology of "as if."* New York: Harcourt, Brace and World.

Van Deurzen-Smith, E. (1997). *Everyday mysteries: Existential dimensions of psychotherapy.* London: Routledge.

Van Etten, M. L., & Taylor, S. (1998). Comparative efficacy of treatments for posttraumatic stress disorder: A meta-analysis. *Clinical Psychology and Psychotherapy, 5,* 126–144.

Velten, E. J. (1968). A laboratory task for induction of mood states. *Behaviour Research and Therapy, 6,* 473–482.

Vontress, C. E., Johnson, J. A., & Epp, L. R. (1999). *Cross-cultural counseling: A casebook.* Alexandria, VA: American Counseling Association.

Vygotsky, L. (1962). *Thought and language.* New York: Wiley.

Wachtel, P. L. (1977). *Psychoanalysis and behavior therapy: Toward an integration.* New York: Basic Books.

Walter, J. L., & Peller, J. E. (1996). Rethinking our assumptions: Assuming anew in a postmodern world. In S. D. Miller, M. A. Hubble, & B. L. Duncan (Eds.), *Handbook of solution-focused brief therapy* (pp. 9–26). San Francisco: Jossey-Bass.

Watkins, J. G. (1971). The affect bridge: A hypnoanalytic technique. *International Journal of Clinical and Experimental Hypnosis, 19,* 21–27.

Watkins, J. G., & Watkins, H. H. (1997). *Ego states: Theory and therapy.* New York: Norton.

Watson, J. B. (1913). Psychology as a behaviorist views it. *Psychological Review, 20,* 158–177.

Watson, J. B. (1924). *Behaviorism.* Chicago: University of Chicago Press.

Watson, J. B., & Rayner, R. (1920). Conditioned emotional reactions. *Journal of Experimental Psychology, 3,* 1–14.

Watts, R. E. (Ed.). (2003). *Adlerian, cognitive, and constructivist therapies: An integrative perspective.* New York: Springer.

Watzlawick, P. (1963). A review of the double bind theory. *Family Process, 2*(1), 132–153.

Watzlawick, P., Beavin, J. H., & Jackson, D. D. (1967). *Pragmatics of human communication.* New York: Norton.

Weakland, J. H. (1962). Family therapy as a research arena. *Family Process, 1*(1), 63–68.

Weakland, J. H. (1993). Conversation—But what kind? In S. G. Gilligan & R. Price (Eds.), *Therapeutic conversations* (pp. 136–145). New York: Norton.

Weiner-Davis, M. (1993). Pro-constructed realities. In S. G. Gilligan & R. Price (Eds.), *Therapeutic conversations* (pp. 149–157). New York: Norton.

Weiner-Davis, M., de Shazer, S., & Gingerich, W. (1987). Building on pretreatment change to construct the therapeutic solution: An exploratory study. *Journal of Marital and Family Therapy, 13*(4), 359–363.

Weishaar, M. E. (1993). *Aaron T. Beck.* London: Sage.

Weiss, F. G. (1974). *Hegel: The essential writings.* New York: Harper & Row.

Weissman, M. M., Markowitz, J. C., & Klerman, G. L. (2000). *Comprehensive guide to interpersonal psychotherapy.* New York: Basic Books.

Weisz, J. R., Donenberg, G. R., Han, S. S., & Weiss, B. (1995). Bridging the gap between laboratory and clinic in child and adolescent psychotherapy. *Journal of Consulting and Clinical Psychology, 63,* 688–701.

Weisz, J. R., Weiss, B., Alicke, M. D., & Klotz, M. L. (1987). Effectiveness of psychotherapy with children and adolescents: A meta-analysis for clinicians. *Journal of Consulting and Clinical Psychology, 55,* 542–549.

Weisz, J. R., Weiss, B., Han, S. S., Granger, D. A., & Morton, T. (1995). Effects of psychotherapy with children and adolescents revisited: A meta-analysis of treatment outcome studies. *Psychological Bulletin, 117,* 450–468.

Welfel, E. R. (2001). *Ethics in counseling and psychotherapy* (2nd ed.). Pacific Grove, CA: Brooks/Cole.

Wells, H. K. (1972). Alienation and dialectical logic. *Kansas Journal of Sociology, 3,* 7–32.

Wessler, R. L. (1992). Constructivism and rational-emotive therapy: A critique. *Psychotherapy, 29,* 620–625.

White, M. (1988). The process of questioning: A therapy of literary merit? *Dulwich Centre Newsletter,* 8–14.

White, M. (1993). Commentary: The histories of the present. In S. G. Gilligan & R. Price (Eds.), *Therapeutic conversations* (pp. 121–135). New York: Norton.

White, M. (1995). *Re-authoring lives: Interviews and esays.* Adelaide, South Australia: Dulwich Centre.

White, M., & Epston, D. (1990). *Narrative means to therapeutic ends.* New York: Norton.

Whitehouse, D. (1984). Adlerian antecedents to reality therapy and control theory. *Journal of Reality Therapy, 3,* 10–14.

Whitney, M. (1985). *A matter of heart: The extraordinary journey of C. G. Jung into the soul of man* [Videotape]. Los Angeles: C. G. Jung Institute.

Wickman, S. A., & Campbell, C. (2003). An analysis of how Carl Rogers enacted client-centered conversation with Gloria. *Journal of Counseling and Development, 81,* 178–184.

Williams, A. M., Diehl, N. S., & Mahoney, M. J. (2002). Mirror-time: Empirical findings and implications for a constructivist psychotherapeutic technique. *Journal of Constructivist Psychology, 15*(1), 21–39.

Wilson, E. O. (1999). *Consilience: The unity of knowledge.* New York: Random House.

Wittgenstein, L. (1968). *Philosophical investigations* (3rd ed.). New York: Macmillan.

Wolberg, L. R. (1995). *The technique of psychotherapy* (4th Rev. ed.). New York: Grune & Stratton.

Wolitzky, D. L., & Eagle, M. N. (1997). Psychoanalytic theories of psychotherapy. In P. L. Wachtel & S. B. Messer (Eds.), *Theories of psychotherapy: Origins and evolution* (pp. 39–96). Washington, DC: American Psychological Association.

Wolpe, J. (1948). *An approach to the problem of neurosis based on the conditioned response.* Johannesburg, South Africa: University of the Witwatersrand.

Wolpe, J. (1954). Reciprocal inhibition as the main basis of psychotherapeutic effects. *Proceedings of the South African Psychological Association No. 5,* 14.

Wolpe, J. (1958). *Psychotherapy by reciprocal inhibition.* Stanford, CA: Stanford University Press.

Wolpe, J. (1973). *The practice of behavior therapy* (2nd ed.). Elmsford, NY: Pergamon.

Wolpe, J. (1987). The promotion of scientific psychotherapy: A long voyage. In J. K. Zeig (Ed.), *The evolution of psychotherapy* (pp. 133–148). New York: Brunner/Mazel.

Wolpe, J., & Plaud, J. J. (1997). Pavlov's contributions to behavior therapy: The obvious and the not so obvious. *American Psychologist, 52*(9), 966–972.

Wong, E. C., Kim, B. S. K., Zane, N. W. S., Kim, I. J., & Huang, J. S. (2003). Examining culturally based variables associated with ethnicity: Influences on credibility perceptions of empirically supported interventions. *Cultural Diversity and Ethnic Minority Psychology, 9*(1), 88–96.

Woody, S. R., Luborsky, L., McLellan, A. T., & O'Brien, C. P. (1990). Corrections and revised analyses for psychotherapy in methadone maintenance patients. *Archives of General Psychiatry, 47,* 788–789.

Worell, J., & Chandler, R. (1996). *Personal progress scale.* Unpublished manuscript, Lexington, KY.

Worell, J., & Johnson, D. (2003). Therapy with women: Feminist frameworks. In R. K. Unger (Ed.), *Handbook of the psychology of women and gender* (pp. 317–329). New York: Wiley.

Worell, J. R., & Rema, P. (2003). *Feminist perspectives in therapy: Empowering diverse women* (2nd ed.). New York: Wiley.

Whenn, C. G. (1962). The culturally encapsulated counselor. *Howard Educational Review, 32,* 444–449.

Wright, L. K. (2002). Book review: Letters to a young feminist. *Women and Therapy, 25*(1), 113–115.

Wubbolding, R. E. (1988). *Using reality therapy.* New York: Harper & Row.

Wubbolding, R. E. (1991). *Understanding reality therapy.* New York: Harper & Row.

Wubbolding, R. E. (1999). Client inner self-evaluation: A necessary prelude to change. In H. G. Rosenthal (Ed.), *Favorite counseling and therapy techniques* (pp. 196–197). Washington, DC: Accelerated Development.

Wubbolding, R. E. (2000). *Reality therapy for the 21st century.* Muncie, IN: Accelerated Development.

Wubbolding, R. E., Al-Rashidi, B., Brickell, J., Kakitani, M., Kim, R. I., Lennon, B., Lojk, L., Ong, K. H., Honey, I., Stijacic, D., & Tham, E. (1998). Multicultural awareness: Implications for reality therapy and choice theory. *International Journal of Reality Therapy, 17,* 4–6.

Wubbolding, R. E., & Brickell, J. (1998). Qualities of the reality therapist. *International Journal of Reality Therapy, 17,* 47–49.

Wubbolding, R. E., & Brickell, J. (2000). Misconceptions about reality therapy. *International Journal of Reality Therapy, 19*(2), 64–65.

Wubbolding, R. E., Brickell, J., Loi, I., & Al-Rashidi, B. (2001). The why and how of self-evaluation. *International Journal of Reality Therapy, 21,* 36–37.

Yalom, I. D. (1980). *Existential psychotherapy.* New York: Basic Books.

Yalom, I. D. (1989). *Love's executioner.* New York: Basic Books.

Yalom, I. D. (2002). *The gift of therapy.* New York: HarperCollins.

Young-Eisendrath, P. (1999). Response to Tougas. *Journal of Analytical Psychology, 44*(3), 39.

Zetzel, E. R. (1956). Current concepts of transference. *International Journal of Psychoanalysis, 37,* 369–376.

Zucker, K. J. (2001). Biological influences on psychosexual differentiation. In R. K. Unger (Ed.), *Handbook of the psychology of women and gender* (pp. 101–115). New York: Wiley.

Author Index

511

Subject Index

ABC model, in behavior therapy, 227
ABCDEF model, in REBT, 265, 268, 271
Acceptance and commitment therapy, 460, 461
Activating event, 265, 268, 280
Adler School of Professional Psychology, 110
Adlerian theory (individual psychology):
  Adler, biographical information on, 75
  basic mistakes and, 23, 83, 90, 91, 95–97, 109
  brief therapy, 106
  discouragement and, 74, 76, 77, 88, 91, 102
  encouragement and, 74, 76, 90, 91, 98, 103–105
  feminism and, 76–78, 108
  historical context, 75–77
  holism, 78, 84, 109
  lifestyle, 23, 74, 82–84, 86–97, 103–105, 108, 109, 140, 141, 268, 313
  multicultural issues, 107, 108
  psychopathology and, 80, 88, 109
  social interest and community feeling, 80, 82, 84, 87, 88, 91, 96, 109, 110, 304, 330, 342
  superiority and inferiority, 7, 78, 80, 84, 85, 88, 89, 91, 102, 103, 109, 140, 150
  tasks of life, 85–88, 109
  theoretical principles, 78–88
  "why use Adlerian theory," 77
Adlerian therapy techniques:
  acting (as if), 98, 103
  advice, suggestion, and direction, 100, 101
  assessment, 90–97, 104
  birth order, 92, 93, 108, 109
  catching oneself, 99, 109
  creating new images, 97, 105, 109
  dream analysis, 92, 94, 95, 109
  early recollections, 75, 92, 98, 104, 109, 110
  family constellation interview, 91, 92, 101–103
  forming the therapeutic relationship, 90, 91
  future autobiography, 96, 97, 109
  "I'll betcha," 101, 109
  initial lifestyle interpretations, 91, 103
  interpretation and insight, 90, 96
  lifestyle assessment, 91–96, 104
  multicultural perspectives and, 106–107

  outcomes research and, 106
  paradoxical strategies (antisuggestion), 100–101, 106, 109
  reorientation, 90, 96, 101, 103
  push-button technique, 98, 99, 109
  the question, 92, 109
  spitting in the client's soup, 99, 105, 109
  stages (phases) of therapy, 74, 90, 100, 109
  task-setting and indirect suggestion, 100, 109
Aetiology of Hysteria, 35, 36, 69, 71, 76
Albert Ellis Institute, 296
Allegiance effect, 67, 167, 205
American Counseling Association, 19, 31, 32, 329, 407, 419
American Psychoanalytic Association, 73
American Psychological Association, 31, 32, 53, 177, 216, 407, 419
Analytical psychological theory (Jungian):
  anima and animus, 118, 119, 123, 131, 133, 136
  archetypes, 117–119, 122, 126, 130–132, 135, 136, 137
  collective unconscious, 114, 116, 117, 131, 132, 135, 136
  complexes, 116, 117, 121,
  God and, 118, 123, 125, 131, 136
  historical context, 112–114
  individuation, 114, 119, 122–124, 126, 135, 136
  Jung, biographical information on, 111–112
  Jung-Freud correspondence, 112–114
  multicultural issues and, 111, 132–134
  outcomes research and, 132
  persona, 117, 118, 122, 123, 128, 130, 131, 136
  personal unconscious, 116, 136
  personality types, 119–121, 127
  psychopathology and, 121, 122, 127, 135, 136
  self, 118, 119, 123, 124, 129–131, 136
  shadow, 118, 119, 123, 129, 131, 136, 144,
  spirituality and, 112, 115, 117, 118, 131, 132, 134–136
  synchronicity, 124, 125, 136
  theoretical principles, 114–122

About the Authors

John Sommers-Flanagan, Ph.D. is a clinical psychologist and assistant professor of counselor education at the University of Montana. He is a former columnist for the Missoulian newspaper, former local public radio show co-host of "What Is It with Men?" and coauthor of over 30 professional publications. John is a long-time member of both the American Counseling Association and the American Psychological Association and regularly presents professional workshops at the annual conferences of both these organizations.

Rita Sommers-Flanagan, Ph.D., has been a professor of counselor education at the University of Montana for the past 13 years. Her favorite teaching and research areas are ethics and women's issues, and she recently became the director of Women's Studies at the University of Montana. She is also a clinical psychologist, and has worked with youth, families, and women for many years.

Together, John and Rita have coauthored five books. More importantly, they have two daughters, whom they have dragged along with them while working in Belize and England. Both John and Rita enjoy professional speaking, exercising, gardening, and eating oat bran pancakes with the family on Saturday mornings.